Ethnic Studies:
Critical Fundamentals

Revised Edition

Revised Edition January 2018
First published August 2017

by Achromous Books
1027 Greenhills Rd., Toledo, OH 43607

Ordering Information:
Desk copies for professional review may be requested from the publisher at achromous@gmx.com.
All other orders see achromous.com

Printed in the United States of America

Library of Congress Cataloging-in-Publication Data

Messer-Kruse, Tim
        Ethnic Studies: Critical Fundamentals / Tim Messer-Kruse
                p. cm.
        Includes illustrations.
        1. Minorities--United States. 2. United States--Ethnic Relations. 3. United States--Race Relations.
        4. Prejudices--United States I. Title

ISBN-13: 978-0692985762
ISBN-10: 069298576X

Typeset in Adobe Carlson, Gill Sans MT, and Minion Pro.

Cover: George Washington with William Lee, a man Washington enslaved, painting by John Trumbull, 1780. Metropolitan Museum of Art, New York City.

Achromous Books
1027 Greenhills Rd.
Toledo, OH 43607

Revised Edition

14 13 12 11 10 / 10 9 8 7 6 5 4

Contents

Preface

This textbook is the product of my decade's experience teaching introductory classes in ethnic studies at Bowling Green State University. During that time I grew increasingly dissatisfied with the books commonly assigned in these courses. These tended to be either focused on the sociology of "race relations," American cultural history, social psychology or physical anthropology. I found myself resorting to picking one of these disciplinary texts as a primary reading for my classes and supplementing it with academic and magazine articles from week to week. If only, I wished, someone would attempt to integrate both the biology of human variation with critical theories of race, social psychology, and the history of racial construction and racism. In the end, I resorted to doing it myself.

When I first set out to organize and write this book, I planned on submitting it to an academic publisher as I had all my other books. But while teaching I had an experience that made me more acutely aware of the costs of traditional publishing. Every year I received a complimentary desk copy directly from the publisher and I'd never bothered to find out how much it cost. Walking through the bookstore one day I was stunned to find that the book I required cost nearly one hundred dollars. Used and rental copies cut this price by a third but this was still more than sixty bucks. I resolved then and there not to assign any more expensive textbooks to my students.

I soon found out that many of my colleagues had reached the same resolution. Some assigned nothing but journal articles that students could access through their library accounts. Others shared collections of various readings with their students through their course management systems. Trying this approach in my own classes proved unsatisfactory. While this work-around had the virtue of providing coverage of a broad scope of topics this advantage was far overshadowed by the problem that most articles written for academic journals are written for fellow academics, not students new to the field. Moreover, journal articles, even review essays, are too specialized to be a substitute for a broad introduction to an idea. Many of my students told me that they had difficulty reading such materials because they all seemed so different, by which I think they meant that they had confusingly different voices, methodologies, and perspectives. One virtue of a textbook, for good or ill, is its consistent authorial voice. Students read and absorb material better once they become familiar with a particular author's style and approach.

Due to the skyrocketing costs of textbooks, an increasing number of instructors have abandoned textbooks altogether in favor of cobbled-together collections of readings. Could it be that out of our concern for our students' pocket books we have skimped on the one thing that might make the biggest impact on our students' learning, namely, the quality of their course materials?

I began filling in the gaps by writing introductory and explanatory essays for the articles I was assigning my students and at some point I realized I wasn't just filling in the gaps, I was beginning to write my own ethnic studies textbook. But when I thought about undertaking such a work in the traditional manner I had done with my previous books, I realized this was no solution either.

The problem was that authors have no influence over the price of their books. Most authors, including this one, are thrilled that a reputable press would accept and publish their works, let alone do so on our own terms. All the negotiating power is in the hands of the publisher and price is not specified when a contract is negotiated. Traditional publishing was clearly not an option if I wanted to publish a book that was actually inexpensive.

One alternative was to simply post chapters to a blog and have students read them online and print them out for class use. I require my students to bring copies with them to class as I've found it is useful to be able to refer to facts, figures, and quotes to spur discussion. Calculating the total number of pages of both my chapters and other articles and sources I'd assigned totaled over thirty dollars at the university's copying charge of five cents per page. This cut the cost in half, but provided no funds with which to pay for editing, proofreading, graphic design, or the costs of recruiting and compensating external reviewers who could provide the sort of academic checks and balances that any serious work required.

I remembered the stories I heard in graduate school of one of my professors who self-published a textbook in the 1970s. At that time, he had to scramble to come up with a sizeable amount of money to get his book printed, warehoused, and distributed. He may have mortgaged his house, according to one story I heard. I am not so bold and my house probably doesn't have enough equity anyway.

Exploring what self-publishing opportunities exist today, I discovered that technology had revolutionized the economics of such a venture. In the 1970s an author interested in self-publishing would have to pay up front to have a printer to run a thousand or more copies. Today, high-speed machines print, collate, and bind a paperback book in a matter of seconds and can make one copy as easily as a thousand. This means that books need not be preprinted by the thousands and warehoused, but can be printed on demand.

Given these realities, it was possible to produce a reasonably well designed and printed textbook for a fraction of the cost that large commercial firms charge. I found I could contract to have the books printed on demand and shipped from distribution centers for less than the cost of a case of beer and still pay all the associated editorial costs associated with a book of this scope. Having found my answer, I undertook this project.

This textbook is not available in an ebook format intentionally because an increasing number of pedagogical studies have documented that information is better learned and retained from traditionally printed books than from screens. Studies have also shown that the relationship between text and images and the stable arrangement of text on a page aids memory and retention. This volume has been richly illustrated to take full advantage of this effect and though ebooks can be illustrated, the relationship between text and image is hard to control in electronic formats. Finally, because print books are easier to visually peruse, students can better estimate the time required for finishing chapters and assignments and better plan their study time with printed texts.

Ultimately, this book is a work of synthesis, not interpretation. I've gathered and benefited from the insights of hundreds of scholars, few of which I mention by name in the body of the text out of concern for this book's readability and accessibilty. Of course, all of the writers and researchers who have influenced this work are listed in the notes and direct quotations are indicated more specifically. I hope I have not overlooked anyone, though in a work of this size I probably have.

I am indebted to many colleagues and scholars for their criticisms and suggestions. Vibha Bhalla, Thomas Edge, Sridevi Menon, and Susana Pena offered helpful suggestions at the earliest stages of conception of this project. Dalton Jones, Abdul Alkalimat, and Donna Stuber, in particular, went out of their way to be helpful and I am grateful for their suggestions and criticisms, though, none of them saw the entire mansucript before publication and, of course, do not neccesarily endorse the perspectives, interpretations, and arguments made in these pages. Connor Messer-Kruse provided the artwork for the Achromous Books logo.

It is my sincere hope that this volume facilitates the teaching and learning of what, unfortunately, in the twenty-first century, remains a vitally relevant and important body of knowledge. Few subjects are as deeply misunderstood and mythologized as is the subject of America's tragic embrace of the idea of races and the even more corrosive belief in their inequality.

Students don't usually come to college with firmly set opinions about chemistry or physics or even literature, but they almost universally arrive on campus believing they understand what races are and how they work. The task of teaching ethnic studies is not simply one of pouring new information into the heads of our students, but combating the falsehoods and myths that reside there. From the start this book has been planned and organized around that challenge. Hundreds of hours of classroom experience and daily interactions with many cohorts of students have informed the selection of topics, their ordering, and the strategies of presentation used here that I believe are some of the most effective in overcoming the common resistance of students to rethinking their assumptions. I hope this book serves those ends.

Figure P-1 The Achromous Books editorial office.

Introduction

How to Think

Mark Twain once wrote that "education consists mainly in what we have unlearned." Learning is not the passive absorbing of new information but the interaction, sometimes the battle, between what we know, what we've come to believe through our own experiences, and what others tell us. Learning is easy when what we are told confirms our beliefs and understandings but turns increasingly difficult the more our assumptions are threatened. Even when faced with convincing evidence that some of our ideas are in error, we resist letting go of them because they are part of who we are, they are pieces of our identity, they define us and help us make sense of our lives.

Dear reader, this book will challenge many of your ideas about how the world works and even about yourself. The information presented here should not be accepted solely because it carries the authority of the author's credentials or because it's heavy with academic references and citations (though noting such things should be part of the way in which any critical thinker should judge the weight of new information), but because it might be a better explanation of what we experience reality to be, or of how our institutions work.

Critical Reasoning

Everyone thinks but few people reason. Most every moment of every waking hour is filled with fleeting thoughts of all sorts. Our minds wander and our ideas are often as unpredictable as wild horses darting across the prairie. All of our worrying, musing, dreaming, and pondering are forms of thinking, but like wild ponies they are not the kind you can ride to your destination. For that, you need a special form of thinking that has purpose and method. We call that form of thinking reasoning. Reasoning differs from ordinary thinking in that it has a specific aim, usually to solve a particular problem or answer a specific question. Critical reasoning is a specific method of thinking in which one teases apart the basis of their ideas and then compares these presumptions to evidence or other ideas with a willingness to adopt the one that appears closer to the truth.

This all sounds good in theory, but in reality reasoning is very difficult, not so much because thinking in this purposeful way is hard, but because we have all developed patterns of thinking that fight changing our beliefs. The subjects of this book will in all likelihood challenge some of the ideas and understandings you hold of how the world works. This is because American society has been built on the denial of certain truths and the assumption of certain falsehoods as obvious beliefs. These beliefs and denials are so widely shared and so deeply embedded in the official founding stories of the nation that to examine them critically feels uncomfortable, perhaps even unpatriotic.

Such discomfort is unavoidable as all critical reasoning begins by doubting. Doubting new information, doubting old beliefs, doubting even those things that seem natural. Unfortunately, this is hard because doubt requires more effort than belief. It is easier to simply float with the current and accept the things most people assume are true. The most difficult thing of all is to doubt the things that most people consider obvious.

Doubting does not mean disbelief, it does not mean discarding old ideas. To doubt is not the same as adopting new ideas. Rather, doubting is putting oneself in a state of mind that nurtures uncertainty. Most people avoid doubt as uncertainty provides no advice for living, no signposts to guide one's direction, no help in fitting in.

Critical reasoning begins by embracing uncertainty. Without uncertainty as a starting point of thought, ideas are adopted not on their own merits but because they agree with earlier beliefs. Much of what passes for thinking is actually rationalizing a reason to continue believing what is customary. Only once one is comfortable holding a position of uncertainty can one perform such mental feats as considering the possibility that two seemingly contradictory ideas may both be true at the same time.

Most of the reasons people believe things have nothing to do with the truth of those beliefs. Sometimes people believe a certain idea because this idea has a long, perhaps even ancient history. But the age or longevity of an idea is really no evidence of its truth. For thousands of years people believed that the world was flat, lightning bolts were tossed from heaven by gods, and diseases were the work of witches. Similarly many also assume that the popularity of an idea increases the likelihood that it is true. One need only glance across history to see that both truthful and false ideas have been popular. Democracy, while perhaps the best system for settling disputes and governing a nation, has a poor record as an producer of truth.

An argument delivered passionately is commonly considered more convincing than one proposed without emotion. An idea that moves or stirs our feelings may seem at the time to have a certain force or power that speaks in its favor, but this doesn't make it more likely to be true. This is the key to the success and power of con artists and demagogues.

The Danger of Common Sense

All of these deceptive and weak reasons for belief are reinforced by a particular way in which they come to be seen as obvious and beyond questioning—they pass into a false certainty that we call "common sense."

Everyone grows up with a habit of mind that manufacturers excuses for believing the ideas that have been passed on to us by those around us, whether parents, siblings, or friends. Such ideas that are inherited at an early age and continually reinforced over time get lodged deeply in one's perception of the world—so deeply that they are shielded from being questioned by being considered so obvious that they require no further explanation or consideration. We call such ideas "common sense."

Sometimes our perceptions and experiences seem to confirm our "common sense" but they are doing nothing of the kind because we have linked certain experiences to certain presumptions about reality that aren't actually tested by those experiences. For example, every day I perceive that the sun moves across the sky, rising in the east and setting in the west. When I sit on my porch beneath the sun it seems to me that I am perfectly still and yet the sun travels its course. I could think that as I am not moving and the sun is, this confirms my common sense idea that the sun orbits the earth (as one-quarter of Americans believe). But it's not my perceptions that are in error, it is the presumptions I brought to those observations—I assumed that if I didn't feel movement in my body that meant that my body was not in motion. Many of our most deeply held beliefs are rooted in presumptions that are hidden from us because we haven't taken the effort to untangle and examine them.

Of course, one reason we don't think critcally about such "common sense" things is that there can be a penalty for questioning them. Such longstanding ideas are usually ones that are widely held in our communities, or in our families, and as such are ideas that if challenged can distance us from those we hold dear. Commonly held ideas are the glue of every society and questioning them comes at a cost, not only for one's belonging to that society, but also for one's understanding of themselves.

Some ideas that are accepted for a large portion of our lives become a part of our identity. Beliefs are part of who we are and how we present ourselves to others. To truly be prepared to reason we have to also be prepared for the consequences of reasoning, for the possibility that what we believe or know can be false. To reason we must risk not only changing our minds, but also changing a piece of who we are.

Philosophers have grappled with this problem for thousands of years. In 1662 the French writer Antoine Arnauld wrote a treatise on thinking and made a very modern

Figure 1.1 The Thinker Statue at Bowling Green State University.

observation: "We judge of things, not by what they are in themselves, but by what they are in relation to us…" Arnauld recognized that it was quite natural for people to be reluctant to question their own ideas and opinions in favor of new ones, no matter how strong the evidence for one over the other, largely because doing so forced people to examine themselves, not just their beliefs. Others have noted that most of our reasoning is not really critical reasoning but is a process of constructing arguments that allow one to go on believing the things one already believes so one can continue being the person they were. So one of the first steps in reasoning critically is to find the courage to separate one's beliefs from one's sense of themselves.

Our beliefs do more than structure the ways we think, they also filter and shape how we perceive the world. Our patterns of thinking do more than simply influence our opinions of things, they filter and interpret our senses. A certain way of thinking is not just a way of thinking about the world, it is also a way of seeing the world. When we question ourselves, when we are skeptical, when we sever our investment in our own beliefs, we are suddenly open both to new ways of thinking and to different perceptions about the world.

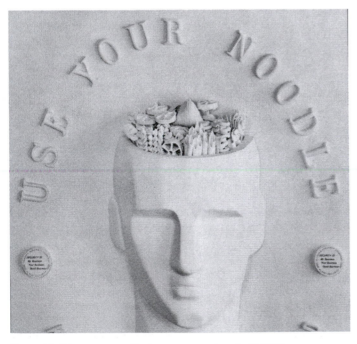

Figure I.2 "Use your noodle, keep security in mind," 1966.

Why White and Black?

The past century has witnessed a revolution in American attitudes about race. For the first 28 years of the twentieth century, the U.S. Congress was all white. Even when Oscar De Priest was elected to the House of Representatives from Chicago in 1928, the official Congressional restaurant refused to serve him and his staff. Prior to the 1960s many states enforced laws limiting where black people could live, socialize, work, go to school, participate in politics, or marry. For the most part it was customary to refuse to serve, employ, matriculate, rent, or contract with a person because of his or her race.

Since that time American attitudes have undergone a wholesale shift. In 1958 a national poll found that 94% of Americans disapproved of "marriage between white and colored people." Twenty years later that number had dropped to 54% though the number of people "unsure" of their attitude toward interracial marriage had climbed from 3 to 10 percent. As late as 1994 a minority of Americans (48%) approved of marriage between blacks and whites while 15% were uncertain. In our own times, while a large majority (82%) now approve of such unions there is a stubborn ten percent that continue to disapprove of interracial marriages and eight percent of people remain unsure whether they approve or not.

While there has been much progress since the 1950s, there remains a curious divergence of attitudes between white and black Americans. In the summer of 2013 the Pew Research Center phoned thousands of Americans and asked them whether they thought the average black person was "better off, worse off, or just about as well off" financially as the average white person. More than half of whites thought blacks were about as well off or better off than whites. Nearly three-quarters of whites thought blacks in their community were treated just as fairly as whites in the workplace, at school, in courthouses, in polling places, or in public accommodations like restaurants.

In contrast to the rosy outlook of most whites, the black people asked these same questions expressed different views. A large majority, 59%, thought the average black person was worse off than the average white person. Most blacks thought black people were treated less fairly on the job, in the courts, in elections, and in schools. More than a third reported having been personally discriminated against because of their race in the previous year.

How can we explain such dramatic differences in outlooks between white and black Americans? If, as most white people believe, race is no longer a powerful factor in American society, how can two groups, defined only by their race, have such opposite outlooks? Is it possible for two groups to experience the same world and view it so

Figure I.3 Black and white people in the District of Columbia, 1962.

collected about our society but such facts are almost always the results and effects of other forces and dynamics that remain invisible to the statistician. Such freely available facts as average life expectancy, high school drop-out rates, or the number of white and black Senators or CEO's tell us nothing by themselves about their causes and we are ultimately curious about which of these things are the results of racism.

Ironically, the very progress that has been made in racial civil rights has actually made it harder to investigate the nature and extent of racism in America. Before there were laws prohibiting racial discrimination and before most Americans disapproved of prejudice, racism was open and obvious. There was no denying its powerful influence in American society and its corrosive impact on the black community. But today, when most acts of discrimination are illegal and the vast majority of white Americans deny that their actions might be influenced by racial thinking it is more difficult to connect unequal outcomes to the racial attitudes or behaviors that might contribute to them. Opinion pollsters have long suspected that today their polls are becoming less dependable because most people, when asked about race or racism, respond with the color-blind answer they think they should say and not the one they really think.

In the end, no one approach or method can answer these questions. The study of race and racism is an interdisciplinary subject because no single discipline, not history, sociology, economics, political science, biology, or psychology can chart and connect the causes and effects of these problems. However, borrowing theories and methods from all of them does provide some insights.

What Should We Call Each Other?

We begin with the seemingly simplest of questions: what should we call each other? What is the appropriate term to use when describing a group of people by their race or ethnicity? Is it acceptable to call someone white or black? Or is it preferable to say caucasian and African American? If color words are acceptable for white and black people shouldn't they also be used for yellow and red folks? What about older terms of respect that were used in the past? Is it wrong to call someone colored, negro, or oriental? And what about people from south of the border? Are they Mexican, Latin American, Latino, Hispanic, Chicano? What is the difference? And what do we call all people who aren't white? Minorities? Non-whites? People of color?

So these are not so simple or easy questions after all. Just as your personal name is one of the most essential parts of your identity, the name by which you are grouped

differently? If not, is one group living in a dream world while the other has its feet set firmly in reality? Or is it possible that both groups' attitudes equally reflect a different truth about America? Like the old fable about the blind men encountering an elephant and one grabs a leg and says it is a tree, another touches an ear and says it is a fan, and a third holds the trunk and says it is a pipe, might white and black Americans see a different part of the whole? Another possibility is that black and white Americans don't just see different aspects of the same reality, maybe there are two Americas, one black and white and these two realities are largely separate.

Determining which of these possibilities is true is a complicated problem because it contains both of the classic problems of knowledge – what is the nature of reality (ontology) and how do people understand that reality (epistemology)? Some things that are the basis of people's opinions can be objectively measured such as the amount of money people make, or the proportion of different races attending college, being elected to office, or going to jail. But other things are difficult to count, such as the number of people denied jobs, promotions, grades, or services because of their race. Frustratingly, much data is routinely

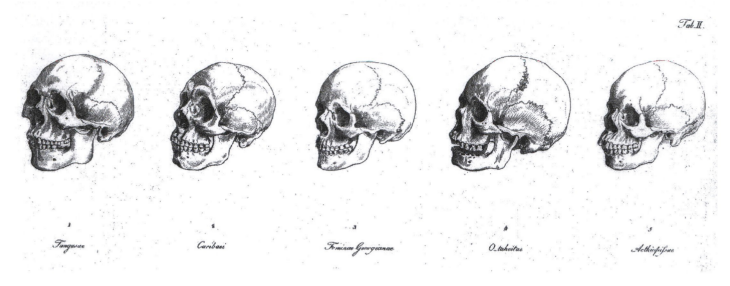

Figure I.4 Engraving of five skulls of different races, from J. Blumenbach, *De generis humani varietate nativa* (Gottingen: Vanderhoek, 1795).

together with other people in society is a powerful force for shaping how you see yourself and how you are viewed by others. There are two fundamental types of group names, those that groups have chosen for themselves and those that have been forced upon them. Throughout history those groups who have dominated other groups have forced names upon those they discriminated while enjoying the privilege of naming themselves as they wish. In America, oppressed groups have had to struggle for the right to be called by names of their own choosing.

White or Caucasian?

For their part the English colonists only rarely used the word "white" to describe themselves. Rather, they tended to describe themselves nationally or just as "Christians" and the concept that their society could be divided by these color words only gradually dawned on them towards the end of the 1600s when slavery and other forms of servitude were made more and more distinct. As slavery became increasingly a status reserved only for people of African ancestry and as the American colonies attracted people from a number of European nations, the idea of "white" as describing a group of people became more common. The word "white" had many positive ancient connotations, related to purity, cleanliness, piety, and honesty, that added to the words attraction. In calling themselves "white," Americans were not only distinguishing themselves from other groups in their society, they were claiming a higher social status for themselves.

However, it is important to note that even as late as the American Revolution and into the decades following, the term "white" did not encompass all the types of people it would come to have in its modern usage. Whiteness itself, as an idea, only first arose in the eighteenth century and then it mostly only encompassed people of northern and western (Protestant and Anglo-Saxon) Europe. Jews, most Catholics, and peoples from southern and eastern Europe were not considered fully "white" until later in the twentieth century.

Well into the nineteenth century, Irish immigrants were not considered "white" by many Americans (though they were in the eyes of the law). Following this pattern, many immigrants seized on the idea of being "white" upon landing in America as a means of claiming a kind of equality with Americans of older stock.

The fact is that the concept of a "white race" has changed substantially over time – excluding and including different groups and defining the characteristics of whiteness with marked variability across historical eras. The issue of Mexicans' "whiteness" under the federal law was not settled until 1897. Armenians weren't declared by the courts to be white until 1909 (*In re Halladjian*), which is especially ironic as the Caucasus mountains which runs through this area are what gave the word "caucasian" its name. Syrians were declared white in federal court in 1909 (*In re Najour*), then declared non-white in 1913 (*Ex parte Shahid*). Asian Indians were legally white in 1910 (*U.S. v. Balsara*) then not white in 1917 (*In re Sadar Bhagwab Singh*) and then white again in 1920 (*In re Thind*) only to darken again in 1923 (*U.S. v. Thind*). Of course, what this means is that whiteness is not some sort of organic heritage, passed down from ancient times, but a modern invention that over its lifespan has been continually reinvented to meet the needs of the nation's most powerful constituencies.

Because the word "white" has been so unstable, including and excluding different groups in different eras, scientists have attempted to devise a more precise term. In the 1700s the German biologist, Johann Blumenbach, collected hundreds of skulls from around the globe for the purpose of devising a classification scheme for human races. When Blumenbach found that his hoard of skulls failed to have any distinctive features by which they could be grouped, he decided to search for the skull that was most "beautiful" on the principle that it must represent the most perfect of all white persons (and therefore the ancestral birthplace of the white race). All other races would then be measured by their "degeneration" from that perfect specimen. The skull Blumenbach thought most beautiful originated from the Caucasus mountains, a region lying between Turkey, Russia, and Iran, between the Black and Caspian seas, hence the name, caucasian.

Though Blumenbach's methods were laughable as science, and his idea of the caucasian skull being beautiful was probably influenced by the historical fact that in the middle ages this area supplied a steady stream of captured men and women who were then sold in the slave markets of Constantinople, Genoa, and Venice. Caucasian women and girls were especially prized in this trade and stories of the enslavement of great beauties became staples of European lore, myth, and art. In fact, we know today that the very skull Blumenbach beheld as the pinnacle of white people actually belonged to an adolescent girl from the Caucasus country of Georgia who was kidnapped by Russian soldiers and died of venereal disease in Moscow.

The concept of a racial group called 'caucasians' was attacked at the turn of the twentieth century not because scholars felt it was inaccurate, but because they believed it obscured great racial differences between caucasians. The entry for "Spain" in the American Standard Dictionary of 1899 stated that the "inhabitants include four distinct races, viz., the Spaniards proper, the Basques, the Moriscoes, and the Gitanos." Early anthropologists argued that Europe was divided into different racial groups variously labelled as Nordics, Alpines, Teutons, Aryans, and Mediterraneans. While popular for a generation, terms such as 'Aryans' fell out of fashion when Nazi Germany embarked on its murderous campaign for world domination under its banner.

Despite having no scientific substance, 'caucasian' has persisted as a term white people employ when they wish to make the fuzzy category of 'white' seem more precise and grounded in nature. It remains commonly used in medical research in spite of its lack of scientific validity.

Hispanic or Latino/Latina?

The 53 million Americans who have some historical

Figure I.5 'Boardwalk benches with shade,' 1978, photo by John Margolies.

Figure I.6 Watching the children's parade at the Charro Days fiesta, Brownsville, Texas, 1942. Photo by Arthur Rothstein.

connection to Spain or Latin America only recently began to be called, and to call themselves, by a single term, either Hispanic or Latino. (As Latino refers to men it is often paired with Latina, the feminine form, as in Latino/a, to be more inclusive and universal. The plural form, Latinos, refers to both genders and is therefore used most frequently in this book.). Historically, most Americans who traced ancestry to a Spanish-speaking country, simply referred to themselves by that nationality. They were Puerto Ricans, Dominicans, Cubans, Mexicans, or one of a dozen other heritages. Most wished to simply be recognized as Americans though that simple designation was usually denied to them.

The term "Hispanic" was actually invented by the United States government in the 1970s. Prior to then, the census only counted "Mexicans" once, in 1930, and that year it was a category listed as a "race." In 1971 a national conference intended to work out some sort of broader advocacy plan that would unite Spanish-speaking communities broke up as Americans of Puerto Rican, Cuban, and Mexican heritages failed to find common ground. A census bureau official later complained, ""People didn't even know what Hispanic meant!"

Some scholars have alleged that the government initiative to create the concept of "Hispanic" was a reaction to the rise of the Chicano identity movement in the 1960s. They allege that "Hispanic" identity was engineered to downplay the particular issues and demands of Mexican-Americans (who were struggling for civil rights) and Puerto Ricans (who were raising issues of the colonial status of their homeland).

Chicano was a term meant to embrace and celebrate not only Spanish and Mexican heritage but also Indian ancestry and culture. Unlike the United States, populated by millions of voluntary or forced immigrants, a relatively few number of Europeans (only about 200,000) and a similar number of African slaves, sailed to Mexico by 1810. As a result most Mexican people today can trace native relatives in their family tree. As in the United States, discrimination against people of more pronounced Indian or African ancestry characterized Mexican society and only with the rise of civil rights and decolonization movements around the world in the 1950s did Mexican and Mexican-American activists begin campaigning for people to celebrate their Aztec and other indigenous heritages. Leaders of this movement reclaimed the word "Chicano," a term that had sometimes been used in a demeaning way, and turned it into a statement of ethnic pride. When labor leader César

Chávez organized farm workers in Texas and California with appeals to Chicano unity, the idea gained great popularity.

Though the term "Hispanic" obscures differences rather than describing shared heritages and experiences, the term did grow in popularity from the 1970s on. The government's definition of Hispanic included national groups, such as Brazilians (who speak Portuguese) and many indigenous people of Central America whose native tongue was not Spanish. Nevertheless, the grouping of such diverse people under one label has continued.

So-called Hispanic communities did face common problems of discrimination especially as a conservative turn in national politics increasingly viewed them as suspected "illegals" rather than as citizens. Organizations representing different Latin American communities began cooperating nationally to an unprecedented extent and found that their national political concerns were best addressed under an inclusive "Hispanic" label. This pan-ethnic movement, the creation of a super identity by combining diverse ethnic communities under one larger name, spread quickly. Today, the majority of people with Spanish or Latin American heritage prefer to be called Hispanics, though many also regularly use Latino/a or their ancestral nationality to describe themselves.

Oriental or Asian?

Just like the term "Hispanic" was invented to lump together many groups of people who had few things in common, the terms "Oriental" and "Asian" created a group that never actually existed in history. Lacking even the tie of common language, prior to the 1960s no Americans who could trace their ancestry to countries in "Asia" thought of themselves as "Asian." To them this idea was just about as descriptive as "Earthling." Rather, Americans who could trace their ancestry to Japan or China or Korea or the Philippines or dozens of other countries, identified with their national heritage. Indeed, for more than a century there was little cooperation and often outright hostility between Americans of Chinese, Japanese, Korean, and Filipino heritage.

The concept of "Asia" (or to use the outdated term, the "Orient") was created by Europeans as they conquered and ruled distant nations to their east. As their colonial possessions spread, European thinkers and artists attempted to understand these vast and diverse lands as sharing some essential qualities. Borrowing from the Latin word orientalis meaning 'sunrise,' educated Europeans imagined an Orient that justified their colonial rule and upheld their assumed racial superiority. These stereotypes erased cultural

Figure I.7 'Young man with Puerto Rican flag,' 1970. Photo by Frank Espada.

Figure 1.8 Wedding Photograph of Wong Lan Fong and Yee Shew Ning, Jan. 27, 1927.

differences and encouraged racism and discrimination against immigrants from these lands. "Oriental" as a name was more commonly used in association with these stereotypes and is now generally considered demeaning.

In America the family trees of many Chinese, Japanese, Korean, and Filipino Americans have deep roots, tracing several generations through American history. Indeed, until 1970 the majority of people called Asian American were born in America. Immigration reforms in the 1960s ended a century of discriminatory laws and policies that had severely limited the numbers people from Asia who were allowed to settle in the United States. As the population of Asian immigrants grew, so did a desire to be recognized as a pan-ethnic community.

Today the term Asian American includes upwards of forty-five different national heritages. Asian Americans have little in common: not language, religion, holidays, favorite foods or traditional dress. What most ties Asian Americans together is an experience common to many

generations of Americans throughout history—the immigrant experience. Today two out of three Asian Americans were born in another country. Many Asian Americans, whether foreign born, or of many American generations, have experienced being viewed suspiciously as an alien presence in American society. These shared experiences, more than shared heritage or culture, cement the identity of Asian Americans today.

Native American or Indian?

The name "Indian" was coined by Christopher Columbus who mistakenly thought he had sailed clear around the world and arrived in the Indies that Marco Polo had written about. Columbus wasn't primarily interested in which side of the world the people he called "Indios" were, only that they seemed well suited for slavery. They were, he wrote back to his Queen, "fit to be ordered about and made to work, plant, and do everything else that may be needed…"

Other European explorers called the peoples they encountered different things. French pioneers called them "sauvages" (savages). The first English settlers at Jamestown called the people who lived nearby "savages" or "infidels." But by the time of the American Revolution, the term Indian had been widely adopted by Americans.

Native peoples are the only ethnic group specifically mentioned in the United States Constitution (which even avoided mentioning the word slave, using the euphemism "persons bound to service" instead). The word "Indian" is used twice in the nation's founding document: once in describing the powers of Congress which shall have the right to "to regulate Commerce with foreign Nations, and among the several States, and with the Indian Tribes" and again in describing how people should be counted to determine the apportionment of representatives to Congress. "Indians not taxed," (meaning most all Indians at the time) were not to be counted when the government totaled up the number of Americans.

Some scholars have pointed out that by using the word "Indian" to refer to native peoples, a word that is a mistake, a confused reference to a far distant place, the people so described are separated from their own lands and their own histories. By being called "Indians" they become a people out of place and out of time and therefore easier to expel from their homelands.

The Census office did not count Indians until 1860 when it began including in its figures "civilized Indians" who were defined as Indians who owned land outside of Indian territories. That year, and for the next two censuses, Indian numbers were reduced by counting any person of mixed Indian and European ancestry who lived in a white community as white. Beginning in 1890 the government began publishing population figures on all Indians, but systematically undercounted native peoples by simply not assigning enough census-takers to do the job. In 1940, for example, there was only one census enumerator assigned to the entire Navajo nation, a land of over 25,000 square miles.

In 1978, the United States government developed uniform rules for how government agencies should classify people by race and these rules seemed to purposely diminish the number of people who could be counted as being Indians. An Indian was defined as "A person having origins in any of the original peoples of North America and who maintains cultural identification through tribal affiliation or community recognition." By including the term "North America" in this definition (and excluding Mexico from North America), many people with native ancestry in Latin America, such as Mayan people from Guatemala, were purposely rendered invisible.

Figure I.9 Gilbert Redsleeves of the White Mountain Apache

Moreover, under these definitions Indians were the only racial group defined not only by heritage but also by culture. Thus a black or white person could never cease being black or white simply because of their social associations, but an Indian could cease being an Indian if they were no longer actively affiliated with a native community. Such a definition gave ample opportunity for bureaucrats to reduce the count of Indians at their whim.

Of course, no one is simply an "Indian." Every native person is primarily linked to the heritage of a tribe or even several tribes. So a native person may refer to themselves as a Lakota or a Navajo or any of hundreds of other tribal affiliations, or they might refer to themselves as an "Indian," a "Native American," or more rarely a member of an indigenous community, depending on the context and who they may be speaking with.

From African to Colored to Negro to Black

For most of American history, whites refused to call black folks by the names they chose for themselves. People of African ancestry participated in the building of the first European settlements in the New World though they certainly weren't called by the names they used for themselves. Some of Christopher Columbus' crewmen with darker skin were called "Moors," meaning Spaniards of African ancestry. At least one of the pilgrims at Plymouth settlement in Massachusetts was a black man and was described in the town's records as the "blackamoor." When the first shipload of enslaved men from Africa arrived in Jamestown, Virginia, in 1619, they were described by colonist John Rolphe in his journal as "Negurs."

In the 1700s and early 1800s black people tried to get others to refer to them as "Africans" or even "African Americans." Free black people in Philadelphia named their first church the African Methodist Episcopal Church and the black community in Boston named its first church the African Baptist Church. New York City's black children attended the African Free School. The choice of the term "African" reflected both an attempt to reestablish a connection to a homeland that had been severed by slavery and a broad acceptance of all people, regardless of their tribal or national heritage, whose lives in America were overshadowed by slavery and racism.

But conditions swiftly changed as the nineteenth century progressed. In 1812, a number of leading American politicians, including Francis Scott Key, the author of the song that would be adopted as the national anthem a century later, founded the American Colonization Society, whose goal was to end racial tensions by sending all free black Americans to Africa. While a small number of black reformers cooperated in the Colonization Society's efforts and even voluntarily emigrated to the newly founded country of Liberia, most free black people viewed the organizations' goals as yet another dangerous threat to their rights and their communities, and they fought the very idea that any country but America was their true home. In order not to be misunderstood as supporting the racist efforts of the colonizationists, black people stopped using the term 'African' to refer to themselves and their communities and instead adopted the term "colored" or "people of color." For example, a congregation in Boston renamed their African Baptist Church the First Independent Church of the People of Color.

It is important to note that the term "colored" was adopted to combat the intensifying viciousness of white peoples' use of language. The ancient Latin word, "niger," meaning "black," had been in use for centuries without having the particularly hateful meanings that it latter carried. Moreover, it had long been used interchangeably with the word "negro" and both words had been spelled in various creative ways. But beginning in the early 1800s, the word nigger began to be used in the American North in an intentionally hurtful and demeaning way. It suddenly accumulated a uniquely heavy burden of new meanings, the common theme of which was that they were the opposite of the virtues and values Americans held. So loathsome and repulsive was this word, that even its cousin, 'negro,' was shunned by black people at first as well. For example, Robert Benjamin Lewis (who described himself as "A Colored Man") wrote in his 1844 book, *Light and Truth*, (which was published in Boston by the "Committee of Colored Gentlemen"):

> The word negro is considered insulting and is used as an epithet of contempt to the colored people. It has been long used by our common enemies in America. It is not only insulting but very improper for any one to make use of it. Our friends the friends of Christ would do well to consider this and never write or publish it again to the world. Let it be remembered that it is as wicked for a Christian to swear as to call a disciple of Christ a negro.

For the first half of the 1800s, 'negro' was used as the polite alternative to nigger mostly by white elites. Using the term 'negro' did not mean that upper class Whites were any less racist than other white Americans. Rather, wealthier whites preferred the softer term because it marked them as being above the white working poor who eagerly used the more viscous term to, in turn, distinguish themselves from black people who shared their neighborhoods and often their poverty.

During the 1800s, while generally using the term 'colored' (usually as an adjective not as a noun) black leaders continued to debate what names would be most effective in fighting the hardening racism they faced. Some leaders argued that the only word that should be used was 'American' because any other word could readily be twisted and made derogatory by whites. Others creatively came up with numerous alternatives including Afric-American, Anglo-African, and Aliened American.

After the Civil War the term 'negro' grew into more common use in the black community, especially among freed men and women whereas 'colored' retained its popularity among northern black folks. Part of the reason for this shift was a deep aspiration to break with a painful past and shape a new identity that struggled for equality without abandoning the unique heritage and experience of black people. The term negro was actively campaigned for as a new standard of address by notable black leaders such as Booker T. Washington.

Meanwhile, the term "colored" (as an adjective) remained acceptable as well. At the dawn of the Twentieth century, both 'colored' and 'negro' were names black folks used for themselves. When activists founded an organization dedicated to fighting racial discrimination in 1909, they named it the National Association for the Advancement of Colored People (NAACP) . At nearly the same time, the charismatic Harlem, New York, radical, Marcus Garvey organized the United Negro Improvement Association.

For much of the twentieth century, whites used different names for black people than black people used for themselves. Most whites could ignore black preferences and sensitivities because it was socially acceptable in white society to ridicule and scorn black folks. While adopting the term 'negro,' most newspapers, magazines, and book publishers refused to capitalize it. Worse, as 'negro' came into more common usage, the hurtful term nigger that had once been primarily the possession of poor whites spread upward through white society and became so common it was spoken by politicians in public speeches, used by companies to brand their products, and even worked into the titles of popular songs.

But white prejudice is not the whole story behind the different language whites used for blacks than blacks used for themselves. There was also a fundamental difference in the logic behind these terms. White people used words to describe black people in an attempt to describe them as sharing some fundamental qualities—in whites' view, black people were a group because they possessed physical features, behaviors, and ancestry that were different from their own. Black people, for their part, didn't think of themselves as group just because they supposedly shared something in their bodies or character (no one knew better than themselves that their communities included all types and sorts of people). Rather to black folks what defined them was not simply ancestrty or some presumed essential physical or behavorial qualities, but the experience of being oppressed, of being thought of as different and treated unequally. Ancestry, and the ways in which ancestry was marked in ones' body, were important parts of this identity, but not for themselves—too much time and distance seperated most black people from their roots in Africa. Ancestry and physical features were important mostly because they drew a line between those who were entitled to all the rights and protections of American society and those who were not.

So though black people insisted on being referred to as "negroes" or "colored people," Whites for much of the twentieth century called them "blacks," "coloreds," or worse. White officials often attempted an impossible scientific precision by giving different names to black folks

depending on the proportion of their white and black ancestors. Offspring of a mixed couple were "mulattoes," people who had one white grandparent were "quadroons" and those with one white great grandparent were "octaroons." These categories were used by census officials from 1890 to 1930.

Prior to the 1960s, black people generally considered the term "black" as being derogatory. Black was a term sometimes used within the African American community to describe low-class or ill-mannered people. Decent peo-

Figure I.10 Sculptor Selma Burke with her bust of Booker T. Washington.

ple did not wish to be called "black" preferring "negro", a term literally meaning the same thing but sufficiently distanced from "black" to connote respectability.

In 1966, Stokely Carmichael, a self-proclaimed "black" radical, successfully urged the adoption of "black" in place of "negro." He did so as a means of more sharply repudiating whiteness and the century-long program of cultural assimilation advocated by such mainstream civil rights organizations as the NAACP. The largely youthful movement embracing "black" invested this word with an autonomy, dignity, and pride that the older word "negro"

Figure 1.11 Rev. Jesse Jackson, 1983. Photo by Warren Leffler.

lost hyphens and described themselves as "German-Americans" or "Irish-Americans", a level field was opened upon which black folks could identify themselves in an equivalent way.

Seizing this moment in 1988, Jesse Jackson, a civil rights activist who had been Dr. Martin Luther King's trusted associate, and who was then seeking the Democratic party's nomination for president, declared that the nation's black leaders and organizations should adopt "African-American" as their preferred term of identity. Jackson's argument was persuasive:

> To be called African-Americans has cultural integrity...It puts us in our proper historical context. Every ethnic group in this country has a reference to some land base, some historical cultural base. African-Americans have hit that level of cultural maturity. There are Armenian-Americans and Jewish-Americans and Arab-Americans and Italian-Americans; and with a degree of accepted and reasonable pride, they connect their heritage to their mother country and where they are now.

African-Americans had begun to shift the focus of their identity from color to heritage.

Over the next few years, most major media outlets and official agencies adopted the term as their standard of address. In 2008 in the midst of Barack Obama's presidential campaign, fellow Democratic Senator Harry Reid proclaimed that Obama was going to win because he was "light-skinned" and had "no Negro dialect." Reid's comment provoked howls of criticism and calls for his resignation. By 2008 a term that had a generation before been considered polite and customary had become taboo.

In early 2013, the U.S. Census Bureau announced that it was dropping the term "negro" from all of its surveys and forms. Census forms had asked respondents whether they were "Black, African American, or Negro" and the federal census had used the term "negro" for official purposes for well over a hundred years, appearing for the first time in the census of 1900. Like most bureaucratic changes, this one had been in the works for years, first set in motion by complaints made over inclusion of the term in the 2010 census and the admission of the bureau's director that no research had ever been done on the feelings of the black community towards the word. It was clear that what held up the change was a fear among census experts that deleting the word "negro" would lead to undercounting the black population as older folks who grew up as "negro" would not respond the same way to "black" or "African American." Under increasing political pressure to remove

had once possessed but which had faded as the term gained currency and widespread use among whites. Though civil rights leaders were torn by this turn of events—many not being entirely comfortable with the term but recognizing its power and militancy—carried along by the intensity of social protest at the time the term gained rapidly, its victory complete by 1968 when James Brown recorded his hit single, "Say it Loud: I'm Black and I'm Proud!" Henry Louis Gates, Jr., today a renowned scholar, wrote on his admission essay to Yale, "My grandfather was colored, my father was a Negro and I am black."

As the passion and fervor of the Black Power movement of the 1960s diminished over the following decades, some activists felt the term's usefulness had passed and argued for new language that underscored the commonalities of blacks and whites rather than their supposed racial differences. During the 1970s many white folks, whose parents and grandparents had struggled to assimilate into mainstream culture by abandoning their immigrant languages and customs, rediscovered their ethnic heritage. Neighborhoods suddenly rebranded themselves as "Little Italy" or "Polish Village" and inaugurated annual ethnic festivals. As white Americans increasingly embraced long the term, the Census Bureau conducted tests to determine how changing labels would impact the numbers and discovered in 2012 that dropping "Negro" had "had no reduction in respondents reporting 'Black or African American.'" The researchers observed that "Across focus groups, which were conducted with many race and ethnic communities, participants felt the use of the term 'Negro' was offensive and outdated, and recommended that the term be removed from the questionnaires."

Looking across this history several things should be evident. First, that words, though seemingly fixed and permanent, actually shift in their meaning as society changes. Words do not "have" meaning in the sense that they contain meaning, they are only symbols upon which people project ideas. This is why they can change so quickly.

Secondly, because of this character of words, they can be a battleground between different social groups each pushing to impose their own ideas and agendas through the meanings of words. Words thus can have importance and power beyond mere language, beyond the ability to convey meaning. They can also be an instrument of power and control over people and can have real consequences in the world.

Figure 1.12 Palace Amusements, Asbury Park, New Jersey, 1978, photo by John Margolies.

The Name "Negro"
by W.E.B. Du Bois from *The Crisis* (March 1928): 96- 97.

South Bend, Ind.
DEAR SIR:

I am only a high school student in my Sophomore year, and have not the understanding of you college educated men. It seems to me that since The Crisis is the Official Organ of the National Association for the Advancement of Colored People which stand for equality for all Americans, why would it designate, and segregate us as "Negroes", and not as "Americans".

The most piercing thing that hurts me in this February Crisis, which forced me to write, was the notice that called the natives of Africa, "Negroes", instead of calling them "Africans", or "natives".

The word, 'Negro', or "nigger", is a white man's word to make us feel inferior. I hope to be a worker for my race, that is why I wrote this letter. I hope that by the time I become a man, that this word, "Negro", will be abolished.
ROLAND A. BARTON

MY dear Roland:

Do not at the outset of your career make the all too common error of mistaking names for things. Names are only conventional signs for identifying things. Things are the reality that counts. If a thing is despised, either because of ignorance or because it is despicable, you will not alter matters by changing its name. If men despise Negroes, they will not despise them less if Negroes are called "colored" or "Afro-Americans".

Moreover, you cannot change the name of a thing at will. Names are not merely matters of thought and reason; they are growths and habits. As long as the majority of men mean black or brown folk when they say "Negro", so long will Negro be the name of folk brown and black. And neither anger nor wailing nor tears can or will change the name until the name-habit changes.

But why seek to change the name? "Negro" is a fine word. Etymologically and phonetically it is much better and more logical than "African" or "colored" or any of the various hyphenated circumlocutions. Of course, it is not "historically" accurate. No name ever was historically accurate: neither "English," "French," "German,"

"White," "Jew," "Nordic" nor "Anglo-Saxon." They were all at first nicknames, misnomers, accidents, grown eventually to conventional habits and achieving accuracy because, and simply because, wide and continued usage rendered them accurate. In this sense "Negro" is quite as accurate, quite as old and quite as definite as any name of any great group of people.

Suppose now we could change the name. Suppose we arose tomorrow morning and lo! instead of being "Negroes", all the world called us "Cheiropolidi",—do

W.E.B. (William Edward Burghardt) Du Bois, May 1919. Photo by C.M. Battey.

you really think this would make a vast and momentous difference to you and to me? Would the Negro problem be suddenly and eternally settled? Would you be any less ashamed of being descended from a black man, or would your schoolmates feel any less superior to you? The feeling of inferiority is in you, not in any name. The name merely evokes what is already there.

Exorcise the hateful complex and no name can ever make you hang your head.

Or, on the other hand, suppose that we slip out of the whole thing by calling ourselves "Americans". But in that case, what word shall we use when we want to talk about those descendants of dark slaves who are largely excluded still from full American citizenship and from complete social privilege with white folk? Here is Something that we want to talk about; that we do talk about; that we Negroes could not live without talking about. In that case, we need a name for it, do we not? In order to talk logically and easily and be understood. If you do not believe in the necessity of such a name, watch the antics of a colored newspaper which has determined in a fit of New Year's Resolutions not to use the word "Negro!"

And then too, without the word that means Us, where are all those spiritual ideals, those inner bonds, those group ideals and forward strivings of this mighty army of 12 millions? Shall we abolish these with the abolition of a name? Do we want to abolish them? Of course we do not. They are our most precious heritage.

Historically, of course, your dislike of the word Negro is easily explained: "Negroes" among your grandfathers meant black folk; "Colored" people were mulattoes. The mulattoes hated and despised the blacks and were insulted if called "Negroes". But we are not insulted—not you and I. We are quite as proud of our black ancestors as of our white. And perhaps a little prouder. What hurts us is the mere rnemory that any man of Negro descent was ever so cowardly as to despise any part of his own blood.

Your real work, my dear young man, does not lie with names. It is not a matter of changing them, losing them, or forgetting them. Names are nothing but little guideposts along the Way. The Way would be there and just as hard and just as long if there were no guideposts, but not quite as easily followed! Your real work as a Negro lies in two directions: First, to let the world know what there is fine and genuine about the Negro race. And secondly, to see that there is nothing about that race which is worth contempt; your contempt, my contempt; or the contempt of the wide, wide world.

Get this then, Rowland, and get it straight even if it pierces your soul: a Negro by any other name would be just as black and just as white; just as ashamed of himself and just as shamed by others, as today. It is not the name—it's the Thing that counts. Come on, Kid, let's go get the Thing!

W.E.B. DU BOIS

Chapter One: Ethnicity and Race

Everyone, at some point, asks themselves the question, "who am I?" Some people try to answer this question by researching their genealogy and looking for their connection to the past, hoping to find the roots that will help them understand their "true" identity. Understanding one's family history can reveal events that shaped the circumstances a person was born into. But knowing the details of one's family history is often misunderstood as discovering some true belonging to a broader group.

For example, many groups today that celebrate their ethnic heritage are not actually recovering or preserving something that once existed and has since faded, but are creatively making identity. Those attending a German-American Oktoberfest, or a Norwegian Nordic festival, probably would be surprised to learn that most of the people from those lands who immigrated to the U.S. never thought of themselves as "German" or as "Norwegian" until after they arrived in America. In the case of "Germans," Germany until the 1870s was a patchwork of over a hundred independent kingdoms and semi-autonomous cities divided by religious and deep regional rivalries. Most "Germans" actually identified with these political divisions, not their common language. On the opposite extreme, Norwegians had a strong central state, but identified with their richly diverse local dialects that rooted them to their village and towns rather than to the nation. However, in America, one ceased being a Hessian or a Valdresian and simply became a German or a Norwegian. As cultural scholar Wilbur Zelinsky famously noted, most American ethnic groups are of very recent origins.

Ethnicity has grown in popularity and importance over the past century. There are two major reasons for this. One, is that some groups who fought against discrimination by claiming inclusion into a generalized whiteness, such as Jews and other marginalized European immigrants, successfully used the idea of ethnicity as a means of distancing themselves from being a race. In America, Jewish leaders, faced with a rising tide of anti-semitism in the first part of the twentieth century, responded by redefining themselves as an "ethnic group" not a "race."

Secondly, many people confronted with the confusion of the modern world—their wrenching transition from rural life to urban life; a mass media that seems to reduce everything to a prepackaged, mass-produced, uniformity; and a technologically-driven pace of change that seems to undermine everything with increasing speed—responded by imagining their own organic connection to something natural, simpler, and wholesome. By the late twentieth century, people began referring to "ethnicity" as a quality that some people had and others did not. But in reality, ethnicity was a way of claiming you were special just like everyone else. The idea of ethnicity traded in a fictitious shared experience; it was usually indicated by generic symbols of belonging that marked a mythical commonality that denied the actual distinctiveness of communities that had deep histories, shared common experiences, and remembered the pain of actual struggles. Ethnicity in the late twentieth century, for many who otherwise identified as white, was a part-time engagement with difference that could be worn and thrown aside as easily as any dress-up costume.

A number of genetics testing companies market their services by promising to help their customers discover their "true" identities. In one of these companies' television commercials, a middle-aged man, Kyle, wearing German lederhosen explains that "growing up we were German…" and he always thought of himself as German, but couldn't find any Germans in his family tree. So he took a genetics test "and big surprise, we're not German at all." Kyle suddenly reappears wearing a Scottish costume, explaining, "fifty-two percent of my DNA comes from Scotland and Ireland. So, I traded in my lederhosen for a kilt!"

The presumption in this commercial is that identity, in this case an ethnic identity, was something that Kyle possessed all along without knowing it. Lurking inside Kyle was his Scottishness just waiting to be discovered and released. His German identity, presumably, was false, a mistaken identity not a real one.

While Kyle sought out his own identity another case that captured national headlines in 2012 involved a woman who was comfortable in her identity but was publicly "exposed" for living a "lie." Rachel Dolezal was the president of the Spokane, Washington, chapter of the National Association for the Advancement of Colored People. She was by all accounts an effective organizer, leading the fight for greater police accountability and rising to chair the city's Police Commission. But in June of 2012, a local reporter published a story about how Dolezal was "really white":

> …her parents, Ruthanne and Larry Dolezal, who are both white and live in the Troy/Libby

Figure 1.1 Rachel Dolezal speaking at a Spokane rally, May 2015

area in Montana, told The Press their daughter is not African-American. They backed up the claim with a copy of their daughter's birth certificate and photos. The images show a younger, pale, blonde-haired, blue-eyed Dolezal who looks much different than the woman with caramel-colored skin now leading the Spokane NAACP and helping review claims of police misconduct in that city.

The overwhelming majority of Spokane's residents identify themselves as white and only 1.9% identify as black. Given these demographics, a majority of the NAACP's members in Spokane are white and the chapter has had white presidents in the past. The issue, therefore, was not that Dolezal was born of white parents, but that she "falsely" claimed to be African American. In other words, unlike Kyle, who is celebrated for choosing to switch his identity from German to Scottish, Dolezal is condemned for abandoning being white and choosing to be black.

Of course, one difference between German, Irish, or Scottish identity, and black identity, is that blackness is marked and visible on the body. Kyle had to wear either leather pants or a tartan kilt to indicate his identity, while for most people who are black their bodies are not a choice but a daily reminder of minority status. However, to be fair, Rachel Dolezal did what she could to mark her own body as "black." Through tanning, hairstyle, makeup, and clothing, Rachel Dolezal achieved an appearance that

"passed" as black. In other words, most people she met in the context of working with the NAACP, the Spokane police commission, or her teaching, presumed she was black. Dolezal voluntarily put herself in the position of being subject to the same sort of racial presumptions, and possibly slights, that most black people experience every day. In that sense, Dolezal, elected to experience what it was to be black in America, though she always had the option of crossing back across the color line and rejoining a white identity.

When Dolezal's story broke in her local newspaper, it was soon picked up by network media outlets and ignited a national flurry of condemnation. Several network nightly news episodes led with the story. Dolezal made headline news in most of America's major newspapers and social media was clogged with posts and angry comments about her. She soon resigned from her office with the NAACP and NAACP leaders made it clear that the issue was not Dolezal's identity—the NAACP welcomes members of all backgrounds and identities—but was the question of her misrepresentations impugning the integrity of the organization.

In 2017 Dolezal clarified her racial odyssey in an interview with CNN and indicated just how tricky and complicated this subject of identity is:

> If I would have had time to really, you know, discuss my identity, I probably would have described a more complex label, pan-African, pro-black, bisexual, mother, artist, activist, but I think the question, Are you African-American?—I haven't identified as African-American. I've identified as black. And black is a culture, a philosophy, a political and social view.

While offering more thoughtful reflections on what identity was, Dolezal ignited another controversy in the book she wrote on her experience. There she described herself as "transracial" and compared this identity to transgender people who make the change from one gender to another. "When it came to sexism, the way people are forced to adopt either a masculine or feminine identity... [was] one of the root problems. Allowing fluidity in gender identity...did not make sexism worse; instead, it improved understanding...Likewise, if people are permitted to adopt 'transracial,'...identities, racism will be weakened..." Scholars were quick to point out that sexual and gender alignments, while not necessarily corresponding to outward bodily form, are unlike race in that they are an expression of an inner orientation that is in-born. Race and ethnicity are literally skin-deep and whatever meanings they possess are attached there by history and culture.

These incidents highlight the way in which races are not natural, biological categories, (though physical bodies are part of the process of race-making) but are ideas, social practices, and even creations of language. To the extent that racial groups are "real" it is because people share historical experiences and because acting and thinking according to race in a society that has been structured by race helps make sense of reality. Most Americans think racially every day. They reflexively note a person's race when they meet them. They mention a person's race when describing them. Race helps most people make sense of their world.

In addition to these practices that create the sense of racial reality, race belief is also generated by the deeply personal process that molds one's own sense of self. Race appears as a natural, commonsensical thing to most people partly because it seems a part of who we are as individuals, it is one of the things that defines us and gives us as sense of belonging, a sense of who we are in the world. It is part of our identity, the way we understand ourselves and the way we are seen by others.

What is Race?

Before progressing any further, it is essential that we clarify some of the key terms of this field, such as the words "race," "ethnicity," and "racism," as they are often used in a way that leads to fuzzy and loose thinking.

"Race" is a word that refers to a particular categorization of humanity. There are an infinite number of ways that people could be grouped and differentiated. Nearly any way that humans differ can be the basis of a system of categorization: humans could be grouped by ancestry, by geographic region, by physical characteristics, by language, by cultural practices, surname or even by zodiac sign. For much of human history, most people viewed some form of family relationship (sometimes expanded to encompass all those native to a region) as the primary and most important way to differentiate humanity.

Sometime in the eighteenth century, European elites began to conceive of another—a category that was a rough combination of ancestry and physical attributes. Over the next two centuries most people in the western world came to believe that a category called "race" and divided into five or so "races" that roughly corresponded with a person's continent of origin, was of fundamental importance.

As we shall see, there is no natural basis for dividing humanity into five or six "races" (there are no greater differences between these five or six "races" and other ways of grouping humans—such as by language or ancestry group—and far less than the differences between extended families). Nevertheless, race as a primary category of differentiating and defining people has become an unavoidable

Figure 1.2 School children, Atlanta, GA, 2014, Photo by Amanda Mills.

part of modern life. It is built into the very fabric of modern society and has seeped deeply into the consciousness and perception of nearly everyone. Yet, it is important to remember that for the most part "race" exists not in nature but in our social structures, our minds, and our behaviors.

Of course it seems very strange to speak about race as being something "constructed", "invented", or "artificial" when it seems so obvious and real to us in our everyday lives. This feeling arises because of the way that our society can make any agreed upon idea seemingly real and natural by simply behaving as if it were. Race is just an idea that some superficial physical differences are important and meaningful, but after a long period of time of people in society behaving as if these differences are significant, these categories become built into the very structures and fabric of our world. The places people live, the way they are educated, the types of jobs they do, the customary ways we interact, and even the ways we view ourselves all become patterned and fixed according to the fiction of racial difference until the differences themselves are real while their source is not.

If race is not natural and biological, then what is it? Is it just an idea? Is it something learned or is it connected to something deeper, something in the way our minds work?

Or is it not in our minds at all but in the ways people interact according to social conventions and customs? If it is just an idea, why is it such a stubborn one? Can we ever escape it?

Race is, on one level, a system of belief. It is a system organized around the idea that humanity is divided into a handful of groups that differ in their behaviors and abilities. This idea is built upon another even more basic one, that membership in a particular group is readily apparent because of obvious physical features peculiar to each group. Race belief is usually also tied together with the idea that group membership is inherited, though the exact mechanism of inheritance need not be clear. Historically, most belief in race has located this mechanism in some sort of biological inheritance, ones "seed" or one's "blood." Modern science, while actually providing strong evidence against the reality of race, has also been easily adapted to it, as "genes" can take the place of "seeds" or "blood" in providing the obscure mechanism by which the supposed qualities of race are handed down from generation to generation.

What all racist ideas have in common is not prejudice, but the false belief that being a member of a particular racial group explains, determines, or predicts something about one's character. Historically, most of these ideas have in fact been prejudicial and demeaning, as the original function of the idea of races was to arrange privilege and power in society. Blackness was a convenient badge of slavery just as whiteness became a convenient badge of privilege once slavery ended. The most vicious forms of racism are those that express the idea that one race is superior or inferior to another, but racism does not need this sort of bigotry to exist. It flourishes anytime anyone attributes any quality or value, positive or negative or indifferent, to the artificial groupings we call "races."

But race belief is not purely an idea because it is a set of ideas that are attached to actual bodies, actual people. Another way of thinking about this is to begin with the body and then move to the idea. Along this line of thinking, race is the meanings or values people map onto particular bodily features. When people see race, they are just seeing parts of bodies that they "read" as meaning something else, something imagined to be significant. In other words, racial thinking treats human bodies as symbols, as signs, meaning other things.

Such widespread practices of associating bodily features and fundamental characters is most commonly dependent on two other false assumptions. First, most people conceive of races as distinct entities each having their own distinct characteristics. This line of thinking holds that the boundary between races might naturally grow fuzzy where people are a combination of two or more races but such "mixed" people are exceptions to the norm of "pure" races.

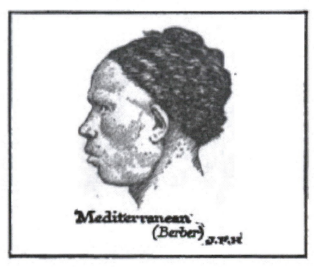

Figure 1.3 "Caucasian Types," H.G. Wells, *The Outline of History: Being a Plain History of Life and Mankind* (New York: Macmillan, 1921), p. 144.

Secondly, it is commonly believed that race characteristics (here think of all the usual stereotypes about a racial group) are passed down from parents to children organically. This second premise of the biological inheritance of racial character, technically known as hypodescent, is common but not actually required to believe in race; in modern times many people substitute some vague idea of "culture" in place of blood, seed, or genetics, as the transmission belt of race.

The idea that races are "pure" and people can be mixtures of them, like dog breeds, has been long encoded into the laws of America. Most states legally defined races in terms of specific proportions of "blood," usually one drop of African blood being sufficient to be classified as black. Some states, such as Louisiana, seeking even greater legal precision, went beyond this one-drop rule and specifically defined a black person as anyone having at least 1/32 African ancestry. As late as 1977, Louisiana employed two full time investigators whose job it was to track down inconsistencies in the race provided on birth certificates so as to ensure their "accuracy" against historical records.

Of course, all such systems of racial determination are equally mythological. Consider the question of a person whose father is one race and mother is considered a different race. It makes no greater sense to assign this person to either race, but in America this person would be considered "black." In Brazil and many parts of Africa, however, such a person would be considered "white."

The difficulty in attempting to make any system of racial assignment consistent is well illustrated by the struggles of the U.S. Census Bureau to count people by their race.

Race in the U.S. Census

The U.S. Constitution requires that the population be counted every ten years. The first census in 1790 was conducted by marshals who submitted their numbers on whatever ledgers or notebooks they had on hand. They were told only to note whether someone was free or slave, white or black, male or female, and over or under the age of 16. In 1820, census takers were ordered to count foreigners and were instructed to identify the class status of "heads of households" so as to distinguish between "that of a master, mistress, steward, overseer, or other principal person," but exactly how to distinguish between white and black was not spelled out. For the 1830 count, the federal government for the first time printed standardized forms for its enumerators to use.

Reflecting the increasingly mixed ancestry of Americans that was weakening the imagined natural boundaries of race (and especially of slavery), the census of 1850 added

Figure 1.4 Poster: "Have your answers ready..." 1917.

a new category, "mulatto," to those of "white" and "black." Administrators seemed worried that their underlings might not be careful to distinguish between these three labels, and underlined their instructions with a plea for diligence: "Under heading 6, entitled "Color," in all cases where the person is white, leave the space blank; in all cases where the person is black, insert the letter B; if mulatto, insert M. It is very desirable that these particulars be carefully regarded." (Enumerators in 1850 were also instructed to count the number of slaves who successfully ran away and the number voluntarily freed.)

Anxiety over the difficulties in determining race only built as time went on. In 1870, the census manual for the first time spelled out that its employees were to follow a one-drop rule of hypodescent in determining if someone was "mulatto" but implied that "black" was an unmixed ancestry. "Be particularly careful in reporting the class Mulatto. The word is here generic, and includes quadroons, octoroons, and all persons having any perceptible trace of African blood." Again reflecting the uncertainty of this attempt to neatly place every person into a racial category, the instructions to enumerators stressed the urgency of taking care in this work of racial distinction, saying, "Important scientific results depend upon the correct determination of this class."

The census generally didn't count native peoples until the later half of the nineteenth century, and when it did its instructions reflected the standard racist views of Indians as primitive people unable to assimilate into white society:

> Indians not in tribal relations, whether full-bloods or half-breeds, who are found mingled with the white population, residing in white families, engaged as servants or laborers, or living in huts or wigwams on the outskirts of towns or settlements are to be regarded as a part of the ordinary population of the country.

Note here how indigenous people can only live outside of white society, their only options being living with their own tribe or perhaps on the "outskirts of towns." Even when part of society, they were just "mingling" with whites. Even in their own homes native people were just "residing in white families."

Census racial categories expanded as governments began to more clearly and distinctly classify people by race near the turn of the twentieth century. As racial segregation was cemented into law, states attempted to draw clearer definitions of races, and because simple categories did not line up with reality, they simply invented more categories in an attempt to capture all the many exceptions to their rules. Pity the enumerators given these instructions in the 1890 census:

> Write white, black, mulatto, quadroon, octoroon, Chinese, Japanese, or Indian, according to the color or race of the person enumerated. Be particularly careful to distinguish between blacks, mulattoes, quadroons, and octoroons. The word "black" should be used to describe those persons who have three-fourths or more black blood; "mulatto," those persons who have from three-eighths to five-eighths black blood; "quadroon," those persons who have one-fourth black blood; and "octoroon," those persons who have one-eighth or any trace of black blood.

Such attempts at anthropological precision must have been a failure as the next census of 1900 collapsed the four racial categories related to African ancestry into one, telling its agents to just "Write..."B" for black (negro or negro descent)..." However, the government showed a greater interest in the ancestry of Indians, asking enumerators to "If the Indian has no white blood, write 0. If he or she has white blood, write 1/2, 1/4, 1/8, whichever fraction is nearest the truth."

Lumping all people into a general category of "negro descent" proved unsatisfactory. In 1910, the census brought back the category of "mulatto," but could not define it, saying only that black meant "all persons who are evidently fullblooded negroes," leaving mulatto to mean anyone who seemed to fall between white and black. Apparently even this simplified system was unworkable because the census added, for the first time, the category of "other," a designation "for all persons not falling within one of these classes..."

The census not only counts people, but identifies them in the sense that it imposes an identity, an association of socially-derived meanings, upon them through the categories it constructs. Take this description from 1910 that constructed native peoples as wavering between two possibilities of savagery and civilization: "If the Indian is living in a house of civilized designs, as a log, frame, brick, or stone house, write "Civ." (for civilized) in this column."

At the end of a decade when Congress passed numerous laws closing its borders to immigrants, the 1930 census defined a new category of Americans and of races, namely the "Mexican." This race was an odd construction in that it was partially defined by ancestry but that ancestry only counted for those "who were not definitely White, Negro, Indian, Chinese, or Japanese..." As if that wasn't confusing enough, ancestry only counted for one generation: "In order to obtain separate figures for Mexicans, it was decided that all persons born in Mexico, or having parents born in Mexico...would be returned as Mexicans (Mex)." Given such rules, in practice enumerators simply used their own biases to pick out who was a Mexican and who was not. The Mexican race vanished in 1940. That year the guidelines stated that "With regard to race...Mexicans were to be listed as White unless they were definitely Indian or some race other than White."

In spite of all the attempts to draw categories that sorted people according to the American system of races, government demographers by 1930 could find no consistent rules to use, resorting to drafting different systems for each race: "Any mixture of White and some other race was to be reported according to the race of the parent who was not White; mixtures of colored races were to be listed according to the father's race, except Negro-Indian..."

The American racial system defined whiteness as narrowly as possible by defining any discernible black ancestry as being black. What came to be known as the "one drop rule" operated by defining black as having any black ancestry no matter how slight. Courts were frequently confronted with the contradiction between a person's white skin and seemingly white appearance and their documented black ancestry. In such cases, American law came down

Figure 1.5 'U.S. Census taking--Wisconsin Indians, 1911.' Photographer unknown.

on the side of ancestry and dismissed claims of whiteness based on appearance alone. "Blood" was legally viewed as an objective fact in comparison with physical appearances which were considered subjective and therefore legally less solid.

In 1866, William Dean was arrested in Michigan and charged with voting illegally. Dean was jailed because local authorities considered him black and Michigan's constitution declared that only white people could lawfully vote. Michigan's Supreme Court observed that:

> If a man is not made white by a mere preponderance of white blood, then the question arises, where is the line to be drawn…we are compelled to discover some mode of classification, and that persons of precisely the same blood should be treated alike, although they differ in their complexions. There are white men as dark as mulattoes, and there are pure-blooded Albino Africans as white as the whitest Saxons. This classification is no doubt a difficult task…

The justices decided that anyone who had fewer than one black grandparent could be considered white.

There is one additional component of racial belief that has gone hand in hand with the concept of race itself since the invention of the idea, though it is not actually required for race belief to persist. This is the idea that races not only have different qualities and characteristics, but that these traits are unequal. Today any claim that some races are superior to others is quickly recognized and condemned as racist. And while this is patently true, it should be remembered that any belief in the existence of races, whether conceived as being equal or unequal in capacities, is also racist. Racism, at bottom, is the belief in races not in their relative merits. Just as a monarchist is someone who believes that kings and queens should rule society, not that certain kings and queens are naturally better than others, a racist is, in one sense, simply someone who believes in the importance and permanence of something called races.

What is Ethnicity?

Most people have difficulty explaining the difference between race and ethnicity. There are many reasons for this confusion. One important reason is that most people inaccurately connect race and culture. When asked to make a list of traits characteristic of any race, most people will list qualities that are not physical, but are beliefs, values or ways of life. Things like beliefs and behaviors are cultural, in other words they are learned or a product of a particular way society is organized, not something inherited like eye or skin color. When trying to understand what 'race' is we need to be sure and examine only those things that are truly physical and inherited through biology (and as we will see in the next chapter, biological facts discredit the idea of races as well.) All other characteristics lie in the world of society and culture and therefore fall under the label 'ethnicity' not 'race.'

"Ethnicity," is a term invented in the mid-twentieth century by academics who rejected the idea of natural races but needed a word to differentiate the complicated combination of ancestry, language, and culture by which many people define themselves. Unlike "race", the term "ethnicity" does not rest upon supposedly natural and physical differences though it may sometimes include them among many other elements that make up an ethnicity. Notice that "ethnicity" is a way of defining groups that is much more open to alteration, adaptation, and change than racial categories which are usually and falsely thought to be permanent and stable.

At the time the term "ethnicity" was coined, the concept of race was under considerable scientific attack. This attack was first launched by black scholars a century before but only accepted in the White scientific community when anthropologists led by Franz Boas and his students in the early 1900s began to reveal its gaps and contradictions. With the rise of Nazism in German in the 1930s, which made racial science a centerpiece of its dictatorial and murderous regime, the idea of race was further tarnished and scholars worked to find a new concept that would not only be a replacement for the old term but one that could better distinguish between things that were natural and biological and those that were artificial, invented by people.

For most of American history, educated people believed that race, nationality, and culture were all the same thing. They viewed nations as being collections of races and saw both race and nation as fundamentally determining a person's character, values, outlook, and abilities. For example, in the 1750s, Benjamin Franklin spoke out against the increasing numbers of Germans (who he referred to as "Palatine Boors") immigrating to Pennsylvania:

Figure 1.6 St. Patrick's Day Girl, photo by Benjamin Miller.

...why should the Palatine Boors be suffered to swarm into our settlements, and by herding together establish their languages and manners to the exclusion of ours? Why should Pennsylvania, founded by the English, become a colony of Aliens, who will shortly be so numerous as to Germanize us instead of our Anglifying them, and will never adopt our language or customs, any more than they can acquire our complexion?

By the beginning of the twentieth century, social scientists used the word "race" to refer both to large continental groupings of people but also to nations, frequently writing of the English, French, or Russian races. In 1910, the U.S. Immigration Service included 39 "races or peoples" in their year-end report, including "Polish, Hebrew, North Italian, Slovak, Greek, Irish" and so on. By using the word race interchangeably with "stock," "nation," and "people," these scientists implied that most of the things that we would today refer to as elements of culture—language, customs, traditions, values, foodways, myths, taboos—were natural expressions of heritage, even biological. For example, a Senate report on immigration in 1911 observed:

> The most interesting fact in immigration is the sudden and recent change in the character of immigration. While up to 1880 it was almost entirely from Europe or in other words composed of races or peoples which now constitute the older American stock, immigration comes mainly at the present time from southern and southeastern Europe; that is, chiefly from Italian, Hebrew, and Slavic stocks that differ widely from the American in language, character, and political institutions.

In 1941, the term "ethnicity" was used for the first time in a scholarly article. The word "ethnic," borrowed from the Greek ethnos that meant "people," had been floating about for a few decades but it was only then that the word was used in the sense of describing the quality of being a people.

The word soon caught on, especially as Americans had come to fancy themselves a nation of immigrants, a vast "melting pot" of different peoples. It seemed a wonderfully democratic term; after all, did not everyone come from somewhere and therefore have an "ethnicity"? Soon ethnicity was used not only to describe groups that shared heritage, customs, and traditions, but also groups that rediscovered these things after having lost or abandoned them. This was one of the advantages of "ethnicity": unlike "race" the term did not require a natural, organic connection to an ancestral homeland. More importantly, ethnicity was an idea that separated culture from the physical characteristics of ancestry.

While ethnicity grew into common scholarly usage, the idea of races did not go away. Rather than being discarded, the concept of 'race' was viewed with ever greater scientific sophistication as it became clear that races were not fixed through time and their boundaries shifted with changing social arrangements. At the same time the idea of ethnicity expanded to include many types of culturally distinct groups, even those whose ties seemed more imagined and invented than based in real historical experience. In other words, both terms became less and less specific over time and as they did the question loomed: what was the difference between race and ethnicity?

Some scholars argued that ethnicity was the primary term and racial groups should be viewed as just one expression of ethnicity. Others have pointed out that this neat arrangement carries the danger of equating the experience of being a member of a racial group with that of being a member of any other ethnic group. They point out that in America, black people have been considered a separate and distinct group whether or not they have adopted the norms and cultural values of the larger society, whereas ethnic groups readily lose their separate (and often subordinate) status when they assimilate to the culture of the majority.

Pierre L. van den Berghe, a sociologist studying the differences between racial practices in the United States and in South Africa in the 1960s, proposed a clever solution to this problem. Ethnic groups, van den Berghe observed, were groups that were socially constructed on the basis of their culture, on their imagined links to an ancestral past. (Think of how 'everyone' gets to be 'Irish' on St. Patrick's day.) Racial groups were different because they were groups socially constructed on the basis of some physical difference.

It is important here to pause and consider that races didn't exist before cultures invented them. As we will see, a race is just a set of rules for lumping people together into a group or excluding people from a group. Such rules do not arise from nature. The bodily features used as the basis for these rules may not be ones that are obvious (Jews were once believed by many Europeans to be a race distinguishable by the slope of their noses) or consistent (many people categorized as black in America are actually lighter skinned than many people categorized as white). So while these racial rules may be based on people's bodies, because bodies don't actually vary the way these rules demand that they do, all such rules are ultimately arbitrary and fall apart at their boundaries.

While seemingly clear-cut, van den Berghe's distinction gets a little fuzzy when you ask the question, how much of a physical difference does it take to be a race rather than an ethnicity? There are two elements in van den Berghe's equation: a distinctive physical feature and the "social construction" of a group on the basis of that difference. But the process of social construction involves not only seeing a difference but shaping how and what to see.

Psychologists have long proven that much of our perceptions are socially defined—our senses are shaped and trained by our culture and we learn certain habits of mind that determine the way we experience the world. As we sense the world, as we see it, hear it, smell it, taste it, we not only feel these sensations, but we immediately decide what they mean, how significant they are, and how they relate to each other. These decisions, many of them unconscious to us in our everyday lives, are molded by our upbringing in a certain society. So people from different societies may perceive a sound differently, one finding it pleasing, the other annoying, which is why certain tonal scales are more popular in one culture than another.

So saying the difference between ethnicity and race is

Figure 1.7 'Bavarian Manor...', 1977. Photo by John Margolies.

that ethnicity is socially constructed on the basis of cultural elements and racial difference is socially constructed on the basis of bodily features is really saying the same thing if "socially constructed" includes the senses. Something is socially constructed or socially defined when people customarily view something the same way and associate that thing with certain meanings and values. Saying that something is "socially constructed" on the basis of a physical characteristic doesn't make that physical characteristic consistent, distinctive, or important. It only makes it commonly perceived and understood a certain way. In the Middle Ages people believed in (and believed they saw) fairies, witches, trolls, and magic, all of which were "socially defined" things.

Moreover, socially defined ideas can be built on things thought to be physical and real but in reality just aren't actually there the way they are thought to be. Witches were thought to be identifiable by their worts and their inability to float. Some women had these features, though that didn't make them witches. Nor did it make them one group with all other people who had pimples and sunk in ponds. So saying race is "socially defined" on the basis of physical appearance is essentially the same thing as just saying "socially defined." This gets us nowhere, unless we like chasing our tails.

While it is tempting to just discard the idea of race altogether and call everything an ethnic phenomenon, doing so would only ignore the unique things about being a member of a racial group that we need a word for so we can understand them. Among the most important of these is that the purpose of defining people into races has been to restrict the rights, power, and opportunities different groups have access to. While this can also happen on the basis of ethnicity, generally when it does societies also invent a way of thinking about that ethnic difference as physical, thereby giving it this same racial quality. So one major difference between race and ethnicity is that race has been not only a system for sorting people into groups but a system for distributing rights and power.

Because for much of American history race has been connected to social status and social opportunities, it has also been imposed upon people rather than chosen by them. Ethnicity, because it is defined more by behaviors and distinctive tastes—languages, accents, foodways, fashion—is something people can choose to adopt or discard. Immigrants may be marked as being different by their customs but over time may choose to adopt the ways of the larger culture, to assimilate, and thereby lose their ethnicity (or more commonly, to set it aside, choosing only to display it during ethnic festivals or holidays). However, people are generally not given the choice of being viewed as a member of a racial group. In America race has been legally defined and membership enforced with the full force of the government. Because of this, the experience of being a member of racial group, especially one that has been denied rights and opportunities on the basis of that membership, is profoundly different from the experience of being ethnic.

So while we can't draw a neat line between the definition of race and ethnicity, we can summarize a few differences that can help distinguish between them:

1. Race is a special aspect of ethnicity, not a completely different social practice or conception. Like all other types of ethnicity, it is invented by a process where society decides certain perceived differences are important and attributes meanings to them.

2. Unlike other forms of ethnicity, races are defined not only according to cultural differences, but by physical ones. Because of the ways that our perceptions are socially influenced, the physical differences that determine racial membership need not be significant, consistent, or even real.

3. Racial categories, much more than ethnic ones, have commonly been used to distribute important social and political benefits like political rights and economic opportunities.

4. While many people have had the choice of their ethnic membership (at least in terms of embracing and expressing their heritage or not), few have had the right to choose which racial group they belong to. Ethnicity is unlike race because it is largely voluntarily embraced or discarded.

The Invention of Races

Races are a modern invention. The idea that humanity was divided into races that corresponded to colors and continents is only a few hundred years old at most. The word "race" was first printed in the English language in a poem published in 1508. For the next two centuries the word was used to refer to categories of both things and people. Only about the time of the American Revolution did the word begin to take on its modern connotation of meaning a distinct group of humans fundamentally different from other humans by means of their heredity.

It is important to consider that racism is not one idea but a complex of several separate and interlocking ideas. One of the reasons that racism took so long to develop, not appearing until relatively modern times, is that it requires each of these components to exist.

First, racism depends on the categorization of people by physical differences. This is the simplest element of racism and something that was evident to travelers and residents of great imperial capitals in very ancient times. But the observation of physical difference goes nowhere without also understanding a second idea, that these physical differences are ancestral, shared, and inheritable. It wasn't until the fifteenth century that some Europeans began describing racial differences as being "in the blood" or being a matter of ancestry.

Racism most heavily rests on a third element, the belief that physical differences are indicators of deeper and more meaningful differences of character, temperament, and behavior. Race could only became racism when it was linked with culture in this way.

A final component built on this concept that physical differences revealed more profound distinctions between people but went beyond it. The capstone of racist thinking was the idea that races were not equal and that some were naturally superior to others. In order for racism to arise all these component ideas had to be invented and to combine together. This took hundreds of years and their combination was only finally accomplished in the crucible of modern slavery.

Just as racism is not one idea but several interrelated ones, racism as a practice consists of several elements. Racism begins as an idea, a theory of the pattern of human differences. This concept can be sophisticated, like the pseudo-scientific explanations of nineteenth century thinkers, or it can be crude prejudice. Racism is also actions and behavior. Once individuals, or even an entire society, begin to behave according to racist ideas, racism becomes a force that impacts the lives of both those targeted by racism and those acting upon it. Finally, if racist behaviors persist over time they can become embedded in the very structures of society. At this stage racism can be expressed by society's institutions, especially through law and property ownership, in ways that go beyond any individual's beliefs or attitudes.

Ideas of Difference in the Ancient World

The ancient Mediterranean world, extending from the African lands of Kush through Egypt and on to Persia in the east and Greece to the north, was a vast crossroads of humanity. Ancients seem to have noted differences in skin color, facial features, and hair textures among different peoples, but did not seem to attribute any particular meanings to these differences. Ancient artists frequently portrayed people with all sorts of different physical features on the mosaics, sculptures, vases and monuments that have survived the eons to the present. Among these there seem to be no patterns of disparagement or caricature, Nubians and Ethiopians are depicted in ways similar to figures from other groups. Ancient texts don't describe those peoples with darker skin as particularly more savage or primitive than any others.

More significantly, color was not used to determine status in the ancient world. Though ancient writers might observe that someone was an "Aethiop" (a term used generally for dark-skinned Africans) they didn't express surprise that they might be highly positioned in society, even the ruler of a great empire like Egypt. Likewise, slavery in the ancient world was color-blind. Slaves were captured and sold out of southeastern European lands more often than they were from nations up the Nile river in Africa. (This is how the modern word "slave" and the ethnic category "slav" arose from the same ancient root.) While color, like other features of body or dress or custom were noted in the ancient world, there is no evidence the ancients had any concept of color as a primary division of humanity, or practiced color prejudice.

Additionally, premodern peoples believed they lived in a world filled with a great variety of human forms. By the time of the Middle Ages in Europe, travel writers filled their accounts with many descriptions of the "savages" that populated the wilds in every direction. A bishop, Adam of Bremen, published an account of his travels to the area of the eastern Baltic sea in the 11th century and wrote of the Amazons who conceive by sipping water and give birth to boys who grow heads out of their chests and ferocious girls. Three hundred years later Sir John Mandeville published his travelogue of journeys to the east which included his detailed description of giant cyclops and men without heads who had an eye on one shoulder and a horseshoe-shaped mouth on the other.

Such medieval monster lore, much of it rediscovered in ancient Greek texts, also often described various types of 'wild men,' hairy beings who seemed to exist midway between beast and man. Wild men were men in appearance (except for the hair covering their entire bodies) but animals in habit and mind. A belief in such wild extremes of humanity, or near-humanity, led these early societies to not put read too much meaning into the ordinary differences of peoples from distant lands.

This is not to say the ancient world was a world of tolerance, quite the opposite. The ancients clearly believed that different nations had fundamentally different

Figure 1.8 *A Moorish Couple on Their Terrace* by Eugène Delacroix, 1832. Metropolitan Museum of Art, New York City.

qualities and Greek and Roman writers were not slow to proclaim theirs superior to all others. However, the Roman empire, built on taxes and tribute rather than missionary zeal, allowed a variety of religious ideas and Gods to be worshiped by its subjects, punctuated at times by horrific outbursts of official persecution. But the adoption of Christianity by Roman emperor Constantine I in 312 CE and the proclamation of Theodosius I making it the empire's sole religion sixty-eight years later, laid the basis for a sharp division of society into the faithful and the heathen.

Upon the consolidation and spread of Christianity, Judaism came under increasing attack. But unlike the religious persecutions of old that were mostly the result of power politics, attacks on Jews seemed to be more about Christian identity than about Jewish power. Early church thinkers emphasized doctrines of "supersession" (that Judaism was obsolete once Jesus was born) and "deicide" (that Jews bear responsibility for the murder of God as Jesus). However, unlike pagan religions that were totally eradicated, the early church permitted Jewish communities to continue—both because of the reliance of Christianity on Jewish traditions, but because the existence of Judaism provided a mirror by which Christians came to know and define themselves. Christians could believe they were a universal faith because they pictured Jewish society as closed and insular. Christians believed their faith was grounded on the spirit and the heavenly kingdom while viewing Jews as more concerned with the debased matters of the physical world.

Christianity washed itself of many of the slanders it suffered in its early years by projecting them onto Judaism. When Christianity began, most all other religions conducted their rituals in great public displays. Because Christians held their services in subdued privacy, they were accused by their neighbors of engaging in human sacrifice and ritual cannibalism. In the middle ages, Christians hurled the same slander against Jews, accusing them of satanic blood sacrifices of kidnapped children.

More significantly, Jews came to be seen popularly not just as a particular faith, but as a particular type of people. This occurred slowly, step by step, as the rights of Jews were restricted and Jewish communities increasingly walled off from Christian ones. Periodic attacks on Jewish communities occurred throughout Europe, especially during the Crusades as Christian armies, fired with evangelical fury, slaughtered the Jews they encountered on their march to Jerusalem.

Though many of the ingredients of racial thinking could be found throughout Europe, the full stew of ideas that became racism first mixed together in the lands that became Spain. The Spanish peninsula was the most religiously and culturally diverse region of Europe. By the Fourteenth century large Jewish communities had flourished there for 1500 years. Spain was a land of successions of invasions: Muslims had settled there since the Moorish invasion of 711 conquered the descendents of Romans who had invaded from the east five hundred years earlier taking lands from the Celts who had invaded from the north some 900 years before. Renewed warfare between Christians, Muslims, and Jews in Spain 1211 prompted the Pope to issue proclamations further restricting the rights of Jews throughout Europe. Jews were prohibited from holding public offices and, most importantly, Jews were required to wear certain types of hats and bonnets so they could be readily identified—an idea borrowed from the ruler of Muslim parts of Spain, Abu-Yussuff Almansur, who a few years earlier ordered Jews who converted to Islam to wear outlandish outfits.

Such rules publicly separating, restricting, and degrading Jews created the conditions under which Jews could be scapegoated for any problem the Christian community faced. When the greatest calamity Europe ever faced, the pandemic known as the "Black Death" broke out in the 1340s, it was blamed on Jews who Christians believed had poisoned their drinking wells. Jews across Europe were massacred and many Jewish communities were completely wiped out. The killings grew to such levels that in 1348 Pope Clement IV was compelled to issue orders prohibiting extrajudicial killing, forced baptisms, or property seizures of Jews.

The same year Columbus sailed westward to find a quicker route to the riches of the Indies, Grenada, the last Moorish (Muslim) stronghold in Spain, fell to Christian armies. Consolidation of Christian power over all of Spain prompted first the mass banishment of Jews who refused to convert, then the mass expulsion of all Muslims. Estimates are that some 300,000 Jews and a million Muslims were expelled from Spain and their property seized by the crown. Forced conversion of the remainder did not allay Christian fears that Jews continued to practice their faith in secret, prompting royal and church authorities to create a bureaucratic apparatus of investigation, the Inquisition, to root out false converts. Over the next three centuries over thirty thousand "conversos" were burned at the stake.

At first the usual techniques of torture and forced confessions were used to uncover false Christians, but eventually even these were deemed ineffective. It was at this point that one of the key ideas of race was invented and made policy—that racial characteristics resided in bodies and were inherited from generation to generation. Spanish rulers resorted to maintaining elaborate genealogies to certify true Christians and mark those with "Jewish blood." By locating race in blood and heredity, here was the first expression of true modern racism in European history.

Figure 1.9 Didacus Valades, *Rhetorica Christiana*, 1579.

The Great Chain of Being

On the eve of the Europe's era of exploration and conquest of the New World, the idea of races of humans did not yet exist. There was a kernel of this word's modern meaning in its use when referring to the nobility of kings and queens. Nobles claimed their right to rule by birth, by their family history. A noble family was entitled to its high offices by virtue of its royal blood, what was often referred to as its 'noble race.' But the word applied only to aristocrats and there were no other races.

However, this idea of a race of nobles did mesh with another ancient conception that later would lend force to the racist belief that distant peoples were not only essentially different, but also unequal in their abilities and character. This idea was known as the "Great Chain of Being," and originated in Greek philosophy but was imported into Christian theorizing about the nature of creation by Augustine.

God's creation, it was said, was both perfect in its continuity and plentiful in its variety, meaning that though God created a vast number of different living things all connected to him like links in a chain rising from the worms in the mud right up into angels in heaven. Each living thing occupied its link—a little lower on the scale of nature than the thing above it, a little higher than that below it. Common humans occupied a place on the chain just below the nobles but above the apes and other beasts. This deeply ingrained and religiously sanctioned doctrine predisposed Europeans to conceive of the world in terms of hierarchies, in terms of things being naturally higher or lower, superior and inferior to others; an idea that proved dangerous later when races were invented.

The Curse of Ham

Before the first naturalists began to apply scientific methods to the study of living things during the Enlightenment of the 17th and 18th centuries, another religious idea was seized upon to explain the different appearances of humans. In the biblical book of Genesis there is a story that explains the origins of different peoples in the world. After God flooded the world, sparing only Noah and his family and the animals brought on the ark, Noah had occasion to consume too much wine and pass out in his tent. His son Ham discovered him lying there naked and did nothing but tell his brothers, Shem and Japheth, who then went and covered their father up without looking upon him. When Noah awoke he cursed Ham's son, Canaan, who he said would be a "servant of servants" to his uncles.

The Bible story of Ham and Noah did not mention anything about color or other bodily features that would have marked Canaan and his offspring as servants. Being a tale wrapped in mysteries (Why was Noah so upset that his son Canaan had seen him naked? Why did Noah curse Ham's son Canaan rather than Ham himself? What did mean by cursing Canaan and his children to be the "lowest of slaves"?) this story proved endlessly adaptable to those who sought justification for their social practices in the Bible. Early church commentators pointed to it as justifying slavery, at a time when slavery was not racial but included people from any nationality and ancestry. By the Middle Ages, aristocrats used the story of Ham as sanction for the system of serfdom. In the late 1500s when Protestants and Catholics tightened their grip on their adherents, the story of Ham became a fable teaching discipline, self-control, and the importance of children being subservient to their parents. Only in the early 1600s, when trans-Atlantic slavery began to spread, did this Bible passage come to be used as an explanation for the different appearances of Africans and Europeans.

Early Christian thinkers, like Saint Augustine, did not read the story of Noah and Ham as explaining racial origins because the idea of race hadn't yet formed. Rather, early theologians thought of Ham's Curse as a story about faithfulness and fidelity. Later commentaries on the Bible interpreted the curse on Ham to be a curse on all his descendents and only much later did some go as so far as to associate this curse with blackness and exile to the lands of Africa.

George Best, an explorer who voyaged with Martin Frobisher to what is today Canada in search of the fabled northwest passage to China, included such a Biblical interpretation of race in his account of these expeditions published in 1578. Having visited many lands and seen the different complexions of men and women, Best speculated on what caused such variety. First he wondered if climate or sunshine could be the cause but dismissed these factors because black people didn't whiten after living for a time in England. The true cause, Best concluded, must be the will of God as revealed in the Bible:

> ...there is some other cause then the Climate or the Sonnes perpendicular reflexion, that should cause the Ethiopians great blacknesse. And the most probable cause to my judgement is, that this blackenesse proceedeth of some naturall infection of the first inhabitants of that Countrey, and so all the whole progenie of them descended, are still polluted with the same blot of infection. Therefore it shall not bee farre from our purpose, to examine the first originall of these blacke men, and howe by a lineall discent they haue hitherto continued thus blacke.
>
> It manifestly and plainely appeareth by Holy Scripture...the wicked Spirite is such, that as hee ...finding at this flood none but a father and three sonnes liuing, hee so caused one of them to transgresse and disobey his fathers commaundement, that after him all his posterity shoulde bee accursed...for contempt of Almightie God, and disobedience of parents, God would a sonne should bee borne...who not onely it selfe, but all his posteritie after him should bee so blacke and lothsome, that it might remaine a spectacle of disobedience to all the worlde. And of this blacke and cursed... came all these blacke Moores which are in Africa...

Such early attempts to divide humanity by color and divine law were not common until after England had firmly established its overseas empire and embraced the slave trade to expand it.

Slavery and the Idea of Races

One of the most common mistakes people make in thinking about where race comes from is to assume that racial differences come first and then the systems that have exploited them followed. Many people believe that in America blacks were enslaved because slavery depended upon easily identifying who was a slave and who was not. In fact, the opposite is true. It wasn't that Africans were enslaved because they were black, but rather that slavery created the idea of "blacks."

There was no clear perception of one people being "black" or "white" before modern slavery. This wasn't because ancient people lacked prejudices but because they tended to view all differences of language, culture, and custom as fundamental. Differences of skin color were regarded as no more significant than the fact that some groups were tall, or dressed in a certain costume, or braided their beards. Because only elites routinely bathed and working people spent most of their time working outdoors, the poor tended to be darker in appearance than the rich. The eighteenth century scientist Johann Blumenbach noted the differences in skin color between elites and commoners in his own society. "The face of the working man or the artisan, exposed to the force of the sun and the weather, differs as much as the cheeks of a delicate [white] female, as the man himself from does from the dark American, and he again from the Ethiopian."

Slavery was not built on race because for thousands of years slavery was practiced among people who would one day believe they were all the same "race." Up to the middle ages in Europe slavery was widely practiced among Europeans. Vikings made slaves of Saxons, Romans made slaves of Britons, Saxons in turn made slaves of Celts, and numerous peoples of Western Europe enslaved people from the Balkans whose collective name "Slav" gave English its word for slave. Undoubtedly people who threw others into chains looked upon them as different, as "other", as "savage" or "uncivilized." Slavery in Europe flourished for a thousand years by chaining people with different languages and customs without any need for skin color. The census of the English realm compiled in 1086 counted nearly one in ten Englishmen as being slaves.

Even as outright slavery later became rare in England, a large part of the population labored in a form of bondage. The Statute of Laborers codified in 1351 bound most workers and laborers to their employers and criminalized unemployment. Until emancipated by Parliament in 1775 coal miners in Scotland were not free to leave their mines and were sold as assets of the mining companies.

Under Islamic law Muslims could not be enslaved. In Muslim societies slavery was not racial, not marked by color or presumptions of physical differences, until the Sultan of Morocco decided to draft all dark-skinned people into his slave army in 1699, an act that provoked courageous protests from Islamic scholars and a formal clerical denunciation, a fatwa, against him.

It is not a coincidence that the great flowering of learning and thought called the Enlightenment and the spread of racial slavery happened at the same time. Europeans were blind to the impact of racial slavery and the contributions of those stolen from Africa on their own achievements. Many of the modern ways of thinking—of conceiving of rights as natural, governments as beholden to people rather than to God, and society as progressing over time—were the direct result of thinking about (often justifying) the nature of slavery and were shaped by the unique perspective of those kept in bondage.

Revolution, Race, and the Enlightenment

The first thinkers to write about human variation borrowed much of their reasoning from the ancient medical philosopher Galen, who divided the body up into four "humors" or essential qualities each corresponding to a natural element and its primary color. The terms black, white, red, and yellow were thereby applied to humanity, even though human skin follows a color spectrum from pinkish to dark brown. Black and white are terms that cannot be blended—to say something is blackish white or whitish black is to say something nonsensical. Grey is a different con-

cept altogether, denoting all the spectrum of color between black and white, thereby preserving the two poles of meaning that can never combine. Thus one unstated but present meaning lurking in the words black and white themselves is a concept of natural and unavoidable separation.

Conceiving of racial groups by primary colors may have begun as a means of connecting what was then known about biology to human populations, but because of the power of language to accumulate meanings over time, these color names soon grew heavy with connotations. Blackness was a word burdened with associations to evil, ugliness, sin and filth, while whiteness was attached to holiness, purity, and beauty. Europeans by the 1800s called Africa the "Dark Continent," a phrase containing many layers of meaning, from a place unexplored (and therefore available to be claimed), to a place filled with evil and savagery, to the brown skin of its inhabitants.

Just as the rise of the scientific method of classification and observation encouraged modern thinking about how humanity could be divided by fundamental differences of color, the rise of new theories of government, law, and society also fostered the idea that different groups were profoundly unequal in their rights and abilities. Enlightenment social theorists like Descartes and Locke sought to base the legitimacy of government on something other than tradition and divine right, but in so doing grounded it upon ideas that further reinforced the idea that humanity was divided into racial groups of deeply different characters and rights.

Figure 1.10 Marchand d'esclaves (slave market), by Victor Giraud, 1900-1920.

In ancient Greece and Rome, citizenship, in other words the definition of who may participate in political life, was not based on race (though it was limited by sex). In the classic Roman republics the right to engage in politics was generally earned by a person's contributions to the state, not the land in which one was born. Later when aristocratic forms of government arose in the middle ages of Europe, most all political rights were hereditary and ancient; an arbitrary justification to be sure but one not supported by a biological or natural understanding of the difference between rulers, ruled, and those considered alien.

It was not until philosophers of the Enlightenment began formulating a more rational basis of government that the seeming natural differences among men became a basis of citizenship. The ancients looked upon nature as savage and chaotic and viewed society and government as its opposite. Enlightenment thinkers like Rousseau and Locke, turned this thinking around and looked to nature

Figure 1.11 "The Chain of Nature," 1802. This illustration shows how old religious ideas of the "Great Chain of Being" were adapted to Enlightenment thinking.

as the realm of pure freedom, while viewing society and government as the source of the corruption and immorality that caused widespread misery. Rights, they wrote, were not granted by kings and charters, but were always part of the natural birthright of men and the unspoken social contract all men agree to when they form a community.

While this theory of natural rights had a tendency over time to extend the idea of political rights to more and more groups in society, it also contained elements that worked against the idea of equality. Most importantly, unlike aristocratic and ancient societies that based rights on noble birth or civic contributions, natural rights flowed from the God-given abilities and qualities of every person. This idea worked to expand rights when those abilities and qualities were assumed to be good, wise, and intelligent. However, for those groups believed to have been endowed by nature with undesirable qualities, natural rights theory justified their exclusion from civic life.

As long as aristocracies ruled Europe, as they did until the American and French revolutions of the late Eighteenth century, these radical ideas circulated freely but had limited social impact. However, once Americans declared independence, conquered British armies, and declared themselves a republic, these ideas were given free reign to organize society. American ideals of independence, freedom, and equality were not meant to be universal ones—they were reserved for those with the proper racial endowments to enjoy them.

Considered in this way, the new American nation's commitment to inequality—its strengthening protections for slavery, its federal requirement that only white immigrants could be naturalized as citizens, its states' proliferating bars to black voting, and its direct commitment to eradicating the land of native inhabitants—was not viewed by its leaders as being hypocritical or contradictory, but in keeping with the spirit of both political philosophy and law.

Though most people assume race is natural and has been a force throughout human history, scholars point out that it is largely absent from thousands of years of written history. The idea of races is a recent idea, one that is only a few hundred years old. The idea that skin color marked fundamental divisions of humanity did not exist in the ancient world and only began to emerge in Europe about the same time that Columbus discovered the New World. Racial thinking did not become common or powerful enough to shape societies until after the founding of the English colonies in North America.

Thomas Jefferson, *Notes on the State of Virginia*, (1784)
Queries 14, 18, 137–43, 162–63

... The first difference which strikes us is that of colour. Whether the black of the negro resides in the reticular membrane between the skin and scarf-skin, or in the scarfskin[1] itself; whether it proceeds from the colour of the blood, the colour of the bile, or from that of some other secretion, the difference is fixed in nature, and is as real as if its seat and cause were better known to us. And is this difference of no importance? Is it not the foundation of a greater or less share of beauty in the two races? Are not the fine mixtures of red and white, the expressions of every passion by greater or less suffusions of colour in the one, preferable to that eternal monotony, which reigns in the countenances, that immoveable veil of black which covers all the emotions of the other race? Add to these, flowing hair, a more elegant symmetry of form, their own judgment in favour of the whites, declared by their preference of them, as uniformly as is the preference of the Oran-ootan for the black women over those of his own species. The circumstance of superior beauty, is thought worthy attention in the propagation of our horses, dogs, and other domestic animals; why not in that of man?

Besides those of colour, figure, and hair, there are other physical distinctions proving a difference of race. They have less hair on the face and body. They secrete less by the kidneys, and more by the glands of the skin, which gives them a very strong and disagreeable odour. This greater degree of transpiration renders them more tolerant of heat, and less so of cold, than the whites. Perhaps too a difference of structure in the pulmonary apparatus, which a late ingenious experimentalist has discovered to be the principal regulator of animal heat, may have disabled them from extricating, in the act of inspiration, so much of that fluid from the outer air, or obliged them in expiration, to part with more of it. They seem to require less sleep. A black, after hard labour through the day, will be induced by the slightest amusements to sit up till midnight, or later, though knowing he must be out with the first dawn of the morning.

They are at least as brave, and more adventuresome. But this may perhaps proceed from a want of fore-thought, which prevents their seeing a danger till it be present. When present, they do not go through it with more coolness or steadiness than the whites. They are more ardent after their female: but love seems with them to be more an eager desire, than a tender delicate mixture of sentiment and sensation. Their griefs are transient. Those numberless afflictions, which render it doubtful whether heaven has given life to us in mercy or in wrath, are less felt, and sooner forgotten with them.

In general, their existence appears to participate more of sensation than reflection. To this must be ascribed their disposition to sleep when abstracted from their diversions, and unemployed in labour. An animal whose body is at rest, and who does not reflect, must be disposed to sleep of course. Comparing them by their faculties of memory, reason, and imagination, it appears to me, that in memory they are equal to the whites; in reason much inferior, as I think one could scarcely be found capable of tracing and comprehending the investigations of Euclid ; and that in imagination they are dull, tasteless, and anomalous.

It would be unfair to follow them to Africa for this investigation. We will consider them here, on the same stage with the whites, and where the facts are not apocryphal on which a judgment is to be formed. It will be right to make great allowances for the difference of condition, of education, of conversation, of the sphere in which they move. Many millions of them have been brought to, and born in America. Most of them indeed have been confined to tillage, to their own homes, and their own society: yet many have been so situated, that they might have availed themselves of the conversation of their masters; many have been brought up to the handicraft arts, and from that circumstance have always been associated with the whites. Some have been liberally educated, and all have lived in countries where the arts and sciences are cultivated to a considerable degree, and have had before their eyes samples of the best works from abroad. The Indians, with no advantages of this kind, will often carve figures on their pipes not destitute of design and merit. They will crayon out an animal, a plant, or a country, so as to prove the existence of a germ in their minds which only wants cultivation. They astonish you with strokes of the most sublime oratory; such as prove their reason and sentiment strong, their imagination glowing and elevated. But never yet could I find that a black had uttered a thought above the level of plain narration; never see even an elementary trait of painting or sculpture.

In music they are more generally gifted than the whites with accurate ears for tune and time, and they have been found capable of imagining a small catch. Whether they will be equal to the composition of a more extensive run of melody, or of complicated harmony, is yet to be proved. Misery is often the parent of the most affecting touches in poetry.—Among the blacks is misery enough, God knows, but no poetry... Their love is ardent, but it kindles the senses only, not the imagination... They breathe the purest effusions of friendship and general philanthropy, and show how great a degree of the latter may be compounded with strong religious zeal. He is often happy in the turn of his compliments, and his stile is easy and familiar, except when he affects a Shandean[2] fabrication of words. But his imagination is wild and extravagant, escapes incessantly from every restraint of reason and taste, and, in the course of its vagaries, leaves a tract of thought as incoherent and eccentric, as is the course of a meteor through the sky. His subjects should often have led him to a process of sober reasoning: yet we find him always substituting sentiment for demonstration.

Upon the whole, though we admit him to the first place among those of his own colour who have presented themselves to the public judgment, yet when we compare him with the writers of the race among whom he lived, and particularly with the epistolary[3] class, in which he has taken his own stand, we are compelled to enroll him at the bottom of the column...The improvement of the blacks in body and mind, in the first instance of their mixture with the whites, has been observed by every one, and proves that their inferiority is not the effect merely of their condition of life... —Whether further observation will or will not verify the conjecture, that nature has been less bountiful to them in the endowments of the head, I believe that in those of the heart she will be found to have done them justice. That disposition to theft with which they have been branded, must be ascribed to their situation, and not to any depravity of the moral sense. The man, in whose favour no laws of property exist, probably feels himself less bound to respect those made in favour of others.... Notwithstanding these considerations which must weaken their respect for the laws of property, we find among them numerous instances of the most rigid integrity, and as many as among their better instructed masters, of benevolence, gratitude, and unshaken fidelity....

The opinion, that they are inferior in the faculties of reason and imagination, must be hazarded with great diffidence. To justify a general conclusion, requires many observations, even where the subject may be submitted to the Anatomical knife, to Optical glasses, to analysis by fire, or by solvents. How much more then where it is a faculty, not a substance, we are examining; where it eludes the research of all the senses; where the conditions of its existence are various and variously combined; where the effects of those which are present or absent bid defiance to calculation; let me add too, as a circumstance of great tenderness, where our conclusion would degrade a whole race of men from the rank in the scale of beings which their Creator may perhaps have given them...

I advance it therefore as a suspicion only, that the blacks, whether originally a distinct race, or made distinct by time and circumstances, are inferior to the whites in the endowments both of body and mind. It is not against experience to suppose, that different species of the same genus, or varieties of the same species, may possess different qualifications. Will not a lover of natural history then, one who views the gradations in all the races of animals with the eye of philosophy, excuse an effort to keep those in the department of man as distinct as nature has formed them? This unfortunate difference of colour, and perhaps of faculty, is a powerful obstacle to the emancipation of these people. Many of their advocates, while they wish to vindicate the liberty of human nature, are anxious also to preserve its dignity and beauty. Some of these, embarrassed by the question "What further is to be done with them?" join themselves in opposition with those who are actuated by sordid avarice only. Among the Romans emancipation required but one effort. The slave, when made free, might mix with, without staining the blood of his master. But with us a second is necessary, unknown to history. When freed, he is to be removed beyond the reach of mixture.

[1]Scarf-skin is an old term for the outermost layer of skin, technically known as the epidermis.
[2]Referring to the comic novel Tristam Shandy by Laurence Sterne (1759) in which the main character narrates his life in a way that never get around to the main topic and digresses as if unable to long hold a single thought.
[3]In this sense meaning 'lettered or educated.'

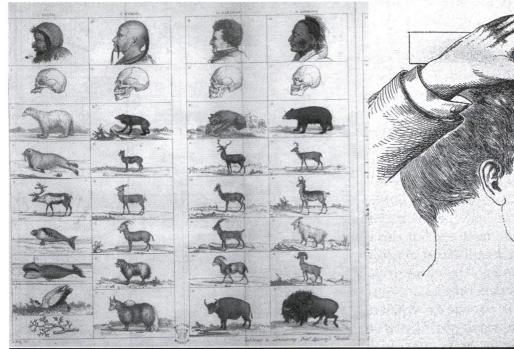

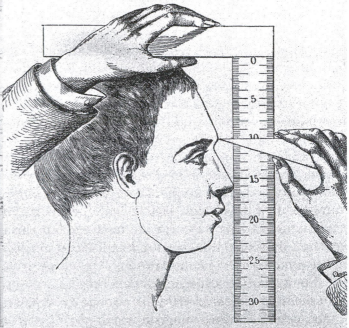

Part One: The Science of Race

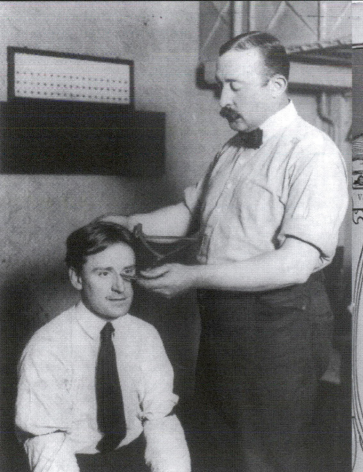

Chapter Two: Human Variation

The idea of 'race' seems to most people natural and physical. After all, it seems fairly easy to identify people by race at a glance. Most people find race to be one of the more obvious of the physical characteristics of any person. To most people, race is fairly simple and uncomplicated—a fixed quantity that one inherits from their parents.

But ask any person how many races there are and they will likely be unsure of the answer. Ask them what features are most important in defining a race and they may have difficulty coming up with a coherent list. Go a step further and ask, 'why are there races?' and you may not get an answer. Race is something nearly everybody thinks they understand but have trouble actually defining.

This chapter we will start to get to the bottom of this question. Our first step is to understand that races are a way of dividing humanity into groups based on some real or imagined natural differences among them. (These differences need to be natural because the concept of race demands that people inherit the qualities they share.) From this definition, we can see that there are two parts to this problem. We need to determine exactly what patterns of natural differences can be found among humans. Secondly, we need to decide whether the categories we call races accurately capture these patterns.

The Human Genome

For centuries scientists have sought an answer to the question of how qualities and characteristics are passed down from parents to child. By the dawn of the twentieth century certain principles of inheritance had been traced, but the exact chemical mechanism that communicated such information remained a mystery. In 1953, James Watson and Francis Crick mapped the structure of DNA, deoxyribonucleic acid, a chemical that had been discovered nearly a century before but whose composition and function had long been a mystery. Watson and Crick revealed that DNA was composed of incredibly long braided strands upon which were strung just four molecules—adenine, guanine, thymine, and cytosine. The blueprints for all animals and plants, it turned out, was written with just four letters (or "bases").

Human DNA is composed of three billion of these bases. A sequence of bases that together function as an instruction for the growth or functioning of the body is

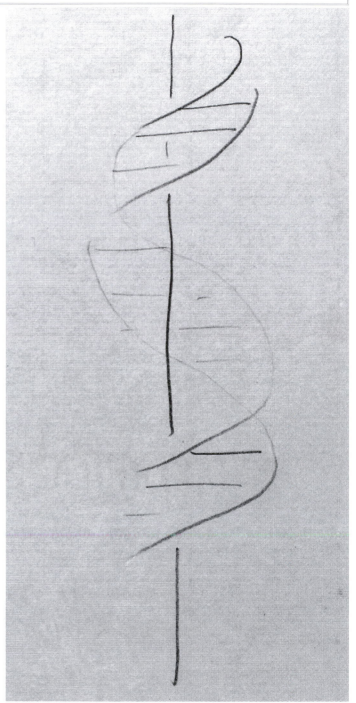

Figure 2.1 Pencil sketch of the DNA double helix by Francis Crick from 1953.

called a gene and the complete collection of all genes in a body is called a genome. So vast is the human genome, it was nearly fifty years before genetic technologies had advanced to the point where it became possible to map it from end to end. Doing so promised to revolutionize our understanding of humanity, for rather than just comparing people on the basis of observed traits, it might become possible to analyze people at their most fundamental molecular unit, the gene.

By the early 1970s genetic technology had advanced to where it was possible to determine the presence or absence of particular variations in genes (known as alleles) in people. An evolutionary biologist, Richard Lewontin set out to use these techniques to estimate how much people actually differed in terms of their genes. Lewontin sampled seventeen genetic markers across people representing racial groups as traditionally defined by scientists (African, Caucasian, Mongoloid, Amerindians, etc.), to estimate the actual distribution of human variation. His findings strikingly indicated that what people called "races" poorly matched the pattern of human genetic variation. He found that most human variation, approximately 85%, was unpatterned and could be found between individuals within any group. Only about 6% of human variation was attributable to differences between what were called racial groups. In other words, people differed far more from others in their so-called race that they did on average with those of another race. This astounding result drew much skepticism but has since been reconfirmed by many other more comprehensive studies.

In June of 2000 President Bill Clinton appeared at a White House press conference surrounded by a group of dignitaries and scientists, including Dr. Francis Collins, Director of the National Human Genome Research Institute, and Dr. Craig Venter, head of the Celera Genomics Corporation, two organizations that had been locked in a race to be the first to chart all three billion bases that make up an entire human genome. After noting that they stood in the same room that Thomas Jefferson used to publicly display the vast map Lewis and Meriwether had charted during their exploration of the Louisiana Purchase, President Clinton announced that the two teams had both completed maps of the human genome. Amidst the usual speech-making about the historic occasion and the many recognitions and congratulations to scientists around the world, the speakers felt compelled to note how this achievement shed light on the issue of racial difference.

President Clinton observed, "I believe one of the great truths to emerge from this triumphant expedition inside the human genome is that in genetic terms, all human beings, regardless of race, are more than 99.9 percent the same." And then Dr. Venter continued, noting that his company had sequenced the genomes of five people (Venter didn't mention it but his genome was the first) and said "We have sequenced the genome of three females and two males, who have identified themselves as Hispanic, Asian, Caucasian or African American. We did this sampling not in an exclusionary way, but out of respect for the diversity that is America, and to help illustrate that the concept of race has no genetic or scientific basis. In the five Celera genomes, there is no way to tell one ethnicity from another. Society and medicine treats us all as members of populations, where as individuals we are all unique, and population statistics do not apply." President Clinton was slightly off. According to the most recent studies using larger sample sizes and better technology, humans are 99.5% genetically identical, but his overall point remains valid.

As the speed, cost, and accuracy of genetic testing has markedly increased over time, so has the ability of scientists to survey larger populations. As the number of samples in a survey have increased from a few dozen to hundreds and even thousands, the calculated average variation between populations has declined. The Human Genome Diversity Panel analyzed over 650,000 genes that are known to vary between individuals (known as single nucleotide polymorphisms or SNPs) from samples taken from 1064 individuals from 51 communities around the world. These results showed even higher levels of variation between individuals in the same population, 88.9% (±0.3) than Lewontin's. In effect, the closer scientists look at the human genome, the more genetically identical humanity looks. Similar results have come from large scale surveys of human genomes that have looked to see if people with certain different genetic traits cluster into distinct groups.

Figure 2.2 The first printout of the human genome filled over 100 volumes, each with 1000 pages. Photo by Russ London.

Even though modern genetics, in spite of its seemingly endless power to uncover the fundamental building blocks of the human body, has piled up an impressive amount of evidence showing that humanity is not naturally divided into races, proponents of racial categories continue to battle through the pages of scholarly journals. One of these schools of thought argues that when a large number of people are sampled across the planet they can be grouped according to the frequency of distinct strings of genes, and these clusters, or "islands," are generally continental, mirroring the old idea of races.

Over the last decade, a number of scientists claimed to have found genetic clusters that largely corresponded to the traditional continental view of races. But for the most part, none of these clustering studies can agree on precisely how many clusters there are or even what counts as a cluster. According to one of the more recent surveys, of the seven distinct clusters of traits that were mapped, five were in sub-Saharan Africa. Does this mean that there are seven "races" and two-thirds of them are African?

No, because as it turns out a different number and variety of clusters are produced depending on what scale of analysis is chosen. This is exactly what one would expect to find in a population that has a high degree of genetic similarity and most of whose variations occur clinally, that is, they vary gradually across distance. In such a situation, the closer one looks, the more groups there are because at the largest levels of abstraction the similarities simply swamp the differences. In the end, those scientists who have tried to use these studies to uphold the concept of race have just forced this data into the preexisting boxes we call race, rather than allowing the facts to speak for themselves, as science should.

Such scientists tend to commit a common error in studying race. They have begun by using the categories that their investigations are supposed to discover. One of the bedrock principles of science is not to presume the nature of the phenomenon examined. This is because when one does so, there is a danger that the results will merely tend to uphold one's presumptions. For example, in 2004, a pair of geneticists at the Max Planck Institute for Evolutionary Anthropology, pointed out that many of the studies of the "island school" that claimed to have found genetic evidence for racial clusters were biased in their fundamental design. In these studies subjects were selected on the basis of their identification with an ethnic group and people who were identified as having "mixed" ancestry were excluded. By sampling only culturally and socially defined groups these researchers essentially created the social differences they then claimed to have objectively discovered. When populations of people are sampled not according to their pre-existing membership in social groups but based solely on their geographic distribution the clusters or islands of difference largely disappear. Rather, what is revealed, is that human traits vary gradually over distance with occasional but small breaks between great natural barriers like oceans and mountain ranges.

A race is theoretically a grouping of people that is physically different from other groupings of people. Of course, individuals within groups also differ. In theory, a race is a group of people that varies from other groups of people more than either group varies within itself. Geneticists have calculated the actual genetic variance between races and among individuals within these groups and the results are startling. On average, individuals within the groups we call races vary twenty times more than the groups themselves.

Most biologists and anthropologists today conclude that almost all the genes in any two people are identical and what variation there is does not clump into distinct groups. Obviously, though, people do vary and there is a pattern to that variation, just not the pattern that we call "races."

Clines versus Clusters (or Clades)

Generally, taxonomists (scientists who put things into their proper categories) use two principles to determine whether seemingly different living things should be put into separate groups. First, they examine whether each of these things share a distinct common ancestry—in other words that the seemingly different organisms share no ancestors except an original common one. As the first is often difficult or impossible to document, a second criteria is even more important: they measure how similar or different they are in their anatomy or their behavior.

Taxonomists divide the living world into eight ranks ranging from the broadest classifications of domain and kingdom to the smallest of family, genus and species. Species are the fundamental level of classification. In mammals, different species are generally unable to mate and produce fertile offspring. Some species, though, have different populations that have the ability to mate but rarely mix and over time have become distinctly different in their physical characteristics. This level of variation below species is called either a sub-species or a race.

Today the word "race" is rarely used by biologists to describe any other organism than humans. Instead, biologists use the terms "demes," meaning a local population, or "ecotype," meaning a group that has adapted to a particular environment, or a "subspecies," the major subdivision of a species. It is important to consider that while demes and ecotypes will exhibit genetic variation, the amount of genetic variation needed to qualify as a subspecies is quite substantial. If every local human population that has slightly different patterns of variation than others were to be considered a race, there would be thousands, perhaps tens of thousands of races.

Geographically distant human populations do tend to vary from each other in their appearance and genetically. But how much difference does it take to be meaningful? How much difference would justify calling two groups different "races?" To classify as being races, different groups must vary in specific ways. Biologists have long relied on Amadon's Rule of 75%: that in two populations mixed together, three quarters of the members of one group must be able to be identified on the basis of some characteristic that can be distinguished from all members of the other group. Another way of expressing this rule is that to be considered races, populations need to vary genetically by at least 25% (this number was derived from studies of well-known subspecies across many species of animals).

For example, our closest mammal relative, the chimpanzee, was for many years assumed to be subdivided into five races due to their differing appearances and their seemingly isolated ranges in various parts of Africa. But genetic testing of the animals revealed that in fact only three of the groups exceeded the 25% minimum of variation (these averaged a robust 30%) and studies of their lineages confirmed that chimpanzees had in the past twice separated into distinct breeding populations, making for three total subspecies (or races). Likewise, nearly a third, 27%, of the total genetic variation in dogs is between their breeds.

Following these scientific criteria, the human species has but two races. You, dear reader, are a member of one of these races, *Homo sapiens sapiens*. The other, *Homo sapiens neanderthalensis*, went extinct forty thousand years ago. Neanderthals were not all that different from you or I, but they were just different enough to constitute being a separate race. None of the other divisions of humanity we call 'races' even come close to the variation required by Amadon's Rule.

Humans have shown a remarkable amount of similarity. Large scale studies of human genetic markers have consistently concluded that human subpopulations, even those on far-flung continents, vary by an average of only 4%. Most of the genetic variation that humans exhibit, about 93% of it, exists randomly between individuals, not in a way that outlines groups. The rate of continental variation is so low that many computer models of human variation end up lumping a significant number of individuals into multiple "races" at the same time!

Additionally, when even this small amount of genetic variation is plotted over a map, no sharp boundaries between populations can be found. Rather the frequencies of different genetic types change slightly and consistently

Figure 2.3 An illustration of an evolutionary tree of humans from H.G. Wells, *An Outline of History,* 1921.

with distance. Human differences are patterned in clines, or gradual variation, not clusters of individuals (or as biologists would term them, clades). The farther one travels from home in any direction, the more human variation they will encounter.

One of the consequences of this clinal pattern of variation is that most all human traits don't fall neatly into a handful of types or categories. Rather, across a large population they vary gradually from one extreme to another with few gaps to distinguish one type from another. Human skin is not one color or another but a full spectrum of shades from light to dark and pink to brown. This creates a problem for dividing people into types for when there are no clear jumps from one characteristic to another, when in any population you could find an example of one ideal type or another but also find every variation in between, there really is no obvious place to draw a boundary between one thing and another.

This is exactly the problem with any characteristic one might choose to define a race. Take skin color for example: sure one could find a person who has very light skin or one who has very dark skin, but looking across the global population you will find people at every conceivable hue in between. For all those people in the middle, who is black and who is white?

The Myth of the Evolutionary Tree

For generations school children have been taught the basics of evolution (at least where the study of evolution has not been banned) through the metaphor of a tree. The trunk of the tree represents an original ancestor that lived long long ago. Each limb and branch denotes an adaptation and a different family of descendents who all share not only unique characteristics but also a separate and common ancestor from every other branch of the tree. But this well-known metaphor has only served to perpetuate false ideas of race. The symbol of the evolutionary tree is not an accurate representation of humanity.

This is because the lack of sharp genetic boundaries between human populations exists not only in space but in time. Unlike chimpanzees and many other mammals, humans have no clearly divided lineages or ancestries that can divide them genetically into separate groups. Humanity's family tree is a more like an overgrown trellis, where vines criss-cross in all directions rather than a branching oak. As one survey of scientific studies on this issue recently concluded, "On a time scale of tens of thousands of years...there is not one statistically significant inference of splitting during the last 1.9 million years."

More confounding to the idea of races is the fact that the genetic pattern of geographic variation does not match the genetic pattern of hereditary differences. Careful comparisons of datasets for the ways in which humans vary by continent and the ways they vary in terms of their ancestry, reveal that the two do not agree. For example, there is more genetic distance between populations in Africa that are descended from hunting and gathering ancestors and their neighbors descended from farmers than there is between those descendants of African farmers and Europeans. In other words, the pattern of genetic variation that can be measured as existing between what most people call "races" has no relationship to people's overall ancestry. So not only are races not "pure" they aren't even collections of people that can be grouped by a shared genetic family history.

Human Origins

Why are humans so unusually similar? The answer lies in the peculiar history of human origins. The seven billion people living on Earth have bodies that vary in many ways, some of these ways tracing the patterns of our species'

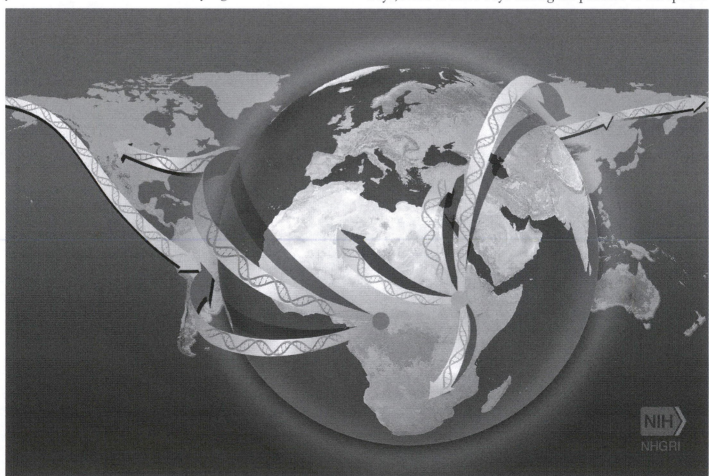

Figure 2.4 Human migration routes out of Africa.

migrations from Africa to all parts of the globe.

The general rule of thumb when thinking about how people evolve over time is this: the more complicated the trait the longer it takes to develop. This is important because humans are actually a very young species and for the vast majority of our species history there was only a small population of humans.

According to the fossil record, half a million years ago one or more of early human-like species, or hominids, that had evolved from earlier apes in Africa, began to spread outward across the Eurasian landmass. Meanwhile, the ancestors of modern humans continued to evolve in Africa until they resembled modern humans around 200,000 years ago. Judging from the available archaeological evidence found scattered in Southern and Eastern Africa, humans quickly developed the use of symbols—beads and pigment for ornamenting their bodies—and complex tools. Linguistic evidence dates the ancestors of modern languages to an early birth in Africa where the greatest variety of language roots still exist. (Today there are approximately 2000 languages from four different language groups spoken in Africa, representing about one-third of all known languages.)

Probably around fifty thousand years ago, modern humans began to rapidly spread out from humanity's cradle into far-flung lands. Fifty thousand years is enough time for humans to expand out from Africa, to inhabit virtually every corner of the globe, but not enough time for anything other than superficial differences to evolve. Many superficial characteristics, such as the shape of one's ears or the particular features of the face, changed for no particular reason other than increasing isolation from other groups as humans increasingly lived over a broader swath of the planet, a phenomenon known as genetic drift. (Genetic drift describes gradual changes in physical features that have no advantage or disadvantage in adaptation to any particular environment, or what biologists call "neutral evolution.")

Of course, no human group could remain truly isolated for very long. Genes have no respect for borders. Populations that appear separate actually exchange and share genes over great distances. This can happen directly by the occasional long-distance travel of people, or indirectly as genes hop from one to another distant spot by using many local populations in between as "stepping stones." In the end, humans have ended up as a species that actually has much less variation among its members than most other mammals.

In the 1980s it became possible to unravel large chunks of the molecular strings of DNA that are the recipe of life. In particular geneticists were for the first time able to survey large numbers of peoples' mitochondrial DNA, a bit of coding in one particular structure of a cell that each person inherits from their mother. These strings of DNA vary slightly but regularly over time, almost clock-like over long periods. By comparing the number of differences in the mitochondrial DNA of many people spread across the globe scientists are able to accurately estimate how many years it must have taken for these differences to arise from a small number of common ancestors. The answer, about 200,000 years, confirmed much of the fossil evidence that had previously been the only way to answer the question, when did modern humans appear?

Genetics has also neatly confirmed the fossil evidence that all humans are descended from African ancestors. By comparing key genetic markers of a number of individuals in a given regional population, the average amount that these individuals vary genetically can be measured and the relative genetic variation within two different populations can be compared. Done across a sample of the entire human population a striking fact is revealed. The most genetically diverse human populations are found in Africa while populations in Eurasia and North America are about one-third as varied.

This difference in genetic variation between Africans and non-Africans is the result of what anthropologists call the Serial Founder Effect. Humans evolved in Africa and had more than a hundred thousand years to break into sub-populations, develop genetic differences, and exchange these varieties before a part of them wandered off toward Eurasia taking with them only a subset of this variation. Then those groups splintered with some of their members pushing further on, taking with them a subset of the second group's variety and so on. Over hundreds of generations the process of spreading over the globe was also a process by which human genetic diversity was reduced as groups moved further in distance and time from the genetic richness of Mother Africa. (Languages also seem to follow a similar serial founder effect, with sub-Saharan Africa having a higher density of distinct language types and more distant regions having fewer.) Genetic studies have confirmed that the loss of genetic diversity and distance from Africa correlate to a very high degree, close to 90%.

Genetic sequencing has also allowed scientists to determine that the ancestral human population for most of human history, before the expansion out of Africa, was the size of a small town, perhaps 12,000 to 15,000 individuals. Then for some unknown reason, between 65,000 and 50,000 year ago, the human population collapsed, according to one estimate to fewer than a thousand individuals. When the population recovered somewhat, the size of the group that inaugurated the migration out of Africa (either by following a coastal path around the Indian ocean or northward towards Eurasia) has been estimated to be between 1,000 and 2,500 people.

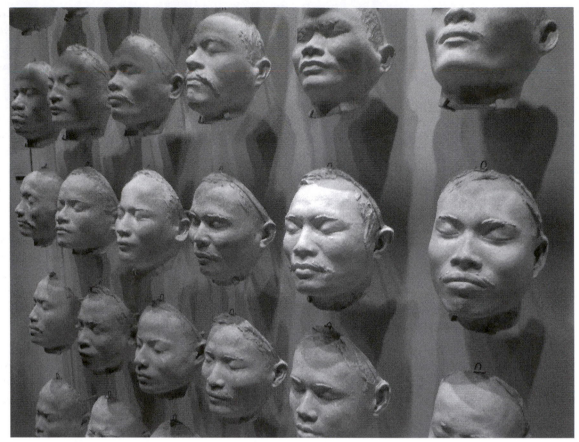

Figure 2.5 Plaster face casts of Nias islanders by J.P. Kleiweg de Zwaan, circa 1910.

As the speed and accuracy of such genetic testing has rapidly improved, it has become possible to recover strings of DNA from the rare fossil remains of long extinct humanoid species, such as the Neandertals. In 1999 the first successful attempts to extract DNA from a Neandertal bone confirmed that Neanderthals were not an ancestor of modern humans but a parallel species, one that evolved separately from a common ancestor of modern humans and for a time lived at the same time as humans. A decade later refinement of these techniques were able to determine that some of the fossils that had been thought to be Neandertal were actually an entirely different parallel species that was named 'Denisovan' after the name of the Central Asian cave where they were found.

By comparing certain portions of the Neandertal genome to human ones, anthropologists were able to determine that at some early point in time there was some exchange of genes from Neandertals to humans after humans spread out from Africa. It was estimated that somewhere between 1.5 and 2.1% of the genes of Eurasians came from Neandertals. Likewise, another 3 to 6% of the genes of people in whose descendents come from Oceania (the tropical islands of the Pacific) were inherited from Denisovans. Anthropologists note that these are very small levels of interbreeding indicating that human contact with these other hominids was limited in scope and of short duration.

One of the common misconceptions about races is thinking that racial groups developed independently of each other. Such a view leads easily to thinking that races are fundamentally different and that the many people who don't seem to easily fit into one or another race are the product of the intermixture of races. Most of the scientific community also held this view prior to the 1940s.

Until the 1960s, most scientists believed that human groups, once similar in makeup, became separated by vast distances and natural barriers such as deserts and mountain ranges, and over time grew apart and developed distinctive characteristics. Modern genetics has rewritten this story, finding much evidence for widespread mixing and sharing of genes between groups supposed to have been isolated over a very long period of time.

In 2015 the first results of the African Genome Variation Project, (AGVP) the most extensive attempt to chart the genetic variety of Africans who lived south of the Sahara desert, were published. The AGVP surveyed the genetics of 1,481 Africans from 18 different ethnic and linguistic groups including sequencing the entire genomes of 320 individuals. Their results confirmed other studies that have indicated that genes have long flowed between the populations of Africa and Western Eurasia. These widespread genetic interactions can be traced from the strongest signal, indicated the greatest exchanges, in Ethiopia in

Africa's northeast, with signatures identifiable all the way to the Cape of Good Hope, Africa's southern tip where the ancient Khoe-San people live.

Interestingly, a large amount of this mixture of Eurasian varieties of genes into Africa occurred well before Europeans began seizing and transporting millions of Africans to their colonies in the New World and well before European nations began conquering and colonizing African nations. Recent studies of genetic diversity between Spain and Algeria, regions divided by the Strait of Gibraltar, showed that there have been high levels of exchange over this natural bridge between Europe and Africa since the stone age. For example, "complex" admixture was evident in the Yoruba people of West Africa that dated to between 7,500 and 10,000 years ago. (This signal included traces of Neandertal genes which up to that point had only been found in Eurasian populations.) It is known that at this particular period in history the North African climate was much wetter, facilitating crossing of the Sahara desert.

Conversely, studies of the genetic diversity of ancient and modern Europeans show that this region was peopled by successive waves of migrants, especially following the invention of agriculture in the "fertile crescent," the area lying between the Euphrates and Tigris rivers in what is today Iraq. Recent surveys of both the genes recovered from ancient human remains found in archeological sites from Spain to Scandinavia have revealed that Europeans became more genetically diverse, not more similar, over time.

Non-Concordance of Traits

Most people incorrectly assume that if a human group develops an evolutionary adaptation different from other groups, that this is proof that humanity is naturally divided into the groups we call races. While it is true that human populations have adapted to different environments by becoming darker or lighter skinned, or taller or shorter, or better able to breath at high altitudes, these adaptations have been shown to be singular and do not reflect other unseen differences. For such adaptations to represent true group distinctions, they must be linked to changes in many other traits as well. Surveys of genetic differences have not shown any such linked differences.

While it is true that researchers have identified many instances where populations have adapted a specific genetic trait to deal with the challenges of their local environmental conditions, such as thin air in high mountains or a limited diet in the arctic, these traits tend to be singular and not connected to the other ways people vary. In other words, each trait tends to vary independently, not in concordance with others. As a result, depending on what trait is selected, a different arrangement of human groups can be created. No one trait consistently draws boundaries between groups of people and each new trait draws those boundaries differently.

Even skin color, which has been long viewed as the key marker dividing humanity into different groups, is a terrible predictor of genetic difference. People from equatorial Africa and from Papua New Guinea have some of the darkest skin color on the planet. Yet because these groups live about as far apart as one can be on a globe, they have a greater degree of genetic difference from each other than either group does with Europeans, whose skin is much lighter in tint.

Biologists have been studying what exactly is physically inherited for more than a century and recently with the rapid advancement of the study of genes we can say with great certainty what and how traits are inherited. Scientists make an important distinction between a particular physical characteristic, or a phenotype, and the genes that make up the recipe for a characteristic, known as a genotype.

One of the most important insights of this research has been to show how even seemingly simple physical traits, like skin color, are not simply determined by a single inherited gene, but are the result of the interaction of many genes. To complicate matters, many traits involve both the interaction of numerous genes and, in turn, their interaction with the environment. As a general rule, the more complicated the characteristic—such as intelligence, the sharpness of senses, or athletic coordination, the greater the number of both inherited and environmental factors that make it up.

Most people assume that racial characteristics are simply passed from parents to children in a mechanical way. It is commonly believed that each parent possesses a seed that contains within it the recipe for shaping a child. In our scientific age, people generally try and sound technically sophisticated and refer to these seeds as "genes" or "DNA," though their understanding of what these terms mean doesn't go much farther than thinking of them as "seeds." It is generally thought that physical features such as skin color or hair texture are passed from generation to generation from either father or mother or, perhaps, by some sort of mixing of qualities from each parent. Those who remember their high school biology lessons may think of Gregor Mendel's pea-pods and poster charts that calculated the frequencies of different colored peas appearing in different pods.

But humans are not pea-pods and the manner in which even the most simple traits are inherited and expressed in humans is far more complicated. While the varieties of Mendel's peas were governed by four "genes," one of two possibilities being given to the offspring by each parent, in humans something as basic as skin color is determined by at least 124 variables (technically speaking, 124 single nucleotide polymorphisms located in 33 different genes). Not only is inheritance complicated by the dizzying number of factors specifying one's hue, some of these factors may be switched on or off, or altered in some way by interactions with the environment. For example, all of the eleven known genes that contribute to eye color are still estimated to account for only half of the variation observed in the appearance of human eyes. The rest, presumably, is due to some sort of environmental interaction. Likewise, genes account for 92% of a person's hair color, the remaining bit being something other than inheritance.

Many observable differences seem to be the result of complex interactions between environment and lifestyles rather than heredity. For example, as early as the mid 1800s biologist Carl Bergmann noted that mammals tended to have larger body masses in higher latitudes with their colder climates than populations living closer to the tropics. Anthropologists later applied "Bergmann's Rule" to humans and attributed these variations to racial heredity. Today, scientists attribute most of this difference not to genes but to the effects of industrialization on human diets and habits.

One recent study went even further and found evidence that not only was diet responsible for regional differences in body mass, but the particular makeup of bacteria in the digestive tract also varied by latitude but did not vary as a result of ethnicity. These results provide a reminder that much of human variation is caused by environmental

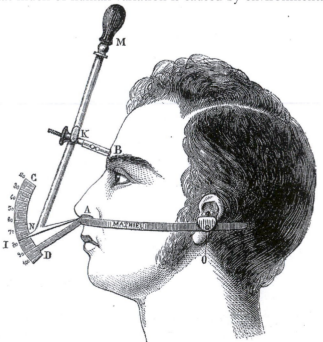

Figure 2.6 A specialized tool for measuring angles of the face developed by Paul Broca 1870.

differences and that "the environment" is not just something "out there" but is also something within us.

Many of the observed physical differences between people are the result of neutral variation, or genetic drift, rather than a result of being selected by some environmental pressure. This is another common mistake of reading meaning into perceived differences—most differences of appearance have no meaning, they reveal nothing deeper or hidden about one's character or makeup. Even when a physical trait is more common in a population due to environmental pressures, its selection can result in changes in a number of other physical features that are connected to the same gene or set of genes but are by themselves superficial. For example, the same gene that regulates the density of hair on parts of the body also affects the size of teeth. While it might be advantageous to have a hairier body in a cold climate, whether one's teeth are slightly larger or smaller probably makes little difference.

Geneticists who have surveyed the full human genome looking for adaptive genes particular to Africans or non-Africans have turned up few candidates. One discovery was that a particular gene that controls the body's ability to digest lactose, the sugar in cow's milk, was found in more than three-quarters of Europeans but virtually absent in Africans. Apparently, the prevalence of this gene spread rapidly with the spread of dairy farming. But the domestication of cattle occurred at a very early point in African history as well and researchers who examined African patterns found that a majority of Africans are just as lactose tolerant and their bodies have a different combination of genes that accomplishes the same thing—digesting milk comfortably.

Skin Color

Of course the most obvious seeming difference between people is skin color. Humans in Africa evolved to have dark skin because of the high levels of ultraviolet radiation present at tropical latitudes that can deplete the levels of folate (B vitamins) in the blood. Low folate levels can interfere with a population's fertility by increasing the frequency of birth defects, something evolution strenuously tries to prevent. A natural pigmenting agent, eumelanin, when concentrated in the skin, acts to block the degradation of the body's levels of folic acid.

It was once believed that dark skin evolved primarily to prevent fatal melanoma (skin cancer) which is more prevalent in people with lighter than darker skin. But large-scale population studies have shown that skin cancer is just rare enough, and tends to manifest at an older age, so its effect on population size was not significant.

It is interesting to consider that human skin color is

one of the consequences of evolving a largely hairless body. Hair and fur effectively block ultraviolet radiation as well but humans' larger brains required higher calorie diets to sustain, which in turn required the ability to reach higher levels of exertion and endurance in order to hunt, and this demanded a better mechanism for cooling the body. Sweating doesn't work well on a furry body. So, in a sense, humanity owes its survival and success to dark skin.

As humans migrated toward higher latitudes, they encountered environments that had lower ultraviolet exposure, decreasing the need for solar protection but also turning darker skin into a liability. One nutrient important to human health, vitamin D3, is synthesized in the skin in the presence of ultraviolet sunshine. Vitamin D3 is crucial to the regulation of the immune system, to proper bone growth, and in the normal functioning of the pancreas. In the tropics sunshine is so abundant and steady that plenty of vitamin D3 can be produced even in the darkest of skin. But where sunshine was highly seasonal, vitamin D3 deficiency was a problem. As a result of these combined pressures of melanoma and vitamin D3 deficiency, skin color shades progressively from the tropics to the Arctic circle.

The mechanisms regulating the amount of skin pigmentation are complicated, being controlled by at least ten genes. Nevertheless, human populations just as readily darkened as they lightened as they migrated from place to place. Populations that had developed lighter skin while living in central Asia and then migrated back to tropical climes in southern India, rapidly darkened. So did groups of east Asians who migrated across the Bering Strait land bridge and into South America.

In addition to skin, a number of other features of the human body vary gradually over distance, or clinally. The anatomy of the sinus cavity varies in a clinal fashion from hot humid climates to dry and cold ones as each environment poses different challenges to respiration.

A few local populations, who have lived for eons in extreme environments, commonly have characteristics that are rare elsewhere. The Himalayas in Asia, the Andes in South America, and the Ethiopian plateau in East Africa, are all places whwere people have lived at high altitudes for thousands of years. A large percentage of people in these regions have gene variants that make them resistant to the effects of hypobaric hypoxia, an illness caused by a chronic shortage of oxygen at high elevations.

Interestingly, recent investigations have revealed that the physiological mechanisms that account for these different groups' resistance to hypoxia, and the genes that are responsible for them, varies in each of the three populations.

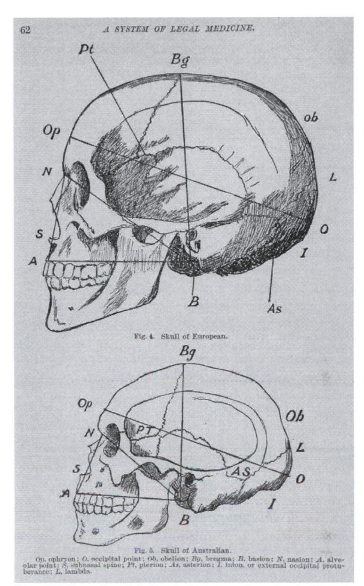

Figure 2.7 Illustration of skull traits from an early textbook of "Legal Medicine."

Forensic Science

American television viewers are regularly presented with crime shows that spread the myth that race is a simple difference in physical traits. In the Fox series *Bones* scientists routinely scrutinize a bone or a skull and pronounce it to be "caucasoid" or "mongoloid." A typical episode, "The Mutilation of the Master Manipulator," that aired in December of 2014, opens with forensic pathologist Temperance Brennan in her FBI lab discussing a small pile of bones on her examining table with her associate Hodgins:

Hodgins: This is it? These are all the remains we have?
Brennan: Yes.
Hodgins: Can you get any kind of an ID from these?
Brennan: Well, the length and lack of curvature of the

femur indicates the victim was a Negroid male, approximately six-foot-two in height.

Hodgins: Nice. But no name?

Brennan: Right.

Such definitive conclusions are not what really happens in the crime lab. Interviewed about the show, Dr. Elizabeth Miller, the consulting anthropologist to the Los Angeles Coroner, described what actually happens:

I usually say something like 'white,' which includes a long list, and then as a caveat, I put, 'This bears no relationship to the race an individual considers themselves, and has no bearing on hair color or skin type...It's the hardest thing to determine, it is the least accurate, and I'm never surprised when I'm wrong...Pardon the pun: It's not a black-and-white issue...

For over a century forensic pathologists have claimed that they could scientifically sort unidentified bones into racial groups based on specific traits that marked specific bones as being "negroid," "caucasoid," or "mongoloid." This field of science was based on research done in the late 1800s by individuals who not only believed races were the natural divisions of humanity but that non-white races were more primitive and animal-like. So strong were beliefs about the natural divisions of race within the ranks of forensic scientists, that the evidence for the field's basic principles went unexamined and untested. Tellingly, the impulse to reexamine the basis of many longstanding forensic scientific formulas came from outside the discipline. In 1993, in the case of *Daubert v. Merrell Dow Pharmaceuticals*, the Supreme Court ruled that forensic evidence was not admissible in court unless it could be shown to be based on sound principles and its procedures were tested and shown to be statistically reliable in peer-reviewed studies. Prior to *Daubert*, the legal standard for the admission of scientific testimony was a 1923 decision that allowed scientific testimony as long as such evidence was the commonly accepted views of the scientific community. Suddenly, the longstanding consensus among forensic practitioners was thrown open to reexamination and this consensus was found to be based on pseudoscience and racist presumptions.

One of the most significant casualties of this reexamination of the bases of the field was the idea that races were defined by "trait lists." These were simply lists of anatomical features, mostly of the bones, whose presence or absence was supposed to distinguish race. This technique, pioneered by anthropologist E.A. Hooten in the early twentieth century, is called the morphoscopic method and it presumes that there are clear anatomical distinctions between people of different races, such as the shape of the sutures across the top of the skull or the shape of the bones that make up the nasal passages.

For example, the shape of the bone surrounding the eye, the orbital, was thought to directly indicate race. Round orbitals were African or Asian, angular orbits were European. But this system, in use for decades, upon actual testing was shown to be a fantasy. In actuality, the shape of the orbital bone reveals very little about a person's ancestry. One recent reevaluation of measurement of the orbital bone revealed that while there may be slight differences in bone shape related to ancestry, the variation within populations was greater than the observed differences between them. Additionally this study revealed that the conscious or unconscious bias of scientists may have skewed their data as these researchers had different technicians repeat the same measurements on the same bones and discovered that the variation in measurement was greater than the factor that was supposed to be attributed to ancestry.

Several other studies of the reliability of morphoscopic techniques concluded that if they worked at all, they were more akin to art than to science. One group of scientists looked at a large sample of bones and applied the textbook collection of six traits to sorting them among four races. Their results agreed with the expected race of the sample as infrequently as 17% of the time and at best 58% of the time. (Keep in mind that dividing samples into four categories would result in a completely random success rate of 25%.) An even larger study that attempted to quantify the actual accuracy of using lists of traits to determine race determined them to be utterly unreliable. Applying a list of eleven common morphoscopic traits to a collection of 747 skulls of known ancestry, these researchers could not find a single skull that displayed all eleven traits as expected. Every skull had at least one trait that textbooks said were indicative of another race. A quarter of the supposedly racial traits, when quantified, did not correlate with the others, meaning that they were not even weakly connected to particular groups at all. Additionally, they found a greater range of variation among all their subjects than science had long assumed existed.

Another study put nine of skeletal indicators to a test by comparing the results obtained by each method on the same skeletons against each other and found them utterly contradictory. In examinations of 20 skeletons using all nine methods, no skeleton was consistently identified as "White," "Black," or "Asian" by all techniques. Only twelve skeletons were identified as one race or another by the majority of the methods. Of the 20 skeletons, all but six were identified as being both White, Black, and Asian when all the methods were used. As the scientists reviewing the results dryly observed of one startling result, "Specimen 18 was identified as White by four methods...Black by three methods...and either Asian, Amerindian, Indigenous Australian or Oceanian by two methods."

Similarly, it was long commonly accepted among forensic investigators that certain characteristics of teeth, their sizes and shapes, could be used to reliably determine a person's race. When this widely-held idea was tested it was found that none of these features reliably distinguished races. The problem was that all features were present in all populations, just in different frequencies. Of ten traits examined, only one proved reliable in distinguishing Black people from others, but this trait is only present in as few as 2% of people of African ancestry.

A second method for assessing race (or what present-day practitioners prefer to call ancestry) from bones is known as the metric method. A metric technique involves carefully measuring the length and dimensions of certain bones, particularly those of the skull, and then to compute ratios and other indexes based on these figures. When compared with a reference group the similarity or variances of the subject can be noted. Note that the metric method does not rely on any particular trait being associated with a particular racial group, but rather uses a comparison of many points of measurement to trace the subtle differences of anatomy that accumulate the more different populations are separated. (Populations can be separated by distance, as in occupying far-flung regions of the globe, or they can be separated by social barriers that prevent groups from mixing in the same community, or they can be separated in time by living in different periods of history.)

Modern forensic investigations on large populations have shown that skull anatomies do vary subtly between widely separated populations. Still only about ten percent of the variation in skull dimensions can be accounted for between populations situated on different continents (in contrast to skin pigmentation, 80-88% of which varies continentally). The rest is just random variation, or genetic drift. Nevertheless, this small degree of variation in bone features found between geographically distant populations has been just enough of a difference to allow forensic anthropologists to statistically compare specimens and infer ancestry.

The ability of anthropologists to sort skulls by race by a metric method has been repeatedly tested and proven. In one of the largest recent studies it was shown that by using 19 specific measurements white and black American skulls could be correctly compared 97% of the time. White, African American, Chinese and Native American skulls were sorted accurately from each other 96% of the time.

Such findings would appear to support the idea that races exist and are biological and real. After all, if race was an illusion why were anthropologists so good at sorting skulls and bones by race? But just because the traditional divisions of race "work" to sort skulls doesn't mean these

Figure 2.8 Man examining skulls, Harris & Ewing, 1926.

categories exist in nature. In a natural pattern of continuous variation any number of ways of categorizing may "work" but don't necessarily mean that distinct groups exist in nature. These metric methods don't work because there exist clear lines and boundaries between groups. Rather, they work because the relative statistical variation that can exist between isolated populations can be compared. When human bodies are looked at individually, not in comparison against some reference group, the high accuracy of racial identification falls apart.

This point was made by an anthropologist who studied an unidentified body, a "John Doe," found in a rural area of Iowa. Using just the measurements taken from the victim's skull and comparing them with published lists of populations with similar dimensions, this individual would have been identified as a member of the tiny community of indigenous Easter Islanders, a place 5000 miles away. However, when compared with the typical metrics of the population of Iowa, it was likely the man would have described himself as "white."

The point is that identification of race cannot be absolute because race is a category created by humans not by nature. By changing the definition of what constitutes a group, in a sense drawing a different line over the natural pattern, nearly any division or order of groups can be created. Researchers have shown that by using the same metric methods that successfully divided skulls into American racial categories, other "non-racial" groups could also be comparatively categorized at a high level of confidence. Chinese, Japanese, and Vietnamese skulls could be distinguished from each other 80% of the time. The skulls of women from the Arikara and Sioux nations, both native to the Dakotas, could be correctly sorted 87% of the time. Skulls from men in Tohoku, in northern Japan, could be separated from those from men from Nagasaki, in southern Japan, with 94% accuracy. Certainly if the most basic division of humankind, as once believed, is that between three broad geographically based groups in Africa, Asia, and Europe, then such geographically close peoples should not be as easy to categorize by their bones as distant ones. What these studies reveal is that the patterns of human variation are complex and can be made to fit into any number of boxes that people care to create.

Forensic scientists now generally accept that use of bones or other body measurements to identify race is fraught with difficulties, not the least being that the categorization of ancestry or race cannot be determined apart from the fickle and arbitrary ways society labels different groups. While people from far-flung parts of the globe do vary physically in many ways and those variations can often be marked and comparatively distinguished from others, such differences do not always (or in many cases even usually) align with the socially-created groupings that we call races or ethnicities.

Ancestry Testing

Over the past decade the plummeting cost of genetic testing has allowed for larger surveys of the relationship between what is written in our genes and how we identify ourselves. Dozens of commercial companies now offer genetic ancestry testing for a relatively low cost (around $100).

To some the ability of DNA to trace ancestry, especially ancestry to the particular continental regions of Africa, Europe, Asia, and the Americas, would seem to confirm that races are natural and real. After all, how could a genetic test be able to sort people into racial groups if racial groups didn't exist in nature? Actually, what these tests confirm is that human genes vary in their frequencies from population to population increasingly as populations grow more distant. These tests do not find that any point along this gradient of genes where one group's characteristics suddenly change into those of another. Rather, when we choose to compare populations separated by great distances we find that the frequencies of genes in each population vary enough to be able to distinguish one from another. But this ability says nothing about these groups being groups and this technique does not show that the fundamental pattern of human variability is among groups.

Moreover, DNA testing of this sort relies mostly on genetic markers from parts of the chromosome that are not linked to particular physical characteristics (most of the human genome does not actually code or control anything, but is a legacy of the long-term evolution of life itself). Thus grouping people by these markers does not imply that these groups share a set of characteristics that others do not. In fact, what these tests confirm is what anthropologists have argued since the early twentieth century: humans vary from place to place, but not by very much and not fundamentally according to the patterns we call races.

Today the accuracy of ancestral genetic tests are severely limited by the relatively small sample sizes of ref-

Figure 2.9 The Genealogical Tree, illustration by Geo. Heiss, n.d.

erence populations. As there are no particular traits that belong to one group or another and individuals within all groups vary significantly, the only way to determine relatedness is to statistically compare a genetic sample with a database of samples gathered from around the world. Because human variation is mostly continual over distance and patterns of variation can be discerned at levels far below those associated with continents or races, the larger the number of reference samples the better.

According to internal documents provided by one of the largest commercial ancestry testing companies, 23andMe, the reference data that they use to calculate a customer's DNA profile is highly skewed toward European samples. When attempting to find a match to a DNA sample, 23andMe compares it to 6842 samples taken from various communities in Europe. That same sample is compared to just 1368 reference samples drawn from Asian and Native American subjects and 621 individuals from Sub-Saharan Africa. A recent paper written by geneticists at 23andMe included the revealing disclaimer, "We note that our cohorts are likely to have ancestry from many African populations, but because of current reference sample availability, our resolution of West African ancestries is outside the scope of our study."

More fundamentally, ancestry genetics, because it relies on finding matches between a customer's spit and the DNA of reference groups around the world, depends on how one defines a group and how society has come to label different peoples as groups. What is a "European" after all? Where does Europe begin and end? Why are people from southern Spain and Northern Finland in the same group, but a Spaniard and a Moroccan (separated by less than 8 miles across the straits of Gibraltar) are not? The "reference European populations" that 23andMe uses include the usual suspects, France, England, and Germany, but also Finland, Russia, Turkey and Iran. Another large testing company for a time lumped together people from the Eastern Mediterranean, those from India, and Native Americans into a single group. Another included matches with West African samples as African but because it didn't have any reference samples among East Africans, a person with such ancestry would have discovered they had no relationship to Africa. The point is that this method of genetic ancestry testing will always tend to reproduce the social labels and categories history has invented, not the ones that nature did.

What these companies call "ancestry testing" does not actually link people in the present to people who lived in the past. Rather, they find statistical (probabilistic) similarities between an individual and samples taken from reference groups around the world. The reference samples used to determine ancestry are not actual historic populations, since no scientists were around to gather blood samples or swab cheeks 500 years ago. Rather they are collections of samples gathered from present-day populations around the world and there is a high likelihood that people, even whole communities, have moved around in that long span of time. Moreover, 500 years is long enough for people's genes to have moved around even if they have not. In other words, a match indicates the probability of some sort of relationship with some group of living individuals elsewhere in the world, not dead ancestors.

Even with a large number of reference samples to compare against, a match of a customer's DNA with a reference sample does not necessarily mean a person is actually related by direct ancestry to that sample population. This is because any single matched genetic variant need not be characteristic of a particular group and probably does not remain the possession of a particular group. Genes like to travel and they can travel directly as human populations migrate or they can move on their own, jumping from person to person in stepping stone fashion over greater distances than any person in that chain ever travelled.

An additional problem with ancestry tests is that the farther back one attempts to look the more ancestors there are to find. As a result of the limitations of analyzing mitochondrial DNA (which is passed unchanged from mother to daughter) or Y chromosome DNA (which is passed mostly unchanged from father to son), ancestry tests can usually only discover relationships to a single ancestor each generation.

The math of this problem is straightforward. One problem of ancestry testing is the sheer number of ancestors each of us has. Every individual who has ever lived has two parents, and each of them has two parents, and so forth. The formula for calculating your ancestry is the simple one of raising 2 to the power of the number of generations back you care to go. These geometric numbers add up very quickly. Ten generations reaches back to about the year 1650 and that far back a person has 1024 ancestors, many more (a total of 2047) if you count all ancestors, not just those alive in 1650. Go back twenty generations and there are 4,194,304 ancestors (and a cumulative total of 8,388,607). In practice few people have that many direct ancestors because prior to the modern era cousins did procreate quite often, but the point still holds—ancestry is not a single point of origin, but a cloud of connections to people in the past.

There is another type of ancestry genetic test, one that looks at a large number of single variations in a region of the chromosome that is known to be highly variable (because it does not actually code for any particular traits and therefore selection pressures do not push them toward a standard expression). This technique while capturing genetic contributions from more ancestors, is still limited by the fact that each generation the genetic contribution of any parent is halved and over many generations the amount of genetic material actually tracked is a very small proportion of the overall contributions of thousands of ancestors. So even this broader method actually measures a relatively small amount of overall relatedness among humans.

In order to represent genetic variation (which is messy) as distinct percentages of national or continental ancestry, genetic testing companies smooth their data to make it more uniform. The actual results of genetic testing are a matter of complicated probability, like a scatter-chart, rather than the clean proportions of a pie-chart. In order to convert the fuzzy nature of probability to something easier to apprehend by the customer (and also more marketable) the testing companies arbitrarily assign confidence thresholds for triggering membership in any particular group. Most companies then report their results as a percentage of continental ancestry, as in "78.3 % Northern European," and "21.7% Sub-Saharan African."

By reporting ancestry results as clean proportions down to one-tenth of a percent of national or continental identity, these companies promote the false idea that races are distinct groups that vary from "pure" (or 100%) membership to "mixed," for all others. Though labelled as "continental" ancestry, these divisions tend to reinforce popular ideas of racial groups as being natural and separate, not products of the sampling that produced those particular reference groups and the social history that gave them certain names and identities. In this way ancestry testing reinforces the usual biases and misunderstandings of race.

While genetic testing "works," in the sense it can provide a rough breakdown of the likelihood of direct ancestral connection to various regions of the globe, that does not mean that such ancestry is what we popularly think of as race. Ancestry does not equal genetic difference even though we are able to read certain genetic markers to trace human connections. In an official statement on ancestry testing released in 2008, the American Society for Human Genetics concluded, "Population genetic inference is ultimately a statistical exercise, and rarely can definitive conclusions about ancestry be made beyond the assessment of whether putative close relatives are or are not related."

Medicine

Doctors have long used race as a tool for diagnosis and treatment for more than a century. Physicians have long believed that certain diseases were linked to racial traits and certain medicines worked better in some races than others.

Unfortunately, for much of the history of medicine, doctors and researchers treated race not as the fuzzy, changing, and contradictory category that it is, but viewed it as a fundamental basis of human difference. Over the past century medical researchers have applied racial labels to their patients and subjects without much concern or care about how people get assigned to various groups. Sometimes research subjects are racially labelled by medical professionals and other times they are allowed to choose their own race and sometimes both methods have been used in the same study! In America, unlike some other societies, a person is considered black if they have even one distant relative who is black, but one is not considered white in a similar fashion. A surprising number of people don't

actually know their own ancestry. One study revealed that more than one in three of people surveyed did not know the identity of all four of their grandparents. Another research project discovered that one-third of subjects changed the race they reported in consecutive years.

One of the most common drugs, Warfarin, a blood thinner, is commonly prescribed in different doses depending on the race of the patient. Various studies had seemed to show that people of different races, particularly Asians, seemed to react differently to the medicine. Researchers understood that this effect was not in fact a consequence of being a member of a certain race, but that the frequencies of certain genes that interacted with the medicine differed across populations and some of this difference was captured by use of the label "Asian." However, once researchers were able to identify the actual genes involved and test their subjects on an individual basis, race was no longer a significant factor compared to knowledge of individual genetic codes. One study concluded that when race was used by itself to determine the best dosing of Warfarin, it explained 14.2% of the variation between individuals. When used in combination with actual genetic information, race explained only 0.3% of variation. In this case race was not a reliable tool for medical diagnosis or treatment.

Sickle cell anemia is a mutation of the red blood cell that limits its ability to carry oxygen through the body. In order to contract this genetic mutation, both of a person's parents must carry a copy of the sickle cell gene. Inheriting a single copy of the sickle cell trait does not lead to anemia but it does provide some protection against malaria, a mosquito-borne parasite which may have collectively killed more people than any other infectious disease. Over time, the sickle cell trait became common among human populations where malaria was widespread, especially in equatorial Africa and in the eastern Mediterranean. Because most African-Americans can trace some part of their ancestry to the western and central parts of Africa, rates of sickle cell disease are much higher among blacks than among whites and for the better part of a century sickle cell has commonly been thought of as a "black" disease.

But sickle cell disease is not limited to black folks. It is also common among people of Greek and Sicilian ancestry, people today commonly considered "white." Notably sickle cell is not common among South Africans, and so the idea of it being a "racial" disease only appears to be the case in the United States because of its peculiar demographic history.

Similarly, doctors had long observed that African Americans disproportionately suffered from high blood pressure (hypertension) and assumed that this had something to do with their race. But a worldwide study of tens of thousands of people with hypertension found

Figure 2.10 Women waiting to see the doctor on a Saturday morning in San Augustine, Texas, in 1939. Photo by Russell Lee.

no correlation between race and the disease. In fact, it noted such facts as that rates of hypertension in Nigeria were much lower than in Germany. Only in the U.S. did hypertension appear to have racial characteristics, calling into question whether the problem was the color of one's skin or the social discrimination that resulted from it.

Biopsychosocial Model of Racism

Many large scale medical studies have documented the link between race and disease, which many medical practitioners have presumed indicates the importance of racial genetics and, therefore, the significance of race itself. According to the Centers for Disease Control, African Americans have lower average life spans, higher rates of infant mortality, and lower birth weight babies than whites. Black children have higher rates of asthma and diabetes, while black adults have higher death rates due to cancer. A black man in Harlem has a lower chance than a man living in Bangladesh to reach the age of 65. Such vast disparities are seen by many as the clearest evidence that racial differences are more than skin deep.

But many researchers have noted that the environmental and social stresses of racism, such as enduring social disapproval and suspicion, poverty, unemployment, work in toxic environments, and being forced to reside in polluted and unhealthy neighborhoods, all take a toll on the body and manifest themselves in physical changes. Scientists have found strong correlations between the stress of racism and the diseases of hypertension, mental illness, auto-immune disorders, diabetes, and other conditions.

Recent research is also documenting that persistent racial discrimination can have effects beyond the individual but can influence subsequent generations as well. This transgenerational effect has been theorized to operate as racial discrimination impacts the health and well-being of mothers who then suffer prenatal malnutrition and prenatal stress of a variety of kinds.

Researchers have shown that various genetic pathways can be switched on or off by environmental effects. It turns out that gene expression can be altered without necessarily changing the arrangement of DNA within genes. As one researcher put it, genes don't just express the genetic code but other mechanisms serve as the volume knob amplifying or muting their expressions. Such "epigenetic" impacts of environment, or even of traumatic experiences, have been shown to alter the developmental biology of the growing fetus. (Intriguing new research also indicates even paternal stress experiences can impact how genes will be expressed.) Because there is this interplay between environment and genetics, social conditions like racial oppression can, in effect, become embodied and physical.

One of the reasons why race continues to be leaned on as an explanation for all sorts of medical issues is that race paints these problems as the result of natural processes. Heredity is something society morally can't do anything about. Thus by assuming a racial component for diseases avoids showing how they are related to class and power, things that society actually could do something about. One recent review of several large scale studies of child psychological disorders noted that most of them relied on biological explanations for the patterns of disorders found without even recording data about their subjects' wealth or education. This in spite of a large weight of evidence that some childhood psychological disorders are highly influenced by the experience of abuse in the home and that impoverished families suffer higher rates of domestic abuse. A psychologist critical of the way his peers dealt with issues of race and inheritance wrote, "Scientists cannot explain most behaviors by describing a brain state created by one or more alleles while ignoring the intermediate phases. Every human allele is part of a genome; every genome is part of a brain–body; every brain–body is in an agent; every agent is in a family; every family is in a community; every community is in a society; and every society is in a historical era."

In 1994 the National Institutes of Health issued a new rule requiring all recipients of federal health research grants to include women and "members of minorities" in all human trials and to include the government-mandated racial categories in their grant proposals and reports. While originally a well intentioned effort to steer cutting-edge treatments and remedies to those historically overlooked, by forcing researchers to use racial categories these guidelines further entrench idea that race is a biologically and medically essential category. This is especially dangerous as many researchers use this term uncritically and without the scientific precision reserved for any other testable category.

Even today the vast majority of medical scientists employ standard racial categories in their research without attempting to define or specify how or why these labels apply, two basic principles of scientific inquiry. A study of National Cancer Institute grant proposals made in the 1990s found that even among those proposals that stated as their goal determining the impact of race on health or treatment outcomes, fewer than one-fifth made any

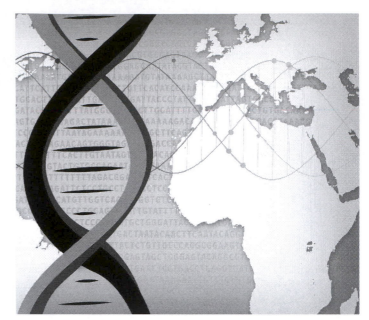

Figure 2.11 Model of a DNA double helix.

attempt to explain why race was a significant category of analysis. Another review of genetics articles published in leading journals from 2001 to 2004 found that fewer than one-tenth even attempted to justify their use of racial terms and none actually defined them. As the lead author of the study noted, "by not explaining what they mean by [racial] terms, authors reinforce the impression that race or ethnicity categories can be consistently distinguished and readily assigned."

Genetic Sampling Bias

Geneticists point out that no large group of humanity has ever been identified that has any characteristic not also found in every other large group. Rather, all that differs among groups is the frequency at which any trait is found. Thus there are no hard boundaries between groups. In fact, depending on what traits are sampled or what frequency threshold is used to define a group, the imagined boundaries of any group or even the number of groups can easily shift.

Much of modern population research depends upon comparing genetic samples to reference populations contained in massive public available databases. The largest and most referenced of these is the Genome Wide Association Study Catalog (GWASC) maintained by the U.S. National Human Genome Research Institute and the European Bioinformatics Institute. The GWASC is continually updated with the data of newly published genetic studies.

Though genetic researchers will readily admit that the study of human population should ideally be based on an even distribution of sample points around the globe, the GWASC, reflecting the ongoing bias in genetic studies themselves, is heavily biased in favor of European populations and poorly represents populations on the African continent or indigenous populations anywhere. As of August 2016, of the 35 million genetic samples archived in GWASC, 81% were taken from European populations. Though most people on earth live in Asia, only 14% of the GWASC samples Asian populations. 1.2 billion people live on the African continent and that continent is known to have the greatest genetic diversity on the planet, but fewer than 4% of GWASC samples come from Africa or from populations, like African Americans, who trace ancestry to Africa.

Such sampling bias causes distortions in the genetic research done on the basis of these datasets. One statistical consequence of limited sampling outside of Europe is to reinforce the idea of continental races as all groups except for Europeans become flattened into less diverse populations than they really are. Persistent sampling bias encourages researchers to describe non-Europeans as undifferntiated masses and to use vague and abiguous labels to describe them. One review of scientific papers found that only 9% of genetic studies even bothered to define the population and regional terms the scientists used. Another review of 80 scientific articles published since 2000 found that only European populations were carefully described according to nationality and region, and the only populations precisely described geographcally, such as "Lazio region of Italy" were Euroepan. Non-European populations were mostly imprecisely described in terms of traditional terms for race, such as "Asian," "African," and "black."

Viewing European populations as specific and unique did not stop these same researchers from assuming that all Europeans shared some quality they called "Caucasian" or "European," and that was assumed to be different from others. In fact, the reviewers faulted researchers for using labels that led them to assume differences that their datasets did not support:

European samples also served more often as the sample of reference in allele frequency comparisons. In such comparisons, the polymorphism frequency observed in European samples was more likely to be described as similar to that reported for other samples of European origin or samples described as "Caucasian," whereas non-European (mostly of Asian origin) sample allele frequencies were described as different from those of Europeans or Caucasians. Although reports of genetic association were only infrequently generalized beyond the specific named population sample, the generalizations we observed nearly always involved a population of European origin and generalization to the category "Caucasian" or to all humans.

The point here is that while the revolution in genetic science, the cracking of the human genome and the rapid spread and ease of genetic testing has given biologists and medical researchers powerful new tools to investigate humanity, the tools themselves do not dictate how they should best be used. Any instrument, no matter how powerful, can be subject to bias because the device does not dictate where it is pointed or how its data is converted into human language and human meaning. As we will see in the next chapter, science has frequently been mislead by the seemingly objective nature of its technologies compared with the invisibility of its own biases.

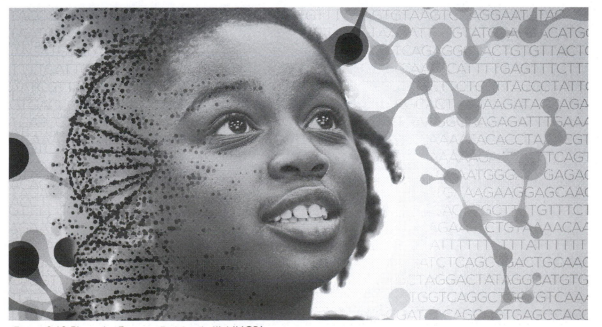

Figure 2.12 Photo by Ernesto Del Aguila III, NHGRI.

"IS GENOMICS THE CURE FOR DISPARITIES?"

A presentation by NHGRI Director Francis Collins to the National Leadership Summit to Eliminate Racial and Ethnic Disparities in Health, January 10, 2006

...I want to give the panel a chance to weigh in on this very important question. Is genomics the cure for disparities? Well let's consider the issue of inheritance and what role it plays in disease and what that has to say about health disparities, conditions that all of us are deeply concerned about and representing it by being here at this meeting.

If you look these young people, you will immediately perceive that they come from different ancestral geographic origins and they faced different futures as far as the likelihood of illness unless we do something about the disparities that are currently deeply disturbing, which brings us all here together for this historic gathering. How much of a difference do they face related to the DNA that they inherited and how much is related to environmental experiences and all manner of other issues that is attached to this very blurry concept called race. That is what I want to try to walk through recognizing that we still don't have a terribly precise answer to that question. We are learning quite a lot especially in the last couple of years.

Of course my focus because it is the thing that I know the most about is going to be on the inherited side of this and that means we need to talk about DNA, this really incredible molecule that exists within each cell of your body carrying information that you have inherited down through the generations and this particular information storage system in each in your body means that there is a complete set of instructions, a series of letters along the DNA code that you are either A, C, G, or T. and three billion of those make the human genome, the human instruction book.

It is a very remarkable thing that until very recently we didn't know a lot about that. We now have a whole instruction book in front us but let's ask the question of what is the nature of variation in that DNA. We are not all identical as we would all be one big set of identical twins and that would be pretty boring. So, what is the nature of that variation?

Well Genome project actually was not set up originally to pay as much attention to variation as it was to try to look at the part that we all share. So when the Human Genome Sequence was announced in its completed form in April of 2003, this was basically a hodge podge of DNA contributed by a number of autonomous individuals but that in itself didn't tell you much about the differences between people because any given segment of DNA came from just one person's chromosome. But clearly we need to understand that variation because varied within that portion of the genome are the risk factors for common illnesses that we really want to understand. And as it turns out that is only 0.1-percent of the DNA, 99.9-percent of the DNA is the same. But that point that 0.1-percent is obviously of great interest. To focus on that another International project was founded just a little over three years ago, the International HapMap project... From the space of just three years, once again coming in sooner than expected, the HapMap delivered a really remarkable picture of DNA variation occurs across all of the chromosomes. As major sent in DNA samples, 270 of them, that while they only represented those 270 people were chosen so that a third of those come from European background, a third from Asian background and a third from West African background. That then gives us a snapshot of something about how variations operate across the world as well as how it operates across chromosomes.

...Well what do we know about genetic variation in general? You know that from all manner of sources of information much from genetics but also from the fossil records and also from history, the migrations of the human species have been occurring in a very irregular way from our original founding population and we were once all Africans as I will come to in a moment, I think we now have very strong evidence that we were all once black Africans living in Africa. Yes? We, white people, as I will tell you in a minute, are actually mutants but we will come that. So, the estimates are that a hundred thousand years ago that there were about ten thousand homo sapiens. This was our founders; all of us, living in Africa and the variation that we see in present day human beings was largely already present in those founders. But that was a large enough group that there was a variation present. There haven't been that many new variations that have cropped up in the five thousand generations since then. Most of what is going as far as how genetic variations are organized around the world relates to the ways in which those genes were spread as people migrated out of Africa to other parts of the world....

On the other hand, a few of the variants that are present in this founder pool might actually have provided a selected advantage in one place or another. We all know the most dramatic example of that is the sickle mutation. If you are a carrier for sickle mutation, you are protected against the most severe consequences of the malarial parasite. So, those who carry that mutation and lived in a malarial area were able to survive better. Therefore that gene occurs with high frequency and whereas, for those who did not live in an area where malaria was prominent the sickle mutation provided no advantage. In fact, it would provide a disadvantage in those who were provided a double dose; those actually would develop a disease that would become sickle cell anemia...

Okay. So that is the story about genetic variations but now let's get really murky. What is the relationship between genetic variations and race? Well, first you have to decide exactly what do you mean by race. If we asked everybody in this room to write on a piece of paper a definition of race, that would be really interesting and I suspect we would get at least a number of definitions that there are number of people in the room and maybe more because some of you might want to provide a couple alternatives. The press hasn't helped us much here in terms of explaining how race and genetics are connected. Depending on which article you read you can read something like this that says that "genes, the study of them prove that race is only a sham. No trace of race in genome project proves nothing biologically separates people". But wait a minute if that is the case how can people be making money right now selling DNA tests that will tell you where your origins are and a lot of people are in fact interested in this information. If there is nothing in DNA that tells you something about ancestry, how is it true to say that there is no biological connection whatsoever to race. Here is one of the websites for one of the places that will do that kind of DNA testing and I gather they are getting lots of customers...

So, what does race mean anyway? I like Evelyn Higginbotham's quote: "When we talk about the concept of race most people believe that they know it when they see it, but arrive at nothing short of confusion when pressed to define it." Try it out on your neighbors and they will fall into confusion, I am quite sure. Most of us if really asked to write this down have that same problem.

Because race has so much baggage it carries with it connotations of history of discrimination. It carries with it cultural and society and dietary practices. It carries a little bit of ancestral geography of course but that in fact is probably the minority of what most people are actually thinking of when the term race appears in a sentence. And is it any wonder therefore as we try to figure out the connection between genetics and race, we have trouble because we are not quite sure what it is that we are connecting to.

So, what do we know about genetics and race? Let's focus on what we know and then I will try to point out the things that we don't know. Well, we know that we are all 99.9-percent the same at the DNA level. That is proven by HapMap and a variety of other types of studies. That is a phenomenal statement. We are much more like each other than other species on the planet. If someone arrived here from outer space and tried to write a little tree up about homo sapiens, one of the things that they would say is wow these people are really all alike. Compared to other species there is more diversity in a small group of chimpanzees living on one hillside than it is in the entire human race because we are so new on the field. It is these five thousand generations separating us from a very small pool of ancestors. That's pretty unprecedented for our species on the planet. But yet isn't that interesting that our characteristic is that we seem so focused on that difference, that 0.1-percent. That 0.1-percent of three billion is still a big number so that leaves a lot of differences between two individuals, most of those fall into places on the genome that isn't doing very much and have no consequence. And most of the variants as I said earlier that we do have were present in our common ancestors. But because of migratory events and a few other things the frequency of a particular variant where you might have a T and I might have a C, could be different depending on where your ancestors came from. Some of that is just drift. Just the sort of chance thing that happened as people migrated from one place to another and maybe brought a T over here and a C over there. And that has been absolutely no particular significance to anybody's health...

Selection however and new mutations are a different story. Selection as we talked about for sickle cell disease operating in a circumstance where a particular variant provides an advantage if you are a carrier for that. New mutations have occurred. For the most part, they appear and then they get lost if they have no advantage or disadvantage the chances of them hanging around for very long is pretty small, which is again why most of the common variation of the genome has been there since our founders and its still there today....

So let's continue our list of what we know about genetics and race. So those differences I just showed you that one but if you look across the whole genome, there are other places where there are quite a difference in frequency of a particular spelling depending upon where your ancestors came from. Most of those just because of drift, some them maybe showing some signs of selection from where we don't know what, and you can in fact use those differences to take a DNA sample and make a guess as to where that person's ancestors came from. But you are not going to be very precise about it especially since as increasingly lots of people don't have all of their ancestors coming from one place. And importantly when people draw out descriptions of human populations, they often draw out this kind as a tree with this rooted sort of foundation in Africa and all of these branches. But that is not really correct. Gene flow don't go in one direction. Genes have been flowing back and forth as long as we humans have been wandering about. In fact, it is probably more appropriate to draw our relationships with each other as a wisteria vine with all of these interconnecting branches.

Maybe that also helps understand why it is incorrect to try to draw boundaries around any particular group and say they are biologically different. That is not justified by the science that we now have in front of us, which means except maybe in a few cases of extreme geographic isolation, the founders of our population groups are going to be blurry and imprecise....

So, in summary here race is a term that carries a whole lot of baggage. I think we all agree. Much is being learned about genetic variation around the world. Neither of these statements is correct. Race has absolutely no biological basis. Not really true. There is a connection in ancestral geographic origin. It's murky but it's not absent. But it is certainly true if you can't draw sharp boundaries around groups based on genetics. So again, if you want to understand health disparities we should go after the proximal causes and not depend upon these muddy and misleading proxies. And to answer the question posed in this session is genomics the cure for health disparities probably not but in some instances, it may play a role in terms of heritable factors but almost always in concert with environmental factors. If we really want to know, we need more data. The good news is in another two or three years we are going to have a lot more data on this subject. I think therefore we will be much better poised to do something about it. Thank you very much.

Chapter Three: Racial Science

Scientists have long misinterpreted the apparent patterns of human variation as suggesting that humanity is naturally divided into subgroups, or races. Scientific attempts to categorize humanity began as a result of a vast intellectual and political upheaval known as the Enlightenment. Beginning in the 1600s, a time of rapid social and political change in Europe due to the discoveries and wealth being extracted from the Americas, Asia, and Africa, and the Protestant Reformation that challenged official religious ideas, many thinkers sought to root truth not in the Bible or church orthodoxy, but in reason and observation. Philosophers and naturalists like Francis Bacon, Galileo Galilei, and Isaac Newton, conceived of nature as a mechanism whose parts and workings could be understood through careful observation and demonstrated the power and practicality of such a method. Political theorists like René Descartes, John Locke, and Voltaire, likewise sought to ground government, laws, and social arrangements in understandings of human nature rather than ancient right and custom. Together these new ways of thinking about nature and society laid the groundwork for the modern world, but they also built the structures of ideas that became race and racism.

The rise of the scientific method was in part a rediscovery and extension of ideas first developed in ancient Greece. Most influential was Aristotle, who first proposed the importance of categorizing of things according to their family and kind, or genus and species. Aristotle held that study of nature was the discovery of the unique essences of things and these qualities distinguished one thing from another. Birds have wings and fish have gills and in this way their fundamental differences are expressed. This view of the world saw reality as a vast collection of essentially different things, not, as nature often is, a continuum of gradual differences. Following this logic, later thinkers and scientists would think of races as being fundamentally, essentially different. All the people of one race shared some qualities that no one in another racial group had. This did not mean that all the people of a race had to be identical, but they were seen to share some essence that people in other races lacked and visa versa.

Scientific Classification

Aristotle's system of categorizing nature (which didn't include human races) stood for more than a thousand years before the Enlightenment spurred a new era of scientific investigation. Carl Linnaeus, a Swedish physician and botanist who developed the system of biological classification that is still used today, was one of the first to expand on Aristotle's system so that it could name and draw connections between all living things. Unlike Aristotle, Linnaeus and his successors, included humanity within their systems of classification not as one type of creature but as a family of distinct species.

Linnaeus identified five species of humans, one of which, the *Homo ferus*, or wild man, was largely based on medieval fables of fantastic and monstrous men. The remaining four "varieties" of humans, that he called "Africanus", "Asiaticus", "Europeanus", and "Americanus," were derived from the ancient theory of the elements, or "humors," that circulated in the human body: phlegm, blood, and bile. Each humor corresponded with a primary element and color of nature, phlegm was white and water, blood was red and air, one type of bile was black and earth, and another type was yellow and fire. (Disease was theorized as an imbalance between the humors, which is why the sick were often bled, sweated, or forced to swallow powerful emetics so as to bring their humors into equilibrium.) Humors were also thought to be the basis of a person's personality; a rash and irritable person was thought to be choleric, a trait associated with fire and yellow bile. Indeed the word "temperament" is derived from the Latin word "temperare" which means "to mix together."

Linnaeus believed that the peoples of the earth had the characters and colors they did because nature gave them a preponderance of a particular humor. Like all the scientists of his day he believed that each of these groups were distinguished both by their geographic origins but, more importantly, by their "characteristics" which included such traits as Americanus being "zealous" and "stubborn" and Asiaticus being "severe" and "greedy." Thus his species of man consisted of the following:

Europaeus albus: white, ingenious, sanguine,
governed by law
Americanus rubescus: red, liberty-loving, tanned
and irascible, governed by custom
Asiaticus luridus: yellow, melancholy, governed
by opinion

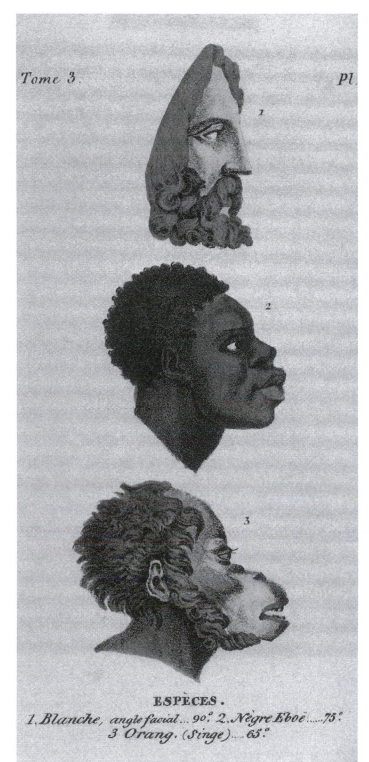

Figure 3.1 Illustration from Julien J. Virey, *Histoire Naturelle du Genre Humain* (Brussels: Aug. Wahlen, 1826), vol. 20, p. 39.

Afer niger: black, lazy, careless, governed by the
will of the master

Writing in 1735, Linnaeus powerfully tied together a number of quite different things—seeming differences in physical appearance, continental origins, psychological characteristics, and social behavior. Here was the essence of racial thinking, that all these things are connected and keyed to the color of bodies, distilled into a seemingly mundane classification scheme. His scientific successors, Blumenbach, Buffon, Kant, Jefferson, and many others, argued for centuries over whether there were four, five, six, or more human races, but none questioned Linnaeus' idea that all these things were bound together.

A generation later, in 1775, Johann Blumenbach improved upon Linnaeus' scheme by adding a fifth race. Blumenbach named his races "Caucasian, Mongolian, Malayan, Ethiopian, and American." While Linnaeus' division of humanity was based entirely on what he imagined different groups' physical characteristics to be, Blumenbach based his system of five races not only on presumed physical differences but on each group's having a different line of ancestors. (A later twentieth century scientist, Julian Huxley, would coin a term for that idea, clade, meaning a biological category in which groups occupy different branches of a family tree, each group sharing a different common ancestor in the deep misty past.)

Monogenesis and Polygenesis

Prior to rise of evolutionary theories of how differences among plants and animals, including humans, arose, scientists had but three possible explanations of why some people were light skinned and others had dark skin. The great English writer, Samuel Johnson, summed up the range of thought in his own day, 1763, to a friend who had asked him why some men were black:

> Why, Sir,… it has been accounted for in three ways: either by supposing that they were the posterity of Ham, who was cursed; or that God at first created two kinds of men, one black and another white; or that by the heat of the sun the skin is scorched, and acquires a sooty hue.

It was this middle possibility, that God created different kinds of men, that eventually predominated among racial scientists. As anatomical interest in the nature of blackness grew in the first decades of the eighteenth century, a new thought dawned on naturalists. Perhaps the physical differences between races were not the result of living in different climates or the consequence of Noah's biblical curse on the sons of Cain. Maybe people were different because there was more than one Adam and Eve? Ironically, this heretical idea was first put forward by a Jesuit priest, August Malfert, who wrote in 1733 of the possibility that different races spring from different origins and moments of creation in a religious journal.

Entangled in this argument were different religious views: did God create man all at once or multiple times in different places? If all humans shared a common origin and gradually grew different over time because they lived in different lands, a theory called environmentalism, then presumably their differences might not be so important or so permanent. But those who believed that races sprung from different Adams and different Eves concluded that races shared little in common and their unlikeness was fixed and timeless.

Both schools of thought, believers in monogenesis (the idea that the was one moment of creation—one Garden of Eden) and believers in polygenesis (those who held that each race was created separately), agreed that races, whatever their origins, were physically, culturally, and morally unequal. Monogenesists had the upper hand as the Bible seemed to be on their side ("[God] hath made of one blood all nations of men." Acts 17:26) But this did not deter the promoters of the idea of polygenesis, such as Lord Kames whose 1774 work, *Sketches of the History of Man,* proposed that there had been multiple divine acts of creation, each individually fitted to a different climate. The Scotsman compared the facts he had gathered about mankind with the Holy Book and found the book wanting, "Though we cannot doubt the authority of Moses, yet his account of the creation of man is not a little puzzling as it seems to contradict every one of the facts…"

Monogenesists, like Johann Blumenbach, thought having an origin theory that threatened to imply that because all people share the same origin they share similar fundamental qualities, sidestepped that possibility. Blumenbach speculated that over time different stocks of humans degenerated away from the perfection of creation so that those people most distant in descent and geography from Adam were the most inferior. Recall that by this principle, Blumenbach attempted to pinpoint the location of the actual Garden of Eden by collecting human skulls. Those skulls that appeared to Blumenbach to be the most beautiful and therefore the most 'perfect' must have originated closest to the place of creation. Blumenbach liked the skull of a teenage slave girl from the Caucuses the best and because of that gave the label "Caucasian" to those people who presumably shared her heritage.

Monogenesists had a more difficult time using their theory of common human origins to explain the human differences that seemed obvious. Polygenesists, after all, didn't need to explain where human differences came from as they could simply chalk them up to the separate origins of various human races, in other words groups were different because they were created differently. But those who followed the Bible and maintained that all people were descended from Adam and Eve, had to identify some mechanism by which different groups became dissimilar over time.

Like Johann Blumenbach, who coined the word "caucasian," many influential naturalists at the end of the 1700s squared their belief that all humanity was descended from one original couple with their equally strong belief that races were utterly and profoundly different from each other by the theory of degeneration. Most explicitly detailed by Georges-Louis Leclerc, Comte de Buffon (sometimes referred to simply as Count Buffon), the theory of degeneration held that groups of animals that became separated from their original stock gradually lost their vitality and decayed into lesser versions of their species. Comparing the animals (that he knew of) common in Europe and in America, Buffon wrote, "all the animals peculiar to the New World…differ from those of the Old Continent, nevertheless have some relations which seem to indicate some common affinity in their formation, and lead us to causes of degeneration more ancient than any of the rest. We have already made the general remark that all animals of the New World, were much smaller than those of the Old. This great diminution in size, whatever may be the cause, is a primary kind of degeneration…"

It was not just America's animals that had degenerated into less strong and fertile versions of the originals, it was also America's native people. Buffon claimed America was "an unprolific land, thinly peopled with wandering savages, who…"

had no property or empire; and, having subjected neither the animals or the elements… nor cultivated the earth…existed as…a kind of weak automaton, incapable of improving…In the savage, the organs of generation are small and feeble. He has no hair, no beard, no ardour for the female…his strength is not so great. His sensations are less acute; and yet he is more timid and cowardly. He has no vivacity, no activity of mind…Their love to parents and children is extremely weak. The bonds of the most intimate of all societies, that of the same family, are feeble; and one family has no attachment to another. Hence no union, no republic, no social state, can take place among them…Their heart is frozen, their society cold, and…cruel.

Interestingly, while Blumenbach was convinced that white people must have been the original people and all other races degenerated from their perfection, Buffon speculated that this might be backwards. Buffon noted that geology indicated that the earth was once much hotter than it was in the 1700s and had cooled. "…and as the negroes are in the human race those whom a strong heat the least incommodes, might we not conclude, according this hypothesis, that earth has continued to decline from its original heat, and that the race of negroes are more ancient than that of white people."

Figure 3.2 Advertisement for exhibition, (New York: n.d.).

should not be confused with the belief that nature should be conserved and protected from pollution and destructive human activities.

Degeneration theory pushed American scientists to side with theories of environmentalism, as this was a way of upholding the vigor and superiority of both the American land and its people. Thomas Jefferson was constantly on the lookout for American varieties of European plants and animals that were larger and stronger than those on the continent. As President, Jefferson even sent to Europe a skeleton of a prehistoric moose that proved that American moose were bigger than European moose.

Environmentalism

Such entanglement of scientific theories and American nationalism peaked after the American Revolution and lead American scientists to believe they had evidence for racial characteristics being readily changeable. Patriot and scientist Benjamin Rush theorized that dark skin was a form of leprosy. Samuel Stanhope Smith, the president of the College of New Jersey (later Princeton), argued in his "Essay on the Causes of the Variety of Complexion and Figure in the Human Species," that all humans were descended from Adam and their color was entirely the result of the climate in which they lived and their "mode of living." Smith took his argument to its natural conclusion: eventually all people living in America will have the same skin color, as those who are dark lighten, and those who are light darken. He even had evidence that the environment was having just this effect: it was well observed, Smith noted, that slaves who worked in their master's houses as domestics tended to be lighter colored than those who worked in the fields. Smith could only conclude from this that the superior culture of white people had bleached them and was blind to other simpler explanations.

The question of how color was formed was not simply an abstract one in those days when race determined the extent of a person's status and rights. Troubling to many were the reports of physicians who documented a succession of cases of black men spontaneously turning white and of parents having babies of different color than themselves or twins of different hues.

To some the idea that black parents could have white children was reassuring of both a certain order of nature and of white racial superiority. The idea that black parents occasionally, and "by accident" had white children was frequently employed in support of the claim that humanity's common ancestor—whether Adam or Noah or Noah's sons—was white and that darkness was a degradation of man's pristine state. In 1785, an essayist in *The Boston Magazine* wrote "We have frequently seen white children

Degeneration theory was far from being a coherent theory of life and nature. It had no clear mechanism by which things degenerated from their original form except a vague idea that something in the soil, or the climate, or the foods people ate, caused their forms to deteriorate over time. This idea that animal and human forms were somehow shaped and determined by their environments is known as environmentalism--though an environmentalism that produced from black parents, but have never seen a black offspring the production of two whites. From hence we may conclude that whiteness is the colour to which mankind generally tends; for, as in the tulip, the parent flock is known by all the artificial varieties breaking into it; from man, that color must be original which never alters, and to which all the rest are accidentally seen to change."

Apart from scientists, most regular people at the time assumed that the world was a place of mysteries, magic, and miracles. Folk beliefs and popular wisdom had the power to explain the wondrous and the mysterious much better than could "science." Popular beliefs allowed for just such possibilities as people changing color and babies born of a color utterly unlike their parents.

The miraculous birth of white babies to black parents and visa versa was periodically reported in medical journals and books throughout the early nineteenth century. In 1835 the *Boston Medical and Surgical Journal* reported on the birth in Berlin of twins "one presenting the color and form of a mulatto." The next issue contained a letter from a Massachusetts physician who knew a black couple who had twins of different colors. A similar report from Virginia cropped up in 1845. A review of a number of books on heredity in 1859 noted the case of a "black woman confined of a white child, and was thereupon in great fear of her [black] husband, and tried to keep the child from his sight as long as she could."

While all the experts expressed great confidence in their scientific understanding of racial inheritance, the fact was that this subject troubled physicians and scientists for much of the nineteenth century. In 1852, Dr. W.L. Sutton, president of the Kentucky Medical Society could only conclude, "Many persons think nothing would be easier than to 'tell a white child from a black one,' but like a great many other things, the more it is studied, the more difficulties start up."

In the nineteenth century, most scientists and doctors, wishing for a natural state of racial order that had long eluded observation, simply asserted a high degree of predictability in the inheritance of racial features. Dr. C. E. Ristine writing in the *Medical and Surgical Reporter* in 1897 proclaimed: "It is well known that the characteristics of skin, hair, etc., are transmitted from the paternal side. For example, the progeny of a white woman and a negro show the negro paternity by the color and character of the skin, while the progeny of the negro woman and a white man evidences the white father in a like manner." Clearly, by this time, the folk beliefs and popular wisdom that had allowed for a world of wonders, monsters, and the power of maternal imagination had lost its force as an alternative to the certainties of scientific categorization. Actual scientific knowledge of human reproduction had not much advanced from the time of the ancient Greeks. It is clear that the development of what passed for medical facts dealing with race were driven mostly out of the need to create firm rules of racial descent and thereby uphold a world rapidly dividing into absolutes of black and white.

The fact was that as the nineteenth century began the old Environmentalist ideas of race, along with the belief in the essential unity of humankind, came under increasing attack. American slavery and European colonialism emerged as the main drivers of economic growth and science bent to the will of the marketplace. Speculations as to the possibility that humans were not merely divided into subgroups, called races, but that Africans, Europeans, and Asians were actually different species, fundamentally alien to one another, first appeared about the time of the American Revolution. Edward Long, included in his influential book, *The History of Jamaica* (1774), his opinion that whites and blacks were different species. "When we reflect on the nature of these men, and their dissimilarity to the rest of mankind, must we not conclude, that they are a different species of the same genus? Of other animals, it is well known, there are many kinds, each kind having its proper species subordinate thereto; and why shall we insist, that man alone, of all other animals, is undiversified in the same manner, when we find so many irresistible proofs which denote his conformity to the general system of the world?"

Edward Long knew that biology had placed a large hurdle in the way of considering races as species. The generally accepted definition of a species required that members of different species not be able to mate and reproduce, or at minimum, have fertile offspring. (Horses and donkeys can reproduce but their offspring, called mules, are incapable of reproducing.) But like so many other scientists of his age, somehow his observations twisted to support the conclusions he desired. Writing of Jamaica's growing "mulatto" population—a term whose latin root means 'mule'—Long observed "The Mulattos are, in general, well-shaped, and the women well-featured....Some few of them have intermarried here with those of their own complexion; but such matches have generally been defective and barren. They seem in this respect to be actually of the mule-kind, and not so capable of producing from one another as from a commerce with a distinct White or Black." Long, of course, was completely and utterly incorrect, but his observations would be repeated for more than a century as scientific evidence of the sexual incompatibility of the races. In fact, the debate about the infertility of human races would continue into the 1930s and one work mentioned it seriously as late as 1974.

So many race scientists of the nineteenth century saw only what their personal interests dictated they even occasionally revealed how their science was fully in the service of the interests of white supremacy, slavery, and colonial domination of the entire world. For example, Theodor

Waitz, Marburg University professor and author of the six volume *Die Anthropologie der Naturvölker* (or 'Science of Natural People'), wrote this in 1858:

> If there be various species of mankind, there must be a natural aristocracy among them, a dominant white species as opposed to the lower races who by their origin are destined to serve the nobility of mankind, and may be tamed, trained, and used like domestic animals, or may, according to circumstances, be fattened or used for physiological or other experiments without any compunction. To endeavor to lead them to a higher morality and intellectual development would be as foolish as to expect that lime trees would, by cultivation, bear peaches, or the monkey would learn to speak by training. Wherever the lower races prove useless for the service of the white man, they must be abandoned to their savage state, it being their fate and natural destination. All wars of extermination, whenever the lower species are in the way of the white man, are not only excusable, but fully justified.

If nineteenth century scientists couldn't explain well how racial inheritance worked, they could claim to measure it. For more than a century (and in some cases even up to the present time) scientists devoted their energies to determining the precise anatomical differences that characterized different races. They repeatedly convinced themselves that in this endeavor they found the differences they sought, though their success in doing so was a result of their use of small sample sizes, predetermining the very categories they then supposedly discovered, misinterpreting their data, and occasionally conducting outright fraud.

Human Exhibitions

Many of the scientific ideas about racial difference were not derived from any particular objective method of investigation, but by the examination and study of people who were seized from far-flung distant places of the globe and exhibited across Europe in traveling shows, fairs, theatres, and even zoos.

Since the beginning of European colonialism, individuals that Europeans encountered were often seized and brought back to Europe to be put on display. Christopher Columbus himself captured native peoples and forcibly hauled them back to Spain to exhibit to the Queen. Danes who explored Greenland seized nine Inuits to parade in the court of Christian IV. Martin Frobisher didn't find the Northwest Passage he sought but he did kidnap three Inuit people from Baffin Island, a man, Calichoughe, a woman, Egnock, and her child, Nutioc, and brought them back to exhibit in England where all of them died soon after arrival.

Exhibitions and traveling shows that displayed peoples brought to Europe from far-flung places were hugely popular and quite lucrative. Chang and Eng, brothers congenitally connected and called the "Siamese Twins" were a sensation in Europe in 1829, as their anatomical anomaly only served to enhance their "exotic" strangeness that so interested their viewers. Through such commercial exhibitions that presented themselves as "scientific" and "educational" displays of uncivilized natives, Europeans became accustomed to thinking about other people as being radically and fundamentally different from themselves, not to mention inferior by all measures of society and culture.

In the 1870s Europe's leading promoter and owner of zoos, Carl Hagenbeck, faced with increasing competition from imitators, experimented with including humans among his exhibits of tigers, giraffes, and zebras. Instead of just purchasing reindeer from "Lapland" for his zoo in Hamburg, Germany, he shipped six indigenous Sami, three men, a woman, and two children as well, and put them all on display (note that in Swedish, the word "lapp" means simpleton or idiot, and the people of "Lapland" call themselves Saami). So many Germans flocked to watch the Saami men erect and pull down their tents, milk the deer, and leer at the women nursing their babies, that extra police had to be called to control the crowds. Hagenback built on his success the following year by exhibiting a group of people from Nubia, in southern Egypt, along with their camels.

In these exhibits - some in zoos and others in fairs, exhibition halls, or traveling shows - the people on display were usually scantily clothed, highlighting their supposed primitive sexuality. Usually advertised as "wild," "natural," or "savage," the people in these exhibits were expected to behave in ways considered indecent by their onlookers. Over time these exhibitions of "exotic" peoples spread ideas about the natural and radical disparities between peoples of different races not only throughout the public, but into the supposedly expert understandings of scientists themselves.

Scientists gathered much of their information about distant people by attending these human shows and making arrangements with zoo promoters to examine the people they displayed. It was not uncommon for a new touring human exhibit to be accompanied by a flurry of scientific articles in anthropological and medical journals.

In 1784, one of Europe's most famed anatomists, Samuel Thomas von Soemmerring, published the work that would serve as the basic textbook of comparative black and white anatomy for the next century, *Über die körperliche*

Verschiedenheit des Mohren vom Europäer (Concerning the Physical Difference between the Moor and the European). The black bodies von Soemmering dissected were all from near Kassel, Germany, where a community of "exotic" Africans had been collected by Duke Frederick II along with leopards, elephants, and camels.

The most famous example of the influence of these traveling displays of racialized persons was the tragic case of Saartjie (Sara) Baartman. Baartman was born in 1789, the daughter of a cattle drover who was orphaned by the time she was reached puberty. She met a young man with whom she had a child, who died in infancy. After her boyfriend was murdered by a Boer (a Dutch settler), Baartman had no other choice but to sell herself into the service of another Boer.

In 1810 she was taken by her master's brother and an English surgeon to England where she was put on display as the "Hottentot Venus." She refused to agree to appear naked, though she did wear flesh-colored tights, wore beads, and smoked a clay pipe. One observer of one of her performances recounted:

> [She was] surrounded by many persons some females! One pinched her, another walked round her; one gentleman poked her with his cane; and one lady employed her parasol to ascertain that all was as she called it, "nattral." This inhuman baiting the poor creature bore with sullen indifference, except upon some great provocation, when she seemed inclined to resent brutality, which even a Hottentot can understand.

Over time her show evolved to include Baartman dancing and playing instruments, but as the novelty wore off, and London society tired of her, she was taken to France and exhibited in increasingly cheaper venues. Eventually she agreed to be studied by Georges Cuvier, a scientist interested in investigating "racial types." When Baartman died suddenly, aged 26, Cuvier dissected her body and donated her skeleton and jars containing her brain and genitals to the Musee' de l'Homme (Museum of Man) in Paris where they were put on public display for the next century and a half. In 1862 her skeleton was remeasured by the famed anatomist Paul Broca. (It took several years of high level talks and the personal intervention of South African president Nelson Mandela plus a unanimous vote of France's National Assembly to convince the Musee' de l'Homme to finally repatriate Sara Baartman's remains to her homeland in 2002.)

Cuvier himself used Baartman's body as the model of all "negroes" for his influential and often cited works on comparative anatomy. Cuvier's observations were shot through with his prejudices as when he explicitly compared

Figure 3.3 "Love and beauty--Sartjee the Hottentot Venus," by Christopher Crupper Rumford (England), 1811.

her anatomy to that of an ape, "I have never seen a human head more similar to that of a monkey's."

At times scientists themselves became showmen. In May of 1847 Dr. Robert Knox, who was then working on his influential book, *The Races of Man*, hosted an evening performance in London's Exeter Hall. Knox lectured on the character of human races and then introduced a troupe of Africans he referred to as "Bushmen" (they called themselves San). The four San paraded around the hall in their native dress, carrying bows, and then staged a "debate" in their language which, of course, none of the hundreds watching them understood.

The popularity of these human exhibits only grew over time. In the last quarter of the nineteenth century, there were at least 50 exhibitions of humans taken from colonies around the world in Denmark alone. Over time the theatrical components of these displays became more sophisticated as promoters invested in elaborate sets, props, and even moving panoramic backdrops to add to the performance's authenticity which audiences seemed to demand. Of course, such authenticity was a sham and served primarily to reinforce stereotypes of savage and primitive people and, by way of contrast, to make Europeans feel superior and entitled.

John Conolly, physician and president of London's Ethnological Society, noted the popularity of these human exhibitions in 1855, writing, "There is scarcely a year in which, among the miscellaneous attractions of a London season, we do not find some exhibition illustrative of the

Figure 3.4 Poster advertising the exhibition of the Hottentot Venus (London: Chester, 1810).

varieties of mankind." Conolly displayed an unusual degree of conscience as he wondered what happened to the Aztec and African children he had seen displayed when their exhibitors were through with them:

> ...what becomes of the illustrations when either the novelty of their exhibition has passed away, and the Town demands fresh wonders, or even when they have grown too big and troublesome to be carried about. The lives of the Aztecs have been insured by their proprietor, to whom they were sold like sheep; but what support is assured to them? Already they are falling into the class of minor shows, and exhibited in the suburbs. If they die, the exhibitor will receive the sum insured on their lives; if they outlive their popularity, what provision is made for them? In what workhouse will they end their days?...If they stay in England, to what depths of want and degradation may they not gradually descend?.... During their long sojourn in this country, it is pitiable to see human beings stared at as mere objects of temporary amusement, to whose subsequent condition all are indifferent.

Such displays proved popular in the United States as well, especially during the period when "World's Fairs" were held nearly every decade beginning with Philadelphia's "Centennial Exposition" of 1876 and extending well into the twentieth century.

Anatomy

For thousands of years European thinkers relied on ancient Greek and Roman medical texts for their knowledge of the human body. This medical theory that predominated for so long is called "Humoral Theory" because it holds that good health is a delicate balance of four fundamental bodily systems or "humors" (the word humor is a translation of the Greek word for "juice"). Each of these humors is associated with a particular bodily fluid, red blood, black or yellow bile, and white phlegm. Each of these substances was then associated with various diseases that arise when one humor falls out of balance with the others.

However, because humoral theory was a complete theory of the body's vital systems it didn't emphasize the importance of one part of the body over others as later medicine would. Most importantly, it did not view the skin as the determinator of the character of a person. To some extent the opposite was true: Medieval writings seem to describe people's "colors" as being equally composed of both their skin complexion and their character. Descriptions of someone being dark, black, yellow, or fair described their temperament and morals as much as their skin color. In other words, skin color was not yet viewed as the key to understanding a person's character.

That skin color was not yet seen as the marker of all other human differences was evident in the way early anatomists investigated the differences between black and white bodies. Humoral medicine viewed the skin as being relatively unimportant, as merely the packaging of the vital organs within. Accordingly, early medical practitioners and writers thought of racial differences as simply a matter of the superficial and relatively unimportant structures of skin. Quite literally, prior to the Enlightenment of the seventeenth and eighteenth centuries, color was only skin deep.

Later when the first scientific naturalists thought about racial differences, they adapted the old humoral theory to their new way of thinking, tying each skin color, red, yellow, black and white, to one of the ancient humors and their temperaments, thus reversing this ancient theory to justify a new division of the world into races. By elevating skin colors over the rest of the humoral system these early "scientists" transformed humoral theory from a theory of disease and human character into a theory of racial difference.

Thinking about color began to change in the seventeenth century as European slave colonies expanded and as scientists began to consider racial differences as being deeper and more extensive than just a tint of skin.

Anatomists began searching for racial differences ever deeper in the body. In 1618, Jean Riolan the Younger, a physician in Paris, conducted experiments on a black man to find the source of his black color. Younger rubbed caustic chemicals on his skin until it bubbled and sliced off a patch to examine, assuming that the source was skin deep. Later that century when Marcello Malphighi sought the source of blackness, he dissected deep into the body.

Marcello Malpighi, the Italian physician considered the father of modern microscopical anatomy, described the anatomy of blacks as being fundamentally different from whites in his treatise on anatomy. Malpighi claimed to have found that the darker skin of blacks extended to the color of their internal organs and even their blood was dark: "The black color resides not only in the fluid which colors the mucous tissue but also in the blood the cortical part of the brain and several other internal parts of the body impregnated with a black tint and what has also been observed by other observers." Malpighi's description of racial differences were repeated in medical textbooks well into the nineteenth century.

Anatomists following Malpighi recorded what they claimed were profound differences in the musculature, tissues, nerves, and bone structure of blacks and whites, again in conformity to the emerging racial stereotypes of the era that blacks were stronger because their bodies were more primitive. They also repeated uncritically and without examination older medical ideas that claimed races had fundamentally different bodies.

In the late 1700s, Berlin anatomist Johann Friedrich Meckel "discovered" that the brains of Africans were darker than those of white men. This falsehood also spread widely and the authoritative *London Medical Dictionary*, published in 1809, described the stem of the brain (the medulla oblongata) as follows: "In a negro the medulla is yellowish, and sometimes a blackish yellow, though in the European of a pure white." Typical of medical books at the time, this compendium found that in addition to having differently colored blood and brains, black people had larger nerves, longer necks, narrower foreheads, longer jaws, larger orbital bones around the eyes, longer forearms, smaller calf muscles, longer achilles tendons, and a different number

Figure 3.5 Guy de Chauliac giving an anatomy lesson, 1300-1370.

of teeth.

Samuel Thomas von Soemmerring, author of the most famed textbook of comparative anatomy for over a century, wrote of many differences he thought he had found between the races. Among the many differences von Soemmerring "found" between the races was his discovery that white buttocks were generally larger than black ones.

French anatomist Julien Virey noted that because black teeth are angled forward they "cannot pronounce the letter R...on the contrary, all inhabitants of northern climates articulate this letter with much facility...Hence, it follows, that the negro is in some respect by his form, the capacity of his skull, the weakness and degradation of his mind, the reverse of the European." Virey did note that slavery was a positive influence: "Generally, the negro is of a merry disposition, even in servitude…" and that black girls are "very lascivious" and "at twelve years of age, they are ripe for marriage."

Medical scientists didn't seem particularly concerned that their list of anatomical differences between the races didn't always agree. Some textbooks claimed black arm bones were longer and others said they were shorter. Others that black people had remarkably flat fleet, others that the curvature of the foot was pronounced. Racism was so natural and seemingly commonsensical to these scientists that most of the claims of previous doctors and anatomists, even those that conflicted and those that were hundreds of years old, went without challenge and were never systematically investigated. As one scientist correctly noted in the *American Journal of Obstretrics* in 1875, after listing many of the "well-known" differences between black and white women, "the present differences of type in the negro and European crania will be admitted probably without discussion."

Craniometry

Scientists believed that racial differences were most clearly seen in skulls. From the eighteenth century on, scientists collected skulls and devised standards of measurements and even specialized tools with which to document how different races had different skull shapes and dimensions. As it turned out, many of the early claims of this science of craniometry were an illusion built upon eurocentric biases and sloppy methods.

In America, early scientific views of human races were most influenced by Samuel G. Morton, a Philadelphia physician who collected nearly a thousand human skulls (many of them probably taken from native peoples killed for bounties) and published several influential books claiming to have found significant and consistent racial variation in cranial capacity in the 1830s and 1840s.

Figure 3.6 Samuel George Morton.

Morton's arguments that racial groups had deep and permanent differences in intelligence, temperament, and physical abilities was comforting to the nation's elites whose livelihoods, whether in the North or the South, depended on the continuation of slavery. Morton's work was hailed for overturning the softer views of scientists (such as Thomas Jefferson) who believed that many racial traits were largely caused by environmental differences in climate, soil, and terrain and provided scientific justification to those who argued that the American republic must exclude nonwhites. The *Charleston Medical Journal* wrote upon Morton's passing, "We can only say that we of the South should consider him as our benefactor, for aiding most materially in giving to the negro his true position as an inferior race."

In 1977, evolutionary biologist Stephen Jay Gould reviewed Morton's research and discovered numerous mistakes, biases, and omissions. Some of Morton's errors were common fallacies of his day, such as his assumption that brain size was an indicator of intelligence. (We know today that brain size and intelligence are not correlated. If they were, larger people would all be geniuses and Neanderthals would have been the most intelligence species of Homo.) Morton did not separate his skulls into different groups on the basis of sex or stature for the purposes of comparison and therefore his data was skewed in favor of those groups in his collection that just happened to include more males and larger bodies. When Gould recalculated Morton's data almost all of the differences Morton claimed to find between racial groups was erased.

Prejudices didn't just skew the research of race scientists, they also influenced what research results were valued and which were quickly forgotten. At about the same time Morton published his works that proved widely read and acclaimed, other scientists published their research showing the opposite results and they were ignored. Friedrich Tiedemann, a doctor at the University of Heidelberg, studied fifty human brains and could find no "racial" differences in overall size. Tiedemann's work had little impact on the scientific community's belief that white brains were the largest of all the races.

Morton trained other influential doctors who would go on to spread ideas of race inferiority beyond the scientific community. Most notably of these was Morton's student Josiah Nott who wrote numerous articles, books and pamphlets defending slavery as the system best suited to the natural constitutions of African Americans. In 1854 Nott co-authored a book collecting all the evidence for such conclusions entitled, *Types of Mankind* that proved to be one of the most widely selling and popular books of the nineteenth century, eventually going through ten editions.

Medical Experimentation

In the American South in 1851, the physician and slaveholder Samuel Cartwright published a widely influential book arguing that whites and blacks were so anatomically unlike each other that they required different medical treatments and suffered from different diseases. Cartwright also conveniently claimed that the unique physiology of black people required hard labor under conditions of slavery for their health. Cartwright even formulated a diagnosis for the problem of slaves running away. He termed this disease "drapetomania," a mental illness that compelled people to flee their masters.

While Cartwright merely scribbled away his fantasies of slave diseases, other southern doctors quickly realized that slavery could provide them with endless subjects for experimentation.

Slavery empowered white physicians to undertake medical experiments and practice surgical procedures upon the bodies of subjects who had no ability to withhold their consent. Medical researchers seized upon this opportunity and inflicted agonizing and dangerous procedures on people for whom the outcome of these experiments, whether they got better or suffered, or sickened and died, mattered little to those wielding the scalpel. For even when their subjects perished from the effects of medical tinkering,

physicians would claim to have gained valuable knowledge. After Dr. A.B. Crook killed one of his own slaves by attempting to surgically remove a benign tumor caused by a fracture on his skull, Crook wrote, "Should such another case present itself, my policy would be attend the general health of the patient, and make no attempt on the brain."

Dr. Harvey L. Byrd, a physician in Georgetown, South Carolina, conducted electro-shock experiments on a twelve-year old girl named Harriet who suffered from epilepsy. Harriet had to be held down by two men as Dr. Byrd applied electricity to her spine. Dr. Byrd first experimented with a shock that lasted four minutes. He later extended this to seven minutes and over the coming days worked up to a shock that caused Harriet to violently convulse and cry out "you are burning my back" for over an hour. Byrd later published his results in the *Charleston Medical Journal and Review* in 1848.

South Carolina's Dr. T. Stillman went further, advertising in southern newspapers to purchase slaves suffering from a list of diseases from their masters. Stillman set his goal of filling his private hospital with fifty enslaved individuals he could test formulas for patent medicines he intended to market. There is no record of what Stillman did with the people he paid for.

However, the cruel experiments of Dr. Thomas Hamilton of Georgia are well documented. Dr. Hamilton sought a cure for heat-stroke, a malady that struck at the ability of masters to drive the people they enslaved for as long as the sun was up. To this end he borrowed a man (history only records his first name, "Fed") owned by a neighbor and constructed a pit in which he made Fed sit with only his head poking out from a mound of wet blankets. Hamilton then lit a fire at the base of the pit and while it smoldered forced Fed to drink different concoctions until he passed out. These experiments were conducted only after Fed had worked a full day of field labor and continued daily for two or three weeks.

The most renowned case of medical experimentation upon people held in bondage was that performed by Dr. James Marion Sims of Montgomery, Alabama. Sims sought a method for repairing a vesico-vaginal fistula, a break in the tissues between the bladder and the vagina. Over the course of four years Sims operated up to thirty times without the aid of anaesthesia on first three enslaved women suffering from the condition (again Sims only recorded their first names, Anarcha, Lucy, and Betsey).

Curiously, though physicians insisted that blacks and whites had radically different bodies and physiologies, making them resistant or susceptible to different diseases and treatments, doctors who experimented on enslaved subjects never questioned that the knowledge gained from their experimentations would apply to their white patients. Indeed, most of those physicians who experimented on

Figure 3.7 J. Marion Sims

black bodies did so with the clear intent of better treating white ones.

Southern medical colleges taught their students how to perform various procedures upon people held in bondage. Such colleges advertised for slave owners to send their ill servants to college infirmaries where they would be treated for low or no cost. The hospital attached to the Medical College of South Carolina treated only black people. Calling for new subjects for their students to practice surgery on, the college advertised in a local paper, "The object of the Faculty...is to collect as many interesting cases, as possible, for the benefit and instruction of their pupils."

During this period many northern medical schools had great difficulty securing cadavers for dissection, both for anatomical instruction and for post-mortem investigations of diseases. Most states passed laws prohibiting human dissection and medical students were known to resort to grave robbing to obtain specimens. But medical colleges in the South enjoyed a steady stream of bodies of those once enslaved to dissect as they wished. French traveler Harriet Martineau observed in 1834, "In Baltimore, the bodies of coloured people exclusively are taken for dissection, 'because the whites do not like it, and the colored people cannot resist.'" As medical colleges often paid slave masters for bodies, they may have actually incentivized brutal treatment by providing a monetary compensation for the premature death of enslaved people.

Once slavery was abolished, dangerous and torturous medical experiments moved to prisons where large populations of people of color could be coerced or forced to comply. While the Philippines was a colony of the United States, Dr. Richard Strong, professor of tropical medicine at Harvard University, conducted experiments with tropical diseases upon death row inmates at the Philippines' Bilibid Prison. His first experiment involving cholera killed thirteen of his patients but survivors were rewarded with cigarettes.

After World War Two, the newly formed National Institute of Health sponsored a program to study the transmission of syphilis and other sexually transmitted diseases. In a two-year experiment, U.S. physicians led by Dr. John Charles Cutler traveled to Guatemala and swabbed the bacteria that causes syphilis into the urethras of prisoners, indigenous members of the military, and mental patients. Cutler freely injected syphilis bacteria into unwitting young women and sometimes wiped gonorrheal pus into their eyes before experimenting with different treatments. Dr. Cutler wrote to his commanders back in Washington, "The experiments need not to be explained at all to the Indians in the Penitentiary, as they are only confused by explanations and knowing what is happening."

Upon returning to the U.S. Dr. Cutler continued his syphilis experiments upon unwitting black subjects in the American south. In 1932, the U.S. Public Health Service (USPHS) medical professionals began a study in Tuskegee, Alabama, pretended to treat 400 black patients already infected with syphilis while secretly withholding treatment and monitoring the progress of their symptoms. Patients were given vitamins or aspirins and told that those pills would fix their "bad blood." Others were given painful spinal taps and told the procedures would relieve their symptoms but they were in fact merely for the purpose of data collection. Though it was widely known that penicillin would cure the disease in most cases, the life-saving drug was withheld from those in the study. In order to chart the progress of the disease in all 400 men through to their deaths, great lengths were taken to keep them enrolled in the study, including paying them $25 per year and secretly pressuring the Macon County draft board not to conscript any of the men during World War Two.

While a similar observational study of men infected with syphilis in Norway was quickly ended in 1910 once treatments were available, the Tuskegee study did not come to an end until a whistleblower in the USPHS contacted a reporter for the *New York Times* in 1972, forty years after the study began. During that time at least 100 of the study participants died an early death from syphilis and unknown numbers of wives, girlfriends, and children were infected with the disease. In 1997, President Bill Clinton formally apologized for the government's shameful conduct, saying, "The United States government did something that was wrong—deeply, profoundly, morally wrong. It was an outrage to our commitment to integrity and equality for all our citizens … and I am sorry."

The racism behind these human experiments connects many of the threads of the history of the science of race to the present. All three officials of the USPHS who were the architects of the Tuskegee syphilis study, were graduates of the University of Virginia School of Medicine who received their training at a time when the fundamental species-level differences between whites and blacks were still taught as scientific fact. The University of Virginia was known as a national leader in "racial medicine." Students at the University of Virginia medical school were taught that blacks were more susceptible to syphilis and other venereal diseases because of their inborn "hypersexuality" and a racial inability to fight the disease like more robust whites. Moreover, all were affiliated with the eugenics movement which viewed syphilis not just as a disease but as "pollution of the bloodline" that had to be eradicated not just with medicine but with the segregation of races.

It should be noted that up to the 1970s, experimentation on prisoners was commonplace in the United States. Both physicians interested in treating various diseases and pharmaceutical companies looking to market new drugs took their experiments to prisons whose large populations could be induced to participate for a low cost. Many dangerous and debilitating experiments were performed on white prisoners as well, including experiments aimed to find the cause of the bone-deforming pellegra (conducted at Rankin Prison Farm in Mississippi), to find a cure for malaria (Statesville Prison in Illinois), or to cure impotence by implanting the testicles of executed men into living ones (California's San Quentin Prison). While all of these projects involved a degree of coercion, in striking contrast with those performed on racial minorities the subjects of these experiments were generally informed of what they were participating in and what was the nature of the treatments or drugs they were given.

Darwin and Lamarck

Charles Darwin published his *On the Origin of Species*

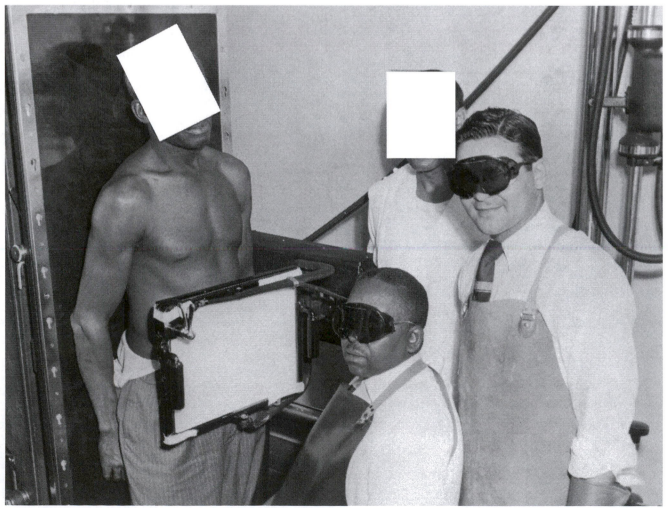

Figure 3.8 Participants in the Tuskeggee Syphilis Study, being x-rayed, 1932.

JEAN BAPTISTE DE LAMARCK.

Figure 3.9 Jean Baptiste Pierre Antoine de Monet de Lamarck,

in 1858 and it was immediately condemned by his fellow scientists on religious grounds. A few years after it appeared a formal statement condemning Darwin and declaring that it was impossible that science should contradict the Bible was signed by 700 scientists including 66 members of the prestigious Royal Society. Darwin's exile from his fellow scientists didn't last long, however, and soon the idea of evolution became quite popular, though in a twisted way Darwin did not approve of.

Darwin's misfortune was to have his theory mixed up with that of Jean Baptiste de Lamarck who a half century earlier had published his own theory that organisms changed over time as they adapted to new surroundings and developed new ways of being. The key difference was that Lamarck proposed that things learned or acquired in one generation were readily passed along to the next. Most lay people and even many scientists made the mistake of confusing Darwin's theory that involved random mutation and then natural selection acting upon populations to eventually shift their composition, with Lamarck's inheritance of acquired traits. Darwin eventually rode to fame and glory by the 1870s not on the strength of his own theories, but on the common mistake of reading Lamarck into them.

This "mistake" was quite popular because Lamarckism provided a powerful support for a racist view of humanity, society, and history that Darwinism did not. Darwinism did not necessarily support the view that humanity was fundamentally divided into races; it did not presuppose that evolution was directed toward ever greater complexity and perfection; and it did not provide a clear mechanism whereby culture and biology could interact. Lamarckism, however, did all of these things.

Lamarckism tightly linked culture and history to biological inheritance and both of them to a divine order that moved toward perfection. According to Lamarck, the things learned or the folkways adopted by one generation were passed along to future ones. In this way social behavior can be viewed as an important element of biological evolution. Here was a theory that provided structure to the general bigotry of white supremacy—Europeans were not just lucky conquerors, they were the pinnacle of evolution whose good and moral habits would lead them ever upward in the divine scheme of progress. All the other peoples of the world were the physical victims of their own bad habits and character. Whether they would languish in their primitive states or rise to civilization depended on the slim hope that they could overcome their own racial inheritance and transcend their own nature.

Lamarckism's linking of culture and race was powerful in a society seeking reasons to continue oppressing others. But such ideas proved dangerous when they were brought together with a view of history as being driven by the competition of societies. The idea that nations were not collections of individuals but personifications of their people's characters can be traced back to the Scottish philosopher David Hume. Other eighteenth century thinkers like Count Arthur de Gobineau built on this philosophy a unifying theory of world history as the rise and fall of empires based on their racial qualities. In the nineteenth century Herbert Spencer, a popularizer of Charles Darwin's ideas (Spencer coined the term "survival of the fittest"), extended the idea that nations rose and fell based on their racial characters to claim that a nation's fate depended on the rise of the fit and the death of the unfit in a process later termed "Social Darwinism."

Intelligence and "IQ"

Prior to the nineteenth century and science's new-found drive to categorize all the ways human races were unequal, the idea of intelligence, as some inherited natural capacity to think and problem-solve that varied from person to person, did not yet exist. Rather, the Christian tradition taught that all men were endowed by God with sufficient reason to understand and follow divine law and seek salvation. Of course in every age some geniuses emerged who were seen as having divine gifts, but the idea that normal people's ability to think varied by measurable degrees awaited its invention.

Craniologists and phrenologists were among the first to think of intelligence as a something each person inherited in differing quantities, as they naturally assumed that the size and shape of a person's head determined how intelligent they were. However, this assumption soon came to be challenged by others who could easily observe that the mental abilities of people with roughly the same size heads could differ dramatically. Clearly there was more to intelligence than merely the capacity of the cranium.

Several scientists in the mid-nineteenth century began devising means of measuring intelligence apart from the skull. Charles Darwin's cousin, Francis Galton, pioneered new ways of judging how much two things are related by calculating the degree to which they vary together. Using this concept of correlation, Galton assigned numerical values to people's "intelligence." At the same time Herbert Spencer, the great popularizer of Darwin's evolutionary theories, included intelligence among the inborn abilities whose variance from person to person drove evolution's continuous improvement of the species through the process of "survival of the fittest."

The greatest progress in quantifying intelligence was made by a French researcher, Alfred Binet, who was not interested in studying intelligence for its own sake, but in developing a method of sorting children by their mental abilities so that those who had learning challenges could be given special lessons and targeted assistance. Binet developed a series of tests and a scale of intelligence based on "mental ages" that other scientists quickly adapted to a more universal purpose.

Binet's work was embraced in America by psychologist Henry H. Goddard who ran a school for the "feebleminded" in New Jersey and believed that Binet's intelligence scale could accurately label the mental abilities of his students. Goddard enthusiastically spread news of this breakthrough with his colleagues across the nation.

At the same time an English statistician, Charles Spearman, invented a means of combining a number of tests and measures into a single quantity he termed "g" for general intelligence. Spearman claimed that his statistical manipulation of various data sets actually measured something that was an essential, and fundamentally biological, basis of all intelligence and not just a specific talent or learned skill (such as vocabulary, memory, or mathematical ability).

Together, the Binet system of testing for intelligence and the Spearman theory that what these tests measured was in fact a core natural quantity that determined every individual's intellectual capacity took the psychological profession by storm. By the time President Wilson steered America into World War One, the idea that IQ tests measured general intelligence was nearly universal in scientific circles. During the War the Army agreed to administer revised IQ tests (called the Stanford-Binet test after the university whose professor Lewis Terman improved on Binet's original measures) to all its soldiers.

Underlying the popularity of this new idea of heritable intelligence was the fact that it was an idea that powerfully justified the existing social and economic order. If it was true that people were born with such different mental endowments, then perhaps the stark inequalities in society were not unjust. Maybe inequality was just the result of the differences in intelligence among people, in which case such unequal outcomes were perfectly natural and unavoidable. (This was the position of Francis Galton who defined intelligence as whatever the ability was that the successful and wealthy had that the poor did not.) Certainly, it was comforting to the white Anglo-Saxon scientists who promoted these ideas that their IQ tests consistently showed white people to have superior intelligence to all other races, western and northern Europeans scoring above southern and eastern Europeans, and wealthier people enjoying a greater endowment of smarts than the poor.

As scientists claimed that intelligence was primarily a fixed biological capacity that was inherited and that they could accurately measure this capacity, policy-makers moved to use these tools to justify racist and elitist policies. Such scientific ideas justified racial segregation (why provide funds for negro schools if black students could not learn?), immigration restriction (why let mentally inferior types into the country?), and laissez-faire economic policies (why fight nature by giving handouts to those will fail anyway?). Largely because these ideas proved so supportive of conservative political policies they went unchallenged for decades.

A few early social critics poked holes in these theories of intelligence, most notably Walter Lippmann who published a series of essays that provoked a fierce backlash from psychologists who compared him to the closed-minded superstitious persecutors of Da Vinci and Copernicus. Lippmann was one of the first to recognize that these scientists had made the seemingly obvious mistake of inventing a way of abstracting collections of data and then treated their model as something real, using this model as the explanation of the causes other phenomenon and effects. Lippmann's objections had little impact and intelligence testing became broadly implemented across U.S. society in the 20th century, coming to govern military commissions, university admissions, and corporate promotions.

After a century of intelligence research, many of the

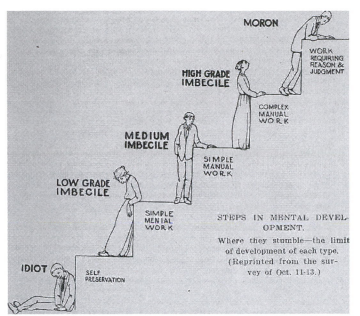

Figure 3.10 "Steps in Mental Development...The Binet-Simon Measuring Scale for Intelligence, 1915

core concepts of the field were later shown to be false. Intelligence researchers going back to Terman in the 1920s have claimed that their results proved that IQ was fixed and stable, it didn't vary over the course of a person's lifetime and was not influenced by environment or society. They claimed that IQ was highly heritable, meaning that most of the differences in IQ between people was the result of the inheritance of specific genes that govern intelligence. While entire runs of academic journals are filled with articles based on these assumptions, none of them rested on solid evidence.

Because no specific set of genes for intelligence could be identified, the genetic contribution to IQ was usually estimated by statistically correlating the scores of related people (who can be shown to share ancestry) with the IQ's of unrelated people. Statistically, related people's IQs vary differently from unrelated people, and the difference between these patterns of variation is assumed to reflect the contribution of genes.

There are many problems with this method, especially that related people tend to live in similar environments raising the question of whether the calculated quantity is actually genetic or environmental. The only certain way to distinguish among these possibilities is to separate related individuals into diverse environments from birth, something done in animal studies of heredity but a method having obvious problems for humans.

Though twin studies and other rough attempts to quantify the heritability of intelligence have been riddled with problems in their methods and interpretations, they failed to shake the long held underlying assumptions that intelligence, whatever it was, was could be easily measured by test and these results applied universally. When the powerful tools of genetic science became available researchers presumed they would find the molecular basis

of intelligence. But after twenty years of comparing IQ tests to genetic samples, scientists have yet to agree that any specific genes are strongly associated with intelligence. As a recent genetic study observed, "The supporting evidence from the molecular findings has not been consistent and many reported candidate–gene associations have not been replicated. A recent study suggested that most reported associations between candidate genes and intelligence are likely to be false." (This observation did not prevent these researchers from claiming that their finding that genes contribute 3.5% of childhood IQ scores was evidence for the genetic basis of intelligence: "Our results suggest that childhood intelligence is heritable and highly polygenic.")

Rather than finding any single gene for intelligence, or even a handful of smart genes, recent broad genetic surveys are finding that hundreds and even thousands of genes seem to contribute small amounts to intelligence. This suggests that whatever is measured by IQ tests is the product of not just specific genes, but is a complex phenomenon that is the result not only of specific genetic factors, but how they interact with each other and with the environment.

Instead of comparing large databases of genetic information to IQ tests, some researchers have used other factors as a stand-in for intelligence. One group of geneticists compared records of levels of education with genetic information for hundreds of thousands of people and estimated that at most genes contributed about 20% to a person's educational attainment.

Scientists have continually refined the tests they use to measure something they call "intelligence." But after more than a century and a half of intelligence research, the central subject of this pursuit remains unclear and undefined. What is this "intelligence" that these researchers claim to measure? Is it the ability to learn? Is it the ability to adapt to changing circumstances? Is it retention and recall of past learning? Does the scale used to measure this thing called intelligence track the analytical, verbal, mechanical, or creative abilities? Does it capture all these different abilities at once? The fact that there remains no agreement on what phenomenon this science claims to observe and quantify is quite unlike any other fields that claim to follow the scientific method.

In 1921 a prominent psychology journal asked a dozen of the leading researchers and scientists of intelligence to define what intelligence was. Each of them gave a distinctly different answer. Sixty-five years later, this undertaking was repeated with the same result; the most prominent scientists couldn't agree on just what it was they were studying. Today researchers studying intelligence disagree on whether intelligence is comprised of two, three or as many as eight different abilities, such as abstract reasoning, spatial perception, and verbal skill. Researchers have not advanced much past the 1923 declaration of psychologist Edwin Boring, "intelligence as a measurable capacity must at the start be defined as the capacity to do well in an intelligence test. Intelligence is what the tests test."

Given that IQ tests admittedly only weigh a person's skill at taking an IQ test, it should not be surprising that numerous studies have documented that IQ tests are culturally and socially biased. Individuals who have been subjected to western-style schools consistently score higher on most IQ tests than those whose experienced other educational systems. This is true of both those IQ tests shown to measure abilities derived more from education and training (vocabulary, arithmetic, comprehension) and those IQ tests designed more to assess abstract reasoning.

Not being able to define what intelligence is, or what their various intelligence tests actually calculate, has not deterred a few IQ scientists from claiming to have discovered significant differences in intelligence between different races. While most intelligence researchers shied away from projects related to racial differences and muted their statements about racial differences in intelligence once the civil rights movement shifted the terrain of acceptable public discourse, a handful of scientists continued to attempt to prove that races had different intellectual capacities. Distinguished psychologists like Arthur Jensen, J. Philippe Rushton, and William Shockley, stubbornly refused to credit evidence that discredited their theories and instead persisted in making unfounded claims linking intelligence and race into the 1970s.

Though few in number, scientists like Jensen had an oversized power to give their pseudo-scientific theories momentum long after such ideas had been shown to be based on false premises, willful misinterpretations, and, in the case of English psychologist Cyril Burt, outright fraud. Together these academics fashioned an echo chamber of their own ideas, citing each other in their articles and founding their own journals to promote their own views.

Most psychologists ignored and shunned cranks like Jensen by the 1980s, but their work later provided the basis for a revival of racist intelligence theory in the 1990s, a time when the neo-conservative politics of America drew policy and opinion makers back to such formerly discredited ideas.

In 1994, Richard Herrnstein and Charles Murray published, *The Bell Curve: Intelligence and Class Structure in American Life*, a hefty volume seemingly filled with proper academic citations supporting their back-to-the-future argument that liberal social welfare programs, even popular ones like the "Head-Start" program that funded early childhood education for poor preschool kids, were a waste of money because the intellectual capacities of the mostly nonwhite children these programs served were fixed, unchangeable, and low grade. *The Bell Curve* rested heavily on both Jensen's previous work (he was cited two dozen times) and on a million dollar grant provided by the Pioneer Fund, an organization founded by eugenicists, segregationists, and nazi-sympathizers, that had long financed Jensen's and other racist scholarship.

Publication of *The Bell Curve* prompted the psychological research establishment to rethink its long toleration of such uses of intelligence testing. Some prominent scholars powerfully rebutted Herrnstein and Murray's central contentions. Particularly effective was Princeton scientist Leon Kamin who recalled some of the absurd early IQ research upon which *The Bell Curve* argument rested, including the large-scale testing of immigrants arriving at Ellis Island in 1917 by one of the towering figures in the field, Henry H. Goddard, who concluded that 83% of the Jews, 80% of the Hungarians, 79% of the Italians, and 87% of the Russians arriving in the U.S. were "feeble-minded."

Eugenics

For most of the nineteenth century and well into the twentieth, most educated Americans believed that science revealed that races were stable, permanent, and profoundly different in character. Cultures were largely understood as manifestations of racial types. By the 1900s most American scientists were so convinced that races shared little beyond their profound dissimilarities, that they encouraged the government to take steps to keep them from mixing. Scientists lent their authority to campaigns to restrict "inferior" European races from immigrating to America (by which they meant Greeks, Slavs, Italians, and most Jews) and supported extending immigration bans on people from China, Japan, Korea, and elsewhere from Asia. Leading scientists supported strengthening bans on interracial marriage, which they called "miscegenation." Many also supported eugenics, programs to "improve" races by forcibly sterilizing habitual criminals, the mentally ill, and people who they determined were of low intelligence or morality.

Eugenics was motivated by the fear that modern society, the labor-saving power of new technologies, the productivity of factories and farms, the advances in medicine and sanitation, and the protections of a welfare state, worked against the vital process of natural selection. Humanity, eugenicists believed, had advanced over thousands of years by the competition and survival of the fittest individuals in a society, and by pitting societies against each other. In their view, in order for humanity to continue to advance and improve, science must determine who best should breed the coming generation, selecting the best to mate and discouraging or preventing the genetically inferior from continuing their line.

Eugenic scientists believed in the then-current theory of "recapitulation," a theory that held that just as an

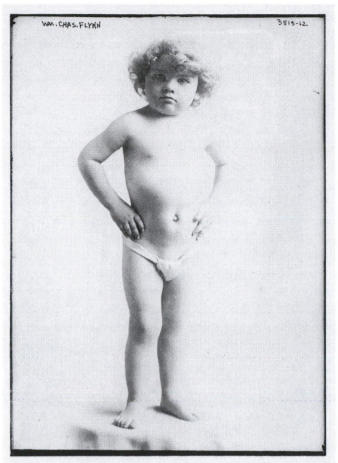

Figure 3.11 William Charles Flynn, a winner of perfect "eugenic baby" contests, ca. 1910-1915.

embryo grows through all evolutionary phases of animal development in the womb, having at various times a tail, gill-like structures, and reptilian features, a human child matures by repeating all the stages of human progress, from the savage, to the tribal, to the civilized thinker. According to this theory, different peoples and societies in the world matured to different levels. Island cannibals and Africans never rose above the childlike savage, while others might have reached into the middle ranks but never reached the stage of reason and civilization.

Eugenic thinking was hopelessly entangled in racism as eugenicists assumed as a truism that whiteness was the indicator of superior intelligence and character. Eugenicists never questioned their basic assumption that a rational science of reproduction would work to encourage the growth of the white population and limit that of non-white groups. When the birth rates of whites in America began to fall around the turn of the century (as generally occurs to all societies experiencing a rapid increase in their standard of living), journalists, politicians, and scientists all warned of "race suicide" and the eventual extinction of the white race. Whites, eugenicists warned, were becoming "over-civilized," becoming weaker in body because of the many devices and machines they had invented to save themselves labor. Modern society, with its luxury, safety, and ease, they warned, was breeding a generation of white

men who had lost the capacity to struggle and fight, and white women who were becoming too weak and fragile to properly birth fit babies.

Eugenicists also made the same mistake as Johann Blumenbach (the biologist who coined the term 'caucasian') of believing that the visible physical "beauty" and "perfection" of a body revealed the greater fitness and higher advancement of its invisible genetic endowment. Never stopping to think that beauty is a creation of culture and varies widely from society to society and from time to time, these scientists encouraged beauty contests and "better baby" contests to promote the procreation of more "genetically fit" individuals.

For eugenic scientists, promoting the breeding of the most fit and beautiful was not enough, the reproduction of the inferior and the unfit needed to be discouraged as well. Beginning with Indiana in 1907, by 1917 sixteen states passed laws requiring the sterilization of people deemed to be mentally or morally defective. The list of conditions justifying surgical sterilization was extensive and in most states included, insanity, drug addiction, mental deficiency, sexual promiscuity, and even epilepsy. In 1927, the constitutionality of such laws was tested in the case of *Buck v. Bell.*

Carrie Buck was born in Charlottesville, Virginia, in 1906, and taken from her single mother when she was an infant and given to a family where she was treated more as a servant than their child. When she turned seventeen, Carrie became pregnant and her foster family initiated proceedings to have her committed her to a state institution, the Virginia Colony for Epileptics and Feeble-Minded. There was no evidence that Carrie lacked intelligence; though she hadn't been allowed to attend much school (she was pulled out of grade school so she could devote more time to her chores) she earned good marks for the grades she did complete. Her last teacher wrote in her report card, "very good—deportment and lessons." But the standards for being declared "feeble-minded" were written in a way that gave full discretion to court officials and doctors to do with poor people whatever they wished, even using a young woman's pregnancy as evidence of her sexual promiscuity. Carrie's foster parents did not tell the court commission the real reason that they no longer wanted Carrie in their home: she had been raped by their nephew.

Virginia not only wanted to sterilize Carrie Buck, as it was routinely doing with hundreds of other criminals and inmates in its asylums, but it wanted to test its right to do so before the high court. Buck's fate was put in the hands of the Supreme Court and its chief justice, Oliver Wendell Holmes, Jr., a man so unsympathetic his official biographer wrote that he was "harsh, and cruel, a bitter and lifelong pessimist," and one whose legal philosophy was to let the majority have its way with the weak, "that is, if the dominant majority...desires to persecute blacks or Jews or communists or atheists, the law, if it is to be 'sound,' must arrange for the persecution to be carried out with, as we might say, due process." Chief justice Holmes was an early and deep believer in Social Darwinism, writing in 1873 that the law "like every other device of man or beast must tend in the long run to aid the survival of the fittest... Why should the greatest number be preferred? Why not the greatest good of the most intelligent and highly developed?"

Not surprisingly, Holmes approved of Carrie Buck's forced sterilization enthusiastically:

> We have seen more than once that the public welfare may call upon the best citizens for their lives. It would be strange if it could not call upon those who already sap the strength of the State for these lesser sacrifices, often not felt to be such by those concerned, in order to prevent our being swamped with incompetence. It is better for all the world if, instead of waiting to execute degenerate offspring for crime or to let them starve for their imbecility, society can prevent those who are manifestly unfit from continuing their kind...Three generations of imbeciles are enough.

Holmes' only regret was that his decision, and the forced sterilizations that came from it would be "confined to a small number who are in the institutions named and is not applied to the multitudes outside..." In this Holmes may have underestimated the power of his decision; by 1941, nearly 36,000 forced sterilizations had been performed across the United States.

While Carrie Buck was a white girl, once states were given the green light to expand their sterilization programs such efforts focused disproportionately on people of color. One careful study of all forced sterilizations in North Carolina over a ten year period from 1958 to 1968, found that "the incidence of sterilization was conditioned on race, as the probability of institutional and total sterilization rose with the black population share." No other factor than race, not income, region, or even health, explained the data.

In California, the focus of eugenicists' efforts to "improve the race" was on people of Mexican origin. From the 1920s on, women of Mexican descent were stereotyped as being hypersexual and unusually fertile. For example, one of the most popular magazines in America, *The Saturday Evening Post*, ran a series of articles warning Americans about the dangers of continued Mexican immigration, describing it as a "race problem," compounded by the "reckless breeding" that would lead to the "mongrelization of America." During the first half of the twentieth century,

thousands of people of Mexican ancestry were sterilized against their will and sometimes without their knowledge.

Though forced sterilizations in state institutions like asylums and prisons were eventually restricted, the practice resumed in public hospitals. While no longer propelled by state programs of "race betterment," coerced sterilizations continued because of the prejudiced views of medical professionals who often saw themselves as patriots helping to stem the tide of immigrants into America, or brown people swelling the welfare rolls. During a closely watched civil trial of a Los Angeles Hospital in 1974, it was revealed that a prominent doctor had complained in a meeting that minorities "were having too many babies" and that this was putting "a strain on society." Such lawsuits in California revealed women of Mexican origin were pressured into agreeing to the procedure, sometimes during labor with the threat of having pain medication withdrawn. Commonly little information was given to laboring women other than the question, "¿Más niños?" (more babies?) and many women were mislead into believing the procedure could be reversed at some future time.

Likewise in the 1970s, native women were targeted

Figure 3.12 Third International Congress of Eugenics held at American Museum of Natural History, New York, August 21-23, 1932,

Figure 3.13 Stop forced sterilization, by Rachael Romero, San Francisco Poster Brigade, 1977.

by medical staff at hospitals of the Indian Health Service and either sterilized without their knowledge during other medical procedures, or coerced into signing consent forms while being threatened that if they didn't they would lose other government benefits.

Though eugenics has long been discredited as a science and no states today mandate sterilization, the practice continues to crop up from time to time. As recently as May 2017, a judge in White County, Tennessee, announced he would reduce by one month the jail sentences of prisoners who agreed to be sterilized, men by vasectomie and women by long-acting birth-control implants. Seventy men and women took the judge up on his offer in its the program's first three months.

Cracks in the Wall of Race

All the racial certainties that had accumulated over a century of biased and slipshod methods were doomed to shatter once they were exposed to actual scientific investigation. But they were so deeply ingrained in scientific circles and so tightly bound to the racist social, economic, and political institutions that pervaded the United States that they would persist in the face of mounting evidence for another fifty years. Even those scientists who uncovered

clear evidence contradicting longheld notions of race had difficulty recognizing the implications of their own research.

In the early 1900s, Aleš Hrdlička was hired to conduct physical measurements of immigrants (known at the time as "new" immigrants) to Ellis Island. Hrdlička later went a step further and enlisted three hundred men and women of "old" white American stock (defined as having all maternal and paternal grandparents who had been born in the U.S.) to be a control group and measured them just as rigorously. Reporting his "striking" findings in 1915, Hrdlička documented that even though all his "old White stock" subjects came from the same racial group, they displayed a "great range of variation… in nearly all all the important measurements." Most complicating the idea of race was Hrdlička's discovery that the skulls of these old stock whites failed to measure as they were supposed to. According to the racial science of the day, white people were supposed to be overwhelmingly "dolichocephalic" (long narrow heads) while "lesser" races bore the more primitive "brachycephalic" (short and broad) head shape. Hrdlička's careful measurements revealed that only one-eighth of the men and one in twenty-five women were dolichocephalic while one in four men and nearly half of the women were brachycephalic. Hrdlička himself failed to recognize that his results contradicted the idea of race: either the white racial type had completely changed in just three generations, or racial categories aren't as solid and natural as one would expect.

That very same year that Hrdlička reported these findings, he also worked as the chief designer of the anthropological exhibit for the 1915 Panama-California Exposition in San Diego. Aleš Hrdlička, by then curator of anthropology at the Smithsonian Institution, created a hall filled with lifelike busts and body casts to illustrate "Man's Variation," though only nonwhite people were represented. As Hrdlička explained,

The main exhibit in this connection is that of twenty large busts showing typical representatives of ten of the subraces, five of the yellow-brown and five of the black stock. These busts...are made with one or two exceptions from the actual facial and body casts of the various people, and are true in every detail. The casts were made, in some instances at much cost, on special expeditions for the Panama-California Exposition. Of the ten pairs those representing the yellow-brown peoples include a typical male and female of the Indian, Eskimo, Formosan, Malay, Mongolian, and the Polynesian Maori; while the series of blacks include the Negro (Zulu), Bushman, African Pygmy, Philippine

Island Negrito, and the Australian.

Not only did the exhibit cement the idea that races were the essential and immutable division of nature, by highlighting only people of color in the hall of "Man's Variation," Hrdlička sent the implicit but direct message that white people were a standard from which all others deviated or, perhaps, fell short. Only those who failed to reach the white norm were curiosities interesting enough to display.

It is hard to overstate the depth and pervasiveness of belief in the existence and fundamental inequality of races by the dawn of the Twentieth century. The president of the American Association for the Advancement of Science at the turn of the century, Daniel G. Brinton, authored a popular book entitled *Races and Peoples* that claimed to be a compilation of the finest and best science of the day. Sadly, it probably was when Brinton wrote that "We are accustomed familiarly to speak of 'higher' and 'lower' races, and we are justified in this even from merely physical considerations….Measured by these criteria, the European or white race stands at the head of the list, the African or negro at its foot." It wasn't until the 1920s that the words "racist" or "racism" were coined by a Belgian librarian who wrote a history of scientific thinking about race.

Besides W.E.B. Du Bois, the most important scholar and scientist whose worked served to undermine the foundations of racist science was Franz Boas, a Jew who fled the persecution of Bismarck's Germany for refuge in America in 1887. Boas had earned a Ph.D. at the University of Kiel and then spent a year living among the Inuit on Baffin Island. His experience among the Inuit convinced him that there was no essential gap in intelligence between different peoples and that humanity was not divided between civilized and primitive but simply between various expressions of cultural complexity.

In America, Boas was a tireless researcher who chose his projects intentionally to bash away at the long-standing certainties of race. His paper on "The Half-Blood Indian," was the first to attack the idea that race mixing produced weak offspring. Boas, trained in the close measurement of human bodies, conducted extensive investigation of immigrants and their children and statistically proved that skulls were not racially fixed but were unstable and varied widely, even among parents and children, depending on their environments. While Boas had to wait fifty years to see the world begin to come around to his views, from his post at Columbia University, Boas went on to train many of the next generation of anthropologists who would finally succeed in piercing scientific racism's armor.

Along with Boas, in the 1930s, a few other scientists began questioning the old scientific certainties about race. Their views would not become accepted by even a minority of scientists until after Americans came face to face with the horrors of the Nazi war machine and its fanatical drive for "Aryan purity."

It was in England in the 1930s, that four eminent scientists and close friends, Julian Huxley, Lancelot Hogben, J. B. S. Haldane, and Alfred Haddon, coordinated a concerted attack on the old idea of races. Like many scientists and scholars of their day, all had once been enthusiastic advocates of eugenics. But as fascism with its extreme racist ideology spread across Europe, they rethought the nature of genetic variety and formulated new arguments that undercut the most important racial principles. Most importantly, they did so in both the scientific and popular press. In addition to their scholarly publishing, Haldane was a frequent contributor to newspapers, Hogben wrote popular science books, and Huxley was a well known essayist for British and American magazines.

In 1935, Huxley and Haddon, with the help of economist A.M. Carr-Saunders, published *We Europeans: A Survey of 'Racial' Problems*, a book that exposed the unscientific basis of racial categories. Huxley and Haddon pointed out that the methods of anthropologists lagged far behind those of biologists who had begun to apply sophisticated statistical methods to understanding variation and taxonomy. Huxley and Haddon didn't attempt to deny that humans varied in their natural endowments or even that some variations might be more common in some groups than others. More fundamentally they pointed out that all variations were expressed in frequencies and probabilities and that the categories called races were derived from history, from cultural, linguistic, and national prejudices, not from the actual scientific investigation of human populations. As they wrote:

> It is difficult to avoid the conclusion that not a few of the anomalies which are encountered by those who have endeavored to trace the 'racial affinities' of the varieties of man have arisen from an a-priori approach to the problem. We have attributed characters to the preconceived type, rather than determined the actual type by its characters.

Racialism, Huxley and Haddon wrote, was a myth, "and a dangerous myth at that."

Huxley, Haddon, and other race debunkers made little headway against the strong current of race belief among both scientists and the public at the time. The popular view was embodied by the permanent exhibit opened in 1933 at the Field Museum of Natural History in Chicago called the "Races of Mankind." In what was probably the richest commission ever given to an American sculptor up to that time, the museum contracted with Malvina Hoffman, an artist who had studied under the great French sculptor

Figure 3.14 Franz Boas, ca. 1915.

Rodin, to produce more than 100 life-sized bronzes. Each statue represented a racial "type" and the pieces were arranged in the hall to represent the progression from the lowest and most primitive type to the highest, namely the "Nordic" European. (Actually, it turns out that Hoffman's model for the "Nordic" man was Tony Sansone, an Italian-American from New York.) All but the Europeans were posed with stone-age tools, loin cloths, and traditional costume. The white man was simply posed like Apollo or a classical Greek hero.

The catalog to the "Races of Mankind" exhibit curiously contains many of the contradictory ideas about race then clashing but not yet resolved into something else. On the one hand it expressed the idea of absolute divisions and distinctions of race, endorsing even the "one-drop rule" that governed how white Americans thought about race: "As a biological type our Negroes belong to the African or "black" race and will always remain within this division; even intermarriage with whites will not modify their racial characteristics to any marked degree." It then went on to endorse the racist view that indigenous people were not only primitive but unable to live in the modern world: "With the advance of civilization and the white man's expansion all over the globe many primitive tribes are now doomed to extinction and are gradually dying out...Many a vanishing race will continue to live only in the statues and busts displayed in this hall."

On the other hand, the same catalog expressed a cultural definition of race that moved away from earlier Lamarckian views that culture was inherited along with other biological characteristics: "Race means breed and refers to the physical traits acquired by heredity, in contrast with experience and the total complex of habits and thoughts acquired from the group to which we belong; in other words, the social heritage called culture. The behavior of a nation is not determined by its biological origin, but by its cultural traditions." That the expert authors of the exhibit's catalog could not agree on what race was or meant was typical of the dissonance creeping into scientific discourse of race in the 1930s.

Over the next thirty-five years, over ten million people streamed through the Hall of Races. So popular was the exhibit that the Field Museum sent part of it on traveling exhibition throughout America. The Museum did not consider closing the exhibit until 1969 after protests against it mounted, including a personal letter from poet Amiri Baraka who called it "white racist pseudo anthropology." When it finally closed the exhibit, the Field Museum did not place all of Hoffman's sculptures into storage but merely scattered them around building as decorative objects, including one aboriginal Australian man who was posted at the doorway to the McDonald's restaurant.

While the white public was content with the idea that races were different and unequal, black activists and scholars had long fought against these notions. The great scholar W.E.B. Du Bois had organized important sociological investigations in Philadelphia, Chicago, and other cities, whose findings disproved racist assumptions about black culture and urban problems. The National Association for the Advancement of Colored People (NAACP) and some important black-owned newspapers, like the Chicago *Defender* and the Pittsburgh *Courier*, publicized this scientific work and lobbied the presidential administrations of Franklin D. Roosevelt and Harry S. Truman to support anti-racist international organizations like the United Nations. Their activism helped to establish a platform and an opening for anti-racist scientists to make their voices heard and respected.

In 1948, the United Nations approved a resolution calling for the United Nations to "to consider the desirability of initiating and recommending the general adoption of a programme of disseminating scientific facts designed to remove what is generally known as racial prejudice." The task was handed over to the United Nations Educational, Scientific and Cultural Organization (UNESCO), whose Director-General at the time was none other than Julian Huxley, who in the 1930s had done pioneering work undermining the fixed biological understanding of race. UNESCO called scientists and scholars from around the world to a conference in Elsinore, Denmark, to hammer out a declaration on the meaning of race. Ultimately, the task of drafting the statement on race fell to a committee of eight, who included Ashley Montagu (a student of Franz Boas at Columbia University), UNESCO's new Director-General, Jaime Torres Bodet (an anthropologist from Mexico), Claude Levi-Strauss (the renowned cultural anthropologist from France), and E. Franklin Frazier (the first black president of the American Sociological Association). Montagu served as the chief editor of the document and after circulating a draft among a dozen other scholars, published it on June 18, 1950.

Much of the UNESCO 1950 Statement on Race mirrored points Montagu had made earlier in his 1942 book, *Man's Most Dangerous Myth: The Fallacy of Race* (which he published after having his mentor Franz Boas, and his colleagues Ruth Benedict and Otto Klineberg read and comment on it). The Statement on Race opened by noting that scientists generally agree "that all men belong to the same species" and that all humans descend from the same original stock. That all differences among them are products of historical isolation of populations and that such differences are less important that the similarities between groups. Rather, race is less biological than social: "To most people, a race is any group of people whom they choose to describe as a race." It notes that culture is not a racial trait and it

urges that the word be dropped altogether when discussing cultural issues and the term "ethnic group" be used instead. Moreover, there is no evidence that any group of humanity is mentally inferior to any other and personality and characters vary equally among them all. Popular ideas that race mixing leads to bad physical effects have been shown to be a complete myth. The statement concludes by calling race "not so much a biological phenomenon as a social myth."

The discovery of DNA in 1953 shifted understandings of the "gene" from being seen as something vague and mysterious like a seed to something precise and ordered like a code. This meant that most of what made any person unique was buried deep inside their bodies and was thus invisible. No longer could anyone suppose that one's outward appearance provided a key to what lurked inside. Heredity was a language written in the cells, not on the surface of the body.

At the same time, biologists innovating what became known as the 'Evolutionary Synthesis,' broke from older ideas of evolution leading to stable forms and instead emphasized the processes of evolutionary adaptation. Moving away from a static understanding of species, evolutionary scientists began thinking in terms of dynamic populations that were always under various pressures and tendencies toward change. The population concept allowed for a greater

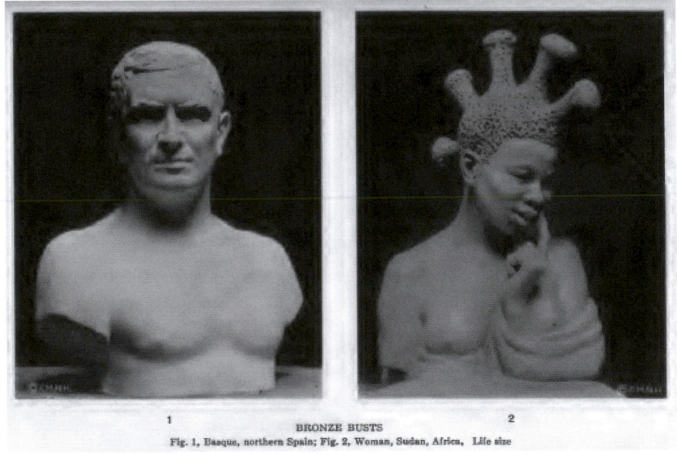

1   2

BRONZE BUSTS

Fig. 1, Basque, northern Spain; Fig. 2, Woman, Sudan, Africa, Life size

Figure 3.15 Detail of bronze busts from Races and Peoples exhibit at the Field Museum of Chicago, 1933.

Figure 3.16 1952 UNESCO General Conference.

appreciation of the patterns of diversity within forms and the recognition that most human traits were characterized by clines of gradual and continuous variation with no fixed boundaries.

Though a few scientific holdouts from the older era remained wedded to the idea of fixed races, such as Ernest Hooten and Carleton Coon, they represented a dwindling minority of opinion that by the 1960s had descended to the level of the crank.

In the early 1960s a number of prominent scientists, Ashley Montagu, C. Loring Brace, Frank Livingstone, and others, building on the earlier work of pioneering anthropologist Franz Boas and his students, published papers arguing that the entire concept of race was flawed and unscientific and must be discarded. They provoked a decade of often bitter debate that raged through the pages *Current Anthropology* and anthropological conferences. But by 1970 it was clear who the winners were. Anthropology textbooks that previously had been written from the assumption that races are real and meaningful began to reverse themselves and argue the opposite. By 1975 the majority of textbooks argued races were a scientific error while only a quarter clung to the old racial views.

Fully half of the North American anthropologists surveyed in 1984 agreed with the statement, "There are biological races within the species Homo sapiens." (40% disagreed and 10% were unsure.) Fifteen years later when the same questions were posed again, the belief in races had dropped by half. In 1999 fewer than one-quarter of the anthropologists polled agreed that there were biological races. (24% yes, 69% no, 7% uncertain).

While scientists apparently became less willing to endorse the concept of races in theory, in practice a large number continued to employ it in their own research. A thirty-year survey of the flagship journal in the field of physical anthropology found that racial concepts were used uncritically and consistently at about the same rates from the 1960s through the 1990s. Overall, about 40% of all the authors researching human variation still used racial categories to describe their findings.

A 2011 survey of 18 English-language anatomy textbooks found that only four even attempted to explain patterns of human variation. Disturbingly, the four that did contain sections explaining why and how human anatomy differs used long outdated and simplistic racial explanations, such as " "Racial differences may be seen in the color of the skin, hair, and eyes, and in the shape and size of the eyes, nose, and lips. Africans and Scandinavians tend to be tall, as a result of long legs, whereas Asians tend to be short, with short legs. The heads of central Europeans and Asians also tend to be round and broad."

Modern science and the concept of race grew up together. Science powerfully reinforced economic and political forces that were weaving notions of racial difference deep into the fabric of society. Conversely, the study of races was among some of the earliest biological topics scientists applied their new methods to understand. Perhaps no other subject better highlights the fact that scientific methods and the tools scientists invent are just as prone to bias and error as the humans wielding them.

Charles. B. Davenport, "Effects of Race Intermingling,"

Proceedings of the American Philosophical Society, 130 (April 1917), pp. 364-368.

The problem of the effects of race intermingling may well interest us of America, when a single state, like New York, of 9,000,000 inhabitants contains 840,000 Russians and Finns, 720,000 Italians, 1,000,000 Germans, 880,000 Irish, 470,000 Austro-Hungarians,, 310,000 of Great Britain, 125,000 Canadians (largely French), and 90,000 Scandinavians. All figures include those born abroad or born of two foreign-born parents. Nearly two thirds of the population of New York State is foreign-born or of foreign or mixed parentage. Even in a state like Connecticut it is doubtful if 2 per cent, of the population are of pure Anglo-Saxon stock for six generations of ancestors in all lines. Clearly a mixture of European races is going on in America on a colossal scale.

Before proceeding further let us inquire into the meaning of "race." The modern geneticists' definition differs from that of the systematist or old fashioned breeder. A race is a more or less pure bred "group" of individuals that differs from other groups by at least one character, or, strictly, a genetically connected group whose germ plasm is characterized by a difference, in one or more genes, from other groups. Thus a blue-eyed Scotchman belongs to a different race from some of the dark Scotch. Strictly, as the term is employed by geneticists they may be said to belong to different elementary species.

Defining race in this sense of elementary species we have to consider our problem: What are the results of race intermingling, or miscegenation? To this question no general answer can be given. A specific answer can, however, be given to questions involving specific characters. For example, if the question be framed: what are the results of hybridization between a blue-eyed race (say Swede) and a brown-eyed race (say South Italian)? The answer is that, since brown eye is dominant over blue eye, all the children will have brown eyes; and if two such children inter-marry brown and blue eyes will appear among their children in the ratio of 3 to 1....

Again, if one parent belong to a tall race—like the Scotch or some Irish—and the other to a short race, like the South Italians, then all the progeny will tend to be intermediate in stature. If two such intermediates intermarry then very short, short, medium, tall and very tall offspring may result in proportions that cannot be precisely given, but about which one can say that the mediums are the commonest and the more extreme classes are less frequented, the more they depart from mediocrity...

What is true of physical traits is no less true of mental. The offspring of an intellectually well-developed man of good stock and a mentally somewhat inferior woman will tend to show a fair to good mentality; but the progeny of the intermarriage of two such will be normal and feeble-minded in the proportion of about 3 to 1. If one parent be of a strain that is highly excitable and liable to outbursts of temper while the other is calm then probably all the children will be excitable, or half of them, if the excitable parent is not of pure excitable stock. Thus, in the intellectual and emotional spheres the traits are no less "inherited" than in the physical sphere.

But I am aware that I have not yet considered the main problem of the consequence of race intermixture, considering races as differing by a number of characters...Any well-established abundant race is probably well adjusted to its conditions and its parts and functions are harmoniously adjusted...

[W]e have races of large tall men, like the Scotch, which are long-lived and whose internal organs are well adapted to care for the large frames. In the South Italians, on the other hand, we have small short bodies, but these, too, have well adjusted viscera. But the hybrids of these or similar two races may be expected to yield, in the second generation, besides the parental types also children with large frame and inadequate viscera—children of whom it is said every inch over 5' 10" is an inch of danger; children of insufficient circulation. On the other hand, there may appear children of short stature with too large circulatory apparatus. Despite the great capacity that the body has for self-adjustment it fails to overcome the bad hereditary combinations.

Again it seems probable, as dentists with whom I have spoken on the subject agree, that many cases of overcrowding or wide separation of teeth are due to a lack of harmony between size of jaw and size of teeth—probably due to a union of a large-jawed, large-toothed race and a small-jawed, small-toothed race. Nothing is more striking than the regular dental arcades commonly seen in the skulls of inbred native races and the irregular dentations of many children of the tremendously hybridized American.

Charles Davenport, 1914.

Not only physical but also mental and temperamental incompatibilities may be a consequence of hybridization. For example, one often sees in mulattoes an ambition and push combined with intellectual inadequacy which makes the unhappy hybrid dissatisfied with his lot and a nuisance to others.

To sum up, then, miscegenation commonly spells disharmony—disharmony of physical, mental and temperamental qualities and this means also disharmony with environment. A hybridized people are a badly put together people and a dissatisfied, restless, ineffective people. One wonders how much of the exceptionally high death rate in middle life in this country is due to such bodily maladjustments; and how much of our crime and insanity is due to mental and temperamental friction.

This country is in for hybridization on the greatest scale that the world has ever seen.

May we predict its consequences? At least we may hazard a prediction and suggest a way of diminishing the evil...

[T]he countries that developed the highest type of civilization occur on peninsulas—Egypt surrounded on two sides by water and on two sides by the desert and by tropical heat, Greece, and Rome on the Italian   peninsula. It is conceded that such peninsulas are centers of inbreeding... [A] period of prolonged inbreeding leads to social stratification. In such a period a social harmony is developed, the arts and sciences flourish but certain consequences of inbreeding follow, particularly, the spread of feeble-mindedness, epilepsy, melancholia and sterility. These weaken the nation, which then succumbs to the pressure of stronger, but less civilized, neighbors. Foreign hordes sweep in; miscegenation takes place, disharmonies appear, the arts and sciences languish, physical and mental vigor are increased in one part of the population and diminished in another part and finally after selection has done its beneficent work a hardier, more vigorous people results. In them social stratification in time follows and a high culture reappears; and so on in cycles... Indeed the result of hybridization after two or three generations is great variability. This means that some new combinations will be formed that are better than the old ones; also others that are worse. If selective annihilation is permitted to do its beneficent work, then the worse combinations will tend to die off early. If now new intermixing is stopped and eugenical mating ensues, consciously or unconsciously, especially in the presence of inbreeding, strains may arise that are superior to any that existed in the unhybridized races. This, then, is the hope for our country; if immigration is restricted, if selective elimination is permitted, if the principle of the inequality of generating strains be accepted and if eugenical ideals prevail in mating, then strains with new and better combinations of traits may arise and our nation take front rank in culture among the nations of ancient and modern times.

WERE WE BORN THAT WAY?

Or Can We Help It? Is Heredity or Environment the Power that Moulds Us? What Science Now Knows About Intellectual Differences, and Their Significance

By LEWIS MADISON TERMAN of the University of California

THE most characteristic thing about our political philosophy of the last two centuries is the increased respect this period accords to the common man. Nowhere has this philosophy more completely ruled the day than in America. ....

However this political philosophy, which every true American accepts, has been interpreted by many as resting on the assumption that there are no inborn differences of intellectual or other mental functions. Generally speaking, the average person in America is likely to believe that the larger differences he sees among those about him are the product of environment: that the successful business man differs from the unskilled laborer chiefly in his opportunity and his luck; that the difference between the college graduate and the illiterate is entirely a matter of education; that the races of men the world over differ only as their opportunities to acquire the arts of civilization have differed.

Of course we have always recognized the existence of idiots and geniuses, but we have regarded these as belonging to distinct species, separated by an impassable gulf from the intermediate-lying normal, who, as far as native endowment is concerned, are supposed to constitute a perfectly undifferentiated mass. Many believe that some such assumption is a necessary presupposition of democracy.

To those who hold this view the findings of individual psychology in the last decade have come as a rude shock. Let us review a few of the facts which have been brought to light and consider their bearing upon social economic and educational theory....

Intelligence tests are based upon the principle of sampling. Just as the value of a mountain of ore can be appraised by assaying a few pocketfuls of material, so it is possible to appraise one's intelligence by sinking shafts at a few critical

GUIDE FOR BINET-SIMON SCALE.   225

Age 7.

27. Show the unfinished pictures one at the time. "What is lacking (or missing) in this face (in this picture, for the standing woman)?" "Look at it carefully." Three correct out of 4 pass. "Eyes" instead of "eye" and "hands" instead of "arms" = +. "One ear" for face without eye, and "one eye" for face without nose = —.

28. "How many fingers have you on your right hand?" "On your left?" "On both hands?" Prompt answers, without counting, in all three cases required. Correct number of fingers, exclusive of thumbs, passes.

29. Ask S. to write the following from copy,

See little Paul

("Copy these words.") Record time. + if legible to one unfamiliar with original.

Examples of Stanford-Binet IQ questions

points and analyzing the samples thus secured. The more varied the range of mental functions tested, the more valid the test. Standard intelligence scales include tests of memory, language comprehension, orientation in time and space, eye-hand coordinations, ability to find likenesses and differences between familiar objects, arithmetical reasoning, resourcefulness and ingenuity, speed, and richness of mental associations, the capacity to generalize from particulars, etc....

Superficially regarded, intelligence tests are likely to appear trivial. Their significance becomes evident only when a subject's responses are compared with norms, or standards. The task of the psychologist is like that of the paleontologist. The latter, through his acquaintance with comparative norms, is able to reconstruct the physical features of a prehistoric man with nothing to guide him but a few fragments of bone which most of us would not recognize as belonging to human remains. So it is with mental tests Responses which signify nothing to the uninitiated are readily interpreted by the psychologist as characteristic of intellectual brilliance, dullness, moronity, imbecility, etc. The most convenient and widely used comparative standard of intellectual ability is the average test performance of normal unselected children of the different ages. This is where we get the term "mental age" which means simply the intelligence level which has been reached by the average child who is any given number of years old.

MENTAL age takes on a very special significance when it is considered in relation to the subject's life age. From this comparison is derived the "intelligence quotient" (IQ), which is simply the ratio of mental age to life age. If a child of ten years has a mental age of eight, his IQ is 80… The ten-year-old with a mental age of twelve has an IQ of 120. In calculating the IQ of an adult subject life age above fifteen or sixteen is disregarded, for strange to say intellectual ability seems to improve little if at all after that age.

The IQ's of idiots are below 25 or 30, those of imbeciles range from the borderline of idiocy to about 50, and those of morons from the borderline of imbecility to 70 or 75…

The IQ is therefore a "brightness index," and as such it is very serviceable even if far from accurate. Its significance lies in the fact that it has a marked tendency to remain constant, thus affording a rough basis for predicting a child's later development….

The IQ is not chiefly a product of formal instruction. Schooling doubtless affects it to some extent; how much psychologists are not agreed. The writer can find little evidence that ordinary inequalities of home environment and school training… invalidate the IQ very materially… Generally speaking, once feeble-minded, always feeble minded; once dull, always dull…

As an exact unit of measure the IQ is anything but satisfactory. Compared to units of measure used by the physicist, for example, it is grossly inaccurate and clumsy. It does seem however to be founded on more than the accidental influences of environment and to reflect, in some degree, the quality of native endowment. When our intelligence scales have become more accurate and the laws governing IQ changes have been more definitely established it will then be possible to say that there is nothing about an individual as important as his IQ… that the first concern of a nation should be the average IQ of its citizens, and the eugenic and dysgenic influences which are capable of raising or lowering that level; that the great test problem of democracy is how to adjust itself to the large IQ differences which can be demonstrated to exist among the members of any race or nationality group.

INTELLIGENCE is chiefly a matter of native endowment. It depends upon physical and chemical properties of the cerebral cortex, which like other physical traits, are subject to the laws of heredity. In fact, the mathematical coefficient of family resemblances in mental traits, particularly intelligence, has been found to be almost exactly the same as for such physical traits as height, weight, cephalic index, etc… The attempts to explain familiar resemblances on any other hypothesis than that of heredity have not been successful. All the available facts that science has to offer support the Galtonian theory that mental abilities are chiefly a matter of original endowment…

THE exact laws which govern the transmission of mental traits have not been determined. It is not surprising, however, that intelligence tests have shown the members of the socially successful classes to have, on the average, better endowment than those of inferior social status… Obviously, therefore, our civilization of a thousand or ten thousand years hence will depend largely upon the relative fertility of our low-grade and high-grade stocks.

Under the primitive economic conditions which prevailed in our relatively new and unformed civilization up to fifty or a hundred years ago, superior ability was more evenly distributed through the population than it is today. As the industrial and social situation becomes more complicated, there is a marked tendency, in any country which tries to give equal opportunity to all, for each individual to gravitate to the social or occupational level which corresponds to his native capacity. The more democratic the country, the more clearly this intellectual stratification tends to appear. In many parts of America it is well advanced….

THE BIRTH-RATE DIFFERENTIAL

UNTIL recently there had not been, at least for hundreds of years, any marked tendency in the civilized countries for one class to produce more rapidly than another. For centuries the average mental endowment of the European and American peoples had held its own. But within the last fifty years a change of sinister portent has taken place. Intellectually superior families are no longer reproducing as rapidly as formerly. Their birth rate is already far below that of the socially incompetent. The average feebleminded individual leaves two or three times as many offspring as the average college graduate. This biological cataclysm, silent but none the less fateful, is rapidly spreading to all civilized countries. If the differential character of our birth rate continues, the day is not many centuries removed when the only surviving stock will be that descended from the least desirable of our present-day population… As a nation we are faced by no other issue of comparable importance. It is a question of national survival or national decay. Unconscious of the danger that impends we haggle over matters of governmental policy that are infinitesimally trivial in comparison with the problem of differential fecundity. The situation will not be fully grasped until we have come to think more in terms of individual differences and intelligent quotients….

RACIAL DIFFERENCES IN INTELLIGENCE

DO races differ in intelligence? A nation which draws its constituents from all corners of the earth and prides itself on being the melting pot of peoples can not safely ignore this question. It is axiomatic that what comes out of the melting pot depends on what goes into it. A decade ago the majority of anthropologists and psychologists flouted the idea that there are any considerable differences in the native mental capacities of races or nationality groups. Today we have overwhelming evidence that they were mistaken. Army mental tests have shown that not more than 15 per cent. of American negroes equal or exceed in intelligence the average of our white population, and that the intelligence of the average negro is vastly inferior to that of the average white man. The available data indicate that the average mulatto occupies about a mid-position between pure negro and pure white. The intelligence of the American Indian has also been over-rated, for mental tests indicate that it is not greatly superior to that of the average negro. Our Mexican population, which is largely of Indian extraction, makes little if any better showing. The immigrants who have recently come to us in such large numbers from Southern and Southeastern Europe are distinctly inferior mentally to the Nordic and Alpine strains we have received from Scandinavia, Germany, Great Britain, and France…

World's Work, 44:6 (Oct. 1922), pp. 655-660.

Walter Lippmann, "The Mental Age of Americans," *New Republic* (Oct.-Nov. 1922)

Because the results are expressed in numbers, it is easy to make the mistake of thinking that the intelligence test is a measure like a foot rule or a pair of scales. It is, of course, a quite different sort of measure. For length and weight are qualities which men have learned how to isolate no matter whether they are found in an army of soldiers, a heap of bricks, or a collection of chlorine molecules. Provided the footrule and the scales agree with the arbitrarily accepted standard foot and standard pound in the Bureau of Standards at Washington they can be used with confidence. But "intelligence" is not an abstraction like length and weight; it is an exceedingly complicated notion which nobody has as yet succeeded in defining.

When we measure the weight of a schoolchild we mean a very definite thing. We mean that if you put the child on one side of an evenly balanced scale, you will have to put a certain number of standard pounds in the other scale in order to cancel the pull of the child's body towards the center of the earth. But when you come to measure intelligence you have nothing like this to guide you. You know in a general way that intelligence is the capacity to deal successfully with the problems that confront human beings, but if you try to say what those problems are, or what you mean by "dealing" with them or by "success," you will soon lose yourself in a fog of controversy. This fundamental difficulty confronts the intelligence tester at all times. The way in which he deals with it is the most important thing to understand about the intelligence test, for otherwise you are certain to misinterpret the results.

The intelligence tester starts with no clear idea of what intelligence means. He then proceeds by drawing upon his common sense and experience to imagine the different kinds of problems men face which might in a general way be said to call for the exercise of intelligence. But these problems are much too complicated and too vague to be reproduced in the classroom. The intelligence tester cannot confront each child with the thousand and one situations arising in a home, a workshop, a farm, an office or in politics, that call for the exercise of those capacities which in a summary fashion we call intelligence. He proceeds, therefore, to guess at the more abstract mental abilities which come into play again and again. By this rough process the intelligence tester gradually makes up his mind that situations in real life call for memory, definition, ingenuity and so on.

He then invents puzzles which can be employed quickly and with little apparatus, that will according to his best guess test memory, ingenuity, definition and the rest. He gives these puzzles to a mixed group of children and sees how children of different ages answer them. Whenever he finds a puzzles that, say, sixty percent of the twelve year old children can do, and twenty percent of the eleven year olds, he adopts that test for the twelve year olds. By a great deal of fitting he gradually works out a series of problems for each age group which sixty percent of his children can pass, twenty percent cannot pass and, say, twenty percent of the children one year younger can also pass. By this method he has arrived under the Stanford-Binet system at a conclusion of this sort: Sixty percent of children twelve years old should be able to define three out of the five words: pity, revenge, charity, envy, justice. According to Professor Terman's instructions, a child passes this test if he says that "pity" is "to be sorry for some one"; the child fails if he says "to help" or "mercy." A correct definition of "justice" is as follows: "It's what you get when you go to court"; an incorrect definition is "to be honest."...

There are, consequently, two uncertain elements. The first is whether the tests really test intelligence. The second is whether the children under observation are a large enough group to be typical... These elements of doubt are, I think, radical enough to prohibit anyone from using the results of these tests for large generalization about the quality of human beings. For when people generalize about the quality of human beings they assume an objective criterion. These puzzles may test intelligence, but they may not. They may test an aspect of intelligence. Nobody knows.

[An intelligence test does] not weigh or measure intelligence by any objective standard. It simply arranges a group of people in a series from best to worst by balancing their capacity to do certain arbitrarily selected puzzles, against the capacity of all the others. The intelligence test, in other words, is fundamentally an instrument for classifying a group of people. It may also be an instrument for measuring their intelligence, but of that we cannot be at all sure unless we believe that M. Binet and Mr. Terman and a few other psychologists have guessed correctly but, as we shall see later, the proof is not yet at hand.

The intelligence test, then, is an instrument for classifying a group of people, rather than "a measure of intelligence." People are classified within a group according to their success in solving problems which may or may not be tests of intelligence. They are classified according to the performance of some Californians in the years 1910 to about 1916 with Mr. Terman's notion of the problems that reveal intelligence. They are not classified according to their ability in dealing with the problems of real life that call for intelligence.

THE RELIABILITY OF INTELLIGENCE TESTS

Suppose, for example, that our aim was to test athletic rather than intellectual ability. We appoint a committee... to work out tests which will take no longer than an hour and can be given to large numbers of men at once. These tests are to measure the true athletic capacity of all men anywhere for the whole of their athletic careers. The order would be a large one, but it would certainly be no larger than the pretensions of many well known intelligence testers.

Our committee of athletic testers scratch their heads. What shall be the hour's test, they wonder, which will "measure" the athletic "capacity" of [Jack] Dempsey, [Ben] Tilden, [golfer Jess] Sweetser, [Boxer "Battling"] Siki, Suzanne Lenglen and Babe Ruth, of all sprinters, Marathon runners, broad jumpers, high divers, wrestlers, billiard players, marksmen, cricketers and pogo bouncers? The committee has courage. After much guessing and some experimenting the committee works out a sort of condensed Olympic games which can be held in any empty lot. These games consist of a short sprint, one or two jumps, throwing a ball at a bull's eye, hitting a punching machine, tackling a dummy and a short game of clock golf. They try out these tests on a mixed assortment of champions and duffers and find that on the whole the champions do all the tests better than the duffers. They score the result and compute statistically what is the average score for all the tests. This average score then constitutes normal athletic ability.

Now it is clear that such tests might really give some clue to athletic ability. But the fact that in any large group of people sixty percent made an average score would be no proof that you had actually tested their athletic ability. To prove that, you would have to show that success in the athletic tests correlated closely with success in athletics. The same conclusion applies to the intelligence tests. Their statistical uniformity is one thing; their reliability another. The tests might be a fair guess at intelligence, but the statistical result does not show whether they are or not. You could get a statistical curve very much like the curve of "intelligence" distribution if instead of giving each child from ten to thirty problems to do you had flipped a coin the same number of times for each child and had credited him with the heads. I do not mean, of course, that the results are as chancy as all that. They are not, as we shall soon see. But I do mean that there is no evidence for the reliability of the tests as tests of intelligence in the claim, made by Terman,4 that the distribution of intelligence quotients corresponds closely to "the theoretical normal curve of distribution (the Gaussian curve)." He would in a large enough number of cases get an even more perfect curve if these tests were tests not of intelligence but of the flip of a coin.

Such statistical check has its uses, of course. It tends to show, for example, that in a large group the bias and errors of the tester have been canceled out. It tends to show that the gross result is reached in the mass by statistically impartial methods, however wrong the judgment about any particular child may be. But the fairness in giving the tests and the reliability of the tests themselves must not be confused. The tests may be quite fair applied in the mass, and yet be poor tests of individual intelligence….

The correlation between the various systems enables us to say only that the tests are not mere chance, and that they do seem to seize upon a certain kind of ability. But whether this ability is a sign of general intelligence or not, we have no means of knowing from such evidence alone. The same conclusion holds true of the fact that when the tests are repeated at intervals on the same group of people they give much the same results. Data of this sort are as yet meager, for intelligence testing has not been practiced long enough to give results over long periods of time. Yet the fact that the same child makes much the same score year after year is significant. It permits us to believe that some genuine capacity is being

tested. But whether this is the capacity to pass tests or the capacity to deal with life, which we call intelligence, we do not know….

TESTS OF HEREDITARY INTELLIGENCE

The first argument in favor of the view that the capacity for intelligence is hereditary is an argument by analogy… It is not necessary for our purpose to come to any conclusion as to the inheritance of capacity. The evidence is altogether insufficient for any conclusion, and the only possible attitude is an open mind. We are, moreover, not concerned with the question of whether intelligence is hereditary. We are concerned only with the claim of the intelligence tester that he reveals and measures hereditary intelligence. These are quite separate propositions, but they are constantly confused by the testers… The facts of heredity cannot be proved by analogy; the facts of heredity are what they are. The question of whether the intelligence test measures heredity is a wholly different matter. It is the only question which concerns us here.

It is possible, of course, to deny that the early environment has any important influence on the growth of intelligence. Men like Stoddard and McDougall do deny it, and so does Mr. Terman. But on the basis of the mental tests they have no right to an opinion. Mr. Terman's observations begin at four years of age. He publishes no data on infancy and he is, therefore, generalizing about the heredity factor after four years of immensely significant development have already taken place. On his own showing as to the high importance of the earlier years, he is hardly justified in ignoring them. He cannot simply lump together the net result of natural endowment and infantile education and ascribe it to the germplasm.

In doing just that he is obeying the will to believe, not the methods of science. How far he is carried may be judged from this instance which Mr. Terman cites as showing the negligible influence of environment. He tested twenty children in an orphanage and found only three who were fully normal. "The orphanage in question," he then remarks, "is a reasonably good one and affords an environment which is about as stimulating as average home life among the middle classes." Think of it. Mr. Terman first discovers what a "normal mental development" is by testing children who are growing up in the abnormal environment of an institution and finds that they are not normal. He then puts the blame for abnormality on the germplasm of the orphans….

How does it happen that men of science can presume to dogmatize about the mental qualities of the germplasm when their own observations begin at four years of age? Yet this is what the chief intelligence testers, led by Professor Terman, are doing. Without offering any data on all that occurs between conception and the age of kindergarten, they announce on the basis of what they have got out of a few thousand questionnaires that they are measuring the hereditary mental endowment of human beings. Obviously this is not a conclusion obtained by research. It is a conclusion planted by the will to believe. It is, I think, for the most part unconsciously planted. The scoring of the tests itself favors an uncritical belief that intelligence is a fixed quantity in the germplasm and that, no matter what the environment, only a predetermined increment of intelligence can develop from year to year. For the result of a test is not stated in terms of intelligence, but as a percentage of the average for that age level. These percentages remain more or less constant. Therefore, if a child shows an IQ of 102, it is easy to argue that he was born with an IQ of 102.

There is here, I am convinced, a purely statistical illusion, which breaks down when we remember what IQ means. A child's IQ is his percentage of passes in the test which the average child of a large group of his own age has passed. The IQ measures his place in respect to the average at any year. But it does not show the rate of his growth from year to year. In fact it tends rather to conceal the fact that the creative opportunities in education are greatest in early childhood. It conceals the fact, which is of such far-reaching importance, that because the capacity to form intellectual habits decreases as the child matures, the earliest education has a cumulative effect on the child's future. All this the static percentages of the IQ iron out. They are meant to iron it out. It is the boast of the inventors of the IQ that "the distribution of intelligence maintains a certain constancy from five to thirteen or fourteen years of age, when the degree of intelligence is expressed in terms of the intelligence quotient." The intention is to eliminate the factor of uneven and cumulative growth, so that there shall be always a constant measure by which to classify children in class rooms....

The effect of the intelligence quotient on a tester's mind may be to make it seem as if intelligence were constant, whereas it is only the statistical position in large groups which is constant. This illusion of constancy has, I believe, helped seriously to prevent men like Terman from appreciating the variability of early childhood. Because in the mass the percentages remain fixed, they tend to forget how in each individual case there were offered creative opportunities which the parents and nurse girls improved or missed or bungled. The whole more or less blind drama of childhood, where the habits of intelligence are formed, is concealed in the mental test. The testers themselves become callous to it. What their footrule does not measure soon ceases to exist for them, and so they discuss heredity in school children before they have studied the education of infants.

But of course no student of human motives will believe that this revival of predestination is due to a purely statistical illusion. He will say with Nietzsche that "every impulse is imperious, and, as such, attempts to philosophize." And so behind the will to believe he will expect to find some manifestation of the will power. He will not have to read far in the literature of mental testing to discover it. He will soon see that the intelligence test is being sold to the public on the basis of the claim that it is a device which will measure pure intelligence, whatever that may be, as distinguished from knowledge and acquired skill.

This advertisement is impressive. If it were true, the emotional and the worldly satisfactions in store for the intelligence tester would be very great. If he were really measuring intelligence, and if intelligence were a fixed hereditary quantity, it would be for him to say not only where to place each child in school, but also which children should go to high school, which to college, which into the professions, which into the manual trades and common labor. If the tester could make good his claim, he would soon occupy a position of power which no intellectual has held since the collapse of theocracy. The vista is enchanting, and even a little of the vista is intoxicating enough. If only it could be proved, or at least believed, that intelligence is fixed by heredity, and that the tester can measure it, what a future to dream about! The unconscious temptation is too strong for the ordinary critical defenses of the scientific methods. With the help of a subtle statistical illusion, intricate logical fallacies and a few smuggled obiter dicta, self-deception as the preliminary to public deception is almost automatic.

The claim that we have learned how to measure hereditary intelligence has no scientific foundation. We cannot measure intelligence when we have never defined it, and we cannot speak of its hereditary basis after it has been indistinguishably fused with a thousand educational and environmental influences from the time of conception to the school age. The claim that Mr. Terman or anyone else is measuring hereditary intelligence has no more scientific foundation than a hundred other fads, vitamins and glands and amateur psychoanalysis and correspondence courses in will power, and it will pass them into that limbo where phrenology and palmistry and characterology and the other Babu sciences are to be found. In all of these there was some admixture of primitive truth which the conscientious scientist retains long after the wave of popular credulity has spent itself.

New Republic 32:412 (Oct. 25, 1922), pp. 213–215; 32:413 (Nov. 1, 1922), pp. 246–248; 323:414 (Nov. 8, 1922), pp. 275–277; 32:415 (Nov. 15, 1922), pp. 297–298; 32:416 (Nov. 22, 1922), pp. 328–330; 32:417 (Nov. 29, 1922), pp. 9–11.

UNESCO Statement of On the Nature of Race and Race Differences 1950

1. Scientists have reached general agreement in recognizing that mankind is one: that all men belong to the same species, Homo sapiens. It is further generally agreed among scientists that all men are probably derived from the same common stock; and that such differences as exist between different groups of mankind are due to the operation of evolutionary factors of differentiation such as isolation, the drift and random fixation of the material particles which control heredity (the genes), changes in the structure of these particles, hybridization, and natural selection. In these ways groups have arisen of varying stability and degree of differentiation which have been classified in different ways for different purposes.

2. From the biological standpoint, the species Homo sapiens is made up of a number of populations, each one of which differs from the others in the frequency of one or more genes. Such genes, responsible for the hereditary differences between men, are always few when compared to the whole genetic constitution of man and to the vast number of genes common to all human beings regardless of the population to which they belong. This means that the likenesses among men are far greater than their differences.

3. A race, from the biological standpoint, may therefore be defined as one of the group of populations constituting the species Homo sapiens. These populations are capable of interbreeding with one another but, by virtue of the isolating barriers which in the past kept them more or less separated, exhibit certain physical differences as a result of their somewhat different biological histories. These represent variations, as it were, on a common theme.

4. In short, the term "race" designates a group or population characterized by some concentrations, relative as to frequency and distribution, of hereditary particles (genes) or physical characters, which appear, fluctuate, and often disappear in the course of time by reason of geographic and/or cultural isolation. The varying manifestations of these traits in different populations are perceived in different ways by each group. What is perceived is largely preconceived, so that each group arbitrarily tends to misinterpret the variability which occurs as a fundamental difference which separates that group from all others.

5. These are the scientific facts. Unfortunately, however, when most people use the term "race" they do not do so in the sense above defined. To most people, a race is any group of people whom they choose to describe as a race. Thus, many national, religious, geographic, linguistic or cultural groups have, in such loose usage, been called "race", when obviously Americans are not a race, nor are Englishmen, nor Frenchmen, nor any other national group. Catholics, Protestants, Moslems and Jews are not races, nor are groups who speak English or any other language thereby definable as a race: people who live in Iceland or England or India are not races; nor are people who are culturally Turkish or Chinese or the like thereby describable as races.

6. National, religious, geographic, linguistic and cultural groups do not necessarily coincide with racial groups; and the cultural traits of such groups have no demonstrated genetic connexion with racial traits. Because serious errors of this kind are habitually committed when the term "race" is used in popular parlance, it would be better when speaking of human races to drop the term "race" altogether and speak of ethnic groups.

7. Now what has the scientist to say about the groups of mankind which may be recognized at the present time? Human races can be and have been differently classified by different anthropologists, but at the present time most anthropologists agree on classifying the greater part of present-day mankind into three major divisions, as follows: the Mongoloid Division, the Negroid Division, the Caucasoid Division. The biological processes which the classifier has here embalmed, as it were, are dynamic, not static. These divisions were not the same in the past as they are at present, and there is every reason to believe that they will change in the future.

8. Many sub-groups or ethnic groups within these divisions have been described. There is no general agreement upon their number, and in any event most ethnic groups have not yet been either studied or described by the physical anthropologists.

9. Whatever classification the anthropologist makes of man, he never includes mental characteristics as part of those classifications. It is now generally recognized that intelligence tests do not in themselves enable us to differentiate safely between what is due to innate capacity and what is the result of environmental influences, training and education. Wherever it has been possible to make allowances for differences in environmental opportunities, the tests have shown essential similarity in mental characters among all human groups. In short, given similar degrees of cultural opportunity to realize their potentialities, the average achievement of the members of each ethnic group is

about the same. The scientific investigations of recent years fully support the dictum of Confucius (551-478 B.C.): "Men's natures are alike; it is their habits that carry them far apart."

10. The scientific material available to us at present does not justify the conclusion that inherited genetic differences are a major factor in producing the differences between the cultures and cultural achievements of different peoples or groups. It does indicate, however, that the history of the cultural experience which each group has undergone is the major factor in explaining such differences. The one trait which above all others has been at a premium in the evolution of men's mental characters has been educability, plasticity. This is a trait which all human beings possess. It is indeed, a species character of Homo sapiens.

11. So far as temperament is concerned, there is no definite evidence that there exist inborn differences between human groups. There is evidence that whatever group differences of the kind there might be are greatly over-ridden by the individual differences, and by the differences springing from environmental factors.

12. As for personality and character, these may be considered raceless. In every human group a rich variety of personality and character types will be found, and there is no reason for believing that any human group is richer than any other in these respects.

13. With respect to race-mixture, the evidence points unequivocally to the fact that this has been going on from the earliest times. Indeed, one of the chief processes of race-formation and race-extinction or absorption is by means of hybridization between races or ethnic groups. Furthermore, no convincing evidence has been adduced that race-mixture of itself produces biologically bad effects. Statements that human hybrids frequently show undesirable traits, both physically and mentally, physical disharmonies and mental degeneracies, are not supported by the facts. There is, therefore, no "biological" justification for prohibiting intermarriage between persons of different ethnic groups.

14. The biological fact of race and the myth of "race" should be distinguished. For all practical social purposes "race" is not so much a biological phenomenon as a social myth. The myth "race" has created an enormous amount of human and social damage. In recent years it has taken a heavy toll in human lives and caused untold suffering. It still prevents the normal development of millions of human beings and deprives civilization of the effective co-operation of productive minds. The biological differences between ethnic groups should be disregarded from the standpoint of social acceptance and social action. The unity of mankind from both the biological and social viewpoints is the main thing. To recognize this and to act accordingly is the first requirement of modern man...And, indeed, the whole of human history shows that a co-operative spirit is not only natural to men, but more deeply rooted than any self-seeking tendencies. If this were not so we should not see the growth of integration and organization of his communities which the centuries and the millenia plainly exhibit.

15. We now have to consider the bearing of these statements on the problem of human equality. It must be asserted with the utmost emphasis that equality as an ethical principle in no way depends upon the assertion that human beings are in fact equal in endowment. Obviously individuals in all ethnic groups vary greatly among themselves in endowment. Nevertheless, the characteristics in which human groups differ from one another are often exaggerated and used as a basis for questioning the validity of equality in the ethical sense. For this purpose we have thought it worth while to set out in a formal manner what is at present scientifically established concerning...group differences.

(a) In matters of race, the only characteristics which anthropologists can effectively use as a basis for classifications are physical and physiological.

(b) According to present knowledge there is no proof that the groups of mankind differ in their innate mental characteristics, whether in respect of intelligence or temperament. The scientific evidence indicates that the range of mental capacities in all ethnic groups is much the same.

(c) Historical and sociological studies support the view that genetic differences are not of importance in determining the social and cultural differences between different groups of Homo sapiens, and that the social and cultural changes in different groups have, in the main, been independent of changes in inborn constitution. Vast social changes have occurred which were not in any way connected with changes in racial type.

(d) There is no evidence that race-mixture as such produces bad results from the biological point of view. The social results of race-mixture whether for good or ill are to be traced to social factors.

(e) All normal human beings are capable of learning to share in a common life, to understand the nature of mutual service and reciprocity, and to respect social obligations and contracts. Such biological differences as exist between members of different ethnic groups have no relevance to problems of social and political organization, moral life and communication between human beings...

Part Two: Race and Nation

Chapter Four: Founding a Racial Republic

One of the many ways America is different from other European nations is that it was founded at the same time that racist thinking first became dominant. As a result, all of America's most basic institutions, its economy, its culture, and its government, were shaped and formed by racism. While racism was certainly present in other European societies, only in America was it the central and organizing principle of everything else.

Most importantly, America was the only European society with slavery at its core. Other nations, most notably England, Spain, France, and the Netherlands, all enriched themselves on the backs of people held in chains and forced to labor, but their involvement with slavery was limited to their overseas colonies. Only in America was slavery primarily a domestic institution at the center of social life.

This fact and this difference from other countries explains many unique aspects of United States history. It explains America's rapid economic growth and its successful revolutionary separation from England. It explains America's unusual representative government and its division of powers between states and a federal center. It explains America's aggressive territorial expansion that rather than forming colonies integrated conquered lands into its home nation. And of course it explains how a nation founded on the liberal ideals of the Enlightenment built the world's most comprehensive legal system of racial discrimination. Racism and slavery were the most important foundation stones of the edifice we call America.

America Before Columbus

The story of North American history begins, not with Columbus or the Pilgrims, but with the people who inhabited this vast land long before any of these conquerors and colonists were born. Sometime between twenty-three and forty thousand years ago (about the same time as humans

THE LANDING OF THE PILGRIMS AT PLYMOUTH, MASS. DEC. 22nd 1620.

Figure 4.1 The landing of the Pilgrims at Plymouth, Mass. Dec. 22nd 1620 (New York: Currier & Ives, 1876).

first arrived at the island chain of Japan and the peninsulas of Scandinavia), the first Americans crossed a land bridge along the Bering Strait from Asia that was exposed due to the unusually cold climate that expanded the polar ice caps and dropped the ocean levels. Successive waves of people spread human settlement southward to the tip of South America (Tierra del Fuego) and eastward to the Atlantic.

Sometime between seven and ten thousand years ago (5,000 - 8,000 B.C.) some of the peoples of North America began to cultivate crops, such as maize (corn), potatoes, and squash, and other plants in addition to gathering wild foods. The invention of agriculture dramatically changed these societies. It allowed for the development of permanent year-round settlements, the concentration of population in larger villages and towns, and created surpluses of food that allowed for trade between settlements. Food surpluses and larger communities allowed people to specialize in their jobs, and some people became artisans: builders, jewelers, tool-makers, merchants, and spiritual leaders. Agriculture also allowed for the development of new cultural traditions and government structures. As groups spent more time in one specific location their ways of life grew more apart from others more distant. Agriculture, because it requires lots of coordinated work and possession of specific plots of land, leads to more formal governing structures. Whereas nomadic bands make many decisions collectively or according to ritual or spiritual ideas, farming communities developed complex governing structures with specific groups of decision-makers.

At least three thousand years ago, in the land we call "America," cities were built that contained several thousand people and relied on extensive networks of trade up and down the mid-continent river systems. In Poverty Point, Louisiana, a village grew to hold as many as 2,000 people. These people buried their leaders in elaborate earthworks, studied the stars and celebrated the annual winter and summer solstices. To the north, first the Adena and later the Hopewell peoples of the Ohio River Valley also buried their dead in great earthen sculptures, one of which, the Great Serpent Mound in Central Ohio is a quarter-mile long. In the southwest, the Hohokam, and later the Anasazi, irrigated cornfields and built increasingly elaborate stone villages or pueblos. All of these communities carried on extensive trade across hundreds and even thousands of miles.

A thousand years ago a great city of people descended from the mound-builders grew up on the banks of the Mississippi River (and therefore called "Mississippian" culture) at Cahokia, Illinois. This city traded far up and down the major rivers that converged nearby and its people built huge temples and earthworks. Its population peaked at around 12,000, but within three hundred years of its founding (1000 A.D.) the city was in ruins, the reasons for

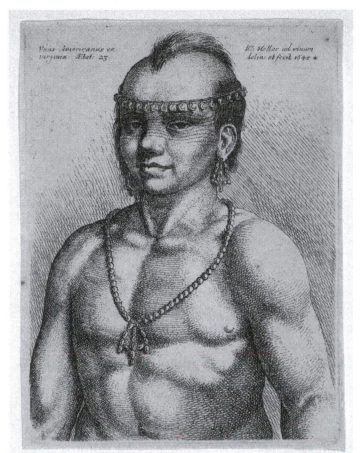

Figure 4.2 "Unus Americanus ex Virginia," by Wenceslaus Hollar, 1645.

its fate still unclear. Hundreds of years later the influence of Mississippian culture could be seen in the Coosa kingdom of Tennessee and Alabama.

Beginning about 1000 A.D. native peoples in the northeast began to blend traditional hunting and gathering with raising corn. Using fire to clear land and fertilize soils had the additional benefit of keeping down underbrush and allowing the growth of stands of tall trees and meadows which in turn allowed for more game. This "woodland culture" proved highly successful and allowed for these societies to flourish prior to European contact.

On the eve of contact with Europeans, a number of growing woodland societies along the eastern seaboard united into large confederations. The Narragansetts united various farming villages in present day Rhode Island. The Powhatans of tidewater Virginia combined many towns under a united government. In New York, the Iroquois forged an alliance of five separate nations. These federations governed peace and war, trade, borders, and other such common concerns of state.

Even before the first Europeans set foot in America, native societies were experiencing rapid growth and change and had a long history of their own. By 1500, what would become the United States was already a land filled with people and diverse cultures. Its population was probably around five million people, perhaps larger. Of these, about half were nomadic and the other half sedentary or only semi-nomadic. Among them they spoke over 350 languages and had as many unique folkways, histories, diets, dress, shelter, tools, religions, and all the other elements of culture.

Why Columbus?

Every American pupil is taught that in 1492 Columbus sailed the ocean blue. But few students are given an explanation of why it was a European and not some other society that ventured out of their homelands to conquer a distant continent. Few are told why this happened in 1492 and not hundreds of years earlier or later. Clearly, technology was not the issue as Leif Erikson made the voyage across the north Atlantic to what is today Canada in 1001 A.D. and other Norse explorers followed over the next century. For hundreds of years before Columbus' voyage, English, Scottish, and Irish sailors routinely sailed westward to harvest cod from the fertile reefs off the coast of Newfoundland, sometimes building temporary camps on Canada's coast.

Long voyages were not unusual before Marco Polo (1271-1295) and Columbus. Arab pilots routinely crossed the Indian Ocean as Vasco de Gama learned when he sailed a few years after Columbus. (Both Vasco de Gama and Columbus employed Arab navigators to lead their fleets). Nearly a century before Columbus sailed Admiral Cheng-Ho of the Ming Dynasty sailed a much larger fleet from the eastern coast of China to west Africa, a voyage about as far as the one from Spain to the Caribbean. Indeed, the great circulating ocean currents of the Atlantic are very reliable and simple compared to those of the South China Sea and the Indian Ocean that Cheng-Ho navigated.

So if Chinese and Arab empires were better sailors and navigators, why were Spanish and Portuguese empires the first to strike out toward the Western Hemisphere? Part of the answer lies in the relative poverty of Europe. When Columbus sailed the largest cities in the world were not in Europe but were in Asia and the Islamic world. In spite of Europe tripling its population between 1000 and 1300, it remained relatively undeveloped, impoverished, and isolated. At the time of Columbus, the largest city in Europe, Paris, had a population of about 200,000, about the same as Constantinople (present day Istanbul, Turkey). Germany's largest city, Cologne, had only about 20,000 people and London had a population of about 50,000. Meanwhile Baghdad had 400,000 and Beijing had grown to nearly a million people.

Both the Chinese and Islamic empires, both at peaks of wealth and power during the European middle ages, had access to all the resources their societies coveted in their own regions. The Indian Ocean was the Arab highway to the far east and to Africa. The seas around China and its vast inland empire also provided a sufficient area of exploitation for their needs. Europeans were the first to venture across the Atlantic in any organized way because they lacked the fine goods they could only secure in trade from larger and more powerful empires to their south and their east.

Historians and anthropologists once universally believed that the European conquest of the Americas was made possible by the extraordinary virulence of European diseases upon native American peoples. They pointed out that Europeans brought to the New World the deadliest diseases ever known to humankind, including the bubonic plague, typhoid, small-pox, measles, yellow fever, malaria, whooping cough, and influenza. (The only significant pathogen that travelled the opposite direction was syphilis.) The "Crowd Theory" of disease holds that extremely deadly diseases can only develop where populations are dense because microbes that kill their hosts need to constantly find new hosts to survive. (For example, it is estimated that measles needs a concentrated population of 250,000 to have developed.) Moreover, populations that harbor such deadly pathogens develop resistance to them, resistance that can be passed onto future generations.

Scholars observed that native populations had few population centers and those that had reached the size of large cities, such as the great centers of Mayan and Incan life, were of relatively recent development. Much of the indigenous population of the Western Hemisphere was dispersed over a large area. As a result, killer diseases did not have a chance to spread far before dying out. Moreover, native societies had few domesticated animals and many deadly human diseases, such as influenza, have evolved by lurking in the guts of the animals humans raise for food. By this logic, native peoples did not have the opportunity to develop the resistance to diseases Europeans enjoyed and consequently these diseases were far more virulent and deadly once they reached the New World.

These seemingly solid facts made possible the historical consensus that it was European diseases, unwittingly carried to the New World, that devastated native populations. Demographers have documented that within a century of Columbus' voyage, or even before, a large proportion of the indigenous peoples of the Western Hemisphere were wiped out. Historians wrote that European colonists moved into a widowed rather than a virgin land. By time Pilgrims landed, it is estimated, 90% of New England's native peoples had already perished from disease. Most of the settlements founded in New England were built on the ruins of native towns where settlers didn't have to undertake the laborious work of clearing trees or breaking fresh fields for crops and pasture.

Figure 4.3 "The March of Myles Standish...with Eight of his Valorous Army Led by Their Indian Guide, By Hobomok, Friend of the White Men."

Beginning in the 2010s, a growing number of specialists have disputed this "Widowed Land Theory." Rather, they point out that native people suffered not simply from disease but from military attack, displacement from their homes, enslavement, and famine. It was not the hidden hand of disease, but the mailed fist of colonial power that drove America's indigenous populations to suddenly decline. Disease was a part of the story, these scholars counter, but native susceptibility to disease could have just as easily been caused by the uprooting of communities, forced labor, and social and cultural changes in response to the threat of attack from Europeans or their Indian allies, as by some genetic predisposition that has never been proved. Also a focus on disease clouds the full picture because the other half of demographic collapse, besides early death, was a decline in fertility and birth-rates which are themselves acutely sensitive to the sort of disruptions colonialism wreaked across native communities. Europeans were themselves not as immune to the diseases they brought with them as has been supposed as epidemics frequently swept through English colonial towns and cities well into the nineteenth century.

Colonists were aware that epidemics decimated native communities, but they had little appreciation for the experiences and particular circumstances that may have led to them. The Pilgrims landed at a spot where native people had abandoned their villages, their crops still standing in the fields. They presumed people had left due to an epidemic but, of course, they did not know any details of what really happened to their departed neighbors. They merely rejoiced at their good fortune and considered it a sign that God approved of their mission. John Winthrop, the Pilgrim leader, was aware that his people were moving into lands abandoned by native peoples who had suffered a horrific loss. Winthrop celebrated this sign from God who "in sweeping away great multitudes of natives...that he might make room for us there" had "hereby cleared our title to this place." Indeed, the "natural" environment that the colonists entered as they stepped off their ships was itself largely the product of the conscious land management of the Indian peoples who landscaped the vast woodlands by regularly setting fires to burn underbrush.

Besides goods, animals, plants, and microbes, ideas and ways of life were exchanged between Old and New Worlds long before Englishmen arrived. Coastal Indian communities traded with Europeans who exchanged metal goods and weapons for furs and fish. In 1534, when Jacques Cartier explored inland along the St. Lawrence river, to his surprise he was invited ashore by Micmac Indians holding aloft furs on long poles. These native peoples already had 50 years of experience in trading with Europeans. In 1542 a Basque whaler reported in his diary that he had dinner with some American Indians who spoke four European languages.

Trade with Europeans profoundly changed how native societies were organized. The expansion of the fur trade shifted power to men in some native communities as the work of men in trapping fur-bearing animals came to be valued over the gathering and farming of women. Trade increased many native communities' dependence on Europeans. Trade drew many native communities into conflict with each other as trade enhanced the power of some tribes over others and changed the balance of nations in the New World. Such conflicts frequently drew colonists into conflict with native peoples who had allied with rival empires. But though from a native perspective such conflicts were limited questions of trading or territorial rights, English colonists again and again seized on these opportunities to expand these skirmishes into total wars of extermination.

Native Slavery

In many ways, England's success in colonizing North America was due not simply to its success at seizing favorable tracts of land from natives, but also in exploiting their labor as well. When English colonies were most vulnerable, in the seventeenth century when their numbers were small and only grew by the addition of new recruits from England, there was a severe shortage of labor. English colonists resorted to Indian slaves to clear forests, and plant crops. Many Indians were simply seized when opportunity presented itself. Others were purchased from natives who had captured tribal enemies in war.

War provided many opportunities to gain slaves. During one of the first serious conflicts with native peoples, Puritans captured hundreds of Pequot men, women and children, many of whom were summarily executed, but many others were enslaved. A few were given to the Puritans' wartime allies, the Narragansetts, as slaves, while at least seventeen women and children were sold off to the slave markets of Bermuda.

By the mid-1600s Virginia and the Carolinas had so many Indian slaves they began passing laws regulating their service. Virginia initially limited the terms of service of Indian children sold into slavery, restricting their service to be no longer than that commonly demanded of English servants. But in 1676 after a number of skirmishes with native peoples provoked Englishmen living in Virginia's frontier to rebel against their colonial governor (who they accused of ignoring their pleas for protection) the colony abandoned any pretense at equal treatment and ordered that "all Indians taken in warr be held and accounted slaves dureing life" and provided that soldiers who captured Indians could keep them for life as a bounty for their service. Largely because Virginia's militia was so effective in killing and driving off the many native communities that once called the lands surrounding Chesapeake Bay home, at most a few dozen native peoples were captured and enslaved for life there.

Further south, in South Carolina, the numbers of native people seized and held as slaves was quite high in the seventeenth century as slaves were key to the colony's economy and colonial leaders organized raiding expeditions on the Indian missions established by the Spanish in nearby Florida. In 1704 alone, Carolina governor James Moore organized a raiding party that included both Englishmen and Creek warriors that ventured deep into Florida and enslaved thousands. Moore boasted that "In this expedition I brought away 300 men, and 1000 women and children, have killed and taken as slaves 325 men and have taken [as] slaves 4000 women and children." Further profitable raids were launched regularly over the next decade until the Spanish mission system collapsed and survivors from many nations added to the growing power of the Seminoles that then served as a barrier to further English attacks.

Most of the people enslaved by Englishmen in Carolina were sold to slave brokers who transported them to the West Indies where they were put to work on sugar plantations. But a large number served as the main labor force of the colony in its critical early years. By 1708 there were 1,400 enslaved Indian people compared to 4,000 slaves of African descent in South Carolina. Together the people held in bondage in that colony outnumbered white colonists by half. One recent historian estimates that as many as 51,000 native peoples were enslaved by Englishmen during just the period from 1670 to 1715.

Enslaved Indian labor helped kick-start the agricultural economies of not only the seaboard regions from Virginia south to the Carolinas, but was also important further west. The French colony of Louisiana relied on Indian slaves before Africans were dragged to the region. Indian slaves were to be found in both Spanish outposts in New Mexico and Texas as well as in some native communities as well (though people held as slaves in native communities were not seen as primarily economic tools, but as tokens of status—many slaves held in Indian hands eventually were incorporated into the kinship structures of the tribe).

Colonization and Slavery

Slavery was the foundation upon which the modern world was built. Slavery produced the first consumer goods, sugar and tobacco, and later supplied Europe with the raw materials, such as cotton, that nurtured industrialisation. The immense profits from plantation slavery developed modern banking and financial practices and tied the Atlantic world together in a web of international finance. Slavery generated such great wealth over such a sustained period of time that it built a new middle class that liberalized most of Europe as it rose. The Enlightenment philosophers who debated natural rights and freedoms in their coffee-houses, did so dressed in their slave-produced broadcloth clothes, smoking their slave-grown tobacco and sipping their hot slave-grown coffee sweetened with slave-grown sugar.

Just looking at history from the widest lens, the European project of colonizing the New World was the creation of one vast slave system. Prior to the nineteenth century, when the slave trade was outlawed, Britain transported three times more Africans than Europeans to the New World.

Slavery's singular importance to American development remains under-appreciated because its truth lies obscured beneath deep layers of myth and misunderstanding. Some of these layers are intentional—they were created to overcome the contradiction between America's ideals of liberty and the primary source of its wealth. They hide the uncomfortable fact that the contours of the fortunes piled up under the crack of the lash are still visible. These myths reinforce the clay feet of America's founding heroes, many of whom held the chains that kept people in bondage. And they spread the lie that race is a fundamental power in the world while claiming the opposite of the force that truly is—history.

The first source of misunderstanding of American slavery is the term itself. The same word, slavery, is used to describe all manner of slaveries through time, even though these institutions vary widely. Most human societies since the beginning of recorded time have practiced slavery. But the customs and purposes of these native practices were nothing like the forms of slavery Europeans brought to the New World. Only a few of the hundreds of slave societies known to history practiced a form of slavery primarily organized as a productive system. And of these, only North American slavery eventually became completely integrated into the marketplace, with all the advanced financial systems of investment, banking, insurance, and management supporting it.

Apologists of American slavery have often excused its horrors by pointing to the fact that many African societies practiced slavery as well. They note that most Africans transported to the New World were not kidnapped and enslaved by Europeans but were already enslaved when they were sold to Europeans. Both points are factual, but misleading. Slavery in Africa took many forms from the market slavery practiced in the north part of the continent where Islamic states ruled, to the domestic-based systems practiced in the rest of Africa where slaves were not a permanent caste of workers, but were tokens of status. In fact, prior to the mid-seventeenth century, there were more English slaves in the Islamic states of North Africa than African slaves in the English colonies of the Americas.

Exchanging Citizens for Horses.   Page 106.

Figure 4. 4 "Exchanging citizens for horses," 1834.

While it may have been true that slavery had its African accomplices, this does not mean that these Africans governed the trade. Europeans created the demand, organized the market, and established the string of forts that served as prisons for collecting enslaved people and embarking them onto ships for their horrific ocean journey. The flow of enslaved people to the Americas ebbed and flowed with the demand for labor. The Atlantic slave trade lasted four centuries but nearly two-thirds of the people transported sailed in the trades' last century.

Most of the native societies Europeans encountered when they invaded the New World practiced slavery. But in most native American societies, slavery was primarily a means of displaying status and power, not an economic system. Slaves were usually enemies captured in battle who were then ritually stripped of all their clothes and adornments, even their name, in an act symbolizing the death of their former selves. Occupying the lowest status of the members of the community and viewed as the property of their capturer, they could be traded or given away as a gift to demonstrate their master's power and influence. In this way slavery in indigenous cultures usually had more symbolic than economic value.

Of course there are exceptions to this. Some native societies that had experienced declines in their population due to warfare or disease or starvation were known to raid and seize captives and incorporate them into their own community. Some native communities that transitioned from primarily farming to primarily buffalo hunting with the introduction of the horse in the sixteenth century (from early Spanish explorers) raided the agricultural settlements of Navajo and Hopi people, capturing women who were then put to the work of curing and sewing buffalo hides into various useful items. Even in these cases, though, slave status was usually not a permanent status and it was certainly not transferred to children into perpetuity as European slavery was.

Spanish colonies in Mexico were well established decades before the English planted colonies to the north. Spaniards organized a transatlantic slave trade in the early 1500s and the first Africans were seized and transported to Mexico in 1527, eighty years before the first permanent English colony at Jamestown was founded. By the time slavery was first being introduced to Virginia, Mexico held over 130,000 slaves, a population greater than that of Spaniards.

Unlike English slavery which progressively became harsher and led to a system whereby slaves had no more rights than farm animals, Spanish slavery trended in the opposite direction, recognizing an increasing number of rights and legal protections for slaves until the institution was abolished in the Mexican Constitution of 1824. Most importantly, under Spanish law, slaves were allowed to marry and such marriages and their offspring, could not be severed, and families separated, as in the English colonies. Moreover, the children of any enslaved man who married a free woman, including the indigenous peoples of the country, were legally free. By 1742, more than a quarter million such free afromestizos were counted in the Mexican census.

Likewise France, which controlled both important

Figure 4.5 "Branding Slaves," William O. Blake (Columbus, Ohio: 1859).

Caribbean islands like Haiti, and the territory of Louisiana to the south, and Canada to the north of English colonies, granted a precious few restrictions on the conduct of slave masters in the Code Noir promulgated by King Louis XIV in 1685. France's slave code prohibited masters from separating husbands from wives, or children from their parents. It prevented masters from benefiting financially from rape by forcing them to forfeit any offspring to the state to either be resold (in the event the rapist was married) or freed (if the father was single). Unlike in most English colonies at the time, where the voluntary freeing of slaves by their owners was strictly limited, in French lands such manumissions were permitted without restrictions.

The extreme difference between American attitudes toward slavery and those of even other European slave states was well illustrated when America purchased Louisiana from the French in 1803. Under French rule, slaves in the territory had the right to purchase their own freedom if they were able to accumulate the means to do so. They also were granted the right to petition courts to be sold away from cruel owners. After the Americans took over these rights were overturned and Louisiana expressly prohibited courts from hearing any complaints from slaves in 1806.

North Carolina State Supreme Court justice, Thomas Ruffin, writing the opinion in the influential case of *State v. Mann* (1829), upheld the complete and absolute power of the master, even over those he didn't directly own. Ruffin wrote "the power of the master must be absolute to render the submission of the slave perfect."

> We cannot allow the right of the master to be brought into discussion in the courts of justice. The slave, to remain a slave, must be made sensible that there is no appeal from his master; that his power is in no instance usurped; but is conferred by the laws of man at least, if not by the law of God. The danger would be great, indeed, if the tribunals of justice should be called on to graduate the punishment appropriate to every temper, and every dereliction of menial duty.

English Slavery

England was much later than its European rivals in pursuing overseas colonies. While Portugal began raiding West Africa for gold and slaves in the 1400s and Columbus sailed westward for Spain towards the end of that century, England did not undertake its first overseas colony in the New World until a century later and didn't establish its first outpost on the African continent until 1631. By the time England established its first permanent colony in America, at Jamestown in 1607, Spanish settlers had already pushed north into native Pueblo lands of New Mexico and their town of Santa Fe de Nuevo México was already nearly a decade old.

England was the last empire to get in on the colonization and conquest competition. But it was more successful at colonizing than any other nation. Between 1600 and 1700 England carved out 17 colonies in the New World with a total population of 400,000 (nearly half of whom were African slaves).

Contrary to elementary school myths, English colonies were not first established in search of liberty and religious freedom. Rather, all the settlements planted along the coast of North America were originally strategic moves in a long contest between the rival empires of Spain, France, England, and the Netherlands. Roanoke, the first attempted English outpost, was primarily to be a base from which freebooters could raid Spanish treasure fleets (and though the settlement failed miserably, its English investors still made a profit from the prizes seized on the way to and from America). Jamestown, the first successful permanent settlement couldn't rely on piracy to turn a profit as King James I made peace with the Spanish, but its investors dreamed they could discover gold or silver like the colonies in Mexico or Peru, or recruit the natives to trap furs, or supply timber, pitch, and rope—vital shipping supplies always in short supply in deforested England. They also harbored hopes that their colonists might chart a northwest passage to China or discover some valuable medicinal plants, such as sassafras which was believed to cure syphilis. Ultimately these hopes proved well founded—it was a medicinal plant that ensured the survival and growth of the Virginia colony, a hardy little weed known as tobacco.

By the 1620s, Virginia was booming on Europe's newfound smoking habit. Thousands of poor Englishmen contracted themselves into servitude for a period of five to seven years in hopes of outlasting their term of service, acquiring a grant of land, and purchasing servants of their own to grow tobacco. Disease, starvation, and war with indigenous peoples ensured that for the first couple decades most servants perished before they earned their freedom.

The first African slaves arrived in 1619, sold from a Dutch slave ship destined for the richer colonies of the Caribbean. But slavery grew slowly in North America as it was initially less profitable than exploiting European indentured servants who died so quickly that most were effectively slaves for life anyway. Over time as food and frontiers became more secure and colonists dispersed out from the pestilential towns, life expectancy steadily increased and an increasing number of servants survived to the end of their indentures. It was at this point, the end of the first half century of English and Dutch colonization, that increasing numbers of African slaves were transported to North America.

Most slaves in North America were concentrated in the Chesapeake region of Virginia and around New Amsterdam (soon to be seized by the British and renamed New York). By 1660, the Chesapeake counted fewer than a thousand enslaved people and New Amsterdam had roughly half that number. But slavery was still not "black." To the south, South Carolina enslaved native peoples as well as Africans. By the beginning of the eighteenth century, nearly half of all the people enslaved in that colony were native people.

In early America, color did not determine one's status as a free person or a slave. In early colonial Virginia both Europeans, native peoples, and people from Africa were held in servitude while some people of African heritage were free citizens. There were important differences to be sure—only enslaved Africans passed their status as slaves on to their children—but neither law nor custom identified "black" with "slavery" and "white" with "freedom." Englishmen certainly harbored many prejudices against Africans (Shakespeare's demeaning depictions of various characters who were "Moors" illustrates that) but such prejudices weren't categorically different from the way they viewed people who were Irish, French, Russian, or Turkish.

Importantly, the process of colonization was itself a key factor in fostering the idea that most Europeans shared qualities beyond their Christian faith. The colonies became an essential corner of a growing international trade that linked many European nations, filling their ports and cities with an increasingly diverse population. As Europe's imperial powers fought each other for lands, trade routes, and strategic alliances with native peoples, they exchanged territories and their own colonists. By the end of the seventeenth century, England had conquered colonies that had previously been French, Dutch, Spanish and Swedish and absorbed their populations under its own rule. Moreover, because these imperial powers attempted to protect their rich coastal plantations by offering land grants to immigrants who would settle along their frontiers, a steady stream of people from Ireland, Scotland, and the German lands of central Europe, added their cultures to the social mix of North America. It was in the New World where the peoples of the Old World confronted each other not as foreigners, but as fellow planters, villagers, militiamen, or colonists.

Out of this ethnic stew a new conception slowly arose - the idea that people from all these places had something in common. Something essential that divided themselves from both the natives they encountered and often fought, and the Africans, most of whom arrived in chains. It wasn't a fully formed notion at first, just the kernel of an idea, but over time it was nourished by the increasing power and

Figure 4.6 Shakespeare's image of a "Moor." Othello (Act 5, Scene 2)

profitability of slavery. This was the idea that Europeans were "white" and therefore physically different from Africans who were "black."

Over time slavery grew in importance with the rising value of colonial crops such as tobacco and sugar, as well as the increasing cost of importing English servants. Colonial governments encouraged this transition partly out of concern with public order and the fear that the poor, both slaves, free black people, and servants, would find common cause and rebel against them as they did during Bacon's Rebellion.

The problem of controlling the poor of the colony was dramatically demonstrated in 1676 when Nathaniel Bacon, a recently arrived aristocrat, led a ragtag army of whites and blacks, servants, slaves, and freemen, and succeeded, for a short time, in overthrowing the government of Virginia. The grievances that Bacon harnessed to form his army were many. Most of the laborers in the colony were indentured servants who had been promised their "freedom dues," a payment upon the end of their five or seven year term of service. For generations those who survived their term of service (and in the early years most did not) could expect that their freedom dues would be enough to purchase a small plot of land to homestead. But as the price of tobacco, the main cash crop, steadily declined as more and more farmers cultivated it, the ruling elites "engrossed" as much land as they could, meaning they hoarded it but did not use it for farming. Instead their aim was to reduce the competition of small farmers by making it more difficult and expensive to purchase land. In this they were aided by Governor Berkeley, a man who had ruled for thirty years, who gave huge grants of land to his wealthy friends and supporters. Increasingly those without political connections or large sums of cash were forced to move west, into the frontier of the colony where they squatted on native lands.

As the numbers of Englishmen living on the fringes of settlement grew, so did tensions with native peoples. English farmers brought with them livestock they allowed to roam freely, trampling and eating native people's crops. Worse, English squatters were quick to kill or kidnap native peoples who strayed too near their settlements. Native people responded in kind and as they did frontier English farmers demanded military protection from Governor Berkeley, who was slow to respond given the costs of a military campaign and the fact that the people they would be sent to protect were not his admirers anyway.

Nathaniel Bacon stepped forward and led the disgruntled colonists of Virginia against the government and his success was largely based on his ability to recruit people of all colors and conditions to his banner. Soon after he forced Governor Berkeley to flee the capital, Bacon succumbed to a fever and died and his movement died with him. When Berkeley returned at the head of a column of British marines, the opposition scattered.

In the years after Bacon's Rebellion, Virginia's government pioneered passing laws that drove wedges between segments of the poor by giving whites a stake in racism. In 1680, the penalty for any black person, whether free or enslaved, who struck a white person was increased to thirty lashes at the whipping post. In 1691, Virginia passed the first laws banning interracial marriage and proscribing harsh penalties for having an interracial child. That same year it was made illegal to voluntary free one's slave (an act termed "manumission") unless the master paid for the freed person's passage out of the colony.

Perhaps the most obvious attempt to recruit the support of poor whites by giving them a stake in slavery, even though they weren't wealthy enough to own another person, came when Virginia prohibited slaves from owning property in 1705. Up to this time, it had not been uncommon for black people who were slaves in Virginia to be given plots of land by their owners to farm for themselves when they weren't serving their master. Some enslaved people were able to not only feed themselves from these plots, but they were able to sell their surplus and accumulate some possessions of their own. Virginia ordered its officers to seize all property and livestock owned by slaves and distribute what they collected among poor whites.

The hardening of slavery by the strengthening of the legal and governmental structures that supported and policed it, powerfully contributed to the idea that there was something fundamentally different and inferior about black people. As the idea of "blackness" became the basis of servitude and as "blackness" became written into the law, it increasingly became a common way of looking at the world. People of African descent came to be viewed not just as different in a world of uncountable differences, but as uniquely different from all others.

In the century leading up to the American Revolution, poor whites found their economic fortunes increasing in absolute terms with the general prosperity of the colony and recognized that their fortunes were closely tied to slavery. But at the same time they felt a declining status as the upper stratums of wealth climbed even higher. Psychologists call this condition "anomie," a feeling of relative social decline. Between the legal encouragement of prejudice in society and those suffering anomie needing to find a scapegoat, racism dug in deeply into American society at the same time as Americans began to raise the banner and take up the call of liberty, independence, and democracy.

Commodity Slavery

Between the middle of the seventeenth century and the middle of the eighteenth, the lands bordering on the Atlantic ocean became the primary arena of European economic, diplomatic, and political rivalry. No area of the world was as central to the economic development of the western world in these years as was the Atlantic.

Over this century, the communities encircling the Atlantic from Europe in the east, North America in the west, and the Caribbean and Africa in the south, became steadily more economically and politically integrated and mutually interdependent. A vast Atlantic economy mobilized goods, capital, and labor, on a scale unprecedented in world history. The Atlantic became the superhighway of human migration as millions of people moved, most of them involuntarily, from one side of the Atlantic to the other.

With the expansion of trade across the Atlantic, the modern world, with its technological progress and its market-driven economies, arose—and it grew upon the backs of enslaved people. It is hard to imagine how the wealth needed to drive these innovations could have been accumulated, or how mass consumer markets could have been created if not for millions of people who were forced to labor for the least possible cost.

Prior to the 1700s, the vast majority of goods needed to sustain life were produced by families for their own needs, or bartered among neighbors and did not circulate in a cash economy. Most people lived upon the land that produced most of what they consumed and exchanged only a minor portion of the products they gathered, grew, or made for money. Relatively few people worked for wages. In the western world, slaves were among the first few people whose entire lives were devoted to producing commodities to be sold for cash in a world market.

Slave-made products were among the first items to entice a large consumer demand. Sugar, tobacco, tea, and coffee, were all pioneering products in luring vast numbers of people to participate in the marketplace, meaning they had to earn money to exchange for these delights. This was especially true as none of them were grown in Europe and all were imported from tropical lands (the refining of sugar from beets did not begin until the early 1800s). All were initially luxury products afforded only by the richest Europeans, but colonial production rapidly expanded and by the mid-1700s they were afforded by people of more modest means and the first true mass markets were formed. The expansion of the market for these commodities stimulated the growth of the infrastructure for producing and distributing them—ship-building, tool-making, insurance and banking, all grew in both scale and sophistication.

The rise of British North America economically in the eighteenth century, and its ultimately successful bid for autonomy from Britain, must be seen within the expansion of the overall Atlantic economy. The colonies that would eventually proclaim themselves the "United States of America," grew wealthy and powerful as a result of their participation in this greater Atlantic economic system, a system whose engine was slavery. Moreover, the ideas and the forces that supplied the American rebellion were the byproducts of the growth of the Atlantic economic system. The communities of sailors, slaves and artisans who were the footsoldiers of the American revolution grew as the Atlantic trade networks expanded. Without the development and expansion of the Atlantic system of trade and the slavery that supported it, America would have remained the poor, weak, isolated agricultural backwater that it began as.

Slavery was shaped by the geography of the southern colonies and visa versa. By the early eighteenth century, South Carolina was the colony that had the most slaves and shared the most similarities to the nearby sugar islands, where slaves were driven to early deaths in search of quick profits. South Carolina was destabilized by the existence of Spanish Florida to its south. Florida provided a beckoning refuge whose growing "Maroon" communities, composed of native peoples and escapees from slavery, offering sanctuary to anyone who could flee their bondage.

To counter this threat, the English Crown granted a charter in 1732 to establish a buffer colony between the slave zone of South Carolina to the north and the sanctuary of Florida to the south. Since it was intended as a

Figure 4.7 "The brave old Hendrick, the great Sachem or chief of the Mohawk Indians…"

buffer zone that would deter slaves from running away, this colony was conceived as the first British colony to prohibit slaves. Instead, its charter mandated that the colony would be populated by white English debt convicts:

> whereas our provinces in North America, have been frequently ravaged by Indian enemies, more especially that of South-Carolina...by reason of the smallness of their numbers, will in case of a new war, be exposed to the late calamities; inasmuch as their whole southern frontier continueth unsettled, and lieth open to the said savages...to protect all our loving subjects, be they ever so distant from us... a regular colony of the said poor people be settled and established in the southern territories of Carolina.... we do by these presents, make, erect and create one independent and separate province, by the name of Georgia... And that all and every person or persons, who shall at any time hereafter inhabit or reside within our said province, shall be, and are hereby declared to be free...

Proving the vital economic importance of slavery,

the Georgia colony languished without slavery until only seventeen years after its founding the ban on slavery was repealed.

In the half century leading up to the American Revolution, the colonial economy not only rapidly grew, but it diversified from its origins as a vast tobacco plantation. In New England old industries like shipbuilding and fishing industries expanded quickly while new ones like distilleries and tanneries grew up. The middle colonies of New York and Pennsylvania became centers of trade for a spreading agricultural frontier. Virginia and the Carolinas expanded acres in production of staple crops like rice, indigo, tobacco, and cotton. Even America's early printing industry was built on the profits of slavery as colonial newspapers drew much of their income from advertisements of slaves for sale or hire.

Propelling all this growth was the great economic engine of the New World, the sugar islands of the Caribbean, San Domingo (Haiti), Cuba, Jamaica, and Barbadoes. In the seventeenth century sugar was the most valuable commodity in world trade and most of Europe's supply was grown and processed on these islands. Even the smallest of these islands were considered more valuable than the vast continental claims of European powers, as evidenced by the fact that when France lost the Seven Years' War (1754-1763) to England and was forced to choose between Canada and the sugar islands of Guadeloupe and Martinique, it chose to hold on to its Caribbean possessions and cede Canada to the British.

Sugar was so profitable, not only because of Europe's insatiable appetite for it, but because growers in places like Barbados had learned how to steadily increase their plantations' productivity by driving the workers they enslaved to ever greater levels of exertion. This they accomplished largely by intensifying their brutality and responding to any insubordination with swift and terrifying punishment. These West Indies islands quickly earned a deserved reputation for being death sentences for those brought there in chains. Unlike the economic reality in most of the American colonies, the price of sugar was usually high enough to make even an enslaved workers' short life profitable to his owner.

Land in the sugar islands was too valuable to devote to farming foodstuffs, so instead sugar plantations became a huge market for wheat, rice, dried fish, salt pork, and other commodities from the American colonies. (The greater distance and higher cost of transport to England and Europe made these products far less profitable in transoceanic trade.) Because the sugar islands maintained a positive balance of trade with England and spent this surplus on American goods, Americans earned the cash with which to import manufactured goods from England.

As a result, the growing export economy of the American colonies allowed for a steadily rising per capita income throughout most of the eighteenth century. Great fleets of ships required to transport sugar to Europe and people from Africa were built in American shipyards. American coopers hammered together the barrels and crates that carried these goods and American distilleries turned much of that sugar into booze. By 1774, Massachusetts alone had sixty-three distilleries producing 2.7 million gallons of rum and neighboring Rhode Island was home to 30 more. When the British in 1763 proposed a tax on sugar and molasses, Massachusetts merchants pointed out that these were staples of the slave trade, and the drag on their trade such a tax would cause would throw 5,000 seamen out of work and idle almost 700 ships.

A few enterprising Americans made fortunes financing the trade in sugar and slavery. John Brown's business as a slave trader and ship owner grew so successful that he was able to found his own bank, Providence Bank, to underwrite his investments in slavery. (Providence Bank eventually evolved into one of the largest financial institutions in New England, Fleet Bank, which was later absorbed by Bank of America.) The profits from Brown's trade in sugar and slaves helped found Brown University.

Indian Land and the American Revolution

By the mid 1700s, the English Lords who governed American colonies realized they could no longer afford the costs of constant war with Indians on their frontiers. When the conflict known in the American colonies as the "French and Indian War" (in Europe it was known as the "Seven Years War") concluded in 1763, the British government moved to eliminate the primary cause of such conflicts that threatened to bankrupt it. Parliament prohibited all further private agreements between its citizens (or even its colonial governments) and native peoples to purchase land. Additionally, it prohibited any settlement west of the Allegheny and Appalachian mountains that stretched like a wall from the border with Canada in the north to nearly the border with Spanish Florida in the south.

British governors understood that the root cause of war with Indians was the unceasing attempts of their subjects to take Indian land. Landless settlers ventured into the frontier and squatted on lands they didn't own, but fought to defend. Even worse were rich speculators who cheated both Indians and Englishmen by using their influence and political connections to amass huge claims at little cost and then to sell them dearly to land-hungry settlers. It was these wealthy speculators who could pressure colonial governments to call out the militia to make good on their claims by driving indigenous communities away.

The Proclamation of 1763 set aside as the exclusive

domain of native people "all the land and territories lying to the westward of the sources of the rivers which fall into the sea…" This proved to be one of the most serious sources of conflict between the English government in London and its colonists in America. English policy provoked violent upheavals among colonists who lived on the western frontier who demanded greater military protection and the freedom to take whatever native lands they wished. Though rarely cited among historians as one of the chief reasons Americans eventually took up arms against the British empire, anger over English policies that restricted Americans' access to Indian lands was a major factor leading to the American Revolution.

This happened most notably in Pennsylvania in the 1760s, as vigilantes calling themselves the "Paxton Boys" protested what they felt was official disregard of the safety of frontier settlers on the part of the colonial government. Organized as unofficial militias, the Paxton Boys marauded through the colony massacring whatever Indians they could lay their hands on, including the Conestogas that had allied with the English to fight the French and had accepted the protection of the governor of the state, John Penn, and were living in English towns.

In December of 1763, a band of Paxton Boys slaughtered six of twenty Conestogas living in the town of the same name. Moravian missionaries helped the survivors escape to nearby Lancaster, where local officials sheltered them in a jail. The Paxton Boys regrouped and attacked Lancaster around noon. In front of many of the townspeople, they broke into the jail and killed all fourteen natives. An eyewitness to the event later wrote of what he saw in a letter:

> I saw a number of people running down street towards the gaol, which enticed me and other lads to follow them. At about sixty or eighty yards from the gaol, we met from twenty-five to thirty men, well mounted on horses, and with rifles, tomahawks, and scalping knives, equipped for murder. I ran into the prison yard, and there, O what a horrid sight presented itself to my view! Near the back door of the prison, lay an old Indian and his squaw, particularly well known and esteemed by the people of the town, on account of his placid and friendly conduct. His name was Will Sock; across him and his squaw lay two children, of about the age of three years, whose heads were split with the tomahawk, and their scalps all taken off. Towards the middle of the gaol yard, along the west side of the wall, lay a stout Indian, whom I particularly noticed to have been shot in the breast, his legs were chopped with the tomahawk, his hands cut off, and finally a rifle ball discharged in his mouth; so that his head was blown to atoms, and the brains were splashed against, and yet hanging to the wall, for three or four feet around. This man's hands and feet had also been chopped off with a tomahawk. In this manner lay the whole of them, men, women and children, spread about the prison yard: shot-scalped-hacked-and cut to pieces.

While Governor John Penn initially placed a bounty on the heads of the perpetrators of this crime, the Paxton Boys proved so popular in the state that he chose to side with them rather than lose an upcoming election. All attempts to punish the Conestoga and Lancaster murderers were abandoned. Instead, Penn agreed to institute a bounty for Indian scalps and issued a proclamation that treated all native peoples as one homogenous group of "Indians": "[w]hereas, it is necessary for the better carrying on Offensive Operations against our Indian Enemies, and bringing the unhappy war with them to a speedy issue, that the greatest Encouragements should be given to all his Majesty's Subjects to exert and use their utmost Endeavours to pursue, attack, take, and destroy our said Enemy Indians."

Pennsylvania's refusal to try any of Paxton Boys for murders committed in broad daylight, in front of scores of witnesses, led to a general attitude that no white man should face consequences for crimes against Indians. Just a few years after the Paxton Boys murders, Frederick Stump, a German settler in Cumberland county, for reasons never fully uncovered, killed two men and their wives from the Seneca nation, as well as two other Mohawk men who had wandered near his cabin. Stump scalped the men and tossed all the bodies through a hole he chipped through ice covering a nearby river. The following day Stump and his German servant walked fourteen miles to an Indian village and murdered a woman, two young girls, and a baby, hacking them and burning them in their own houses. Stump and his servant were arrested by colonial marshals but were freed from jail by an armed mob of his neighbors. Authorities in Philadelphia chose to drop the matter rather than incite more frontier protest.

The royal official in charge of Indian affairs in Pennsylvania was forced to admit to his superiors in London that "from the present disposition of our People we can expect little Justice for the Indians. . . . neither our Laws, nor our People are much Calculated for redressing Indians, and we are in the utmost want of some method for doing them effectual Justice."

Land-hungry American settlers pushed across the mountains of Virginia in the 1770s but were prevented from penetrating very far westward by the power of the

Shawnee and the Mingo peoples who had extensive settlements along the Ohio River and south through eastern Kentucky. As more and more Americans squatted upon native lands, in violation of the British Proclamation line intended to maintain peace with the Ohio Valley's native peoples, violence flared between the natives and the American newcomers. John Heckewelder, a missionary who is generally considered the most reliable eye-witness at this time, recounted:

> The [illegal] sale of the lands, below the Conhawa river, had opened a wide field for speculation. The whole country on the Ohio river, had already drawn the attention of many persons from the neighbouring provinces; who generally forming themselves into parties, would rove through the country in search of land, either to settle on, or for speculation; and some, careless of watching over their conduct, or destitute of both honour and humanity, would join a rabble, (a class of people generally met with on the frontiers) who maintained, that to kill an Indian, was the same as killing a bear...and would fire on Indians that came across them by the way; nay, more, would decoy such as lived across the river, to come over, for the purpose of joining them in hilarity;

and when these complied, they fell on them and murdered them.

In the summer of 1774, some of these Virginian land speculators schemed to provoke a war with the nearby Shawnee. Their idea was that such a war would force Virginia's governor to send an army to protect the colony's western settlements and thereby secure their shaky claims and titles to the rich Kentucky and Ohio lands they desired. They also had reason to believe Viriginia's governor, Lord Dunsmore, would seize the chance to distract his rebellious colonists with a war that would unite all Englishmen against the savages. Hatching their plot a group of settlers ambushed a Shawnee family rowing down the Ohio River in a canoe, murdering one man and nine women and children, ripping the fetus from the belly of one of the women and sticking it on a pole. As the slaughtered were the family of a Technedorus, son of Shawnee chief Shikellamy, the settlers soon had their war. William Preston, a Virginia militia commander and land surveyor, wrote excitedly "the opportunity we have so long wished for, is now before us."

Governor Dunsmore reacted exactly as expected and led a large force of 2000 militia to the frontier and destroyed Shawnee villages all along the river. The decisive battle came at Point Pleasant on the Kanawha River on October 10, where Dunsmore army defeated the Shawnee

LOGAN FINDING HIS MURDERED FAMILY.

Figure 4.8 Logan finding his murdered family. Wood engraving ca. 1873.

and forced them to cede all their claims over the lands of southern Ohio and Kentucky.

But what seemed like a great triumph for the colonial land speculators was suddenly put in jeapordy. Dunsmore was rebuked by his superiors in London and ordered to withdraw. At the same time Parliament passed a law, the Quebec Act, that granted all the lands west of the Ohio to the province of Quebec, endangering land titles and grants that had been made in Virginia and Pennsylvania.

The Quebec Act of 1774 was as provocative of protest in the colonies as any other Parliamentary law. As soon as it was passed an American in London wrote home and asked:

> I am very anxious to hear, what reception the latter wanton strokes of government here have met with in America, particularly that detestable Quebec Bill, which is so evidently intended as a bridle on the northern Colonies - That act is looked upon in the most unfavourable light here of any of them;

Another correspondent in England, wondered, "As to America, I presume I can add very little to your own feelings; such oppression must rouse a Stoic; you are by this time in possession of the infamous Popery bill, for the colony of Quebec; if this don't rouse the most lethargic man among you, I shall be amazed" One writer urged action against the Quebec Act and recalled a minister's sermon from before the last war with France who thundered:

> What Course shall we pursue in Defence of our Native Rights and Privileges, when these Dogs of Hell, Popish Superstition and French Tyranny, dare to erect their Heads, and triumph within our Borders? Shall we not rise up as one Man, and with united Hearts and Hands vindicate our Religion and Liberties; our Protestant Religion and our British Liberties?

The Continental Congress protested the Quebec Act, along with the Coercive Act (which closed the port of Boston) as "cruel, and oppressive," condemning the measure "extending the province of Quebec, so as to border on the western frontiers of these Colonies, establishing an arbitrary government therein, and discouraging the settlement of British subjects in that wide extended country…" In protest, the Congress announced it was urging all Americans to boycott British goods thereby launching the powerful nonimportation movement.

Parliament's Indian policies were a serious obstacle to the speculative plans of many of the men who would become leaders of the American Revolution. George Washington, Thomas Jefferson, Patrick Henry, and George Mason all speculated heavily in lands west of the Ohio river, in spite of the fact that these lands were legally restricted from ownership or settlement by Royal proclamation.

As the agitation against England progressed, these rebel leaders glimpsed the possibiility that a successfull revolution would open these lands to settlement and, more importantly to them, speculation. In 1772, George Mason purchased rights to fifty thousand acres in the Ohio Valley. Jefferson invested in a company that controlled ten thousand acres in 1773. Richard Henry Lee, another member of the Continental Congress, had interests in the Mississippi Land Company that claimed over two million acres of land. George Washington had purchased land claims from poor veterans of the Seven Years War for pennies on the dollar and has sent surveyors into the area just months before Dunsmore's War. Thomas Jefferson owned stakes in three different land companies controlling seventeen thousand acres. Patrick Henry was an investor in at least five land companies holding an unknown amount of western land.

The independent American government that emerged victorious from the Revolutionary War proved incapable of satisfying the demands of frontier settlers and newly formed state governments for a more aggressive Indian policy. Just as the Paxton Boys had registered their protest by massacring native people, Americans who coveted the Shawnee and Wyandot lands across the Ohio river from Pennsylvania and Virginia, grew increasingly willing to use violence to achieve their ends.

A Revolution for Slavery

As has been seen, the role that American land hunger played in the Revolution has long been downplayed by patriotic historians. Likewise, historians' obsessive focus on the role of new taxes obscures the even more fundamental economic disagreements between England and her colonies that revolved around the institution of slavery. All historians date the beginnings of American independence in the changes in commercial and tax policies instituted by the English Crown in the 1760s to recoup the vast expenses of defending the colonies from France in the Seven Years War (also called the French and Indian War). But these policies, most notably the Sugar Act and the Stamp Act, were not only about raising revenue for the crown, they were also an attempt to restrain the rapid growth of the American slave trade, a dimension of these policies rarely discussed in the textbooks.

To fully comprehend this point, one needs to begin with the fact that in the 1600s Great Britain reserved the

Figure 4.9 Boston Tea Party.

Take for example, the Sugar Act (formally titled the "American Revenue Act or the American Duties Act"), a measure history textbooks generally only discuss in terms of its provoking anti-tax protests in the 1760s and being one of the major stepping stones to the American Revolution. Few mention that Americans protested not just the increasing enforcement and collection of taxes, but that the act prohibited them from importing sugar from the non-British colonies in the West Indies. Massachusetts merchants who petitioned for Parliament to reconsider their law noted that the measure would destroy not just their rum industry and other principal industries, like their fisheries, but also the slave trade. In fact, all of these were interconnected as the French (their largest trading partners) required that all imports to their island colonies be paid for in molasses.

The importation of sugar to be distilled into rum was the cornerstone of New England's economy. New England was by far the leader of transatlantic commerce among the American colonies and a majority of its ships were dedicated to the West Indies trade. These Spanish, French, and Dutch islands were the primary market for the export of its fish, lumber, and grains. In the early 1770s, the closest years that solid figures are available, Boston imported over a million gallons of molasses from French, Dutch, and Spanish sugar islands, but only 23,000 gallons from British West Indian plantations.

Most American rum was produced not for domestic consumption, but for export because it was the best trade good to sail to the coast of Africa and swap for slaves. The price of slaves was generally denominated in barrels of rum. Human cargoes were then transported to the West Indies where they were in constant demand because of the brutally short lives of enslaved sugar workers. In just one year, Boston distilled and exported 58,700 gallons of rum while its neighbor to the east, Rhode Island, produced and traded an extraordinary 153,000 gallons. (For perspective, New York and Charleston together distilled 22,000 gallons.) New England's rum accounted for more than three-quarters of all English colonial trade with Africa in the 1760s.

It was the Sugar Act, according to the patriot John Otis, that "set people a-thinking in six months, more than they had done in their whole lives before." Out of these protests against the Sugar Act emerged the peculiar American rhetoric of slavery. Americans charged that England, by restricting their commercial freedom to trade in sugar and slaves, had reduced them to "slavery." John Dickenson, an American revolutionary from Pennsylvania, argued, "Those who are taxed without their own consent...are slaves. We are taxed without our consent...We are therefore—SLAVES." Again and again over the next ten years of revolutionary protest, free white Americans will argue

most lucrative part of slavery, the buying and selling of slaves themselves, to a royal monopoly, the Royal Africa Company. The growth of slavery in the American colonies was choked by this royal monopoly on the slave trade that kept the price of Africans artificially high and cut American shippers out of the business. But in the wake of the political upheaval in England known as the Glorious Revolution that overthrew King James II, Americans seized their chance and petitioned the new government for a change of policy. American merchants wrote to London pointing out that if they were "sufficiently supplied with Negroes, they would produce twice the quantity they do now," because "the shortage of slaves was hindering the development of the tobacco colonies."

When the Crown eventually granted their request in 1696, it had a doubly powerful impact on all the American colonies. For southern planters, it lowered the cost of importing slaves and spurred a tremendous increase in the transatlantic slave trade. For enterprising northern traders, the slave trade business was wildly profitable and soon became the engine of the entire New England economy. By the middle of the eighteenth century, the Americans had cut themselves into a sizeable share of the transatlantic slave trade. The American colonies benefited from lower slave prices and rapidly replaced the old system of indentured servitude of Europeans with the slavery of Africans.

that they were fighting against their slavery, by which they meant that their freedom to hold others in bondage and buy and sell them for a profit, was being unfairly restricted. The British Tory, Samuel Johnson, fed up with such hypocricy, asked, "How is that we hear the loudest yelps for liberty among the drivers of negroes?"

In the end, Parliament backed down and repealed its Sugar Act in the face of both colonial protest and the enormous economic damage it was bound to cause in the colonial triangular trade. But though they had avoided ruining their colonial economies, these British policies had lit the fuse that would smolder to the Revolution.

The Somerset Case

While the scuffle over the Sugar Act demonstrated how the interests of the English empire were diverging from those of Americans, a decade later a civil trial in an English courtroom threatened to undermine the very foundation of American society—slavery—and further fanned the flames of revolution.

Though he is largely lost to history, perhaps no individual is as important to the course of American history as was James Somerset. James Somerset was born in Africa and somehow seized and taken on the long middle passage to America, arriving in 1749 in Virginia. Standing on the auction block, he was purchased by a Norfolk merchant, Charles Steuart. Steuart moved with Somerset to Boston, and then to Britain. At some point Somerset escaped from Steuart and before long was recaptured. Steuart, having had enough of Somerset's determination for freedom, sold him to a trader who planned to take him to Jamaica where Somerset could expect to live a short, brutal life of labor on a sugar plantation. Before Somerset's ship sailed for the West Indies in 1772, he was discovered chained in the hold by English abolitionists.

Somerset's English friends initiated a suit for habeas corpus and won an order demanding that Somerset's owners bring him before the court for examination. Somerset's case eventually landed on the docket of England's highest tribunal. In an extraordinary ruling issued in August of 1772, Lord Mansfield, the Lord Justice of England's High Court, ruled that Somerset was a free man because England had no affirmative laws upholding slavery. In effect, Lord Mansfield had with one ruling freed all of England's fifteen thousand slaves because Parliament, unlike English colonies, had never bothered to pass a slave code governing property in humans.

Lord Mansfield's ruling was of minor significance in England where slavery was an insignificant part of the economy. But in the American colonies it represented an earthquake that shook their allegiances to their core. Practically every newspaper in the American colonies reported on the Somerset ruling and slave-holding Americans viewed it with alarm. While the ruling only applied to slavery in England proper, colonists worried that this principle could be extended to America as well, threatening to overturn their legal authority to continue enjoying the profits of enslaved labor.

A New York correspondent wrote that the Somerset ruling "will occasion a greater ferment in America (particularly in the islands) than the Stamp Act itself." A letter in the *Virginia Gazette* first reported on news of Lord Mansfield's Somerset ruling and then commented bitterly, "Every Evil with which the Nation is affected is owing to the Weakness and Wickedness of this Administration. The Nation has no Confidence in this Set of Men....Lord Mansfield [is] known to hold principles incompatible with the Freedom of this country." Repeatedly in the coming decade, the name Mansfield was recited by American patriots listing their grievances against the empire.

Revealingly, one of the protests against the Somerset decision by a "West Indian" slaveholder, though arguing for his right to keep people enslaved, thought it best to avoid using the word "slave":

I must now then apprize your Lordship, that from this instant it is my intention to drop the term slavery. It is an odious word, that engendered this law suit, and how seeds and supports it with the fuel of heated passions and imaginations. Instead then of such prejudiced and unpopular ground, whereupon the case has hitherto been made to stand, I shall take the liberty to remove its situation, to change its point of view, and to rest it on the land of property; from hence, perhaps, it will be seen, not only in a less offensive light, but where also it may find a foundation more solid and substantial for its support.

"West Indian" made a point that struck to the root of the thinking of American slaveholders: legally, slaves were mere property, chattel like horses and cows. Abolition, in their minds, was not just an act of granting rights to a person, it was the taking of their property without trial or compensation. Clearly, in this sense, the Somerset decision was seen as a greater threat to these Americans "natural rights" than was even British taxes, which have been overly credited with being the grievance that ignited rebellion.

England's actions to abolish slavery were well known on both sides of the Atlantic, especially among those most concerned by these developments, enslaved people themselves. Joseph Martin, a poor man who fought for American independence and kept a detailed memoir of his experiences, recounted meeting one enslaved man who

Figure 4.10 George Washington (with his servant Billy Lee),

Compounding American fears that their government no longer protected their property in slaves, were proposals debated in Parliament to grant rights to slaves and even to abolish slavery in the colonies as a means of punishing the growing rebellion. In 1775 the House of Commons debated extending the right of trial by jury to American slaves. Also that year a measure to abolish slavery completely for the purpose of "humbling the high aristocratic spirit of Virginia and the southern colonies," was proposed.

Of the seven most popular college history textbooks, not one mentions the Somerset Case of 1772. However, each of these American history textbooks discuss at length all of the taxes and commercial restrictions, the Sugar Act, the Stamp Act, the Townshend Acts, the Tea Act, etc., that pushed the American colonists into revolution against "taxation without representation." But none mention British actions to restrict slavery and the slave trade that according to some contemporary sources provoked just as much anger among white Americans.

Dunmore's Proclamation

As Americans intensified their protests against the Crown, culminating in the skirmishes at Concord and Lexington in April of 1775, British colonial governors garrisoned troops in most major ports. Some of these units were drawn from Caribbean islands and from Florida and many of these regiments included black soldiers, fueling American suspicions that their governors were willing to recruit slaves to crush their protests.

Such suspicions were worsened when soon after the fighting in Massachusetts broke out, the governor of Virginia, Lord Dunmore, sent marines to seize the stores of gunpowder held in a Williamsburg armory. Enraged Virginia officials, including many members of the House of Burgesses, demanded the powder's return and convinced Dunmore to return it on the grounds that it was essential to their safety for without it they would not be able to put down a slave revolt. Dunmore fumed, "by the living God, if any insult is offered to me, or to those who have obeyed my orders, I will declare freedom to the slaves, and lay the town in ashes." Dunmore then wrote to the Secretary of State in London that he was planning "to arm all my own Negroes and receive all others that will come to me whom I shall declare free."

Nothing frightened American slaveholders more than the possibility that their slaves would be encouraged to revolt. Many of the most prosperous counties of Virginia and the Carolinas were ones in which slaves vastly outnumbered free colonists. Colonists followed closely news of recent slave uprisings in Jamaica whose horrors they knew could spread to the mainland, especially if such

clearly understood the geopolitics of his situation:

> The man of the house where I was quartered had a smart looking negro man, a great politician; I chanced one day to go into the barn where he was threshing. He quickly began to upbraid me with my opposition to the British. The king of England was a very powerful prince, he said, a very powerful prince; and it was a great pitty (sic) that the colonists had fallen out with him; but as we had, we must abide by the consequences. I had no inclination to waste the shafts of my rhetoric upon a negro slave. I concluded he had heard his betters say so. As the old cock crows so crows the young one; and I thought, as the white cock crows so crows the black one. He ran away from his master, before I left there, and went to Long-Island to assist king George; but it seems the king of terrors was more potent than king George, for his master had certain intelligence that poor Cuff was laid flat on his back.

revolts were encouraged and even armed by their own government.

In the summer of 1775 wild rumors of slaves plotting with royal spies spread throughout the southern colonies. Remembered one Charleston resident, "The newspapers were full of publications calculated to excite the fears of the people—massacres and instigated insurrections were the words in the mouth of every child." A traveler to the region noted that whites believed that the Governor had promised "every Negro that would murder his master and family that he should have his master's plantation."

In August a free black man, Thomas Jeremiah, well known locally as a ship pilot, was seized in Charleston and accused of organizing a slave revolt. Jeremiah was hastily put on trial, the only evidence against him being that he was overheard to say that he would pilot the King's ships into Charleston harbor. South Carolina's governor who wrote to a friend that "my blood ran cold when I read on what grounds they had doomed a fellow creature to death," attempted to intervene but backed down when patriots threatened to nail Jeremiah's body to the governor's door. Condemned and paraded into the public square before a large crowd who had gathered to watch the symbol of their fears destroyed, Jeremiah was hung and then his body was set aflame.

As conditions worsened for loyalists and British officials through that summer and fall of 1775, the governor of Virginia, Lord Dunmore, encouraged by influential members of Parliament, acted on the plan he had sent to London of offering freedom to slaves who joined his forces. From his quarters on the ship William anchored in Norfolk harbor (as it was unsafe for the governor to run the colony from shore), Dunmore wrote his declaration instituting martial law and proclaiming:

> I do hereby further declare all indented servants, Negroes, or others...free, that are able and willing to bear arms, they joining His Majesty's Troops as soon as may be, for the more speedily reducing the Colony to a proper sense of their duty, to His Majesty's crown and dignity.

Dunmore had only to wait a week to see the fruits of his new policy. A squad of Redcoats that included some men who had escaped their masters defeated a unit of Virginia militia south of the city, taking two militia commanders prisoner, including Joseph Hutchings who was captured by two men who Hutchings had considered his own property. Shortly thereafter, Aggy, Billy, Eve, Sam, Lucy, George, Henry, and Peter, eight of the men and women that Peyton Randolph enslaved, escaped and joined the British. Randolph was one of Virginia's delegates to the Continental Congress. Less than a month after Dunmore made his proclamation, George Washington's cousin, Lund, who he had left in charge of the management of his plantation at Mount Vernon while he went off to general the Continental Army, wrote to George about trouble with their slaves, "there is not a man of them but would leave us, if they could make their escape..." Robert Carter, one of the largest patriot slave owners in Virginia, threatened the people he kept chained that if the British won, he would sell them all off to the sugar plantations of Jamaica, a near-certain death sentence at the time.

In just a few weeks, between eight hundred and a thousand men, women, and children fled their masters and joined Dunmore's growing "Ethiopian Regiment." Women sewed sashes for the Ethiopian troops emblazoned with the motto "LIBERTY TO SLAVES." On December 9, Dunmore's forces marched out from Norfolk, half of their number consisting of the three hundred strong Ethiopian Regiment. They battled the Virginia militias at Great Bridge and though the Ethiopian Regiment fought hard, "with the intrepidity of lions," Dunmore's troops were forced to retreat back to their ships, making it harder for additional enslaved people to escape and join them.

Dunmore's success was imitated elsewhere. Sir Henry Clinton, Dunmore's counterpart for Georgia and the Carolinas, organized men who escaped bondage into the "Black Pioneers" company of the English army. Clinton expanded Dunmore's terms by offering freedom to any person who escaped slavery and fled to his protection, not just those who joined his regiments.

Though the American Revolution was not fought over slavery, slavery was at stake in the war, as the English attempted to undermine the power of the colonists by weakening slavery which was at the base of their economy. Twenty-five thousand enslaved people, about one-in-twenty of all people enslaved in America, expressed their feelings with their feet when they fled to British lines or even fought on the British side during the Revolutionary War in exchange for their freedom. Thomas Jefferson lost thirty of his several hundred slaves. When the British evacuated Charleston and Savannah at the end of the war, over fifteen thousand men and women who had escaped ther slavery accompanied them.

While the English army and navy had long recruited black soldiers, and with Dunmore's Proclamation had moved to foment slave uprisings and resistance by offering freedom to loyal slaves who fought against the American rebels, the Americans rejected those black patriots who rallied to their banner. In the Revolution's first serious and prolonged fight, the Battle of Bunker Hill, a number of black men fought bravely defending their lines on Breed's Hill. George Washington, later inspecting his victorious troops, was angered to find that there were black soldiers in his army and ordered them expelled.

Many urged Washington to relent and change his policy but he held fast, until, at least, the effectiveness of Dunmore's recruitment policies were made evident and he relented and agreed to accept free black soldiers into the Continental Army. However, Washington vetoed proposals to recruit slaves on the same terms as the English—namely, offering them their freedom in return for their service. Instead, Virginia's House of Delegates passed a recruitment bill that promised every white volunteer for the Continental army a bounty of "one able bodied healthy Negroe slave between the age of ten and forty years."

Even during the last uncertain years of the war Washington refused to agree to a plan to recruit black slaves from South Carolina, apparently prioritizing white supremacy and slavery over American independence. Eventually, pressed by continuing defeats, Washington agreed to a plan to raise black troops by promising them their freedom in return for three years service. (After the war, states often refused to honor these promises.) It was, ironically, the largely black First Rhode Island Regiment that turned the tide at a decisive moment at the battle of Yorktown.

Though a significant number of black Americans ended up fighting on the patriot side, the simple fact was most black people in America viewed England as their beacon of hope for freedom, not America. Black Americans were well aware of the hypocrisy of their white neighbors' cries for liberty. In 1765 the Charleston, South Carolina, members of the Sons of Liberty were shocked when during a protest against the Stamp Act when they shouted "Liberty and No Stamps" slaves and free black workers began a parade shouting simply "Liberty, Liberty!" Felix Holbrook, a man enslaved in Massachusetts, petitioned the Massachusetts legislature in 1773 to end slavery in the commonwealth, writing, "We have no Property! We have no wives! No children! We have no City! No Country!" The holding of one out of five Americans in bondage while screaming for liberty was clearly a contradiction evident to all by the years of the Revolution.

American history textbooks attempt to polish the image of the founding fathers by noting that they passed laws in their colonial legislatures to prohibit the further importation of slaves. They generally fail to put these laws into context where they can be viewed not as moral steps toward abolition but as self-interested measures to protect against slave uprisings. Such laws were only considered after a series of slave uprisings in the Caribbean, first in Antigua in 1729 and 1736, then in the Danish West Indies in 1733, and in Jamaica in 1760, that highlighted the ever-present danger posed by keeping people in bondage. In 1739 a group of Africans from the Congo organized a powerful rebellion against their masters in South Carolina, an uprising that led to the deaths of over forty whites and more blacks. This so-called Stono Rebellion seemed to

Figure 4.11 "Blow for blow," by Henry L. Stephens, 1863.

confirm the widely held belief that those having just experienced enslavement and the middle passage, native Africans, were the most likely to rebel. Thus, banning importations of slaves from Africa was broadly seen as protecting public safety and thereby securing slavery, not weakening it.

At a time when slave populations in the American colonies were becoming healthier and growing rapidly, slave owners could end the practice of slave importation without hurting their bottom line. In fact, banning the importation of slaves actually shifted wealth and power upwards into the hands of the largest planters as they, having more people in bondage than they needed, were well positioned to profit from the increasing sale price of enslaved people.

That advocating for an end to the slave trade and supporting slavery were comfortably compatible, is illustrated in the actions of Thomas Jefferson. In 1769 a young Thomas Jefferson joined the Virginia colonial legislature and he there he offered a bill to gradually emancipate the colony's slaves. That same year Jefferson also spent time trying to recapture a man who had gained his freedom by running away from him. Jefferson put an advertisement in a local paper offering a reward for the man's capture:

> Run away a Mulatto slave Sandy, 35 years, complexion light, shoemaker by trade, can do coarse carpenters work, a horse jockey, when drunk insolent and disorderly, swears much, and his behavior is artful and knavish. Took a horse. Whoever conveys the said slave to me shall have reward… THOMAS JEFFERSON

Slavery's troubling existence at the center of the American colonies and therefore the center of the American Revolution is evident in the pains the patriots took to distance themselves from the institution they depended on. This is evident in the first draft of the Declaration of Independence where Thomas Jefferson attempted to blame King George for forcing the institution of slavery upon the colonists:

> [The King has waged] cruel war against human nature itself, violating its most sacred rights of life and liberty in the persons of a distant people who never offended him, captivating and carrying them into slavery in another Hemisphere or to incur miserable death in their transportation thither…Determined to keep open a market where MEN should be bought and sold, he has prostituted his negative for suppressing every legislative attempt to prohibit or to restrain this execrable commerce; and that this assemblage

of horrors might want no fact of distinguished die, he is now exciting these very people to rise in arms among us, and to purchase that liberty of which he deprived them, by murdering the people upon whom he also intruded them; thus paying off former crimes committed against the liberties of one people, with crimes which he urges them to commit against the lives of another.

While his fellow patriots in the Continental Congress were eager to heap every charge they could at the feet of King George, Jefferson's claims too implicitly condemned slavery and were too much for a gathering of mostly slave owners and was dropped from the Declaration of Independence. By this time all the patriots understood that the success of their Revolution depended upon slave labor, for it was slavery that produced the cash with which they purchased weapons from the French and freed up their men from farming so they could go fight the British. Instead they settled on alluding to the King having "excited domestic insurrections amongst us…" meaning, of course, slave rebellions and desertions. And they blamed King George for putting native people in the way of their westward expansion: "[he] has endeavoured to bring on the inhabitants of our frontiers, the merciless Indian Savages whose known rule of warfare, is an undistinguished destruction of all ages, sexes and conditions."

Independence in a Slave Republic

Thousands of black soldiers fought on both sides of the battle of Yorktown, though those fighting for England's Lord Cornwallis knew that if they were defeated

Figure 4.12 The British surrendering their arms to General Washington after their defeat at Yorktown, October 1781.

they would not only be prisoners of war but would be returned to their lifelong chains. As soon as Cornwallis surrendered to the patriots, planters descended on the area claiming their "property." Soldiers in Washington's army were paid bounties for recapturing the black soldiers who had fled into the woods and swamps. George Washington himself recaptured two of the many men and women who had escaped his bondage and dragged them back to Mount Vernon. Washington continued to search for another fifteen people he claimed as his chattel. Washington did his fellows a favor and brought Thomas Jefferson back some of his slaves, including Isaac, who was just a boy at the time.

Not surprisingly, many of the black men who fought bravely and carried the day for Washington's army, who had been recruited on the promise that if they fought for the American side they would be freed when the war was won, were betrayed. Even James Armistead, a black man who at great risk volunteered to enter the British service and spy for the patriots; who had given critical intelligence about the British positions at Yorktown that helped win the battle; even Armistead was reclaimed by his former master and enslaved after the battle. (The French general Lafayette learned of Armistead's fate and intervened, shaming the Virginia legislature into releasing him five years later.)

After the war, Washington demanded that the defeated British forces renege on the promise of freedom they made to the 80,000 slaves who fought on the loyalist side and to return them to chains. Even after the British offered full monetary compensation to their former owners instead, Washington and other leaders of the new republic insisted on the re-enslavement of these emancipated men and women. Eventually the British refused to waver on this point and pushed to choose between reclaiming their slaves and returning to war, the patriots backed down and accepted payment instead.

In the end, the American Revolution defended and secured the future of slavery. When bells tolled from Massachusetts in the North to Georgia in the South celebrating victory at Yorktown and the achievement of independence from England, every state and territory in the young nation practiced and legally protected slavery.

While the British blockade and the Revolutionary War halted Rhode Island's lucrative slave trading for the duration of the conflict, as soon as peace returned at least half a dozen slave ships sailed out of Newport headed for Africa. Even passage of a state law prohibiting the trade was little more than a paper tiger, as the slave merchants defied the ban. As the federal official in charge of the port of Newport observed, "an Ethiopian could as soon change his skin as a Newport merchant could be induced to change so lucrative a trade…" Freed from all colonial restraints, in a short period, New England slave merchants out-competed even the slave trade centers of Liverpool and Bristol. Americans took over as the leading carriers of human cargo in the world, expanding their trade in human misery across the Caribbean islands and into Brazil. To give but one of many examples, by 1790, American slave traders had doubled the number of people enslaved on the island of Hispaniola from a quarter to half a million souls.

Nineteen of the fifty-five delegates to the Constitutional Convention held in Philadelphia in the summer of 1787 were slave owners. America's founding fathers had few doubts that whites were by nature superior and that America was and should always be a white nation. While it is true that the word "white" does not appear in the Constitution, it was freely used during the debates that produced it. On June 15, 1787, the notes taken by representative King during the convention noted that the apportioning of representatives would be done on the basis of "Whites [and] 3/5ths of all others." A month later, debating how to apportion representatives and taxes, Madison's notes revealed the delegates discussed the black and white populations of the various states.

While the U.S. Constitution never uses the words "white" or "black" and even avoids the word "slave" by instead referring to "other persons" or a "person held to service or labour" it gave powerful support to slavery. The radical abolitionist, William Lloyd Garrison, described the U.S. Constitution as a "covenant with death" and an "agreement with hell." Garrison pointed out that the Constitution was a document drafted with the intention of strengthening the institution of slavery and protecting it from democracy. Most famously, the three-fifths clause (Art. 1, Sec. 2) and the Electoral College (Art. II, Sec. 1) enhanced the political power of slave states while the "direct tax clause" (Art. 1, Sec. 9) limited slave-holders' tax burden. The fugitive slave clause (Art. IV, Sec. 2) took away states' rights to shelter or protect runaway slaves by requiring all states to return runaways on the demand of their "owners."

Many clauses on their face did not appear to involve slavery unless the context of their times is considered. Art. 1, Sec. 8 gives Congress the power to call "forth the militia" to "suppress insurrections" a fear that at the time primarily was one of slave owners who lived in terror of the men and women they held in bondage. This militia was also menioned in the celebrated Second Amendment protecting gun ownership so that slave owners could also organize armed patrols to police enslaved people and catch runaways. (This purpose was further reinforced a year later when Congress passed the Uniform Militia Act of 1792 that restricted militia service to "every free able-bodied white male citizen," a law that threw black men out of several state militias.)

Art. 1, Sec. 9 and Sec. 10 included provisions restricting the ability of Congress and the states to tax exports, a measure only understandable as a protection against attempts to undermine slavery by taxing the products made by slaves. Finally, federal courts were limited in their jurisdictions to "Citizens of different States", not the inhabitants of the nation, thus excluding most black people from access to the courts.

Constitutional signer Charles Pinckney later defended the document he helped to craft to his South Carolina legislature, saying, "In short...we have made the best terms for the security of this species of property (slavery) it was in our power to make. We would have made better if we could; but on the whole, I do not think them bad."

Likewise when the Constitutional Convention resolved to allow the international slave trade until at least 1808, President Washington wrote a friend gleefully that Congress "was as favorable as the proprietors of that species of property could well have expected considering the great dereliction [criticism] to Slavery in a large part of this Union." So skewed in favor of the South and slavery was America's Constitutional system of national representation that eleven of the first sixteen presidents, and two thirds of the first Speakers of the House were southerners. Additionally, four of the first five presidents were slave owners (as were eight of the first dozen). By the 1850s, every committee in Congress would be chaired by a southern congressman and southerners controlled the Supreme Court as well.

America was not only the first European colony to successfully revolt and form an independent republic, it was the first modern nation founded with slavery as one of its bedrock principles and institutions. For the nearly its first century of existence, the United States would be an outlier among even slave-holding nations, wielding its growing economic and military power to expand the horizon of slavery at a time when other nations struggled to contain it.

Moreover, the United States was unique in the degree to which its racist principles dictated its system of government. The nation was constructed with whiteness as its central principle, as native peoples and those of African ancestry defined as outsiders and excluded from the category of citizen. Again, as the unusually blunt Charles Pinckney recalled, "at the time I drew that constitution, I perfectly knew that there did not then exist such a thing in the Union as a black or colored citizen, nor could I then have conceived it possible such a thing could have ever existed in it; nor, notwithstanding all that has been said on the subject, do I now believe one does exist in it..."

The United States' distinctiveness among other European nations is perhaps best seen in its ongoing clashes with England, conflicts rooted in the question of slavery. Abolitionist sentiment grew rapidly in England in the late 1700s and by 1793, while the U.S. Congress speedily passed a harsh Fugitive Slave Act to strengthen the hand of masters and better secure their "property," English Canada declared that any slave setting foot on Canadian soil was free.

English policy makers routinely refused to hand back to the Americans fugitives from slavery. In fact, England provided cannons, muskets, powder and shot to the communities of runaway slaves and native Americans referred to as Seminoles who successfully resisted American armies for decades in Florida. Many of the forces England sent against the Americans in the War of 1812 were the Americans' own former slaves. At least a tenth of the Redcoats who faced Andrew Jackson in the Battle of New Orleans were black (Jackson also recruited free black soldiers into his army, though estimates of their numbers are wildly exaggerated in American textbooks. A close scrutiny of all available muster lists and rosters find fewer than 300 black men in Jackson's ranks.)

Native Peoples and the New Republic

In 1780, Thomas Jefferson personally ordered William Clark (later famous for exploring the west with Meriwether Lewis) to exterminate or drive from their land the Shawnees and other native people who occupied the lands around the Ohio river that Congress planned to redistribute to veterans of the Revolutionary War (and to enrich themselves through land speculation). Jefferson wrote to his military commander, "I think the most important object which can be proposed with such a force is the extermination of these hostile tribes... The Shawanese, Mingos, Munsies, and Wiandots can never be relied on as friends, and therefore the object of the war should be their total extinction, or their removal beyond the [Great] lakes or the Illinois river..." Later when Jefferson was President he instructed his Secretary of War to show no mercy to hostile Indians: "...if ever we are constrained to lift the hatchet against any tribe, we will never lay it down till that tribe is exterminated, or driven beyond the Mississippi... In war, they will kill some of us; we shall destroy all of them."

In 1782, a group of Pennsylvania militiamen, searching for Indian bands who had attacked white travelers in the area, surrounded an Indian village called Gnadenhutten that had been established by missionaries. While the Christian Indians sang and prayed, they took each native man, woman, and child in turn and killed them by smashing their heads with a heavy mallet. Before nightfall they had hammered to death nearly one hundred people, including thirty children. (Native memory of this horrifying event ran deep and led to bloody recriminations against American captives for years, including the torture execution of captured militia commander William Crawford.)

Figure 4.13 Gnadenhutten massacre.

Increasing frontier tensions and the conflicting claims of states over Indian territories were major issues helping to drive adoption of a revised charter for the federal government, the 1787 Constitution of the United States. The Constitution was seen as a step towards solving these problems as it clearly handed over to the central government sole authority for regulating commerce and agreements with Indian nations, and it gave the federal government the independent means to raise and fund armies without having to depend on voluntary contributions of the states as before. In this sense, the U.S. government was structured so as to best dispossess native people of their land and break their considerable power.

Between the Revolution and the Civil War (1776-1861) some one billion acres of native lands were taken, three-quarters of which were obtained by the pretense of some 374 treaties.

Without vast native lands to seize, it is doubtful the newborn republic would have survived. The need to coordinate efforts to control these western lands was the glue that united and held together the squabbling states. By selling off chunks of Indian land, the young government was able to retire its wartime debt, provide bonuses for its soldiers, and keep pay for its operations without raising the taxes its citizens would have opposed. The frontier helped establish order in a war-torn and disorderly society by providing an opportunity for the poor to provide for themselves and a distant haven for dissidents and dreamers. Indian lands were a safety valve venting the frustrations of those resentful that the revolution had not also elevated the status of workers. Grants of native lands built public schools, great colleges, roads, canals, and later the railroads that would drive an industrial economy.

With independence from Britain, speculation in Indian lands turned from being a savvy business practice of a few well-connected insiders into a national mania. Independence freed Americans from the constraints of the British Crown, erasing the boundary between legal and illegal land ownership that ran down the spine of the Allegheny and Appalachian mountains. The cost of fighting the British empire had piled up huge debts for the newborn American government; debts that could only be paid in one of two ways: either levying heavy taxes on its citizens or seizing and selling at a profit huge tracts of Indian land. Americans who had rebelled against taxes (and land restrictions) they felt were unjust were in no mood to tax themselves so their governments encouraged the fast sale and settlement of lands. One contemporary observed in 1798, "The Land Mania is a frequent disease in every part of America. It broke out with peculiar violence in most of the states immediately after the peace and has continued to be more or less the epidemic of our country ever since." Another wrote in 1792, "The Americans seem possessed with a species of mania for getting lands, which have no bounds. Their Congress, prudent, reasonable, and wise in other matters, in this seems as much infected as the people."

One of the most famous of these land speculators was George Washington, who had first gotten into the land speculation business by sending agents to purchase land grants that had been given to veterans (most of whom, not having the resources to actually homestead in the distant Ohio valley, were happy to realize some cash from their deeds) at a steep discount. Before he became president, Washington formed a partnership with the governor of New York state to purchase 6,000 acres of Mohawk land in the northern part of the state, eventually doubling his investment when he sold it nine years later. Washington eventually accumulated deeds to 45,000 acres in Indian territories west of the Allegheny mountains.

In the first decades of the United States, most new states were persuaded to sell the lands they accumulated through forced Indian treaties in the form of single deals to individual speculators or land companies rather than to settlers and citizens directly. This became an obvious source of corruption as speculators and land companies made sure to include powerful politicians in their syndicates so as to ensure the most advantageous terms with the government.

Thomas Jefferson and George Mason lobbied for a law in Virginia that would prevent such corruption in land sales by establishing a state land office that would sell small parcels directly to citizens, but this bill was voted down repeatedly by legislators who had stakes in land companies.

Figure 4.14 The Chief of the Little Osages.

The Treaty Myth

Federal officials in the young American republic understood well that they could not afford to militarily defeat all the native peoples they wished to remove from their midst. It was cheaper to attempt to induce Indian nations to sell tracts of land, especially as this could often be accomplished by false promises, cultivated misunderstandings of what "selling" meant to white society, or even negotiating with members of tribes who weren't the recognized leaders of their own governments.

Americans insisted on formalizing Indian surrender of their lands in the form of treaties not because they felt bound by such agreements (most of the hundreds signed in the first century of the United States were quickly disregarded and broken) but because they deeply desired to pretend that they weren't actually conquering and expelling indigenous people from their homes, but coming to peaceful agreement with them. American identity was formed more through negation than affirmation; Americans understood themselves as being 'not-Spanish,' 'not-French,' and 'not-English.' Unlike the crowned heads of Europe

who simply planted their flags and claimed dominion over vast empires, Americans thought of themselves as upholding higher ideals of fair-play, justice, and law. Simply taking native lands would have erased that crucial distinction from the Old World that Americans deeply desired, so instead they insisted that the people who they had maneuvered into a position where they had no other option but to concede, should pretend that they were giving over their ancient homelands of their own free choice.

In this way the signing of treaties was made into a great public pageant: one historian described treaty ceremonies as Americans' first stage plays. Americans insisted that the signing of treaties be done publicly, sometimes literally on a stage, with crowds of witnesses and much speech-making. Such ceremonies were then popular subjects for illustrators, sculptors, and painters whose romantic images of these events adorned government buildings and private homes alike. Benjamin Franklin printed full texts of both the treaties themselves but also the speech-making around them in the hopes, as he put it, they would illustrate "the method of doing business with these barbarians."

In private, American leaders could admit that treaty-making was not the free act of a free people they publicly proclaimed it to be. In the summer of 1789 Secretary of War, Henry Knox, wrote a briefing paper for President Washington on how to rid the frontier of the troublesome native peoples who lived in Indiana. He calculated the cost of simply raising an army "with the view of extirpating them, or destroying their towns" at $200,000, "a sum exceeding the ability of the United States to advance…" Purchasing their land, Knox thought, would cost only a tenth that much. Buying their agreement to move was not only cheaper, but probably would achieve the same ends as "extirpating" them:

> When it shall be considered that the Indians derive their subsistence chiefly by hunting, and that, according to fixed principles, their population is in proportion to the facility with which they procure their food, it would most probably be found that the expulsion or destruction of Indian tribes have nearly the same effect: for if they are removed from the usual hunting grounds, they must necessarily encroach on the hunting grounds of another tribe, who will not suffer the encroachment with impunity—hence they destroy each other.

Americans wanted to have it both ways: they wished to imagine themselves the stewards and protectors of native peoples, treating with them in fairness and just respect for their original claims, and they wanted them to vanish, ceding their vast lands to them. The first Congress included in its law for the territories such ringing principles:

> The utmost good faith shall always be observed toward the Indians; their land and property shall never be taken from them without their consent; and in their property, rights, and liberty, they never shall be invaded or disturbed, unless in just and lawful wars authorized by Congress; but laws founded in justice and humanity shall from time to time be made, for preventing wrongs being done to them, and preserving peace and friendship with them.

But many of the founder's policies meant to ensure peace and order on the frontier had the unintended consequence of encouraging corrupt dealings with native peoples and ensured their lasting poverty. The U.S. Constitution reserved to the federal government the right to regulate trade with Indian nations and in 1790 Congress outlawed native people selling their lands to anyone but the federal government (The Indian Trade and Intercourse Act). This measure effectively guaranteed that the federal government could pay as little as it cared to for Indian land. Instead of being able to sell land at a market price, Indian people were given a 'take it or leave it' deal with government agents. Native leaders only alternative to agreement was a crowd of land-hungry squatters and an army to protect them. By ensuring that the federal government would only pay pennies per acre for lands worth dollars, this system encouraged corruption on the part of government officials.

A persistent problem was white settlers attacking, killing, and stealing from Indians, or squatting on their lands and defending their illegal homesteads with arms. During the 1780s, some 80,000 settlers invaded Shawnee lands in the Ohio valley that had been guaranteed to them in exchange for other lands they had ceded. The Shawnee were subsequently forced to hastily move and rebuild their communities progressively westward four times.

Figure 4.15 Penn's Treaty with the Indians, ca. 1788. Metropolitan Museum of Art, New York City.

Whites knew they could thieve and murder with impunity as Federal courts refused to allow tribal courts jurisdiction over whites, even for crimes committed on their recognized lands. Instead, whites would be tried in courts in their own communities with all-white juries of their own neighbors.

The federal government did formally try to restrain both individual settlers and individual states from negotiating with native nations or purchasing their lands. The Constitution reserved to the federal government the right to make treaties with Indians and Congress established an Office of Indian Affairs (as part of the War Department) that sent Indian agents into the field to act on their behalf. But Indian agents were never supplied with the resources they needed or the authority to police the agreements entered into with native peoples. Most of the funds Congress allocated "for the purpose of providing against the further decline and final extinction of the Indian tribes...and for introducing among them the habits and arts of civilization" went to subsidize Protestant missionaries to convert the "heathens" to Christianity.

In practically every case, federal efforts to police established boundaries with native people were tragically weak. In Ohio a single government agent was posted to police a border between white settlers and native peoples hundreds of miles long. That agent in 1812 resorted to simply advising the Shawnee and other people's of the area to stay miles back from their agreed upon border otherwise they were likely to be killed by lynch mobs. He could do nothing to retrain the "armed parties of our people out in all directions breathing destruction against the Indians indiscriminately."

Even such hopeless attempts to uphold the agreed upon Ohio and Indiana borders were only made when British forts and forces in Detroit gave native peoples leverage over the Americans. Americans observed their treaties for a brief time only out of concern that if they seemed like more of a threat to Indians than the British, they might push all the native nations into a powerful alliance with their imperial rivals. Once the Americans defeated the British on Lake Erie and in Michigan in 1813, their commitment to upholding treaties or protecting native communities from settler violence evaporated. As soon as British power was broken, politicians and settlers in the valley of the Ohio river demanded the renegotiation of established treaties.

Slavery in the Northwest Territories

Even though slavery was not as tremendously profitable as it once had been, it remained extremely useful to some. Western settlers who in the 1780s began to push across the Appalachian mountains into Indian lands of Kentucky, Tennessee, Western Virginia, and Western Georgia, relied on forced labor to do much of the exhausting and dangerous work of felling trees, pulling stumps, digging ditches, grading roads, and erecting fences in what was essentially hostile territory. Further to the northwest, Africans had been forcibly dragged into the lands of the upper midwest governed by France since at least 1717. Their enslaved descendants represented a significant population and labor force of the region.

In 1783, Timothy Pickering, Washington's quartermaster general, petitioned Congress for a grant of land upon which poor veterans could settle. Pickering had his eyes on the vast lands of the Northwest Territory and included in his proposal the idea that this area not only be set aside for veterans of the Revolutionary War, but that these lands be emancipated of slavery so these farmers could better compete economically. Thomas Jefferson, a slaveholder himself, opposed Pickering's petition and instead proposed that slavery be protected for at least sixteen years, to the year 1800, upon which time the citizens of the territory would be free to decide for themselves whether to hold slaves or not. Instead of Pickering's petition, Congress drafted the Articles of Confederation which effectively nationalized

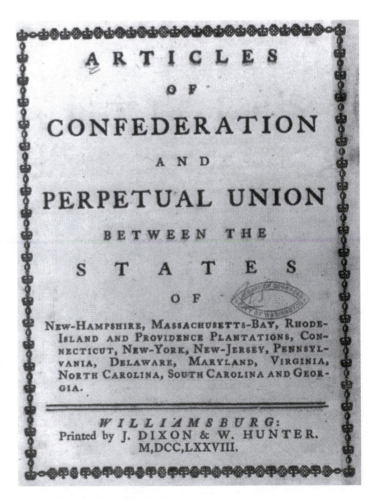

Figure 4.16 Articles of Confederation

Figure 4.17 Arthur St. Clair, painting by Charles Willson Peale, 1780.

slavery by guaranteeing the right of every slave-holder to take their enslaved workers to any state without restriction.

The only national law restricting slavery that the founding fathers ever supported, was passed without debate in a hurried meeting of Congress. In 1787, still reeling from the devastation of the Revolutionary War, with a bankrupt treasury, huge war debts, and a confederated structure of government that made passing any law extraordinarily difficult, Congressmen agreed to include an antislavery provision in the law organizing the new territories west of the Appalachian mountains and north of the Ohio river. A syndicate of investors had pooled their funds and were prepared to pay Congress an impressive sum for control of millions of acres of prime land that they would then sell to settlers for a tidy profit. Knowing that poor New England farmers would be hesitant to move to an area where they would have to compete with slave labor, the investor syndicate desired the anti-slave clause as a marketing tool. Even southern representatives went along without protest, believing those northern territories had climates unfavorable to slave products and more importantly confident that when it came time to organize the richer lands west of Virginia and the Carolinas, slavery would be permitted.

In spite of the seemingly iron-clad language of the Northwest Ordinance, Congress quickly reinterpreted it so as to allow as much slavery as possible. Almost immediately after its passage, James Madison, later to become author of the Bill of Rights, headed a committee that concluded that Congress had really not intended to completely ban

slavery. According to the committee territorial governments created by the act retained the power to protect their citizens slave property, "anything in the said Ordinance to the contrary notwithstanding."

While in theory slave-owners from other states were restricted in their ability to carry their "property" into the area, slaves already in the territory and even slaves imported from British Canada into the Northwest territories were allowed under this interpretation of the law.

What weak restrictions remained in the Ordinance were largely ignored by the founding President, George Washington, and his Secretary of State, Jefferson, who chose not to enforce the anti-slavery articles. Washington's own pick for territorial governor, Arthur St. Clair, brought his slaves with him when he trekked west to establish his headquarters in a place he named Cincinnati. St. Clair officially allowed slaveholders in the territory (which included the present day states of Wisconsin, Illinois, Indiana, Michigan, and Ohio) to continue their bondage. In spite of his defiance of the letter of the ban on slavery, St. Clair was re-appointed by the next two presidents.

When Ohio was granted statehood in 1803, the single Northwest Territory was split into four separate territories each of which was free to determine its own position regarding slavery.

On the eve of Indiana's statehood in 1816, several hundred enslaved people worked within its new borders. Indiana's constitution contained strong language prohibiting slavery, "There shall be neither slavery nor involuntary servitude in this state, otherwise than for the punishment of crimes, whereof the party shall have been duly convicted. Nor shall any indenture of any negro or mulatto hereafter made, and executed out of the bounds of this state be of any validity within the state." Yet for several decades past statehood, some black men, women and children labored as slaves in the Hoosier state. Illinois also largely ignored Congress' prohibition of slavery, even passing legislation regulating and protecting slave owners who mostly lived in the southern tip of the state and kept slaves there until passage of the Thirteenth Amendment after the conclusion of the Civil War.

The Temporary Decline of Slavery

Though slavery was the pillar of the world economy in the 1700s, by the end of the American Revolution its profitability in the old established areas of America was declining. International prices for America's chief export, tobacco, had fallen and remained low while most of the oldest farms in Virginia and the Carolinas suffered from declining yields due to the exhaustion of their soils. In the largest cities of the Northeast, Philadelphia, New York, and

Boston, growing populations of poor laborers were cheaper to hire and easier to dispose of when unwanted. Slavery in the cities was shifting from manufacturing to domestic service while in the South states loosened restrictions on manumissions (the voluntary freeing of one's slaves). Many observers predicted that slavery was on the slow path to extinction.

For example, the population of slaves peaked in Boston in 1752 when 1541 enslaved people resided in the city, about a third of the total for the Massachusetts Bay Colony. Over the next half century the total steadily declined as the colony's economy suffered from England's imperial wars and masters sold younger slaves to southern or Caribbean colonies or freed older ones to unburden themselves of the obligation of their support.

It was in this last half of the eighteenth century that the myth of the paternalistic slave owner was born. In the long-established slave colonies, like Virginia, conditions for enslaved people were healthier and more stable than in the murderous sugar islands of the Caribbean. Slave owners began to credit themselves with their great benevolence for not casually breaking up families by selling husbands, wives, or children to distant lands. Some credited themselves with providing religious instruction, for beating and whipping people sparingly, or allowing their property to cultivate their own gardens and keep or sell their harvest.

In reality, none of these gestures were either freely given or altruistic. Enslaved people struggled hard and strategically to keep their families together and to wring other concessions from their oppressors. They found ways to limit their productivity when they were disgruntled, from feigning sickness or misunderstanding of orders, to breaking tools, or doing shoddy work. More serious resistance, such as fighting masters and overseers or running away, though uncommon, had the salutary effect of forcing these possibilities into their owners' calculations.

Anti-slavery sentiment at this time was not primarily an expression of compassion toward those held in chains, but a fear that the institution would prove incompatible with a republican form of government or even with the nation's economic prospects. Some influential colonists (such as George Washington) began to fear that the southern colonies' dependence on slave labor would undermine their long-term economic prospects. Such men wanted to diversify the economy of the plantation colonies, to move them away from reliance on a single cash crop like tobacco or rice, a move they thought required free wage labor to achieve the sort of specialization of industries and economic flexibility a modern economy required.

In the decade following the Revolutionary War, a number of northern state legislatures responded to the slow decline of slavery in their states by passing gradual emancipation laws. These laws were not motivated by the sort of moral concern that would later fuel the abolitionist movement, but rather were intended to end slavery (which was seen as public nuisance) without destroying the wealth of slave-owners or burdening taxpayers with the support of emancipated and impoverished people. Typical was the opposition to slavery of John Adams who wrote, "I wish to see the day that Slaves are not necessary. Whites and Negroes cannot work together. Negroes are Goods and Chattells, are Property. A Negro works under the impulse of fear—has no Care of his Masters Interest."

Gradual emancipation laws were more or less gradual, depending on the profitability of slavery in an area. Emancipation occurred swiftly in New England where slavery had long been economically unimportant. But in New York and New Jersey many of the farms that fed the growing metropolis of New York City were worked by slaves as they had been since when it was a Dutch colony and one-fifth of the population were enslaved. By 1820, there were still over ten thousand people held in bondage in the state of New York. In New Jersey the gradual emancipation law had been so gradual that one-quarter of the state's black population, approximately 3,000 people, remained enslaved in 1830. Only about one in seven New Jersey masters voluntarily freed the people they enslaved and most of those freed were aged or infirm. Those who still had the youth and energy to be profitably exploited were kept in chains. Even when the state legislature, under pressure from the rising tide of abolitionism, passed an "Abolition Act" in 1846, the law merely reclassified slaves as "apprentices for life" and kept them bound to their masters.

In New Jersey, where slavery had long been an important foundation of the area's economy, slavery persisted nearly as long as it did in the Confederacy. Hannah (she was never given a last name), a girl born into slavery in New Jersey on March 27, 1844, was not freed until her birthday on March 27, 1865, three months after Congress passed the 13th amendment to the U.S. constitution banning slavery (but nine months before it was technically ratified by the required three-quarters of states on December 18).

Even Vermont, renowned for being the first American state to abolish slavery in 1777, only freed those men older than 21 and women above the age of 18, not children. Vermonters turned a blind eye to the persistence of slavery in their communities, especially as it was generally the wealthiest and most powerful families in the state that refused to free their slaves. Levi Allen, the brother of the American patriot Ethan Allen, purchased a black man named Prince from a business partner in New York seven years after slavery was supposedly banned. In 1802, four years after the last possible person (someone born in 1777) could have legally been kept a slave, one of the three members of the state supreme court was sued by the town of Windsor for having "discarded" his elderly slave Dinah (who he had purchased illegally in 1783 when she was thirty) who by then, in the words of the indictment, was "infirm, sick and blind." Windsor's town officials did not want to expend the funds for Dinah's care and sued to have the state justice pay for her on the principle that she was his property.

Every fourth day of July Americans celebrate their independence. They do so without remembering that this momentous event was propelled by settlers and speculators who wanted to free themselves from Parliamentary restrictions on stealing Indian lands, merchants who wanted a larger share of the international slave trade, poor Protestants who feared the power of Catholic Canada, and southern planters whose fortunes were threatened by England's steady movement toward the abolition of slavery. For those colonists in America who were not enslaved, independence was a step towards securing their economic future. But for the one-quarter of Americans who existed as the legal property of others and for the uncounted numbers of native people, independence was a tragedy of Biblical proportions. Free of English restraints, the newly independent state of America were now free to dispossess and devastate indigenous nations and expand the realm and cruelty of slavery to the ends of the continent.

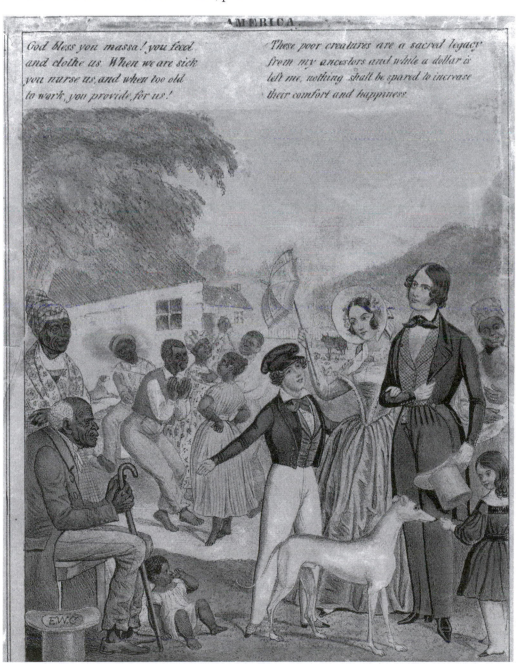

Figure 4.18 "America," by Edward Williams clay, 1841.

Figure 4.19 Frederick Douglass.

WHAT TO THE SLAVE IS THE FOURTH OF JULY?
AN ORATION, AT ROCHESTER, JULY 5, 1852.
Frederick Douglass, *My Bondage and My Freedom* (New York, 1857)

Fellow-Citizens — Pardon me, and allow me to ask, why am I called upon to speak here to-day? What have I, or those I represent, to do with your national independence? Are the great principles of political freedom and of natural justice, embodied in that Declaration of Independence, extended to us? and am I, therefore, called upon to bring our humble offering to the national altar, and to confess the benefits, and express devout gratitude for the blessings, resulting from your independence to us?

Would to God, both for your sakes and ours, that an affirmative answer could be truthfully returned to these questions! Then would my task be light, and my burden easy and delightful. For who is there so cold that a nation's sympathy could not warm him? Who so obdurate and dead to the claims of gratitude, that would not thankfully acknowledge such priceless benefits? Who so stolid and selfish, that would not give his voice to swell the hallelu-jahs of a nation's jubilee... I am not that man...

But, such is not the state of the case. I say it with a sad sense of the disparity between us. I am not included within the pale of this glorious anniversary! Your high independence only reveals the immeasurable distance between us. The blessings in which you this day rejoice, are not enjoyed in common. The rich inheritance of justice, liberty, prosperity, and independence, bequeathed by your fathers, is shared by you, not by me. The sunlight that brought life and healing to you, has brought stripes and death to me. This Fourth of July is yours, not mine. You, may rejoice, I must mourn. To drag a man in fetters into the grand illuminated temple of liberty, and call upon him to join you in joyous anthems, were inhuman mockery and sacrilegious irony. Do you mean, citizens, to mock me, by asking me to speak to-day? If so, there is a parallel to your conduct. And let me warn you that it is dangerous to copy the example of a nation whose crimes, towering up to heaven, were thrown down by the breath of the Almighty, burying that nation in irrecoverable ruin! I can to-day take up the plaintive lament of a peeled and woe-smitten people.

"By the rivers of Babylon, there we sat down. Yea! we wept when we remembered Zion...For there, they that carried us away captive, required of us a song; and they who wasted us required of us mirth, saying, Sing us one of the songs of Zion. How can we sing the Lord's song in a strange land?..."

Fellow-citizens, above your national, tumultuous joy, I hear the mournful wail of millions, whose chains, heavy and grievous yesterday, are day rendered more intolerable by the jubilant shouts that reach them. If I do forget...those bleeding children of sorrow this day, "may my right hand forget her cunning, and may my tongue cleave to the roof of my mouth!" To forget them, to pass lightly over their wrongs, and to chime in with the popular theme, would be treason most scandalous and shocking, and would make me a reproach before God and the world... I do not hesitate to declare, with all my soul, that the character and conduct of this nation never looked blacker to me than on this Fourth of July. Whether we turn to the declarations of the past, or to the professions of the present, the conduct of the nation seems equally hideous and revolting. America is false to the past, false to the present, and solemnly binds herself to be false to the future. Standing with God and the crushed and bleeding slave on this occasion, I will, in the name of humanity which is outraged, in the name of liberty which is fettered, in the name of the constitution and the bible, which are disregarded and trampled upon, dare to call in question and to denounce, with all the em-phasis I can command, everything that serves to perpet-uate slavery—the great sin and shame of America! "I will not equivocate; I will not excuse;" I will use the severest language I can command....

At a time like this, scorching irony, not convincing argument, is needed. Oh! had I the ability, and could I reach the nation's ear, I would to-day pour out a fiery stream of biting ridicule, blasting reproach, withering sar-casm, and stern rebuke. For it is not light that is needed, but fire; it is not the gentle shower, but thunder. We need the storm, the whirlwind, and the earthquake. The feeling of the nation must be quickened; the conscience of the nation must be roused; the propriety of the nation must be startled; the hypocrisy of the nation must be exposed; and its crimes against God and man must be proclaimed and denounced.

What to the American slave is your Fourth of July? I answer, a day that reveals to him, more than all other days in the year, the gross injustice and cruelty to which he is the constant victim. To him, your celebration is a sham; your boasted liberty, an unholy license; your na-tional greatness, swelling vanity; your sounds of rejoicing are empty and heartless; your denunciations of tyrants, brass-fronted impudence; your shouts of liberty and equality, hollow mockery; your prayers and hymns, your sermons and thanksgivings, with all your religious parade and solemnity, are to him mere bombast, fraud, deception, impiety, and hypocrisy—a thin veil to cover up crimes which would disgrace a nation of savages. There is not a nation on the earth guilty of practices more shocking and bloody, than are the people of these United States, at this very hour.

Go where you may, search where you will, roam through all the monarchies and despotisms of the old world, travel through South America, search out every abuse, and when you have found the last, lay your facts by the side of the every-day practices of this nation, and you will say with me, that, for revolting barbarity and shame-less hypocrisy, America reigns without a rival.

POLITICAL DESTINY OF THE COLORED RACE ON THE AMERICAN CONTINENT
Address of the National Emigration Convention of Colored People To the Colored Inhabitants of the U.S.
by Martin R. Delany
Cleveland, Ohio, Aug. 24, 1854

Martin Delany was a complex figure whose life spanned many eras of struggle against oppression. In his youth he studied to become a doctor and was one of the first black men accepted to Harvard Medical School but was expelled when white students protested. Delany assisted many fugitives from slavery to escape to Canada and worked as an assistant editor on Frederick Douglass' newspaper, The **Northstar.** *But Delany was a person of action, not just words. In advocating for emigration he traveled to Nigeria. He conspired with John Brown. When the army finally allowed black enlistments, Delany joined up as did his teenage son, Toussaint L'Ouverture Delany (named for the leader of the Haitian Revolution), and become the first black Major in the U.S. Army.*

Fellow countrymen The duty assigned us is an important one, comprehending all that pertains to our destiny and that of our posterity--present and prospectively…Our object…shall be to place before you our true position in this country--the United State--the improbability of realizing our desires, and the sure, practicable and infallible remedy for the evils we now endure.

We have not addressed you as citizens--a term desired and ever cherished by us--because such you have never been. We have not addressed you as freemen--because such privileges have never been enjoyed by any colored man in the United States. Why then should we flatter your credulity, by inducing you to believe that which neither has now, nor never before had an existence. Our oppressors are ever gratified at our manifest satisfaction, especially when that satisfaction is founded upon false premises; an assumption on our part of the enjoyment of rights and privileges which never have been conceded, and which, according to the present system of the United States policy, we never can enjoy.

The political policy of this country was solely borrowed from, and shaped and modeled after, that of Rome. This was strikingly the case in the establishment of immunities, and the application of terms in their civil and legal regulations….Such, then, is the condition, precisely, of the

Figure 4.20 Martin Delany

black and colored inhabitants of the United States; in some of the States…having the privilege of voting, to elevate their superiors to positions to which they need never dare aspire, or even hope to attain.

There has, of late years, been a false impression…that the privilege of voting constitutes, or necessarily embodies, the rights of citizenship. A more radical error never obtained favor among an oppressed people….

Let it then be understood, as a great principle of political economy, that no people can be free who themselves do not constitute an essential part of the ruling element of the country in which they live. Whether this element be founded upon a true or false, a just or an unjust basis, this position in community is necessary to personal safety. The liberty of no man is secure who controls not his own political destiny…To suppose otherwise is that delusion which at once induces its victim, through a period of long suffering, patiently to submit to every species of wrong; trusting against probability, and hoping against all reasonable grounds of expectation, for the granting of privileges and enjoyment of rights which never will be attained. This delusion reveals the true secret of the power which holds in peaceable subjection all the oppressed in every part of the world.

In other periods and parts of the world, as in Europe and Asia, the people being of one common, direct origin of race, though established on the presumption of difference by birth, or what was termed blood, yet the distinction between the superior classes and common people could only be marked by the difference in the dress and education of the two classes. To effect this the interposition of government was necessary; consequently, the costume and education of the people became a subject of legal restriction, guarding carefully against the privileges of the common people….

In the United States, our degradation being once--as

it has in a hundred instances been done--legally determined, our color is sufficient, independently of costume, education, or other distinguishing marks, to keep up that distinction.

In Europe, when an inferior is elevated to the rank of equality with the superior class, the law first comes to his aid, which, in its decrees, entirely destroys his identity as an inferior, leaving no trace of his former condition visible.

In the United States, among the whites, their color is made, by law and custom, the mark of distinction and supe-riority; while the color of the blacks is a badge of degrada-tion, acknowledged by statute, organic law, and the common consent of the people.

With this view of the case--which we hold to be correct--to elevate to equality the degraded subject of law and custom, it can only be done, as in Europe, by an entire destruction of the identity of the former condition of the applicant. Even were this desirable--which we by no means admit--with the deep-seated prejudices engendered by oppression with which we have to contend, ages incalculable might reasonably be expected to roll around before this could honorably be accomplished; otherwise we should en-courage and at once commence an indiscriminate concubi-nage and immoral commerce of our mothers, sisters, wives, and daughters, revolting to think of, and a physical curse to humanity....

But we have fully discovered and comprehended the great political disease with which we are affected, the cause of its origin and continuance; and what is now left for us to do is to discover and apply a sovereign remedy--a healing balm to a sorely diseased body--a wrecked but not entirely shattered system. We propose for this disease a remedy. That remedy is emigration....

Were we content to remain as we are, sparsely interspersed among our white fellow countrymen, we never might be expected to equal them in any honorable or respectable competition for a livelihood. For the reason that according to the customs and policy of the country, we for ages would be kept in a secondary position, every situation of respectability, honor, profit, or trust, either as mechanics, clerks, teachers, jurors, councilmen, or legislators, being filled by white men, consequently our energies must become par-alyzed...for the want of proper encouragement....

It would be duplicity longer to disguise the fact that the great issue, sooner or later, upon which must be disputed the world's destiny, will be a question of black and white; and every individual will be called upon for his identity with one or the other. The blacks and colored races are four sixths of all the population of the world; and these people are fast tending to a common cause with each other. The white races are but one third of the population of the globe, or one of them to two of us, and it cannot much longer continue that two-thirds will passively submit to the universal domination of this one-third. And it is notorious that the only progress made in territorial domain in the last three centuries by the whites has been a usurpation and encroachment on the rights and native soil of some of the colored races....

We regret the necessity of stating the fact, but duty compels us to the task, that for more than two thousand years the determined aim of the whites has been to crush the colored races wherever found. With a determined will, they have sought and pursued them in every quarter of the globe. The Anglo-Saxon has taken the lead in this work of universal subjugation. But the Anglo-American stands pre-eminent for deeds of injustice and acts of oppression, unparalleled, perhaps, in the annals of modern history.

We admit the existence of great and good people in America, England, France, and the rest of Europe, who desire a unity of interests among the whole human family, of what-ever origin or race.

But it is neither the moralist, Christian, nor philan-thropist whom we now have to meet and combat, but the politician--the civil engineer and skilful economist, who direct and control the machinery which moves forward, with mighty impulse, the nations and powers of the earth. We must therefore, if possible, meet them on vantage ground, or, at least, with adequate means for the conflict.

Should we encounter an enemy with artillery, a prayer will not stay the cannon shot; neither will the kind words nor smiles of philanthropy shield his spear from piercing us through the heart. We must meet mankind, then, as they meet us--prepared for the worst, though we may hope for the best. Our submission does not gain for us an increase of friends nor respectability, as the white race will only respect those who oppose their usurpation, and acknowledge as equals those who will not submit to their rule. This may be no new discovery in political economy, but it certainly is a subject worthy the consideration of the black race.

Should anything occur to prevent a successful emigra-tion to the south--Central, South America, and the West In-dies--we have no hesitancy, rather than remain in the United States, the merest subordinates and serviles of the whites, should the Canadas still continue separate, in their political relations from this country, to recommend to the great body of our people to remove to Canada West, where, being politically equal to the whites, physically united with each other by a concentration of strength, when worse comes to worse, we may be found, not as a scattered, weak, and impotent people, as we now are, separated from each other throughout the Union, but a united and powerful body of freemen, mighty in politics, and terrible in any conflict which might ensue in the event of an attempt at the disturbance of our political relations, domestic repose, and peaceful firesides.

Now, fellow countrymen, we have done. Into your ears have we recounted your own sorrows; before your own eyes have we exhibited your wrongs; into your own hands have we committed your own cause. If there should prove a failure to remedy this dreadful evil, to assuage this terrible curse which has come upon us, the fault will be yours and not ours, since we have offered you a healing balm for every sorely aggravated wound.

("Report of the Select Committee on Emancipation and Colonization," U.S. House of Representatives, 37th Cong., 2d Sess., Rep. 148, (1862), pp. 37-59.")

Chapter Five: An Empire for Slavery

George Washington, President and Enslaver

The young American republic's reliance on slavery is well illustrated by George Washington's treatment of the men, women, and children he kept in bondage. When his father died when he was a boy, George Washington inherited eleven enslaved men and women. Like other rich Virginians Washington worked to accumulate slaves throughout his adult life, including purchasing some off the auction block in nearby Williamsburg. Washington helped organize a raffle to recover a debtor's liabilities in which an entire enslaved family was broken apart and given to different men holding winning tickets. When Americans like Washington revolted against England for freedom and independence, Washington owned nearly 150 men and women. By the time he died in 1799, his inventory of the men, women and children he held in bondage counted 317.

Nevertheless, even Washington wished he could rid himself of his status as an enslaver. As early as 1778 he wrote that he wished he could "get quit of Negroes." But the people he owned were the main source of his wealth, comfort, and security, and Washington never freed a soul during his lifetime, even his loyal personal man, William Lee, who bravely served him throughout the war.

Following his credo, "lost labour can never be regained," Washington was a shrewd plantation manager, squeezing the most profit from his enslaved workers by keeping careful records of each person's activities and output, having shirkers whipped, and providing but the barest rations of food, the coarsest clothing and bedding, and the cheapest shelter. Like other enslavers, Washington used the threat of separating loved ones to enforce his will, which he could easily do as he owned five different plantations. One historian calculated that at any one time, more than half of the married couples held in bondage were broken up among Washington's different properties. A few defiant men who actually challenged Washington's orders he sold to slavers in the West Indies, a place where sugar was so profitable that it paid to work slaves to death. When Washington needed a set of dentures to replace his own rotten teeth he used teeth yanked from the mouth of a slave. Yet a few of Washington's friends thought his treatment of his slaves was kinder than most Virginians, one claiming Washington provided much better provisions than the usual master who "give to their Blacks only bread, water, and blows."

Throughout his life many of the people Washington enslaved struggled to free themselves from his mastery. In 1761, Washington distributed handbills offering a reward of forty shillings for help in securing the recovery of four people, Peros, Jack, Neptune, and Cupid, who had escaped. When the war for independence from England broke out, Washington's enslaved stable-keeper, Harry, fled to the British lines seeking his freedom. Harry was eventually granted land by the Brits in Nova Scotia, a farmstead he later swapped for resettlement in Sierra Leone on the coast of west Africa, the land from which his ancestors had been stolen.

When Washington moved to Philadelphia to take up his duties as President he brought many of slaves with him even though Pennsylvania had passed laws establishing a timetable for the gradual emancipation of all the state's enslaved people. Exploiting a loophole in Pennsylvania's abolition law that freed any slave brought to the state for more than six months, Washington rotated his slaves between Virginia and Philadelphia every few months before the clock ran out. He and Martha repeatedly lied to the men and women they enslaved about the existence of this law. Once, having kept one of their enslaved entourage too long in the state, Martha hurriedly drove with him across the border into New Jersey just for an hour to skirt the law.

As President Washington supported measures that strengthened slavery, putting his signature to a bill making helping or sheltering a fugitive slave a federal crime in 1793. Three years later, he had occasion to benefit from his own law when one of the nine slaves he and Martha dragged around as their personal servants escaped. Ona Judge, a young woman of twenty-two, stole out of the Washington's Philadelphia townhouse. Washington personally pursued Judge northward until her trail grew cold.

What Ona knew she faced was a life of economic and sexual exploitation. Like his friend Thomas Jefferson, who fathered two children with his slave Sally Hemmings, Washington may have fathered children with slaves, as Martha's first husband did and as his own children later did. There is some evidence that Washington may have been the father of West Ford, a boy whose mother, Venus, was owned by Washington's brother, though determining this with certainty is extraordinarily difficult as both George and Martha burned nearly all their letters and personal papers.

Martha Washington's father had at least one child

with one of his slaves, Martha's half sister, Ann Dandridge, who Martha kept as her own slave. Like most young enslaved girls, Ann was raped, the sexual prey of Martha's son Jacky who fathered her first child, a boy named William.

Four years after Ona Judge escaped Washington's clutches, the President's personal chef, a man known only as Hercules, threw his apron aside and fled. Just before he died, another of the people Washington held in bondage attempted to free himself. Christopher Sheels ran off in 1799 but was recaptured.

In the last years of his life Washington grew more ashamed of his life as an enslaver and to his credit he made arrangements to free many, but not all, of his slaves. Unlike Jefferson, whose last will and testament freed only five of the people he enslaved and auctioned the remaining two hundred, or James Madison, one of the authors of the Constitution who freed none of the people he held in bondage, even upon his death, Washington drafted a will freeing some of the people he owned. But not immediately, only upon the death of Martha. Those slaves that Washington obtained when he married Martha were not

to be freed. Ultimately, only 126 of the 317 people enslaved on Washington estates were freed. The rest realized their worst fears, first split up among four grandchildren upon Martha's death, then many were sold to slave traders who drove them in neck chains to the cotton frontier of the Mississippi valley.

At the time of the American revolution slavery was an important but stagnant institution. Approximately 400,000 people were held in bondage, primarily within a short distance of the Atlantic coast. After independence from England was achieved and the new American government protected and promoted it, slavery rapidly expanded across the continent. Over the next century the number of enslaved people would grow exponentially, reaching four million before Union armies put an end to it.

A common error in thinking about slavery is to think of it as a single static institution. In fact, slavery changed and adapted to the industrializing American economy and as it did so the conditions under which its victims lived and labored degraded as well. From the beginning of the nineteenth century until emancipation in the mid-1860s,

Figure 5.1 George Washington--The farmer, painting by Junius Stearns (Paris : Lemercier, c1853).

slavery grew to be much more harsh, brutal, and degrading, largely as it became wildly more profitable with the rise of a new cash crop.

The Cotton Boom Saves Slavery

While the early plantation crops of tobacco, rice, and sugar were important but declining in profitability, they were all quickly eclipsed by the rise of cotton at the beginning of the nineteenth century. Cotton cloth had been one of the principal items of trade between Europe and Asia since medieval times, most of it being spun and woven near where it was grown in India and China. Little cotton was grown in the Western hemisphere as it took a great deal of labor to raise, to separate the seeds, to spin into thread and to weave into cloth. All but the richest Europeans made do with coarse woolen clothes.

Two developments at the end of the 1700s revolutionized this industry. The one, Eli Whitney's cotton gin, a device that quickly separated cotton seeds from the usable fiber, allowed for the mass production of cotton on North American plantations. The other, automatic spinning and weaving machinery, scaled up cloth production in the world's first true factories. As the volume of cotton cloth being produced increased and the price fell it came within reach of ordinary Europeans and another rapidly expanding commodity market was created.

By the first years of the nineteenth century a cotton boom was in full swing with vast fortunes to be made for anyone who could command land and labor. Labor, in the form of slavery was readily available in North America, especially since the U.S. Constitution prohibited Congress from restricting the slave trade for twenty years. Consequently, a slave trade rush ensued and more slaves were imported to America between 1787 and 1807 than in any comparable period in American history. 100,000 men, women, and children from Africa were landed in the United States in these years; thousands of others perished during the journey including many who died while rebelling onboard their ships. (One careful estimate counts that those chained below decks in these ships rebelled and fought their crews at least every tenth journey.)

Land, however, was actually in short supply as the young American republic was bottled up and surrounded by the land claims of European empires and powerful native nations who England, Spain, and France had allied with. For the most part, the ridge of mountains that began as the Alleghenies in Massachusetts and New York and reached as the Appalachians into the Carolinas and Georgia, marked America's western boundary. America maintained a few scattered western outposts, such as Fort Pitt in western Pennsylvania, but controlled little of the surrounding territory, especially south of the Ohio river.

Prior to the revolution, worried that continued settlement would provoke costly wars with other European and native powers, the English Parliament had declared the lands beyond that line of mountains off limits to American colonists. Popular resentment against a policy that seemed to many American colonists as a violation of their right to conquer and exploit the frontier was one of the grievances that fueled an independence movement. When independence was achieved the same public pressures motivated the new U.S. Congress to hastily attempt to organize and open new western territories to settlers. This proved a much more difficult and costly undertaking than anyone could have expected at the time, indeed, it lead directly to wars with England, Mexico, dozens of native nations and, ultimately, a civil war that cleaved the nation in two. Deep beneath these grand movements of history, driving the pressures that caused their lurching movements like tectonic plates, was the lure of cotton profits.

The policymakers of the young nation saw the tremendous potential of promoting a continental system of commerce but also saw the chokepoints that threatened its growth. Foremost among them was the fact that the lynchpin to the whole system, the port of New Orleans that allowed cotton growers access to the world's markets and slave markets access to the nation's cotton growers, was in the hands of foreign powers. New Orleans was originally part of the Spanish claims to the coastal swath stretching from Florida to its possessions in Texas and New Mexico. The city was one of the most important centers of commerce in the New World when Jefferson sent a delegation to France with orders to offer a sum greater than the entire U.S. government's annual budget, 10 million dollars, to buy it. To their astonishment, Napoleon offered to sell not only the city, but the entire territory of 828,000 square miles, an expanse greater than the rest of the American nation combined, for 15 million.

Of course, the American government didn't have that sort of cash, so Jefferson's Louisiana Purchase was made possible by the underwriting of British banks, especially that of Thomas Baring, whose bank underwrote the bonds that paid off the French government. It was no coincidence that Baring was also one of the leading cotton merchants in England.

So the American west was purchased on the promise of cotton profits which were high due to the forced labor of enslaved people. But more fundamentally, the deal was made possible because Napoleon's own plans to expand slavery were foiled by the largest revolt of enslaved people in modern history. Enslaved people rose up against their French masters in 1794. Led by the brilliant general Toussaint L'Ouveture, Haitian rebels first defeated an invasion of British Redcoats (even imperial rivalries could be put

Figure 5.2 General Toussaint L'Ouveture

Planters, investors, and speculators who pushed into western Georgia and then further west into the new territories of Alabama, Mississippi, Tennessee, and Louisiana, aimed to profit directly from the production of cotton. Those settlers who flooded out of the old communities of New England and the Mid-Atlantic states and into the new northern territories drained by the Ohio river sought their fortunes in the commerce generated by the spread of cotton plantations to the South.

Cotton's economic potential seemed limitless. By 1807, cotton exports amounted to more than one-fifth of all U.S. exports. Twelve years later they had climbed to account for one-half. The American South produced two-thirds of the world's cotton by 1850. Three-quarters of all southern cotton went to England where it was exchanged for cash and served as collateral for loans. It was easily the nation's leading export and provided the crucial foreign exchange and capital that allowed the country to develop manufacturing and diversify its economy.

The new economics of cotton revived slavery in the U.S. and decisively ended any talk of abolition. Thomas Jefferson understood well that the period of debate over slavery was over: "We have the wolf by the ears and we can neither hold him, nor safely let him go. Justice is on one scale, self-preservation on the other." Jefferson, who had previously vowed to emancipate his own hundreds of slaves upon his death, recanted and instead willed them to his heirs.

Cotton was so valuable a crop that it was more profitable to purchase northern food than squander acres growing it on the plantation. Settlers in Ohio, Indiana, Kentucky, and Illinois raised wheat, corn, and hogs and shipped them south on great flatboats that were broken up and sold for lumber once they reached their destination. So many hogs were butchered in Cincinnati by the 1820s that the first assembly lines were invented there to process and pack the salted meat. The great quantities of salt these factories needed for their operations came from the saline springs and salt works in southern Illinois that were actually worked by hundreds of enslaved laborers in flagrant disregard of the technicality that Illinois, like its neighboring states north of the Ohio river, was supposedly a "free" state. By the 1830s, one-third of all the transportable goods produced in the northeast were sent to slave states in the south and west. This is not surprising given that at this time half of all American economic activity was dependent on slavery.

Lasting fortunes were made in the trade in manufacturing goods or providing services in support of slavery. Brooks Brothers, today a retailer of expensive suits and fine clothes, got its start selling shoddy clothing to slave traders and plantation owners. Many banks and insurance

aside to subdue an uprising against slavery) then defeated the French who had sent the largest invasion fleet to ever cross the Atlantic to their island. The failure of the Haitian campaign denied Napoleon a base from which to secure his other valuable possession, New Orleans and forced him to sell all of Louisiana to the Americans. The Haitian people declared their own independent republic on January 1, 1804.

When he acquired Louisiana, Thomas Jefferson congratulated himself for having given the American people "room enough for our descendents to the thousandth and thousandth generation." Within two decades settlers were finding the purchase lands "crowded" and were beginning to infiltrate the less settled national domains to the south. In 1846 the U.S. went to war with Mexico and stole half of its territory for itself. The territory thus gained constituted the greatest acquisition of natural wealth in American history, dwarfing even the Louisiana Purchase. But the cost of this conquest proved high. No other single event contributed as significantly to Mexico's underdevelopment in the modern era as did its conquest by the United States in 1848. Moreover, no single event was as responsible for dividing the nation or altering the terrain of its politics and leading to the Civil War.

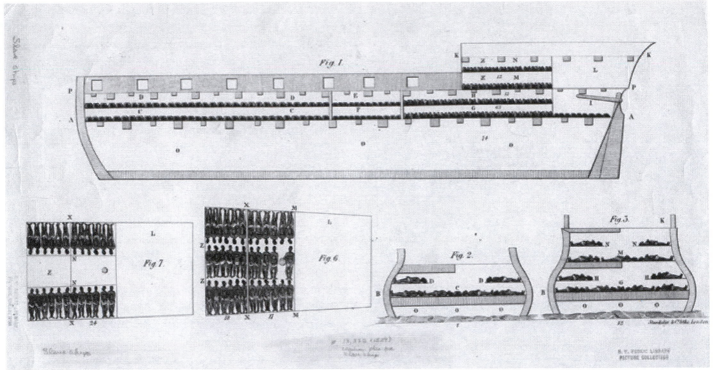

Figure 5.3 Schematic drawing of an English slave ship, possibly the Brookes, 1839.

companies still in operation today, Chase, Wachovia, Aetna, New York Life, and others, can trace their genealogies back to companies whose primary business involved the financing or insuring of slavery.

Perhaps the most vicious and calculating part of this business was selling insurance to slave traders transporting people seized in Africa to slavery in the Americas. Policies were sold at a high price that covered "loss of cargo," meaning people, in the event of storm or shipwreck as well as in the event of piracy or insurrection. So finely tuned were these businesses that by the late 1700s policies issued by Lloyd's and other English insurers were estimated to cost £3.8 per slave, roughly 12.6% of the average slave's value upon sale at their destination (£30). A figure remarkably close to the 13% estimate of the total proportion of people who died while being forcibly transported across the Atlantic in the last half of the 1700s.

Knowing they were covered by insurance encouraged owners and speculators in humans to be even less concerned with the welfare of their "property" than they otherwise would have been. In the late summer of 1781, the Zong, a ship carrying 442 men, women and children as cargo, drew anchor off the coast of west Africa (Sao Tomé) and headed for Jamaica. Even for a slave ship the Zong was seriously overcrowded as the ship master and crew stood to financially gain by shoving more people into the hold. By the eleventh week when its island destination was sighted, sixty Africans (13.5%) had died chained in the dark bottom of the ship. The insurance policy that backed the Zong, did not pay out upon the routine death of those chained on shipboard, but only in cases of natural calamity, piracy, or shipwreck. While still at sea, but within striking distance of Jamaica, the captain of the Zong ordered his crew to drag topside about a quarter of the remaining men, women and children, 132 of them and toss them into the sea. Owners of the Zong later submitted their insurance claim on the basis that provisions had run too low and the "cargo" had to be "jettisoned" to prevent the greater calamity of the loss of the entire ship. Eventually, the case wound its way through the English courts and resulted in a judgement in favor of the insurers who alleged there was no necessity for "jettison" in this case. (English abolitionists led by escaped slave Olaudah Equiano and reformer Granville Sharp, successfully sought an indictment of murder against surviving crewmen, but they were ultimately found not guilty.)

America and Transatlantic Human Trafficking

One of the common myths about slavery is that the federal government effectively outlawed the horrific transatlantic trade as soon as the Constitution allowed for it to do so in 1807. It is true that Congress banned the importation of slaves beginning on Jan. 1, 1808. But this ban was not only ineffective for another decade, a crucial ten years when great areas of western cotton cultivation were opened, but it was designed in a way to uphold slavery itself.

In enforcing the prohibition on the slave trade, the federal government carefully upheld the institution of slavery. When on rare occasion a federal coast guard ship would seize a ship smuggling slaves into the country, the federal government would begin court proceedings to confiscate the ship and its cargo from the smuggler. If successful, such prosecutions resulted in all these assets being disposed at public auction, including the men, women and children held in chains. From the perspective of an African dragged across the Atlantic in the hold of a slave ship, Congress' so-called ban on the slave trade made no difference whatsoever. It was only a financial inconvenience to the small number of shippers unlucky enough to be caught. (It wasn't until 1819 that Congress adopted a law returning confiscated slaves to Africa rather than auctioning them off in the U.S.)

Federal courts were ineffective in prosecuting cases of human trafficking. One study of prosecutions in the most active smuggling region, Louisiana, found that convictions were secured in fewer than a quarter of prosecutions. Even in cases of civil forfeiture, the easiest cases to prosecute as the evidentiary requirements were quite low, smugglers avoided having their human property seized about a quarter of the time.

Moreover, the federal prohibition on the slave trade was never strictly enforced. Soon after the ban was effective, President Jefferson's administration granted a waiver to thousands of French planters who had fled the slave revolution in Haiti and allowed them to immigrate to the United States along with their 3,200 slaves. Some slave-shippers exploited a loophole in maritime law that allowed any ship "in distress" to seek shelter in an American port without penalty. This is how the pirate captain of the *Massavito*, avoided having his cargo seized in 1810 when he made port in Louisiana, took on provisions, and sold his cargo of 105 people to a local slave dealer and how a Spanish slave ship, the *Alerta*, disembarked its 170 slaves later that year in New Orleans. In 1815, President Madison formalized this loophole by declaring a policy of neutrality with Spain, allowing its slave ships free access to American ports as long as they claimed "distress."

Some unsettled territories on America's borders provided havens for human trafficking that federal officials ignored. In the late 1810s, the port of Galveston, in a region disputed and claimed by Spain, Mexico, and the U.S., became an open international slave market supplying many enslaved people to the expanding cotton lands of the Mississippi delta area. James Bowie, later to distinguish himself at the Alamo, successfully imported 180 enslaved people making a sizeable fortune in 1820. Likewise, Amelia Island, in Spanish territory just a mile over the Georgia line, became a smuggling destination that was assisted by a federal policy of not interdicting and inspecting vessels smaller than 5 tons. Smugglers would land their human cargoes on Amelia island, then force enslaved people onto skiffs and row themselves in groups of two or three to shore.

Throughout this period, Spain continued to import enslaved people directly from Africa to its remaining colonies in the New World, particularly Cuba where more than 100,000 enslaved people were dragged in the decade following America's outlawing of the trade. This meant that it was fairly easy for American smugglers to purchase slaves in Cuban markets and ship the short distance to the growing cotton regions along the gulf coast.

Calculations of the number of slaves imported directly to America from Africa after Congress prohibited the trade in 1808 vary widely because of the lack of historical documentation. Federal officials documented approximately 4,100 enslaved people being smuggled between 1810 and 1821, a number that certainly was a small percentage of the total as most smugglers were not caught. Conservative estimates begin at 1,000 people brought into America per year, though some reputable scholars have made cases for as many as 14,000 smuggled annually, which would represent a total of three-quarters of a million people by the time of the Civil War.

The Cherokee Treaties

Soon after the United States was formed, the young government devoted much of its energy and time to forcing native peoples to give up as much of their territory as they could be persuaded to surrender. Government agents quickly developed an effective formula for persuading native peoples to sign treaties giving up land. They would point out the fact that the tribe was suffering from the attacks and illegal settlement of white squatters and these would only grow more serious as time went on. If the tribe would surrender a portion of their land, the U.S. government promised to use its power to prevent settlers from trespassing on the land they retained. Once the formal boundary between the U.S. and the tribe was surveyed and clearly established, the U.S. would guarantee the security and peaceful ownership of the remaining lands in Indian hands for all time to come. Further inducements of cash payments or annual grants of seed, tools, or other valuable goods would often be offered to seal the deal.

How sincerely these agreements were offered and observed can be seen in the treaties made with the Cherokee. The Cherokee were a numerous and powerful nation at the time of the American Revolution whose territory included most of western Georgia. Upon conclusion of the war with England, America's founding fathers were eager not only to take the fertile Cherokee lands but also to recover the many slaves who had taken advantage of the disruptions of the war and fled their captivity by taking refuge in Indian communities. In 1785, the Cherokee agreed to cede a large

Figure 5.4 Cherokee War Chief.

portion of their lands and to return all slaves in exchange for clear and definite boundaries and a promise that the U.S. would respect and protect the smaller territory where they remained. The treaty concluded as most treaties did, "The hatchet shall be for ever buried, and the peace given... shall be universal..."

That universal, everlasting agreement lasted only six years before the U.S. returned to the Cherokee and demanded more land. A new treaty, pledging a "permanent" and "perpetual peace and friendship" was pressed upon the Cherokee. Again "in order to preclude forever all disputes relative to the...boundary" the U.S. agreed to protect the Cherokee in the lands they retained as long as they ceded another vast area to the federal government. "The United States solemnly guaranty to the Cherokee nation all their lands not hereby ceded."

Over the next few years government surveyors failed to undertake the promised mapping and marking of the agreed upon boundaries and white settlers continued to freely claim homesteads on land that was by agreement reserved to the Cherokee. Finally in 1798, U.S. agents offered the Cherokee more protection in return for their ceding another great stretch of land and another "perpetual" treaty signed in which the newly restricted "limits and boundaries of the Cherokee nation...shall be and remain the same" permanently.

At the same time the U.S. government was pledging

to respect the much reduced territory of the Cherokee for all time, it was negotiating with the state of Georgia to give up its ancient colonial claims to all the land between it and the Mississippi river. In 1802 Georgia agreed to cede these lands to the federal government as long as the national government pledged to force the Cherokee to surrender all their lands to the state of Georgia. President Washington's appointed commissioner, James Madison, agreed "that the United States shall...extinguish the Indian title to all the other lands within the state of Georgia."

Federal agents returned to the Cherokee and pressured them to give up more lands in 1805, twice in 1806, twice in 1816 (the second time in the Treaty of Sept. 14, the U.S. ordered that if the Cherokee refused to negotiate it would consider that to be an agreement: "if they do not assemble at the time and place specified, it is understood that the said commissioners may report the same as a tacit ratification..."), 1817, 1819, 1824. Pressured by the U.S. army and Andrew Jackson's swift and brutal campaign against the Creeks to their west, one group of Cherokee agreed in principle to swap their lands for new territories in the far west, outside the borders of the United States. In 1819 U.S. agents pressured another band of Cherokees to give up all their claims in exchange for homesteads of 640 acres.

While Andrew Jackson like many other white Americans simply wanted to be rid of people they considered "savages," others sought a means by which the ideals of human equality enshrined in America's founding documents could be squared with the ongoing oppression of Indians and Africans. Many white Americans believed the government should foster the "civilization" and "christianizing" of Indians. In this spirit, the federal government encouraged native people to abandon their collective tribal society and adopt the ways of European society. Congress approved the "Indian Civilization Act" in 1819 that allocated $10,000 annually to Christian missionaries to "civilize" the Indian tribes. American leaders claimed Indian tribes that moved toward assimilation into white society would gain the protection of the federal government.

Some Cherokee communities attempted to do just that and divided up their collective lands into individual plots, adopted European dress and religion, and established a school system. The Cherokee innovated a written form of their language and organized a representative form of government, not unlike that of the state of Georgia that surrounded them.

However, whites in Georgia coveted the rich lands of what they called the "Five Civilized Tribes." Georgia's leaders demanded that the federal government expel the Choctaw, Chickasaw, Muscogee-Creek, Seminole, and Cherokee nations from the state and President Jackson supported removing all Indians to the distant territory of

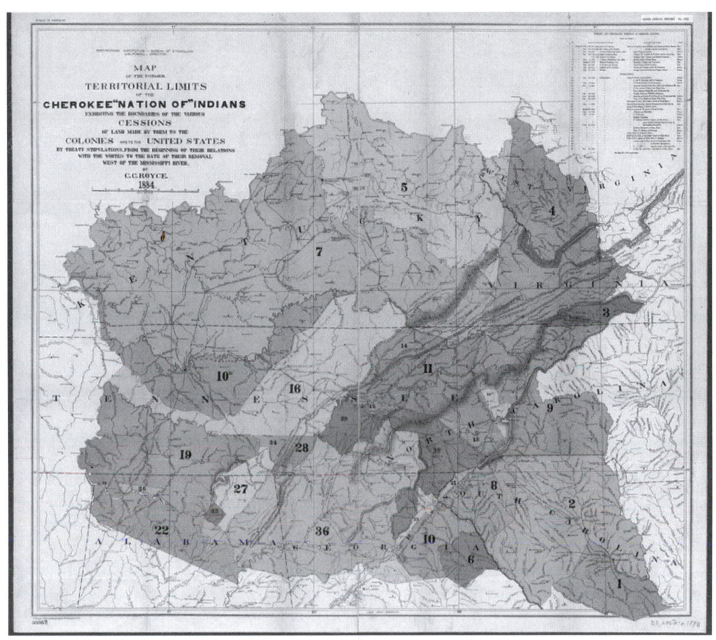

Figure 5.5 Map of the former territorial limits of the Cherokee Nation, 1884.

Louisiana. Southern Indian nations refused such plans and attempted to secure their rights through the federal courts.

After gold was discovered in Cherokee territory in 1827, thousands of white prospectors invaded the Cherokee nation and began digging up as much precious metal as quickly as they could. Georgia and federal officials not only turned a blind eye to this obvious treaty violation, but did what they could to protect the white trespassers. President Andrew Jackson ordered federal troops out of the area. In 1828 Georgia prohibited its courts from allowing any Indian to testify in a case involving a white man. Georgia also claimed jurisdiction over criminal cases between native peoples on their own lands. When the U.S. Supreme Court agreed to hear the case of a Cherokee man, George Tassel, who had been tried and condemned by a Georgia court for murdering a Cherokee within the borders of the Cherokee nation, Georgia officials publicly hanged him in defiance of the highest court. In spite of Georgia's conflict with the U.S. Supreme Court, Georgia's determination to extinguish all treaty rights and extend its authority over all the lands within its borders was actually consistent with the long-term policies of the federal government.

Buried in the U.S. Constitution was an ambiguity, a critical passage whose meaning was not nailed down and which, if interpreted in one reasonable way would have undermined the ability of the government to easily claim Indian lands. Buried in the wording of the famous Commerce Clause (Art. 1, Sec. 8) was a potential time bomb lurking for the right interpretation to blow up American excuses for appropriating native lands. The clause reads:

"The Congress shall have Power… To regulate Commerce with foreign Nations, and among the several States, and with the Indian Tribes…" One reading of the clause distinguishes between these three different entities—foreign nations, states, and Indian tribes—and supposes that they were listed separately because they had different powers, rights, and status. But another way of viewing this passage was that all three of these entities are listed together because they shared the quality of possessing sovereignty—the right and authority to rule themselves. By this second interpretation of the clause, the Constitution recognizes the sovereignty of Indian peoples and therefore the government can't simply extend its laws and its power over Indian lands.

This reading of native sovereignty posed a dire threat to the project of dispossessing Indian people of their lands and removing them out of the nation. If Indian nations were sovereign they had the right, as all states and foreign nations do, to regulate their own affairs, which would include subjecting alien trespassers and squatters to their own courts of justice. America's legal fiction that Indian nations were both sovereign (because they could sign treaties surrendering their lands) and subject to the laws of the states that surrounded them (as Georgia and other states insisted) was a contradiction that Americans happily lived with.

In 1831 the Supreme Court accepted a case, *Cherokee Nation v. Georgia*, that demanded that this legal contradiction be resolved. In his ruling Chief Justice John Marshall resolved this ambiguity:

> It may well be doubted whether those tribes which reside within the acknowledged boundaries of the United States can, with strict accuracy, be denominated foreign nations. They may more correctly, perhaps, be denominated domestic dependent nations. They occupy a territory to which we assert a title independent of their will, which must take effect in point of possession when their right of possession ceases; meanwhile, they are in a state of pupilage. Their relations to the United States resemble that of a ward to his guardian. They look to our Government for protection, rely upon its kindness and its power, appeal to it for relief to their wants, and address the President as their Great Father.

Chief Justice Marshall's ruling that the Cherokee and all other Indian nations were "domestic dependent nations" invented a new legal status that had never before existed. It was like having to chose between a square and circle and choosing a triangle. Of course what was really happening

Figure 5.6 Silhouette Portrait of John Marshall.

was that Marshall was ruling that Indian nations were not sovereign, that they were conquered nations that the U.S. could do with whatever it chose, but he was sympathetic enough to the crimes committed against native peoples that he couldn't bring himself to admit that this was the effect of his ruling.

The denial of sovereignty to native peoples was not only a legal and political blow to their chances of maintaining the integrity of their communities, it also became a significant element of the way whites conceived of native peoples. Indians came to be viewed as a people without the power of self-determination, a people without a legitimate claim to self-rule. They were seen as essentially dependent people, unable to care for themselves, needing the U.S. government's protection in the same way children must rely on their parents for safety. In this way the denial of native peoples their innate sovereignty as nations was an element of their racialization.

Indian Removal

White Americans could not imagine a place in their new nation for either Indians or Black people and from a very early date began laying plans to remove them from the boundaries of the nation. President Thomas Jefferson had advocated that part of the Louisiana Purchase (1803) be used to resettle Indians out of the borders of the United States. Once America forced England to abandon its western forts in the War of 1812, Michigan's governor Lewis Cass demanded that the federal government remove all Indians from his state to outside the borders of the United States. Secretary of War John Armstrong advocated such a policy not just for those native nations that had sided with the British, but for those in particular that had been America's allies, "the Wyandots, Delawares, and Shawonese," calling for their "relinquishment of their former settlements," and "removal to the country" far west. Cass framed such a move as being in the native's own interests:

> I am convinced that this must be there [sic] ultimate destination and that no other measure will secure them from the exterminating pressure of our progressive settlements. In the immense woods and prairies of that boundless Country, they may hope to preserve for a long succession of years their manners & Customs their wild independence and their ferocious spirit…

President Monroe enthusiastically supported Cass's plan, stating, "'The great object is to remove altogether these tribes beyond the Mississippi. If that is accomplished, every difficulty is removed; there then ceases to be any question about the tenure by which the Indians shall hold their lands." Monroe wrote to Missouri's territorial governor and instructed him to make ready to receive Ohio and Michigan's Indians. In 1818, the Delaware Indians, who had legal possession of most of central Indiana from a treaty of 1795, were forced to surrender their homes in exchange for an unspecified parcel in the west. All the treaty promised was "to provide for the Delawares a country to reside in, upon the west side of the Mississippi, and to guaranty to them the peaceable possession of the same." Missouri eventually resettled them in the swamps of the southwestern portion of the state where hunting and farming proved too poor to sustain the community and they were forced to move on to Kansas.

In 1825 President James Monroe proposed to Congress a "removal act" that would "induce" Indians to "relinquish the lands on which they now reside and to remove to those which are designated." Congress passed such a law five years later and it was enthusiastically signed by President Andrew Jackson.

The law had been controversial because of a large degree of sympathy many whites had developed for the "Christianized" Indians, such as the Cherokee, who seemed to have successfully transformed themselves into a nation of farmers and tradesmen. In order to garner support, removal advocates framed their proposal as one that would in the words of President Monroe, "protect their families and posterity from inevitable destruction." Removal advocates including Andrew Jackson emphasized that new Indian lands would be "guaranteed to the Indian tribes as long as they shall occupy it."

With the passage of the Indian Removal Act, federal and state interests aligned to force native communities to leave the United States. William Henry Harrison, who was territorial governor of Indiana before rising to the presidency in 1841, encouraged Indiana's legislature to do more to push Indians west:

> Although much has been done towards the extinguishment of Indian titles in the Territory, much still remains to be done. We have not sufficient space to form a tolerable State. The eastern settlements are separated from the western by a considerable extent of Indian lands, and the most fertile tracts that are within our territorial bounds, are still their property…Is one of the fairest portions of the globe to remain in a state of nature, the haunt of a few wretched savages, when it seems destined by the Creator to give support to a large population, and to be the seat of civilization, of science, and true religion?

One group of native people managed to cling to a diminishing grant of land till the 1840s. The Wyandot ceded most of their land but retained a portion that became one county in Ohio along the Upper Sandusky river. There they cleared fields and adopted European ways of farming and living. Like many of the Cherokee in Georgia, they adopted Christianity, western dress, and set about being as enterprising as any of their English neighbors. Nevertheless, the presence of a native people, a group increasingly despised as a "degenerate race," was not tolerated and under intense pressure they agreed to move west. Because they were farmers and had built homes, barns, mills, and dug ditches and carved roads through the area, they demanded and won in their removal treaty an agreement that the government would pay them the value of the improvements they had made to the land. The assessors appointed by the war department reported their figure of $127,094.24, a sum Congress refused to appropriate. In flagrant disregard for the treaty they had just approved, Congress instead voted the sum of $20,000 and the Secretary of War instructed his agent to the Wyandot to tell them this was just the first installment so they would continue with their migration out of the state. Twenty years later the Wyandot, now in Kansas, were still petitioning the government not only to pay their original promised amount, but just to pay them the interest on it. A new treaty agreeing to pay $83,814.40 was signed in 1867 (and by which the Wyandot agreed to surrender their now valuable lands near Kansas City and move to Oklahoma). Most of that sum hadn't been appropriated by Congress as late as 1894.

At the time Congress passed the Indian Removal Act, about one hundred thousand native survivors of centuries of attempted genocide remained within the borders of the United States. The Indian Removal Act was enforced with ruthless disregard for the health and welfare of the people evicted from their homes and forcibly moved beyond the borders of America. Choctaws were forced to leave Mississippi in 1830. Muskogee Creeks were pushed west in 1834. Beginning in 1836 different groups of Seminole peoples walked out of Florida to points far west.

At least four thousand Choctaws, seven hundred Creeks, and eight thousand Cherokees perished on their forced march to Oklahoma in the 1830s. Thousands more died from starvation and disease in their first year in Oklahoma territory.

More than 60 native nations were ultimately forced to leave the United States over the course of the nineteenth century. But even the territories beyond American borders provided for them by treaties that were to be in force "as long as the river flows and the grass grows," were taken back as soon as a sufficient number of white settlers demanded land or once corrupt government officials could maneuver a deal to their own advantage.

At the time Jefferson concluded negotiations for the purchase of Louisiana, there were already thousands of Indians, Cherokee, Choctaw, Chickasaw, Shawnee, Miami, and Delaware, living there who had been forced from their homelands further east. When Arkansas was officially designated a territory in 1819, most of its area was officially ceded to native peoples through various treaties in which they agreed to relinquish their claims to vast lands in the east for new areas in Arkansas. But just a couple years later, as soon as it was discovered that much of Arkansas was excellent land for cotton production, one of the most valuable crops in the world at that time, Congress pressured the native communities that they had just swapped lands with to sign new treaties surrendering these lands for ones even further west in Oklahoma, where cotton didn't grow well.

It wasn't just homesteaders and pioneers that coveted Indian lands, ambitious politicians and speculators hatched schemes to convert native territories into fortunes for themselves. For example, Arkansas territorial delegate (the equivalent of a U.S. member of the House of Representatives) Henry W. Conway, proposed to officials in Washington that for a payment of $50,000 the Quapaws could be induced to give up their tract of land in the northern part of the state. Conway also mentioned that he could then sell

YAHA-HAJO.
A SEMINOLE CHIEF.

Figure 5.7 Yaha-Hajo. A Seminole chief.

those lands for at least $500,000, implying that he would spread some of those profits around to those who helped him with his scheme. (The Quapaws were then extorted to sign away their lands for $17,000.)

Federal officials aided the theft and misappropriation of money allocated to comply with existing treaties. The treaty forcing the Choctaws to give up their valuable farming lands ordered that funds from the public sale of those lands be kept in trust by the government and used to aid the Choctaw people's difficult trek to Oklahoma. A fortune, $300,000 quickly accumulated in the account and these funds were deposited in a newly chartered Arkansas bank (most of whose directors were members of the Arkansas legislature who created it). The bank's directors used these funds to support their own businesses and land purchases, taking out large loans they never repaid. The Choctaw nation never received the bounty their lands had earned.

Seminole Wars

While all the efforts of federal and state governments in the South to take native lands were tied to the demands of slave owners to expand their empire, one struggle in particular highlighted the intersection of slavery and native dispossesion. Known as the "Seminole Wars" this title is a misnomer that obscures the important fact that for at least a century many people who escaped slavery headed south to Spanish Florida rather than north to British Canada and there became integrated into native tribes. In the 1700s, people who had stolen themselves out of slavery were known as "maroons" and they were powerful enough to keep both the Americans and the Spanish at bay.

Determined to destroy Seminole communities whose continued existence inspired slaves to run away from the expanding cotton lands of Alabama, Georgia and South Carolina, in 1812 the U.S. army invaded Florida to destroy what they then called Seminole refuges. A military disaster for the invaders from beginning to end, Seminole fighters routed the U.S. Marines, a defeat that kept the Americans at bay for another twenty years.

In 1835, President Jackson sent a second military expedition to crush Seminole independence. Planned as a three month campaign, Seminole resistance stretched it into a grinding seven-year war. American general Thomas Sidney Jessup wrote to Washington when the campaign began observing, "This you may be assured is a negro, not an Indian war." In the end, after 1,600 U.S. troops and an undocumented number of native and black fighters perished, the Seminoles were forced to agree to move west, beyond the borders of America to Indian territory.

Expanding Slavery into the Mississippi Delta

Securing the southeast from Florida to New Orleans not only opened up the vast fertile delta lands to cotton cultivation, it secured the defeat of the resistance of southeastern native peoples to encroachments on their lands. But these new lands required a tremendous amount of labor even to prepare them for cultivation. Forests had to be felled, stumps and stones torn and scratched out of fields, and roads and ditches dug. After 1807 it was no longer legal to import enslaved people directly from Africa (though every year smugglers would successfully bring more—the last being landed months before the Civil War broke out). But the traffic between states, within America, remained unrestricted and largely unregulated. As slavery's profitability had declined with the exhaustion of soils in the oldest states, like Virginia, Maryland, and the Carolinas, while the population of those held in bondage rapidly increased with rising fertility rates, brokers and traders exploited the imbalance and organized a complex network for transporting people to the west.

Figure 5.8 The Coffle Gang, 1864.

Between 1820 and 1860 more than a million enslaved people were sold, separated from family and friends, and forcibly driven to the new territories. Even founding father, James Madison, author of the Bill of Rights, faced with mounting debts in his old age, sold sixteen of the people he enslaved to a relative in Louisiana.

For hundreds of thousands of people their worst fears were realized as married couples were split apart and children were taken from parents. One recent estimate is that the forced movement of people in this period tore apart one-third of all married couples in bondage in the upper South. One-half of all people enslaved in the upper South experienced the loss of a spouse or a child to the interstate traffic.

Stories of husbands fighting to the death to avoid leaving their families, and mothers smothering their children rather than sending them away, began to circulate. Enslavers fearful of resistance if the impending separation of a loved one was known generally seized children when parents weren't nearby or shackled a husband or wife after they had been sent some distance on an "errand." As a result, few of those separated ever had the opportunity to say goodbye.

Such sights troubled even some who benefited from slavery. Just before the Civil War broke out Mary Chestnut, who followed events closely from her high vantage point in a rich South Carolina slave-holding family, wrote in her diary: "A mad woman, taken from her husband and children. Of course she was mad—or she would not have given 'her grief words' in that public place. Her keepers were along. What she said was rational enough—pathetic, at times heart-rending... It excited me so—I quickly took opium, and that I kept up..."

Most of those moved from seaboard states in the east to the Mississippi delta states were forced to walk the hundreds of miles to their destinations. Large groups of people were assembled and then chained at the neck and made to walk in file. These formations were known as "coffles" and became a common sight before the war that ended them.

A few large scale speculators operated their own fleets of coastal ships to transport enslaved people from eastern ports, especially Baltimore, to New Orleans. These ships, while not as large as the specially constructed ships that plied the "middle passage" from Africa to the Americas, were just as cramped with people chained below decks shoulder to shoulder in tiers less than two feet high.

An entire infrastructure had to be built in towns throughout the South to accommodate this movement of people. Major cities erected elaborate slave markets to conduct sales and towns throughout the South constructed "slave pens," jails that held people being transported overnight or longer if they were awaiting ships in harbor. A

Congressional panel described such "pens" as "dungeons" where people were "confined in their filth." Private speculators built so many of these jails in Natchez, Mississippi by 1833 that the townspeople complained of the noise and passed an ordinance requiring all new pens to be located outside the city limits.

A majority of whites did not own slaves and their stake in the system was not well grounded. While they enjoyed the benefits of believing themselves superior, these privileges did not put food on the table. While some whites were recruited into the slave system as overseers or guards and patrolmen of various types, most poor whites to a greater or lesser degree understood that the existence of slavery undermined their own wages and limited their job prospects. This was repeatedly made clear when the plots of slaves planning uprisings were revealed or betrayed and often involved poor white allies.

One institution that served to cement the interests of both slave-owners and poor whites who didn't possess slaves was the militia system. Service in the militia was a responsibility of white male citizens dating back to the American Revolution and continued as a tradition that prevented the tyranny of standing armies. The second amendment to the U.S. Constitution sanctioned this practice by declaring that "A well regulated Militia" was "necessary to the security of a free State" and therefore "the right of the people to keep and bear Arms, shall not be infringed."

In slave-holding areas (which it should be remembered every state except Vermont was when the Constitution was adopted) such militias principal duty was not to defend the borders against foreign invasion but to guard against slave revolts and to catch those escaping their bondage. Militia duty was a burden on the poor as militia members often had to pay for their own weapon and uniform and militia members had to muster, or assemble and drill, on certain designated 'muster days.' One victim of these militia musters remembered:

It was always the custom to have a muster every year. On that occasion every white man shouldered his musket. The citizens and the so-called country gentlemen wore military uniforms. The poor whites took their places in the ranks in every-day dress, some without shoes, some without hats….It was a grand opportunity for the low whites who had no negroes of their own to scourge. They exulted in such a chance to exercise a little brief authority, and show their subserviency to the slaveholders; not reflecting that the power which trampled on the colored people also kept themselves in poverty, ignorance, and moral degradation.

Those who never witnessed such scenes

can hardly believe what I know was inflicted at this time on innocent men, women, and children, against whom there was not the slightest ground for suspicion...The dwellings of the colored people, unless they happened to be protected by some influential white person, who was nigh at hand, were robbed of clothing and every-thing else the marauders thought worth carrying away. All day long these unfeeling wretches went round, like a troop of demons terrifying and tormenting the helpless. At night, they formed themselves into patrol bands, and went wherever they chose among the colored people, acting out their brutal will. Many women hid themselves in woods and swamps, to keep out of their way. If any of the husbands or fathers told of these outrages, they were tied up to the public whipping post, and cruelly scourged for telling lies about white men. The consternation was universal. No two people that had the slightest tinge of color in their faces dared to be seen talking together.

Slavery and Capitalism

One of the most common myths about slavery held by both scholars and the wider public was that slavery was a backward institution that lacked the innovation and entrepreneurial energy of northern industry. According to this myth, with each passing year slavery was falling behind economically to the dynamic free labor system of the North. Slavery, it is said, was becoming increasingly irrelevant to a modern, technological society and it was doomed to be overwhelmed and swept away by the rise of American capitalism. For a time, historians even debated whether the Civil War was unnecessary to ending slavery, as slavery was on the road to extinction due to its own inability to compete with modern business practices.

This longstanding myth, largely based on the idea that slavery could not compete with the free market because the capital invested in enslaved people could not be easily shifted or reallocated to take advantage of new opportunities, the same way employers could easily hire or fire employees who worked for a wage. Slaves, it was believed, were less productive than free workers because they had no incentives to exert themselves beyond the least effort they could get away with as they received no benefit from their labors. Wage workers, though poorly paid and insecure, were nonetheless motivated to work hard because they had opportunities to rise, to earn a raise, to win a promotion, or even to discover a better way of doing something and going into business for themselves.

Figure 5.9 Old Slave Market, Charleston, S. C.

Historians too fed this myth by describing capitalism as the opposite of slavery. Capitalism unlike slavery, scholars long argued, was an economic system that rapidly grew by allocating capital to its most productive uses and by innovating new financial arrangements that shared and limited risk among larger numbers of investors. Capitalism invented management techniques to measure the cost of labor and steadily improve its productivity.

New research has exploded these myths by documenting that slavery and capitalism were not opposites but allies. Innovations in financial markets such as the development of reserve banking and banking syndicates, state-guaranteed bonds, and new forms of insurance, were all primarily applied to the expansion of slavery in the nineteenth century. Modern scientific systems of personnel management were used more routinely and in a more sophisticated manner in the slave South than in the free North. Markets for slaves themselves became more standardized, more integrated nationally, and increasingly

"efficient" as time went on. In some ways the slave South was even more quick to adapt new technologies than the free North, as by the 1830s, more steam boats (one of the most advanced technologies of the day) plied the waters of slave states than free ones and many southern cities were adapting the steam engine to the pressing of cotton into bales and the refining of cane into sugar. By the eve of the Civil War, the South was rapidly catching up to the North in the size of its railroad network. Where the South had only about a quarter of the track the North did in 1850, a decade later it had increased its share to nearly a third. For the year of 1860, more new track was laid in the South than in the North.

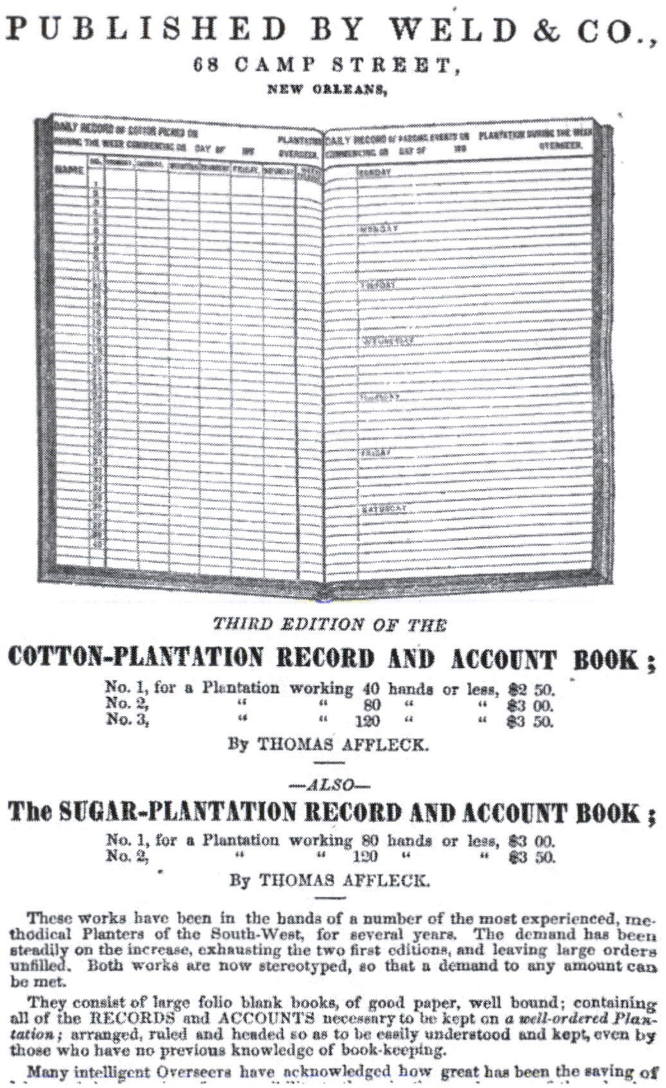

Contrary to the theories of economists, which were influenced by racist stereotypes of sluggish and lazy black workers and imagined slavery as a stagnant system, slavery proved able to innovate and even increase its productivity (a key measure of the amount of goods produced per unit of time worked). Remarkably, between 1800 and 1830, the productivity of workers held in bondage in agriculture quadrupled. This is an annual growth rate of approximately 5.5%, about double the rate for the rest of the century (2.8% from 1840-1900), a time that saw the introduction of new farm machinery including steam powered tractors. How was it that a period in which there were no new tools or machinery (the cotton gin was invented in 1793) grew far more quickly in terms of output per worker than a period in which the invention of new machinery and labor-saving devices was legendary?

Without new tools, machines, or other labor-saving devices, the only way to increase agricultural productivity was for the workers themselves to labor harder. Somehow agricultural laborers were made to work more intensively, to push themselves to dig, hoe, pick and carry more and to do so faster and without interruption over the course of a lengthening work day. People are generally driven to work harder one of two ways: by either increasing rewards for work (such as paying workers bonuses for reaching higher goals), or by threatening punishments for failing to meet rising quotas.

In areas where slavery had long existed, as in Virginia and other coastal states, over time the culture of elite society had set customary limits on the regime of discipline a master could employ without risking the disapproval of his or her friends and neighbors. People held in bondage used what little leverage they had to strike bargains between a small degree of autonomy and fulfilling their masters' demands. It was not uncommon in older communities rooted in slavery for masters to set aside plots for slaves to grow their own food, or allow them to keep their own chickens, or even work for neighbors for goods or cash they could keep. These arrangements grew more common, especially as the prices of many farm commodities dropped in the last

PUBLISHED BY WELD & CO.,

68 CAMP STREET,

NEW ORLEANS,

THIRD EDITION OF THE

COTTON-PLANTATION RECORD AND ACCOUNT BOOK ;

No. 1, for a Plantation working 40 hands or less, $2 50.
No. 2,   "   "   80   "   " $3 00.
No. 3,   "   "   120   "   " $3 50.

By THOMAS AFFLECK.

—ALSO—

The SUGAR-PLANTATION RECORD AND ACCOUNT BOOK ;

No. 1, for a Plantation working 80 hands or less, $3 00.
No. 2,   "   "   120   "   " $3 50.

By THOMAS AFFLECK.

These works have been in the hands of a number of the most experienced, methodical Planters of the South-West, for several years. The demand has been steadily on the increase, exhausting the two first editions, and leaving large orders unfilled. Both works are now stereotyped, so that a demand to any amount can be met.

They consist of large folio blank books, of good paper, well bound; containing all of the RECORDS and ACCOUNTS necessary to be kept on *a well-ordered Plantation*; arranged, ruled and headed so as to be easily understood and kept, even by those who have no previous knowledge of book-keeping.

Many intelligent Overseers have acknowledged how great has been the saving of

Figure 5.10 Record book for calculating how much cotton enslaved people harvested each day.

decades of the eighteenth century and there was no quick profit to be made by driving workers to exhaustion.

But with the new economics of cotton and the opening of vast western lands to slavery, the old bargains were quickly broken. Plantations carved out of the wilderness in the west tended to be isolated from the community norms that placed some weak restraints on the actions of masters and overseers. Worse, as most everyone rushing to set up farms in the newly opened lands were speculators and profit-seekers interested in getting rich quickly rather than setting down roots and building stable communities, the culture of these places was harsh and violent, more like that of western boom-towns than that of the gentrified parishes of Virginia or Maryland.

Speculators setting up plantations in Mississippi, Alabama, or Louisiana could make fantastic profits in a relatively short time if they could force those they enslaved to work to the very ends of human endurance. This they learned they could do by tying a worker's daily output to the threat of physical torture. At harvest time the amount of cotton each laborer picked was weighed and anyone falling below some set quota was tied to a post and mercilessly beaten with a whip. Whipping became not a punishment for bad or insubordinate behavior, but a production tool that made possible the pushing of men, women, and children to unimaginable levels of effort.

Under American slavery, there were practically no limits on what cruel things an owner could do to the people he held in bondage. Only one state, Louisiana, because of its French and Spanish legal tradition, that provided some rights to slaves and some limits on enslavers' behavior, even bothered to include in its legal code a prohibition on cruel punishments. Louisiana's law bared punishments performed with "unusual rigor...so as to maim or mutilate him, or expose him to the danger of loss of life, or to cause his death." The penalty for an infraction was a fine, not a jail sentence. (In contrast, someone who cruelly beat a horse or mule to death in Louisiana was subject to a six month jail sentence.)

However, even this weak law contained several large loopholes that effectively rendered it useless. One was that all beatings performed with "a whip, leather thong, switch or small stick" were legal. The other was that the punishment had to be "unusual" which quickly ceased to be the case once the cotton economy grew up. Other state courts, like North Carolina's in the famed case of *State v. Mann* (1829), specifically ruled that owners could not be punished for assault or battery against the people they enslaved because the absolute power of the master was necessary "to render the submission of the slave perfect." Over the entire course of slavery in the nineteenth century only a handful of masters, most of them free blacks themselves, were ever held to account for cruelty, even torture and murder, before

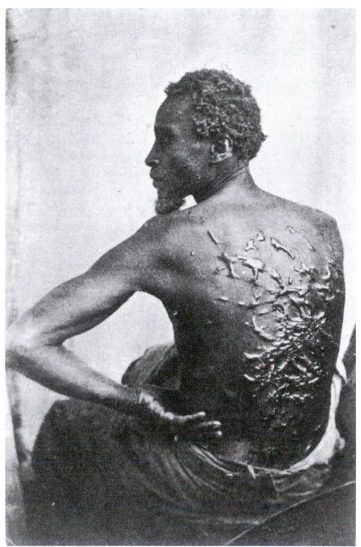

Figure 5.11 "The Scourged Back - The furrowed and scarred back of Gordon, a slave who escaped from his master in Mississippi and made his way to a Union Army encampment in Baton Rouge, Louisiana, 1863."

the courts.

It is nearly impossible for anyone today to appreciate the daily cruelties that were a routine element of slavery. Masters summoned enslaved people the same way they called animals, with shrill whistles. Larger plantation households were known to keep a stock of "gagging irons," bands of metal that were locked around a cook's head and prevented her eating the food she prepared.

One southern farming magazine contained the following suggestions for slave masters:

> In the management of negroes there should always be perfect uniformity of conduct towards them; that is, you should not be too rigid in your discipline at one time and too lax at another. They should understand that real faults will not go unpunished; but at the same time moderate

punishment, with a certainty of its succeeding a fault, is much more efficient in producing good conduct, than severe punishments irregularly inflicted…It is the certainty of punishment, and not its severity, which deters misconduct…

On the eve of the Civil War slavery was the central economic institution in the United States and its most valuable asset. The collective value of all the men, women, and children held in bondage was more than the combined worth of all the nation's factories, railroads, and banks. The number of enslaved people had grown to exceed one-third the entire population of the American south. As a consequence, the South was where most of the nation's wealthiest people lived; two-thirds of all Americans with estates worth more than $100,000 lived in the South.

Slave Resistance

Such cruelties and denial of the basic humanity of women and men could not go on for long without provoking organized and violent resistance. Armed rebellions of enslaved people were a regular occurance throughout the age of slavery, but became more daring and far-reaching as the frontier of slavery expanded.

In 1800 Gabriel, an enslaved blacksmith who secured his own jobs and paid a share to his owner, organized a network of other slaves across Virginia and laid plans to militarily seize the city of Richmond. Unlike many other rebels against slavery who were religiously inspired, Gabriel and his fellow conspirators saw themselves as "democrats" carrying out the promise of the American Revolution, even preparing to carry a banner inscribed "Death or Liberty." When one of their fellow rebels betrayed them, state authorities rounded them up and swiftly executed twenty-five men including Gabriel. Virginia's leaders were deeply alarmed by the breadth of Gabriel's conspiracy and were most upset by Gabriel's expectation that poor white Virginians would join him, which was a dire threat to their racial order. On the gallows, one of the rebels cried out: "I have ventured my life…to obtain the liberty of my countrymen." Though Gabriel and his fellow rebels paid the ultimate price, his organizing work spawned two subsequent rebellions over the next several years and forced Virginia's legislature to seriously debate and come close to passing a law gradually outlawing slavery in the state.

Gabriel's plans for rebellion were still a fresh memory when the enslaved people of the island of Haiti, led by the slave rebel Toussaint L'Ouverture, successfully overthrew French rule and defeated a large French army to establish the independent republic of Haiti in 1804. Whites refused to recognize the military achievements of L'Ouverture and his black army, as doing so would destroy their docile image

Figure 5.12 Illustration in, *Authentic and Impartial Narrative of the Tragical Scene which was witnessed in Southampton County* (New York, 1831).

of the people they held in chains. A Philadelphia newspaper typically described the Haitian military victory as the result of environment rather than Haitian resolve: "It is not to the military skill alone of this negro population, that this effectual defeat of a powerful and inveterate adversary should be attributed; the nature of the climate, with the inevitable severities of the service, induced diseases, rapidly extended them throughout the army and rendered them peculiarly fatal."

In 1822, a free black carpenter, Denmark Vesey, who had managed to scrimp and save and finally purchase himself, prepared an elaborate plan to revolt and sail for Haiti. Vesey spent four years planning and crafting weapons regularly preaching to the enslaved, reading the story of Moses and the exodus from the Bible. Before Vesey's plans were exposed, he had established a network of hundreds of allies and even written to the Haitian government seeking aid.

Of the hundreds of plots and rebellions against slavery, none did more to strike fear into the hearts of enslavers than the uprising lead by Nat Turner. On a summer Sunday evening in 1831, Nat Turner, a man enslaved on a Virginia plantation, gathered with six of his most trusted friends in wooded area away from white ears and agreed to rebel. Turner had been dreaming of this day for years, to the point of having prophetic visions that charged his actions with divine authority. The men broke into Turner's master's house and slayed the family of five with axes and hatchets. Arming themselves with a few old muskets and some horses, they moved from farm to farm, picking up recruits along the way. Over the next forty-eight hours the rebel band, that had grown to about two dozen, attacked a dozen farms and killed 58 whites, many of them children. The band fought a brief skirmish with a militia unit, held their own and moved on to another plantation where they encountered determined and organized resistance that scattered the rebels and led to the capture of many. A few, including Nat Turner, eluded their pursuers for weeks, while white militia units terrorized the region, indiscriminately torturing and killing any black person, free or slave, who seemed the least bit suspicious to them.

One militia unit in hot pursuit of a reported rebel encountered Alfred, an enslaved blacksmith, along the road, and wanting to interrogate him but not having time to do so, slashed the tendons in his legs so he could not walk and left him. A second unit arriving a short time later, shot Alfred on the spot, severed his head and put it on a roadside pike as a warning to others. That road that runs near Courtland, Virginia, still carries the name "Blackhead Signpost Road."

Turner himself was not captured until late October, and was held for less than a week before he was executed, just long enough for a writer to record his confession.

After he was hanged, Nat Turner's body was carved up for souvenirs and wallets and other leather goods were made from his skin.

While maintaining their public belief that blacks were simple, childlike, and contented with their status, after Nat Turner's rebellion southerners quickly moved to reinforce their ability to police black people and to further restrict their activities. Virginia promptly prohibited teaching any black person, free or slave, to read or write, black people were banned from holding religious services at night, and the printing or circulating of any publications advocating against slavery was criminalized. A bill to expel all free blacks from the state of Virginia failed by a handful of votes, though one prohibiting entry into the state passed (as did similar laws in Maryland, Tennessee, Louisiana, Alabama, and Delaware). Georgia limited to seven the number of black people who could attend church together which was two more than Alabama allowed. North Carolina outlawed black preachers completely. Most southern states moved to prohibit free black people from possessing firearms. In addition to all of these, South Carolina also restricted free black people from working as salespersons in any shop, store, or trading post.

Myths of the Civil War

Few events in American history are as important or as misunderstood as the Civil War. Northerners have long thought of the war as a glorious undertaking to free slaves while southerners have described it as an act of northern aggression against their states' rights as guaranteed in the Constitution. In an odd twist of reality, both views contradict what their own heroes said and did at the time. Northern politicians, most notably Abraham Lincoln, disavowed any intention of interfering with slavery where it existed. Southern statesmen just as loudly proclaimed their struggle was not to defend some abstract constitutional interpretation but to defend and strengthen slavery. In hindsight, with the bloody war behind them, both sides found it convenient to misinterpret what they stood for when the war began. Once the war destroyed slavery, northerners pretended that was always their glorious mission. Once they were defeated, southerners tried to invest their Lost Cause with more legal and principled spirit than it actually had. Both sides are mirror images of each other in their refusal to recognize that slavery was actually destroyed by enslaved people themselves.

Abraham Lincoln was considered a racial radical by the standards of his day. But this did not mean that he believed in any sort of equality between races. Rather, he shared many of the racial beliefs common to whites at this time. During his famous debate with Stephen Douglas, his challenger for the Senate in 1858, Lincoln declared:

> I am not, nor ever have been, in favor of bringing
> about in any way the social and political equal-
> ity of the white and black races, that I am not,
> nor ever have been, in favor of making voters or
> jurors of negroes, nor of qualifying them to hold
> office, nor to intermarry with white people; and
> I will say in addition to this that there is a physi-
> cal difference between the white and black races
> which I believe will forever forbid the two races
> living together on terms of social and political
> equality ... I will add to this that I have never
> seen, to my knowledge, a man, woman, or child
> who was in favor of producing a perfect equality,
> social and political, between negroes and white
> men.

When he ran for President in 1860, Lincoln was not an abolitionist, but instead stood for limiting slavery to the states in which it currently thrived, and reserving new territories, such as Kansas, for free settlers. At the same time southern slave-owners were more aggressively demanding ever greater federal guarantees that slavery would be supported and protected. Southern politicians pushed Congress to establish slave codes for territories that didn't protect the interests of slave-owners, to lift the federal ban on the international slave trade, to purchase Cuba from Spain and eventually make it a slave state, and for stricter laws that enhanced their ability to pursue and reclaim any people who escaped to the north.

For the first time, because of the faster growing population in the north that gave them more seats in Congress, northern politicians managed to block such measures and in response leading southerners, shocked at not having their way in Washington, began advocating their states secede from the union as the best course of defending slavery. Tensions escalated quickly as evidenced by one Senate debate in February of 1858 that ended with a an all-out brawl that included some thirty Senators throwing punches in the Senate chamber. By the following year most Congressmen began coming to sessions armed. One observer said at the time: "the only persons who do not have a revolver and a knife are those who have two revolvers."

Lincoln won the most votes, but not a majority of them, in a three-way race that saw the Democratic party split and the Republicans unite. Lincoln repeatedly reassured the nation that neither he nor his party had any intention of attacking slavery. He called it an "unmixed and unmitigated falsehood" that he wanted to alter slavery in any way. In one letter to a Chicago editor Lincoln explained, "I have declared a thousand times and now repeat that, in my opinion, neither the General Government, nor any other power outside of the slave states, can constitutionally or rightfully interfere with slaves or slavery where it already exists."

In the months between the presidential election in November and Lincoln's inauguration in March, seven southern states officially left the United States and formed the Confederate States of America and Congress considered a package of measures intended to lure them back into the union. Northern politicians offered to amend the U.S. Constitution to protect slavery in all the territories in the southwest (including any future conquests of Central America), to prohibit the federal government from abolishing slavery in D.C. or any federal facility or to restrict the interstate slave trade, and to provide at public expense federal compensation of slave-owners who could not recover their escaped slaves due to local opposition. Republicans narrowly defeated this attempt to enshrine slavery into the U.S. Constitution for all time, a provision that ironically would have been the 13th amendment.

When a South Carolina state convention voted to secede from the union its declaration made it clear that its sole reason for doing so was to protect the institution of slavery:

> We affirm that these ends for which this Gov-
> ernment was instituted have been defeated, and
> the Government itself has been made destruc-
> tive of them by the action of the non slave-
> holding States. Those States have assumed the
> right of deciding upon the propriety of our do-
> mestic institutions; and have denied the rights
> of property established in fifteen of the States
> and recognized by the Constitution; they have
> denounced as sinful the institution of Slavery;
> they have permitted the open establishment
> among them of societies, whose avowed object
> is to disturb the peace and to eloign [take away]
> the property of the citizens of other States. They
> have encouraged and assisted thousands of our
> slaves to leave their homes; and those who re-
> main, have been incited by emissaries, books
> and pictures to servile insurrection.
>
> On the 4th March next this party will take
> possession of the Government. It has an-
> nounced that the South shall be excluded from
> the common Territory; that the Judicial Tri-
> bunals shall be made sectional, and that a war
> must be waged against slavery until it shall cease
> throughout the United States...

Mississippi, in its formal statement of secession, took an even less legalistic approach and simply appealed to the

FREEDOM TO THE SLAVES
Proclaimed January 1st 1863, by ABRAHAM LINCOLN, President of the United States.
"Proclaim liberty throughout All the land unto All the inhabitants thereof" ___ LEV XXV 10.

Figure 5.13 "Freedom to the slaves," lithograph by Currier & Ives, probably between 1863 and 1870.

importance of slavery to their economy:

Our position is thoroughly identified with the institution of slavery—the greatest material interest of the world. Its labor supplies the product which constitutes by far the largest and most important portions of the commerce of the earth. These products are peculiar to the climate verging on the tropical regions, and by an imperious law of nature, none but the black race can bear exposure to the tropical sun. These products have become necessities of the world, and a blow at slavery is a blow at commerce and civilization. That blow has been long aimed at the institution, and was at the point of reaching its consummation. There was no choice left us but submission to the mandates of abolition, or a dissolution of the Union, whose principles had been subverted to work out our ruin.

Alexander H. Stephens, after being elected the provisional vice president of the Confederate States of America, told the convention gathered at Montgomery that "...African slavery as it exists among us—the proper status of the Negro in our form of civilization. This was the immediate cause of the late rupture and present revolution."

On April 12, 1865, Confederate batteries in Charleston, South Carolina, opened fire on a federal fort in the Charleston harbor, Fort Sumter. Within a week four more states seceded to the Confederacy. The day after the attack on Fort Sumter, Lincoln called up 75,000 state militia to serve a period of 90 days. Though thousands of black citizens rushed to enlist in the northern states, they were refused the opportunity to serve.

President Lincoln made it clear, in both words and deeds, that the war was not aimed at destroying the institution of slavery or of white supremacy. In August his commander in the Missouri district, General John C. Fremont, issued an order freeing the slaves of any individuals rebelling against the government. Lincoln reversed Fremont's order and then fired him for taking an action that would "alarm our Southern Union friends, and turn them against us." Six months later Lincoln's Secretary of War included in his annual report a proposal to begin enlisting black soldiers. Lincoln ordered the passage rescinded. The following May General James H. Lane was denied permission to begin recruiting escaped slaves and native peoples into his First Kansas Volunteer regiment. (General Lane defied orders and did so anyway.) Then a week later, General David Hunter commanding troops in coastal Georgia, issued a field order declaring slaves in his district free and encouraging their enlistment. Lincoln immediately annulled both of General Hunter's orders. At a July cabinet meeting, Lincoln continued to oppose enlisting and arming black troops, a step he said "would be productive of more evil than good."

With his usual depth of insight, Frederick Douglass summed up the situation at the war's beginning as acutely as one could: "It was begun, I say, in the interest of slavery on both sides. The South was fighting to take slavery out of the Union, and the North fighting to keep it in the Union; the South fighting to get it beyond the limits of the United-States Constitution, and the North fighting to retain it within those limits; the South fighting for new guarantees, and the North fighting for the old guarantees;—both despising the Negro, both insulting the Negro."

As the war dragged on and as the numbers of casualties mounted, Lincoln took the unpopular step of issuing his Emancipation Proclamation which was initially released in a draft form in the hopes it would not have to take effect. It was essentially an ultimatum to the rebel states: either quit and return to the union and keep your slaves, or

Figure 15.14 Contrabands Aboard U.S. Ship Vermont, Port Royal, South Carolina, 1861.

continue fighting and risk losing them. By issuing a draft of the proposed emancipation order two months prior to making it effective, Lincoln was giving the South time to salvage slavery. Moreover, the proclamation did not end slavery anywhere but in those areas in rebellion, preserving slavery for the million people held in bondage in the border states of Kentucky, Maryland, Delaware and Missouri.

In between the time Lincoln issued his draft Emancipation Proclamation and when it was to go into effect, Lincoln issued his second annual message to Congress (Dec. 1862) and he devoted the bulk of it to advocating for a Constitutional Amendment to end the Civil War and the crisis of slavery. Lincoln's proposed constitutional amendment offered to pay slave owners for freeing their slaves. It was clearly motivated by his desire to end the war and restore the union. But reading more deeply into his remarks reveals that it was also part of his belief that America was, and should always remain, a white nation. In short, this "Thirteenth Amendment" was a solution not only to the intractable problem of slavery and the rebellion and war it caused, but to the problem of a white country possessing a large population of blacks. When Lincoln defended his plan by observing that "there is great diversity of sentiment and of policy in regard to slavery and the African race amongst us" he recognized this.

Lincoln proposed a slow road to emancipation—thirty-seven years before slavery was to be abolished—not only because he hoped the South might consider such a conservative policy, but also because he believed that black people were not fit for freedom and had no other place in America. "[This] emancipation will be unsatisfactory to the advocates of perpetual slavery, but the length of time should greatly mitigate their dissatisfaction. The time spares both races from the evils of sudden derangement... it really gives them [slaves] much. It saves them from the vagrant destitution which must largely attend immediate emancipation in localities where their numbers are very great..."

Besides ending the war, Lincoln advocated gradual emancipation because it would reduce the number of black people in the country by encouraging their emigration. "I can not make it better known than it already is that I strongly favor colonization," Lincoln wrote. He boasted that his administration had been actively pressuring countries in the "Tropics" and European nations that have "tropical" colonies, to accept America's black emigrants. But, Lincoln complained, only Liberia in Africa and Haiti in the Caribbean were willing to accept black American "colonists" and, more troubling, black Americans were not clamoring to leave.

Black leaders opposed such colonization schemes as

they struggled to claim belonging in a nation whose majority of people didn't want them as fellow citizens. In order to justify their place in America they pointed out an obvious but much overlooked and denied fact—black Americans were Americans and shared more culturally with the majority than they did with Africa.

After Lincoln issued his preliminary Emancipation Proclamation in September, the Democrats rallied opposition to it and to Lincoln's party. A favorite Democratic slogan in the midterm election that year was "the Constitution as it is; the Union as it was; the Negroes where they are." Republicans replied by branding Democrats the party of "Dixie, Davis and the Devil." The 1862 Congressional elections proved a defeat for Lincoln's administration and in many ways a popular rejection of the Emancipation Proclamation. Rolling to victory the Democrats gained 32 seats in the House and took over two state assemblies, one in Indiana and one in Lincoln's home state of Illinois.

But Lincoln stuck to his plan, not primarily out of sentimental concern for those chained, but because he learned from his generals that the war that began with his promise not to change the institution of slavery where it was rooted had become a war that could only be won by

doing so. Over the course of the war's first year as Union forces advanced on the periphery of slaveholding regions, tens of thousands of men, women and children fled their captivity by crossing into Yankee army camps. At first local military commanders were ordered by Lincoln's generals to return these "fugitives" to their owners who claimed them. But soon it became obvious that the actions of these brave and hopeful people were the key to victory.

This fact was first pointed out by the pioneering scholar W.E.B. Du Bois in 1934. Du Bois observed that the Confederate army and the Confederate cause was utterly dependent on southern enslaved labor. Slavery allowed a larger proportion of the white male population to join the army without disrupting the essential production of goods. Though the South had less than a quarter of the white population of the North, it was at the start of the war able to field an army of the same size. But even this seeming parity is deceptive as southern armies had a larger proportion of their soldiers in combat units, as most of the support work of hauling goods, digging trenches, pitching camp, and cooking rations were done by slaves—work that soldiers did in northern units.

Northern generals seized on the opportunity to

Figure 5.15 Black Soldier in Camp, photo possibly by Alexander Gardner, 1863.

supplement the number of workers performing the jobs essential to keep their armies moving, armed, and fed. They stopped calling the people who escaped to their camps "fugitives" and started calling them "contrabands," as in rebel property that they could legally seize. Each "contraband" that escaped was one more worker for the union war effort and one less for the rebels. Without slaves to do their dirty work, fewer Confederate soldiers were available to do the actual fighting and without enslaved farm workers back home, there were fewer crops to eat and less cotton to sell abroad to purchase arms. Lincoln's cabinet turned a blind eye to the practice of employing runaways in support of the army, neither authorizing or prohibiting it. Radicals in Congress pushed through a bill in July, 1862, granting permission to the army to do what they were quietly doing already. By the summer of 1864, Lincoln's War Department reported that 41,150 former slaves were employed in the service of their armies. Another 72,500 had fled behind union lines and most of these, 62,300 of them, had been resettled into self-supporting communities. (The remainder who were directly dependent on the government for support were children, elderly, and the sick.)

As the war dragged on and as the numbers of casualties mounted, the number of people volunteering for service dwindled and the federal government was forced to pass a conscription law to fill the army. The law was much hated, especially because it exempted anyone who could hire a substitute or pay a $300 bounty. Over 160,000 men would eventually dodge this hated draft. It was not, however, the first draft in American history. The South began forcing its young men into the Confederate army a year earlier. Like the north's draft it was biased to favor the social elite: a man was exempted if he provided a substitute or owned more than 20 slaves.

Conscription uncovered the depths of white attitudes against a war that had turned into a campaign against slavery. On July 13, 1863, as the first names of those on the draft lists were being announced, New York City erupted into violence. Mobs targeted both symbols of federal power and wealth, but, especially, African Americans who symbolized the equality they did not favor. Mobs lynched a dozen black men and burned the Colored Orphan Asylum to the ground. This uprising, one of the deadliest urban riots in American history, was finally put down by federal troops at a cost of over a hundred lives. New York City bought off future dissent by agreeing to budget two million dollars to pay for the bounties of its poor residents.

Conscription was only half the solution to the north's dwindling forces, the other came five days following Lincoln's final Emancipation Proclamation. On January 6, 1863, the Secretary of War granted the request of the Governor of Massachusetts to accept black volunteers into a combat regiment. This was not the first time black soldiers had lined up and fought to destroy slavery.

Local commanders had several times raised companies of black soldiers on their own initiative in defiance of Washington. In the summer of 1862 General John W. Phelps, who defended the approaches to New Orleans, armed some of the men who had escaped bondage and fled to his lines. The War Department ordered him to use these recruits only for "cutting wood." Phelps immediately submitted his letter of resignation, writing, "I am willing to prepare African regiments for the defense of the government against its assailants. I am not willing to become the mere slave-driver which you propose, have no qualifications in that way." A month later Phelps' fellow commander, General Benjamin Butler, pressed hard by the advance of southern forces on Baton Rouge, welcomed the volunteering of a regiment of free-black soldiers, who were initially organized into the Confederate Army and switched sides as soon as the Yankees arrived.

General Hunter whose unreinforced contingent of

Figure 5.16 Willis Winn, a former slave, with horn with which slaves were called, near Marshall, Texas.

just 11,000 men were stretched to patrol hundreds of miles of coastline from Florida to the Carolinas, told his superiors in Washington that he was "forming a Negro regiment, and compelling every able-bodied black man in the department to fight for the freedom which could not but be the issue of our war." The War Department immediately sent a message asking Hunter to clarify whether he was defying orders and raising a troop of fugitives. Hunter replied, "No regiment of 'fugitive slaves' has been, or is being, organized in this department. There is, however, a fine regiment of loyal persons whose late masters are fugitive rebels." Washington asked no more questions and let the matter drop, though the Confederate government hearing of Hunter's action declared him subject to immediate execution upon capture.

After Lincoln's administration gave permission to recruit black troops, states had difficulty organizing them as quickly as they had volunteers. There can be no question that the 186,017 black troops organized into 154 regiments turned the tide of the war and secured the Union's victory. Their freedom was not bestowed on them but was hard won.

While slavery allowed Europe to become liberal and modern, it won America its independence and conquered its westward empire. It shaped Americans' outlook, thinking, values, and culture more than any other single factor. Slavery influenced every aspect of the young American republic, from its geography to its federal political structure to its conception of private property. More than a century and a half since slavery was legally abolished, its traces can still easily be found in both the South and the North, if one knows where to look.

Its imprint remains in our national symbols and rituals. The National Anthem, for example, was written by a man, Francis Scott Key, who kept many men and women in bondage himself and believed that African Americans, free or slave, had no place in America and was an early advocate of shipping them all to Africa. Though Key over the course of his life freed a handful of the people he enslaved, unlike many national leaders of his generation, Key did not provide for freeing any slaves upon his death, rather leaving them to his wife. When the Civil War broke out all of Key's family and descendants supported the Confederate cause.

The lyrics Key wrote in 1814 to an old English drinking song ("Ode to Anacreon"), renamed the *Star-Spangled Banner*, reflect the fact that this song was written during a war with England, largely over the right of Americans to dispossess native peoples in the western territories the English empire still controlled. Buried in the never-sung third verse of Key's anthem is a line reflecting his age's commitment to slavery:

No refuge could save the hireling and slave
From the terror of flight or the gloom of the grave,
And the star-spangled banner in triumph doth wave
O'er the land of the free and the home of the brave.

Key's lyric referred to a British regiment of black soldiers, formerly enslaved, who had been recruited on the promise of their freedom. Just as had been true a generation before during America's war for independence, it was once again fighting men who were themselves fighting for their literal freedom. To Key, like most white men of his time, America was their land, a land for and of free white men at war with those who would unbind the Africans they kept as their property.

ETHIOPIA SALUTING THE COLORS

WHO are you, dusky woman, so ancient, hardly human,
With your woolly white and turban'd head and bare, bony feet?
Why, rising by the roadside here, do you the colors greet?

('Tis while our army lines, Carolina's sands and pines,
Forth from thy hovel door thou Ethiopia com'st to me,
As under doughty Sherman I march toward the sea.)

Me master years a hundred since from my parents sunder'd
A little child they caught me as the savage beast is caught,
Then hither me across the sea the cruel slaver brought.

No further does she say, but lingering all the day,
Her high borne turban'd head she wags and rolls her darkling eye,
And courtesies to the regiments the guidons moving by.

What is it, fateful woman, so blear, hardly human?
Why wag your head with turban bound yellow, red and green?
Are the things so strange and marvelous you see or have seen?

--Walt Whitman (1867)

President Abraham Lincoln's Inaugural Address, March 4, 1861

In compliance with a custom as old as the Government itself, I appear before you to address you briefly and to take in your presence the oath prescribed by the Constitution of the United States to be taken by the President "before he enters on the execution of this office."

I do not consider it necessary at present for me to discuss those matters of administration about which there is no special anxiety or excitement.

Apprehension seems to exist among the people of the Southern States that by the accession of a Republican Administration their property and their peace and personal security are to be endangered. There has never been any reasonable cause for such apprehension. Indeed, the most ample evidence to the contrary has all the while existed and been open to their inspection. It is found in nearly all the published speeches of him who now addresses you. I do but quote from one of those speeches when I declare that--I have no purpose, directly or indirectly, to interfere with the institution of slavery in the States where it exists. I believe I have no lawful right to do so, and I have no inclination to do so.

Those who nominated and elected me did so with full knowledge that I had made this and many similar declarations and had never recanted them; and more than this, they placed in the platform for my acceptance, and as a law to themselves and to me, the clear and emphatic resolution which I now read:

'Resolved', That the maintenance inviolate of the rights of the States, and especially the right of each State to order and control its own domestic institutions according to its own judgment exclusively, is essential to that balance of power on which the perfection and endurance of our political fabric depend; and we denounce the lawless invasion by armed force of the soil of any State or Territory, no matter what pretext, as among the gravest of crimes.

I now reiterate these sentiments, and in doing so I only press upon the public attention the most conclusive evidence of which the case is susceptible that the property, peace, and security of no section are to be in any wise endangered by the now incoming Administration. I add, too, that all the protection which, consistently with the Constitution and the laws, can be given will be cheerfully given to all the States when lawfully demanded, for whatever cause--as cheerfully to one section as to another.

There is much controversy about the delivering up of fugitives from service or labor. The clause I now read is as plainly written in the Constitution as any other of its provisions:

No person held to service or labor in one State, under the laws thereof, escaping into another, shall in consequence of any law or regulation therein be discharged from such service or labor, but shall be delivered up on claim of the party to whom such service or labor may be due.

It is scarcely questioned that this provision was intend-

ed by those who made it for the reclaiming of what we call fugitive slaves; and the intention of the lawgiver is the law. All members of Congress swear their support to the whole Constitution--to this provision as much as to any other. To the proposition, then, that slaves whose cases come within the terms of this clause "shall be delivered up" their oaths are unanimous. Now, if they would make the effort in good temper, could they not with nearly equal unanimity frame and pass a law by means of which to keep good that unanimous oath?

There is some difference of opinion whether this clause should be enforced by national or by State authority, but surely that difference is not a very material one. If the slave is to be surrendered, it can be of but little consequence to him or to others by which authority it is done. And should anyone in any case be content that his oath shall go unkept on a merely unsubstantial controversy as to 'how' it shall be kept?... [But] in any law upon this subject ought not all the safeguards of liberty known in civilized and humane jurisprudence to be introduced, so that a free man be not in any case surrendered as a slave?...

It is seventy-two years since the first inauguration of a President under our National Constitution. During that period fifteen different and greatly distinguished citizens have in succession administered the executive branch of the Government...I now enter upon the same task for the brief constitutional term of four years under great and peculiar difficulty. A disruption of the Federal Union, heretofore only menaced, is now formidably attempted....

I hold that in contemplation of universal law and of the Constitution the Union of these States is perpetual...It follows from these views that no State upon its own mere motion can lawfully get out of the Union...and that acts of violence within any State or States against the authority of the United States are insurrectionary or revolutionary, according to circumstances....

One section of our country believes slavery is 'right' and ought to be extended, while the other believes it is 'wrong' and ought not to be extended. This is the only substantial dispute. The fugitive-slave clause of the Constitution and the law for the suppression of the foreign slave trade are each as well enforced, perhaps, as any law can ever be in a community where the moral sense of the people imperfectly supports the law itself. The great body of the people abide by the dry legal obligation in both cases, and a few break over in each. This, I think, can not be perfectly cured, and it would be worse in both cases 'after' the separation of the sections than before. The foreign slave trade, now imperfectly suppressed, would be ultimately revived without restriction in one section, while fugitive slaves, now only partially surrendered, would not be surrendered at all by the other....

....I understand a proposed amendment to the Constitution--which amendment, however, I have not seen--has passed Congress, to the effect that the Federal Government shall never interfere with the domestic institutions of the

States, including that of persons held to service. To avoid misconstruction of what I have said, I depart from my purpose not to speak of particular amendments so far as to say that, holding such a provision to now be implied constitutional law, I have no objection to its being made express and irrevocable.

....Such of you as are now dissatisfied still have the old Constitution unimpaired, and, on the sensitive point, the laws of your own framing under it; while the new Administration will have no immediate power, if it would, to change either. If it were admitted that you who are dissatisfied hold the right side in the dispute, there still is no single good reason for precipitate action. Intelligence, patriotism, Christianity, and a firm reliance on Him who has never yet forsaken this favored land are still competent to adjust in the best way all our present difficulty.

In 'your' hands, my dissatisfied fellow-countrymen, and not in 'mine', is the momentous issue of civil war. The Government will not assail 'you'. You can have no conflict without being yourselves the aggressors. 'You' have no oath registered in heaven to destroy the Government, while I shall have the most solemn one to "preserve, protect, and defend it."

I am loath to close. We are not enemies, but friends. We must not be enemies. Though passion may have strained it must not break our bonds of affection. The mystic chords of memory, stretching from every battlefield and patriot grave to every living heart and hearthstone all over this broad land, will yet swell the chorus of the Union, when again touched, as surely they will be, by the better angels of our nature.

Figure 5.17 Harry Stephens and his family photgraphed after the Civil War. Stephens and his family were once enslaved by Alexander H. Stephens, once vice-president of the Confederate States and, at the time of this photograph, a U.S. Senator.

"Cornerstone Speech" by Alexander H. Stephens, Vice-President of the Confederacy,
March 21, 1861, Savannah, Georgia

The new constitution has put at rest, forever, all the agitating questions relating to our peculiar institution African slavery as it exists amongst us the proper status of the negro in our form of civilization. This was the immediate cause of the late rupture and present revolution. Jefferson in his forecast, had anticipated this, as the "rock upon which the old Union would split." He was right. What was conjecture with him, is now a realized fact. But whether he fully comprehended the great truth upon which that rock stood and stands, may be doubted. The prevailing ideas entertained by him and most of the leading statesmen at the time of the formation of the old constitution, were that the enslavement of the African was in violation of the laws of nature; that it was wrong in principle, socially, morally, and politically. It was an evil they knew not well how to deal with, but the general opinion of the men of that day was that, somehow or other in the order of Providence, the institution would be evanescent and pass away. This idea, though not incorporated in the constitution, was the prevailing idea at that time. The constitution, it is true, secured every essential guarantee to the institution while it should last, and hence no argument can be justly urged against the constitutional guarantees thus secured, because of the common sentiment of the day. Those ideas, however, were fundamentally wrong. They rested upon the assumption of the equality of races. This was an error. It was a sandy foundation, and the government built upon it fell when the "storm came and the wind blew."

Our new government is founded upon exactly the opposite idea; its foundations are laid, its corner- stone rests, upon the great truth that the negro is not equal to the white man; that slavery subordination to the superior race is his natural and normal condition. This, our new government, is the first, in the history of the world, based upon this great physical, philosophical, and moral truth. This truth has been slow in the process of its development, like all other truths in the various departments of science. It has been so even amongst us. Many who hear me, perhaps, can recollect well, that this truth was not generally admitted, even within their day. The errors of the past generation still clung to many as late as twenty years ago. Those at the North, who still cling to these errors, with a zeal above knowledge, we justly denominate fanatics…

In the conflict thus far, success has been on our side, complete throughout the length and breadth of the Confederate States. It is upon this, as I have stated, our social fabric is firmly planted; and I cannot permit myself to doubt the ultimate success of a full recognition of this principle throughout the civilized and enlightened world.

As I have stated, the truth of this principle may be slow in development, as all truths are and ever have been, in the various branches of science…May we not, therefore, look with confidence to the ultimate universal acknowledgment of the truths upon which our system rests? It is the first government ever instituted upon the principles in strict conformity to nature, and the ordination of Providence, in furnishing the materials of human society. Many governments have been founded upon the principle of the subordination and serfdom of certain classes of the same race; such were and are in violation of the laws of nature. Our system commits no such violation of nature's laws. With us, all of the white race, however high or low, rich or poor, are equal in the eye of the law. Not so with the negro. Subordination is his place. He, by nature, or by the curse against Canaan, is fitted for that condition which he occupies in our system. The architect, in the construction of buildings, lays the foundation with the proper material-the granite; then comes the brick or the marble. The substratum of our society is made of the material fitted by nature for it, and by experience we know that it is best, not only for the superior, but for the inferior race, that it should be so. It is, indeed, in conformity with the ordinance of the Creator. It is not for us to inquire into the wisdom of His ordinances, or to question them. For His own purposes, He has made one race to differ from another, as He has made "one star to differ from another star in glory." The great objects of humanity are best attained when there is conformity to His laws and decrees, in the formation of governments as well as in all things else. Our confederacy is founded upon principles in strict conformity with these laws. This stone which was rejected by the first builders "is become the chief of the corner" the real "corner-stone" in our new edifice. I have been asked, what of the future? It has been apprehended by some that we would have arrayed against us the civilized world. I care not who or how many they may be against us, when we stand upon the eternal principles of truth, if we are true to ourselves and the principles for which we contend, we are obliged to, and must triumph.

Sept. 27, 1856.] THE ILLUSTRATED LONDON NEWS 315

SLAVE AUCTION AT RICHMOND, VIRGINIA.

Figure 5.18 A slave auction in Richmond, Virginia (*Illustrated London News*, Sept. 27, 1856).

Description of a Slave Auction, from Josiah Henson, *Father Henson's Story of His Own Life* (Boston: John P. Jewett & Co., 1858), pp. 10-13.

For two or three years my mother and her young family of six children had resided on this estate; and we had been in the main very happy. She was a good mother to us, a woman of deep piety, anxious above all things to touch our hearts with a sense of religion. How or where she acquired her knowledge of God, or her acquaintance with the Lord's Prayer, which she so frequently taught us to repeat, I am unable to say. I remember seeing her often on her knees, trying to arrange her thoughts in prayer appropriate to her situation, but which amounted to little more than...the repetition of short phrases which were within my infant comprehension, and have remained in my memory to this hour.

Our term of happy union as one family was now, alas, at an end. Mournful as was the Doctor's death to his friends it was a far greater calamity to us. The estate and the slaves must be sold and the proceeds divided among the heirs. We were but property—not a mother, and the children God had given her.

Common as are slave-auctions in the southern states, and naturally as a slave may look forward to the time when he will be put up on the block, still the full misery of the event—of the scenes which precede and succeed it—is never understood till the actual experience comes. The first sad announcement that the sale is to be; the knowledge that all ties of the past are to be sundered; the frantic terror at the idea of being sent "down south;" the almost certainty that one member of a family will be torn from another; the anxious scanning of purchasers' faces; the agony at parting, often forever, with husband, wife, child—these must be seen and felt to be fully understood. Young as I was then, the iron entered into my soul. The remembrance of the breaking up of McPherson's estate is photographed in its minutest features in my mind. The crowd collected round the stand, the huddling group of negroes, the examination of muscle, teeth, the exhibition of agility, the look of the auctioneer, the agony of my mother—I can shut my eyes and see them all.

My brothers and sisters were bid off first, and one by one, while my mother, paralyzed by grief, held me by the hand. Her turn came, and she was bought by Isaac Riley of Montgomery county. Then I was offered to the assembled purchasers. My mother, half distracted with the thought of parting forever from all her children, pushed through the crowd, while the bidding for me was going on, to the spot where Riley was standing. She fell at his feet, and clung to his knees, entreating him in tones that a mother only could command, to buy her baby as well as herself, and spare to her one, at least of her little ones. Will it, can it be believed that this man, thus appealed to, was capable not merely of turning a deaf ear to her supplication, but of disengaging himself from her with such violent blows and kicks, as to reduce her to the necessity of creeping out of his reach, and mingling the groan of bodily suffering with the sob of a breaking heart? As she crawled away from the brutal man I heard her sob out, "Oh, Lord Jesus, how long, how long shall I suffer this way!" I must have been then between five and six years old.

Dr. Samuel A. Cartwright, "Report on the Diseases and Physical Peculiarities of the Negro Race,"

New Orleans Medical and Surgical Journal, 7 (1851), pp. 691-715.

DRAPETOMANIA, OR THE DISEASE CAUSING NEGROES TO RUN AWAY.

...It is unknown to our medical authorities, although its diagnostic symptom, the absconding from service, is well known to our planters and overseers...In noticing a disease not heretofore classed among the long list of maladies that man is subject to, it was necessary to have a new term to express it. The cause in the most of cases, that induces the negro to run away from service, is as much a disease of the mind as any other species of mental alienation, and much more curable, as a general rule. With the advantages of proper medical advice, strictly followed, this troublesome practice that many negroes have of running away, can be almost entirely prevented, although the slaves be located on the borders of a free state, within a stone's throw of the abolitionists...

If the white man attempts to oppose the Deity's will, by trying to make the negro anything else than "the submissive knee-bender," (which the Almighty declared he should be,) by trying to raise him to a level with himself, or by putting himself on an equality with the negro; or if he abuses the power which God has given him over his fellow-man, by being cruel to him, or punishing him in anger, or by neglecting to protect him from the wanton abuses of his fellow-servants and all others, or by denying him the usual comforts and necessaries of life, the negro will run away; but if he keeps him in the position that we learn from the Scriptures he was intended to occupy, that is, the position of submission; and if his master or overseer be kind and gracious in his hearing towards him, without condescension, and at the sane time ministers to his physical wants, and protects him from abuses, the negro is spell-bound, and cannot run away...Before the negroes run away, unless they are frightened or panic-struck, they become sulky and dissatisfied. The cause of this sulkiness and dissatisfaction should be inquired into and removed, or they are apt to run away or fall into the negro consumption. When sulky and dissatisfied without cause, the experience of those on the line and elsewhere, was decidedly in favor of whipping them out of it, as a preventive measure against absconding, or other bad conduct. It was called whipping the devil out of them.

If treated kindly, well fed and clothed, with fuel enough to keep a small fire burning all night--separated into families, each family having its own house--not permitted to run about at night to visit their neighbors, to receive visits or use intoxicating liquors, and not overworked or exposed too much to the weather, they are very easily governed--more so than any other people in the world. When all this is done, if any one of more of them, at any time, are inclined to raise their heads to a level with their master or overseer, humanity and their own good require that they should be punished until they fall into that submissive state which it was intended for them to occupy in all after-time... They have only to be kept in that state and treated like children, with care, kindness, attention and humanity, to prevent and cure them from running away.

DYSAETHESIA AETHIOPICA...A DISEASE PECULIAR TO NEGROES--CALLED BY OVERSEERS, "RASCALITY."

Dysaesthesia Aethiopica is a disease peculiar to negroes, affecting both mind and body in a manner as well expressed by dysaesthesia, the name I have given it, as could be by a single term. There is both mind and sensibility, but both seem to be difficult to reach by impressions from without. There is a partial insensibility of the skin, and so great a hebetude of the intellectual faculties, as to be like a person half asleep, that is with difficulty aroused and kept awake. It differs from every other species of mental disease, as it is accompanied with physical signs or lesions of the body discoverable to the medical observer, which are always present and sufficient to account for the symptoms. It is much more prevalent among free negroes living in clusters by themselves, than among slaves on our plantations, and attacks only such slaves as live like free negroes in regard to diet, drinks, exercise, etc. It is not my purpose to treat of the complaint as it prevails among free negroes, nearly all of whom are more or less afflicted with it, that have not got some white person to direct and to take care of them...I propose only to describe its symptoms among slaves.

From the careless movements of the individuals affected with the complaint, they are apt to do much mischief, which appears as if intentional, but is mostly owing to the stupidness of mind and insensibility of the nerves induced by the disease. Thus, they break, waste and destroy everything they handle,--abuse horses and cattle,--tear, burn or rend their own clothing, and, paying no attention to the rights of property, steal others, to replace what they have destroyed. They wander about at night, and keep in a half nodding sleep during the day. They slight their work,--cut up corn, cane, cotton or tobacco when hoeing it, as if for pure mischief. They raise disturbances with their overseers and fellow-servants without cause or motive, and seem to be insensible to pain when subjected to punishment. The fact of the existence of such a complaint, making man like an automaton or senseless machine, having the above or similar symptoms, can be clearly established by the most direct and positive testimony. That it should have escaped the attention of the medical profession, can only be accounted for because its attention has not been sufficiently directed to the maladies of the negro race. Otherwise a complaint of so common an occurrence on badly-governed plantations, and so universal among free negroes, or those who are not governed at all,--a disease...having its peculiar and well marked symptoms and its curative indications, would not have escaped the notice of the profession. The northern physicians... have noticed the symptoms, but not the disease from which they spring. They ignorantly attribute the symptoms to the debasing influence of slavery on the mind without considering that those who have never been in slavery, or their fathers before them, are the most afflicted...The disease is the natural offspring of negro liberty--the liberty to be idle, to wallow in filth, and to indulge in improper food and drinks.

Part Three: Racializations

Chapter Six: Inventing the Indian

Americans remember the conquest of the New World with two deceptive holidays. Columbus Day celebrates Columbus as an explorer, as though he sailed for knowledge rather than gold. Thanksgiving memorializes the Mayflower and the Pilgrim settlers it carried who sought the freedom to follow their religious principles and their peaceful cooperation with the native people they encountered. These holidays have flourished because they obscure the past rather than recall it. They erase the fact that all the European colonies planted in North America were commercial ventures, even the company that sponsored the Pilgrims, or that most Englishmen who clamored onto boats did so seeking their fortunes, not their liberty.

While some English settlers wished for peaceful relations with neighboring Indians so they could, in the words of the charter of the Massachusetts Bay Company, "wynn and incite the native of country, to the knowledge and obedience of the onlie true God and Savior of mankind, and the Christian fayth," the leaders of these settlements were mainly interested in conquest and control. The directors of the Massachusetts Bay Company sent private orders to Governor John Winthrop requiring that all of his men should be trained to use firearms and to prohibit Indians from entering any of the colony's towns. English colonists hoped for peace, as peace was cheaper, but prepared for war to expand their foothold in the New World.

Between the hope for peace and the willingness to force native peoples from their lands with violence, the story of America was written. From the beginnings of small settlement towns hugging the coastlines of Massachusetts and Virginia, Americans sought to expand their holdings westward. At first their ambitions were thwarted by the powerful Indian societies they dealt with from a position of weakness and insecurity. But with English numbers so did their ambitions grow until the colonists began demanding greater concessions of land and even began seizing native peoples as slaves.

As fighting erupted more and more frequently on their frontier, English attitudes toward native people slowly changed. Once seen as noble and admirably independent people, they came to be viewed as savages, wholly unlike themselves. Centuries later, when Indian power was broken, their savagery was downplayed and they were seen as dependent children, wards of the new American state. As Americans pushed even the most peaceful and cooperative native nations from their borders, intolerant of any "primitive" people in their young white nation, they began to view them as a people doomed by their own simple nature to extinction, thus excusing themselves of any guilt for their decline. Not until the twentieth century would even a minority of white Americans consider Indian culture something worth preserving.

Becoming Red

Early European colonists did not see or think of race the way that modern people do. Their ideas of human relatedness and division were based more on ideas of shared kinship rather than shared physical features. They saw physical differences not as markers of group identity, but as accidental products of different environments and circumstances. For them, people's appearances varied widely—even Englishmen came in different colors depending on their class and occupation. To them, Indians were different not because of how they looked, but because of how and where they lived.

The idea that Indians were "red" men and "red" women, arose hundreds of years after Europeans first encountered them. At first, English described Indians' skin the same way they described peasants and farm laborers in England, as "swart [swarthy], tawnie or Chestnut." John Smith proclaimed that the Indians were "borne white" and other first Englishmen in Virginia described Indians as "faire."

"Red" was not an observation of indigenous people's physical differences, but a category invented and then hardened when English society abandoned the idea that Indians could be made into Englishmen and instead were to be dispossessed, driven away, and destroyed. Historians argue over the obscure source for the term "Red," some arguing it derived from the red paint some native people's decorated their bodies with, others finding some indigenous leaders in the Carolinas describing themselves as "Red," which in their language meant something equivalent to ambassador (these communities had two leaders, one "white" who was in charge of domestic affairs and one "red" who represented the tribe in foreign matters). Some historians also point to the early development of racial science, particularly Carl Linnaeus who divided humanity into four colors (red, white, black, and yellow) that according to ancient medical

Figure 6.1 'Natural inhabitants' of the Antilles of America. From Jean Baptiste Du Tertre, *Histoire generale des Antilles habitées par les François* (Paris: T lolly, 1667)

wisdom corresponded to the four "humors" or vital fluids of the body. In any case, "red" was not a description of the skin of native peoples—but a general name for original Americans. Only later, when Indians were being excluded from American society, did the need arise to pretend they were strikingly physically different from others.

The idea of native people's being "red," or any particular color, served another purpose which was to lump all indigenous people into one idea of an "Indian" race. While the first colonists were very aware of the cultural and linguistic differences between the people they encountered, making clear distinctions between the Pequot, Narragansett, Iroquois, and others, over time white Americans erased these differences and increasingly just referred to "Indians." For example, many of the conflicts with native peoples in the first century of colonization were named for the particular native nation that was fought. Massachusetts Puritans fought the Pequot War, the Virginians fought the Powhattan War, New Yorkers fought the Tuscarora War, and Carolinians fought the Yamasee War. But by the 1760s the major conflict that engulfed all the colonies and included native peoples both as allies and enemies was simply referred to as the "French and Indian War."

This lumping of all native people into the category of Indian had more severe consequences than merely producing vague and inaccurate language. It promoted violence on any native community in retaliation for attacks perpetrated by another "Indian" group. Repeatedly throughout American history, peaceful native towns and people were assaulted by neighboring whites outraged at news of murders committed by entirely different native nations.

The Noble Savage

During the colonial era, when English and Dutch and French settlers clung uncertainly to their coastal forts and towns, their views of native peoples swung between the extremes of seeing them as God's children waiting and yearning for Christian awakening, or as primitive devils living in a sinful and savage state.

European observers of native American societies tended to project their own dreams and longings upon them. At a time when oppressive monarchies ruled throughout Europe; when social roles and identities were fixed by tradition; when vicious religious wars raged for the better part of a century and both sides regularly burned heretics; indigenous societies in America seemed relatively free of both governmental, social and religious oppression. Europeans began seeing in Indian societies a model of the absolute liberty and freedom they began to idealize. In this way native peoples were drawn and described as 'noble savages.'

Early Englishmen who first encountered native peoples described them in ways that emphasized their childlike character. Early explorers frequently described native men as being "beardless." They assumed that the smooth faces of the native men they encountered was a natural physical difference from themselves, not appreciating that in many native societies men plucked hair from their faces from puberty. This was more than just a mistake, more than just a cross-cultural misunderstanding. Beards in western culture had come to signify masculine power and to connote wisdom and leadership. By declaring indigenous men as being naturally beardless, Europeans were also marking them as being childish and effeminate, not quite men, and lacking in those qualities of higher reasoning and strategic thinking that they associated with authority. (This tradition can still be seen up to the time of the American Civil War when most generals on both sides flourished bushy beards.)

Indians were seen as living in a carefree (though primitive) state of freedom that in many ways appealed to people whose own society was becoming increasingly restrictive. In 1795, the American revolutionary, Thomas Paine, favorably compared the freedom of Indians to Europeans:

To understand what the state of society ought to be, it is necessary to have some idea of the natural and primitive state of man; such as it is at this day among the Indians of North America. There is not, in that state, any of those spectacles of human misery which poverty and want present in our eyes in all the towns and streets in Europe....The life of an Indian is a continual holiday, compared with the poor of Europe.... the fact is, that the condition of millions in every country in Europe, is far worse than if they had been born before civilization began, or had been born among the Indians of North America...

Being a part of nature carried with it both positive and negative connotations. On the positive side, the imagined naturalness of Indians was viewed as something that gave them an uncorrupted sense of justice and morality, a healthful and vigorous constitution, and a deep spirituality. Such virtues were more than offset by Indians also being seen as childlike, naive, irresponsible, and lacking in self-control.

But the idea of the noble or natural savage came with a cost: it was based on the related idea that Indians lived in a state of nature, or, more accurately, were themselves part of nature like other wild untamed animals. The 'noble savage' was noble because he was untainted and uncorrupted by nature's opposite--civilization. Native peoples were seen as living in a natural state like Adam and Eve enjoyed in their Eden, but unlike that original couple they could not survive outside of their garden.

Such ideas were evident among the educated European elite in the 1700s, but became more specific and refined in the early nineteenth century when naturalists such as James Cowles Prichard drew parallels between American Indians and other 'beasts of the wild'. "The Barbarous races of America...are essentially untamable [and] submit to extermination, rather than wear the yoke under which our Negro slaves fatten and multiply." (Of course, the other implication of this idea, that native peoples should be left alone to enjoy their lands free from the conquest, theft, and enslavement of Europeans, was never considered.)

This scientific theory quickly became a national ideology that native peoples were incapable of adapting to the modern world and instead would naturally pass into extinction along with the wild plants and animals that retreated from the expanding line of settlement. Such ideas spread quickly and sunk deeply into American culture because they so neatly justified the expulsion of native peoples from their lands and their concentration into designated

Figure 6.2 Philip alias Metacomet, chief of Wampanoags.

areas called "reservations." American politicians, ministers, editors, scientists, and other opinion-makers, proclaimed that removing Indians from their lands was a policy of mercy and charity. Reservations, Americans believed, protected native peoples from the corrupting touch of civilization and allowed them to continue their barbarous lives in peace, protected from the modern world in which they could not possibly survive. Reservations, in a twisted sense, were the American government's first program to conserve nature, though in this case the wilderness being preserved from development and kept from extinction were native peoples themselves.

There was one glaring problem with this ideology of the vanishing Indian. Many native peoples refused to vanish and some rapidly adapted to the culture that white Europeans called "civilization." One of the reasons federal and state governments focused so much attention and effort in uprooting the Cherokee from their homes in Georgia and surrounding states, forcing them to march out of the country along the "Trail of Tears", was that the Cherokee were the living proof that the presumptions behind the ideology

of the vanishing Indian were false. Cherokee peoples had adopted western dress and western systems of private land ownership and farming techniques. They had innovated a written language and published a newspaper. They operated western-style courts and governed themselves in a republican manner. Worse, their population was not tipping into extinction as expected. Cherokee success at assimilation struck directly at the lies justifying the land theft and crimes committed against native peoples and for this their towns had to be destroyed and they had to be forcibly reduced to the poverty and decline that the theory predicted they would naturally fall into.

Ultimately, English colonists and later Americans embraced the image of the Indian as a blank page upon which they could write all their desires and anxieties. Indians could be seen as savages, when thinking of them as bloodthirsty served to excuse military attacks upon them. Or they could be seen as innocent and childlike when viewing them as dependents was advantageous, as governments assumed powers over them and deprived them of rights commonly granted others. In practice, Indians were pictured as noble, independent and proud when they lacked power, and savage scalp-hunters when they possessed some leverage.

Toward Segregation

By the time English adventurers and Pilgrims splashed ashore in Virginia and Plymouth native peoples along the Atlantic coast already had generations of experience in dealing with Europeans. Spaniards had occupied St. Augustine further south on the coast (in what is today Florida) for forty-two years, Puerto Rico for over a century, and had a string of settlements reaching across the continent. England's first permanent settlement at Jamestown, Virginia, was founded in the same year that the Spanish empire founded a provincial city nestled in the Sangre de Cristo mountains of what is today New Mexico. By that time it had been 66 years since the French founded Quebec with 400 settlers, four times as many colonists as landed at Jamestown.

The religiously fervent Englishmen who dominated the settlement of New England regarded themselves as far more humane toward the native peoples they encountered than rival imperial powers, such as the Spanish, had been. By the early seventeenth century many tales of the dark deeds of conquistadors, especially Bartolomé de las Casas" *Brevísima Relación de las Indias* that exposed horrific examples of Spanish cruelty and exploitation, circulated widely in England. Promoters of English colonization of the New World claimed that their fairer policies would win over native peoples so completely that Englishmen would be greeted as liberators and friends.

English expectations of peaceful coexistence with natives drew on Christian ideas that all men were descended from Adam and were equal in the eyes of God. They also leaned on philosophical principles that people differed not essentially but because of the different environments in which they lived. In this way early English explorers and some colonists looked upon the natives as not differing categorically (as in developing notions of racial difference) from themselves.

While colonists could think of Indians philosophically as being men and women like themselves, they could not imagine them having the same rights or privileges as they did, even if they did adopt Christianity. The policy of restricting Indians to particular areas set aside for them, later to be known as reservations, began quite soon after the English began to colonize North America. In 1675 Massachusetts ordered all native people to live within the boundaries of three "praying towns." According to the law, any Englishman discovering an Indian outside of those towns was permitted to "to kill and destroy them as they best may or can."

In the American colonies, laws defining races were first passed to separate whites and Indians, not whites and blacks. The first law prohibiting whites and Indians from marrying and prohibiting whites from voluntarily living among Indians, was passed in Connecticut in 1642. It would be another generation before Virginia became the first colony to outlaw intermarriage between whites and blacks.

Such legal attempts to force the separation of English and native people were prompted by the growing numbers of colonists who preferred to live among natives. A number of colonists taken prisoner by native people refused to be "liberated" from their captivity and some who did return to English society wrote narratives of their experiences that compared Indian ways and character favorably to those of England. Attempting to prevent continued defections of English colonists to native societies, Virginia in 1612 made running away to join the Indians punishable by death. Connecticut was more lenient, proscribing whipping, fines, and three years imprisonment for living among the Indians.

From Innocent Primitive to Savage Beast

Seizing land from natives was the lynchpin of the entire colonial project. The colonies had an insatiable appetite for land, both for their own settlements and plantations but also as buffers against other imperial powers and as the basis of their labor system. Besides enslaved Indians, the colonies depended on the labor of indentured servants brought from Europe. Some of these came involuntarily as they were criminals given the choice between death and transportation to America. Most were volunteers who were recruited to the dangerous venture by the promise of land. In exchange for seven years of labor, indentured servants were given their freedom and a parcel of land. Though in the first decades few servants survived long enough to claim their "freedom dues," the dream of doing so served to keep a steady flow of workers coming to America and to maintain social order among those already there.

Once the English colonists were committed to wiping out their Indian neighbors, they found support for considering indigenous people utterly different and alien from themselves in the very sources from which they had earlier drawn ideas of equality. The Bible proved adaptable to both purposes, providing the story of Noah's sons, one of whom, Ham, was punished by God for disrespecting his father, a curse that the Bible stated continued on through all of Ham's descendents. In this way one early English advocate of colonization wrote that "some conceive the Inhabitants of New-England to be Chams posterity, and consequently shut out from grace by Noahs curse" while about the same time one of the petty officials of Virginia wrote, "as for convertinge of the Infidells itt was an attempt impossible they being descended of ye cursed race of Cham." Over time the idea that native people and English people were fundamentally different grew along with the increasingly formal and legal separation of the two communities.

English leaders were not shy to openly state that extermination was their goal. After a particularly costly attack upon the colony, the Virginia Company's governors demanded "a sharp revenge upon the bloody miscreants, even the measure that they intended against us, the rooting them out for being longer a people uppon the face of the earth." New England's famous minister Cotton Mather prophesied that the Indians would eventually be destroyed. "There is a Voice coming from almost every side of us...a Voice as Loud as that in the Heavens, which gave Terrour to all this Land a few Months ago. What says this Voice, but this, They are going to be Cut down for ever." Connecticut's English settlers quickly resolved to eradicate their native neighbors, the Pequot people, who they telling referred to as "Pequod Amalecks." The Amalecks were a people of the Old Testament Bible that God told the Israelites to utterly destroy, leaving no man, woman or child or even a "remembrance" of them for all time.

English ideas of Indians were built by comparison with England's experiences attempting to conquer and rule Ireland. Beginning in the fourteenth century, English rulers had sponsored numerous attempts to subdue the Irish. English invaders viewed Irish society, organized as it was by dense kinship networks and ancient traditions, as primitive. When Irish people resisted attempts to drive them from their lands and reduce them to servants of English lords, English writers described them as "wild" and "savage." Irish people were stereotyped as being lazy and so satisfied with their poverty that they would rather starve than work the fields.

English commanders pursued a scorched earth policy in Ireland, sparing no one so as to open lands to English settlers. Sir Humphrey Gilbert lined both sides of the road leading to his tent with piked Irish heads. Gilbert and several of the other military leaders of the English invasion of Ireland later participated in colonizing America. Not sur-

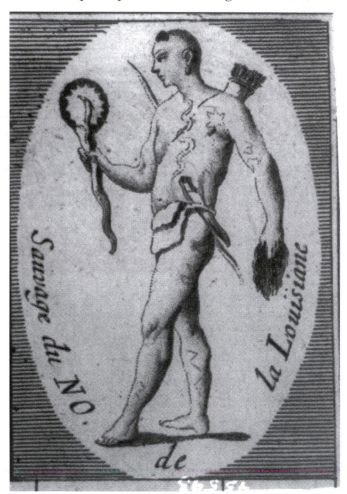

Figure 6.3 "Sauvage du NO. de la Louisiane" (native of New Orleans, Louisiana).

prisingly, when conflict flared with the people of the New World, English colonists drew on their experience fighting the "wild" Irish to understand it. When Mayflower passenger and the Plymouth colony's commander, Miles Standish, killed native leader Wituwamat, he ordered his severed head to be set on a stake on the wall of the fort as a warning to other natives.

English colonists believed they were morally permitted to destroy native peoples and take their land because Indians had failed to follow God's desire that man improve and cultivate the land. Mayflower passenger Robert Cushman expressed this idea most clearly when he wrote in 1622:

> ...our land is full, to them we may go, [as] their land is empty. This then is a sufficient reason to prove our going thither to live lawful: their land is spacious and void, and they are few and do but run over the grass, as do also the foxes and wild beasts. They are not industrious, neither have [they] art, science, skill or faculty to use either the land or the commodities of it; but all spoils, rots, and is marred for want of manuring, gathering, ordering, etc. As the ancient patriarchs therefore removed from straiter places into more roomy, where the land lay idle and wasted and none used it, though there dwelt inhabitants by them (as in Gen. 13: 6, 11, 12, and 34: 21, and 41: 20), so is it lawful now to take a land which none useth and make use of it.

Rev. John Winthrop expressed nearly identical thoughts seven years later, "As for the Natives in New England, they inclose noe Land, neither have any setled habytation, nor any tame Cattle to improve the Land by, and soe have noe other but a Naturall Right to those Countries, soe as if we leave them sufficient for their use, we may lawfully take the rest, there being more than enough for them and us." Though such thinking originated with Puritan ministers, it proved so useful that more secular thinkers like John Locke incorporated it into their theories of property. English perceptions of "empty lands" and native peoples who merely occupied them rather than cultivating them were powerfully warped by the many waves of epidemics that ravaged native communities rapidly decreasing their populations.

Such justification for killing native peoples and dispossessing them of their lands proved remarkably durable through American history. John Quincy Adams, America's sixth president, wrote, "What is the right of the huntsman to the forest of a thousand miles over which he has accidentally ranged in quest of prey?... Shall the exuberant bosom of the common mother, amply adequate to the nourishment of millions, be claimed exclusively by a few hundreds of her offspring? Shall the lordly savage not only disdain the virtues and enjoyments of civilization himself, but shall he control the civilization of the world?"

In 1622, after years of extorting food and other tribute from the neighboring Powhattan Confederacy of native tribes, the Virginia colony finally pushed the Powhatan leader Opechancanough too far. Opechancanough led a massive assault on English settlements that killed 350 colonists. Afterwards the colony's leaders vowed to use all means to "to roote out from being any longer a people" including "famine in burning their Corne" and unleashing war dogs "Mastives to seaze them." Englishmen spoke less about Indians being "noble" or "gentle" or "innocent" and described them increasingly as "naked, tanned, deformed Savages."

The following year Virginia's leaders invited Opechancanough and his lieutenants to a peace meeting at a native village on the Potomac (or in the Algonquin language, the Patawomeck) river. At the conference Opechancanough agreed to release the remaining English prisoners he held and the colonists then threw a feast for the several hundred Indians gathered there. Captain William Tucker who led Virginia's delegation offered a toast and in the spirit of friendship gave many flagons of wine to Opechancanough's people. Prior to the conference Captain Tucker had arranged with one of the colony's physicians to lace the wine with poison and this concoction worked to deadly effect, killing at least half of the native people who drank it. Tucker ordered his men to murder the remaining fifty or so Indians who were incapacitated but had not succumbed. Somehow Opechancanough himself managed to escape the poison massacre.

The use of poison or other indiscriminate means of killing was not used in warfare between European powers at this time and was reserved only for the killing of people considered inherently inferior. In 1763 when Ottawa commander Pontiac and his troops threatened Fort Pitt, the Americans' westernmost outpost deep in the wilds of Pennsylvania (later to become Pittsburgh), the fort's commander agreed to meet with a delegation from the Delaware tribe to discuss peace. The commander later wrote to a colleague boasting of what he did next, "out of our regard for them, we gave them two Blankets and a Handkerchief out of the Small Pox Hospital. I hope it will have the desired effect." It did and a small pox epidemic raged through the Delaware community. Similar tactics were used by other British commanders, most notably General Jeffrey Amherst who ordered one of his colonels to distribute smallpox infected blankets to native peoples. Amherst urged, "You will do well to try to inoculate [meaning infect] the Indians by means of blankets, as well as to try every other method that can serve to extirpate this execrable race."

Both French and English colonial governments offered bounties for the killing of "enemy" Indians, to be paid upon presentation of the skin and hair cut from a victim's skull. Salem, Massachusetts, tacked the scalps it collected on the wall of its courthouse. French governors in Canada traded Indian scalps for beaver pelts. In 1689, three of New England's colonies paid an eight pound bounty for each native head. Four years later Massachusetts began paying a higher bonus for the scalps or heads of native children "under the age of fourteen years." In the season from 1703 to 1704 Massachusetts paid for 208 scalps. Most English colonies in the eighteenth century paid scalp bounties with

Figure 6.4 "Redmens' Diploma Legendary & Historical Chart" for the Society of Red Men," (Philadelphia: Burk & McFetridge, c1889).

Maryland budgeting the huge sum of ten thousand pounds to fund its purchases in 1755. That same year the Massachusetts colonial legislature ordered "his Majesty's Subjects of this Province to embrace all Opportunities of pursuing, captivating, killing and destroying all and every" Indian. Even Quaker Pennsylvania immediately resorted to sanctioning the murder of natives, including children, once war broke out on its frontier in 1756. Pennsylvania's council offered bounties for scalps for Indians over the age of 10.

States continued paying bounties for the killing of native people for the next century. Illinois paid fifty dollars per scalp in 1814. The U.S. government paid bounties for the killing of Seminoles in Florida. Minnesota enacted a scalp bounty in the 1860s while Arizona clung to its murderous program until the 1880s.

The gathering of trophies from the bodies of slain Indians continued for hundreds of years. Andrew Jackson, who commanded the army that defeated the Creek nation over a year's-long campaign, rewarded his men for their killings of native people and accounted for his army's successes by collecting noses. Jackson's men sliced 557 noses from the faces of fallen Creek people after the Battle of Horseshoe Bend. Soldiers were also known to flay the bodies of warriors and tan the skin into useful objects, such as a set of bridle reins that Jackson held as he rode down Potomac Avenue during his inauguration as President. The U.S. army troops that indiscriminately murdered hundreds of men, women, and children at Sand Creek, Colorado, in 1864, mutilated the bodies for souvenirs and their commander, John Chivington, proudly strung over a hundred human scalps across the stage of the Denver Opera House. (One of these souvenirs, a tobacco pouch made from a man's scrotum, was passed down across generations of one family and was reportedly used by a member of the Colorado state legislature.)

Indians and American Identity

Through this tragic history, Americans came to understand themselves as a people and a nation by way of the figure of the Indian. American stereotypes of native people were not only driven by their land hunger and the need to disguise the immorality of their treatment of Indians, but were also shaped by Americans own desire to distinguish themselves from the European societies they had left. Americans appropriated the idea of the Indian to define who they were; to them Indians represented the natural liberty and morality they themselves aspired to. White Americans smeared themselves in war paint and adorned themselves with feathers to express the ways they were not English.

Americans developed a special attraction to the idea of being an Indian, because being Indian was a convenient way of distinguishing what was otherwise indistinguishable—namely, themselves from other English people. When Americans first grew angry with their English leaders, when they resisted policies and taxes levied and imposed from across the ocean, they were not a united people, they were not "Americans." Rather, they were a group of distinct colonies, each with somewhat different populations and distinctly different customs, religions and outlooks. What tied them together and made them different from other English people? This was a question upon which rested the prospect of independence itself. The answer was close at hand—what made Americans distinct from English people was their relationship to Indians. They were the people who lived among the "savages."

When it was convenient to do so, rebellious colonists could express their distinct separation from the English by dressing up as Indians, by pretending to be Indians; what in their minds was the complete opposite of civilized society and therefore clearly not English. Most famously American tax rebels painted their faces, donned feathers, and wore buckskins before boarding ships in Boston harbor and dumping crates of tea into the sea.

Likewise, some of the first American social organizations adopted Indian symbols and names to better separate themselves from social clubs, like the St. Andrews Society, that supported the English crown. These clubs called themselves Saint Tamina clubs, named for Tamenend, a chief of the Lenni Lenape (Delaware) nation who agreed to cede lands to William Penn near what is today Philadelphia. When independence was achieved, these St. Tamina clubs quickly spread, a version popping up in most major cities. Many became active in the new nation's politics, and one eventually became the Tammany club that ruled New York city's politics and was influential in the Democratic party decades later.

Giving each other pretend Indian names, wearing feathers and skins, painting their faces and dancing with abandon, members acted out their fantasies of what Indians were. Such clubs' pretend Indianness expressed a newfound patriotism and gave their members license to indulge themselves as Indians in ways they might not have as white men. Believing that Indians lived in a state of natural liberty, free to indulge their every whim, Tammany clubs revelled in drunken excess, even instructing members to "force" those of their brothers who were reluctant "to do as they pleased." Drinking started early and continued well past the time the "council fires" were lit late at night.

Where they didn't become the kernel of political parties, Tammany societies morphed into fraternal organizations, including the first truly American fraternal organization, the Society of Red Men founded in 1813. Later when the temperance movement began to gain strength in the 1830s, the Red Men become the Improved Order of Red Men ("improved" because they discouraged drinking and established death and disability benefits for their members). This organization grow to be one of the largest fraternal organizations in America. In the 1840s and 1850s, it proved particularly popular with German immigrants to America who joined the Improved Order of Red Men seeking a distinctively American organization and nothing was more American than white men dressing up as Indians.

Typical of the requirements of maintaining a fictional Indian world of assumed Indian names, invented Indian songs and dances, and feathery costumes, actual Indians or any other people of color were not allowed to be members. The organization's rules dictated that "No person shall be adopted into a Tribe of the Order except a free white male of good moral character and standing of the full age of twenty one great suns who believes in the existence of a Great Spirit the Creator and Preserver of the Universe…"

The Vanishing Indian Myth

Americans came to explain what they saw of Indian life by considering it similar to their own ancestors' ways. Just as those living in England and Germany had been considered savage tribes by the Romans who in many places subdued and "civilized" them, so in comparison to themselves were Indians. In this way Europeans thought of Indians as people living in the past, their own past perhaps, but the past nonetheless. By the eighteenth century philosophers and scientists had begun to develop such prejudices into formal theories of human social development and theorized that all societies progressed through stages of complexity from simple savagery to advanced European civilization. The difference between them was that their racial characters limited the pace or height of their advances.

This idea would eventually be used to justify policies that segregated native peoples from other Americans or forced them out of the country altogether. One implication of thinking that Indians were a primitive people trapped in some common past, was that they cannot be brought to civilization all at once, but only gradually, over the course of generations. Contact with white civilization was too disruptive to their gentle constitutions and only served to drive them more quickly to extinction. Forcing them to leave their homelands and march west beyond America's borders, or later to move again onto reservations was therefore justified as a necessary protection of the Indians themselves.

Ideas of Indians being a people of the past, a stone age people wholly unsuited to the modern world, also served

Figure 6.5 Henry W. Longfellow, photo by Frederick Gutekunst, 1876.

to obscure the fact that they had been systematically destroyed by white colonization. Indians did not suffer defeat and decimation at the hands of land-hungry colonists, but rather were depicted as people whose decline was "natural." Indians weren't killed off, they "vanished."

One of the most persistent of all Indian stereotypes is the myth that native people are genetically or biologically more prone to alcoholism. This myth is built on the common fable that alcohol was unknown in the New World until Europeans introduced Indians to "firewater." In fact, the fermentation of various beverages was widely practiced in the Americas long before contact with Europeans and alcoholic drinks were used in religious and seasonal ceremonies and festivals long before Columbus arrived. Aztec people fermented the Agave plant for centuries before the Spanish conquerors arrived and to their south various groups brewed an alcoholic drink from cacao. Mayans enjoyed balche, which was similar to mead. Corn, of course, was widely known to produce a sweet juice when its stalks were crushed that was easily fermented into a potent beverage. Corn was grown everywhere from the Iroquois regions in the north all along the seaboard to Florida. Ralph Lane, who was part of the earliest English expeditions to Virginia in 1585, noted the great fields of corn being grown there by the native people, whose "cane maketh very good and perfect sugar." When early Europeans traded their brandies, rums, whiskies, and wines with indigenous people, native peoples simply substituted these more powerful drinks for the traditional brews they had used in various rituals and ceremonies.

While sources for the earliest periods of contact are scarce, some indicate the opposite of the myth of the drunken Indian. Thomas Hariot, an early explorer of the Americas, described Indians as being "verye sober in their eatinge, and drinkinge, and consequentlye verye longe lived because they doe not oppress nature."

While alcoholism certainly became a problem in many native communities, the degree to which this was any different than colonial societies is highly debatable. English colonists were known to love their strong drinks to excess. Among the most prominent of the supplies brought on the Mayflower was a large supply of beer. Within a short period in New England even the smallest villages had a tavern. Puritans viewed wine and rum as such basic necessities of life that grog rations were included among the meager goods given to the indigent and poor.

By the time of the American Revolution, due partly to rising incomes, the per capita consumption of strong liquor was astounding. The best records indicate that by the eve of the American Revolution, on average, colonists guzzled the equivalent of 3.5 gallons of alcohol from all sources per person every year. (In 2014, U.S. per capita consumption was estimated at 2.3 gallons.) John Adams took a tankard of hard cider each morning with breakfast. European travelers to America, well accustomed to heavy drinking back home, were surprised at the amount of alcohol Americans regularly downed. The image of Indians racially prone to drunkenness persisted because it fed the myth of their natural decline.

Americans' response to the Indian's vanishing was to mourn and memorialize them. In American literature and other arts, Indians were portrayed as gently fading into history. Stoically facing their certain doom and riding off into the setting sun. James Fenimore Cooper famously wrote his classic novel, *The Last of the Mohicans*, seemingly oblivious to the thousands of Mohicans who lived around him in upstate New York. President Thomas Jefferson struck this theme in his second inaugural address as he

Figure 6.6 Hiawatha's departure (New York: Currier & Ives, c1868).

Figure 6.7 Stick Indian Natives of Copper River, members of Bellums Indian Tribe, near Kotsina Crossing, Alaska, 1899.

eulogized people that were very much alive:

> The aboriginal inhabitants of these countries I have regarded with the commiseration their history inspires. Endowed with the faculties and the rights of men, breathing an ardent love of liberty and independence, and occupying a country which left them no desire but to be undisturbed, the stream of overflowing population from other regions directed itself on these shores; without power to divert, or habits to contend against, they have been overwhelmed by the current, or driven before it; now reduced within limits too narrow for the hunter's state, humanity enjoins us to teach them agriculture and the domestic arts; to encourage them to that industry which alone can enable them to maintain their place in existence, and to prepare them in time for that state of society, which to bodily comforts adds the improvement of the mind and morals.

According to one careful estimate made in the nineteenth century, there were approximately 471,036 native peoples inside the borders of the United States

when Congress voted to provide funds to Christianize and "civilize" Indians who they assumed were naturally vanishing. The text of the Indian Civilization Act of 1819 set forth that its purpose was "of providing against the further decline and final extinction of the Indian tribes…"

When Henry Wadsworth Longfellow decided to set his epic poems and novels in the American frontier, the Indians he imagined were of the noble and conveniently vanishing variety, not the bloodthirsty devils that earlier colonists dreaded. Longfellow's *Hiawatha* (1855) perfectly captures this combination of nobility, naturalism, and extinction and wraps it within an upward (and seemingly inevitable) trace of America's progress. Hiawatha is a prophet and hero to his people and most of the poem relates his exploits in slaying the evil sorcerer Pearl-Feather and falling in love with the maiden, Minnehaha. But in the last chapter, a canoe approaches Hiawatha's town bearing black-robed priests, symbolizing the progress and inevitability of white civilization. Hiawatha graciously welcomes the visitors and quietly prepared to leave forever, as all noble savages were supposed to do:

> On the shore stood Hiawatha,
> Turned and waved his hand at parting;
> On the clear and luminous water

Launched his birch canoe for sailing,
From the pebbles of the margin
Shoved it forth into the water;
Whispered to it, "Westward! westward!"
And with speed it darted forward.
 And the evening sun descending
Set the clouds on fire with redness,
Burned the broad sky, like a prairie,
Left upon the level water
One long track and trail of splendor,
Down whose stream, as down a river,
Westward, westward Hiawatha
Sailed into the fiery sunset,
Sailed into the purple vapors,
Sailed into the dusk of evening...

Longfellow was not the only poet depicting his hero slinking off to extinction rather than becoming part of the modern world. Oliver Wendell Holmes, Sr., along with Longfellow one of the most acclaimed poets of his day, delivered a widely reprinted oration in 1855 that located the source of the Indians' inevitable demise in their own "racial" character:

Look at the aboriginal inhabitants of the land we occupy. It pleased the Creator to call into existence this half-filled outline of humanity; this sketch in red crayons of a rudimental manhood; to keep the continent from being a blank until the true lord of creation should come to claim it. Civilization and Christianity have tried to humanize him, and he proves a dead failure. Theologians stand aghast at a whole race destined, according to their old formulae, to destruction, temporal and eternal. Philanthropists mourn over them, and from time to time catch a red man and turn him into their colleges as they would turn a partridge in among the barn-door fowls. But instinct has its way sooner or later; the partridge makes but a troublesome chicken and the Indian but a sorry Master of Arts, if he does not run for the woods, where all the ferae naturae impulses are urging him. These instincts lead to his extermination; too often the sad solution of the problem of his relation to the white race. As soon as any conflict arises between them, his savage nature begins to show itself. He dashes the babes' heads against their fathers' hearthstones—as at our Oxford—a heap of stones still shows you where he did it; or flings them out of windows, as at Haverhill; he mutilates his prostrate enemy; he drives away the women like beasts of burden. Then the white man hates him, and hunts him down like the wild beasts of the forest, and so the red crayon is rubbed out, and the canvas is ready for a picture of manhood a little more like God's own image.

In the 1850s Henry David Thoreau, the famed author of *Walden*, began compiling extensive notebooks (nearly 3,000 pages of them) for a book he was planning to write about Indians but never did. Thoreau idolized Indian life because he imagined that being closer to nature than civilized men, Indians had a deeper wisdom and insight into the mysteries of the natural world and an unspoiled morality that modern society corrupted. *Walden*, was in many ways the chronicle of Thoreau's attempt to "go native" and "regress" from civilization to nature—to experience the existence of Indians.

By the time Thoreau had compiled his dozen notebooks and wanted to actually see Indians living as he imagined Indians lived, he traveled out west to do so. In 1861 Thoreau traveled to Minnesota to see Indians but he actually didn't need to go so far as many lived nearby in New England. Like most whites, Thoreau was probably mislead by the intentional effort to hide the fact that native peoples were not cooperating in vanishing or going extinct.

U.S. government census policy was to hide the true size of the native population. Census takers did not count Indians in the first seven censuses because the Constitution excluded from representation all "Indians not taxed." In 1870 the federal government instructed census takers to count as white any Indians they thought were of mixed ancestry or who had assimilated into "civilized" life: "Where persons reported as "Half-breeds" are found residing with whites, adopting their habits of life and methods of industry, such persons are to be treated as belonging to the white population." (At the same time the government had the opposite policy toward black people—they counted as "black" anyone with any discernible black ancestry.) In 1853 an appendix to the census did not include any estimate for the population of Indians in New England, instead simply appending a note reading, "Of late years these tribes have either become extinct or so reduced in numbers as to be lost sight of by the government in their tribal character." However, in the 1860 census, the government suddenly found nearly a thousand Indians "retaining their tribal character" in nearby Maine and another 3,785 in New York.

The fact was that Indians were not cooperating in their own vanishing. In spite of great adversity, disease, dispossession, and at least 55 massacres of between 26 and 1000 indigenous people that took place in a total of 31 states between the first European colonization of North America and 1870, Indians remained numerous and a serious obstacle to white American plans for development of the West.

The West

In spite of promises made to those native communities uprooted from the east and forcibly marched to "Indian territory" across the Mississippi river in the 1830s and 1840s, almost as soon as their new towns and farms were laid out, federal, state and local governments began plotting to uproot them and take their new lands.

About the same time eastern native groups were forced west, thousands of white settlers inspired by fantastic stories of the riches of Oregon and California, embarked on their own long overland trail. Guidebooks and magazine editors advised white settlers to heavily arm themselves before venturing west and to shoot first and ask questions later when encountering Indians. In spite of such prejudices, documented instances of pioneers indiscriminately shooting at any natives they saw, and the large number of wagon trains of such settlers pouring across the Great Plains, skirmishes and fighting was remarkably rare prior to the 1860s. In fact, the most famous and worst attack upon settlers venturing along the Oregon Trail was the slaughter of 120 pioneers by a Mormon militia unit at Mountain Meadows in 1857. (Typically, the Mormon forces tried to disguise themselves as Indians and then blame the massacre on their neighboring Paiutes.)

One of the peculiarities of American genocide of indigenous people, unlike that in other colonial areas such as Australia, was that much of the violence against native people was organized and wielded by private citizens, popular volunteers as it were, who weren't directed or coordinated by the government. This was seen most nakedly in California where soon after thousands of white settlers began pouring across the Sierra mountains in the 1840s and 1850s, bands of murderous militias formed whose only connection to the California government was the official permission and sanction to hunt Indians. But vigilante killings were common throughout the American West.

Even while the Civil War was raging, the federal government diverted significant forces to suppress an uprising of Sioux people in Minnesota, sparked, as nearly all these conflicts were, by white squatters and officials who turned a blind eye to their trespassing. Sioux warriors killed hundreds of settlers attempting to reclaim their land.

When U.S. Army general John Pope ordered his troops into Minnesota in 1862, he proclaimed:

> There will be no peace in this region by virtue of treaties and Indian faith. It is my purpose utterly to exterminate the Sioux if I have the power to do so and even if it requires a campaign lasting the whole of next year. Destroy everything belonging to them and force them out to the plains, unless as I suggest, you can capture them. They are to be treated as maniacs or wild beasts, and by no means as people with whom treaties or compromises can be made. Urge the

Figure 6.8 Execution of the thirty-eight Sioux Indians at Mankato Minnesota, December 25, 1862.

Figure 6.9 Ponca Indians between 1865 and 1880.

campaign vigorously; you shall be as vigorously supported and supplied.

In September of 1862 General Pope eventually rounded up all the Sioux he could find, 1,700 of them, and chained them together and pushed them on a three-day march to Fort Snelling. White settlers lined the roads and jeered, beat, and tore at the prisoners with pitchforks as they passed through their towns. The prisoners were kept in Fort Snelling, exposed to the elements for the duration of the winter (over a hundred died during that time). In the meantime, 393 Sioux men were tried for murder before a military tribunal, their average hearings lasting just ten minutes. All but two were sentenced to death, setting a new and unsettling precedent for American warfare: defeated soldiers who surrendered would be charged for murder for the actions they committed during a war. President Lincoln, considering the vast implications of this policy, decided to commute most of the sentences. In the fort at Mankato, Minnesota, on the day after Christmas, 1862, 38 Sioux warriors were simultaneously executed in the largest mass hanging in American history. In May, some of the Sioux were transported in chains to Camp McClellan in Davenport, Iowa, while others were sent to a camp in South Dakota.

After the Civil War the pace of seizures of land in the west quickened. The federal government punished Indian nations that had sided with the Confederacy by claiming such actions negated their treaties and forfeited their lands. (A similar punishment was not given to the actual white leaders of the Confederacy, most all of whom were pardoned and their lands and property restored after the war.) During the war, Lincoln's Republican party, desperate to hold onto its restless voters and maintain support for a war that became unpopular once it turned from being a war for the union into a war for emancipation, promised to open the west for whites. It passed a Homestead Act that guaranteed free homesteads and farm lands to western settlers. It enacted measures subsidizing the building of a transcontinental railroad with subsidies of thousands of square miles of land grants. It rewarded loyal states with land grants for the construction of colleges. Of course, all these promises depended on the swift displacement of the many indigenous people living on those already allocated lands.

The pressure upon the government to obtain land finally dislodged the long-running legal fiction that such lands were purchased from Indians according to contracts called "treaties." At first the Interior Department, charged with obtaining lands by such agreements, attempted to keep up with the demand and submitted dozens of treaties to the Senate for ratification. When the Senate refused to allocate funds to pay for the meagre sums promised in exchange for these lands, the great fraud was over. President Grant in 1871 signed a law negating all treaties and declaring all Indians wards of the state, and all Indian territories public lands.

As settlers, ranchers, and railroads steadily encroached on the lands of many different western peoples, conflicts flared throughout the west. A sad and common cycle was repeated again and again over the next thirty years. Whites encroaching on Indian lands would be attacked, often with horrific consequences. American politicians would demand protection (just before he was elected to be president, General Ulysses Grant declared, "the settlers and emigrants must be protected, even if the extermination of every Indian tribe is necessary to procure such a result.") and the army (now much better equipped and more capable because of the recent Civil War) would be dispatched and a brief, intense war would end with native people being formally dispossessed of their land and usually imprisoned in stockades and forts.

This cycle of violence and dispossession happened to the Comanche in 1875, the Sioux in 1876, the Arapaho and Kiowa in 1875, the Nez Perce in 1877, the Cheyenne in 1878, the Ute and the Ponca in 1879. Wars frequently broke out in the last third of the nineteenth century until the last uprising of the Sioux was put down with a massacre of hundreds of mostly women and children at Wounded Knee in 1890.

The Indian Wars that raged across the western plains aroused a greater degree of sympathy for native people than earlier conflicts had. While colonial wars had forged the idea of the noble savage and a romantic mourning for the ill-fated vanishing Indian, the wars of the later nineteenth century fostered a new sense that native people had been unjustly treated. Partly, this was due to the fact that the killing and dying was being done far away from the centers of population in the east. Also, day to day news of events in the post-civil war west were better reported in the expanding newspaper syndicates. Finally, because the federal government had abandoned the fiction that land cessations were voluntary acts of sovereign nations, the land-grabs of the west were nakedly matters of conquest.

A particularly strong public response occurred in response to the saga of the Ponca nation, a small community surrounded by the much larger Sioux nations. In 1877, the federal government decided to settle a dispute with the Ponca's Sioux neighbors by granting them the land the

.312. Gov't School for Indians. Pawnee Reservation.

Figure 6.10 Government school for Indians on the Pawnee reservation, n.d..

Ponca owned. The Ponca were forced to move to a malaria-infested patch of Indian Territory in Oklahoma where a quarter of their population soon perished. Starving and determined to claim their lands, a group of 30 Ponca, led by Standing Bear, a man who had promised his young son on his deathbed to bury him on their old lands, left and walked north to their homeland, until they were intercepted by the U.S. army and arrested for having left their designated reservation.

Jailed in Fort Omaha, word of their arrest reached sympathetic reformers back east and a movement for their release was organized. A legal defense committee was organized to carry Standing Bear's case and in 1879, for the first time, a judge granted a native person standing before a federal court and ruled him a "person" (though not a citizen) before the law. Following their legal triumph, Standing Bear's elite friends took him on a speaking tour of Chicago, Boston and New York where he was met with enthusiastic crowds cheering his cause.

Like Black Hawk before him who was also paraded around eastern cities to great acclaim, much of Standing Bear's popularity came from the fact that he told white people exactly what they wanted to hear: that Indians craved their white civilization and if only given half a chance they would rapidly become farmers and citizens like them. Popularized reports of Standing Bear's testimony stressed these elements. Standing Bear was widely reported as testifying:

In every tribe of Indians there are two parties. First, those who understand that it is necessary, if the Indians are not all to be exterminated, to go to work, to learn to read and write and count money, to be like white men. Those who think about these things at all, know that the game is all gone, and that our mode of life must change. Then there are always some who believe in the old traditions, who think the Great Spirit will be displeased with them if they do like white men. They want to retain their old habits and religion They hate to work. They want to lie in the shade in the summer, and near the fire in the winter, and make their women wait on them...I represent in the Ponca tribe the foremost of those who want to support themselves, to send their children to school, to build houses, to get property and all kinds of stock around us, and to be independent. It may be that those lazy, bad Indians told the Commissioner that I had no influence. They would do so if they had a chance. But if I could go down to the Territory, and tell all the tribe to follow me who wanted to work and send their children to school, nine out of every ten would come with me.

One of those inspired by Standing Bear's story was a young author, Helen Hunt Jackson, who made the Indian tragedy the subject of her best-selling book, *A Century of Dishonor* (1881). Jackson prefaced her work by saying her purpose was to "simply show our causes for national shame in the matter of our treatment of the Indians...If there be one thing which [Americans] believe in more than any other, and mean that every man on this continent shall have, it is 'fair play.' And as soon as they fairly understand how cruelly it has been denied to the Indian, they will rise up and demand it for him."

Figure 6.11 Group portrait of the Carlisle Indian School football team, 1899.

The Dawes Act of 1887 and Assimilation

Jackson's book and a changing public mood prompted Congress in 1887 to pass landmark legislation that was intended to solve the "Indian Problem" once and for all. This law, known as the Dawes Act or the Indian Severalty Act of 1887, followed the logic of Standing Bear's words by moving to make independent farmers and citizens out of native people whether they wanted to be or not. The law broke up existing reservations into individual parcels of land to be divided up among households. As Senator Dawes himself put it, breaking up the reservations was "the beginning of the end of the Indian as an Indian."

But since Indians were not yet quite 'civilized,' not yet to be trusted with their own affairs, the title to these lands would be held by the government for twenty-five years. "Excess" land beyond that needed to give each head of household 160 acres would be sold to settlers and, again, the proceeds held in trust by the government. (Though the government could give these monies to missionaries and other agencies working to Christianize and educate Indians.) Lands were 'excess' because no reserves needed to provided for future generations as once Indians were "civilized" they ceased to be Indians, thus the beauty of the plan in the eyes of the politicians who devised it was that it both freed up more lands for whites and it got rid of the Indian by turning savages into homesteaders. Notably no provision was made to gain native nations' consent to these measures; rather, they were simply imposed upon them. In 1898 Congress dissolved the longest running native governments, those of the "Five Nations" in Indian Territory (soon to be Oklahoma) and broke up their reservation lands without their permission.

The Dawes Act policy dovetailed with the government's attempt to 'kill the Indian and save the man' by alienating children from their culture. Beginning in 1879, the federal government began seizing native children from their families and confining them to boarding schools where they were to be "civilized." Native children were stripped of their culture, forced to stop speaking their native languages or observing their religious rituals, and converted to protestant Christianity. By the 1920s nearly 80,000 Indian children were being raised apart from their families and their cultures in over 200 boarding schools.

Once begun, the logic of "civilizing" reached absurd lengths. Concerned that Indians did not work (overlooking the inconvenient fact that there were few jobs to be had in most Indian communities), in 1901 the Bureau of Indian Affairs began striking any Indian who didn't have a job from receiving federal aid. In 1902, the federal government embarked on renaming all the Indians on its official rolls to give them "proper" Christian names in place of their own

Figure 6.12 Harris, Beebe & Co.: Pocahontas Chewing Tobacco, 1868

names. Renowned novelist and editor Hamlin Garland was recruited to head the project even though Garland expressed his doubts that "a stone age man can be developed into a citizen of the United States in a single generation." In 1923, the government banned Indian dancing, with one Senator praising the plan for its work to "bring the Indian into the fullness of Caucasian civilization."

Promises of assimilation proved hollow when Congress refused to combine their civilizing project with citizenship. This was, after all, the highpoint of the era of Jim Crow segregation and few whites were enthusiastic with the idea of seeing native peoples possess equal rights to themselves. As long as native people swallowed their second-class citizenship with good humor they were accepted into American popular culture, if not society. In 1910, only eight states prohibited marriages between whites and Indians (compared with 26 that barred whites and blacks from marrying. By 1950, that number had dwindled to five states banning white and Indian marriage.) In World War One, native soldiers were not segregated from whites as black soldiers were.

While native people were victims of racism as other non-whites were, the racism directed against them was structured differently. The acceptance or rejection of native people was in proportion to the degree that they abandoned everything about themselves that was Indian. In other words, by the twentieth century, whites tolerated Indians as long as they rejected and discarded everything Indian. Indians were admitted into the highest realms of American sport, though not without being constantly subjected to jeers and shouts of "chief" and fans mimicking war chants. The Carlisle (Pennsylvania) Indian School football team, coached by Glenn "Pop" Warner and starring Jim Thorpe, drew national fame and acclaim when it beat the collegiate powerhouse, the U.S. Military Academy in 1912. Both teams in the 1911 World Series fielded starting players who were Indians, both of whom had Christianized names and tried in every way to fit in with the other players.

Government efforts to terminate the powers of Indian governments and breakup tribal lands into private plots finally overreached when Congress considered giving the lands of New Mexico's Pueblo nation to white trespassers. Pueblo title to these lands extended back to Spanish land patents and were legally guaranteed by the Treaty of Guadalupe Hidalgo that settled the Mexican-American War. Nevertheless, white squatters had taken thousands of acres of rich Pueblo lands without payment or permission and then used their political clout to enlist the state and federal governments to secure their false claims. As Pueblos were not citizens and could not vote, New Mexico's Republican Senator, H.O. Bursom, sponsored legislation granting clear title to 60,000 of the Pueblo's 340,000 acres to white squatters.

The Bursom bill stirred the reform movement that had fallen silent since the passage of the Dawes Act in 1887. Unexpectedly, opposition to Bursom's land grab materialized in Congress and in the editorial pages of American newspapers. A sympathetic campaign in favor of Indian rights gathered force and not only defeated the Bursom bill, but pressured Congress into finally granting citizenship to native people in 1924. Within a few years the public mood had changed and a new attitude that Indian culture had value and was worth preserving emerged.

JOHNNY APPLESEED.

Figure 6.13 Jonathan Chapman, illustration 1862.

Indians in Popular Culture

While most Americans in the early nineteenth century feasted on tales of Daniel Boone and Davy Crockett fighting Indians without the slightest twinge of guilt or regret, by the end of that century there were some who viewed native peoples with some sympathy, though without understanding. They comforted themselves with romantic stories of noble savages giving speeches as they vanished into history or tales of pioneers who did what they could to protect Indians who succumbed to their destiny in spite of the white man's best efforts at salvation.

The most popular characters in American playhouses for much of the nineteenth century were mythic Indian figures. A majority of staged plays were about Indians who went against their own people to protect English colonists. Squanto, Massasoit, and most of all, Pocahontas, were comforting myths that excused white Americans of their responsibility for uprooting, killing, and driving away native tribes. Plays featuring Indian characters tragically vanishing or willing to sacrifice themselves to save settlers were staged at least forty times between 1825 and 1860. Pocahontas was playing at the National Theater in Washington, D.C. in 1836 when a delegation of Cherokee leaders arrived to protest legislation being passed to remove them from their lands in Georgia.

Also typical of this class of stories was the story of Johnny Appleseed. Johnny Appleseed, so the story goes, was an eccentric and solitary pioneer who ventured deep into the wilderness sowing apple seeds that would grow into life-sustaining orchards by the time the horizon of white settlement arrived. Indians did not molest him, sensing his spiritual innocence and his gentle nature. One poem celebrated Johnny by describing: "The forests were infested with murderous savages, but there was always a welcome for Johnny at their wigwam and village." Reformer and writer Lydia Maria Child was one of Johnny Appleseed's first popularizers, writing a widely published poem of his humble mission:

> Poor Johnny was bended well nigh double
> With years of toil, and care, and trouble;
> But his large old heart still felt the need
> Of doing for others some kindly deed.

Following the logic that white civilization gives and Indians take, Child's poem, like most all accounts of Appleseed, depict him as instructing native peoples in both the wonders of tree planting and of thinking past one's immediate gratification.

> Sometimes an Indian of sturdy limb
> Came striding along and walked with him;
> And he who had food shared with the other,
> As if he had met a hungry brother.

> When the Indian saw how the bag was filled,
> And looked at the holes that the white man drilled,
> He thought to himself 't was a silly plan
> To be planting seed for some future man.

Historical fact portrays a different flesh and blood Jonathan Chapman who complained when Indians stole his horses and sided with his fellow Americans against them in the War of 1812. He was certainly not an ascetic as land records show he bought and sold and sometimes defaulted on parcels he owned. Some evidence suggests he later worked as a bill collector squeezing money from the last remaining villages of the Delaware.

In any event, his myth has served to further reduce native peoples in American's memories to helpless dependents, waiting for a white to tutor them in survival. To this day, communities throughout Ohio and Indiana continue to credit the existence of the oldest fruit trees to his handiwork, overlooking the obvious fact that native peoples participated in their cultivation and spread since the seventeenth century when they were first introduced.

These new attitudes toward native societies grew out of a complex mixture of politics and cultural shifts. On the one hand, by the late 1920s it had been a generation since any white Americans felt directly threatened by the resistance of native peoples. On the other, since the end of the nineteenth century, Indian culture had been increasingly romanticized, commercialized, and appropriated by whites who now began to view it as a source of manly strength and an important counterweight to the "emasculating" tendencies of modern urban and industrialized life.

Advertisers had long profited from American's beliefs that Indian people were closer to nature and therefore had developed both healing knowledge and an earthly wisdom. Images and names of native peoples are used so commonly in marketing products that become invisible. The frequent naming of products by Indian names and the repetition of mythic pictures of Indians living in the past were among the earliest stereotypes used in marketing.

White Jealousy of the 'Savage'

By the late nineteenth century white men, particularly middle and upper class white men, grew obsessed with what it meant to be man. Many worried about whether they were manly and how manhood itself was changing.

Earlier generations of white men understood manhood to mean independence. Independence meant not being under the rule or control of another man. Slave owners were quite secure in their manhood as were rich men who controlled their employees. Poorer men strived to master a trade and thought of their skills as the basis of their independence.

Independence was not only something to be struggled for out in the world, but also something to be won inside. Manhood meant having a strong will that was shown by acts of self-control. In this way ideas of manliness reinforced and were in turn reinforced by religion that stressed morality and fighting temptation to sin. A manly man in the early nineteenth century was one who minded his own business, abstained from alcohol, and kept his emotions in check.

As the nineteenth century progressed that ability of men to feel independent and in control of their own selves was eroded by industrialization that steadily reduced artisans into factory workers and small business owners into middle managers in ever growing bureaucracies.

There was a deep paradox in white men's anxiety about their manhood and identity. Their whiteness told them that they were the product of the highest achievement of all human history, civilization. But modern civilization for all its virtues and technological progress, was seen as feminizing men by insulating them from nature;

Figure 6.14 Boy Scouts - Outside tent with headdresses, c. 1935-1945.

making them soft with its luxuries and weak with its ease and order, endangering their manhood by robbing men of their independence.

As the possibility of being independent or in command of others diminished, men turned to other models of manliness to imitate. They became fascinated with physical strength and prowess. They redoubled their efforts to distinguish themselves from women, in dress, in manners, in all ways (no more powdered wigs or knickers). Body builders, like Eugene Sandow, who billed himself as the "perfect man" toured America, displaying their bodies and performing feats of strength. Professional men stuck in their offices developed a new fondness for paintings and sculptures of working class men physically laboring in the factories.

Scientists, like the influential psychologist G. Stanley Hall, theorized that to overcome the potentially debilitating effects of modern luxury, white boys needed to be allowed a period of life when they could express their inner savages.

Popular culture at the end of the nineteenth century emphasized the importance of naturalistic experiences to develop boys into men. Speaking of Kit Carson, Daniel Boone, and Johnny Appleseed, one author of a book for boys wrote: "Men of this description are not the product of an over-refined civilization. At times they might be and, indeed, are called barbarians. They are essentially boyish; like boys they have restless minds and are noisy, energetic, fun-loving creatures, and, while ready at any time to prove their true manhood, it cannot be denied they often lack the stiff, artificial deportment that sometimes masquerades as real dignity."

Beginning in the 1880s, a number of 'summer camps' began serving the children of well-to-do families on the east coast. These emphasized the educational, physical, and spiritual values of sending boys into the woods to learn woodcraft and other "Indian skills" and to commune with nature. As one camp boasted, "The design of the camp is to furnish boys with a rational and healthy outdoor life…

[where they can develop] other manly sports form and cultivate good habits and build up their bodily strength."

The most popular manifestation of these ideas was the founding of an organization dedicated to instilling in boys these naturalistic and 'primitive' values by having them pretend to be Indians. Ernest T. Seton a popular author and self-proclaimed 'naturalist,' founded the "Woodcraft Indians," an organization for boys he hoped would prevent them from becoming "flat chested cigarette smokers, with shaky nerves and doubtful vitality." Seton, like so many of his generation, believed that the antidote to modern man's weaknesses was imitating Indian "woodcraft" so to obtain the Indian's vigor. In fact, doing so was neccesary to save the white race:

No one who studies man's beginnings in the light of modern research can doubt that Woodcraft was the earliest of our sciences. It was Woodcraft indeed that constructed man out of the crude and brutish stuff that was then the best live product of the earth. We can see a little of the process to day in our children... And weightier yet it seems to me that

Woodcraft, in its broad entirety, more than any other activity, is calculated to save our species from decay.

The Camp Life is the climax of all Woodcraft and the man who leads us there who blazes the trail who teaches us the fords that grow less fearsome as we follow is a heal worker for our race.

...The blue sky life is associated with mighty benefits... The benefits are beyond question--all the glorious purification of sunlight, the upbuild of exercise with the zest of pleasure, the balm of fresh air at night, the blessedness of sleep, the nerve rest, and change of daily life....

Seton eventually combined his faux Indian ethic with the militarized boys club founded by Lord Robert Baden-Powell to become the Boy Scouts. Seton wrote most of the first Boy Scout Handbook emphasizing the importance of boys reclaiming their primitive natures by pretending to be Indians, adopting fake Indian names, memorizing Indian folklore he had imagined, and performing fake Indian rituals.

Figure 6.15 Washington Redskins start training. Washington, D.C. Aug. 28, 1937. In air, left to right: Millner (Notre Dame), Rentner (Northwestern) and Peterson (West Virginia-Wesleyan).

Pretending to be Indian also appealed to the fans of a new rising sports culture that offered another physical and gladitorial solution to the problem of the weakening white race. Eagle scout Lester Leutwiler drew on his extensive experience playing Indians in the Boy Scots to invent the University of Illinois' Indian mascot Chief Illiniwek in the 1920s. Indeed, the first four "Chief Illiniweks" were not only former scouts, but studied directly under scoutings' self-declared 'expert' of Indian lore, Ralph Hubbard. Dozens of other college sports teams adopted Indian mascots at the same time, seeing in them a combination of primitive physicality and an organic connection to place and land that their transient and largely immigrant spectators found satisfying.

The spectacle of a white man dressed as an Indian chief, performing a made-up dance at the halftime of a football game before tens of thousands of white spectators, was a ritual that claimed rightful possession of the land the athletes played upon. Mascots had to be made-up, invented Indians, not real ones, because by being fake they conveyed the message that there were no more real Indians, they had all vanished, along with their claims to their land. Mascots both appropriated Indian virtues and denied Indian rights at the same time.

Movie Indians

In the early years of movie-making, Indians were a favorite subject but they were portrayed with more variety and perhaps even more sympathy than they would once filmmaking consolidated into a handful of studios by the 1920s. Among the silent films featuring depictions of Indians were many literary adaptations: *Pocahontas* (1908), *Hiawatha* (1909), *The Death of Minnehaha* (1910), *Ramona* (1911) and in 1912 an Indian-themed Romeo and Juliet titled unimaginatively, *An Indian Romeo and Juliet*. Doomed romances between Indians and whites was a popular theme in the silent era, D.W. Griffith, the famed director of *Birth of a Nation*, filmed thirty movies about Indians, most of them portraying Indians as noble savages, sympathetic characters who tragically were completely unsuited to modern life and unable to live in the white man's world.

Interestingly, during the silent film era movie companies sought out and employed native actors to fill their Indian roles. One production company, the New York Motion Picture Company, contracted with the Bureau of Indian Affairs to relocate groups of Oglala Sioux from South Dakota to Santa Monica, California, for six month stints of filmmaking. This partnership produced some eighty movies between 1912 and 1917. Success attracted imitators and the Universal Film Manufacturing Company relocated several hundred Navajo people to California's San

Figure 6.16 Movie poster for "The Way of the Redman Blood of his Fathers" (Chicago: Goes Lithograph Co., 1914).

Fernando Valley. Another film company, Pathé, outdid the others by both recruiting a large native troupe of actors and hiring a native director, James Young Deer, to film them. (Another native director, Edwin Carewe, a Chickasaw native of Texas, filmed dozens of pictures between 1914 and 1931.)

The movies produced in this era were relatively short, one or two reels of film or between fifteen and thirty minutes in length. Such short movies were cheap and made quickly thus encouraging more risk-taking and variety as less money was staked on each one. But beginning in 1914, the industry began to shift toward feature-length films of six reels. These required far more investment, planning and risk and as a result discouraged departures from proven formulas.

The very first of these new longer western movies was an Indian-themed drama, *The Squaw Man* (1914). *The Squaw Man* was adapted from a play staged a decade earlier that repeated one of the most common storylines of the old western dime novels, the ill-fated marriage of an Indian maiden and a white man that inevitably leads to her death. (The underlying message being that whites and Indians must be kept apart for the good of the Indian.) While being the first of the new feature-length westerns, *The Squaw Man* was one of the last movies to cast a native actress in the leading role as director Cecil B. DeMille insisted a "real Indian" play the part and hired actress Lillian St. Cyr who was Winnebago.

In 1923, Paramount studios invested heavily in an epic movie, *The Covered Wagon,* and its record-breaking success drove other movie-makers to imitate its depiction of cowboys fighting Indians along the Oregon Trail. Westerns came to mean action-packed movies where white heroes fought Indians and saved the girl. The one big-budget feature that bucked this trend, *The Vanishing American* (1925), a film that faulted white greed and corruption for the decline of the Indian and ends with the Indian heroine dying while clutching a Bible, was a commercial flop. Instead, by the 1930s, formula cowboy and Indian epics dominated the silver screen and epics like *Texas Rangers* (1936), *The Plainsman* (1937), *Stagecoach* (1939), and *Geronimo* (1939), simplified their storylines by depicting Indians as savage obstacles to America's manifest destiny.

By the 1930s, when as many as two-thirds of all the Indians depicted in westerns were non-natives in wigs and makeup, the decline in the use of actual native actors in Hollywood drove the remaining few Indian actors to unionize and form the Indian Actors Association (IAA). The IAA unsuccessfully demanded that only Indian actors be cast in Indian roles and that the pay between Indian and non-Indian extras be equalized (Indian extras usually were paid half the wages of white actors).

While western movies portrayed Indians as two-dimensional stock characters, as interchangeably nameless bloodthirsty, war-whooping, savages, one popular Indian character became a household name, Tonto, sidekick of the Lone Ranger. *The Lone Ranger* series was first developed for radio in 1932 by the owner of Detroit's WXYZ, George Trendle. In 1949, after being adapted to two motion pictures, a weekly comic strip (that would run until 1971) and a long-running comic book series, it made the transition to television.

Even without his shining white hat, or his white horse, Trigger, the Lone Ranger embodied whiteness in his masculine purity. Never needing a shave, never to be seen in dirty clothes, the Lone Ranger's only motivation was to fight for justice against evil. As the voice-over announcer intoned in the episode explaining how the Texas Ranger became the Lone Ranger, after the ambush that killed most of his Ranger unit:

> ANNOUNCER: Tonto was amazed at the sudden strength that seemed to surge through the wounded man. He seemed to be transformed by some strange alchemy into the composite of all six Rangers. In his eyes, there was a light that must have burned in the eyes of knights in armor—a light that, through the ages, lifted the souls of strong men who fought for justice, for Christianity.

The Lone Ranger works outside the structure of law and society and operates as a white vigilante who sees himself as fighting for 'justice and Christianity.' In embodying these principles, the Lone Ranger mirrored an organization that grew rapidly to national proportions around the same time and also proclaimed itself carrying on a vigilante fight for white Christian justice—the Ku Klux Klan.

The Lone Ranger's sidekick, Tonto (a name which means "fool" in Spanish), in contrast to the Ranger and his shining white horse Trigger, rides a mottled pinto horse, symbolic of his mixed ancestry. Tonto's backstory follows the long-established idea that he was part of a vanishing race, when, as a child, he was saved by The Lone Ranger after an enemy tribe wiped out his family and all of his people (illustrating the lawless savagery of Indians that was the opposite of The Lone Ranger's quest for law and order). Like James Fenimore Cooper's Uncas, the young man who was the last Mohican, Tonto was his tribes' only survivor.

In spite of his having spent all his life around English speakers, Tonto speaks in only broken, pidgin English, consistently misusing pronouns and verb tenses: "While me in town, Kemosabe, me follow crook's tracks .. Me show you where we pick up trail outside town."

Figure 6.17 Sign in bar window, Sisseton, South Dakota, 1939.

Figure 6.18 Longest Walk Indian Teepee at the Washington Monument grounds, July 11, 1978.

The Indian New Deal

The horrors of World War One caused deep changes in western culture. It destroyed one of the cornerstones of white claims of European society being superior to all others, while revolutionary anthropologists like Franz Boas and Claude Levis-Strauss demonstrated the sophistication and complexity of cultures long thought of as "primitive." In 1928, a government report for the first time described Indian society and culture as something not to be suppressed and extinguished, but as something of value, and recommended that Indian communities be given the right to choose whether to assimilate or preserve their cultures. Of course, even such new expression of the relative value of all cultures could at this time only be expressed through the lens of race:

Leadership will recognize the good in the economic and social life of Indians in their religion and ethics, and will seek to develop it and build on it rather than to crush out all that is Indian. The Indians have much to contribute to the dominant civilization, and the effort should be made to secure this contribution, in part because of the good it will do the Indians in stimulating a proper race pride and self-respect.

Such ideas were given full attention once the national economic disaster known as the Great Depression struck and President Franklin Roosevelt's administration had the opportunity to experiment with radically new policies. By 1934, the amount of land held by Indians just prior to passage of the Dawes Act breaking up reservations had been reduced by two-thirds. Roosevelt suspended all additional sales of Indian land and supported passage of the Wheeler-Howard Indian Reorganization Act that provided a fund for restoring reservation land and fostered the organization of Indian tribal governments. Roosevelt's administration ordered an end to government interference in Indian religious ceremonies and prohibited the suppression of native languages among Indian children in government schools. Indian arts were promoted as both a means of preserving culture and a step toward economic development. While FDR's reforms of government policies toward native peoples did not resolve all the thorny issues accumulated over centuries of colonial domination, they did mark a landmark where the government, at least in principle, recognized Indian nations rather than just saw individual Indians as dependent children to be tutored and disciplined.

All good ideas can be taken too far and by the 1950s the logic of freeing native nations from government oversight led to a drive to terminate all government relationships and responsibilities to indigenous peoples. Congress passed several bills phasing in a termination of all government services and withdrawing all supervisory powers over various tribal governments. In practice those nations first subject to these termination policies, the Klamath in Washington and the Menominee in Wisconsin, were simply cut loose without the economic resources to fully support their communities and the result was the further fragmentation and loss of their tribal lands. Many observers compared the new termination policies to the failed Dawes Act of 1887 and by the early 1970s pressure mounted to end the government's policy of neglect.

Fighting these policies were a number of Indian organizations. But while the Civil Rights Movement grew into a transformative force in the 1950s, Indian rights activists were barely visible. However, in the summer of 1961 nearly 500 delegates from tribes and native nations gathered in

Chicago, the largest such meeting in the twentieth century, and hammered out a "Declaration of Indian Purpose," a lengthy manifesto that called for greater government respect for Indian self-determination and autonomy. Soon after this meeting a number of Indian college students met in New Mexico and formed a new organization, the National Indian Youth Council whose young activists would soon began calling their movement one for "Red Power," and this was a movement that attracted headlines.

Red Power youth activists departed from the older native rights organizations by criticizing the larger structures of racial oppression as well as their own tribal representatives. Clyde Warrior, one of their leaders and a member of the Ponca tribe of Oklahoma told a Congressional hearing in 1967:

> We are not free. We do not make choices. Our choices are made for us; we are the poor. For those of us who live on reservations these choices and decisions are made by federal administrators, bureaucrats, and their "yes men," euphemistically called tribal governments. Those of us who live in non-reservation areas have our lives controlled by local white power elites. We have many rulers. They are called social workers, "cops," school teachers, churches, etc...

More importantly, Red Power activists were tired of the slow work of lobbying and backroom politicking that had characterized the older native civil rights organizations. One of these, Richard Oakes, a San Francisco State University student from the St. Regis Mohawk community, led a symbolic "takeover" of Alcatraz Island in San Francisco Bay in 1969. Oakes was inspired by an earlier effort on the part of Lakota (Sioux) activists to claim the island under the terms of the Fort Laramie Treaty of 1868 that promised that any unused land taken by the government would be returned to the Lakota nation. Alcatraz had ceased operating as a federal prison in 1963 but neither the federal government or California had developed any specific plans for redeveloping the area.

On a chilly morning in November, Oakes and two dozen other members of the newly formed group, Indians of All Tribes (IAT), an umbrella group that brought together seven Indian organizations including the American Indian Movement (AIM) organized a few months earlier. Launching their occupation by boat, Oakes and a few others symbolically swam the last yards through the cold waters to the island. That night they evaded the mothballed prison's lone security guard and a coast guard boat that searched for them. IAT's occupation lasted nineteen months as supporters ran coast guard blockades with supplies and committed IAT activists refused to accept various

Figure 6.19 RCA black/white Indian Head test card, used from 1940 until the advent of color television.

deals brokered with federal officials. So organized were the IAT members that in addition to caring for daily needs on the island with cooking, laundry, and childcare chores divided up among the occupiers. There were classes in various subjects and a newsletter written and edited on the island. Volunteers visited the island to offer their help, such as tradesmen who opened up the prison's old water lines and a doctor and nurse who provided health care. Celebrities like Jane Fonda and Anthony Quinn made publicized visits to the island and the band Creedence Clearwater Revival donated a boat.

Inspired by the occupation of Alcatraz, young native activists used similar tactics to highlight longstanding injustices and denial of treaty rights elsewhere. Native activists demanded the restoration of native fishing rights by occupying Seattle's Fort Lawton, the restoration of lands seized by utility companies from the Pit River tribes of California, and conducted the Trail of Broken Treaties, a dramatic four-mile long auto caravan protest from Seattle to Washington, D.C. in 1972.

The following year hundreds of armed AIM members occupied Wounded Knee, a village on the Pine Ridge Lakota reservation in South Dakota. Federal officials treated this occupation more severely than the one at Alcatraz and soon surrounded the town with agents from various federal justice agencies including the FBI. Over the course of the 71 day standoff, firefights erupted several times and at least two native activists and an FBI agent were killed. Two leaders of the protest, Dennis Banks and Russell Means were tried in federal court on charges of conspiracy and acquitted after a nearly nine month trial in which the presiding judge condemned the government for "aggravated" prosecutorial misconduct. Lakota leader Leonard Peltier was convicted of murder in the death of a federal agent and sentenced to life without parole.

Direct action and more visible protests succeeded in pushing President Nixon to order the restoration of government services to terminated tribes, establishing a status quo that has held since. Today most tribal governments have a limited autonomy in exchange for a range of health, legal, educational and economic development services provided by the federal government.

Modern Day Stereotypes of Native People

By the mid-twentieth century white Americans continued to think of native people as living in the past and being unsuited to the modern world. That they were still widely and deeply associated with a 'vanishing race' that a drawing of a Indian chief in full headdress became the most visible element in television's sign-off card that marked the end of that day's broadcast. A test pattern featuring the Indian was shown at the end of each broadcast day by the major television networks and their local affiliates from 1939 to the 1960s when color TV's simple chromatic bars replaced him.

Native people had clearly not lived up to the expectations of white Americans and vanished. Though the census had tried its best to ignore them, (researchers in the 1960s documented systematic undercounts of up to 20,000 Navajo by comparing census rolls to Bureau of Indian Affairs records) by the end of the twentieth century it was indisputable that native populations were growing. In the 2000 census, 2.5 million people reported identifying as American Indian or Alaskan native.

In addition to a steadily increasing population, the last half of the twentieth century also saw the increasing urbanization of Indian peoples. Many native people moved from rural areas to urban ones in search of work and other opportunities and by the end of the century a majority of native people lived in cities. In fact, outside of the Navajo reservation, the largest concentration of native people are the 111,000 native people who live in New York City. Today, only about a quarter of native Americans live on reservation lands.

Though the reality for most native people is not one of living on a reservation or maintaining ancient practices, most whites still think of Indians in the stereotypical ways invented centuries ago. Though images of Indians as "savages" have become uncommon, native people continue to be depicted in ways that mark them as living in the past rather than fitting into the modern world. Native people are still widely thought of as natural mystics, possessing a spiritual and healthful knowledge that white people covet. Beginning in the 1960s and 1970s, a "New Age" movement of mostly middle class whites commercialized crystals and dream catchers and consciousness-raising seminars into a billion-dollar a year industry.

White people's desire to escape the constraints of their whiteness by pretending to be Indians continued into modern times. In 1991 a book published a dozen years earlier, Forrest Carter's *The Education of Little Tree*, hit the nonfiction best-seller lists selling over a million copies. *The Education of Little Tree* was an account of a boy raised in rural Tennessee by his native grandparents who taught him Indian ways and values, including a deep distrust of white man's government and respect for all natural things. *The Education of Little Tree* was especially popular in the "New Age" community that celebrated multiculturalism, native spirituality, and alternative lifestyles.

After Carter's death his fans learned that Carter was not the child of native grandparents but of white Confederates. He was not even from Tennessee. His real name was Asa Earl Carter and he was from Alabama. Carter was a lifelong white supremacist who during World War Two joined the Navy so he wouldn't have to fight what he considered to be his racial brothers, the Germans. He fought the Civil Rights movement as editor of the pro-segregation magazine, *The Southerner*, and worked as a speechwriter for Alabama Governor George Wallace, for whom he wrote the famous lines "Segregation now! Segregation tomorrow! Segregation forever!" As late as 1971, Carter was still trying to organize a white-supremacist paramilitary organization to fight civil rights.

Carter reinvented himself as a Cherokee writer in the mid-1970s after he felt abandoned by his old racist supporters and wrote a number of books including one, *The Outlaw Josey Wales*, that Clint Eastwood turned into a popular movie. Cherokee critics immediately saw through Carter's disguise, especially as Carter made up all the Cherokee words he used in *The Education of Little Tree*.

As they were in the 19th century, Indians continued to be used in advertising as symbols of natural wisdom, a throwback to the old "noble savage" ideas of the colonial era.

One of the most famous advertising campaigns of the 1970s, a government public service message discouraging littering, depicted an Indian man fringed in buckskin, paddling his birch bark canoe past mounds of trash. As the voice over announcer solemnly intoned, "Some people have a deep abiding respect for natural beauty that was once this country. And some people don't." The native actor, Iron Eyes Cody, then turned to face the camera for a close-up revealing a solitary tear rolling down his cheek.

This 1971 "Keep America Beautiful" commercial

proved to be a powerful cultural moment because it combined the image of the Indian as stoic and noble with his purported naturalism and mixed in his living in the past. Few knew at the time that it also illustrated well the long-standing desire of white men to 'play Indian.' Only upon his death was it revealed that Iron Eyes Cody was not Cree and Cherokee at all, as he claimed, but was actually Oscar DeCorti, son of Francesca Salpietra and Antonio DeCorti, Italian immigrants who settled in Kaplan, Louisiana and opened a grocery store.

European Americans, from their first contacts with native peoples, projected onto them their own fears, desires, and beliefs instead of seeing them as people. When needed, Indian communities were made allies and granted a grudging respect. When an obstacle to European American goals, they were betrayed, conquered, and scattered, only to be romanticized once their power was broken. Through it all European Americans rooted themselves in their new homeland by memorializing Indian nations who were not actually in need of memorials as they were still very much alive. Whether viewed as innocents, as noble primitives, as savages, as the vanishing people of the past, or as innately spiritual beings, Indian stereotypes have always had one quality in common. They all serve to deny the simple fact that indigenous nations are nations whose rights to sovereignty and self-determination have never been respected.

Figure 6.20 Actor "Iron Eyes" Cody

Figure 6.21 U.S. Census Poster, 2010.

Approved by General Assembly resolution 260 A (III) of 9 December 1948. Entry into force 12 January 1951. (Note: The U.S. Senate blocked US ratification of this convention for 30 years until 1988, making it the 146th nation to adopt this law.)

Convention on the Prevention and Punishment of the Crime of Genocide

The Contracting Parties,

Having considered the declaration made by the General Assembly of the United Nations in its resolution 96 (I) dated 11 December 1946 that genocide is a crime under international law, contrary to the spirit and aims of the United Nations and condemned by the civilized world,

Recognizing that at all periods of history genocide has inflicted great losses on humanity, and Being convinced that, in order to liberate mankind from such an odious scourge, international co-operation is required,

Hereby agree as hereinafter provided:

Article I

The Contracting Parties confirm that genocide, whether committed in time of peace or in time of war, is a crime under international law which they undertake to prevent and to punish.

Article II

In the present Convention, genocide means any of the following acts committed with intent to destroy, in whole or in part, a national, ethnical, racial or religious group, as such:

Killing members of the group;

Causing serious bodily or mental harm to members of the group;

Deliberately inflicting on the group conditions of life calculated to bring about its physical destruction in whole

or in part;

Imposing measures intended to prevent births within the group;

Forcibly transferring children of the group to another group.

Article III

The following acts shall be punishable:

Genocide;

Conspiracy to commit genocide;

Direct and public incitement to commit genocide;

Attempt to commit genocide;

Complicity in genocide.

Article IV

Persons committing genocide or any of the other acts enumerated in article III shall be punished, whether they are constitutionally responsible rulers, public officials or private individuals.

Article V

The Contracting Parties undertake to enact, in accordance with their respective Constitutions, the necessary legislation to give effect to the provisions of the present Convention, and, in particular, to provide effective penalties for persons guilty of genocide or any of the other acts enumerated in article III.

Article VI

Persons charged with genocide or any of the other acts enumerated in article III shall be tried by a competent tribunal of the State in the territory of which the act was committed, or by such international penal tribunal as may have jurisdiction with respect to those Contracting Parties which shall have accepted its jurisdiction.

Article VII

Genocide and the other acts enumerated in article III shall not be considered as political crimes for the purpose of extradition. The Contracting Parties pledge themselves in such cases to grant extradition in accordance with their laws and treaties in force.

Article VIII

Any Contracting Party may call upon the competent organs of the United Nations to take such action under the Charter of the United Nations as they consider appropriate for the prevention and suppression of acts of genocide or any of the other acts enumerated in article III...

Washington Irving, "The Traits of Indian Character"
from *The Sketch-Book of Geoffrey Crayon*, 1820 (originally published in *Analectic Magazine*, 1814).

THERE is something in the character and habits of the North American savage, taken in connection with the scenery over which he is accustomed to range, its vast lakes, boundless forests, majestic rivers, and trackless plains, that is, to my mind, wonderfully striking and sublime. He is formed for the wilderness, as the Arab is for the desert. His nature is stern, simple and enduring; fitted to grapple with difficulties, and to support privations. There seems but little soil in his heart for the support of the kindly virtues; and yet, if we would but take the trouble to penetrate through that proud stoicism and habitual taciturnity, which lock up his character from casual observation, we should find him linked to his fellow-man of civilized life by more of those sympathies and affections than are usually ascribed to him.

It has been the lot of the unfortunate aborigines of America, in the early periods of colonization, to be doubly wronged by the white men. They have been dispossessed of their hereditary possessions by mercenary and frequently wanton warfare: and their characters have been traduced by bigoted and interested writers. The colonist often treated them like beasts of the forest; and the author has endeavored to justify him in his outrages. The former found it easier to exterminate than to civilize; the latter to vilify than to discriminate. The appellations of savage and pagan were deemed sufficient to sanction the hostilities of both; and thus the poor wanderers of the forest were persecuted and defamed, not because they were guilty, but because they were ignorant.

The rights of the savage have seldom been properly appreciated or respected by the white man. In peace he has too often been the dupe of artful traffic; in war he has been regarded as a ferocious animal, whose life or death was a question of mere precaution and convenience. Man is cruelly wasteful of life when his own safety is endangered, and he is sheltered by impunity; and little mercy is to be expected from him, when he feels the sting of the reptile and is conscious of the power to destroy.

The same prejudices, which were indulged thus early, exist in common circulation at the present day. Certain learned societies have, it is true, with laudable diligence, endeavored to investigate and record the real characters and manners of the Indian tribes; the American government, too, has wisely and humanely exerted itself to inculcate a friendly and forbearing spirit towards them, and to protect them from fraud and injustice.* The current opinion of the Indian character, however, is too apt to be formed from the miserable hordes which infest the frontiers, and hang on the skirts of the settlements. These are too commonly composed of degenerate beings, corrupted and enfeebled by the vices of society, without being benefited by its civilization. That proud independence, which formed the main pillar of savage virtue, has been shaken down, and the whole moral fabric lies in ruins. Their spirits are humiliated and debased by a sense of inferiority, and their native courage cowed and daunted by the superior knowledge and power of their enlightened neighbors. Society has advanced upon them like one of those withering airs that will sometimes breed desolation over a whole region of fertility. It has enervated their strength, multiplied their diseases, and superinduced upon their original barbarity the low vices of artificial life. It has given them a thousand superfluous wants, whilst it has diminished their means of mere existence. It has driven before it the animals of the chase, who fly from the sound of the axe and the smoke of the settlement, and seek refuge in the depths of remoter forests and yet untrodden wilds. Thus do we too often find the Indians on our frontiers to be the mere wrecks and remnants of once powerful tribes, who have lingered in the vicinity of the settlements, and sunk into precarious and vagabond existence. Poverty, repining and hopeless poverty, a canker of the mind unknown in savage life, corrodes their spirits, and blights every free and noble quality of their natures. They become drunken, indolent, feeble, thievish, and pusillanimous. They loiter like vagrants about the settlements, among spacious dwellings replete with elaborate comforts, which only render them sensible of the comparative wretchedness of their own condition. Luxury spreads its ample board before their eyes; but they are excluded from the banquet. Plenty revels over the fields; but they are starving in the midst of its abundance: the whole wilderness has blossomed into a garden; but they feel as reptiles that infest it.

How different was their state while yet the undisputed lords of the soil! Their wants were few, and the means of gratification within their reach. They saw every one around them sharing the same lot, enduring the same hardships, feeding on the same aliments, arrayed in the same rude garments. No roof then rose, but was open to the homeless stranger; no smoke curled among the trees, but he was welcome to sit down by its fire, and join the hunter in his repast. "For," says an old historian of New England, "their life is so void of care, and they are so loving also, that they make use of those things they enjoy as common goods, and are therein so compassionate, that rather than one should starve through want, they would starve all; thus they pass their time merrily, not regarding our pomp, but are better content with their own, which some men esteem so meanly of." Such were the Indians, whilst in the pride and energy of their primitive natures: they resembled those wild plants, which thrive best in the shades of the forest, but shrink from the hand of cultivation, and perish beneath the influence of the sun....

But if courage intrinsically consists in the defiance of danger and pain, the life of the Indian is a continual exhibition of it. He lives in a state of perpetual hostility and risk. Peril and adventure are congenial to his nature; or rather seem necessary to arouse his faculties and to give an interest to his existence. Surrounded by hostile tribes, whose mode of warfare is by ambush and surprisal (sic), he is always prepared for fight, and lives with his weapons in his hands. As the ship careers in fearful singleness through the solitudes of ocean;- as the bird mingles among clouds and storms, and wings its way, a mere speck, across the pathless fields of air;- so the Indian holds his course, silent, solitary, but undaunted, through the boundless bosom of the wilderness. His expeditions may vie in distance and danger with the pilgrimage of the devotee, or the crusade of the knight-errant. He traverses vast forests, exposed to the hazards of lonely sickness, of lurking enemies, and pining famine. Stormy lakes, those great inland seas, are no obstacles to his wanderings: in his light canoe of bark he sports, like a feather, on their waves, and darts, with the swiftness of an arrow, down the roaring rapids of the rivers. His very subsistence is snatched from the midst of toil and peril. He gains his food by the hardships and dangers of the chase: he wraps himself in the spoils of the bear, the panther, and the buffalo, and sleeps among the thunders of the cataract.

But I forbear to dwell on these gloomy pictures. The eastern tribes have long since disappeared; the forests that sheltered them have been laid low, and scarce any traces remain of them in the thickly-settled states of New England, excepting here and there the Indian name of a village or a stream. And such must, sooner or later, be the fate of those other tribes which skirt the frontiers, and have occasionally been inveigled from their forests to mingle in the wars of white men. In a little while, and they will go the way that their brethren have gone before. The few hordes which still linger about the shores of Huron and Superior, and the tributary streams of the Mississippi, will share the fate of those tribes that once spread over Massachusetts and Connecticut, and lorded it along the proud banks of the Hudson; of that gigantic race said to have existed on the borders of the Susquehanna; and of those various nations that flourished about the Potomac and the Rappahannock, and that peopled the forests of the vast valley of Shenandoah. They will vanish like a vapor from the face of the earth; their very history will be lost in forgetfulness; and "the places that now know them will know them no more forever." Or if, perchance, some dubious memorial of them should survive, it may be in the romantic dreams of the poet, to people in imagination his glades and groves, like the fauns and satyrs and sylvan deities of antiquity. But should he venture upon the dark story of their wrongs and wretchedness; should he tell how they were invaded, corrupted, despoiled, driven from their native abodes and the sepulchers of their fathers, hunted like wild beasts about the earth, and sent down with violence and butchery to the grave, posterity will either turn with horror and incredulity from the tale, or blush with indignation at the inhumanity of their forefathers.- "We are driven back," said an old warrior, "until we can retreat no farther- our hatchets are broken, our bows are snapped, our fires are nearly extinguished:- a little longer, and the white man will cease to persecute us- for we shall cease to exist!"

Washington Irving

Maxi'diwiac's Account

(A few words should now be said of informant and interpreter. Maxi'diwiac, or Buffalobird- woman, is a daughter of Small Ankle, a leader of the Hidatsas in the trying time of the tribe's removal to what is now Fort Berthold reservation. She was born on one of the villages at Knife River two years after the "smallpox year," or about 1839. She is a conservative and sighs for the good old times, yet is aware that the younger generation of Indians must adopt civilized ways. Ignorant of English, she has a quick intelligence and a memory that is marvelous. To her patience and loyal interest is chiefly due whatever of value is in this thesis. In the sweltering heat of an August day she has continued dictation for nine hours, lying down but never flagging in her account, when too weary to sit longer in a chair. Goodbird's testimony that his mother "knows more about old ways of raising corn and squashes than anyone else on this reservation," is not without probability...

Edward Goodbird, or Tsaka'kasakic, the writer's interpreter, is a son of Maxi'diwiac, born about November, 1869. Goodbird was one of the first of the reservation children to be sent to the mission school; and he is now native pastor of the Congregational chapel at Independence. He speaks the Hidatsa, Mandan, Dakota, and English languages...

Indians have the gentle custom of adopting very dear friends by relationship terms. By such adoption Goodbird is the writer's brother; Maxi'diwiac is his mother....)

My tribe, as our old men tell us, after they got corn, abandoned their villages at Devils Lake, and joined the Mandans near the mouth of the Heart River. The Mandans helped them build new villages here, near their own. I think this was hundreds of years ago. Firewood growing scarce, the two tribes removed up the Missouri to the mouth of the Knife River, where they built the Five Villages, as they called them. Smallpox was brought to my people here, by traders. In a single year, more than half my tribe died, and of the Mandans, even more. Those who survived removed up the Missouri and built a village at Like-a-fishhook bend, where they lived together, Hidatsas and Mandans, as one tribe. This village we Hidatsas called Mu'a-idu'skupe-hi'cec, or Like-a-fishhook village, after the bend on which it stood; but white men called it Fort Berthold, from a trading post that was there.

We lived in Like-a-fishhook village about forty years, or until 1885, when the government began to place families on allotments. The agriculture of the Hidatsas, as I now describe it, I saw practiced in the gardens of Like-a-fishhook village, in my girlhood, before my tribe owned plows....

I was too small to note very much at first. But I remember that my father set boundary marks— whether wooden stakes or little mounds of earth or stones, I do not now remember —at the corners of the field we claimed. My mothers and my two grandmothers began at one end of this field and worked forward. All had heavy iron hoes, except Turtle, who used an old fashioned wooden digging stick....

It was our Indian rule to keep our fields very sacred. We did not like to quarrel about our garden lands. One's title to a field once set up, no one ever thought of disputing it; for if one were selfish and quarrelsome, and tried to seize land belonging to another, we thought some evil would come upon him, as that some one of his family would die...

This that I am going to tell you of the planting and harvesting of our crops is out of my own experience, seen with my own eyes. In olden times, I know, my tribe used digging sticks and bone hoes for garden tools; and I have described how I saw my grandmother use them. There may be other tools or garden customs once in use in my tribe, and now forgotten; of them I cannot speak...This that I now tell is as I saw my mothers do, or did myself, when I was young. My mothers were industrious women, and our family had always good crops;

Mrs. Good Bear, a Hidatsa woman, 1908.

and I will tell now how the women of my father's family cared for their fields, as I saw them, and helped them.

...The first seed that we planted in the spring was sunflower seed. Ice breaks on the Missouri about the first week in April; and we planted sunflower seed as soon after as the soil could be worked. Our native name for the lunar month that corresponds most nearly to April, is Mapi'-o'ce-mi'di, or Sunflower-planting-moon.

Planting was done by hoe, or the woman scooped up the soil with her hands. Three seeds were planted in a hill, at the depth of the second joint of a woman's finger. The three seeds were planted together, pressed into the loose soil by a single motion, with thumb and first two fingers. The hill was heaped up and patted firm with the palm in the same way as we did for corn.

Usually we planted sunflowers only around the edges of a field. The hills were placed eight or nine paces apart; for we never sowed sunflowers thickly. We thought a field surrounded thus by a sparse-sown row of sunflowers, had a handsome appearance.

Of cultivated sunflowers we had several varieties, black, white, red, striped, named from the color of the seed. The varieties differed only in color; all had the same taste and smell, and were treated alike in cooking. White sunflower seed when pounded into meal, turned dark...

To harvest the larger heads, I put a basket on my back, and knife in hand, passed from plant to plant, cutting off each large head close to the stem... My basket filled, I returned to the lodge, climbed the ladder to the roof, and spread the sunflower heads upon the flat part of the roof around the smoke hole, to dry...When I was a girl, only three or four earth lodges in the village had peaked roofs; and these lodges were rather small. All the larger and better lodges, those of what we deemed wealthier families, were built with the top of the roof flat, like a floor. A flat roof was useful to dry things on; and when the weather was fair, the men often sat there and gossiped....

To make sunflower meal the seeds were first roasted, or parched. This was done in a clay pot, for iron pots were scarce in my tribe when I was young. The clay pot in use in my father's family was about a foot high and eight or nine inches in diameter, as you see from measurements I make with my hands. This pot I set on the lodge fire, working it down into the coals with a rocking motion, and raked coals around it; the mouth I tipped slightly toward me. I threw into the pot two or three double-handfuls of the seeds and as they parched, I stirred them with a little stick, to keep them from burning. Now and then I took out a seed and bit it; if the kernel was soft and gummy, I knew the parching was not done; but when it bit dry and crisp, I knew the seeds were cooked and I dipped them out with a horn spoon into a wooden bowl...The parching done, I lifted the pot out, first throwing over it a piece of old tent cover to protect my two hands. Parching the seeds caused them to crack open somewhat. The parched seeds were pounded in the corn mortar to make meal. Pounding sunflower seeds took longer, and was harder work, than pounding corn... Sunflower meal was used in making a dish that we called do'patsamakihi'ks, or four-vegetables-mixed; from do'patsa, four things; and makihi'ks, mixed or put together. Four-vegetables-mixed we thought our very best dish...Four-vegetables-mixed was eaten freshly cooked; and the mixed corn-and-sunflower meal was made fresh for it each time. A little alkali salt might be added for seasoning, but even this was not usual. No other seasoning was used. Meat was not boiled with the mess, as the sunflower seed gave sufficient oil to furnish fat.

We Hidatsa women were early risers in the planting season; it was my habit to be up before sunrise, while the air was cool, for we thought this the best time for garden work. Having arrived at the field I would begin one hill, preparing it, as I have said, with my hoe; and so for ten rows each as long as from this spot to yonder fence; —about thirty yards; the rows were about four feet apart, and the hills stood about the same distance apart in the row.

The hills all prepared, I went back and planted them, patting down each with my palms, as described. Planting corn thus by hand was slow work; but by ten o'clock the morning's work was done, and I was tired and ready to go home for my breakfast and rest; we did not eat before going into the field. The ten rows making the morning's planting contained about two hundred and twenty-five hills.

I usually went to the field every morning in the planting season, if the weather was fine. Sometimes I went out again a little before sunset and planted; but this was not usual.

It was usual for the women of a household to do their own planting; but if a woman was sick, or for some reason was unable to attend to her planting, she sometimes cooked a feast, to which she invited the members of her age society and asked them to plant her field for her.
The members of her society would come upon an appointed day and plant her field in a short time; sometimes a half day was enough. There were about thirty members in my age society when I was a young woman. If we were invited to plant a garden for some sick wom-an, each member would take a row to plant; and each would strive to complete her row first. A member having completed her row, might begin a second, and even a third row; or if, when each had complet-ed one row, there was but a small part of the field yet unplanted, all pitched in miscellaneously and finished the planting.

When our corn was in, we began planting beans and squashes. Beans we commonly planted between corn rows, sometimes over the whole field, more often over a part of it.

Hoeing time began when the corn was about three inches high; but this varied somewhat with the season....Corn and weeds alike

grew rapidly now, and we women of the house hold were out with our hoes daily, to keep ahead of the weeds. We worked as in planting season, in the early morning hours.

Our corn fields had many enemies. Magpies, and especially crows, pulled up much of the young corn, so that we had to replant many hills... Spotted gophers would dig up the seed from the roots of young plants. When the corn had eared, and the grains were still soft, blackbirds and crows were destructive....

We made scarecrows to frighten the crows. Two sticks were driven into the ground for legs; to these were bound two other sticks, like out stretched arms; on the top was fastened a ball of cast-away skins, or the like, for a head. An old buffalo robe was drawn over the figure and a belt tied around its middle, to make it look like a man....

A platform, or stage, was often built in a garden, where the girls and young women of the household came to sit and sing as they watched that crows and other thieves did not destroy the ripening crop. We cared for our corn in those days as we would care for a child; for we Indian people loved our gardens, just as a mother loves her children; and we thought that our growing corn liked to hear us sing, just as children like to hear their mother sing to them....

Girls began to go on the watchers' stage to watch the corn and sing, when they were about ten or twelve years of age. They contin-ued the custom even after they had grown up and married; and old women, working in the garden and stopping to rest, often went on the stage and sang.
Two girls usually watched and sang together. The village gardens were laid out close to one another; and a girl of one family would be joined by the girl of the family who owned the garden adjoining. Sometimes three, or even four, girls got on the stage and sang together; but never more than four. A drum was not used to accompany the singing.

The watchers sometimes rose and stood upon the stage as they looked to see if any boys or horses were in the field, stealing corn. Older girls and young married women, and even old women, often worked at porcupine embroidery as they watched. Very young girls did not embroider.

Most of the songs that were sung on the watchers' stage were love songs, but not all. One that little girls were fond of singing —girls that is of about twelve years of age—was as follows :

You bad boys, you are all alike !
Your bow is like a bent basket hoop;
You poor boys, you have to run on the prairie barefoot;
Your arrows are fit for nothing but to shoot up into the sky !

This song was sung for the benefit of the boys who came to the near-by woods to hunt birds.

Here is another song; but that you may understand it I shall first have to explain to you what ikupa' means. A girl whom another girl loves as her own sister, we call her ikupa'. I think your word chum, as you explain it, has about the same meaning. This is the song:

"My ikupa', what do you wish to see?" you said to me.
What I wish to see is the corn silk coming out on the growing ear;
But what you wish to see is that naughty young man coming !

These songs from the watchers' stage we called mi'daxika, or gardeners' songs. The words of these I have just given you we called love-boy words; and they were intended to tease.

Gilbert L. Wilson, *Agriculture of the Hidatsa Indians: An Indian Interpretation* (Min-neapolis: Univ. of Minnesota, Studies in the Social Sciences, No. 9, Nov. 1917).

To Acknowledge a Long History of Official Depredations and Ill-Conceived Policies by the United States Government Regarding Indian Tribes and Offer an Apology to All Native Peoples on Behalf of the United States, S.J. Res. 14, 111th Cong., 1st Sess., 2009.

To acknowledge a long history of official depredations and ill-conceived policies by the Federal Government regarding Indian tribes and offer an apology to all Native Peoples on behalf of the United States.

IN THE SENATE OF THE UNITED STATES April 30, 2009...JOINT RESOLUTION

To acknowledge a long history of official depredations and ill-conceived policies by the Federal Government regarding Indian tribes and offer an apology to all Native Peoples on behalf of the United States.

Whereas the ancestors of today's Native Peoples inhabited the land of the present-day United States since time immemorial and for thousands of years before the arrival of people of European descent;

Whereas for millennia, Native Peoples have honored, protected, and stewarded this land we cherish;

Whereas Native Peoples are spiritual people with a deep and abiding belief in the Creator, and for millennia Native Peoples have maintained a powerful spiritual connection to this land, as evidenced by their customs and legends;

Whereas the arrival of Europeans in North America opened a new chapter in the history of Native Peoples;

Whereas while establishment of permanent European settlements in North America did stir conflict with nearby Indian tribes, peaceful and mutually beneficial interactions also took place;

Whereas the foundational English settlements in Jamestown, Virginia, and Plymouth, Massachusetts, owed their survival in large measure to the compassion and aid of Native Peoples in the vicinities of the settlements;

Whereas in the infancy of the United States, the founders of the Republic expressed their desire for a just relationship with the Indian tribes, as evidenced by the Northwest Ordinance enacted by Congress in 1787, which begins with the phrase, "The utmost good faith shall always be observed toward the Indians";

Whereas Indian tribes provided great assistance to the fledgling Republic as it strengthened and grew, including invaluable help to Meriwether Lewis and William Clark on their epic journey from St. Louis, Missouri, to the Pacific Coast;

Whereas Native Peoples and non-Native settlers engaged in numerous armed conflicts in which unfortunately, both took innocent lives, including those of women and children;

Whereas the Federal Government violated many of the treaties ratified by Congress and other diplomatic agreements with Indian tribes;

Whereas the United States forced Indian tribes and their citizens to move away from their traditional homelands and onto federally established and controlled reservations, in accordance with such Acts as the Act of May 28, 1830 (4 Stat. 411, chapter 148) (commonly known as the "Indian Removal Act");

Whereas many Native Peoples suffered and perished—

(1) during the execution of the official Federal Government policy of forced removal, including the infamous Trail of Tears and Long Walk;

(2) during bloody armed confrontations and massacres, such as the Sand Creek Massacre in 1864 and the Wounded Knee Massacre in 1890; and

(3) on numerous Indian reservations;

Whereas the Federal Government condemned the traditions, beliefs, and customs of Native Peoples and endeavored to assimilate them by such policies as the redistribution of land under the Act of February 8, 1887 (25 U.S.C. 331; 24 Stat. 388, chapter 119) (commonly known as the "General Allotment Act"), and the forcible removal of Native children from their families to faraway boarding schools where their Native practices and languages were degraded and forbidden;

Whereas officials of the Federal Government and private United States citizens harmed Native Peoples by the unlawful acquisition of recognized tribal land and the theft of tribal resources and assets from recognized tribal land;

Whereas the policies of the Federal Government toward Indian tribes and the breaking of covenants with Indian tribes have contributed to the severe social ills and economic troubles in many Native communities today;

Whereas despite the wrongs committed against Native Peoples by the United States, Native Peoples have remained committed to the protection of this great land, as evidenced by the fact that, on a per capita basis, more Native Peoples have served in the United States Armed Forces and placed themselves in harm's way in defense of the United States in every major military conflict than any other ethnic group;

Whereas Indian tribes have actively influenced the public life of the United States by continued cooperation with Congress and the Department of the Interior, through the involvement of Native individuals in official Federal Government positions, and by leadership of their own sovereign Indian tribes;

Whereas Indian tribes are resilient and determined to preserve, develop, and transmit to future generations their unique cultural identities;

Whereas the National Museum of the American Indian was established within the Smithsonian Institution as a living memorial to Native Peoples and their traditions; and

Whereas Native Peoples are endowed by their Creator with certain unalienable rights, and among those are life, liberty, and the pursuit of happiness: Now, therefore, be it

Resolved by the Senate and House of Representatives of the United States of America in Congress assembled,

SECTION 1. RESOLUTION OF APOLOGY TO NATIVE PEOPLES OF THE UNITED STATES.
(a) Acknowledgment And Apology.—The United States, acting through Congress—

(1) recognizes the special legal and political relationship Indian tribes have with the United States and the solemn covenant with the land we share;

(2) commends and honors Native Peoples for the thousands of years that they have stewarded and protected this land;

(3) recognizes that there have been years of official depredations, ill-conceived policies, and the breaking of covenants by the Federal Government regarding Indian tribes;

(4) apologizes on behalf of the people of the United States to all Native Peoples for the many instances of violence, maltreatment, and neglect inflicted on Native Peoples by citizens of the United States;

(5) expresses its regret for the ramifications of former wrongs and its commitment to build on the positive relationships of the past and present to move toward a brighter future where all the people of this land live reconciled as brothers and sisters, and harmoniously steward and protect this land together;

(6) urges the President to acknowledge the wrongs of the United States against Indian tribes in the history of the United States in order to bring healing to this land; and

(7) commends the State governments that have begun reconciliation efforts with recognized Indian tribes located in their boundaries and encourages all State governments similarly to work toward reconciling relationships with Indian tribes within their boundaries.
(b) Disclaimer.—Nothing in this Joint Resolution—

(1) authorizes or supports any claim against the United States; or

(2) serves as a settlement of any claim against the United States.

Red Cloud., photo by Edward Curtis, 1905.

Chapter Seven: Imagining Blackness

Racism is a complex idea composed of many elements. It took a long period of time to develop into a system of thought shared by more than a small segment of Europe's most elite and educated people. At the beginning of the 1700s, English Americans rarely used color words to describe their differences with other groups. Fifty years later they routinely called Indians "red" and Africans "black" and themselves "white." Prior to the war for American independence, most people living on the fringes of the English empire on the North American continent had rather fluid racial beliefs quite unlike the fixed attitudes and rigid boundaries that hardened later. One has only to read Shakespeare to find examples of some crude racial stereotypes that would have existed years prior to the founding of Jamestown in 1607. But other evidence suggests that these stereotypes were lightly held by Britons who seemed to heap more scorn and bias upon immigrants from rival nations, such as France and the Netherlands, than those from Africa.

Before the 1700s, there were more white servants than black slaves in Virginia, the largest of the American colonies. While some discriminatory laws were passed distinguishing between the rights of whites and blacks, such as Virginia's law of 1670 stating that free blacks could not own white servants, there is much evidence that few whites yet equated blackness with slavery or believed that free black colonists were an unnatural presence in their society, as they would later.

After 1700, the pace of slave importations quickened and most of the southern colonies shifted to an even greater dependence on enslaved black people. As society increasingly depended upon slavery, the role and status of free black colonists diminished. Virginia passed a law in 1723 stripping free blacks of many of their rights including that of voting, a watershed moment after which the rights and status of free black Americans would be increasingly narrowed. Noting this point in the history of the development of American racism is useful in providing a mark against which to measure the rate and depth that American ideas would descend over the next century.

Figure 7.1 Watson and the Shark by John Singleton Copley, 1778.

In the oldest settled areas of English control, such as tidewater Virginia or New England, by the mid-1700s, slavery had become fully interwoven into the fabric of society. However, it is important to note that at this point in time the vast differences in rights and privileges between whites and blacks did not promote their physical separation. In New England, blacks and whites worked alongside each other along the docks, the shipyards, the merchant warehouses, and on the ships that connected all points around the Atlantic world. Virginians of all colors celebrated the coming of the harvest, the Christmas holiday, and Easter in integrated gatherings. Men of all classes and colors gathered to gamble on cockfights and horse races or dance to fiddle music. While congregations in Virginia were segregated, a notable number in Massachusetts were not. It was not uncommon for whites and blacks to gather together for weddings, funerals or christenings. Enslaved nannies cared for white babies and children.

All this is not to say that these societies were moving toward a more equitable relationship—quite the contrary, even the most paternalistic masters would one day perform an act of benevolence and another flog or sell a person they considered their property. The point is to emphasize that human interactions worked to pull racist beliefs toward reality, the reality that enslaved people were just like free ones in all the fullness of their human feelings, behaviors, characters, and desires. Racism, as a system of myths defining a group, was to some extent held in check by the direct interactions of most people in these early slave societies.

The Hardening Lines of Race

In the first years of the new American republic whites were conflicted and uncertain about the place of black people in their new nation. Their new federal union was founded on the principle that slavery was to be forever strongly protected in those states that relied on it, while each state was free to decide for itself whether to maintain it as an institution. Northern and southern states adopted opposite positions: all northern states except Vermont (which outlawed slavery in its 1777 constitution) enacted gradual emancipation laws while all the states south of Pennsylvania and New Jersey passed laws protecting the right of whites to hold others in bondage.

During the last quarter of the 1700s, slavery's growth in America stalled. Slavery's most profitable crop, tobacco, steadily declined in price as too much of it flooded markets. As enslaving people was no longer as profitable as it had once been, the thought of giving up slavery or of it dying a natural economic death became a frequently discussed idea. Americans who believed slavery was passing away felt no urgency to square the contradiction of their republic of

Figure 7.2 The Battle of Bunker's Hill, lithograph by Johann Gotthard Muller after painting by John Trumbull, 1798.

liberty holding so many people in bondage. This also meant that they didn't feel the urgent need to think of black people as being completely unsuited to freedom and self-government, as they would later on when slavery revived and expanded. In this period artists and writers commonly depicted black people having some shared humanity with whites and even at times acting heroically.

In 1778, the American artist John Singleton Copley painted "Watson and the Shark," a painting notable for the sturdy and strong black man that is at the center of the composition. Likewise, in 1776, a Philadelphia publisher illustrated the cover of a book with an image of the death of patriot Joseph Warren at Bunker Hill, an illustration that included an image of a black soldier by Warren's side. This presumably was Peter Salem, a black fighter who heroically stood his ground and shot a British commander turning the tide of the battle. Again, the figure of the black man is depicted in rough equality with other white figures in the picture.

Ten years later, however, such artistic equality began to wane. Painter John Trumbull also included Peter Salem in his epic painting of the battle that he composed in 1786. By this time, though, the artist decided to partially obscure Salem by the figure of another soldier, though Salem is armed and part of the fight. By the twentieth century, schoolbook illustrations of the battle would erase Salem's presence entirely.

By the dawn of the nineteenth century, white artists and writers were exhibiting in their works a greater inequality in depictions of black people. Most likely this change was driven by many factors, not least the growing black presence in northern cities. By the 1790s a number of states adopted gradual emancipation laws and the number of masters freeing the people they held in bondage, many in their wills, jumped. The populations of free black Americans rose in most major cities, those of Philadelphia and New York became especially well-organized and prominent.

The growing visibility of free black Americans fueled whites' determination to distinguish themselves even further from those who now shared at least one aspect of their status—liberty. When slavery drew a bright line between white and black, whites did not go out of their way to characterize the people they kept in chains as being entirely different from themselves. But when this clear boundary between white (free citizen) and black (slave) grew foggy, whites invented ideas of black character that helped to restore their superior place in their own understanding of the world.

Educated whites in Jefferson's day could consider the possibility that black people shared much with whites, but were merely inferior because of their environment and circumstances. As Jefferson, replying to a letter from the black scientist, Benjamin Banneker, wrote in 1791, "No body wished more than I do, to see such proofs as you exhibit, that nature has given to our black brethren talents equal to those of the other colors of men; and that the appearance of the want of them, is owing merely to the degraded condition of their existence…" But by the turn of the nineteenth century, whites in both the north and the south were insisting that blacks were by their nature less capable, less intelligent, and less virtuous than themselves. In this they had the support of learned naturalists, like Charles White's popular book, *The Regular Gradation of Man* (1799), in which he described "the African" as "nearer to the brute creation than any other of the human species…"

Americans by this time even displayed less tolerance for black actors on their stages than did English audiences. In 1787, a play revolving around the romance of an enslaved girl (Yarico) and a white man (Trudge) on the sugar island of Barbados was a hit and played 164 performances over three seasons in London. The play ends with the island's governor freeing Yarico who then marries Trudge. When the play moved to America and premiered in Philadelphia, the nation's capital in 1790, the theatre managers changed the characters for American tastes. Trudge remained a low class cockney Englishman but Yarico was switched from being black to being, in the words of the playbill, "an Indian savage maiden."

Likewise, discomfort with displays of black equality were evident in a review of the opening of a play in 1813 Boston that began:

> Among the productions of Mr. Reynolds, the comedy of Laugh When You Can is certainly one of the most pleasing…were it not that he has introduced one character, which has no prototype on earth, we could see the representation with unceasing delight. But the character of Sambo, a West Indian negro, who talks morality, religion, and law, with more fluency and copiousness than half the lawyers and clergymen of the state, is an outrage upon common sense; and directly opposite to the character of the whole tribe.

Whites' increasingly biased views of their black neighbors were dramatically revealed in Philadelphia, the city of brotherly love and the new nation's capitol, in 1793. That summer and fall the city was struck by an epidemic of Yellow Fever that soon reduced it to near-anarchy. Thousands died in a city with fewer than 30,000 residents. Most wealthier families closed their businesses and fled to the countryside leaving a city (and the nation's government) in collapse. Many of those struck with the disease were abandoned and so many unburied corpses rotted in the heat that the stench of death filled the city.

White Philadelphians blamed their black neighbors for the tragedy. It was widely believed that the disease was carried northward from tropical islands by slave-made goods and by slaves or free blacks who had arrived in the city and swelled its black population to six percent of the total. A white politician, Mathew Carey, published a pamphlet accusing black Philadelphians of extorting sufferers' last pennies in exchange for care or provisions and then fleeing their responsibilities. Carey claimed black gangs looted vacant houses and robbed refugees. Whites generally (and wrongly) believed that blacks were immune to the disease and therefore their supposed dereliction of duty and opportunism could not be excused by any risks they assumed.

RIGHT REV. RICHARD ALLEN.
First Bishop of the A. M. E. Church.
Founder of that Faith That Once Nestled in a Blacksmith Shop, But Now
Encircles the World.

Figure 7.3 Right Rev. Richard Allen

Philadelphia's black leaders, such as Rev. Richard Allen, founder of the African Methodist Episcopal church (AME), responded with pamphlets of their own, pointing out that Carey could not have seen the things he claimed as he was one of the first to flee the city. Meanwhile members of the AME church, along with the renowned physician Benjamin Rush, never faltered and stayed in the city to care for the sick, shelter orphans, and bury the dead. Dr. Rush's own African servant, Marcus, nursed him back to health when he was struck with the disease.

As white Philadelphians endured the crisis of the epidemic, they erased all the differences and distinctions between their black neighbors they had been careful to note before. In their eyes blacks ceased being individuals but became submerged into one despised group of blackness. Even Dr. Rush, though saved by a black man, wrote of blacks as a group that "the sick are nursed by blacks ignorant of their business, and frequently asleep or out of the room." Though this one event was not responsible for driving racial attitudes generally, it highlights how racism was always available as a tool for white interests to use in times of social stress.

The Rise of Whiteness

Up to the early eighteenth century, English colonists liked to call themselves "Christians" and the term "white" first became popular in South Carolina where slavery was most concentrated, most socially and economically tied to the sugar islands of the Caribbean, and oriented to the production of export-crops.

The idea of stark differences between black and white people most likely developed first on the British sugar island of Barbados. There a society grew up based almost entirely on plantation agriculture worked by enslaved people brought directly from Africa. As a result there were few European farm workers or servants occupying a middle social position between masters and slaves. In Barbados the lines between class and race ran parallel to each other and there color served as a code indicating both status and ancestry. In a 1681 book, the author, a minister from the island, had to explain to his English readers that the word "white" was "the general name for Europeans."

The American Revolution, by creating the necessity of inventing a new national identity, fostered the growth of the idea of "whiteness" as an American identity. For the founding fathers, whiteness was not only the opposite of blackness (more on that later), but also a political identity that expressed the ideals of the new republic: individual independence, self-sacrificing citizenship, and rational behavior. Such ideals became the theoretical basis for citizenship and voting in the young nation.

On the same day the Declaration of Independence was proclaimed, July 4, 1776, Ben Franklin, Thomas Jefferson, and John Adams were appointed a committee to formulate the design for a symbol for the new nation, a "Seal of the United States of America." After consulting with a French painter living in Philadelphia, the founding fathers recommended that the national symbol should be a shield held aloft by two women representing justice and liberty. The shield was to be divided into six parts, each part containing a symbol "pointing out the countries from which these States have been peopled." Arrayed around the shield was a rose representing England, a thistle for Scotland, Ireland of course got her harp, France its "flower de luce," Germany its eagle, and Holland a lion. Surrounding the shield was the motto, e pluribus unum, which literally means "out of many, one," a phrase that in this context must be seen as referring to not just any sorts of people, but northern and western Europeans in particular. Above the women and the shield was the "Eye of Providence" looking down on that which God most favored.

Because of more pressing matters, like fighting the British, the committee's recommendation was not adopted and over the next six years two more design committees were charged with the task. When Congress could not agree on any of the designs, the whole matter was left to Congress' secretary to come up with something and he sketched the eagle familiar today. However, the original motto of the first committee, e pluribus unum, was retained, forever to be mistaken as representing more types of people than ever intended, as historians misinterpreted the motto to mean from thirteen colonies comes one country. The simple fact is that these founding fathers envisioned and intended their new nation to be a white one and they viewed whiteness as the natural heritage and possession of only Anglo-Saxon Protestants.

Jefferson clearly used the word "white" one way to describe those who were not "black" but then also thought of the term more narrowly at other times. For example, he stated that he thought "Saxons" were the superior race and even advocated that the great seal of the United States should feature Hengist and Horsa, the Saxon chiefs. Benjamin Franklin famously observed:

> ...the number of purely white people in the world is proportionably very small. All Africa is black or tawny; Asia chiefly tawny; America (exclusive of the new comers) wholly so. And in Europe, the Spaniards, Italians, French, Russians, and Swedes, are generally of what we call a swarthy complexion; as are the Germans also, the Saxons only excepted, who, with the English, make the principal body of white people on the face of the earth. I could wish their numbers were increased. And while we are, as I may call it, scouring our planet...why should we...darken its people? Why increase the sons of Africa by planting them in America, where we have so fair an opportunity, by excluding all blacks and tawnys, of increasing the lovely white and red?

Historical archaeologists have observed that in the decades following the Revolutionary War, white consumers developed a mania for all things white. This was a time when the status of black Americans was suddenly uncertain as northern states passed laws gradually abolishing slavery and free black communities grew in most major cities. It was at that moment that household goods and ornaments, previously preferred in as many colors as were available, became mostly white. Even those who could afford it chose imported white marble for their gravestones over the locally available and previously universal grey slate. At the same time the goods, clothes and dishes, produced in bulk for the use of slaves darkened in color. The physical

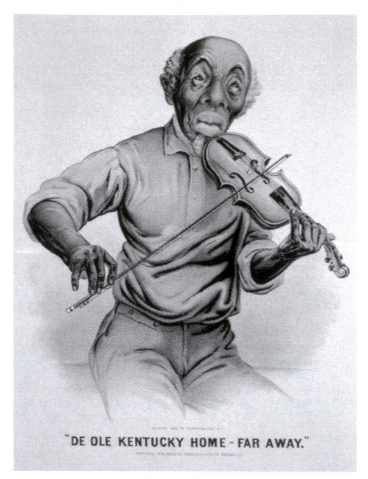

"DE OLE KENTUCKY HOME - FAR AWAY."

Figure 7.4 "De ole Kentucky home--far away" 1885.

environment of white Americans' houses came to reflect their increasing self-definition as 'white' as white became the most popular color of house paint.

The Sambo and Mammy Stereotypes

Ironically, it was the moral threat posed by the small but vocal abolitionist movement that provoked white Americans to openly and defiantly express the racism that they had practiced for at least a century. The movement for the abolition of slavery found early supporters among the Quakers in the 1700s, and some American revolutionaries, such as Tom Paine, supported it, but oppression of slavery's opponents increased with the rising profitability of slavery in the first decades of the 1800s. Prior to the Civil War, the abolitionists were a small, vocal, and intensely hated group of Americans. The abolitionist movement grew more prominent with the founding of *The Liberator* in 1831, a newspaper devoted to the cause and edited by William Lloyd Garrison. Two years later Garrison and others founded the American Anti-Slavery Society, a group dedicated to the immediate and total abolition of slavery. Soon abolitionists had raised alarm across the South, especially as Harriet Tubman and others helped slaves escape north

Figure 7.5 "Mammy," n.d.

prone to vice; that his mind is heavy, dull, and unambitious; and that the doom that has made the African in all ages and countries, a slave—is the natural consequence of the inferiority of his character.

Such rationalizing of the injustice of slavery had its cultural counterpart in the appearance of new racist stereotypes of black men and black women. The so-called "Sambo" and "Mammy" caricatures became popular in the 1830s. The "Sambo" character was essentially a loyal, happy slave. Mammy was similar in that she too was contented with her bondage, but because she was portrayed as laboring in the service of the white mistress of the plantation and lived in the 'big house,' she was portrayed in ways that hid or downplayed her sexuality as a woman (so as not to appear as being sexually available to the master or other young men in the white family). Sambo and Mammy were simple-minded, lazy, and quite satisfied with the simplest and rudest of life's pleasures.

Much of the power of these black stereotypes arose from the way white society redefined womanhood generally in the nineteenth century. In colonial times women were expected to take an active part in economic activities, whether it was doing chores on the farm or assisting with tasks in the family workshop. A rising middle class in the early 1800s began to stress the importance of clearly separating men's and women's work and, indeed, their entire spheres of life. Men were to venture out into the dog-eat-dog competitive world while women were to remain in a domestic sphere, responsible for the moral instruction of children and overseeing the running of the home (which for middle class and elite women often depended on the labor of black servants).

Such an ideal was oftentimes unreachable for many working class whites, who depended on the wages or enterprise of women to make ends meet. But this ideal was impossible to achieve for people enslaved and forced without regard to sex or age to stoop and labor in the field. Rather than acknowledge the fundamental violation of this domestic ideal of femininity caused by slavery, whites ridiculed blacks for their inability to conform to the conventions of gender. Thus, men were seen as lazy for allowing wives and daughters to work in the field and women were depicted as masculine for doing so. By attributing this reversal of gendered roles to black nature, rather than racial oppression, whites once again excused themselves of responsibility for their cruelties.

Sambo first appeared on a theatrical stage in the play *Triumphs of Love* that premiered in 1795. That production's Sambo character spoke in a dialect filled with grammatical mistakes and slang that had already become a common

and to freedom in Canada.

Abolitionists pointed out the hypocrisy of America's claim to being a land of liberty yet practicing the most severe slavery. This provoked an outpouring of pamphlets and speeches, mostly, but not exclusively, from southerners, who defended slavery on the grounds of black inferiority. William Drayton's pamphlet, "The South Vindicated from the Treason and Fanaticism of the Northern Abolitionists," printed in 1836, was typical:

It may be justly doubted, whether, under the most favourable auspices, the negro character is adequate to the task of self elevation and support, whether he can, when left to himself, win or retain the advantages of civilization and self control; and it is certain that, where the circumstances are adverse, he must sink, when the supporting hand of the white man is withdrawn, into barbarity and wretchedness...Personal observation must convince every candid man, that the Negro is constitutionally indolent and parody of black people by that time. Sambo spoke lines like "I has the bess massa in e world" and he played fiddle and danced as part of the show. In the play, Sambo is eventually granted his freedom by his kind master and he promptly celebrates by drinking to excess. A white character then takes the stage and says, "I am afraid our friend Sambo, will make a bad use of his liberty...So much for...liberating those people. The greatest number of them, after they are set free, become vicious."

Here was the key to the success and longevity of the Sambo and Mammy stereotypes; in a nation that thought of itself as being founded on the theory of human equality and the promise of liberty, slavery gnawed at the cornerstone of American values and exposed white Americans to the obvious charge of hypocrisy. Later in the 1820s and 1830s, when slavery was legally abolished in northern states but was replaced by racially discriminatory laws making blacks second-class citizens, the same discordant clash with the ringing principles of America's founding ideals exposed the lie of freedom and democracy. Sambo (and Mammy) solved this problem by displaying how supposedly unsuited black men and women were for freedom or citizenship. The image of Sambo was an argument that blacks could only be happy and peaceful when leashed and restrained by the civilized white hand. Liberty and democracy were, therefore, not being denied to America's black minority, for they could not properly use such things even if they were given to them.

White Americans were so invested in believing that the Sambo character was real, that people who were enslaved were so simple and contented that they would break into song or dance at almost any time, that they insisted black people perform for them. Masters forced those they owned to dance and sing for visitors and slave auctioneers were noted for forcing those about to be sold to dance. Black street performers danced and sang in the ways whites expected to earn their spare change.

If there is any truth to the old saying that within every stereotype is a grain of truth, then the kernel at the heart of the Sambo stereotype was not some truth about black people's nature or behavior, but was the reality that American slavery tolerated no deviation from white expectations. To the extent that anyone ever acted as Sambo supposedly did, their behavior was a performance staged for the benefit of the whites who had been conferred absolute power over them by the customs of society and the laws of the state. Frederick Douglass, who escaped from slavery at the age of twenty, described how:

> slaves, when inquired of as to their condition and the character of their masters, almost invariably say that they are contented, and their

Figure 7.6 "The Two Platforms," campaign poster from 1866 Pennsylvania gubernatorial race.

> masters are kind...[among them there is] the maxim, that a still tongue makes a wise head. They suppress the truth rather than take the consequence of telling it, and, in so doing, they prove themselves a part of the human family.....It is a blessed thing, that the tyrant may not always know the thoughts and purposes of his victim.

Slavery was known as the "peculiar institution" for more reasons than just that it was unique. It was also peculiar in inverting the ethical universe and turning every decent impulse of a person enslaved into something prohibited and immoral. As a slave did not own themselves, did not possess themselves, anything they did for themselves was suspect, especially the most human and natural of actions, seeking to better their own lives. Benjamin Franklin sensed this when he wrote that a slave "was by nature a thief." He didn't mean black people compulsively stole things, but rather that slavery converted the natural needs of people into crimes. A slave was a thief if he or she ran away. A slave was also a thief if they took time away from their assigned chores and did something for themselves, like go fishing or cultivating a hidden garden.

American slavery's unique social organization facilitated an atmosphere of pervasive control. Most slaves did not live on massive plantations with hundreds of other slaves (a quarter of enslaved people lived on farms with more than 50 other slaves). Nine out of ten farms operated by the labor of enslaved workers had fewer than 30 hands, a number that allowed for close and direct supervision by the owner of the property. The generally small size of slavery farms molded the character of America and made it distinct from other slave-societies in the Western Hemisphere where absentee owners tended to own massive plantations managed by hired overseers. American slavery thus made for a closer and more intense relationship between masters and slaves where whites interfered in the daily lives of slaves to a far greater degree than in any other society. White enslavers spent much of their time supervising and suppressing every vestige of slave independence they could. Typically masters established rules governing everything from the time the people they kept in bondage woke up to when they went to sleep. Societal customs and mores tightly regulated and patrolled all aspects of enslaved people's behavior in public. Thus it is not surprising that whites observed black behavior following their own warped expectations and stereotypes of what black character was supposed to be.

In spite of whites' attempts to totally control all aspects of their lives, slaves did not passively accept their lot in life and resisted white tyranny as best they could. Resistance to slavery was an everyday act of slaves and it took innumerable forms such as feigning misunderstanding and stupidity, which, by playing into the master's own stereotypes, seemed plausible but nevertheless frustrated the master's orders. Planters often failed to disassociate slave resistance from their own racist belief in slave inferiority. One planter, plagued by the frequent breaking of tools, wrote in his diary: "(My slaves) break and destroy more farming utensils, ruin more carts, break more gates, spoil more cattle and horses and commit more waste than five times their number of white laborers do. They are under instruction relative to labor from their childhood, and still when they are gray-headed they are the same heedless botches; the negro traits predominate over all artificial training." In this way enslaved people exploited white's stereotypes about them to undermine the system that kept them in bondage.

Beyond such daily acts of resistance were more serious challenges to the slavery system and to the racist stereotypes it promoted. The most powerful challenge to the Sambo image of enslaved people was the act of outright rebellion.

Racism in the North

That keen observer of all things America, Alexis de Tocqueville, noted that prejudice and slavery were not tied together. "Whosoever has inhabited the United States must have perceived, that in those parts of the Union in which the negroes are no longer slaves, they have in nowise drawn nearer to the whites. On the contrary, the prejudice of the race appears to be stronger in the States which have abolished slavery, than in those where it still exists; and nowhere is it so intolerant as in those States where servitude has never been known." de Tocqueville continued:

In the South, where slavery still exists, the negroes are less carefully kept apart; they sometimes share the labor and the recreations of the whites; the whites consent to intermix with them to a certain extent... In the South the master is not afraid to raise his slave to his own standing, because he knows that he can in a moment reduce him to the dust at pleasure. In the North the white no longer distinctly perceives the barrier which separates him from the degraded race, and he shuns the negro with the more pertinacity, because he fears lest they should some day be confounded together.

Where white southerners secretly feared the black people they held in bondage, knowing deep in their being the simmering resentment and yearning for liberty in the black community, they also had no idea how to live without their labor. White northerners, on the other hand, had no similar dependence on black labor and while white southerners couldn't imagine a future without slaves, white northerners dreamed of a future without black people. Such dreams of an all white nation, though partially accomplished by the forced expulsion of Indians beyond the borders of America, were at odds with the reality of the slow but steady growth of free black populations in the North.

Many northern states took action to limit or suppress slavery but paired these measures with laws that narrowly restricted the freedom of blacks. Only one state, Massachusetts allowed black men to serve on juries. Five states did not allow black witnesses to testify in court if a white man was one of the parties in the case. An Ohio judge bound by these rules protested from his bench, "The white man may now plunder the Negro, he may abuse his person; he may take his life: He may do this in open daylight...and he must go acquitted, unless...some white man [was] present." Oregon outlawed black ownership of property. In addition to all these bans, most northern states also prohibited blacks from holding public offices, from voting, from serving in the state militia or from practicing law in the state.

With his usual sharp insight, Frederick Douglass explained the hollowness of northern freedom for black folks: "In the Northern states, we are not slaves to individuals, not personal slaves, yet in many respects we are the slaves of the community."

The Invention of Blackface Minstrelsy

The growth of free black communities in the North created a highly creative environment for new and distinct cultural forms. Unlike slaves in the South, because of northern practices and laws establishing segregation, black northerners tended to be live in separate and dense neighborhoods. Within these communities many cultural influences combined, both from centuries of experience as Americans, from those fleeing slavery in the South, and from a trickle of people continually arriving from Africa. New forms of music, speech, fashion, dance, and thought flourished into a rich expression that was probably the first uniquely American art. Out of this came new styles of Christian worship, new holidays (first Pinkster and later Juneteenth), and a manner of performance that was so powerful that it was immediately imitated and stolen by white entertainers.

Black performers brought some of these unique songs and dances into the streets, entertaining for pennies or sometimes being hired by businessmen to attract traffic to their markets. Much innovation happened in New York City, in 1800 the largest center of black population in the northern states with 5,865 free and slave residents. One reminiscence of that time vividly described the creativity of black street performers in the city's public marketplace:

The first introduction in this city of public "negro dancing" no doubt took place at this market. The negroes who visited here were principally slaves from Long Island, who had leave of their masters for certain holidays, among which "Pinkster" was the principal one... as they had usually three days holiday, they were ever ready, by their "negro sayings or doings," to make a few shillings more. So they would be hired by some joking butcher or individual to engage in a jig or break-down, as that was one of their pastimes at home on the barn floor, or in a frolic, and those that could and would dance soon raised a collection; but some of them did more in "turning around and shying off" from the designated spot than keeping to the regular "shake down" which caused them all to be confined to a "board," (or shingle, as they called it,) and not allowed off it; on this they must show their skill; and being several together in parties, each had his particular "shingle" brought with him as part of his stock in trade. This board was usually about five to six feet long, of large width, with its particular spring in it, and to keep it in its place while dancing on it, it was held down by one on each end. Their music or time was usually given by one of their party, which was done by beating their hands on the sides of their legs and the noise of the heel. The favorite dancing-place was a cleared spot on the east side of the fish market in front of Burnel Brown's Ship Chandlery. The large amount collected in this way after a time produced some excellent "dancers;" in fact, it raised a sort of strife for the highest honors, i.e., the most cheering and the most collected in the "hat."

Prior to the theft of black music and dance by white performers, there was a brief flowering of black theater in the 1820s. The African Grove theater opened in 1821 to serve black New Yorkers who were prohibited from most theaters or restricted to dingy balcony areas in the few where they were allowed. While the African Grove specialized in Shakespeare and other popular plays of the day, between acts black musicians and dancers performed. African Grove was a sensation and a success and quickly grew, purchasing a neighboring hotel for more room. At the peak of its popularity, the African Grove Theater was shut down in the midst of its second season by the city authorities on the excuse that it was too disorderly.

In the early 1830s a number of white performers began imitating songs, dances and mannerisms they encountered in those parts of the city (namely the markets and wharfs) that were most racially mixed. T.D. Rice, a New York actor who spent much time touring down the Ohio Valley, took not only the song he heard an elderly black stable-hand sing, but bought the clothes of another black man to perform in. When he applied burnt cork to his face and hands Rice walked out onto a stage as the world's first "minstrel" act in Pittsburgh in 1830. Stephen Foster learned the style of songs that he made enduringly popular from his servant Olivia Pise, who was said to be "a member of a church of shouting colored people." The famed blackface performer E.P. Christy adopted his style from a man known as "One-Legged Harrison," who sang in a black church in Christy's hometown of Buffalo. Soon blackface performances became standardized with the stock characters of "Jim Crow," a figure modeled on the stereotypes of the plantation Sambo, and "Zip Coon," a caricature of a free cityfied black man. (The name "Jim Crow" came from a rhyme popular among black children.)

Through the blackface of minstrelsy whites could enjoy black music yet separate themselves from black people. Soon minstrel music was the most popular music in America. "It is truly wonderful, and we cannot help thinking that it is a matter well worth the attention of musical professors and composers, the popularity of the Negro Melodies of our time. You hear them in all our streets—you hear them at every party—they are danced after a thousand times a week in every city in the Union..."

The key element of the explosive success of minstrelsy was, of course, its application of blacking to white faces, a mask that gave permission to white entertainers to

Figure 7.7 "Jim Crow" 1836.

perform black songs and dances (and white audiences to enjoy them) without risking being seen as enjoying or celebrating black culture. Minstrel performances were racist and demeaning to be sure, but they were also the way in which white people expressed their interest and fascination with black culture. Minstrelsy reveals that the boundaries between white and black were drawn so sharply that the only way in which whites could explore the music, poetry, humor, or dancing that black people had created was to ridicule it. The reason why the blackface minstrel show was so immensely popular, and remained so for so long, lies in both its ability to continually redraw the lines marking race and to give whites permission to cross them.

Minstrelsy and the Working Class

Blackface minstrel performances had a particular importance and meaning for white urban workers. Such workers were just experiencing the impact of the industrial revolution when minstrel acts first appeared. Urban workers, though always poor, had once prided themselves on the independence that their mechanical skills secured. At a time when most production was centered in small workshops, urban workers could reasonably dream of the day when they would go into business for themselves and no longer sell their labor by the day. But as factories grew in scale, and the financing and organization required to compete in an expanding market grew along with them, such workers faced the prospect of being a permanent underclass.

Workers responded to the narrowing of their liberty and their futures in numerous ways. They organized the first trade unions in the 1820s. They demanded and won the right to vote and to hold office in most states. They also redefined themselves and claimed a measure of greater social status by seizing upon the idea of being "white."

In other words, at a time when workers were forced

Figure 7.8 White man in blackface, ca. 1890-1910.

they could no longer as legitimately claim to be future businessmen in waiting, race provided a means of distinguishing themselves as worthy citizens of the nation. Slavery and blackness provided a necessary contrast for white workers to measure themselves against. Rather than seeing themselves as the dependent servants of their industrial masters, they thought of themselves as independent and free "workers." They stopped calling their employers "masters" and themselves "servants," as was common in the colonial period, and instead reserved those words exclusively for slaves. Instead they called their employers "boss" (the Dutch word for "master") and themselves "hands," "help," "mechanics," or "workers." Even in describing the sexual division of labor that formally gave working class men domestic authority they would call themselves the "head" of the household rather than its "master."

While such twisting of language may have provided a more comforting identity for white workers, it didn't solve another more vexing problem they faced—the double bind of respectability. The double bind of respectability was a product of workers aspiring for acceptance according to the new ideals of the young republic. Such ideals demanded that citizens follow a civic and moral code of responsbility to the community, to put public interest ahead of private gain, and to be honest, forthright, and always working toward self-improvement, while avoiding the traps of corruption and vice. This unwritten code of citizenship put workers into a bind because it allowed no room for the collective actions, like strikes and protests, that were neccesary for them to improve their lives. Moreover, this "republicanism" (as scholars sometimes refer to it) was incompatible with the ways the actual, natural ways that people lived their lives which often involved a continuous cycle of hard work and carefree release rather than steady rectitude and self-restraint.

Blackface shows, and racism in general, offered white workers a solution to this double bind. By the act of blacking up, an actor could enact all sorts of otherwise dangerous and subversive ideas that were not socially acceptable outside of the theater. Because these transgressive performances were enacted as the expressions of those inherently outside social norms, namely black people, they were placed at a critical distance for their white audiences to enjoy without fear of being confused for them. As one scholar insightfully observed, "it was through blackness that class was staged..." In other words, white workers came to see themselves, to define themselves, as both a race and a class, by the blackface characters on stage that they loved to watch, and laugh to, and sing along with, and clap and shout over.

While blackface performances could disguise what were radical and subversive themes, they were also available for the opposite use. For the next century cities and their

to consider that what defined them was their labor (and they increasingly referred to themselves as "mechanics" emphasizing this fact) they had also to contend with the question of what divided them from the degraded status of being a slave? Weren't slaves also workers? How were they different?

A generation earlier ones' status as a worker was a matter of law: some workers were enslaved, some indentured servants, others apprentices, some debt prisoners, and a fortunate few free laborers. In such a system one's status was measured in degrees of independence and bondage. But as the system of indentures and apprenticeship declined, all that was left was the stark contrast between freedom and slavery. According to the beliefs spread by the American Revolution, not only was freedom the opposite of slavery, but free men could not enslaved because they were willing to fight for their liberty. The solution to this dilemma, of course, was the idea that what divided white and black workers was their innate natural character, their race. By this line of logic, only whites could be workers, because to be black was to be a slave.

At a time when workers were losing status because

industries would grow by drawing men and women out of the countryside, taking people off of American farms, and attracting them from rural areas across the ocean. Each wave of newcomers faced the same wrenching change in their lives, of entering a world governed by the clock, the machine, and the crowded city block. Blackface minstrelsy adapted to soothe their heartache for a simpler rural life by singing about the bygone days of their lost natural pleasures. As such pleasures as loafing, drinking, fishing, and acting foolish were no longer as socially permissible in this new city world of industrial discipline, when a white man pretending to be a black man sang about indulging in them, it was both satisfying and deniable to a white audience.

Blackface minstrel shows were powerful vehicles for spreading and deepening racist ideas and images and its influence was soon seen in virtually every depiction of black people. White minstrel performers were not unaware of the effects of their racist mimicry. T.D. Rice exclaimed from a stage in Baltimore that his act "effectually proved that negroes are essentially an inferior species of the human family and they ought to remain slaves." Even putting aside the obvious racist ridicule of minstrel songs, jokes, and dances themselves, the central fact of this dramatic form, of putting on a disguise of blackness, was that it taught people that whiteness was meaningful and important.

Minstrelsy was probably the most popular form of entertainment among the working class, but its reach extended into the heights of elite society as well. Blackface minstrels performed at the inauguration of President John Tyler, in front of Queen Victoria, and for President Lincoln. When Commodore Matthew Perry sailed the first American ships into Tokyo bay, the Shogun entertained the American delegation with a Kabuki play and Perry returned the favor by displaying something just as authentically representative of his country—a blackface minstrel show. Christy's Minstrels, one of the most popular troupes, performed 2,792 times over a single decade.

Just as minstrelsy exploited stereotypes of black people on stage, publishers and journalists followed the same conventions in print. Newspapers and magazines reported any statement made by a black person in the form of the exaggerated slang of the minstrel performer. For example, a mock letter to the editor written by "Sambo" read: "I tink, misser printer, he Nited State berry good country—better, great deal, den Africa. And I like e wite people company, better, great deal, den a wild neeger...I guess you no cibilize him berry quick...."

Such minstrel representations of black speakers was popular even among antislavery reformers and can be seen in the most popular novel of the age, Harriet Beecher Stowe's *Uncle Tom's Cabin*. Stowe's abolitionist masterpiece included a number of characters who could have stepped directly from the minstrel stage onto the pages of her book, such as Topsy, a tumbling, dancing, smiling, thieving girl, and, of course, Uncle Tom himself who personified much of the romanticized stereotype of the simple, good, and faithful servant.

As early as 1837, well before advances in printing technology allowed for cheaper mass produced images, a black minister in Boston noted whites' fondness for degrading images of black people (known as "cuts" from the "woodcuts" that were used in early printing) :

> Cuts and placards descriptive of the negroe's deformity, are every where displayed to the observation of the young, with corresponding broken lingo, the very character of which is marked with design. Many of the popular book stores, in commercial towns and cities, have their show-windows lined with them. The barrooms of the most popular public houses in the country, sometimes have their ceiling literally covered with them. This display of American civility is under the daily observation of every class of society, even in New England. But this kind of education is not only systematized, but legalized. At the south, public newspapers are teeming through the country, bearing negro cuts, with remarks corresponding to the object for which they are inserted.

Claiming Citizenship Through Whiteness

While racism proved a useful lever with which white workers redefined themselves, and, in the process, defined the working class itself as "white" in America, racism was also a lubricant easing the assimilation of European immigrants into the American nation. Blackness served as a reference point against which every European immigrant group could imagine itself as superior and belonging to the larger white nation.

While an Irish Catholic like Charles Carroll, who was one of the delegates to the Constitutional Convention, may have been legally white, it did not make him "white" in social or cultural life. Carroll, like other Irish Catholics for the next generation, would be viewed with suspicion and considered of a questionable character because he was not Anglo-Saxon.

The mass immigration of Irish refugees from the famine that wracked Ireland in the 1840s, provoked vehement opposition among white Protestant Americans who viewed Irish newcomers as beastial and uncivilized. Most Irish immigrants were Catholic, a religion American Protestants feared for what they saw as its superstitious and servile adherents. Though Irish immigrants were white in terms of the laws, their whiteness and therefore their ability to be naturalized citizens was never questioned in the courts, socially they were often seen as falling outside the boundaries of whiteness. Irish immigrants to America, being poor, were often crowded into the same neighborhoods with free black folk.

Anti-Catholicism predated the mass immigration of the Irish by a decade, indicating that it was not the numbers of Irish that was perceived as a problem but their "racial" character. Whereas native white Protestants were mostly "Anglo-Saxons," the Irish were derided as "Celts," then viewed as a vastly different and inferior breed. The influential essayist Thomas Carlyle, called Ireland "a human dog kennel," while Oxford University professor Charles Kingsley described the Irish as "white chimpanzees." Samuel Morse, the famed inventor of the telegraph, devoted an entire book, *Foreign Conspiracy against the Liberties of the United States*, to the grave racial threat posed by the Irish in America:

> The Irish Catholics in an especial manner clan together, keep themselves distinct from the American family, exercise the political privileges framed to them by our hospitality, not a Americans, but as Irishmen, keep alive their foreign feelings, their foreign associations, habits, and manners. Is this mixture and these doings favorable or unfavorable to American character, and national independence?

Pioneering "race scientist" Robert Knox, determined that all the religious deficiencies of the Irish man were in-

THE IRISH DECLARATION OF INDEPENDENCE THAT WE ARE ALL FAMILIAR WITH.

Figure 7.9 Illustration by Frederick B. Opper in *Puck*, (May 9, 1883).

born: "Civilization but modifies, education effects little; his religious formula is the result of his race; his morals, actions, feelings, greatnesses, and littlenesses, flow distinctly and surely from his physical structure; that structure which seems not to have altered since the commencement of recorded time."

As early as 1830, prominent Protestant ministers railed against the Catholic church as a despotic and corrupt institution that controlled its members and through its control of Catholic voters threatened to undermine democracy by surrendering the republic to the Pope. In 1834 a mob, inflamed by rumors of wicked rituals and orgies at Boston's Ursuline Convent and School, burned the structures to the ground while fire companies stood by and watched.

America's second best selling book prior to the Civil War was the lurid memoir of a Catholic nun who claimed she and other nuns were kept in seclusion only to be sexually used by priests who then murdered and discarded the babies they bore. Though the *Awful Disclosures of Maria Monk: The Hidden Secrets of a Nun's Life in a Convent Exposed* (1836) was quickly shown to have been a fabrication, it sold 300,000 copies and was serialized in a number of large daily newspapers. Massachusetts even held hearings and sent a committee to investigate the "secret chambers" of its local Catholic institutions - though, of course, none of the allegations were proven to be true.

In 1835, opponents of immigration in New York City organized a "Native American Party." In a couple of years this "Native American Party" captured control of New York's city council and Mayor's office. Similar parties sprung up around the country and on July 1845, delegates from 13 states met in Philadelphia and soon founded a national Native American Party that ran candidates for national office. The Native American Party, known derisively as the "Know-Nothings," demanded restrictions on immigration and on office-holding by foreign-born, eradication of parochial schools, and support for slavery.

Other nativists worked in the fraternal arena. Later that year, Philadelphia's Protestants founded "The Order of United Americans" (OUA), a secret society pledged to unify "true-born Americans," to check the progress of immigrant politicians, and to save the republic from Popish schemes. By 1852, the OUA claimed 30,000 members. Copycat organizations also flourished in the 1840's with names as the United American Mechanics, the United Sons of America (and United Daughters of America), the Sons of Liberty, the Order of the Star-Spangled Banner, etc. Four national journals of Know-nothing opinion were published in these years, *The Republic* (begun Jan. 1851), *The Know-nothing and American Crusader*, *The Wide-Awake and the Spirit of Washington*, and lastly *The Mystery* (that claimed it was "published nowhere, sold everywhere, edited by Nobody and Know-nothing."

Where black people were mocked and ridiculed by blackface minstrels, Irish people were subject to their own milder stereotypical depictions on the stage by the 1850s. Stock Irish caricatures included Mose, the Bowery boy (or "B'hoy" as it was pronounced in a feigned Irish brogue), a well-dressed cityfied ruffian who comically aspired to a status far above his working class station in life. Commonly actors pasted little "Galway" beards on their chins and donned red wigs and carried a shillelagh, an oak club, to indicate their Irish otherness.

Irish immigrants seized upon whiteness as a means of distinguishing themselves as Americans. National circumstances at the time of their mass arrival, namely the closeness of competition between the major political parties and the increasing sectional split between North and South, provided an opening for the Irish to emerge as one of the most important voting blocks in the nation. Initially shunned by the Federalist Party whose pro-English and anti-immigrant attitudes pushed the Irish away, Irish voters drifted toward the party of Jefferson. Later, when Jeffersonian factionalism became the Democratic Party, the Irish were naturally attracted to its support for eliminating property requirements for voting and easing the restrictions on naturalization. Once cemented into the Democratic Party they provided the keystone of the northern alliance with southern slavery, an alliance that propagated the idea that whiteness and blackness mattered and that slavery was natural and neccesary.

The Spectre of Miscegenation

While abolitionists posed a rhetorical challenge to slavery, by the 1850s they posed less a threat to the slave system than its own logic. After several generations of the unbridled power of masters and their tendency to use that power to sexually assault and exploit the women they held in bondage, the proportion of slaves with lighter skin grew dramatically. An increasing number of enslaved people were white in appearance, confusing the system's ability to mark a person's status by their superficial features. In the last decade before the Civil War, the population of people of mixed ancestry increased 70%, to 412,000 people.

Though divided by questions of the political power of slavery, whites on both sides of the Mason-Dixon line grew more anxious about 'race-mixing' as a result. The free black community in the North grew 15% in the 1850s and one-third of northern states banned interracial marriage. Eventually, every state in which more than five percent of the population was black eventually passed laws outlawing marriage or sexual relations between whites and blacks.

Such shared fears on the part of both northern and

Redeemed in Virginia

By Catherine S. Lawrence. Baptized in Brooklyn, at Plymouth Church, by Henry Ward Beecher, May, 1863. Fannie Virginia Casseopia Lawrence, a Redeemed SLAVE CHILD, 5 years of age. Entered according to Act of Congress, in the year 1863, by C. S. Lawrence, in the Clerk's Office of the district Court of the United States, for the Southern District of New-York.

Photograph by Renowden, 65 Fulton Av. Brooklyn.

Figure 7.10 Fannie Virginia Casseopia Lawrence, a Redeemed Slave Child, 5 years of age, 1863.

southern whites was one of the few things uniting them politically. Not surprisingly, the spectre of interracial mating became a powerful political tool. A new term "miscegenation" was coined in 1863 by opponents of President Lincoln's reelection to refer to procreation between people of different races. First printed in the political pamphlet, "Miscegenation: The Theory of the Blending of the Races, Applied to the American White Man and Negro," the term was incidental to the author's main purpose of associating Lincoln and emancipation with the spectre of racial mixing. Probably because of its air of precision and scientific authority, the term quickly supplanted the older term for the same thing, "amalgamation."

By the 1850s, with the rapid growth in the number of biracial people, the question of how to define whiteness frequently arose in the southern court system. One scholar counted at least 68 cases that reached southern state supreme courts that turned on the question of whether a defendant was white or black.

Lacking clear standards of what constituted blackness or whiteness, courts came to rely on a wide assortment of markers that they considered indicative of race. Quite often, southern judges allowed testimony as to a man's performance of various acts that were considered white, such as serving in the militia, voting, or having served on a jury. In other words, courts, frustrated by their inability to readily see whiteness or blackness, fell back to using the privileges of whiteness as its measure.

In everyday life, southerners responded to the gradual breakdown of the association of color and slavery by claiming that their other senses besides sight that could distinguish "true" black people, even when they looked white. Particularly slavery apologists claimed race was deeper than color and could be smelled. Hermann Burmeister, a celebrated anatomist, included in his 1853 treatise on the comparative anatomy of the black man, titled *The Black Man*, the claim that the body of Africans has "a disagreeable property...the disagreeable smell emitted by their perspiration." Such ideas only spread and increased in popularity after emancipation.

From Sambo to Savage

More serious was an undertone in the southern myth of Sambo and Mammy, that though presently childlike and content, any relaxation of the discipline of slavery would unleash their savage natures. As one "Southern Lady" explained in the South's most-read magazine, *De Bow's Review*, "The negro...has his peculiarities which are kept in abeyance by his association with, and subjection to the white man. Check that association and subjection, and how rapidly do we see him falling back to...barbarism!" Such thinking had been held in check by slavery's need to depict its victims as happy and cheerful servants but after the Union Army destroyed slavery and freed men and women began struggling to build their communities in a hostile nation, these images of savagery became prominent.

The bitter irony was that there was savage barbarity in the years immediately following the surrender of the Confederacy, but the perpetrators were overwhelmingly members of the white majority who used tactics of terrorism to prevent any meaningful steps towards political, economic, or social equality. Various white vigilante groups employed violence to destabilize state governments that had been elected by coalitions of poor white and black voters, destroying schools that taught black children, burning new churches erected by black congregations, and as much as possible forcing free black farmers back into a position of dependence and poverty. Though records are incomplete, the best estimates are that more than two thousand black people were murdered in northern Louisiana in just the year 1865. At least another thousand white supremacist killings occurred in Texas in the three years following the war. In 1869, white terror groups coalesced into a single organization called the Ku Klux Klan and succeeded in using violence to return most southern states to all-white governments.

In the 1880s, lynching grew into its modern ritualistic form where hundreds, sometimes thousands of whites gathered to watch the spectacle and the horrific mutilation of the victims. Violence against black people was nothing new, but in preceding decades it tended to be political and collective—attacks were made on entire communities in order to terrorize people into retreating from voting or expressing their dreams. But later the victims of white violence were almost always accused not of voting or organizing, but of raping, molesting or even just disrespecting white women.

Popular newspapers of the period that were subject to increasing censorship in the name of fighting obscenity, soon discovered that while they could not publish illustrations of white women exposing their pale ankles, government censors allowed lurid pictures of black 'brutes' attacking white women. As a result the number and luridness of illustrated stories of black men raping white women, most of them imagined, increased. Between 1882 and 1927, at least 4,951 black men (and a few women) were lynched by white mobs.

From the end of the 1870s to the middle of the twentieth century, America was a society that strictly confined its black citizens to inferior opportunities and

Figure 7.11 "Alligator Bait," n.d..

rights. Legally and politically this was accomplished by extremely narrow and formalistic interpretations of the three amendments passed after the Civil War guaranteeing citizenship, equal protection of the laws, and voting rights for men. Culturally, this was accomplished by dehumanizing black men, women and children as is seen in the refusal of whites to recognize the adulthood and maturity of black men and women by calling them "boy" or "girl" or in the increasing numbers of demeaning images Americans produced and consumed.

As printing technology improved in the 1880s and transcontinental railroads allowed manufacturers of household products to expand their distribution of their goods nationally, the number of visual images encountered by the average American multiplied rapidly. Among the earliest and most popular were trade cards, advertisements printed on cardstock about the size of playing cards that were distributed as bonuses to purchasers. Many families began collecting these cards and arranging them in albums. Lithographic companies found themselves unable to keep up with demand even as they printed millions of the cards.

Card printers featured a dizzying array of subjects of all kinds, but one of the most common images was of black people, especially children, shown in various situations that

THE TEN LITTLE NIGGERS.

Ten Little Nigger Boys went out to dine;
One choked his little self, and then there were Nine.

Figure 7.13 "Ten Little Niggers," (London: Dean & Sons, 1867).

highlighted their supposed backward and primitive qualities. One theory as to why racist themes were so often the subject of advertising is that consumer companies placed a high value on being able to market their goods to both the north and south and racism was a value that white people in both halves of the country found comforting and familiar. Beyond the ability of racist humor to unify whites across the sectional divide, producers of goods whose claim was convenience found images of cheerful black servility a quick means of identifying the value their products. As the target consumer was usually a middle-class white woman, images of "dirty" or "savage" natives provided a measure against which they could imagine themselves as "pure" and "civilized."

Children's Books

With slavery destroyed, whites seemed to compensate for the rising social status of black Americans by strengthening their racist stereotypes and ideas of blackness. One of the more tragic elements of this effort was the extension of racist figures and images into books and materials written for children. Children's books and magazines (and later movies and cartoons) with racist themes were hugely popular from the late nineteenth century to well into the twentieth.

A flood of racist children's books began with *Ten Little Niggers* published in 1867 and reissued regularly for decades. Later also published as *Ten Little Injuns*, it established the racist stereotype of the "pickaninny," a black child who roams uncared for by their parents getting into trouble and harm's way. In this racist depiction, the black child's life is so devalued that humor is built on the

Figure 7.12 "The original child's book. Kids of many colors," ca. 1895-1911.

imaginative variety of ways he or she can be killed. Game-maker Parker Brothers exploited the popularity of this book by publishing a board game of the same name in 1895.

One of the most important adaptations of racist stereotypes to children's literature was the Uncle Remus books of Joel Chandler Harris. Though Harris was a white Georgian born in poverty, raised by his single mom who worked as a seamstress, Harris nevertheless developed a fondness for the old plantation days and set his adaptations of African American folktales in a pleasant and happy vision of slavery. Harris' narrator, the elderly slave Uncle Remus, lovingly tells his tales to a young boy, the son of Uncle Remus' master, a setting that appealed to white readers for its celebration of Uncle Remus' submissiveness and his satisfaction with his servile life. Naturally, both Harris' black narrators and the animal characters whose stories they tell are written in a form of dialect spelling that marks them as being inferior and unintelligent, no matter how clever the main character, Brer Rabbit, could be. Pulitzer-prize winning novelist Alice Walker, whose family was from the same small town as Harris, condemned his work not only as racist, but as theft. "As far as I'm concerned, he stole a good part of my heritage. How did he steal it? By making me feel ashamed of it."

In 1946, the Walt Disney company adapted Harris' stories to the cinema and produced *Song of the South*. Even more than Harris' original books, the movie highlighted Uncle Remus and the wonderful bucolic world of the Old South. So much so that in spite of its commercial success and award-winning song, as times changed with the Civil Rights movement, Disney embarrassingly locked the movie away in its vaults, never to be released again.

Harris' *Uncle Remus: His Songs and His Sayings*

Figure 7.14 Booker T. Washington, ca. 1890-1910.

appeared in 1880 and soon he had many imitators. Most popular was Louise Clarke Pyrnelle whose 1882 childrens' book, *Diddie, Dumps & Tot*, used the word "nigger" fifty-eight times. Likewise, Helen Bannerman's *Little Black Sambo* appeared in England in 1899, a book whose story was supposedly about an East Indian boy who confronts tigers but whose illustrations in American versions showed the usual grinning pickaninny characters. Langston Hughes described *Little Black Sambo* in 1932 as "amusing undoubtedly to the white child, but like an unkind word to one who has known too many hurts to enjoy the additional pain of being laughed at."

Other popular children's books that did not have a consistently racist theme often brought into their plots occasional characters that upheld racist stereotypes. Hugh Lofting's Dr. Dolittle series relied on "Prince Bumpo" for comic relief, though at the expense of one of the few Africans to appear in a speaking role. In one story Dr. Dolittle agrees to transform Prince Bumpo into a white man so he can marry Sleeping Beauty. Though peppered with racial epithets, *The Voyages of Doctor Dolittle* won the Newberry Medal, the highest award for children's literature in 1923.

Towards the end of the nineteenth century the old racist stereotypes were updated by literary entrepreneurs looking to cash in on white readers' nostalgia for the lost social order of slavery and their fears of free black people. Uncle Tom, who once quietly bore his captivity with resigned selflessness, now freed from his shackles became the black brute, Moses, driven by his savage desire for white women in Thomas Nelson Page's *Red Rock* and later, more famously the lustful villain, Gus, in Thomas Dixon's novel *The Clansman*.

By then a few black writers had cracked open the door to the literary world and counterposed these vicious stereotypes with realistic portrayals of black life. Charles Chesnutt and Paul Dunbar (and later Jean Toomer and Zora Neal Hurston) all employed the black slang that white readers expected in order to undermine the stereotypes they believed.

Booker T. Washington Comes to Dinner

By the turn of the twentieth century, most white Americans' views of their fellow black citizens had descended as far as they could in denying not only their place in the nation, but their simple humanity. Many historians refer to this time and the decades that followed as the "Nadir," a term that attempts to capture the fresh intensity of racism in this era.

One potent illustration of white America's intolerance was the reaction to a seemingly uncontroversial event that is confusing in its ferocity. On Oct. 16, 1901, President

Theodore Roosevelt sat down to dinner at the White House with his wife, Edith, his three sons and daughter, and two invited guests, an old western hunting partner and Booker T. Washington, the author of *Up From Slavery* and founder of the Tuskegee Institute in Alabama. Roosevelt had made no announcement about Mr. Washington's visit and that it happened at all was only noted because one enterprising reporter had a habit of looking over the presidential guest book every day.

Roosevelt probably enjoyed the most support from the South for any Republican president. His mother's family was from Georgia and he had two uncles who had served the Confederacy. Moreover, in his first months in office he had appointed as federal judge a conservative Democrat and former well-liked Alabama governor, Thomas G. Jones. Southern newspaper editors praised Roosevelt's bipartisanship and predicted he would succeed in advancing the Republican party in the South.

But when news broke that the President had dined with black man in the White House a storm of protest broke out. Predictably, southern newspapers were most shrill in denouncing the President, but even the liberal *Springfield Republican* called the dinner "an indiscretion." According to the *New Orleans Picayune*, President Roosevelt was "the worst enemy to his race of any white man who has ever occupied so high a place in this republic." *The Richmond Times* editorialized, "It means the President is willing that negroes shall mingle freely with whites in the social circle - that white women may receive attentions from negro men; it means that there is no racial reason in his opinion why whites and blacks may not marry and intermarry, why the Anglo-Saxon may not mix negro blood with his blood."

A flood of threatening letters, many of them promising death, inundated the White House and Washington's Tuskegee office. For weeks after the dinner the Secret Service kept Roosevelt away from crowds, prohibiting him from shaking hands with strangers as he liked to do. U.S. Senator Ben Tillman roared, "The action of President Roosevelt in entertaining that nigger will necessitate our killing a thousand niggers in the South before they will learn their place again." Even some of Washington's closest friends thought his action selfish and counterproductive. Father Edgar G. Murphy wrote Washington and surmised: "The average man in the street can see nothing in the incident but a deliberate attempt on the part of the President and yourself to force the issue of inter-marriage and amalgamation!!!"

Roosevelt's own view on the incident, revealed in a private letter to a close friend, is chilling in its mixture of a liberal attitude toward the rights of black citizens with a racist view that it would be better if they all could just go away.

When I asked Booker T. Washington to dinner I did not devote very much thought to the matter one way or the other. I respect him greatly and believe in the work he has done...it seemed to me that it was natural to ask him to dinner to talk over this work, and the very fact that I felt a moment's qualm on inviting him because of his color made me ashamed of myself and made me hasten to send the invitation. I did not think of its bearing one way or the other, either on my own future or on anything else. As things have turned out, I am very glad that I asked him, for the clamor aroused by the act makes me feel as if the act was necessary.

I have not been able to think out any solution of the terrible problem offered by the presence of the negro on this continent, but of one thing I am sure, and that is that inasmuch as he is here and can neither be killed nor driven away, the only wise and honorable and Christian thing to do is to treat each black man and each white man strictly on his merits as a man, giving him him no more and no less than he shows himself worthy to have.

Figure 7.15 "The coon with the big white spot," ca. 1895.

Figure 7.16 "Aunt Jemima's pancake flour," n.d.

Like most other liberal politicians, Roosevelt believed in equality of opportunity for those, like Booker T. Washington, who had demonstrated their talents and capacities, not the equality of races. As far as races were concerned, Roosevelt never budged from his rock-solid belief in the inferiority of the black race which he called, "a perfectly stupid race" that "can never rise to a very high plane."

Rise of Mass Media

The turn of the twentieth century saw the innovation of new forms of media, music recording, radio, and movies, all of which built their audiences by exploiting the ongoing popularity of minstrel-like ridicule of black people. Sheet music publishing, which preceded but also competed with music records, built its market upon what were called "coon songs" after the smash success of Ernest Hogan's "All Coons Look Alike to Me," published in 1896. White control of the publishing and recording industry meant that many African American musicians and composers, like Hogan, were forced to conform to the racist templates of white expectations in order to make a living.

Thomas Edison invented motion pictures and one of his first series of movies was entitled *Ten Pickaninnies* and featured black children dancing and playing. This theme carried throughout the movies, appearing in *Our Gang* in 1922 (sometimes also called "The Little Rascals") a series that pushed boundaries by showing black and white children interacting equally, but doing so with the confining racial stereotypes of black children. The two most famous characters, Farina and Buckwheat, were shown craving watermelon and being easily frightened. (The term "pickaninny" was so usual and acceptable that America's favorite singer, Kate Smith, sang "Pickaninny Heaven," in the 1933 film, *Hello Everybody*.)

The further removed they were from the days of slavery, the more white people, both northern and southern, expressed a romantic fondness for it. Such reminiscent feelings are evident in the popularity of images of slavery at the turn of the century. A businessman turned a bankrupt flour mill in St. Joseph, Missouri, into a national success by selling pancake flour featuring the image of Aunt Jemima on the box, an image taken from a traveling minstrel show that had passed through town. In 1923, the United Daughters of the Confederacy laid plans to erect a memorial in Washington, D.C., to commemorate the "mammy," the "long-lost southern icon" of devoted domestic service.

Mass media images of subservient blacks proliferated as modern advertising expanded. By the 1950s, advertising images were unavoidable as they filled landscapes of billboards, most pages of magazines and newspapers, and crowded the airwaves. A 1950 industry survey found that only one-half of one percent of magazine advertisements included an image of a black person, and they were shown in the service of a white person nearly two-thirds of the time. By 1968 this proportion of magazine ads had grown to two percent while on television four percent of advertisments showed black people. It wasn't until the 1980s that African Americans were depicted in advertising in anything close to their proportion of the population (in 1982, nine percent of ads showed African Americans).

Movie-Made Blackness

Just as advertising built its audience through racist images in the nineteenth century, the movie industry was founded upon racist stereotypes that allowed despised immigrants to imagine themselves part of a broad white community by laughing at black people. Movies in their first decade catered to immigrant working class audiences, most of whom were viewed as culturally and racially inferior by old stock white protestants. These movie-goers crowded into nickel theaters, often little more than benches in a storefront room, where for a nickel they could watch eight or ten one-reel shows (originally, movies were at most 10 or 12 minutes long). In those early years movie producers employed the most base stereotypes as they were popular and they did the work of quickly informing audiences about the nature of their characters by simply recruiting their own prejudiced assumptions. Film companies churned out westerns featuring savage Indians and remakes of popular books, like *Uncle Tom's Cabin*, whose characters were well-known because they had already been recycled by minstrel productions for more than half a century. Movies featuring Sambo characters, known as "Rastus" films, were most common just before World War One. Another popular character included the "tragic mulatto," a child of mixed parentage who, according to racist ideas common at the time, were sickly because of their racial mixture but were, at the same time, sexual promiscuous.

Before the movie industry became monopolized in the late 1920s as production studios integrated with national chains of cinemas, there were opportunities and niches for independent film companies to prosper. In the 1910s and early 1920s there were as many as a dozen black-owned movie companies that turned out hundreds of one-reelers and a few longer feature films. These production companies attempted to create films that more accurately portrayed the complexity and variety of the black community. Leading this movement was Oscar Micheaux whose Harlem Studios produced two dozen feature and short films that were widely shown at Jim Crow theaters that reserved one day a week when black patrons could buy a ticket. But ultimately none of these companies could compete with the financial giants of Hollywood who were able to flood American screens with their epic-scale dramas.

Of all the silent era movies, one stands out for its

technical innovation and its far-reaching popularity unmatched by any other film. Hollywood's first full-length production, its first feature film to introduce many of the basic elements of cinematography still in use today, and its most influential movie was a celebration of the rise of the Ku Klux Klan and their role in restoring white supremacy in the South after the Civil War. *Birth of a Nation* opened in 1915 and was immensely popular with white moviegoers. The NAACP unsuccessfully attempted to prevent the film from showing in many cities on the grounds it would incite rioting. President Woodrow Wilson had a private screening in the White House and told reporters it was "like writing history with lightning, and my only regret is that it is all so terribly true." Thomas Dixon, author of the novel, *The Clansman*, upon which it was based, was open about his intention for his book and the film to increase sympathy for the South's lost cause of slavery: "The real purpose of my film was to revolutionize Northern audiences that would transform every man into a Southern partisan for life."

Dixon may have well obtained his wish as Birth of a Nation inspired William J. Simmons, a failed preacher from Atlanta, to revive the old Ku Klux Klan that had died out in the 1870s and reinvent it as a fraternal organization with a broader purpose of protecting what he saw as the ideals of a white Protestant America that were increasingly threatened not only by black activism but by the increasing numbers of Catholics and Jews immigrating to the U.S.

Birth of a Nation was an unusually political film and after its success, rather than make more openly white supremacist movies, Hollywood churned out less controversial movies whose racism was everywhere but usually incidental to the plot.

Blackface minstrelsy remained popular into the twentieth century, first on the vaudeville stage and then in movies. White people's ease and comfort with racism, its utter pervasiveness into all aspects of American life, was evident in the number of major Hollywood stars who appeared with their faces smudged black and their lips drawn large. Of course Al Jolson is famous for having introduced the sound era of film with his blackface portrayal in *The Jazz Singer*. Less known is the fact that this movie was remade three times with other actors rubbing on the burned cork: Danny Thomas in 1952, Jerry Lewis in 1959, and Neil Diamond in 1980. Laurel and Hardy in *Pardon Us* (1931), Eddie Cantor in *Kid Millions* (1934), Shirley Temple in *The Littlest Rebel* (1935), Fred Astaire in *Swing Time* (1936), Martha Raye in *College Holiday* (1936), the Marx Brothers in *A Day at the Races* (1937), Mickey Rooney in *Babes in Arms* (1939), Bing Crosby in *Holiday Inn* (1942) and again in *Dixie* (1943), all blacked up for their starring roles.

Figure 7.17 "The Birth of a Nation."   Gus (played by white actor Walter Long in blackface) from director D.W. Griffith's 1915 movie.

Even children's cartoons, down through the 1950s regularly placed their characters in blackface. Both cartoon characters Mickey Mouse and Felix the Cat were originally envisioned as animals that echoed blackface appearance and humor. Tom and Jerry, Bugs Bunny, and many others had adventures that ended with them in blackface and in Bugs' case, even singing "Dixie" while playing the banjo. Such depictions were rendered unacceptable in the Civil Rights era and in the 1960s a group of the eleven most racist Merrie Melodies and Looney Tunes cartoons were finally taken out of circulation.

Movies provided more opportunities for black actors to perform than previous mass entertainments, but most of these roles were cast in the mold of the existing stereotypes. In spite of the limitations presented by stock characters, black actors found ways to humanize their characters. But lurking above every performance were the fixed racial stereotypes that exerted their presence even, or perhaps especially, when actors pushed against them. Brilliant acting and creativity were often not enough to escape the presence of the corrosive images of the clownish coon, the simple mammy, the childish Tom, the savage buck, and the tragic mulatto. Again and again, throughout cinema history, these stock types reappeared, limited, or compromised the freedom of black performers.

The novelist, James Baldwin, remembered going to the movies as a boy and failing to see anyone on the screen who seemed familiar:

> It is not entirely true that no one from the world I knew had yet made an appearance on the American screen: there were, for example, Stephin Fetchit and Willie Best and Manton Moreland, all of whom, rightly or wrongly, I loathed. It seemed to me that they lied about the world I knew, and debased it, and certainly I did not know anybody like them—as far as I could tell; for it is also possible that their comic, bug-eyed terror contained the truth concerning a terror by which I hoped never to be engulfed.

Amos N' Andy

In 1926, two white radio actors hit upon the idea of making a serial comedy from the stock caricatures of black people. Both actors had ties to the South: Freeman Gosden was born in Richmond, Virginia, the son of a Confederate soldier who refused to surrender with the rest of Lee's army. Charles J. Correll was born in Peoria, Illinois, but counted Confederate President Jefferson Davis among his ancestors. Gosden and Correll hit upon a remarkable possibility inherent in the new technology of radio that no one

else had thought to develop. Radio allowed them to perform a blackface comedy without having to actually apply the greasy makeup. The key to their performance was not just their exploitation of all the standard racist stereotypes of the age, but the fact that listeners knew they were hearing white men perform this mimicry. With this formula, Gosden and Correll created *Amos N' Andy*, the most popular radio show in the history of radio, and made themselves the highest paid actors in the business.

National syndication of *Amos N' Andy* began in 1929 (sponsored by Pepsodent toothpaste that promised the whitest teeth) and soon dominated the airwaves and American culture. For fifteen minutes each night except Sunday, Amos and Andy shucked and jived and mispronounced their way into white American's hearts. So popular was the show that movie theaters rearranged their movie schedules so as not to conflict with it. Many restaurants closed for the half hour the show aired. AT&T reported that telephone traffic across the nation fell precipitously when the show was on.

Gosden and Correll hired many talented black actors for supporting roles in the show, including Dorothy Dandridge (who was the first African American actress to be nominated for the best actress Academy Award in 1954 for her role in Carmen Jones), Ernestine Wade, Lillian Randolph, Johnny Lee, and even an occasional appearance by Sammy Davis Jr.. The fact that *Amos N' Andy* provided virtually the only employment for black actors in nationally syndicated radio earned Gosden and Correll some support within the black community. But after several years of being ridiculed on a nightly basis, the black community was fed up.

The nationally distributed black newspaper, the *Pittsburgh Courier*, launched a campaign to drive *Amos N" Andy* from the radio. In 1931, the newspaper organized a petition drive that garnered three-quarters of a million signatures and printed hundreds of letters from readers criticizing the program, but failed to make any impact on the most popular, most profitable, show in America. *Amos N' Andy* ran nightly for fourteen years, then weekly for another twelve—more than a quarter century in all. CBS bought the rights and adapted the radio show to television in 1951.

CBS, knowing it had a potential number-one show in *Amos N' Andy*, initiated an unprecedented national search for black actors to fill out the cast. Many of the actors, including the leads, Spencer Williams, who played Andy, and Alvin Childress, as Amos, were leery of playing yet another eye-popping, mispronouncing, foolish minstrel-like character and only agreed after reassurances that this was not the intention of the producers. However, when production began, Gosden appeared on the set and demanded that Williams use the same stereotypical slang and comic mispronunciation that he had made the hallmark of his radio

Figure 7.18 Spencer Williams playing Andy in the Amos n' Andy Show, n.d.

show. Williams stood his ground and later recalled:

> We couldn't get together on this use of dialect...
> He wanted me to say 'dis here and dat dere,' and
> I just wasn't going to do it. He said he 'ought
> to know how Amos N' Andy should talk,' but I
> told him Negroes don't want to see Negroes on
> TV talking that way. Then I told him I ought to
> know how Negroes talk. After all, I've been one
> all my life. He never came back on the set.

Williams and Childress also insisted that their characters wear neat and clean clothing, rather than the torn and raggedy comic outfits the studio first proposed.

The cast of *Amos N' Andy* eventually performed eighty-one episodes before anxious sponsors withdrew their support and the show was cancelled in late 1954. However, the show remained in local syndication until 1966, when civil rights protests finally pushed it into the archives.

Gosden and Correll were paid 2.5 million while the black leads of the series were paid $300 per week while filming the show. Because of the lack of opportunities for black actors in Hollywood, television studios were under no pressure to pay them more than minimum scale for their talents. Neither star of the show, Neither Williams (Andy) or Childress (Amos) were paid enough to lift them out of poverty. When the show went into syndication none of the black actors received royalty payments and when some formed a traveling troupe to continue acting their characters, they were sued by CBS and forced to cancel their tour. Williams lived out his days relying on his military pension, having served as an intelligence officer in France during World War One. After the show was cancelled, Childress could not find any other roles as an actor, in spite of having a resume of Broadway performances and being a college graduate. He eventually found work as a temporary clerk in the Los Angeles County Assessor's office.

Gosden and Correll adapted their Amos and Andy routine one last time as a Saturday morning cartoon called *Calvin and the Colonel*, a show that put Gosden and Correll's mimicry of black speech into characters that were drawn as animals. In this case the Colonel, a lazy fox, was simply a repeat of Amos and his friend Calvin was none other than a reprise of Andy. The blackness of the characters existed wholly in their minstrelsy speech and not in the color of their fur, and just to make sure the audience understood that the Calvin and the Colonel were supposed to be black, the series opened with Calvin being arrested and booked into jail by an unseen and presumably white policemen who spoke proper English.

After *Amos N' Andy* was canceled in 1954, no television network would cast a black actor in a starring role for over a decade. Cautious network executives feared a show with a black cast that didn't do all the stereotypical things white audiences expected would be unpopular, while one that did might risk protests from the increasingly powerful civil rights movement.

Figure 7.19 Mayberry R.F.D. Pictured are Ken Berry (Sam Jones), Buddy Foster (Mike Jones), and Andy Griffith (Sheriff Andy Taylor).

In 1960, at the very peak of the Civil Rights Movement and the massive white resistance to it, a new show debuted in the prime time family hour whose fictional location, a small town in the deep South, would have been experiencing the turmoil of change. Instead, the town depicted, in what would become the top-rated prime-time series throughout its eight year run, had no segregation, no racism, and practically no black people at all.

Fictional Mayberry was based on Andy Griffith's own hometown of Mount Airy, North Carolina, a place that in 1960 had a significant black population, separate water fountains in the downtown Sears store, whites-only counters at the diner, and only allowed blacks to sit in the balcony at the town's only movie theater. Americans who observed Mayberry through their television sets saw a very different portrait of a southern town. One in which there were few black residents (only a handful of black extras could be glimpsed in crowd scenes), no Jim Crow, and in which only one out of 249 episodes did a black actor (playing a visiting football coach) speak. Indeed, many observers at the time and since have speculated that the show's great popularity may have been because its glaring whiteness erased the troubling reality of America.

At times the *Andy Griffith Show* played immediately after the nightly news with its actual newsreel footage of black children being beaten, set upon by dogs, and blasted with fire hoses in Birmingham, Alabama, whose outspoken sheriff, Eugene "Bull" Connor, was the opposite of everything Andy Griffith was on the small screen. Connor was threatening, uncompromising, and violent. Griffith was soft-spoken, folksy, gentle and so non-violent he did not carry a sidearm. In one sense, as the Civil Rights Movement successfully exposed the racism and violence that whites had long refused to see, the *Andy Griffith Show* served to repress this white cognitive dissonance by restoring the image of a simpler South free of strife and racial oppression.

Likewise, rival prime-time television sitcoms set in the South, *Green Acres* and *Petticoat Junction*, imitated the *Andy Griffith Show*'s formula of painting an all-white South free of racism, violence, and protest.

It wouldn't be until 1965 when Bill Cosby debuted on *I Spy* as Robert Culp's spying partner that a black actor would be featured again on television. Twenty years later it was Bill Cosby again making television history when, in 1984, *The Bill Cosby Show* debuted and rocketed to the top of the ratings. By the 1980s, America was ready for a show that depicted an affluent black family, even one whose storylines carefully avoided issues of racism.

TOM DIXON'S CLANSMAN: A Contemptible Slander
The Crisis, vol. 10, no. 1 (May 1915), pp. 19-20

Of...Dixon's latest attack on colored people, Jane Addams says: "The producer seems to have followed the principle of gathering the most vicious and grotesque individuals he could find among colored people, and showing them as representatives of the truth about the entire race," she said in describing her impressions of the play. "It is both unjust and untrue. The same method could be followed to smirch the reputation of any race. For instance, it would be easy enough to go about the slums of a city and bring together some of the criminals and degenerates, and take pictures of them purporting to show the character of the white race. It would no more be the truth about the white race than this is about the black."

Rabbi Stephen S. Wise said in a recent sermon: "Most serious of all is the circumstance that this play constitutes a deliberate attempt to deepen and justify within the hearts of men the more or less instinctive prejudices which it is the business of an enlightened democracy ceaselessly to challenge and to combat. If but the author and the producers had the courage to declare that of which I accuse them, of designing to foster hate and to intensify prejudice, to make it impossible for two races to live side by side in this republic upon the basis of peace and good-will, one could almost respect their frankness and courage and not be moved to despise them for their cowardice as one loathes them for their shame.

Figure 7.20 "Birth Of A Nation" movie poster.

"The general effect of the play is to present the Negro of a generation ago as a foul and murderous beast. Therefore, I call this play a crime against two races. The men who are responsible for it are coining prejudice and bitterness and every unholy instinct of men into money.

"If thirty or forty years ago Europe had set her face like flint against the initial causes which inevitably brought about the campaigns that ultimately ended in war, the war that now is upon us need never have been fought. The time to protest is not when race assassination has come to pass. The time to do that is now, when an attempt is deliberately made to foment it. It may become too late; and if too late and we have been silent, the blood will be upon our own heads, for we shall have suffered the soul of our city and our nation to be poisoned day by day by the fatal and ineradicable poisoning of race prejudice and race assassination."

The *Brooklyn Standard Union* says: "If a whole race, other than the Negro race, were slandered as the Negroes are slandered in the current moving picture play, it would not run two nights in New York or in any other city... Baiting the Negro and attributing to a whole class of people, all the evils that minds of a certain type can think of, has been prevalent in many parts of the country for some time. It will be disgusting and discreditable if such should become the sentiment of this community..."

Walter Ben Hare, *The Minstrel Encyclopedia*
(Boston: Walter H. Baker Co., 1921).

PART 1 HOW TO PRODUCE A MINSTREL SHOW

No form of amateur entertaining is more popular than the minstrel show. Year after year the black-face comedians appear before the public to packed houses of pleased patrons. The spontaneous good humor, the quick repartee, the harmony singing, the "local" stories, the bright end-songs and well rendered ballads attract an audience when all other forms of entertaining fail. Men naturally love minstrel shows, and the obliging ladies naturally love what the men love; and that is the secret of the popularity of the burnt-cork performance.

We have elaborate professional minstrel shows with parades, brass bands, complete orchestras, a hundred performers, tons of scenery! Elk's Minstrels, Shrine Minstrels, K. of C. Minstrels, College Minstrels, Y.M.C.A. Minstrels, High School Minstrels, Ladies' Minstrels, Children's Minstrels, Church Minstrels and Club Minstrels. Some day, doubtless, we shall have Kindergarten Minstrels and Baby Minstrels. Probably in the future some enterprising director will stage a First Part Performance with the infant actors wheeled around the stage in perambulators, all wailing tunefully to the Nurse Bottle Rag. "The youngest chorus of broilers on record, positively guaranteed, Ladies and Gents, a grand potpourri of melody from a band of enthusiastic minstrels, the oldest member of which has not reached the mature age of fourteen months!"

At any rate the minstrel show is here and it is here to stay.

The object of this book is chiefly to supply the amateur world with material from which to select a minstrel performance suited to the particular wants of the participants. While nearly all of the jokes are original, the author has borrowed from the old-time and modern minstrel stars who have been his friends and associates during an experience of four years as featured comedian with one of the very largest minstrel shows in the country....

HOW TO MAKE UP

Moisten the face with a little water, take a lump of cork the size of a small walnut in the palm of your hand; make a thin paste of it with water. Dip the forefinger of the right hand into the black and draw a line around each eye, leaving about one-eighth of an inch of white showing. Be very careful not to leave any more; better cover the eye with black than leave too much white visible. Then draw a circle around the mouth in the same

way. Jolly's mouth is rather large and slopes upward at the corners. Kolly's mouth slopes downward. Take plenty of pains with the eyes and the mouth and the rest is a cinch. Rub palms together and wash your face, neck and ears in black, being careful not to overrun the eye and mouth circles. Let it dry while you wash your hands. Then remove surplus cork with a bit of cotton. Have the end-men look each other over to see if the cork is evenly distributed. Never mix burnt cork with anything but water.

Put on your wigs and see if black meets black; no white spots must be visible, except around the mouth and under the eyes.

I advise you not to paint the lips at all, but several successful professional minstrels apply No. 1 grease paint to the lips, making them a pale pink. The white lips or pink lips make a much better contrast with the cork than do the bright red lips so often seen in amateur shows....

OLD DARKIES

Old darkies should use bald or semi-bald gray or white wigs, gray eyebrows, whiskers and mustache. Large spectacles add to the make up. Wrinkles are not needed. Any shaped nose may be made with nose putty, worked pliable and then corked. Stein's nose putty is 25 cents a box. Stein's spirit gum for attaching whiskers, etc. is 35 cents a bottle, with brush included....

MERRY CHRISTMAS MINSTRELS - For the Children

Have three adults, one for Santa Claus (interlocutor) one for Silly Willie and one for Old Mother Hubbard (end-men). Fill in with children. Use simple jokes and songs and marches. Run the show about twenty minutes, end with Santa showing the Christmas Tree....

PICKANINNY STUNT

Have the end-man sing a song about some "little black coon" and at the end have three or four sure-enough little coons come in, rush to him, clasp his knees and call "Papa!"....

IMPROMPTU MINSTRELS - For Interlocutor Male Quartet and Four End Men

A Minstrel Show that may be given anywhere, as no scenery is necessary, not even a front curtain. Nine chairs, a piano, rag-bag costumes and very few properties are all that are necessary. Six rehearsals are enough to put this entertainment over "big," if every one gets

down to work. All the performers black up, and all wear comedy misfit clothes. This is a sort of a happy-go-lucky show, but if carefully managed and prepared it will prove as big a success as a much more elaborate entertainment.

It was written for the Boys' Literary Society of the Springfield, Mo., High School and has been successfully produced from manuscript in all parts of the country....

MALE QUARTET

(*Sing two numbers, using well-known selections. "Way Down Yander in the Cornfield," "Sailing Away on the Henry Clay," "Darktown Strutters Ball," "Old Black Joe," "Swing Low, Sweet Chariot," "Sweet Adeline," "A Perfect Day," "Darling Nellie Gray" —have been wonderful hits in the most successful minstrel shows. Do not sing too loud; harmonic effects are most successful when sung softly.*)

Pete: Did you ever go to school, Mr Brown?
Inter: Why, certainly, Pete. I have a college degree. Did you ever attend college?
Pete: Yassir, I done went to college. Took a letter up there once to the president's office. But I went to nigger night school, too. Met all kind of smart men up there at the night school.
Inter: Indeed? Who were they?
Pete: (*counts on fingers*) Well, there was old George

Gravey.
Inter: I suppose you are referring to geography.
Pete: Yas, dat's de time. Den there was old Matthew, old Matthew, I done disrecommember his last name.
Inter: You mean mathematics.
Pete: Dat's de time. And Algy, Algy was there, too.
Inter: Algy Bray.
Pete: Dat's de time. And Jimmy Nastycuss he was there, too.
Inter: Gymnastics.
Pete: Yassir, Jim Nasty-tricks. I didn't learn none of them things, though. I jest learned spelling. Inter: And what can you spell, Pete?
Pete: I got as far as (*Spells*) M-U-D.
Inter: That's mud.
Pete: And that's where I stuck. The teacher was all the time spanking me.
Inter: He chastised you, did he?
Pete: Dat's de time. Nearly every day he'd lambast me with a paddle. And the worst thing about it was there was a nail in that paddle.
Inter: That's very sad, Pete.
Pete: Sad ain't no name for it, it was lamentable. One day I take old Georgy Gravey and put him right back here. (*Hand to hip.*)
Inter: You put the geography there to protect you, did you?
Pete: Dat's de time. Teacher lambasted me jest the same. But old book wasn't no protection agin dat paddle wif a nail in it. Whack, went de paddle. I felt it clean through the United States and over into China. Whack went de paddle, clean through Asia and down into Australia. Whack, went the paddle--and right there was where I exploded. Dat nail went clean through the Pacific Ocean and pierced into the interior of Africa, and I ain't sot down since.
Inter: Melancholy, are you ready to sing?
Kolly: Is you all ready to listen to me?
Inter: Of course, we ve all been vaccinated. (*Rises.*) Mr Kolly will now paint the stage a deep mournful blue by singing "The St Louis Blues."

Chapter Eight: Making the Foreigner

It is often said that America is a nation of nations, a country of immigrants. In spite of our national myth that America has been a uniquely welcoming nation for immigrants, the actual historical record is far more complicated. America's immigration policies have largely been driven by racist fears of those who did not share the Anglo-Saxon heritage of the republic's first politicians. Racism, not the yearning for liberty, has been the most powerful agent in how the U.S. has opened or barred its national gates since its founding.

One of America's most famous and powerful symbols of its character as a land welcoming of immigrants is the Statue of Liberty, a monument marking the entrance to New York harbor, where, between its construction in 1886 and 1924, nearly 14 million immigrants first arrived in their adopted land. Auguste Bartholdi's statue of a 151 foot "Libertas," the Roman god of liberty, was intended to symbolize American freedom, from her torch held aloft to the broken chains coiled around her feet. But in 1886 that freedom was not meant to be one sheltering refugees from tyranny but a freedom spreading outward and toppling tyrants everywhere.

Bartholdi based his sculpture on an earlier design he had made for a figure meant to tower over the harbor in Cairo, Egypt, that he called, "Progress: Egypt Carrying the Light to Asia." In this sense it becomes clear that Liberty's

Figure 8.1 Aerial view of Lady Liberty's feet and pedestal, Statue of Liberty, Liberty Island, Manhattan.

light was not meant to beckon those fleeing to American shores but to enlighten the masses and topple the despots across the waves. Bartholdi himself hoped his towering creation would strike a symbolic blow against his own tyrant, Napoleon III of France, as well as everywhere monarchies reigned. This is why it's official and original name was "Liberty Enlightening the World."

Only in the early years of the twentieth century, after millions of new immigrants from Europe had arrived, was Lady Liberty rethought of as a monument to their arrival. In 1903, a bronze plaque was bolted to the statue's plinth bearing a poem written by Emma Lazarus twenty years earlier but disregarded at the time:

Not like the brazen giant of Greek fame,
With conquering limbs astride from land to
    land;
Here at our sea-washed, sunset gates shall stand
A mighty woman with a torch, whose flame
Is the imprisoned lightning, and her name
Mother of Exiles. From her beacon-hand
Glows world-wide welcome; her mild eyes
    command
The air-bridged harbor that twin cities frame.
"Keep ancient lands, your storied pomp!" cries
    she
With silent lips. "Give me your tired, your poor,
Your huddled masses yearning to breathe free,
The wretched refuse of your teeming shore.
Send these, the homeless, tempest-tost to me,
I lift my lamp beside the golden door!"

In 1883, Lazarus' view of America's identity as one beckoning to the world's "huddled masses" was not a popular one. Lazarus herself was not an immigrant but a wealthy fourth-generation New Yorker whose father had owned a sugar business in Louisiana operated by men and women lashed and chained. The same week that a model of the proposed statue was exhibited in Congress, the *New York Times*, speaking of the increasing numbers of Poles, Italians, and Russian Jews arriving in the U.S., editorialized, "This country is already overstocked with people whose capital consists of their arms and legs and just enough intelligence to do what they are told in their own language to do… Human rubbish does not cease to be rubbish when it is dumped upon the western coast of the Atlantic…"

The Founders' Immigration Policy

America's founders clearly intended for their young country to grow westward with a steady influx of immigrants. But these same leaders conceived of their country as a nation of and for whites alone and organized their laws regarding immigration as a mechanism by which their racial majority could be preserved and even increased. In substance, America's immigration laws were aimed primarily at social-engineering a white republic by excluding from citizenship anyone who was not considered white.

While it is well known that the Constitution prohibited Congress from restricting the importation of slaves for twenty years, it is not as well remembered that the same provision also prevented Congress from restricting the flow of immigrants. Charles Pinckney, who participated in the convention that hammered out the Constitution, recounted, "The reasons for restraining the power to prevent migration hither for twenty years, were, to the best of my recollection…[that] it was of very great consequence to encourage the emigration of able, skillful, and industrious Europeans." In other words, the drafters of the Constitution thought they were crafting a political framework that would guarantee the growth of the white population.

When the first United States Congress met in Philadelphia in 1790, its first order of business was defining who was and who was not eligible to become a citizen of the new republic. The representatives of the thirteen states argued over whether Catholics should be allowed to become citizens, some arguing that their religion with its loyalty to a pope in Rome was incompatible with democracy. Others worried about European nobles coming to America and reestablishing an aristocracy and proposed requiring all nobles to renounce their titles before becoming naturalized. A handful of legislators proposed barring slaveholders, but this suggestion was quickly defeated.

There was much argument as to the probationary term prior to earning citizenship and other administrative practices, but not one word of discussion was provoked by the requirement that citizens must be "free white persons." That America was to be a nation populated and ruled by whites alone was assumed by all, and even when the naturalization law was taken up again and amended in 1795 and 1798, the requirement that citizens be "white" was left undiscussed and unquestioned. For the next eighty years, this law restricted who was eligible to become an American to those considered "white".

Citizenship was no small or symbolic matter. For most of U.S. history it meant more than the right to permanently reside in the country, vote, or serve on a jury. Beginning in the nineteenth century, most other rights that states or courts granted were tied to citizenship. In most places non-citizens could not hold office, or be a public employee. While foreigners were usually welcome to serve in the military, only citizens were eligible to promotion to officer rank. In many states only citizens were allowed to obtain licenses to run a business or own land, possess a firearm, or pursue a professional occupation. Some states even restricted hunting and fishing licenses to citizens.

Over the course of America's first century as an independent nation, its government did nothing to restrict the overall numbers of immigrants who could enter the country. Immigration rates doubled from 1820 to 1830, tripled from 1830 to 1840, and then nearly tripled again from 1840 to 1850. By 1860, more than 13% of the American population was foreign-born (more than today).

Rather than regulating the number of immigrants, federal, state, and local laws were solely aimed at keeping out certain sorts of people, primarily travelers sickened with communicable diseases, criminals being dumped upon American shores by European states eager to be rid of them, or people considered racially inferior. Of these three groups, non-white races were considered even more dangerous than those bearing diseases or foreign criminals because while Congress acted many times to bar the immigration of people of color throughout this period, it didn't prohibit the importation of convicts until 1875 or bar entry to the diseased until 1891.

Most states took it upon themselves to ban all free black people from entering their borders. South Carolina and a few other southern coastal states went a step further and required free black sailors arriving in port to be held in the local jail at their shipmaster's expense until their ships sailed. But some northern states clung to similar regulations just as tightly as did those of the South. Illinois enforced its statewide ban on the entrance of any free black person even while fighting the Civil War, its Supreme Court upholding this statute in 1864. In 1803 Congress strengthened all these state prohibitions by passing a law making it a federal crime to transport any "any negro, mulatto, or other person of colour" into states where their migration was prohibited.

Only non-Europeans faced such total bans. When Irish people fleeing English persecution and later an epic famine began arriving in large numbers, they provoked a wave of nativist opposition. Orators, editors, and politicians denounced the "savage" Irish who threatened American democracy with their supposed servile obedience to their Catholic bishops and their violent habits. But even as this tide of opposition became a significant political force, federal and state governments never considered banning the Irish, who even their worst enemies and the courts begrudgingly conceded were "white." States and the federal government only responded by passing laws establishing fees and bonds for immigrants, or setting standards of minimum accommodations to raise the cost of ocean travel. In the end, millions of Irish men and women immigrated in the nineteenth century and most were naturalized to the equal rights of full citizenship.

Mexican Americans

America's expansion westward across the continent posed a unique challenge to the founding vision of a white republic. With the annexation of Texas in 1846 and then the United States conquest of Mexico from 1847 to 1848, the American republic was faced with the prospect of incorporating a large non-white and non-slave population. Ultimately the hunger for an American empire outweighed fears of racial subversion.

Because racism is fundamentally mythical, it is endlessly adaptable to different causes. Though imperial expansion compromised the nation's blueprint of white citizenship, its proponents crafted arguments defending it on racial grounds. Chief among these was the idea that America's "manifest destiny" or God's plan for the nation, was to rule inferior peoples until they could be tutored up to the standards of civilization.

Many Americans opposed the war with Mexico, and the Treaty of Guadalupe Hidalgo of 1848 that ended it, because they feared the incorporation of a large population of non-white people, most of whom were Catholics, into their nation that they believed was naturally the home of white Protestants. The treaty declared that all Mexicans within the territories ceded to the United States were to become U.S. citizens. When the treaty was debated in Congress, Senator James Buchanan criticized the idea that Mexicans should be allowed the rights of citizenship, especially voting or holding office. "[O]ur race of men can never be subjected to the imbecile and indolent Mexican race…" Opposition to non-whites as citizens was one policy that united both Northerners and Southerners at this time. Rhode Island Senator Albert Greene declared that the Constitution was "framed for an Anglo-Saxon race," not Mexicans, while South Carolina's John C. Calhoun thundered, "ours is the government of the white man."

Democratic Senator Daniel Dickinson defended the Mexican treaty by pointing out that "new races are presented for us to civilize, educate, and absorb." God, Dickinson argued, had willed that Mexicans "give way to a stronger race." Fellow Democratic Senator Lewis Cass supported the absorption of former Mexican provinces because the Mexicans were racially unable to progress. They were an "ignorant, feeble, and, if not retrograding, stationary," people. Tennessee Senator John Bell supported the annexation of Mexican territory as the expression of the "natural superiority of [the Anglo-Saxon] race" over a "degraded, dependent, melancholy race."

Logic can work some surprising and counter-intuitive conclusions as when the combination of the Treaty of Guadalupe Hidalgo and American naturalization law were forced to reckon with each other. By the treaty, all Mexicans

Figure 8.2 "Miscegenation," photo by Fitz W. Guerin, 1902.

whose lands and communities were incorporated into United States territory were declared citizens. But by the naturalization laws of America, only white people could be citizens. The only solution was to declare that all Mexicans were white and this is what the federal government did.

For all formal and legal purposes, the federal government considered Mexicans to be white. Government census takers were instructed to count Mexicans as white and the published census totals that included Mexicans under the columns labelled "white." Mexican Americans' legal whiteness was often challenged in courts where important property issues such as land deeds and contracts were worked out until 1897 when a federal court declared Ricardo Rodriguez was legally white because of the Treaty of Guadalupe Hidalgo, regardless of his "anthropological" race.

However, prior to passage of the Fourteenth Amendment in 1868, that defined birthright citizenship for all purposes, states were free to restrict citizenship differently than the federal government. Most states with significant Mexican American populations crafted constitutions and passed legislation that limited the rights of large numbers of Mexican Americans. California and Arizona limited

voting to whites and denied the right to vote to Mexican Americans who were considered "Indians" or of mixed ("mestizo") ancestry.

Though the courts upheld the principle that Mexican Americans were citizens, most white Americans were not prepared to grant that equality. Both popular and academic writings at the time portrayed people of Mexican descent as racially inferior "greasers" whose mixed ancestry had left them weak-willed, impulsive, cruel, and generally unfit to participate in the self-rule required of democracy. Army captain and popular author of the West, John G. Bourke, writing in the popular magazine *Scribner's* in 1894, compared the Rio Grande to the Congo, not because of its waters, but because of the race of its people: "Through the centre of this unknown region, fully as large as New England, courses the Rio Grande, which can more correctly be compared to the Congo than to the Nile the moment that the degraded, turbulent, ignorant, and superstitious character of its population comes under examination....we have cast the precious pearl of the ballot before swine, and nowhere more freely than on the Rio Grande."

American policymakers' deep-seated belief that the United States was a white nation whose whiteness should be protected shaped not only immigration policy but the very contours and extent of the country itself. Because of their large native and Mexican populations, Congress was reluctant to admit the southwestern territories of New Mexico and Arizona into the union. Oklahoma and Alaska were kept in territorial status for decades because of congressional concerns that their large indigenous populations were not suited for self-government.

Politicians from both parties were concerned and uncertain how any such new territorial additions to Congress might upset the close balance between the Democrats and Republicans but they especially feared admitting into the halls of the legislature people of Mexican ancestry. President Theodore Roosevelt even proposed combining the two territories into one, a suggestion clearly meant to reduce the Spanish-speaking influence in the Senate. (Roosevelt's proposal was rejected by Senators who, as Georgia's Alexander Clay explained, "I oppose the blending of the two states because a large per cent of the people of New Mexico are Mexicans, while the population of Arizona, with the exception of the Indians, is almost entirely American. The population of New Mexico and Arizona have different habits and customs...the two are not likely to come together in brotherly love. Experience and observation have taught me that racial differences and antagonisms are hard to overcome.")

For these territories, statehood meant a greater degree of autonomy to determine their own affairs. Territorial citizens did not have the ability to elect their own governor and any legislation their territorial assembly passed was subject to a veto by the U.S. Congress. Just as importantly, statehood would give New Mexicans and Arizonans a significant share of national power by giving them representation in Congress with the addition of their congressional delegations and four senators.

The people of New Mexico territory first campaigned to become a state within a couple of years of having been annexed to the United States in 1848. During the Civil War, Arizona, which had a larger Anglo population, broke away from New Mexico and was recognized by Congress as its own territory. As one Senator recalled, that decision was made because "the population of the New Mexican portion of the Territory...was almost entirely Mexican. They spoke the Spanish language. Their customs and their institutions differed very seriously from those that were in process of development by the American settlers in the Arizona section..." That Senator called the prospect of forcing the "Americans" of Arizona into union with the "Mexicans" of New Mexico, "disagreeable, distasteful, and abhorrent." For the rest of the nineteenth century, both territories regularly sent petitions to Washington requesting statehood status, but these pleas were not seriously considered.

In the meantime, other mostly white territories were rapidly advanced to statehood. Nebraska, for example, was organized as a territory in 1854 and admitted into the union as an equal state in 1867. Congress' swift embrace of Nebraska had much to do with its overwhelmingly white demographics. According to the census of 1870, Nebraska had 122,993 residents, only 790 of them "free colored" (half of whom lived in a single community) and 87 "Indian."

Nevada was rushed to statehood even though its population fell far beneath the 60,000 threshold Congress had established for a territory to be considered as a state. This was primarily a politically motivated move on President Lincoln's part to help ensure his electoral college reelection victory in a bruising three-way race in 1864. But it should be noted that Nevada's nearly all-white population removed race as an issue during its fevered rush to statehood. (Congress even poached a significant slice of Arizona territory and gave it to Nevada so as to provide Anglo mining interests access to the Colorado river.)

For New Mexico and Arizona, though their populations were much larger than those of neighboring territories granted statehood, statehood status was not even debated in Congress until after the Spanish American War of 1898 and the conquest of vast overseas territories raised new and troubling questions about America's racial identity. America's politicians and high courts had to determine how Cuba, Puerto Rico, the Philippines, and the other Pacific islands captured in the war were different from the existing territories of Oklahoma, Arizona, New Mexico, Hawaii, and Alaska. The Supreme Court ruled in *Downes v. Bidwell* (1901) that Congress could treat territories any way it liked, and could provide for different paths to statehood for different groups of territories or simply keep them in a permanently subject status if it wished.

By 1900, more than half of New Mexico's citizens were of Mexican ancestry, while in neighboring Arizona fewer than one in five were Mexicano and a similar number were native peoples, though they were not recognized as citizens nor granted voting rights until 1924. Because of these ratios, Arizona was looked upon much more favorably for statehood than was New Mexico. Senator Thomas Patterson of Colorado, during the debates on statehood, proclaimed, "I doubt if there is a more intelligent, a more patriotic, a more industrious, or a more ambitious people to be found upon the face of this continent than is the population of Arizona...that population...stands about four to one—four parts being what is denominated "American population" and the one being "Mexican." Unfortunately, continued Patterson, "there is a vast difference in the quality of the people" of New Mexico who were characterized by "his indifference, his ignorance, and gullibility."

These statistics were well known to Senator Albert J. Beveridge of Indiana who held the chairmanship of the Committee on Territories and was a staunch opponent of granting statehood to territories that were mostly nonwhite. Beveridge toured the area with other members of his committee and drafted a report in which he seemed shocked to find that most people in New Mexico not only spoke Spanish but conducted their public and legal dealings in that language as well. He described with the revulsion the "mud houses" that Mexicans lived in which Beveridge thought reminded him of "the common and usual homes of the Chinese people..." On the Senate floor, Beveridge asked a rhetorical question:

> Now...what are some of the reasons against this bill? In the first place it is said that there is a difference in population. I have heard that more in the last two years than anything else. The cry which, perhaps, has had most influence has been, "It is unjust to load upon the Americans of Arizona the 'greasers' of New Mexico."

New Mexicans struggled to publicly convince the nation that they were, in fact, good citizens of good Spanish stock. Leaders of the statehood movement tried to reassure skeptics of their ability to assimilate and to promote an open society where both Anglo and Spanish cultures could coexist and even flourish together. Across the territorial border, Arizona politicians made the case that their state actually was mostly white and that the Mexican population was not growing and therefore their new state was racially safe. Finally, by 1910, these arguments won over a sufficient number of members of congress to narrowly approve laws providing for statehood for both territories. In one last act of discrimination, the statehood law for the two territories contained a step never before required of a territory to become a state: both Congress and the president had to give their approval to the state's draft constitution.

The End of White-Only Citizenship

The federal ban on all non-white immigrants from becoming citizens stood until well after the burning question of slavery was settled on the battlefield. Even five years after the defeat of the Confederacy, the idea that America would welcome any but white immigrants was extremely unpopular. On Monday, July 4, 1870, the radical abolitionist Charles Sumner rose in the Senate and and proposed striking out the word "white" from the law relating to the naturalization of aliens "so that hereafter in naturalization there shall be no distinction in race or color." Sumner's proposal was met with fierce opposition. According to one journalist, "Had a bomb shell exploded among the senators from the Pacific coast it would hardly have excited them more." In the end, Sumner attracted only fourteen votes of the forty-four senators present for his proposal to strike the word "white." In the end, instead of dropping the word "white" from the naturalization law, a proposal to add a clause extending naturalization to "aliens of African nativity and to persons of African descent" passed narrowly by a single vote.

It was clear from the record of the debate that most senators feared that striking the word "white" would open the door for immigrants from China, or indeed most of the world, to one day become Americans and this they were not prepared to imagine. A senator from Minnesota spoke against striking the word "white" because doing so might confer "citizenship upon the cruel savages who destroyed peaceful settlements," by which he meant the Sioux Indians his state had recently violently expelled from their borders. Another senator from the West coast explained why "Asiatics" should never be permitted to become American citizens: "those people have no appreciation of [republican]... government; it seems to be obnoxious to their very nature; they seem incapable of either understanding or carrying it out." Such sentiments lingered long in America as every federal naturalization law passed for the next eighty-two years retained the qualification that a person must be white to be an American citizen (unless, after 1870, they were of African ancestry).

Figure 8.3 Charles Sumner, photo by Mathew Brady, ca. 1861-1874.

Chinese Immigrants

Beginning in the 1840s, a steady stream of migrants from China began to arrive on the west coast of America. Almost all of them were Cantonese speakers from the area around the delta of the Pearl River in Guangdong province, where the rapid growth in the population and political unrest had made it customary for families to send their sons to distant parts of China and other countries in search of work. Most of these men left from the port of Macao, after either paying for their own passage, or signing a contract that obligated them to perform a certain term of labor in exchange for their ticket. This was a system not unlike that which brought a large proportion of the European immigrants to the east coast in the centuries leading up to the American Revolution called "indenture."

Chinese workers were particularly sought after by railroad construction companies building the first transcontinental roads, both for their skills, but also because their migration networks were highly organized and reliable. One of the biggest challenges of railroad construction was supplying the labor camps that had to provide all necessities for thousands of workers in remote wilderness areas. Chinese workers were recruited and supplied by Chinese labor companies that not only paid the worker's transportation costs and their wages, but supplied all their provisions and charged the railroads a single fee.

Other workers that railroads recruited, especially citizens, or those eligible for naturalization, were hard to retain as they were likely to quit whenever other opportunities, claiming a homestead, joining a cattle drive, or rushing to pan for gold, presented themselves.

White workers charged that Chinese workers were "coolies," a word that implied that these workers were practically enslaved by the Chinese labor companies that recruited them. While it is true that many immigrant Chinese workers were bound by the terms of their contract to work for a certain period of time in order to pay back the cost of their ocean voyage and the supplies advanced to them, this was only part of the story of their situation. For most Chinese workers a lack of freedom was not simply a result of their being obligated to complete their labor contracts, it was largely the result of the racist environment in America that gave them no other options.

While abuses of Chinese migrants by unscrupulous recruiters and brokers were not uncommon and conditions shipboard on a journey three times as long as that between London and Boston were terrible, Americans' view that Chinese "coolies" were willing slaves was a racist exaggeration. Contrary to white stereotypes of Chinese being docile and servile, Chinese railroad workers fought for higher wages in several dramatic strikes. While most railroad strikes were failures in nineteenth century, Chinese workers forced the Northern Pacific Railroad to increase their wages by one-half in 1879.

Most Chinese immigrants who came to America in the 1840s and 1850s were not contract laborers but independent merchants and adventurers seeking their fortunes in the gold fields. In those early decades as many as 70% of Chinese workers in California worked independently panning for gold. It was only later that most Chinese immigrants were forced into wage labor. Many western states passed laws prohibiting people of Chinese ancestry from owning land at a time when farming was the most common occupation. California levied a heavy tax on any immigrant not eligible to become a citizen who worked in the state's gold mines, which, of course, was aimed specifically at Chinese workers.

Since the arrival of the first Chinese miners in California in the 1840s, western states passed progressively harsher laws limiting their freedoms and opportunities. In 1861, the state of Nevada outlawed marriage between whites and Chinese. Eventually fourteen other states would adopt similar laws banning whites from marrying or forming families with Chinese men or women. Many

Figure 8.4 "A Chinese Vegetable Peddler, San Francisco, Cal." ca. 1898-1931.

cities prohibited Chinese people from living anywhere except in certain designated areas. In California and other states high courts ruled that Chinese victims or witnesses to crimes could not testify in court against whites.

Few employers would hire Chinese workers as white workers, especially unionized workers, would protest and strike if they did. White workers did not appreciate that when they charged Chinese workers with being "coolies" that they themselves were a major reason they lacked the freedom white workers enjoyed. Nor did they appreciate that the presence of Chinese workers allowed them to occupy the higher supervisory positions denied to the Chinese. One reporter observing railroad construction in 1869 noted:

> The majority of the men employed are Chinese, the white men on the road being bosses and superintendents. There has been some fuss about the Chinese being employed on the road, but as long as there is to every gang of these laborers a white man sitting above on the bank doing nothing but "bossing" we don't see any need to find fault. We presume that few of our people would care to take the place of the Chinese and do the work they are doing...

For these reasons, Chinese workers came to dominate railroad construction in the west. In 1882 the four thousand Chinese workers who built the Northern Pacific line in Montana represented twice that states' Chinese population. A year later when they drove the line into Washington state their numbers topped 10,000. Nine-tenths of the labor force constructing the Central Pacific Railroad that pushed east from San Francisco were Chinese workers, numbering at least 12,000 at construction's peak. But on May 10, 1869, at Promontory Point, Utah, when the "golden spike" was driven in the last iron rail marking the completion of the transcontinental railroad, all the Chinese workers were hustled away from the ceremony and none appear in the picture of that historic event. Similarly, a painting depicting the laying of the last rail on the Northern Pacific line that hangs in the Montana capitol building shows President Grant, railroad tycoon Henry Villard, and many workers, none of them Chinese.

Archeological studies of Chinese railroad workers contradict the idea that the Chinese were "coolies" who were happy to subsist in a poverty of meager rations and hard work. Rather, because Chinese goods were relatively cheap, due to an imbalance of trade between the United States and China that kept the costs of shipping goods from China extremely low, Chinese workers often enjoyed a wider variety of food and other provisions than white workers. One survey of the relative provisions found in the

Figure 8.5 Photograph of Golden Spike Ceremony at Promontory, Utah, May 10, 1869.

Chinese and "American" sides of one labor camp found:

> The workers camps were well stocked with Chinese provisions: Dried oysters and fish, tea, rice, poultry, pork, vegetables, dried bamboo shoots, dried seaweed and Chinese sugar. White railroad workers usually consumed a monotonous diet of beef, beans, bread, butter and potatoes. The Chinese railroad workers probably had a more balanced diet than their white counterparts, and certainly did not have a lower living standard.

The Anti-Chinese Movement

Agitation against the Chinese flared up in New England when a handful of Chinese shoe workers arrived in North Adams, Massachusetts, in 1870. Newspapers screamed of a Chinese menace and labor unions lobbied their legislators to take action prohibiting the importation of "coolies." At the time, there were fewer than 500 people of Chinese ancestry in the entire country east of the Mississippi river.

Congress responded to this outcry and attempted to restrict Chinese entry into the U.S. with the Page Act of 1875, the first federal law restricting immigration. The Page Act prohibited the immigration of any Chinese workers bound by contract to a particular employer and also attempted to bar Chinese women by prohibiting the entry of women for "lewd or immoral purposes." (Given the racist stereotypes prevalent at the time, all Chinese women were considered excludable as prostitutes.)

Immigration policy was traditionally more restrictive for women than men. In the early years of the American republic, womens' immigration status was usually tied to that of man, either husbands or fathers. From the middle of the nineteenth century until 1907, a woman was naturalized upon marriage to an American citizen. However, that year in a fit of immigration restriction, Congress moved to strip citizenship from any American woman who married an alien man. In 1922, Congress allowed women to marry aliens and keep their citizenship, but only if those aliens were racially qualified themselves to potentially become American citizens, that is, as long as they weren't Asian.

The Page Act was a drastic departure from the long-standing pattern of allowing states to regulate travelers across their own borders, yet it failed to satisfy the demands of those demanding a total ban on Chinese immigrants. This in spite of the fact that the Chinese amounted to a very small proportion of America's immigrants. Fewer than one in twenty of the immigrants who had entered the U.S. since the Civil War were Chinese.

The early leaders of the American labor movement threat to the American laborer.

Of course, pressure from workers alone would not have been enough to jar Congress to action. Rather, popular hysteria over the prospect of large-scale Chinese immigration reached a fever pitch by the 1880s. National magazines featured spurious stories of an epidemic of "white slavery"—white women who were abducted and enslaved in Chinatown brothels. In 1880, Pierton W. Dooner's novel, *The Last Days of the Republic*, depicted Chinese immigrants as subversive agents who eventually overthrew American democracy and placed the country under the rule of the Chinese emperor. Congress responded in 1882 and passed a near total ban on Chinese immigration, the Chinese Exclusion Act.

The Chinese Exclusion Act prohibited all Chinese workers from entering the country and reaffirmed that no Chinese person, even those who had been residents for decades, could become citizens. This was the first federal law

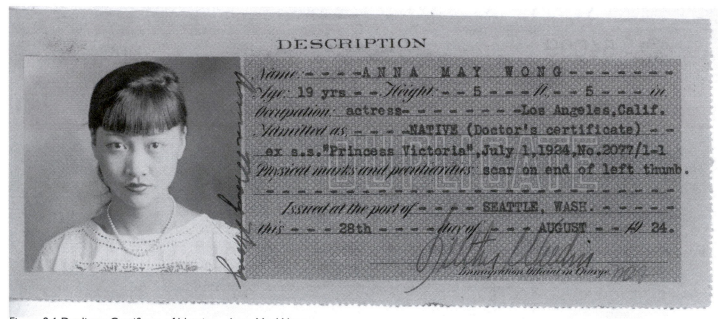

Figure 8.6 Duplicate Certificate of Identity -- Anna May Wong.

were especially vocal advocates of the total restriction of the Chinese and their arguments hinged on how the supposed racial character of the Chinese drove down wages—a clever argument that bypassed the objection that because of their few numbers these immigrants' impact on wages was negligible. The problem, said labor leaders, was not that there were too many Chinese, but that the Chinese were willing to work for wages that no other white worker would accept. Ultimately, argued labor spokesmen, wages were not a matter of the supply or demand for workers, but were set to the minimum that workers would tolerate before rebelling. Because the Chinese, in the words of Samuel Gompers, founder of the American Federation of Labor, were happy to live on "rice and rats" they posed a unique

banning any group from immigrating to the United States on the basis of their race. (The Naturalization Act of 1790 restricted eligibility for citizenship to "whites" but not their ability to enter the country.) Congress tightened these restrictions further in 1898, broadening the classes of Chinese excluded to include everyone but students, tourists, teachers and businessmen. Originally passed to be effective for a period of ten years, the law was renewed in 1892 and finally made permanent in 1902.

Stereotypes of Asian Men and Women

Prior to the Chinese Exclusion Act it occasionally happened that Chinese residents were able to obtain an uncertain citizenship. For example, in 1878 a New York judge granted an application of citizenship to a Chinese man who had lived in New York for eight years. The reporter who watched the court proceedings noted, "The new citizen is a Chinaman of unusual intelligence and ability. When he appeared before Judge Larremore for naturalization he was becomingly dressed in a thorough American costume, and but for his long black hair and copper colored visage, would readily have been taken for a sturdy Anglo-Saxon." Afterwards the judge described Wong Ah Lee as "a bright, intelligent man, and talked English as well as I do." But the conventions of American racism prohibited Wong Ah Lee being depicted as intelligent or well-spoken. The headline of this article was "Made a 'Melican." The following day the same paper ran another reporter's more typically demeaning description of Wong Ah Lee that conformed to the convention that all non-white people fail to command the English language.

> "And how does it feel to be a citizen of this great Republic?" asked the reporter when he had introduced himself.
>
> "All light! Me good Melican mad!" he responded, showing two rows of polished white teeth.
>
> "How long have you lived in this city, Mr. Yee?"
>
> "Six yees in New Yolluck; I live before that two yoes in Calafoin'."
>
> "What did you become a citizen for? Do you want to hold real estate?"
>
> "Yesh; and I go in business too. Me keepee slop for Chinee..."
>
> At this point the pot upon the stove boiled over, making a cloud of steam, and the host rushed to secure its contents from harm.

The reporter implied that Mr. Ah Lee was cooking either rats or cats, noting that in a nearby chair was "an enormous rat cat—suspiciously fat, indeed..."

One Chinese American bravely tried to dispel the prejudices against his fellow Chinese immigrants. Wong Chin Foo, came to America when he was seventeen to attend college, and then returned to China to promote grassroots political organizations. Foo was too successful and was soon hounded from the country by the Qing government. Fleeing back to America in 1873, Wong Chin Foo toured giving lectures (delivering eighty in one year) dispelling the widely held prejudices against Chinese Americans. Wong explained his crusade in a letter to a local editor:

> To the Editor of the Herald:
> Since I have been in this country teaching the

Figure 8.7 Barnum and Bailey, By the Hair of their Heads, 1916.

religion and describing the social life and political affairs of my native land, China, I have been slandered, abused and swindled in many places. I have tried to show the Christians how an honorable Chinaman looks and talks. You send your missionaries to us and we listen to them. Is it unfair for me to ask them to hear what we have to say? They say that we, heathens, are to be eternally damned, no matter how honest, moral and sincere we may be. We think Christians will be damned if they behave like very wicked Buddhists, and on Monday night I will tell the reason why...

(Signed) Wong Chinfoo, The Heathen.

In New York City, where he set up permanent residence, Wong Chin Foo started the first Chinese American newspaper on the east coast, *The Chinese American*. This was a paper whose title itself was a refutation of the widely held belief that Chinese people could never be Americans and were incapable of not serving the Chinese empire. He then organized the relatively small number of Chinese Americans who had won their citizenship, before the Chinese Exclusion Act and a series of court rulings closed the door on naturalizations. Wong Chin Foo hoped that by organizing Chinese American citizens into a club they would win greater "recognition in American politics."

Wong Chin Foo fought an uphill battle, both within and without the Chinese American community. His paper lasted less than a year, failing to sell enough subscriptions to sustain it. In 1880, only about a thousand Chinese Americans held American citizenship. The organizations he founded were also short-lived, as some other Chinese Americans who had adopted Christianity were upset at what they saw as Wong's advocacy of Buddhism. But other organizations continued the struggle. In 1895, Chinese Americans fought for their rights by organizing the Native Sons of the Golden State. In 1897 a convention held in Chicago founded the Chinese Equal Rights League of America and chose Wong Chin Foo its president.

Few white Americans paid attention to such Chinese activism and instead spread stereotypes of Chinese men as politically disloyal and Chinese women as passionately loyal to white men. Such popular novels as *The Mystery of Dr. Fu Manchu* spread stereotypes of inscrutable and devious Chinamen and seductive yet submissive Chinese women

through literature. Fu Manchu pulp fiction was adopted to the movies with the popular Fu Manchu films in the 1920s and 1930s. Competing with the villainous Fu Manchu was the good Chinese detective Charlie Chan who starred in nearly fifty movies through the 1930s and 1940s. Until retired after the attack on Pearl Harbor in 1941, Chan movies had imitators in the form of the mysterious Mr. Moto, a Japanese detective played in several films by Peter Lorre, who not only solved crimes, but like Chan, dispensed ancient wisdom in the form of little aphorisms.

Charlie Chan, like nearly all Asian men depicted in Hollywood productions, was notable for his lack of any romantic involvement whatsoever. Though having children, he was never depicted as most all other detectives were, in sexual tension with female characters. Likewise, television Asians throughout the 1950s and 1960s featured Chinese men who were bachelors and either effeminate or asexual: the cook, Hop Sing (played by Victor Sen Yung) who appeared in more than one hundred episodes of *Bonanza*; hotel worker Kim "Hey Boy" Chan (played by Kam Tong)

Figure 8.8 Examining Passengers Aboard Ships, Vessel is the Shimyo Maru, Angel Island, California, 1931.

was in as many episodes of *Have Gun Will Travel*; or the chauffeur Chao-Li (played by Chao-Li Chi) in 1980s *Falcon Crest*.

Asian women were characterized as tragically sexual, unable to live without white men. This theme was most famously displayed in *Madame Butterfly*, first an opera but adapted into a movie in 1915, then remade into a hit play *Miss Saigon* in the late 1980s. A Japanese woman would rather kill herself than live without a white soldier in *Sayonara*, a hit in 1957. In *The World of Suzie Wong* (1961), a white businessman meets a Chinese hooker in a bar and in this typical fantasy of an "exotic" woman, she quickly discovers she can't live without him. Almost never in American cinema do Asian women fall in love with Asian men.

Chinese characters experienced a brief era of sympathetic portrayals during and immediately after World War Two as America's official enemies, the Japanese, invaded and occupied much of China. Congress in 1943 repealed the Chinese Exclusion Act of 1882, but set the annual quota for Chinese immigrants at the minimum of 105. With a new national enemy, the evil Fu Manchu ended his run of successful films and was replaced instead by images of "Japs" who eagerly sacrificed themselves in kamikaze attacks for their emperor and relished torturing prisoners.

While Fu Manchu was a devious criminal he was at least still human. During the war both Hollywood and government propaganda reduced the Japanese to beasts, portraying them as subhuman. At the same time America's other enemies, the Germans and Italians, were depicted as men and women, tragically mislead by their dictators.

Japanese Immigrants

Though most white Americans used the term "Chinese" to refer to all people from East Asia, lawyers and courts understood the word specifically and usually interpreted the Chinese Exclusion Act to block only citizens of that country from immigrating to the U.S. By the end of the nineteenth century the dwindling population of Chinese people in America had retreated to a handful of urban enclaves in the face of white discrimination and attacks. At the same time, the agricultural and fishing industries of the west coast boomed, creating a labor shortage that was only partially met with seasonal migrants from Mexico. By the turn of the century a steady influx of Japanese immigrants filled the gap.

Like the Chinese who came before them, Japanese immigrants were stereotyped as being perpetual foreigners to America. Whites considered them a race of people so tightly bound to their own cultures and governments that they could never switch their national loyalties. Subservience to their ancestors, their families, and their emperor

was viewed as a racial trait, part of their inner being, that could never change, no matter how apparently "American" they were in their bearing or appearance. The *San Francisco Chronicle* summed up this idea well in 1920 when it editorialized:

> ...the naturalization abroad of a Japanese subject is a thing unthinkable. Imperial ministers, nobles, and commoners alike agreed that it is not possible to alienate the allegiance of a son of Nippon. Japanese law does not recognize foreign naturalization of a Japanese subject. But stronger even than law is the Japanese family and clan system, under which no individual exists except as part of a family which is part of a larger group, which in its turn makes part of the State, and a State with a divine origin in the sun goddess. No individual can transfer his allegiance to a foreign government without repudiating his racial traditions and cutting all his family ties, a thing...abhorrent to filial piety and absolutely unthinkable to a Japanese....every member of a Japanese family is a child of the Yamato race and a subject of the sun goddess and her line...no Japanese can ever be anything else.

Figure 8.9 Immigration Interview on Angel Island, 1923.

White prejudices against the Chinese were simply redirected to the new Japanese immigrants, disregarding the significant cultural and historical differences between them. Popular anti-Japanese lobbying succeeded in 1907 and 1908 in pressuring Theodore Roosevelt's administration to secure a diplomatic agreement with Japan to limit the number of Japanese immigrants coming to America. Japan agreed to cease issuing passports to those seeking work in America and the U.S. agreed to allow Japanese family members to immigrate so as to reunite with their relatives in America.

It was at this time that the federal government opened a central immigration processing and detention facility in San Francisco bay that allowed greater control over those arriving by sea. Angel Island Immigration Facility was patterned after Ellis Island that had opened twenty years earlier but unlike that east coast predecessor, it seemed to more harshly find reasons to exclude than admit. Even American citizens of Chinese or Japanese ancestry who traveled abroad with U.S. papers and returned to the west coast were often detained and interrogated for long periods at Angel Island.

Though immigration restrictions dramatically curtailed the growth of the Japanese population in California, the Democratic party pushed for even further legislation intended to drive the Japanese from the country. In 1909 the California legislature considered a raft of discriminatory measures to deny Japanese people the right to own property, to serve as directors of corporations, to require them to live in specific zoned neighborhoods of cities, and prohibiting their children from attending public school. Republicans, pressured by powerful business interests in the state that had come to rely on Japanese workers, especially the expanding orchard and wine industries, narrowly defeated most of these bills, though the prohibition on Japanese children in public schools passed the legislature. This was such a harsh measure that even President Roosevelt urged the governor to veto it, writing, "This the most offensive bill of all...can it not be stopped?" The governor used his influence to kill the bill, an action that Democrats campaigned on in the next election and won additional seats the legislature. Democrats then pushed through a law that restricted Japanese land ownership which settled the issue for a few years as the world descended into the chaos of World War One.

In 1919, Democratic politicians, relying on the old formula of winning office by scapegoating immigrants, called for tightening the anti-Japanese land law that they claimed was full of loopholes and was being widely evaded. Wanting to maximize the political impact of the issue, the Democrats, rather than passing the law, instead added a new anti-Japanese property ownership referendum to the ballot in the upcoming election, a move they knew would help turn out their base and secure their seats for another term. California's official voters' guide to this issue explained the question in this way:

Through the measure California seeks, as is her inherent right, to preserve her land for Americans...Its primary purpose is to prohibit Orientals who cannot become American citizens from controlling our rich agricultural lands. ..Orientals, and more particularly Japanese, [have] commenced to secure control of agricultural lands in California....once the land is occupied by Japanese the whites move away... Control of these rich lands means in time control of the products, and control of the markets. Control of the products of the soil by a unified interest such as the Japanese will lead to economic control of the country. That will be followed in time by political control through force of numbers induced by the heavy birth rate.

Figure 8.10 Victory Liberty Loan, by Howard Chandler Christy, 1919.

That condition is now at hand in Hawaii. Rather than invite such disaster, better let some land lie idle, and a few large landholders make less profit, and even see production decrease somewhat as opponents claim…

By the 1920s, all the states east of the Mississippi river allowed foreign land ownership while most of the states in the west moved to outlaw it, with measures aimed primarily at Japanese, Chinese, (and in some cases Mexican) landowners. Arizona, New Mexico, Colorado, Texas, Nebraska and Washington passed laws restricting foreign land ownership in 1921. That year Nevada voted to repeal the measure in its Constitution allowing foreigners to own land. Oklahoma wrote its prohibition into its state Constitution. Minnesota in 1913, in a fit of liberalism, voted to allow foreign residents to own up to 90,000 square feet, or two acres, of land.

Courts View Asians as Perpetually Foreign

Tokutaro Slocum, being an Issei (the Japanese term for someone born in Japan but who immigrated to America) was not required to submit to the military draft but enlisted anyway. Slocum had arrived in Minnesota when he was ten and when World War One broke out he volunteered and was sent overseas as part of the 328th Infantry. Slocum fought in several key battles in France. When he returned to his hometown of Minot, North Dakota, in 1921, he applied for citizenship, which under the Army Act of 1918 was to be conferred automatically to foreigners who had honorably served in the U.S. armed forces.

Though the examiner noted Slocum's exceptional character and army record, he refused to grant his application because he was an "alien ineligible for citizenship" and because he was not white (or black). Slocum fighting back tears, and probably wheezing from the effects of the gas attacks he suffered that plagued him all his life, replied, "I know what you mean; you mean that I am yellow. I may be yellow in face, but I am not yellow at heart."

While recent European immigrants took advantage of this law to claim citizenship, those from Asia were excluded. In just two years nearly a quarter million immigrants were converted into citizens (and, more importantly, from the perspective of Democratic politicians, voters). The eurocentric bias in Americans' view of the participation of foreigners was evident in the posters created for a government campaign to sell war bonds. Entitled "Americans All!" it featured an "honor roll" of foreign-sounding names, all of them identifiable as those of European immigrants. Federal officials urged the courts to interpret the 1918 Army Act as narrowly as possible and to deny citizenship

Figure 8.11 Tokutaro Slocum in front of the Japanese American Citizens League headquarters, before leaving for internment camps, 1942.

to all members of the "yellow race" including Turks, "Hindoos", Syrians, and others.

Lacking a clear Supreme Court ruling, American courts in different districts ruled haphazardly, granting citizenship to some Japanese and Chinese veterans and denying them to others. But even those who were granted citizenship were not able to hold it securely. In 1919, war veteran Ichizo Sato sued the Sacramento county clerk for refusing to register him as a voter even though he submitted the citizenship papers he had been granted when he lived in Hawaii. Zato's case meandered all the way to the California Supreme Court who turned him down on the basis that he was a member of the "yellow race" and therefore his naturalization was illegal.

It took till 1925 for a case testing the citizenship of these war veterans made its way up to the U.S. Supreme Court. Hidemitsu Toyota, was a native of Japan who had served in the U.S. Coast Guard for a decade and who had been granted his citizenship under the 1918 law by a federal court in Boston. In *Toyota v. United States* all but one of the justices ruled that the law's clauses that "any person of foreign birth" or "any alien" who had served honorably in the military were to be granted citizenship were not intended to weaken the long-standing bar against the naturalization of non-whites. The court's ruling cancelled Mr. Toyota's citizenship. It wasn't until the Japanese American Citizens League, led by Tokutaro Slocum, allied with veterans organizations to lobby in the 1930s to correct this injustice, and in the midst of the flurry of legislation that was the New Deal, that Congress passed the Nye-Lea Act that granted Asian vets like Slocum their citizenship. Like other Japanese Americans, Toyota was later forced into an internment camp in 1941 for the duration of World War Two.

Toward a Racial Quota System

In the decades following the Civil War both the numbers of immigrants and the range of places they came from increased. A stream of Catholic, Jewish, and Orthodox immigrants from southern and eastern Europe steadily grew to rival the numbers of those arriving from northern and western Europe by the 1890s.

As the religion and nationalities of America's newcomers shifted, a growing popular movement called for restricting immigration and naturalization. Congress responded by requiring all immigrants arriving from overseas to enter through a designated federal facility where immigrants could be screened. In 1892 the first and largest of these immigrant processing centers, Ellis Island, opened in New York harbor adjacent to the island upon which was perched the Statue of Liberty. Over the next thirty years, seventy percent of all immigrants filed through its corridors and were inspected and registered by its staff.

European immigrants arriving in the last decades of the nineteenth century were drawn by American industry's voracious need for labor in a rapidly industrializing economy. But as mechanization and a postwar recession temporarily reduced the need for immigrant labor in the early 1900s, prominent politicians began calling for the creation

Figure 8.12 "At a Russian boarding house, Homestead, Pa., 1909."

of an entirely new and "modern" immigration system that would protect America from the tide of "unfit" and "inferior" racial stocks flooding onto its shores.

At the Paris meeting where the heads of state from around the world met in early 1919 to discuss how to establish a lasting peace after the world's most devestating war, the Japanese delegation proposed adding a provision to the peace treaty creating the League of Nations that would prohibit any government from discriminating against "alien nationals" in their countries and guaranteeing "equal just treatment in every respect, making no distinction either in law or in fact, on account of their race or nationality." President Woodrow Wilson, who chaired the meeting, used his considerable influence to veto this proposal and to eliminate all such language from the treaty.

Likewise, in 1921, Vice-President, and soon to be President, Calvin Coolidge, advocated immigration restriction on the basis of race and ethnicity in the popular magazine, *Good Housekeeping*. Noting that "On every hand we hear that the quality of immigration is not what it used to be," Coolidge continued:

> American liberty is dependent on quality in citizenship. Our obligation is to maintain that citizenship at its best. We must have nothing to do with those who would undermine it. The retroactive immigrant is a danger in our midst.... We might avoid this danger were we insistent that the immigrant, before he leaves foreign soil, is temperamentally keyed for our national background. There are racial considerations too grave to be brushed aside for any sentimental reasons. Biological laws tell us that certain divergent people will not mix or blend. The Nordics propagate themselves successfully. With other races, the outcome shows deterioration on both sides. Quality of mind and body suggests that observance of ethnic law is as great a necessity to a nation as immigration law.

Such ideas were supported by some of the most powerful scientific and philanthropic institutions in the country. The Carnegie Foundation supported the "Eugenic Record Office," a laboratory at Cold Spring Harbor, New York, that was the nerve-center of eugenic research in the United States, and, prior to the rise of the Nazis, the world. Much of their work in the early 1920s was in support of restricting immigration and making more efficient the systems for deporting undesirables already in the country. As the Carnegie Foundation annual report summarized it, this research was necessary for "the prevention of contamination of future American stocks by the permanent introduction of excessive amount of defective alien germ-plasm."

THE ONLY WAY TO HANDLE IT.

Figure 8.13 "An Alien Anti-Dumping Bill" in The Literary Digest, 1921.

Congress acted and passed a series of laws severely limiting immigration except from northern and western Europe. The Immigration Act of 1917 established a literacy test for all adult immigrants and expanded the existing Chinese Exclusion Act by banning all immigration from an area called the "Asiatic Barred Zone," a swath of the planet from Arabia in the west to Polynesia in the east. Congress followed this up four years later with a Quota Act that capped overall annual immigration at 355,000 and within that total capped each nationality at 3 percent of their group's existing proportion of the American population.

Finally, Congress enacted the centerpiece of this flurry of restrictive laws, the National Origins Act of 1924 that reduced the immigration cap to 165,000 and further lowered the ethnic proportion limit from 3 to 2 percent. Reinforcing the restrictions on people from Asia, the law also specified that those "ineligible for citizenship," in other words anyone who was not "white" or "African," was banned from U.S. shores. Though not specifically declaring Africans as ineligible immigrants like other colored peoples, the law set an annual quota of 500 individuals for the entire continent of Africa. While firmly closing the door to most of the world, at the behest of powerful agricultural and industrial interests in the southwest, no limitations were put on immigration within the Western Hemisphere, thereby preserving the free flow of people back and forth across the Mexican border.

Immigration restriction had a profound and immediate effect on American society, slashing immigration to historically low levels (while nearly 24 million immigrants came to the U.S. between 1880 and 1920, only about a quarter as many, 6 million, immigrated from 1920 to 1965). Its cultural impact was larger than even these numbers would indicate. By defining all acceptable immigrants as either white or black, it reinforced the idea that all Asians were perpetually foreign, never really American no matter where they were born or to what country they gave their allegiance. By drastically reducing the numbers of southern and eastern Europeans allowed to enter the country, but not declaring them "ineligible," the law drew clear lines of belonging between all European "nationalities" as a group and the rest of the world. In this it promoted the idea that all Europeans were more alike than different, an idea seriously contested just a decade before. Such hyphenated Americans, like Polish-Americans, Italian-Americans, Jewish-Americans, and dozens of others, were thus aided in thinking of themselves, and being accepted as, simply Americans, though the path to doing so was by embracing

Figure 8.14 "Jap Trap," World War II Posters, 1942-1945,

the idea that they were "white" or "Caucasian."

New immigrants' road to whiteness was blazed with their votes. By the 1930s the block of new immigrants, mostly Catholic and Jewish voters, had risen to national power within the Democratic party. Five million of these voters re-elected Roosevelt by a comfortable margin in 1936 cementing the reforms of the New Deal.

Though considered alien and dangerous at the time, American culture has since celebrated the arrival of the "new" European immigrants as the model of immigrant success. Once the doors of immigration were closed (and especially after the federal government spread propaganda during wartime stressing American ethnic unity), many white Americans of older stock began to view the Italians, Poles, Catholics and Jews that they once feared would overrun the country and destroy the republic as examples of how immigrants should behave. In this view, "new" European immigrants proved that the idea of assimilation, that to be good Americans newcomers must lose their ethnic distinctiveness and blend into the great American "melting pot." By the 1950s, advocates of this idea could point to "new" immigrants economic achievements as well as their successful abandonment of their old world ways in claiming that their experience proved that America was an open and equitable society, the land of opportunity.

Such praise was not really aimed at those who successfully melted into the American pot, rather, it proved a useful standard by which to judge all other minority groups struggling for inclusion and equality. Beneath this fable of immigrants who overcame many hardships and struggles lurked the implication that any group that was slow to climb the economic ladder, or win acceptance as American, failed because of some inherent fault of their own, not because America society blocked their rise. Turn-of-the-century European immigrants were seen as the model for all other groups to follow and by which all other minority groups struggling for acceptance were measured.

But such comparisons were at best unfair and at worst dishonest. Turn-of-the-century European immigrants had several advantages over other minorities from the fact of their timing, their geography, and their racialization.

First, they arrived during the most rapid period of American economic growth in its history. Between 1880 and 1920 when over fourteen million immigrants arrived from Europe, the United States experienced the greatest period of growth in its history. Manufacturing employment for that forty-year period exploded by four hundred percent. The value added by manufacturing and mining even exceeded that multiplying five-fold. It was a time when the availability of industrial jobs more than kept pace with the millions of arriving immigrants.

Secondly, European immigrants overwhelmingly settled in the most dynamic urban areas and not in rural places as older immigrants had done. While rural incomes stagnated urban incomes steadily rose and with them opportunities in new whole new sectors of the economy driven by a cascade of inventions from electricity and automobiles to the mass communications of movies, radio and sound recordings.

Lastly, and most importantly, Europeans may have been viewed by older stock Americans as inferior European races with undesirable characteristics but legally they were categorized as being white and therefore able to claim the citizenship, legal protections, and political power denied to other minority groups.

Japanese Internment

On December 7, 1941, the Japanese Navy bombed Pearl Harbor, Hawaii, killing 2,345 American service men and women and 57 civilians. Though just 1.6% of the population of California at the time, Japanese Americans were suddenly thrown under suspicion for disloyalty and potential subversion. False reports circulated widely of mysterious gatherings of Japanese Americans in the California desert or signalling ships at sea. Both American media outlets and official government spokespeople described Japanese Americans as potential spies and saboteurs because their racial ties to Japan could never be broken. General John DeWitt, who commanded the west coast defense effort, told the public, "A Jap's a Jap, and that's all there is to it….In the war in which we are now engaged racial affinities are not severed by migration….The Japanese race is the enemy race and and while many second and third generation Japanese born on United States soil, possessed of American citizenship, have become 'Americanized,' the racial strains are undiluted…" Public sentiment was echoed by one well-read columnist for the Hearst syndicate of newspapers who wrote:

I am for immediate removal of every Japanese

Figure 8.15 Japanese families form a line outside Civil Control Station, San Francisco, Apr. 25, 1942. Photo by Dorothea Lange.

on the West Coast to a point deep in the interior. I don't mean a nice part of the interior either. Herd 'em up, pack 'em off, and give 'em the inside room in the badlands. Let 'em be pinched, hurt, hungry, and dead up against it… Personally, I hate the Japanese. And that goes for all of them.

In February of 1942, President Franklin Roosevelt issued an executive order that led to all Americans citizens of Japanese ancestry living on the West Coast to be incarcerated in internment camps far inland. That Roosevelt acted more to placate public fears than out of military necessity was evident by his decision to not confine the larger number of Japanese Americans who lived in Hawaii, even though Hawaii was the site of the deadly attack. There military authorities relied on the labor of Japanese American workers to support their Hawaiian bases and so detained just 1,440 "dangerous" people of Japanese descent on the island. Even J. Edgar Hoover, Director of the Federal Bureau of Investigation, wrote to his boss, the U.S. Attorney General, expressing his opinion that a general internment of Japanese Americans was not warranted on security grounds. President Roosevelt also rejected a proposal to also intern Germans and Italians on the East Coast.

More than 110,000 men, women, and children, most of them American-born citizens, were ordered to leave their homes with only the personal items they could carry and gather at assembly points where they were loaded onto trains and transported to distant camps. Most Japanese Americans cooperated as best they could under impossible circumstances. Many were forced to hastily sell their homes, businesses and possessions. Most forfeited jobs, investments, bank accounts, and securities. (Estimates later totaled some 70 million dollars worth of farms and farm equipment, 35 million dollars worth of orchard lands and at least a half billion in other property was lost due to the internment.) Some veterans, like Tokutaro Slocum wore their old uniforms to report to the assembly centers. A handful of others, such as Fred Korematsu, refused to comply citing their constitutional rights as American citizens and were arrested and imprisoned. Korematsu's case eventually wound its way to the Supreme Court and in December of 1944, the court ruled 6-3 that imprisoning Americans without cause or due process was justified by military necessity. This decision came in spite of the fact that not a single Japanese American was ever accused, indicted, or convicted of any act of espionage or other spying crime for the duration of the war.

Ten internment camps scattered across seven states were hastily erected to house the thousands of detainees. In wood and tin barracks twenty feet wide, as many as six families were squeezed together. Guard towers, armed guards, and barbed wire fences surrounded the camps. Daily life was regimented according to military schedules.

After a few months in the camps, government officials began systematically questioning each internee, filling out a "loyalty form" that would later be used to allocate work details and privileges to each person, but also to determine which of the young men were eligible to be drafted into the U.S. armed forces. Though initially the government designated all Japanese Americans as "enemy aliens" ineligible for military service, the administration reconsidered when it learned that Japanese propagandists were successfully damaging America's reputation throughout Asia by charging that Americans only fought for white supremacy in a racial war. Ultimately 33,000 Japanese Americans enlisted and served in the war, most of them in segregated units, including the all Japanese-American U.S. 442nd that was the most decorated combat unit of World War II.

Ultimately, internees spent an average of 900 days in captivity. For four decades following this tragedy, the Japanese American community largely bore their injustice quietly, rebuilding their lives and reintegrating into their communities. By the mid-1970s, in the wake of the Civil Rights movement and a general uprising of activism, many Japanese American activists launched a campaign to win an admission from the government that internment was unnecessary and racist. President Gerald Ford in 1976 issued a formal apology to victims of the wartime internment and symbolically reversed Roosevelt's internment executive order. In the last months of his presidency, Jimmy Carter established a commission (the Commission on Wartime Relocation and Internment of Civilians or CWRIC) to study the episode and make recommendations for redress. But when Ronald Reagan assumed office he told his staff he had little use for "left-over Carterisms like the CWRIC." Nevertheless, Reagan didn't cancel the commission and over the next three years it held hearings where it heard the testimony of 750 witnesses and systematically excavated an archive of War Department records. Among the bombshells it uncovered was clear evidence that Justice Department officials had suppressed evidence and lied to attorneys preparing the government's case on Fred Korematsu. On the strength of this new evidence Korematsu and a handful of other Japanese American citizens successfully sued in federal court to have their convictions reversed, though the Supreme Court ruling authorizing the government's actions continued to stand.

In 1984 Congress considered H.R. 442 (named for the army's famed Japanese American 442nd regiment) that would compensate each internee with a $20,000 payment and require a review of all criminal convictions for internees refusing to comply with camp orders. Though pushed by a

Figure 8.16 "White squadron," (Currier & Ives, 1893).

bipartisan group of legislators, President Reagan fought the measure because he was worried, as his Attorney General put it, that it "could establish a bad precedent for other groups who feel they have suffered injustices." When the legislation passed overwhelming in both houses in 1987, Reagan threatened a veto and dragged his feet for nearly a year, but with his party locked in a hard-fought election campaign he reversed himself and signed the legislation in August of 1988.

Imperialism and Immigration

In the 1890s Americans hotly debated the benefits and costs of building an overseas empire. Those favoring imperialism and colonies pointed out the obvious benefits to American manufacturers, farmers and workers as American merchants expanded into new markets. They also noted the need to keep pace with European rivals who had already carved up among themselves most of the globe's lands and peoples.

Anti-imperialists warned that grabbing foreign territories would inevitably lead America into overseas wars and was fundamentally unchristian and contrary to democratic principles. But alongside these moral arguments, many Americans were wary of overseas expansion out of fear that such a policy would open the door to waves of non-white "savage" and "inferior" immigrants.

Imperialists carried the day and after emerging victorious from a swift war with Spain, the U.S. seized a string of island colonies from the Caribbean to Asia. Most populous of these was Puerto Rico and Cuba to the South and the Philippines in the far Pacific. Suddenly the legal status of millions of new territorial subjects of the U.S. was a burning question. Did they enjoy constitutional rights like other Americans? Were their children citizens by reason of the Fourteenth Amendment which said, "All persons born or naturalized in the United States, and subject to the jurisdiction thereof, are citizens of the United States..."? Were residents of US territories eligible to freely immigrate to the mainland?

Congress decided to treat its colonies in different ways depending on their size. The largest, Cuba and the Philippines, were designated to be gradually granted their independence. Smaller possessions, like Guam, Samoa, and Puerto Rico, were to remain as U.S. territories. Determined to hold onto these islands that were viewed as strategically vital (they provided important bases and refueling stations for a global navy), Congress reluctantly granted their peoples U.S. citizenship. The people of the largest and most important of these countries, Puerto Rico, were made citizens by the Jones Act of 1917. Residents of the Virgin Islands had to wait another decade before Congress, almost as a casual afterthought, granted them citizenship in 1927. The people of Guam were declared citizens by Congress in 1950, the residents of the Northern Mariana Islands followed in 1976, and the people of Samoa have never been granted citizenship and remain in the status of "U.S. Nationals," free to travel to the U.S. but only eligible to be nationalized on an individual basis.

It should be noted that some anti-colonial activists opposed any steps that would tighten the relationship between their nations and the United States. In 1928, Vicente Géigel Polanco, a journalist who later became Puerto Rico's attorney general, condemned the U.S. Congress granting citizenship to the Puerto Rican people as "not an act of justice, but rather, an imposition of the American government." But most were supportive or indifferent to the change as a total of only 288 Puerto Ricans legally refused American citizenship.

American leaders viewed the colonies in the Pacific as being racially more alien than those in the Caribbean. Filipinos and other Pacific islanders were seen as "Asiatics" who could never be assimilated into American society and whose great and growing populations would only pose a competitive threat to American white workers. Representative Francis Newlands, a native of Mississippi who represented Nevada in Congress, and an outspoken advocate of repealing the Fifteenth Amendment giving black men the right to vote, described what he saw as the differences between Puerto Rico, that he described as "...one island near our coast, easily governed, its people friendly and peaceful," and the Philippines that he characterized as "an archipelago of seventeen hundred islands 7,000 miles distant, of diverse races, speaking different languages, having different customs, and ranging all the way from absolute barbarism to semicivilization."

Continuing, Newlands thundered:

...It can be easily imagined what will be the effect of putting inside of our governmental and industrial system 9,000,000 people possessing a high degree of industrial aptitude and accustomed to a scale of wages and mode of living appropriate to Asiatics.

To a round of applause from his fellow congressmen, John Dalzell of Pennsylvania seconded Newlands' concerns, saying he feared "to see the wage-earner of the United States...put upon a level and brought into competition with the cheap half-slave labor, savage labor, of the Philippine Archipelago."

Curiously, it appears congressional support for Puerto Rican citizenship was fueled in part by a widespread impression at the time that most of the island's population were directly descended from Spaniards, and, unlike Mexicans, relatively unmixed with indigenous people or Africans. This was partly an ironic consequence of the way that journalists had whitewashed their depictions of the island in order to whip up popular support for the Spanish-American war. These war hawks suspected, probably accurately, that few Americans would have cared about the Spanish tyranny of people of color. Americans were stirred to come to the rescue of oppressed Puerto Rican whites, not Indians or blacks. By the time Congress debated the status of Puerto Rico in 1900, these impressions remained strong. Representative Sereno Payne of New York, described the people of Puerto Rico as "generally full-blooded white people, descendants of the Spaniards, possibly mixed with some Indian blood, but none of them negro extraction."

Congress' constitutional ability to incorporate territories but deny their people equal status under the law was quickly taken up by the Supreme Court because the standing legal precedents did not allow it. An earlier Supreme Court in 1856 had declared that the Constitution prohibited conquering foreign territories and ruling their people as subjects in remarkably clear language:

There is certainly no power given by the Constitution to the Federal Government to establish or maintain colonies bordering on the United States or at a distance, to be ruled and governed at its own pleasure; nor to enlarge its territorial limits in any way, except by admission of new States . . . . [No] power is given to acquire a Territory to be held and governed [in a] permanently [colonial] character.

But in 1901, in a group of suits collectively called the "Insular Cases," a slim majority of the high court found no constitutional prohibition on seizing foreign territories and putting their people in an unequal and inferior status. They based their decision on the supposed racial inferiority of these lands. Justice Henry B. Brown wrote that granting "alien races" constitutional rights could prove "fatal" to the American republic:

It is obvious that in the annexation of outlying and distant possessions grave questions will arise from differences of race, habits, laws and customs of the people, and from differences of soil, climate and production, which may require action on the part of Congress that would be quite unnecessary in the annexation of contiguous territory inhabited only by people of the same race, or by scattered bodies of native Indians....

If those possessions are inhabited by alien races, differing from us in religion, customs,

Figure 8.17 Filipino lettuce laborer. Imperial Valley, California, 1939.

laws, methods of taxation, and modes of thought, the administration of government and justice, according to Anglo-Saxon principles, may for a time be impossible; and the question at once arises whether large concessions ought not be made for a time, that, ultimately, our own theories may be carried out, and the blessings of a free government under the Constitution extended to them. We decline to hold that there is anything in the Constitution to forbid such action.

Puerto Ricans discovered that even having the benefit of citizenship did not diminish the colonial relationship between the U.S. and themselves. For most of the twentieth century U.S. trade and tax policy kept Puerto Rico's economy dependent on the single crop of sugar for the benefit of U.S. corporations and investors. American companies eventually would control nearly three-fifths of all farmland on the island and pay their Puerto Rican cane workers 50-60 cents per day. When the sugar economy languished after World War Two, Puerto Ricans began a mass immigration to the U.S. where the benefits of U.S. citizenship could be realized. Ultimately, about a third of all Puerto Ricans found their way to the United States, half of whom concentrated in New York City, mostly in East Harlem and the Bronx.

With the United States conquests in Cuba and the Philippines, it extended its racial exclusion of Chinese immigrants to its new empire. Though Cuba had long maintained a policy of open borders to foreign laborers, its U.S. governor barred Chinese migrants from entering the island in 1902.

Soon after the American conquest, a number of Filipino men began to arrive in California and other western states in search of work. Filipinos were technically able to bypass immigration restrictions as U.S. "nationals," a second-class status conferred on those whose countries had been conquered and claimed as a territory of the United States in 1898. But being a "U.S. national" did not mean equal treatment. California, where three-quarters of Filipinos lived in the 1930s, legally classified Filipinos as "Mongolians" a status that made it illegal for them to marry whites.

White resentment of Filipino workers, who largely replaced the Japanese and Chinese workers who once did much of the labor in California's vast farms, grew in the 1920s. An American Legion post in the San Joaquin Valley organized vigilante patrols whose self-proclaimed mission was to keep white and Filipino youth from socializing. In October of 1929, after a fight between a white and a Filipino boy in the San Joaquin Valley town of Exeter, a white mob led by the local sheriff raided a farm beating Filipino workers and burning a barn. Later that year, the town of Watsonville burst into a week of violence as white gangs randomly beat any Filipino men they spotted, and killed one man, twenty-two year old Fermin Tobera, by shooting him from a passing car.

By the 1930s, nativists pressured Congress to establish a program to rid western states of their Filipino communities. The Repatriation Act of 1935 provided cash payments and paid passage back to the Philippines for any Filipino in America. More than two thousand Filipinos accepted the government's offer. Such pressures combined with an independence movement in the Philippines to prompt Congress to establish a framework for full Philippine independence, the Tydings-McDuffie Act, whose price tag was a near total ban on the immigration of Filipinos to the U.S..With passage of the Tydings-McDuffie Act any Filipinos living in the U.S. who returned to the Philippines to visit family or friends, was barred from reentering America, leading to the forced separation of many families.

Japan invaded the Philippines in 1942 and many thousands of Filipinos enlisted in the U.S. armed forces to liberate their homeland. When the war ended the hypocrisy of Filipino soldiers and sailors being denied entry into America because of their nationality moved Congress to pass the Luce-Cellar Act that granted naturalized status to more than one hundred thousand Filipino soldiers and their spouses and children.

Due to the long and strong cultural and political ties

between the U.S. and the Philippines and the long period of restrictions on the immigration of Filipinos to America, once these historic barriers were lifted Filipinos became the second largest group of immigrants to America from 1971 to 2000.

The Question of Refugees

American whites remained determined to maintain their country's racist immigration system even in the face of the desperate uprooting of millions of people by the rise of fascism in Europe and the global war against it in the 1930s and 1940s. In May of 1939 a passenger ship carrying nearly a thousand Jewish refugees left Germany, most of whom had applied for visas to enter the U.S. and hoped to find sanctuary in America. However, because of quota limits on the admission of immigrants to the U.S., the ship planned to dock in Cuba where passengers could wait for permission to come to America. However, when news of the ships voyage reached Cuba large antisemtic demonstrations pressured the government to turn the St. Louis away. The St. Louis sailed close enough to the coast of Florida that passengers could see the lights of Miami but the Roosevelt Administration refused to make an exception to its strict immigration laws and the St. Louis was forced to return to Europe, where England, Holland, Belgium and France agreed to accept equal numbers of the refugees. However, the refugees who resettled on the continent were later trapped by fascist armies and only half of them survived the Holocaust.

Public opinion ran so highly against immigration the year that the St. Louis sailed that a bipartisan bill to make an exception to immigration laws and allow 20,000 Jewish children from Germany into the country failed to garner the votes needed to pass.

It wasn't until late in the war, January of 1944, that President Roosevelt took action to deal with the growing crisis of refugees throughout the world and his first step was limited and tentative, the creation of a War Refugee

Figure 8.18 Border Patrol Agents Blocking a Road in Gainesville, Florida, 1926.

Board to coordinate the efforts of various charitable relief agencies.

To be fair, President Roosevelt was steering a course between irreconcilable forces. On the one hand were the anti-semitic attitudes of many Americans who feared and opposed bringing European refugees to America, primarily because most of them were Jews. On the other was a growing awareness of the immense scale of Nazi atrocities and a growing sympathy for its victims. In the summer of 1944, FDR took the measured step of designating an upstate New York military base as a temporary haven for a small number of refugees who, it was publicly promised, would be returned to their homelands after the war. Though fewer than 1000 mostly Jewish refugees were sheltered, their presence set a precedent for a reconsideration of America's closed door immigration policies.

At first treated like the hundreds of thousands of Japanese Americans who were confined behind barbed wire in hastily constructed camps in the West, namely like prisoners, these European refugees were quickly granted privileges Japanese American citizens were not. After a short time they were allowed day passes to visit the nearby city of Oswego, then their children were bused to public schools.

In spite of the sympathetic press the refugee haven in Oswego received, including a much publicized visit by the first lady Eleanor Roosevelt, immigration restrictionists condemned Roosevelt for bypassing immigration laws and when the war ended the House of Representatives passed a resolution demanding the camp be closed and its residents returned to Europe. Harry Truman who inherited this issue when FDR died in April 1945, chose not to challenge immigration restriction directly and instead tiptoed to a solution by busing the refugees temporarily to Canada where they could legally apply for visas and be readmitted back to the US.

Mexican-Americans in the 20th Century

Long after the territories conquered from Mexico were incorporated into the United States, the two-thousand mile border between the nations went unpoliced and open to travel both northward and southward. Such was a natural consequence of long established social networks and patterns of exchange connecting communities across this arbitrary line. Cross border mobility was so vital to these areas that it was not until 1909 that federal officials attempted to keep track of how many people crossed the border each year.

The federal government paid little attention to its border with Mexico until the long and devastating war known as the Mexican Revolution broke out in 1911. Over the course of several years somewhere between 1.5 and 2 million Mexicans lost their lives. At the dawn of the twentieth century the population of Americans of Mexican descent was about 400,000. The outbreak of the Mexican Revolution, pushed nearly four times this number of people northward. So deep and disruptive was the Mexican Revolution that during the course of the 1920s, one out of every eight Mexicans fled to the United States and the Mexican government initiated a program to pay the costs of repatriating hundreds of thousands back to Mexico.

It wasn't until 1919 that the United States required people crossing its southern border from Mexico to enter through a designated border post. A decade earlier when Congress first required people entering the country to first register with the federal government, it exempted those coming from Mexico. Though Congress exempted Mexico and other nations of the western hemisphere from the national quotas it established in 1924, it nevertheless tightened entrance requirements, instituting a head tax and a visa fee for all those crossing northward. Most importantly, it created a special federal police force to patrol the Mexican border for the first time, the Border Patrol.

When the economic crisis of the Great Depression swept the world in the 1930s, western states moved to exclude and deport Mexican migrants. Colorado Governor "Big" Ed Johnson, ordered the state police to patrol its southern border and summarily "deport" to New Mexico all "alien" Mexicans they apprehended. Vigilante groups were encouraged by the Governor to distribute posters throughout Colorado reading: "WARNING ALL MEXICAN AND ALL OTHER ALIENS TO LEAVE THE STATE OF COLORADO AT ONCE." Southern California counties employed a combination of police repression and offers of free transportation to push thousands of Mexicanos back over the border. Other officials throughout the West and Midwest copied this effort and by the end of the 1930s over 400,000 Mexicans were expelled.

States were not always careful to distinguish between Mexicans and American citizens of Mexican ancestry. According to one survey, as many as 60 percent of those returned to Mexico were American citizens by birth. Even officials of the Immigration and Naturalization Service were critical of the careless attitude of state officials to the question of citizenship. Summoned to investigate a supposed group of "illegals" working in a sugar factory in Michigan, the INS found none of the two hundred workers were in the country illegally and that nearly two-thirds were citizens who had been born in Texas.

Such deportation campaigns were fueled by the influx of white farm laborers who were suddenly available to work the corporate farms and factories. As the human tragedy called the "Great Depression" deepened, millions of small farmers went bankrupt and hundreds of thousands of farm families from the deep South, especially from Texas and Oklahoma, pulled up stakes and moved west to the promised land of California. This migration of largely rural white southerners westward could not have come at a worse time for long established Mexican-American communities in the Golden State. Newcomers crowded into the same areas and competed for the same farm labor jobs, driving down wages even further. Prior to the 1930s, whites accounted for only one-fifth of the agricultural labor force but by 1936 they had taken over 85 percent of the work. White migrants from the U.S. South were quick to view their Mexicano neighbors as "aliens" and "foreigners" even though most of them had lived in the area far longer.

Between the Mexican Revolution and the Great Depression, America's vast southern border had shifted from being a land where people freely moved for work and family on a seasonal basis to being one divided by a hardening line that determined both identity and rights. Those who crossed northward were increasingly thought of as being alien, illegitimate, and out of place. Such characteristics soon attached not just to nationality, but to physical and cultural characteristics, essentially racializing all Mexicans and Mexican-Americans into one suspect race of "illegals" by the 1930s.

So one effect of tightening the borders in the 1920s was to associate the ideas of illegality, mixed ancestry, and foreignness, in contrast to the bonding of Americanness, citizenship, and whiteness. Mexicans and Asians were treated as if their nationality and their race were the same thing while immigrants from Europe were readily allowed to divide these identities and blend into an increasingly homogeneous whiteness. In keeping with this trend, the 1930 federal census counted Mexicans as a "race," not a nationality or ethnic group. In that same decade many of the largest cities in Texas reclassified its Mexican-American residents from the category "white" to that of "colored." When some Congressmen proposed that the Mexican race be dropped from the 1940 census, the Census Bureau's chief statistician objected, writing, "...there are fundamental biological differences between the average American and the average Mexican in the way in which they react to disease as well as great differences in the rate of multiplication."

The Rise of Mexican-American Activism

Mexican workers had eagerly come north in the years following World War One to take jobs in the rapidly expanding steel industry. By the 1930s they were a significant segment of the mill labor force and responded enthusiastically when organizers from the Steel Workers Organizing Committee (SWOC), a new union effort to represent unskilled workers in the industry formed. SWOC would

Figure 8.19 Mexican Farm Workers Applying for Farm Labor in the U.S. through the Braceros Program, ca. 1942-1945.

eventually break away from the AFL to form the more radical national union, the Congress of Industrial Organizations (CIO). In the steel crescent from South Chicago to Gary, Indiana, Mexican steel workers made up 5% of the workforce.

For workers like Mexican Americans, the CIO was a means of not only representing their interests as workers, but also as discriminated minorities. Like most industrial workplaces, steel factories were sharply segregated by race, with the dirtiest, hottest, most dangerous, and lowest paying jobs reserved for nonwhites. Through the CIO, many workers were able to fight against the racist barriers and discriminations many minority workers experienced on the job.

It was Mexican workers employed by corporate farms in California and other southwestern states that first organized in the midst of the Great Depression and launched the massive strike wave that would eventually succeed in organizing the center of the industrial economy. Mexican men and women for the first time found labor allies who recognized their dual struggles of race and class (though, unfortunately, not always of gender) but these labor allies were connected to the Communist Party, a problem later when the full might of the government was enlisted to undermine domestic communism during the Cold War.

Mexicanos were prominent leaders and rank and file activists in farm worker organizing throughout the southwest, staging over fifty strikes in the center of the industry, California's central valleys, in 1933 and 1934 alone. By the end of the decade as the economy picked up, growers began demanding that government allow them to recruit more workers from Mexico even though there was no actual labor shortage, only a shortage of those willing to work for what the growers wanted to pay. Washington immigration officials, holding to the nation's official policy of keeping the borders mostly closed, resisted these demands but relented when the Second World War erupted.

In 1942, the U.S. government broke with over fifty years of precedent and authorized the importation of Mexican workers under contract to American agribusinesses. Calling the initiative the "Bracero" program (Bracero is Spanish for laborer), the U.S. began importing Mexicans mostly to work in agriculture, but some hired for work on the west's vast railroad system. The Mexican government cooperated with the U.S. to coordinate the program, successfully demanding that none of its nationals be allowed to work in Arkansas, Missouri, or Texas, the three states with the worst practices of segregating and discriminating against anyone of Mexican ancestry (though the US successfully lobbied to end this ban within a few years). The program expanded after the war and from 1948 to 1964 approximately 200,000 Mexicans were brought north under the program every year comprising about one in five of

Figure 8.20 Man in the Solidarity Day march, with a picket sign, 1981.

all seasonal farm workers.

Estimates are that at least ten percent of those brought to the U.S. each year under the Bracero program left their employers and sought other employment, which was a violation of their contract but a right most all people expect. This dynamic aligned the interests of the large agribusinesses and federal immigration authorities to more actively pursue and deport "illegal" Mexicans. Mexican American communities continued to grow both through natural increase and from the influx of new migrants, but all faced the prejudice of being associated with being "illegal" and, according to the newly popular bigoted word of the 1940s, being "wetbacks."

Though the Second World War was hailed as a victory over Nazism and its mad nationalist bigotry, racism survived throughout America. In 1948, the remains of one of America's soldiers, Felix Longoria, who was killed by a Japanese sniper's bullet, were discovered lying in the Philippine jungle. Longoria was drafted in 1944, leaving behind his young wife and four-year old daughter and was assigned to a segregated "Mexican" company of soldiers.

Longoria's bones were shipped home and eventually arrived in the town of his birth, Three Rivers, Texas.

Three Rivers was a typical southern small town and typically prohibited blacks and "Mexicans" from living in the white part of town. Longoria's widow, Beatrice, attempted to arrange a proper funeral for her fallen husband in the town's only mortuary, but the local mortician refused, saying (according to notes of the conversation preserved by his own secretary) "You know how the Latin people get drunk and lay around all the time. The last time we let them use the chapel, they got all drunk and we just can't control them - so the white people object to it, and we just can't let them use it." The mortician suggested instead the family do what Mexican-Americans had always done in Three Rivers, hold a private wake in their home and bury their loved one in the "Mexican"-only graveyard.

Longoria's family contacted a newly formed organization of Mexican-American veterans called the American G.I. Forum who organized a protest and enlisted the newly-elected Texas senator, Lyndon Johnson, to address this wrong. As news services across America took up the Longoria story and many Americans expressed outrage at the treatment of a man who paid the ultimate price to defend the nation, Senator Johnson arranged to have Longoria interred at Arlington Cemetery. On February 9, 1949, Lyndon and Lady Bird Johnson stood with the Longoria family at Arlington as Felix was finally given a hero's final salute. Many scholars credit the Longoria's refusal to knuckle under to their town's racist traditions and the activism of the American G.I. Forum with forcing white Americans to pay attention to the second-class treatment of Americans of Mexican ancestry for the first time.

After the war, deportations resumed and became institutionalized as a means of keeping labor costs low. While deportations themselves theoretically threatened to put upward pressure and wages by reducing the pool of potential workers, this effect was more than offset by the power of the threat of deportation had to prevent workers from organizing or bargaining for better pay and conditions. Mass deportations were a regular occurrence in the southwest and in 1954 President Eisenhower authorized "Operation Wetback," a vast police sweep that in its first three months detained and deported 170,000 workers and their family members and forced them back to Mexico.

At the same time federal border control and deportation efforts became more intensive in policing the border with Mexico, plans were being laid to liberalize immigration policies that had kept Europe's and other nation's refugees and migrants out since 1924. Truman, Eisenhower, and Kennedy all advocated scrapping the old racial quota system. But it fell to President Lyndon Johnson to finally sign the Hart-Cellar Act of 1965 that ended America's racist immigration system. When the United States finally abandoned its racially-based system of immigration in 1965, it was the last country in the western hemisphere to do so.

A Civil Rights Revolution in Immigration Law

Senator Philip Hart who had long fought to revise the racist quota system proposed that it be replaced by new immigration limits that both reflected the existing immigrant makeup of the United States and the proportionate size of each country's population. The Kennedy and Johnson administrations, however, were reluctant to create new country-by-country formulas and instead pushed for an equal cap of 20,000 immigrants for every country, no matter its size or historical relationship to the U.S. Under pressure by civil rights groups to wipe away all the vestiges of the racial prejudices inherent in the old system, Hart agreed and the law that passed in 1965 under his name was founded on this principle of equality.

But equality is not the same as justice, and the new immigration limits set by the Hart-Cellar Act (20,000 from

Figure 8.21 President Johnson delivers his speech before signing the Immigration Act, Liberty Island, New York City, Oct. 3, 1965.

any single nation and a global limit of 290,000 per year) disadvantaged many of the same groups historically most discriminated against in America's immigration history. While Congress had earlier repealed the "Asiatic Barred Zone" that had carved out most of humanity as being ineligible candidates to be Americans in 1952, the Hart-Cellar Act paid no attention to the size of any country's population. China, India, and the Philippines with their hundreds of millions of people and large communities of ex-patriots in the United States were severely limited by country caps that had been set so as every country, large or small, would be equal.

While the Hart-Cellar Act represented a giant step toward a more liberal immigration policy it had contradictory and unintended consequences for the most fraught area of immigration policy, America's southern borderlands. For the first time it established a firm ceiling on the number of immigrants from Mexico, and Central and South American nations, allowed into the country each year. At first the limit for all of the western hemisphere was arbitrarily set at 120,000 per year, a forty percent reduction from existing levels. While the western hemisphere was excluded from the overall 20,000 limit of immigrants from any one country, in 1976 Congress extended this cap to all countries, and Mexico, that had long provided the vast majority of all migrants from the western hemisphere alone, was allowed but a fraction of the visas that had been provided before. Indeed, the global limit about equalled the number of Mexicans who migrated to the U.S. each year, most of whom came temporarily in pursuit of seasonal agricultural employment.

When these new limits were put into place, deportations to Mexico soared to a record 781,000 in one year. This intensified a regularized system of policing that routinely and regularly deported people back to Mexico. Over the next twenty years, nearly as many people (85%) arriving from Mexico were deported south.

Instead of country quotas, the new law established a schedule of groups to be given priority in applications for immigrant visas, such as those who already had family members in the United States. These family reunification provisions, was projected to favor Europeans, simply by reason of their overwhelming proportion of the population. Asian Americans, who represented less than one percent of the U.S. population, could take full advantage of these family reunification provisions, but not at the rates that European Americans could. At the time of the law's passage, the Johnson administration estimated that twelve times more Europeans than Asians would be able to immigrate under this rule and this projection helped attract support for the bill from reluctant congressmen.

However, politics tends to follow the laws of unintended consequences and the Hart-Cellar Act had more than its share. If the old system was designed to discriminate on the basis of race, the new system of priorities gave preference on the basis of class; the wealthy and privileged were favored at a time when America had an interest in recruiting the world's most highly trained and talented to help outpace the Communists in a technological arms race and Cold War.

Preferences for professionals written into the Hart-Cellar Act of 1965 particularly benefited immigrants from the Philippines, Hong Kong, Pakistan, and India where an extensive English-language university system had long produced many graduates, especially in the medical fields. As it turned out, many Indian, Pakistani, and Filipino professionals filled a crucial gap as America suddenly had need of a great many health workers as a result of the passage of the Medicare and Medicaid laws that gave millions of people access to the health system. By 1970, one out of seven of all foreign physicians and one-half of all foreign nurses working in the U.S. were Filipino. (American medical professionals successfully lobbied Congress to curtail the growth in immigrant medical workers by sharply limiting the number of visas granted each year in 1978.)

By the 1970s, the fastest growing minority group were Asian-Americans, though having begun with relatively small numbers this is as much a statistical phenomenon as a meaningful trend. Nevertheless, the system's preferences for immigrants with wealth, education, and technical skills increased the cultural visibility of professional immigrants from Asian countries. Popular magazines and other media outlets began featuring stories about Asian immigrants being the "Model Minority." The Christmas issue of the *U.S. News and World Report* for 1966, included a story entitled, "Success Story of One Minority Group in U.S." that began:

> At a time when Americans are awash in worry over the plight of racial minorities--one such minority, the nation's 300,000 Chinese-Americans, is winning wealth and respect by dint of its own hard work. In any Chinatown from San Francisco to New York, you discover youngsters at grips with their studies. Crime and delinquency are found to be rather minor in scope. Still being taught in Chinatown is the old idea that people should depend on their own efforts--not a welfare check--in order to reach America's 'promised land.'

This "Model Minority Myth" was repeated regularly in the U.S. media and by politicians eager to implicitly criticize other people of color by heaping praise on another. This myth served the purpose of combating African American, Native American, and Latino demands for economic justice by implying that poverty in these communities was no one's fault but their own. It also served to create new "Asian" stereotypes that erased the huge cultural and historical differences between the many nationalities and groups that immigrated to the U.S. from Asia.

Since the 1960s, increased immigration has dramatically changed the demographic patterns of the nation. Latinos and Latinas are now the largest minority group, having surpassed African Americans in numbers.

In 1986, Congress reached a historic compromise to deal with the large number of immigrants from Mexico who had set down roots in America but had been unable to regularize their status with the authorities. A system was established to facilitate applications from those lacking documentation for permanent resident status. In exchange, opponents of immigration won agreement to make it a crime for businesses to hire employees lacking documentation and to boost the funding for border protection. This business hiring provision was a largely symbolic one as it contained loopholes that nearly ensured that it was unenforceable, but was, nevertheless, the first measure of its kind ever passed by Congress.

After Congress tightened its border controls in the 1980s, the United States and Mexico agreed to a broad new trade agreement called the North American Free Trade Agreement (NAFTA) in 1994. Both countries agreed to reduce the tariffs it levied on goods imported from the other. While overall the agreement stimulated quicker growth of both economies, it also exacted a high cost on industries and communities long dependent on trade protection to survive.

Most significantly, Mexico was forced to stop subsidizing its small farmers. Millions of Mexican families were dependent on plots of land that were sufficient for survival within the Mexican market, but were unable to compete with the scale and mechanization of American farms. In a short period an estimated 1.5 to 2 million Mexican farmers lost their livelihoods and were forced off their land. Naturally, many of those displaced migrated into Mexican cities and a large number moved across the northern border in an attempt to earn a livelihood.

Congress responded by pouring still more money into border policing and deportations. Congress repeatedly increased border patrol and security funding as part of every immigration bill over the next twenty years. From 1993 to 1996, funding for the border security more than doubled. By the 2000s, funding for US immigration enforcement and border security was larger than all other federal law enforcement agencies (FBI, DEA, ATF, & U.S. Marshalls, etc.) combined. America's border enforcement policies fall unequally on different nationalities. Mexicans, for example, represent about 58% of the estimated undocumented population in the U.S. but are 70% of those deported each year.

One effect of hardening the southern border is that it deters people from moving back to Mexico. During the century in which the border was relatively open, movement was seasonal and in both directions. But as the border closed, many who crossed north without permission decided it wasn't worth the risk to visit or work at home and then later attempt another risky crossing. Today most people in the United States without formal permission have lived in the country for a long time—more than four-fifths have resided in the U.S. for more than seven years.

Between 2000 and 2012, more than fourteen million immigrants entered American society bringing the total number of Americans who were born abroad to one in four of all Americans.

In 2014, after years of small but significant declines in the number of people crossing into America without authorization, Congress came close to passing a package of comprehensive immigration reform that would have provided legal status for undocumented people brought to the U.S. as children and a pathway for regularized status for other undocumented immigrants. But the legislation was voted down signalling a further hardening of the public's attitudes toward immigrants.

Such rising anti-immigrant attitudes were evident as several states passed tough measures that attempted to withhold state services from undocumented immigrants and to make it easier for police to detain and deport them. Alabama's 2011 law, H.B. 56, was the most sweeping, permitting any police officer to ask for documentation of citizenship and requiring proof of legal status to receive any state service, including admission of children into public schools. (The Obama administration successfully sued in federal court to block most of the provisions of H.B. 56, relying on a 1982 Supreme Court decision, *Plyler v. Doe* that upheld all children's right to an education regardless of immigration status.)

Since the 1980s politicians appealed to voters by proclaiming their intent to crack down on illegal immigration, but in the 2010s a small but vocal segment of conservatives went a step further and began arguing that legal immigration should be restricted as well. In 2013, Senator Jeff Sessions of Alabama surprised his colleagues by introducing legislation to curb the total number of immigrants admitted into the country. It failed to attract even a single vote, besides Senator Session's own, in committee. But three years later the same sort of hostility not just to "illegal" but to all immigration would become the winning platform in the Presidential campaign.

By 2015, Senator Sessions was publicly praising the immigration act of 1924 with its restrictive (and racist) quotas as having been "good for America." The Senator's plan for immigration restriction was incorporated into Donald Trump's immigration plan that was the cornerstone of his presidential campaign in 2016.

Even the older style of thinking that Asian Americans are not true Americans and can never truly be "real" Americans was on display during the 2016 election. During a debate Republican Senator Mark Kirk of Illinois responded to his challenger, Tammy Duckworth, a decorated combat veteran who had just spoke of her pride in being from a family that had served in the U.S. armed forces since the Revolutionary War, saying to her in front of the video cameras, "I forgot that your parents came all the way from Thailand to serve George Washington." (Rep. Duckworth's mother was from Thailand.)

In July of 2016, in the thick of the Presidential campaign, Republican Congressman Steve King of Iowa remarked on a national news show: "This whole white people business, though, does get a little tired. I'd ask you to go back through history and figure out where are these contributions that have been made by these other categories of people that you are talking about. Where did any other subgroup of people contribute more to civilization?" Several years earlier, Rep. King said that for every illegal immigrant child "who's a valedictorian, there's another 100 out there who weigh 130 pounds and they've got calves the size of cantaloupes because they're hauling 75 pounds of marijuana across the desert." King won reelection in 2016 and a few months later praised a far-right Dutch politician who has fought the continued resettlement of Muslim refugees in the Netherlands because he "understands that culture and demographics are our destiny. We can't restore our civilization with somebody else's babies." He later defended his statement saying "Western civilization" is "a superior civilization," and "I'd like to see an America that's just so homogenous that we look a lot the same, from that perspective."

With Donald Trump's election, white nationalism was legitimized and empowered. One of Trump's first appointments was tapping Steve Bannon, editor-in-chief of the white nationalist website *Breitbart News*, to be his senior counselor and strategist. Bannon was also the founder of the National Policy Institute, an organization that describes itself as protecting the "heritage, identity, and future of people of European descent in the United States, and around the world."

The Trump phenomenon indicated that the previous norms of a color-blind nation had begun to weaken. Since the 1970s the ideals expressed in Dr. Martin Luther King, Jr.'s "I Have a Dream Speech"—of a world in which "children will one day live in a nation where they will not be judged by the color of their skin but by the content of their character,"—had powerfully dominated public speech, thought, and discussion. Trump's campaign punctured this color-blind consensus and opened a space for white nationalist advocacy.

President Trump, in his first major foreign policy speech, echoed King's ethnocentric view of the world. Speaking in Warsaw, Poland, to a crowd of supporters of the right-wing nationalist government bused in for the occasion, President Trump struck the same themes of the superiority of the "West" compared with the "South" and the "East." It was a theme Calvin Coolidge would have understood and applauded.

Figure 8.22 Trump's Presidential Visit to Poland, 2017, photo by SPC Kevin Wang,

William Z. Ripley, "Races in the United States"
The Atlantic Monthly, 102:6 (December 1908), pp. 745-759.

A few general observations upon the subject of racial intermixture may now be permitted. Is the result likely to be superior or an inferior type? Will the future American two hundred years hence be better or worse, as a physical being, because of his mongrel origin? …

For the continent of Europe, it is indubitable that the highly mixed populations of the British Isles, of Northern France, of the Valley of the Po, and of Southern Germany, are superior in many ways to those of outlying or inaccessible regions where greater purity of type prevails…Viewed in a still larger way, is it not indeed the very beneficence of Nature in these regards which has induced, or permitted, a higher evolution of the human species in Europe than in any of the other continents? …What leads to the survival of the fittest, unless there be the opportunity for variation of type, from which effective choice by selection may result. And yet most students of biology agree that the crossing of types must not be too violently extreme. Nature proceeds in her work by short and easy stages.

.… The significance of the rapidly increasing immigration from Europe in recent years is vastly enhanced by other social conditions in the United States. A powerful process of social selection is apparently at work among us. Racial heterogeneity, due to the direct influx of foreigners in large numbers, is aggravated by their surprisingly sustained tenacity of life, greatly exceeding that of the native-born American. Relative submergence of the domestic Anglo-Saxon stock is strongly indicated for the future. "Race suicide" marked by a low and declining birth-rate, as is well known, is a world-wide social phenomenon of the present day. Nor is it by any means confined solely to the so-called upper classes. It is so notably a characteristic of democratic communities that it may be regarded as almost a direct concomitant of equality of opportunity among men. To this tendency, the United States is no exception; in fact, together with the Australian commonwealths, it affords one of the most striking illustrations of present-day social forces.

.… Is it any wonder that serious students contemplate the racial future of Anglo-Saxon America with some concern? They have seen the passing of the American Indian and the buffalo; and now they query as to how long the Anglo-Saxon may be able to survive.

.… At the outset, confession was made that it was too early as yet to draw positive conclusions as the to probable outcome of this great ethnic struggle for dominance and survival. The great heat and sweat of it is yet to come. Wherever the Anglo-Saxon has fared forth into new lands, his supremacy in his chosen field, whatever that may be, has been manfully upheld. India was never contemplated as a centre for settlement; but Anglo-Saxon law, order, and civilization have prevailed. In Australia, where nature has offered inducements for actual colonization, the Anglo-Saxon line is apparently assured of physical ascendancy. But the great domain of Canada, greater than one can conceive who has not traversed its northeastern empire, is subject to the same physical danger which confronts us in the United States,—actual physical submergence of the English stock by a flood of continental European peoples. And yet, after all, is the word "danger" well considered for use in this connection? What are the English people, after all, but a highly evolved product of racial blending?…And the primary physical brotherhood of all branches of the white race, nay, even of all the races of men, must be admitted on faith,—not the faith of dogma, but the faith of scientific probability. It is only in their degree of physical and mental evolution that the races of men are different.

Great Britain has its "white man's burden" to bear in India and Africa; we have ours to bear with the American Negro and Filipino. But an even greater responsibility with us, and with the people of Canada, is that of the "Anglo-Saxon's burden,"—so to nourish, uplift, and inspire all these immigrant peoples of Europe that, in due course of time, even if the Anglo-Saxon stock be physically inundated by the engulfing flood, the torch of its civilization and ideals may still continue to illuminate the way.

Remarks by President Trump to the People of Poland, July 6, 2017
Krasiński Square, Warsaw, Poland

Americans, Poles, and the nations of Europe value individual freedom and sovereignty. We must work together to confront forces, whether they come from inside or out, from the South or the East, that threaten over time to undermine these values and to erase the bonds of culture, faith and tradition that make us who we are. If left unchecked, these forces will undermine our courage, sap our spirit, and weaken our will to defend ourselves and our societies.

But just as our adversaries and enemies of the past learned here in Poland, we know that these forces, too, are doomed to fail if we want them to fail. And we do, indeed, want them to fail. They are doomed not only because our alliance is strong, our countries are resilient, and our power is unmatched. Through all of that, you have to say everything is true. Our adversaries, however, are doomed because we will never forget who we are. And if we don't forget who are, we just can't be beaten. Americans will never forget. The nations of Europe will never forget. We are the fastest and the greatest community. There is nothing like our community of nations. The world has never known anything like our community of nations.

We write symphonies. We pursue innovation. We celebrate our ancient heroes, embrace our timeless traditions and customs, and always seek to explore and discover brand-new frontiers.

We reward brilliance. We strive for excellence, and cherish inspiring works of art that honor God. We treasure the rule of law and protect the right to free speech and free expression.

We empower women as pillars of our society and of our success. We put faith and family, not government and bureaucracy, at the center of our lives. And we debate everything. We challenge everything. We seek to know everything so that we can better know ourselves.

And above all, we value the dignity of every human life, protect the rights of every person, and share the hope of every soul to live in freedom. That is who we are. Those are the priceless ties that bind us together as nations, as allies, and as a civilization.

What we have, what we inherited from our...ancestors has never existed to this extent before. And if we fail to preserve it, it will never, ever exist again. So we cannot fail.

This great community of nations has something else in common: In every one of them, it is the people, not the powerful, who have always formed the foundation of freedom and the cornerstone of our defense. The people have been that foundation here in Poland—as they were right here in Warsaw—and they were the foundation from the very, very beginning in America.

Our citizens did not win freedom together, did not survive horrors together, did not face down evil together, only to lose our freedom to a lack of pride and confidence in our values. We did not and we will not. We will never back down....

We have to remember that our defense is not just a commitment of money, it is a commitment of will. Because as the Polish experience reminds us, the defense of the West ultimately rests not only on means but also on the will of its people to prevail and be successful and get what you have to have. The fundamental question of our time is whether the West has the will to survive. Do we have the confidence in our values to defend them at any cost? Do we have enough respect for our citizens to protect our borders? Do we have the desire and the courage to preserve our civilization in the face of those who would subvert and destroy it?

We can have the largest economies and the most lethal weapons anywhere on Earth, but if we do not have strong families and strong values, then we will be weak and we will not survive....

Our own fight for the West does not begin on the battlefield—it begins with our minds, our wills, and our souls. Today, the ties that unite our civilization are no less vital, and demand no less defense, than that bare shred of land on which the hope of Poland once totally rested. Our freedom, our civilization, and our survival depend on these bonds of history, culture, and memory.

And today as ever, Poland is in our heart, and its people are in that fight. Just as Poland could not be broken, I declare today for the world to hear that the West will never, ever be broken. Our values will prevail. Our people will thrive. And our civilization will triumph.

Acts of Congress.

Jersey, two hundred dollars; the marshal of the district of Pennsylvania, three hundred dollars; the marshal of the district of Delaware, one hundred dollars; the marshal of the district of Mary-land, three hundred dollars; the marshal of the district of Virginia, five hundred dollars; the mar-shal of the district of Kentucky, two hundred and fifty dollars; the marshal of the district of North Carolina, three hundred and fifty dollars; the marshal of the district of South Carolina, three hundred dollars; the marshal of the district of Georgia, two hundred and fifty dollars. And to obviate all doubts which may arise respecting the persons to be returned, and the manner of making returns,

Sec. 5. *Be it enacted,* That every person whose usual place of abode shall be in any family on the aforesaid first Monday in August next shall be returned as of such family; and the name of every person, who shall be an inhabitant of any district, but without a settled place of residence, shall be inserted in the column of the aforesaid schedule, which is allotted for the heads of families, in that division where he or she shall be on the said first Monday in August next, and every person occasionally absent at the time of the enumeration, as belonging to that place in which he usually resides in the United States.

Sec. 6. *And be it further enacted,* That each and every person more than sixteen years of age, whether heads of families or not, belonging to any family within any division of a district made or established within the United States, shall be, and hereby is, obliged to render to such assistant of the division, a true account, if required, to the best of his or her knowledge, of all and every person belonging to such family respectively, according to the several descriptions aforesaid, on pain of forfeiting twenty dollars, to be sued for and recovered by such assistant, the one half for his own use, and the other half for the use of the United States.

Sec. 7. *And be it further enacted,* That each assistant shall, previous to making his return to the marshal, cause a correct copy, signed by himself, of the schedule, containing the number of in-habitants within his division, to be set up at two of the most public places within the same, there to remain for the inspection of all concerned; for each of which copies the said assistant shall be entitled to receive two dollars, provided proof of a copy of the schedule having been so set up and suffered to remain shall be transmitted to the marshal, with the return of the number of persons; and in case any assistant shall fail to make such proof to the marshal, he shall forfeit the compensation by this act allowed him.

Approved, March 1, 1790.

———

An act to establish a uniform rule of naturalization.

Be it enacted, &c., That any alien, being a free white person, who shall have resided within the limits and under the jurisdiction of the United States for the term of two years, may be admitted to become a citizen thereof, on application to any common law court of record in any one of the States wherein he shall have resided for the term of one year at least, and making proof, to the satisfaction of such court, that he is a person of good character, and taking the oath or affirmation prescribed by law, to support the Constitution of the United States, which oath or affirmation such court shall administer; and the clerk of such court shall record such application, and the proceedings thereon; and thereupon such person shall be considered as a citizen of the United States. And the children of such persons so naturalized, dwelling within the United States, being under the age of twenty-one years, at the time of such naturalization, shall also be considered as citizens of the United States. And the children of citizens of the United States, that may be born beyond sea, or out of the limits of the United States, shall be considered as natural born citizens. *Provided,* That the right of citizenship shall not descend to persons whose fathers have never been resident in the United States. *Provided, also,* That no person heretofore proscribed by any State shall be admitted a citizen aforesaid, except by an act of the Legislature of the State in which such person was proscribed.

Approved, March 26, 1790.

———

An act making appropriations for the support of Government, for the year one thousand seven hundred and ninety.

Be it enacted, &c. That there be appropriated for the service of the year one thousand seven hundred and ninety, to be paid out of the moneys arising from the duties on imports and tonnage, the following sums, to wit: a sum not exceeding one hundred and forty-one thousand four hundred and ninety-two dollars and seventy-three cents, for defraying the expenses of the civil list, as estimated by the Secretary of the Treasury, in the statement annexed to his report made to the House of Representatives on the ninth day of January last, including therein the contingencies of the several executive officers, which are hereby authorized and granted; and, also, a sum not exceeding one hundred and fifty-five thousand five hundred and thirty-seven dollars and seventy-two cents, for defraying the expenses of the Depart-ment of War; and the further sum of ninety-six thousand nine hundred and seventy-nine dollars and seventy-two cents, for paying the pensions which may become due to the invalids, as esti-mated in the statements accompanying the afore-said report.

Sec. 2. *And be it further enacted,* That all the expenses arising from, and incident to, the sessions of Congress, which may happen in the course of the aforesaid year, agreeably to laws heretofore passed, shall be defrayed out of the moneys arising from the aforesaid duties on imports and tonnage.

Sec. 3. *And be it further enacted,* That the President of the United States be authorized to draw from the Treasury a sum not exceeding ten thousand dollars for the purpose of defraying the

The Naturalization Act of 1790 defined American citizenship as being available only to "white persons."

Part Four: Identity, Perception and Prejudice

Model No. 132

Model No. 131

Chapter Nine: Prejudice and Identity

Social scientists first asked the question, "where does prejudice come from," at the turn of the twentieth century. One answer was that it was an evolutionary adaptation. As one scientist put it: "The earliest movements of animal life involve, in the rejection of stimulations vitally bad, an attitude which is the analogue of prejudice... the microorganism will approach a particle of food placed in the water and shun a particle of poison..." Prejudice was seen as a natural outgrowth of intense competition for food and mates in the evolution of the human species. According to these scholars, an innate "consciousness of kind" was hardwired into the human mind. Consequently, prejudice was a permanent fact of life. It was an instinct and "cannot be reasoned with, because, like the other instincts, it originated before deliberative brain centers were developed, and is not to any great extent under their control." Some scientists believed that the objects of prejudice were not fixed and prejudicial instincts could be reassigned from one group to another or that the intensity of prejudice could be lowered through the advancement of the despised group. But ultimately, prejudice was seen as a steady natural force.

Additionally, prejudice was seen as being proportional to the differences between one race and another. It was to be expected that frictions between Anglo-Americans and Italian immigrants would lessen over time because ultimately the two "races" were thought of as being quite close together on the evolutionary scale. But the vast difference in human development between whites and blacks, these scientists argued, was what produced the depth of hatred between them. As Mississipian Alfred Stone wrote in 1908:

It is the practical question of differences—the fundamental differences of physical appearance, of mental habit and thought, of social customs and religious beliefs, of the thousand and one things keenly and clearly appreciable, yet sometimes elusive and undefinable—these are the things which at once create and find expression in what we call race problems and race prejudices, for want of better terms. In just so far as these differences are fixed and permanently associated characteristics of two groups of people will the antipathies and problems between the two be permanent.

In those early years of the twentieth century, only the great black intellectual W.E.B. Du Bois pointed out that for all the books and papers published on the subject of racial prejudice, there was no actual scientific data to back any of it up:

How great is this incompatibility and repugnancy of qualities between white and black Americans? ...As I have often said before, it is a matter of serious disgrace to American science that with the tremendous opportunity that it has had before it for the study of race differences and race development, race intermingling and contact among the most diverse of human kinds right here at its doors, almost nothing has been done....this is then primarily a scientific question, a matter of scientific measurement and observation; and yet the data upon which the mass of men, and even intelligent men, are basing their conclusions today, the basis which they are putting back of their treatment of the Negro, is a most ludicrous and harmful conglomeration of myth, falsehood, and desire.

Du Bois then speculates, what if the difference between whites and blacks is not really so great? How then do we explain the phenomenon of prejudice?

Unfortunately, Du Bois' voice was ignored by virtually all his academic colleagues who continued to rest their conclusions on ludicrous conglomerations of "myth, falsehood, and desire." Ironically, at this very time, the field of sociology began to be revolutionized by the influence of researchers such as Robert Park at the University of Chicago who emphasized a more rigorous objectivity based on the careful accumulation of data. (Du Bois was actually an earlier pioneer of this method in his Atlanta and Philadelphia projects, but his work was overlooked because of his color.) In 1925, one of Park's students, Emory Bogardus, embarked on a project to actually measure racial prejudice. Bogardus conducted interviews with 248 people in order to determine if there were patterns in their views of different ethnic groups. First, each subject was asked if they had friendly, neutral, or adverse feelings toward each of thirty-nine groups. Then they were asked to rank all the friendly groups, all the neutral groups, and all those they had an aversion to. Rankings were then converted to a numerical scale and from such calculations Bogardus developed what he called the Social Distance Scale.

The usefulness of Bogardus' Social Distance Scale was not what it revealed when he first used it in the 1920s, but its ability to uncover differences across time and space. It seemed particularly useful in measuring how consistent prejudices were across large populations and how they varied by region, occupation, education, age, and other demographic factors. The year following its publication, researchers at two dozen other universities repeated Bogardus' method, expanding his data set nationwide. Bogardus himself then repeated the survey every decade through the 1960s, charting shifts in American racial attitudes across one of its most significant times of change.

Bogardus was interested in developing a measurement to gauge prejudice because he, like most all sociologists and psychologists of his day, assumed that prejudice was an aspect of personality. Clearly, not all people were equally biased, and even more obviously, not all people acted on their biases to the same degree. Some people were outspoken in their social hatreds while others harbored varying intensities of prejudice or tolerance. Investigators wanted to know what elements made for such differing degrees of bias and

assumed that such things as childhood experiences, social problems, and maybe even in-born personality might be at their root. In other words, prejudice was a pathology, a deviation from what should be a well-adjusted personality and therefore a matter of individual psychology.

Group Position Theory

By the 1950s sociologists had begun to speculate that perhaps prejudice was not an individual phenomenon, but a social one. Evidence contradicting the idea that prejudice was a function of personality began to surface. Several large opinion surveys discovered not only that racial prejudice was stronger in the south than in the north, but also that in those states, like Louisiana, where whites measured the highest levels of racism towards blacks, rates of prejudice towards Jews was remarkably low. This seemed to suggest that prejudice did not just spring from a certain type of personality, but was a reaction to particular social contexts and environments.

Herbert Blumer and other scientists built on these observations and theorized that prejudice was not the expression of a deviant or disordered personality but a

Figure 9.1 Protest against the integration of Central High School at the Arkansas capitol, Aug. 20, 1959.

common response to the perception of the relative power and status of racial and ethnic groups. Blumer's theory primarily applied to dominant groups; in America's case the white majority, rather than the minority groups (one exception would be if a minority group grew to become a dominant majority). This "Group Threat Theory" hypothesized that prejudice among people in a dominant majority strengthened as the relative population, social position, status, and political or economic power of a subordinate group increased.

Blumer's first paper outlined how viewing racism as related to group identity and perception changed the way scientists should think about prejudice:

> In this paper I am proposing an approach to the study of race prejudice different from that which dominates contemporary scholarly thought on this topic. My thesis is that race prejudice exists basically in a sense of group position rather than in a set of feelings which members of one racial group have toward the members of another racial group. This different way of viewing race prejudice shifts study and analysis from a pre-occupation with feelings as lodged in individuals to a concern with the relationship of racial groups. It also shifts scholarly treatment away from individual lines of experience and focuses interest on the collective process by which a racial group comes to define and redefine another racial group. Such shifts, I believe, will yield a more realistic and penetrating understanding of race prejudice.

By thinking about prejudice not as an individual phenomenon but as a group effect, Blumer could begin asking questions such as how are groups constituted? How do individuals come to identify themselves with a group? How do they come to perceive different groups? Blumer theorized:

> Race prejudice presupposes, necessarily, that racially prejudiced individuals think of themselves as belonging to a given racial group... Thus, logically and actually, a scheme of racial identification is necessary as a framework for racial prejudice. Moreover, such identification involves the formation of an image or a conception of one's own racial group and of another racial group...

Such theories moved the field from thinking about prejudice as an individual issue to a thinking about it as a "collective process." Rather than simply asking what caused

a person to become a bigot, researchers after Blumer were able to ask the wider question of how is identity shaped and influenced throughout society? More importantly, by no longer assuming that prejudice is a condition resulting from childhood experiences and only affecting some people but seeing it as a shared social experience, researchers were able to think about prejudice as a matter of identity and perception.

Researchers soon found evidence supporting this "Group Threat Theory." In 1959, Thomas Pettigrew of Howard University conducted extensive surveys of residents of eight towns, half northern and half southern. Pettigrew specifically chose four southern towns that had a variety of proportions of black and white population, ranging from 10 to 45%. Pettigrew used a survey that measured three axis of outlook: one standard measure of "authoritarianism" (called the "F scale") and scales of anti-semitic and anti-black attitudes. When the results were compiled, it turned out that the F-scale index of authoritarianism did not vary by region. Among all the variables tested, age, sex, education, church-going, class, military service, political affiliation, the variable that unexpectedly emerged most strongly in predicting prejudice was the relative size of the black population in a community. White attitudes seemed to be a response to their perception of the strength of the subordinated group. Other researchers examined whether these group threat effects were stronger in the once-segregated South than the North and found little difference between regions.

Data supporting this group threat effect began accumulating. Several studies that aggregated large national surveys undertaken during the 1970s revealed that white support for integration policies varied negatively with the size of the black community. In cities that had larger proportions of black residents, support for racial integration was lower than in places with smaller relative black communities.

While researchers first documented this correlation between black population size and white racial attitudes in the 1950s during the time when legal segregation was common, this effect has persisted in spite of the success of the civil rights movement and a tidal shift in public attitudes toward racism. Analysis of a massive national attitude survey undertaken in 2000 (the General Social Survey) revealed that the racial outlook of whites continued to vary according to the relative size of the black and white population in a local community.

Herbert Blumer had proposed that prejudice was a product of a social group's sense of their relative position. Blumer thought prejudice was built from four ingredients: feelings of superiority, a perception that a subordinate group is inherently different, claims to a right of privilege

Figure 9.2 Children on their way to school in New York City pass mothers protesting the busing of children to achieve integration, 1965.

and advantage over the other group, and fear that the subordinate group aims to challenge and replace the dominate one. This theory advanced beyond those that presumed conflict was natural by making group interactions a product of history, but Blumer still thought of groups as natural and stable entities.

Allport Contact Hypothesis

In 1954, Gordon Allport theorized that one important factor determining the intensity of bias was the degree of contact between two groups. Allport developed what he called the 'Contact Hypothesis' that held that more regular and casual contacts between defined groups would serve to lessen bias. Subsequent laboratory and field research confirmed this effect, but only under certain conditions. The catch was that contact across racial lines, to have the effect of reducing prejudice, had to take place in conditions that

were not common in American society. Parties to the interaction had to be of equal status, they had to be pursuing a common goal, they had to work together cooperatively, and the whole interaction needed to be supported by the surrounding social institutions. Other psychologists subsequently added to Allport's Contact Hypothesis by demonstrating the effectiveness of intimate contact or the necessity for the interaction to be sustained and regular.

The opposite situation seemed true as well: bias was strengthened simply by "we," or the ingroup, having more cooperation, interaction, and common goals than "they," or the outgroup. Such ingroup favoritism was not only easily fostered, but it effectively maintained itself by assuming ingroup members had certain qualities and a higher level of trust, thereby encouraging even more ingroup contact. Such dynamics can be seen in the lengths white people go to live in all-white communities and other social spaces.

Allport's Contact Hypothesis seemed to explain

some aspects of American racism but not all of them. Most importantly, these and other older explanations of prejudice rested upon the presumption that races, ethnic groups, and nationalities were real, objective things. Scholars assumed that people were members of such groups because they were born into this membership as one more link in a chain whose other end extended back through time into the mists of antiquity. In other words, they began their research from the belief that racial and ethnic groups (or for anthropologists maybe tribes and clans) were just an expression of nature, a fixed foundation of the world.

Well into the twentieth century scientists assumed that what divided people of different races or ethnicities was their shared ancestry, their shared characters, and their common behaviors or cultures. But in the 1960s anthropologist Fredrik Barth pointed out that most of these features of groups are largely mythical and subject to rapid change. Moreover, the boundaries between one group and another are far from fixed; rather, what defines groups was the ongoing struggle of drawing this line itself. Freed from the idea that studying race or ethnicity was like staring at a specimen in a museum display case, scholars began charting the process of group formation, or put another way, how group identities are imagined, implemented, and enforced. In other words, the question, then, was not where bias comes from but where the ideas of "we" and "they" come from.

Subsequent psychological experiments demonstrated that prejudice could arise from just about any social setting in which people are organized into separate and competing groups. Laboratory experiments with participants who were arbitrarily divided, led to members of different groups acting more favorably to others of their group and in a discriminatory manner to those viewed as being in another group. While at first it was thought that the differences between in-groups and out-groups had to be substantial to produce these effects (with much bonding and team-building as part of building the feeling of belonging to the group) subsequent experiments found that even slight differences were sufficient to provoke people to behave differently to those they considered outsiders.

Such studies highlighted how the key part of group conflict was not the terms and circumstances of conflict but the process of creating and defining groups in the first place. While earlier researchers had assumed that groups were natural and given and conflict was the key variable to study, it turns out that the reverse was true. The processes of group formation were themselves the drivers of conflict.

Once scholars realized that groups were not a natural given, they reoriented their work to examine how groups were formed and how they were maintained. They quickly established that there were two separate but related processes at work. Groups were the product of two processes: a process of identity, or self-categorization, and a process of identification, or the sorting of others into different categories. Thus, groups are not things, they are not something people "are," rather, they arise as a product of how people behave, how they interact. As sociologist Rogers Brubaker and his colleagues put it, "ethnicity is fundamentally not a thing in the world, but a perspective on the world."

By moving away from seeing groups as natural and concrete, researchers could begin to appreciate that the process of forming an identity, or identifying someone else, were dependent on deeper aspects of the mind. They were phenomenon linked to issues of perception and how our minds organize the information coming from our senses, two issues that will be explored more fully in chapter 10.

Personal and Social Identity

The science of human behavior was pioneered by economists and not by psychologists. Perhaps this is better put by saying economists were the first psychologists. In the early 1700s, a number of philosophers began asking why people make different choices when faced with the same chance of gaining or losing money. Why were some people more fearful of risk and choose safer but much less rewarding options while others seemed eager to gamble even at long odds?

In 1738, Daniel Bernoulli published a paper that provided the beginnings of a mathematical and psychological answer to this problem. Bernoulli observed that though two people might have exactly the same odds of winning a lottery, they measured their possible gains or losses not by the probabilities alone, but by the impact of winning or losing upon their personal circumstances. Bernoulli noted that rich men were far more willing to take chances to win big than poor men who always took a sure bet with a small pay-out over a risky large one.

Bernoulli's observation might seem simple and unsurprising but it had deep psychological implications that are still today being explored. Bernoulli had discovered that equally rational people perceiving the same situation in an equally objective way—both the rich man and the poor man calculated the odds of their winning or losing accurately—can reach wildly different conclusions. In other words, people don't just perceive the world but perceive it through the lens of their own circumstances, or to put it another way, their identity.

Until very modern times people didn't think of having or developing an "identity." One's character and role in society was largely static and fixed. One's "identity" was a simple matter of a person's relationship to their family and community and these relationships were not easily changed in agricultural, traditional societies. Most areas of life that today are viewed as being open to choice, such as religion, occupation, or where one lives, were very rarely subject to change.

As late as the 19th century American culture was resistant to the idea that identity was subject to change. Most Americans valued the ideal of "authenticity," of being true to one's nature and presenting this inborn, natural self, honestly to others. Those who assumed new identities, who embraced a different religion, changed their careers, or simply moved frequently, were suspected of having evil or predatory motives, of being frauds, charlatans, and swindlers.

However, in the 20th century, as a majority of Americans experienced being uprooted and moving to cities and towns, either as immigrants or migrants within the nation, the ideal of being "self-made," of advancing socially and economically by adopting new beliefs, habits, and social roles, replaced the older distrust of anyone who seemed to

Figure 9.3 Unidentified man in a studio photograph seated before two mirrors placed at right angles to provide five images, ca. 1866-1899.

try to be something new or different (or as this older generation would view it, those who tried to be 'something they were not.') Where the 19th century most valued "character," an unshifting truth of one's nature and being, the 20th century praised "personality," a superficial presentation one exhibited to others.

In 1950, Erik Erikson became one of the first psychologists to comprehensively theorize the nature of this new idea of 'identity.' Identity occupied a middle position between the poles of the idea of natural and honest character and shallow, flighty personality. According to Erikson, identity was something built and developed over time rather than something inborn. Identity was a powerful and important part of any individual's growth and development through the stages of life from childhood to adulthood. Erikson recognized that in modern society the stage of life known as adolescence was a particularly important time for the development of personal identity. In that stage, identity was formed through a process of testing and shifting one's ideas about oneself through the interactions and reactions of others, especially of peers. In this way, Erikson offered a theory that explained the rebellious alienated youth that had just started to be referred to as "teenagers."

One consequence of this adolescent testing and molding of identity was that groups of individuals all behaving in this way tend to become powerfully interested in defining themselves by carefully distinguishing between those like themselves and those they rejected as outsiders.

Gender theorist, Judith Butler, in thinking about the ways in which gender was an identity and not a natural fact, pointed out that one shouldn't think that gender is expressed, as that would mean that gender is something given and true and fixed that is either merely allowed to come out and be shown or is suppressed. Rather, gender should be thought of as existing only as an action, as things people do in the context of social expectations and norms. As a series or pattern of actions, in other words, gender can be thought of as a performance that creates identity rather than the expression of something essential and inner. This "performance" is only meaningful and understandable because its follows or breaks the rules, definitions, and forms already proscribed by society. Seen this way, identity can be understood not as something natural and inherited but as something created by social norms and the ways in which individuals behave in relation to them.

A common misunderstanding of the connection between race and identity is believing that race or ancestry is the basis of one's identity. Actually, this idea is backwards; race is not the foundation of identity but, rather, the processes and dynamics of identity formation are the foundation of race. The pioneering cultural theorist Stuart Hall wrote in 1990, "instead of thinking of identity as an already accomplished fact, which the new cultural practices then represent, we should think, instead, of identity as a 'production', which is never complete, always in process, and always constituted within, not outside, representation."

All of us have multiple identities that influence the way we behave, the way we see the world, and the way we are seen by others. Each of us has a personal identity which is each individual's sense of themselves. Some aspects of our identity are temporary—you might be a college student today but years from now you might be a social worker, a nurse, a writer, or an entrepreneur. Some aspects are freely chosen, the music you enjoy, the clothes you like to wear, the foods you like, and these express something about who you are.

But much of one's identity is not subject to a free choice. Personal identity, one's own self-image, is actually formed of two parts: from a person's own qualities and characteristics and from the relationships and interactions a person has with other people. Our social roles, as sister, father, friend, boss or neighbor, also help define who we are. Some social roles, such as family relationships, are thrust upon us—it has long been said you don't get to choose your parents. Other relationships, such as who your friends, neighbors or romantic partners are, we have some choice in but not as much as we might think. A few social roles, such as who you work for or work with, we have a limited ability to determine. Our personal identity is a product of many social interactions.

Alongside and interwoven with our personal identity is a second form of identity called social identity. Social identity is the part of one's self made up of larger associations with social groups. Most people think of themselves as citizens of the nation in which they were born and this national identity is an important aspect of most people's social identity. Fans of particular sports teams engage in public displays of social identity when they wear their team's colors and the jerseys of their favorite players. Assumptions about someone's race or ethnicity often play a large role in determining social relationships.

Society plays a fundamental role in one's own understanding of themselves, both by providing the web of roles and relationships in which we exist, but also by holding up the mirror by which we can see ourselves. We come to know ourselves not only by what we think about ourselves, but by the way other people view and treat us. This aspect of identity has been called the "looking glass self," in that we form it based on what we think others see in us.

Part of the process of shaping your identity is testing assumptions about yourself against the reactions of others. This process starts from an early age and continues throughout life as our relationships and social roles change. Ultimately who we are, at the most personal interior level,

Figure 9.4 Young women modeling, 1902.

is not something we have, something static that we own, but is a dynamic product of our interactions with other people. Taking this idea to its logical extreme, some thinkers, such as sociologist George Herbert Mead, proposed a century ago that without social relationships reflecting ourselves back at us, without other people responding and reacting to us, we wouldn't have a sense of self at all. Mead theorized, "Selves can only exist in definite relationships to other selves."

In America race has been one of the most powerful of all social identities, shaping the outlook and self-image of most people. Part of the power of race as an identity arises from the high stakes society has placed upon it. Historically, one's racial identity has limited or expanded the scope of actions allowed by society and even today one's racial associations have been shown to dramatically impact one's opportunities. As a result, categorizing the identity of other people is a nearly automatic reflex; most of us do it all the time without even giving it much thought. But as we habitually categorize others into racial groups, we are reinforcing our own racial identities. Ultimately, who we think we are is a product of how we see and group others (and the reverse is true as well).

We usually think that we categorize ourselves in the world, and categorize others, through recognizing similarities and differences between others and ourselves. But when we make such discriminations we are not simply seeing difference as much as we are employing systems of difference-making. They are systems because how we define the group we call 'us' is largely based on the things we think 'they' are and visa versa. Membership in a group then becomes largely built on a shared belief about how others don't belong in that group. In other words, what people in a group most have in common is a shared agreement in the qualities that keep others out, not similarities of their own.

This process of group definition also influences the way we perceive ourselves and others. Once we perceive that another person bears the mark that we define as the sign that they are like us, that they are member of our group, we tend to see their differences as aspects of their individuality. But when we think we see the feature that puts another person in a different group, we then tend to mostly see difference as difference and not as individuality. We comprehend the world differently depending on how we identify others.

Belonging and Identity

One of the strongest of all human motivations is to belong to a social group. Humans are fundamentally social animals and instinctually seek membership in groups and affirmation that these relationships are shared and stable. People crave strong social relationships in order both to have access to resources but also to form their sense of themselves: people understand and define who they are, their own sense of self, in relationship with others. Researchers call this a "belonging need" and have shown that when people perceive their social relationships to be weak and uncertain, they respond by selectively working to strengthen those bonds they feel have the best chance to be shared rather than trying to reinforce all their human connections.

Belonging needs have been shown to reinforce the divisions between social groups by encouraging people to value relationships with people considered members of their own groups (ingroup relationships) more than connections with people considered outside their own group (outgroup relationships). This effect has been shown to strengthen when people experience social rejection or perceive other threats to their social belonging. Moreover, in situations where groups possess different amounts of power and privilege, members of the more empowered groups tend to exert more effort defining the boundaries of their group and are more likely to assume a stranger is not a member of their group. Conversely, those in underprivileged groups put less stress on marking the boundaries of their group and are more likely to assume strangers belong. In America with its racial social structure, this means that white people tend to assume an unknown person is a member of an outgroup while black people have a greater tendency to assume they are part of the ingroup.

It has been shown in controlled research settings that this marking of ingroup or outgroup is not entirely a conscious and purposeful act. White subjects who experienced more social exclusion were more likely than other whites to categorize pictures of men's faces as black, indicating that they were responding to stress by hardening the lines they drew between in and outgroups. In contrast, black subjects were more likely than whites to categorize ambiguous faces as members of their own group, rather than presume they belonged to an outgroup. Social uncertainty thus had opposite effects on white and black people, strengthening the boundaries white people drew around whiteness and loosening black people's criteria for blackness.

System Justification Theory

Just as individuals become invested in justifying the actions and outlooks of a group that they view as being essential to their personal identity (largely from the 'Belonging Needs' discussed earlier) most individuals also have a tendency to view their society as being just, fair and natural. These various forms of thinking that allow individuals to view their society as as being legitimate, even in the face of obvious inequalities and contradictions of that society's governing principles, is called "system justification."

Not suprisingly, system justification reasoning is particularly strong among those who benefit from social inequalities and contradictions. What is surprising is that such thinking is not limited to those privileged by the system being justified. While system justification is not universal, it is a strong and common component of social identity.

One of the first scholars to explore this phenomenon was the Italian political theorist, Antonio Gramsci. Writing during the time when fascism and communism gripped Europe, Gramsci attempted to explain system justification not as an aberration, as the result of propaganda and brainwashing, but as a normal psychological response. Gramsci theorized that this bias in favor of existing social systems was the result of a lack of seemingly viable alternatives:

> The existing social order is presented as a stable, harmoniously coordinated system, and the great mass of people hesitate and lose heart when they think of what a radical change might bring…. They can only imagine the present being torn to pieces, and fail to perceive the new order which is possible.

Since when Gramsci wrote from a prison cell in the 1930s, researchers have documented that even some of those individuals who are least advantaged, privileged, and powerful, nevertheless may also display support for the status quo. This counter-intuitive effect has been explained as being driven by a need for psychological self-protection against the mental confusion and distress caused by believing one thing but experiencing another, a condition referred to as "cognitive dissonance." In the face of a seemingly solid and permanent reality whose existence conflicts with deeply held values and even aspects of one's own identity, the mind becomes more receptive to explanations and justifications that resolve these contradictions. Controlled studies have demonstrated that even very poor people harbor strongly held beliefs that economic inequality is necessary and legitimate. One survey even found that poorer people had higher levels of support than richer subjects for the proposition that big pay differentials were needed to "get people to work hard."

But such observations that system justification is not limited to the beneficiaries of the system only go so far as most evidence also seems to show a stronger relationship between privilege and system justification. This seems to be especially true when race is factored in along with economic issues in considering what is the system being justified. Many studies now show that system justification is stronger among the wealthier and the whiter in America.

Partly, this alignment of race and class in system justification is the product of the interaction of system biases and in-group biases. White Americans can harmonize their group identity with their economic position in supporting the status quo by denying the reality of racism. However, this option is not as available to black Americans for whom a similar system justification would conflict with their group identity as African Americans. As one group of researchers put it, "Group differences in perceptions of racism among high status groups may be partly explained by the fact that system justification motives and group justification motives work in parallel for members of high status groups [whites] but in opposition for members of low status groups [blacks]."

The entangled nature of race and class was perhaps nowhere as tragically and suddenly exposed as when Hurricane Katrina struck New Orleans on August 29, 2005. The city's wealthy and white residents largely managed to escape the worst of the historic flooding the engulfed the Crescent City, while the city's black residents were left behind. Trapped and ignored, the death toll mounted while federal and local officials failed to mount a significant rescue effort. Not surprisingly, when carefully surveyed years later, black Katrina survivors attributed the government's slow response to the hurricane far more readily to racism than white New Orleanians.

Whiteness as Identity

Whiteness is different from other social identities. The complex of ideas and myths of white qualities was the only racial system invented by any people for themselves, all the rest were imposed on others. White people developed and upheld all the other social representations and stereotypes through their control of social institutions. While they projected racist stereotypes and ideas upon other groups, white people had the power and position to fashion their own racial identity.

The dynamics of how white identity arose differed from other racial ideas. As white people aimed to be the standard against which all others are judged they required an opposite by which to define themselves. Other groups were imagined, characterized, and stereotyped according to the perceptions, beliefs and even needs of powerful white elites. Whites invented the idea of race and the qualities of particular races within that system. But they defined whiteness not by some absolute system of values but by contrasting themselves with the others they had constructed. Whiteness emerged from a pattern of imagining what white people are not rather than what they are. It was a product of binary racial thinking.

The power of language to fix and limit our perception of the world is exaggerated the fewer the number of categories for things it provides. The extreme case is when for some reason, usually political and historic, a society limits its range of choices to just two. In such cases where the world is to be divided into two, so many different things are swept up into the same category that it becomes nearly impossible to characterize it by reference to the actual nature of things contained in it. The structure of language provides a clever and devious solution to this problem of inconsistency. Instead of attempting to describe what qualities characterize each group and makes it different from the other, an impossible task because both groups have just as many similar representatives as different ones, it simply depicts one group however it wishes and then defines the other group as its opposite. Various qualities are attributed to one group while the other becomes simply "not the other."

In America the basic logic of race born from the interaction of Europeans and Africans created what scholars call the black/white binary. Binary means a system comprised of two parts and in this case it is a system that produces meaning. In this case each of these two terms developed and accumulated their meaning, the sum total of all the ideas and impressions these words conveyed or connoted, only by comparison to the other. The qualities of what came to be called white folk were the opposite of the qualities these people attributed to black folk and

Figure 9.6 Model No. 702. Young men's two-button notch lapel style,

visa versa. Many concepts are paired in binaries—up/down, hard/soft, day/night—but the difference between these opposites and black/white is that these contrasting pairs exist in the physical world and their qualities are more perceived than imagined.

Whiteness itself had no properties other than being the opposite of the characters and behaviors it stereotyped in others. White colonists defined their freedom as being the opposite of the slavery they imposed on Africans. White laborers defined the working class as being the opposite of both the idle luxurious elite above them as well as the 'naturally' servile black people below. Elite white womanhood was built out of ideas that proper women didn't do manual labor because black women did field work and were thereby masculine. White men were to be self-controlled and responsible, plan and save for the future, and avoid idle pastimes because whites thought of blacks as sensual, impulsive, and lazy.

As whiteness was defined as the negation of bad characteristics and because it was the identity constructed by the powerful and privileged majority for themselves, it had the unique quality of being both a racial idea and a social standard. Because white people in America lived in a society that was built on formal and official white supremacy, they were able to establish a pattern that assumed

whiteness as the standard of values and behavior. Once such a pattern was ingrained, even when the formal aspects of white supremacy that supported it were removed, the habits and informal expectations persisted and it became self-sustaining. Individuals who looked white and lived in such a society that assumed whiteness as the standard enjoyed the immediate assumption that they carried these values as well. In effect, those with bodies considered white were assumed to share the virtues and values of whiteness until proven otherwise. Those without such bodies had to always prove they possessed such qualities, they were never presumed to have them.

In this way, white people eventually came to think of themselves as being outside the racial system they themselves had constructed. They wore their whiteness not as a racial identity but as other ideas, as "being a citizen" or "being a good person" or "being an American." The more they thought of whiteness as "normal" the less visible it became. Eventually, whiteness passed into a strange invisibility to white people themselves. They began thinking of race as something "others" have. White people still don't like being reminded of the fact that within the racial categories developed in America they are "white." White people are generally uncomfortable being called white.

Obviously, one of the properties of whiteness is that it is associated with a particular group of people and not others. It is what scholars refer to as an "embodied idea," a set of beliefs and meanings that attaches to particular bodies. People who confidently inhabit bodies that carry whiteness usually develop a particular way of being and acting in society that is difficult or even denied to those who do not possess such physicality. Such people are acculturated from a young age into an expectation of whiteness and the privileges it can claim. Living whiteness in a world structured for white people leads to a succession of reinforcing experiences that further develops a certain set of behaviors that express and exploit privilege.

In some ways whiteness has become more powerful in the post-Civil Rights Era. Where whiteness in earlier eras directly conferred formal rights and legal privileges, since the 1970s it has lost most of these advantages. While direct and official privileges have largely been swept away, most of the informal and systematic benefits, especially material ones, remain. Whiteness serves a unique role in a society that proclaims itself to be colorblind because it simultaneously operates to perpetuate systematic privileges while denying that these advantages exist. Whiteness as an ideology, a mechanism of ideas, perpetuates and justifies inequality. But its greater strength, its superpower, is that it explains and frames reality in such a way that its own existence is made invisible to those who claim it.

Whiteness because it defined itself as the ideal, as

the touchstone and the standard by which others are to be judged by their distance from itself, renders itself invisible to those who considered themselves to be white. Whiteness exists for white people as what they consider natural and normal. In this way only deviations from its standards are notable and therefore visible to whites. White people are not reminded of their race as they go about their daily business. Their race does not burden them with struggles to avoid confirming others' negative stereotypes of them. Whiteness, for most whites, barely seems to exist at all.

Black Views of Whiteness

Black folks have long studied and scrutinized whites both out of curiosity and the importance of such knowledge to survival in a society where whites held all the cards. In many ways whites were unable to see how others saw them because of their presumed "normality," a quality that denies the characteristics particular to itself. Knowing white ideals to be false or hypocritical by the very fact of their own existence, black observers enjoyed a keen insight into the deeper psychology of the white community.

Standing outside white people's presumptions, black observers did not share white people's assumption that white and purity and goodness were all wrapped together. Though for white people such associations were rooted both in language and a long Christian tradition of equating white with light and godliness and black with darkness and sin, black people's personal experience with whiteness broke these connections. As essayist Richard Dyer observed, "white people...do not imagine that the way whiteness makes its presence felt in black life, most often as terrorizing imposition, a power that wounds, hurts, tortures, is a reality that disrupts the fantasy of whiteness as representing goodness."

James Baldwin, with his characteristic sharp insight, pointed out that the black perspective's ability to puncture through the myths of whiteness posed a psychological threat to white people. Baldwin observed that a great deal of white people's overreaction to black people's demands for civil rights or even the simple presence of black people was irrational. It could not be explained even by political or economic motives. Rather the source was deeper and psychological. Baldwin theorized that "...a vast amount of the energy that goes into what we call the Negro problem is produced by the white man's profound desire not to be judged by those who are not white, not to be seen as he is."

This deep white unease with being seen by those who they considered beneath and inferior to them was read by many black observers as white people's fear of seeing themselves. Brooklyn teacher William J. Wilson, writing under the pseudonym "Ethiop" in 1860, perceptively

described how white people knew in their hearts something was amiss but they can't face it: "They feel that something is wrong, that a screw is somewhere loose in the general machinery of society. Standing by, they dare not bind what they find loosed, and they dare not loosen what they find bound."

Double Consciousness

In W.E.B. Du Bois' classic essay, "The Souls of Black Folks," he described the unique psychological and social insight of black people in America:

...the Negro is a sort of seventh son, born with a veil, and gifted with second-sight in this American world,—a world which yields him no true self consciousness, but only lets him see himself through the revelation of the other world. It is a peculiar sensation, this double-consciousness, this sense of always looking at one's self through the eyes of others, of measuring one's soul by the tape of a world that looks on in amused contempt and pity. One ever feels his two-ness, an American, a Negro; two souls, two thoughts, two unreconciled strivings; two warring ideals in one dark body, whose dogged strength alone keeps it from being torn asunder. The history of the American Negro is the history of this strife-this longing to attain self-conscious manhood, to merge his double self into a better and truer self. In this merging he wishes neither of the older selves to be lost. He does not wish to Africanize America, for America has too much to teach the world and Africa. He wouldn't bleach his Negro blood in a flood of white American-ism, for he knows that Negro blood has a message for the world. He simply wishes to make it possible for a man to be both a Negro and an American without being cursed and spit upon by his fellows, without having the doors of opportunity closed roughly in his face.

What Du Bois termed "double consciousness" is one of the most intimate effects of being marked as the racial other in a racist society. In such a situation one's identity is split; in language, culture, ideals and beliefs, African Americans were far more American than African. But America viewed black people as not being part of the nation, as not being "really" Americans. Thus racism set the two essential elements on either side of the hyphen connecting African-American identity at odds.

In this way one's deepest identity, a person's

Figure 9.7 James Baldwin at the March on Washington, D.C., 1963.

ideals of equality and liberty, they proclaimed these ideals were universal truths, ignoring the obvious and glaring exceptions in their own households. Black folks, however, lived a reality that confirmed at every turn that these ideals were not universal.

Even more deeply, Western Enlightenment thinking began from the belief that the universe operated on natural laws. A world that ran like a machine meant that all truths were fixed and unchanging. But from the perspective of people who had been forced from their homes and prodded onto ships and transported thousands of miles to a new land where at any time they could be sold and forcibly moved again, the world was not fixed and unchanging. People who were dislocated generation after generation, those who suffered enslavement and later a double consciousness, glimpsed a truth unavailable to the privileged, that truth was not fixed—that everything depended on where one stood. Meaning was not settled it was relative.

James Baldwin viewed double consciousness as both a burden, but also a liberating and enlightening perspective: "The American Negro has the great advantage of having never believed that collection of myths to which white Americans cling…"

Embodiment and Identity

Racial identification is a particularly powerful, pervasive and persistent type of identity. Race, like gender, is a uniquely powerful identity because it not only exists as a designation or title we are given in certain situations, but it is an intimate part of our own understanding of ourselves. It is a language written upon our bodies and our bodies are real things.

Race and gender are meanings drawn onto our bodies. They are the process of taking a feature or characteristic of our physical selves and associating this thing with larger social implications and ideas. By attaching ideas to bodies, such ideas, meanings and values seem more solid, more real and more permanent. After all, we can't easily change our bodies and it is easy to overlook the fact that the body is not the source of the ideas connected to it. By linking ideas to bodies, race becomes a thing that not only seems to exist "out there," in society and its institutions, but also exists "in here," in our personal view of ourselves, in our private sense of who we are.

One of the first to explore this problem of embodiment was Frantz Fanon. In 1952, Fanon, a psychiatrist who worked in Algeria, published *Black Skin, White Masks*, a work that first discussed in depth the psychology of whiteness and blackness. Fanon had a great deal of experience in the subject, not only having been born a black child in the French colony of Martinique (an island in the West

consciousness of herself, was divided and set at odds. Du Bois described how though a black person looked out at the world as an American they could not avoid being aware that they were viewed by white society as a group outside of the definition of the nation. Their American consciousness was viewed by the larger majority as illegitimate, as a counterfeit. This cognitive dissonance, this condition of living with conflicting identities, poses psychological burdens upon people of color that whites barely perceive, let alone appreciate.

On the other hand, the struggle to understand and reconcile these divided identities fueled a degree of intellectual insight and clarity about American society and even western civilization that was unique. Africans across the Atlantic world were the first people to think deeply about the irreconcilable of values in western civilization: the clash between the ideals of liberal nations and their practice of slavery. Americas founding on a language of natural rights (As the Declaration of Independence begins, "All men are created equal and endowed by their creator with certain inalienable rights…") grew up alongside a strengthening and expansion of slavery and a counter-philosophy of racist inequality. White people were almost universally tone deaf to these contradictions while black people were keenly aware of them as they governed their daily lives. For example, white American patriots not only claimed certain

Indies), but lived under fascist rule when Martinique was taken over by pro-German forces. Fanon fled Martinique so he could volunteer and fight for the liberation of France in World War Two and later studied psychiatry and moved to another French colony, Algeria.

Fanon documented how the culture, beliefs, and practices of whites were universalized as the norm and standard by which all people were judged. Nonwhite people who wished to, or had to, keep company in white society were forced to assume an identity that was not themselves—what Fanon called a "white mask." By this Fanon meant that because white society had for centuries mythologized itself as uniquely superior, as representing ideals and values opposite to those of the rest of the world (when, in fact, many of those ideals were actually universal), brown and black skinned people who embraced these values were subtly reminded that they wore them as one does a costume rather than their own clothes. Black and brown people in the western world are not quite allowed to be themselves as they are viewed as out of place or imitators. According to Fanon, this alienation is most powerfully felt when these thoughts are internalized not imposed; when they erupt from within oneself rather than from without.

Fanon, the highly educated doctor of psychiatry, the veteran who fought for France, the distinguished and cultured French gentleman, felt all these accomplishments, this hard earned identity, shaken under the gaze of whites who looked upon him first as the other, as a black man. As he described the experience, "…I am being dissected under white eyes, the only real eyes. I am fixed…they objectively cut away slices of my reality. I am laid bare." Fanon writes, "All I wanted was to be a man among other men." But instead, "I was responsible at the same time for my body, for my race, for my ancestors. I subjected myself to an objective examination, I discovered my blackness…"

This is a process Fanon called "epidermalization… of inferiority," the linking of black and brown bodies to negative qualities and their distancing from positive associations. Because such meanings are marked by the darker hue of one's skin, they are inescapable and ever present. In such a circumstance a person is forced to be more aware of their body, to be conscious of their body. Writing as a psychologist, Fanon described this as a situation where the consciousness of one's body negates a person's subjectivity (the natural feeling we have when we are simply experiencing the world) and turns the body into an object (as though it were something apart from oneself).

Fanon recognized that black children raised up in a racist white world learned to love the same stories, heroes, and values as white ones, but in doing so learned that the heroes of books and movies didn't look like themselves. James Baldwin observed in his essay *The Fire Next Time*

that racism not only sets the boundaries and possibilities of life for those targeted by it, but seeps inward and corrodes the way people think of themselves. "Negroes in this country…are taught really to despise themselves from the moment their eyes open on the world. This world is white and they are black."

The Clark Doll Experiments

Such theoretical insights into the caustic effect on the identity and self-esteem of a person racialized as "other" in society were given laboratory confirmation by two psychologists whose work not only revolutionized their field, but helped undermine the foundations of racial segregation.

Mamie Clark was only sixteen when she was accepted into Howard University to study mathematics. Raised in Hot Springs, Arkansas, and educated in segregated black schools, Clark understood deeply the nature and problems in American society and, by the end of her first year at Howard, had switched to social psychology, where she could formally investigate them. In 1938, Clark began her Master's thesis, exploring the impact of racism on the self-identification of young children. By the time Mamie graduated two years later, four of her research papers (three co-written with her newlywed husband, Kenneth, who had just begun his doctoral program as the first black man admitted to the Ph.D. program in psychology at Columbia University) were published in prestigious journals and she and Kenneth had won a substantial grant to expand this line of research into a full-time project.

Mamie and Kenneth Clark's most important research was, like most great research projects, elegantly simple. 250 black children, between the ages of 3 and 7, half from Arkansas and half from Massachusetts, evenly divided between boys and girls, were given a selection of four dolls to play with, each identical in every respect except two were tinted brown with black hair and the others were white with blond hair. They noted which doll the children chose to play with, and they also asked the children to indicate which doll was the "good" or "bad" doll, which was the "white" doll, which was the "Negro" doll, which was the "colored" doll, which was the "nice" doll, and which was most like themselves (note the questions were designed to gauge racial identification, racial preferences, and racial self-identification).

Children, even the youngest, had little difficulty sorting the dolls by racial category, more than 90% reliably indicated which was the "white" or "colored" doll. However, when asked which doll most looked like themselves, one-third of the children selected the white doll. In the dry language of observation, the study noted, "some of the children who were free and relaxed in the beginning of the

Figure 9.8 Jay Street, No. 115, Brooklyn, 1936.

Mr. Brown, and nineteen other black families from Topeka, chose not to make the argument that the Browns were denied the equal facilities that was supposedly the compromise of segregation, but that segregation itself was inherently, and unavoidably, unequal because it harmed the development of children like Linda Brown. A unanimous Supreme Court agreed:

> We come then to the question presented: Does segregation of children in public schools solely on the basis of race... deprive the children of the minority group of equal educational opportunities? We believe that it does....Segregation of white and colored children in public schools has a detrimental effect upon the colored children...for the policy of separating the races is usually interpreted as denoting the inferiority of the negro group. A sense of inferiority affects the motivation of a child to learn. Segregation with the sanction of law, therefore, has a tendency to [retard] the educational and mental development of negro children and to deprive them of some of the benefits they would receive in a racial[ly] integrated school system....Whatever may have been the extent of psychological knowledge at the time of Plessy v. Ferguson, this finding is amply supported by modern authority....We conclude that in the field of public education the doctrine of "separate but equal" has no place. Separate educational facilities are inherently unequal.

The first "modern authority" cited by the court as support for this interpretation was the doll study by Mamie and Kenneth Clark.

The Clarks' findings have been replicated many times since their first publications in the 1940s. Not surprisingly, those studies that repeated their methodology in the 1950s, when Jim Crow still reigned, largely duplicated their results. While one would suspect that these effects should have lessened with the successes of the Civil Rights movement and the movement toward a more tolerant society since, studies as recently as 2009 still showed about the same proportion of black children selected a white figure as being like themselves as the Clark's found seventy years earlier.

experiment broke down and cried or became somewhat negativistic during the later part when they were required to make self-identifications. Indeed, two children ran out of the testing room, unconsolable..."

Further observations of which dolls children thought "good" or "bad" or "nice" and which they wished to play with revealed clear preferences for whiteness. More than two-thirds of the children wanted to play with the white doll, 59% thought the white doll was "nice" and an equal proportion thought the brown doll was "bad."

An interesting aspect of the Clark's research was the finding that rates of identification with the white doll were significantly higher among northern children than southern children who lived in legally segregated communities. Southern kids were more willing to see brown dolls as "nice," "good," and like themselves.

Mamie and Kenneth Clark's papers had been published for over a decade before they attracted much attention which came in an unusual and dramatic form. In 1954, the Supreme Court considered the case of Oliver L. Brown of Topeka, Kansas, whose daughter, Linda, had to walk six blocks to a bus stop and wait for a school bus that would take her another mile to her all-black elementary school. Meanwhile, an all-white elementary school was about as far from her house as the bus stop she walked to. For the first time, the NAACP legal team that represented

Intersecting Identities

This chapter has purposefully simplified the question of identity and focused on black and white identity in order to illustrate the basic dynamics of racial identity and identification. But the world is a far richer and fascinating place where people hold multiple identities at the same time. Many of these identities intersect, meaning that their combination changes the meaning and dynamics of one, both, or many identities at the same time.

To give but one classic example, race and gender have powerfully combined in the experiences of black women, altering both the circumstances of their femininity and the workings of their blackness. When Congress, after the Civil War, debated enfranchising former slaves, they meant only men and the Fifteenth Amendment they passed to do this was the first measure specifying that only men could enjoy its protections in the Constitution. A century later when a new wave of feminism and a civil rights movement both rose into prominence in the 1960s, "Second Wave" feminists talked about "women's issues" as if all women were white and "Black Power" activists discussed racism as if all minorities were men. Somehow either race had eclipsed sex, or sex had negated race, in both these debates, leaving black women floating alone. But black women were not just black or just women, the issues deriving from their race and sex could not be disentangled.

Everyone exists in the intersections of their identities. For many, the effect of these overlapping identities are hidden—just as whiteness is rendered invisible because it is defined as "normal." A white, heterosexual man walking down the street may not realize how these multiple axes of identity interact to produce his privileges because all three are considered normative. Intersections become "issues" and socially problematic when they include identities that deviate from longstanding norms.

Social norms that affect one axis of identity often impact others. Employers have been allowed by courts to proscribe certain makeup and grooming requirements to more clearly mark and orient sex and gender. But such specific rules for hairstyles and makeup, though focused on sex and gender, have had different consequences and burdens for blacks and whites. Black women spend three times as much every year on cosmetics than do white women, partly as a means of redressing the fact of living in a society that has historically considered black women masculine.

Sex and race are not the only identities that intersect in ways that are socially and politically relevant. In fact, the inventory of such identities and social positions is long, but

Figure 9.9 Bella Abzug, Betty Freidan, and Billy Jean King accompanying torch relay runners in Houston, n.d.

in recent years has also famously focused on gender and sexual orientation, age, ability, class, immigration status, and religion.

When identities intersect, they don't just overlap but they interact to alter their nature. Being black and female does not mean that one simply has the burdens or advantages of being black and being a woman, but that one's blackness also changes the character of each identity. One side of a person's multiple identities may act to enhance or to diminish the effects of another.

For example, data amassed by social scientists reveals one of the powerful interactions of the intersection of race and class. For most of the world, health is a function of social class. Class status is the leading worldwide predictor of whether someone will contract disease, the quality of medical care one receives, and the likelihood of early death. But in America, while middle and upper-class men and women enjoy significant health advantages over working class men, for white people class makes a far larger difference in health than it does for blacks. For example, white female college graduates are six times less likely to die of heart disease than white women who dropout of high school. But black women who have earned college degrees are only half as prone to fatal heart disease as black women without a highschool diploma. At every income and educational bracket, on average, whites suffer from lower rates of common diseases and had longer lives than blacks with similar socioeconomic standing. Even white physicians were shown in a 25 year study to have lower rates of cardiovascular disease, diabetes, and mortality than black doctors. Clearly, in America, race interacts to blunt the privileges and benefits of class.

Stereotypes

In 1922, the renowned journalist Walter Lippmann, searched for a term that would capture the sense of an idea, contained and packaged within the image of a social group, that was repeated again and again and transmitted throughout a culture. Lippmann borrowed a word from his own experience, from the printing machines that clattered in the bowels of the buildings where he wrote. Stereotyping was a printing process invented by the French printer and philosopher Diderot in the 18th century that allowed a picture to be repeatedly reproduced. Lippmann coined the word and offered some insight into the process:

> For the most part we do not first see, and then define, we define first and then see. In the great blooming, buzzing confusion of the outer world we pick out what our culture has already defined for us, and we tend to perceive that which we

Figure 9.10 Walter Lippmann, ca. 1905-1945.

have picked out in the form stereotyped for us by our culture....We are told about the world before we see it. We imagine most things before we experience them. And those preconceptions, unless education has made us acutely aware, govern deeply the whole process of perception.

Lippmann was far ahead of his time in linking the culturally produced ideas of stereotypes with the cognitive process of perception. Since then psychologists have charted the many ways that bias operates not as a conscious series of beliefs and decisions, but more deeply in the mind. Stereotypes are collections of symbols that have the ability to invoke complexes of belief by mobilizing a larger structure of social representation.

In one basic sense, a stereotype is a collection of ideas that define the character of a kind of person. But the key element of a stereotype is not that they describe some particular trait or characteristic but that they hide and eliminate all alternatives. Stereotypes flatten a rich and varied reality into a one-dimensional representation that then obscures all other variety. They misrepresent what is real by limiting its possibilities.

Stereotypes are mechanisms of radical simplification. They take what is a messy and complicated world and reduce it to a single image or single idea, thus making the world more understandable and predictable. Such simplification makes the world seem more orderly and stable than it actually is.

This property of stereotypes, like social representations more generally, of rendering reality as fixed, stable and orderly, is useful to those groups and those institutions who desire to maintain currently existing social arrangements. Stereotypes are deeply conservative in nature because by depicting their subjects as having only one character, they deny that alternatives exist and therefore that change is possible. For this reason, stereotypes are supported, propagated, and defended by groups that the current organization of society benefits.

Stereotypes are powerful because they pretend to reveal more than they obscure. Stereotypes seem to show the specific inner nature or essence of the group they depict. It is this illusion of accuracy that makes stereotypes appealing as they solve the problem of knowing how society works and provide a guide for navigating the shifting, confusing modern world.

It is for this reason that some historians link the multiplication and strengthening of stereotypes to the rise of a modern, urbanized, and industrialized society in the late 19th century. This was a time when American society was becoming more culturally diverse with a rush of new immigrants from far-flung regions of Europe, challenges to the seemingly settled certainties of men's and women's roles, and the restructuring of labor with new technologies. Reducing people to flattened group qualities through stereotyping made the world more familiar, even if this familiarity was based on myths and distortions.

The ability of stereotyping to shape culture, consciousness, and behavior is dependent on a society's capacity to produce and circulate images. Prior to the rise of the printing press and the widespread availability of books and literacy, cultural images could only be rooted in language and their spread and strength was constrained by the nature of verbal communication. As communication technologies improved from oral to written to forms of mass communication, images could not only be spread farther and faster, but, because of the centralized nature of broadcasting, gained authority as well. Racial stereotypes were propagated by every innovation in communication technologies, from crude cartoons in early American newspapers, to minstrels on the stage, to advertising caricatures selling products in magazines, to the Amos N' Andy radio and then television shows. Each new technology was more centralized, more connected to the seat of power and finance, than that preceding and as a result produced images that appeared more stable, more real and more true.

Figure 9.11 Hillbilly Hot Dogs, West Virginia Route 2, May, 9, 2015.

How Stereotypes Cause Harm

Stereotypes contribute to behavior and policies that treat groups with less power unfairly or harshly. Negative images of another group can do more than merely foster bias, they can also dehumanize members of the group in the eyes of those with power.

This process (termed "moral exclusion") works by defining certain qualities and characteristics as being the norm of the dominant group. If, most, or perhaps all of these qualities are viewed as being absent in the subordinate group, that group is seen as alien, as Other, to the powerful group. If the qualities and characteristics seen as being possessed by the dominant group and absent to some extent, from the Other, are considered essential to what it is to be fully human, then the stereotyped group is distanced from humanity. They are considered less as people and more as objects. Once objectified in this way, individuals in the group are excluded from the moral world the dominant group created.

Following this process of moral exclusion all sorts of actions that would be considered illegitimate or immoral if done against members of the dominant group can be taken against members of the subordinate group without compromise. Moral exclusion not only grants permission to treat Others unequally and unfairly, it absolves such actions from condemnation because they fall outside the realm of morality altogether.

Moral exclusion is thus both a process of definition and of application. Every person develops a conception of a moral sphere that defines who is entitled to a certain rights and protections. For example, most people divide animals into different categories of moral protection, having no ethical problem with raising and slaughtering cows or pigs for food but would be outraged at similar treatment of dogs and horses. The boundaries and terms of these moral spheres are largely set by society. Though individuals may be able to push them a little wider or constrict them a bit more narrowly, the primary distinctions between who falls outside these borders are strongly dictated by shared social norms.

While anyone can be stereotyped, the force and impact of a stereotype is directly related to one's power in society. Individuals with political, economic, or social power are not as susceptible to stereotypes as they have the means to easily move beyond the boundaries and expectations set by the stereotype. But those without such power find that stereotypes restrict their opportunities and their freedom as the expectations and meanings built into stereotypes come to define them in the eyes of others, especially others who have political, economic, or social power over their lives. This is why stereotypes about white people don't have the bite or the force of stereotypes of people of color. Middle class white folks can shrug them off, as they know that a stereotype about their lack of skill in dancing, or inability to dunk a basketball, is not going to make any difference in their daily lives.

On the other hand, even white folks who lack wealth and power, just like other poor people, can be harmed by stereotypes as these can impact their chances of getting a good job, getting into college, or being treated fairly. Poor white folks are often stereotyped as "white trash," a phrase that stings because it unfavorably compares them to successful and prosperous white people and explains their failure to be properly rich, as white people are supposed to be, as some deep personal fault or deficiency.

Understanding the implicit operation of cognitive categories and the explicit workings of stereotypes helps explain how it is that racist modes of thinking persist even though many of the legal and formal structures of racism have been dismantled. Patterns of racial thought might no longer be policed and enforced as they once were, but they still remain deeply embedded in our society and culture. One way they persist is not only by acts of social definition, by individuals lumping and grouping others into categories of kind, but also by the way in which people come to define and identify themselves. In our next chapter we will explore the process of identity formation and how our answer to the question, 'who am I,' can work to maintain racial divisions.

Social Representation Theory

Social scientists in the 1920s and 1930s viewed biases and social beliefs as being the result of pre-packaged, industrially produced propaganda that was formulated to control society. At a time when authoritarian rulers in Moscow and Berlin (as well as a government in Washington rapidly expanding its scope) first seized upon the power of mass media to manipulate public attitudes, this top-down propaganda model of prejudice seemed fitting. But by the 1950s and 1960s when popular attitudes seemed to fragment in numerous directions, and governmental images and messages were eclipsed by commercial ones, scholars began to rethink where shared social beliefs came from. Were they manufactured and distributed like so many bars of soap or cans of soup? Or were people themselves somehow a partner in the fabrication of their own shared illusions?

In the 1960s, a psychologist named Serge Moscovici proposed what he called Social Representation Theory. This theory attempted to explain how shared systems of belief arise among particular social groups. Such systems of ideas helped define the boundaries between members inside a group and those considered outside of it. Moscovici defined social representation as:

> systems of values, ideas and practices with a two-fold function; first, to establish an order which will enable individuals to orientate themselves in their material and social world and to master it; secondly, to enable communication to take place amongst members of a community by providing them with a code for social exchange and a code for naming and classifying unambiguously the various aspects of their world and their individual and group history

Moscovici proposed that such systems of social representation are the "contact point" between the deep processes of the mind that form the categories that shape individual perception and social relationships (see ch. 10). Such a point of contact implies a mutual influence between the cognitive and social realms; what are perceived as "social realities" become embedded in cognitive categories and ways of seeing the world influence what we believe to be true. In America similar theories were extended by Peter Berger and Thomas Luckmann in their influential 1966 book, *The Social Construction of Reality*.

Because social representations are not imposed upon society by powerful institutions, but are built on the interaction of individual cognition, group identity, and social values and stories, they are not stable, but are constantly being pushed and pulled, stretched and refashioned, as a consequence of the struggle between groups. (This idea was later incorporated into the racial formation theory of Michael Omi and Howard Winant, who described how beliefs about races are produced by competing social interests and positions.) This is why not only the beliefs surrounding races are different at various points in time, but that the very idea and arrangement of the social groups we call races change over time.

Though social ideas and representations change over time, they are not experienced that way. Rather, because they arise out of everyday experiences (which are themselves shaped and filtered through the cognitive categories structured to see race in this way) social representations seem to be self-evident; they appear as "common-sense." This feeling, that certain ideas and symbols so well represent reality that they are beyond critical thought, beyond question, is usually generated by experiences that seemingly confirm these ideas at every turn because of the current arrangements of power and privilege. But some social representations become "common sense" precisely because they provide satisfying explanations as to why reality does not seem to agree with deeply held principles.

Racism is the prime example of this phenomenon. The idea of race has been strengthened because it provided a satisfying explanation as to why a large minority of American citizens were denied the ideals of American citizenship. By the twentieth century it was plainly evident that black citizens were excluded from the basic protections of the Constitution and the bounty of American prosperity. Social representations of blacks, such as the longstanding stereotypes embodied in Sambo and Mammy explained black people's failure to rise economically—the fault was in their bodies and their inborn character. Likewise, ideas and images of black men as savage beasts provided an answer to the charge that American democracy was a sham. Where powerful national principles were involved, myths upon which the entire social structure rested, racist ideas explained away the contradictions and dissonances in reality and by their necessity passed into the "common sense" of social representation.

Identity and Stereotype Threat

Stereotypes are not just ideas that alter how people perceive others, they have the power to negatively impact a targeted person's ability. Controlled laboratory experiments have shown that when people are aware that they may be judged or viewed through a negative stereotype they experience anxiety and perform complicated tasks less well than when such stereotypes are not in play.

Psychologist Claude Steele and his colleagues were the first to document this effect in experiments they did with women asked to take a challenging mathematics exam and black students who were given a verbal test. For each group, performance consistently suffered when subjects were made aware that they might be subject to a negative stereotype, in this case that women are worse mathematicians than men, and black people are less intelligent. Steele found that negative stereotypes can be activated by very subtle cues. In this case, merely suggesting that a test was one that measured "intellectual ability" as opposed to being merely "problem-solving" was enough to cause a significant drop in the performance of minority students.

Steele determined that the effect he was measuring was not the classic explanation of "internalization," that those subject to discrimination "internalized" these ideas and viewed themselves negatively. Rather, Steele found no correlation between the belief in stereotypes and the susceptibility to a stereotype effect. Instead, Steele theorized that what caused poor performance was exactly the opposite, a conscious effort to distance the self from association with false stereotypes. Somehow, as the stakes of the task were raised by the need to outperform a negative stereotype, so was the stress and difficulty of the task. This was evident as the most highly motivated students suffered the worst drops in their test scores under conditions in which they perceived a stereotype threat.

Stereotype threat effects can be measured not just in terms of test scores, but also physiologically. One group of researchers found a consistent rise in blood pressure when subjects took a test under a stereotype threat condition compared to when the stereotype threat was absent.

Controlled studies have repeatedly shown that the verbal cues, testing environment, and the identities of students and test proctors can all significantly impact minority students performance on academic tests. In one large review of data from a national survey that involved over a thousand participants who completed a vocabulary test administered by an in-person interviewer, researchers found that black people tested higher when the test was administered by a black interviewer. In keeping with the theory of stereotype threats, that subjects must be aware of the possibility of being judged negatively by some social belief, the race of the interviewer had no impact on the performance of white test takers.

Stereotype threat situations help account for one element in the persistent academic testing gap between whites and blacks in America. Hundreds of studies have documented the negative impact on minority scholastic achievement given the long history of stereotypes of minorities being intellectually less able and the subtle constant reminders that minority students are so viewed. One group of social scientists estimated that stereotype threat alone accounts for one-third of the total gap in SAT scores between whites and black and Latino/a students.

Researchers found this effect to hold in physical as well as mental tasks. In one study, researchers assembled a pool of forty white and forty black students, none of whom were proficient at the game of golf, and asked them to putt a ball up an incline and into a cup. One group read that the purpose of experiment was to test "one's natural ability to perform complex tasks that require hand—eye coordination..." The other group was told that the experiment measured "personal factors correlated with the ability to think strategically during an athletic performance." Half of the test subjects were further primed to think about race by being asked to complete a questionnaire that asked how much they thought standardized tests were "biased," and upon which they had to indicate their race. As predicted, blacks did substantially worse when they were told the task was one to measure the "ability to think strategically" and whites did substantially worse when they thought the test was one of "natural ability."

Some scholars have theorized that one of the reasons that stereotype threat effects are so large is because stereotypes not only threaten to define the individual, but because in a racist society groups themselves are judged by individual behavior. White presumptions about a minority group are believed to be confirmed when someone deemed to be a representative of that group acts according to the stereotype. By this means, every member of a minority group is made to represent the group raising the stakes for their own performance. Not only will failure result in being negatively assessed themselves, falling short of a goal impacts the group by confirming the biases of the racial majority. The stakes are raised because failing to transcend a stereotype only deepens and strengthens it.

Identity, then, is not a thing people possess, it is not simply something we can discover lurking in our family tree. But being the product of social processes and relationships doesn't make it any less real or any less important in people's lives. Only those whose identity is privileged have the luxury of regarding it casually.

Figure 9.12 Navy Seaman Chanthorn Peou of San Diego, Calif., takes his Scholastic Aptitude Test (SAT).

"THE SOULS OF WHITE FOLK" by W.E.B. Du Bois

From *Darkwarter: Voices from Within the Veil* (New York: Harcourt, Brace and Company, 1920)

High in the tower, where I sit above the loud complaining of the human sea, I know many souls that toss and whirl and pass, but none there are that intrigue me more than the Souls of White Folk.

Of them I am singularly clairvoyant. I see in and through them. I view them from unusual points of vantage. Not as a foreigner do I come, for I am native, not foreign, bone of their thought and flesh of their language. Mine is not the knowledge of the traveler or the colonial composite of dear memories, words and wonder. Nor yet is my knowledge that which servants have of masters, or mass of class, or capitalist of artisan. Rather I see these souls undressed and from the back and side. I see the working of their entrails. I know their thoughts and they know that I know. This knowledge makes them now embarrassed, now furious. They deny my right to live and be and call me misbirth! My word is to them mere bitterness and my soul, pessimism. And yet as they preach and strut and shout and threaten, crouching as they clutch at rags of facts and fancies to hide their nakedness, they go twisting, flying by my tired eyes and I see them ever stripped,—ugly, human.

The discovery of personal whiteness among the world's peoples is a very modern thing,—a nineteenth and twentieth century matter, indeed. The ancient world would have laughed at such a distinction. The Middle Age regarded skin color with mild curiosity; and even up into the eighteenth century we were hammering our national manikins into one, great, Universal Man, with fine frenzy which ignored color and race even more than birth. Today we have changed all that, and the world in a sudden, emotional conversion has discovered that it is white and by that token, wonderful!

This assumption that of all the hues of God whiteness alone is inherently and obviously better than brownness or tan leads to curious acts; even the sweeter souls of the dominant world as they discourse with me on weather, weal, and woe are continually playing above their actual words an obligato of tune and tone, saying:

"My poor, un-white thing! Weep not nor rage. I know, too well, that the curse of God lies heavy on you. Why? That is not for me to say, but be brave! Do your work in your lowly sphere, praying the good Lord that into heaven above, where all is love, you may, one day, be born—white!"

I do not laugh. I am quite straight-faced as I ask soberly:

"But what on earth is whiteness that one should so desire it?" Then always, somehow, some way, silently but clearly, I am given to understand that whiteness is the ownership of the earth forever and ever, Amen!

Now what is the effect on a man or a nation when it comes passionately to believe such an extraordinary dictum as this? That nations are coming to believe it is manifest daily. Wave on wave, each with increasing virulence, is dashing this new religion of whiteness on the shores of our time. Its first effects are funny: the strut of the Southerner, the arrogance of the Englishman amuck, the whoop of the hoodlum who vicariously leads your mob. Next it appears dampening generous enthusiasm in what we once counted glorious; to free the slave is discovered to be tolerable only in so far as it freed his master! Do we sense somnolent writhings in black Africa or angry groans in India or triumphant banzais in Japan? "To your tents, O Israel!" These nations are not white!

After the more comic manifestations and the chilling of generous enthusiasm come subtler, darker deeds. Everything considered, the title to the universe claimed by White Folk is faulty. It ought, at least, to look plausible. How easy, then, by emphasis and omission to make children believe that every great soul the world ever saw was a white man's soul; that every great thought the world ever knew was a white man's thought; that every great deed the world ever did was a white man's deed; that every great dream the world ever sang was a white man's dream. In fine, that if from the world were dropped everything that could not fairly be attributed to White Folk, the world would, if anything, be even greater, truer, better than now. And if all this be a lie, is it not a lie in a great cause?

Here it is that the comedy verges to tragedy. The first minor note is struck, all unconsciously, by those worthy souls in whom consciousness of high descent brings burning desire to spread the gift abroad,—the obligation of nobility to the ignoble. Such sense of duty assumes two things: a real possession of the heritage and its frank appreciation by the humble-born. So long, then, as humble black folk, voluble with thanks, receive barrels of old clothes from lordly and generous whites, there is much mental peace and moral satisfaction. But when the black man begins to dispute the white man's title to certain alleged bequests of the Fathers in wage and position, authority and training; and when his attitude toward charity is sullen anger rather than humble jollity; when he insists on his human right to swagger and swear and waste,—then the spell is suddenly broken and the philanthropist is ready to believe that Negroes are impudent, that the South is right, and that Japan wants to fight America.

After this the descent to Hell is easy. On the pale, white faces which the great billows whirl upward to my tower I see again and again, often and still more often, a writing of human hatred, a deep and passionate hatred, vast by the very vagueness of its expressions. Down through the green waters, on the bottom of the world, where men move to and fro, I have seen a man— an educated gentleman—grow livid with anger because a little, silent, black woman was sitting by herself in a Pullman car. He was a white man. I have seen a great, grown man curse a little child, who had wandered into the wrong waiting-room, searching for its mother: "Here, you damned black—" He was white. In Central Park I have seen the upper lip of a quiet, peaceful man curl back in a tigerish snarl of rage because black folk rode by in a motor car. He was a white man. We have seen, you and I, city after city drunk and furious with ungovernable lust of blood; mad with murder, destroying, killing, and cursing; torturing human victims because somebody accused of crime happened to be of the same color as the mob's innocent victims and because that color was not white! We have seen,—Merciful God! in these wild days and in the name of Civilization, Justice, and Motherhood,— what have we not seen, right here in America, of orgy, cruelty, barbarism, and murder done to men and women of Negro descent.

Up through the foam of green and weltering waters wells this great mass of hatred, in wilder, fiercer violence, until I look down and know that today to the millions of my people no misfortune could happen,—of death and pestilence, failure and defeat—that would not make the hearts of millions of their fellows beat with fierce, vindictive joy! Do you doubt it? ….

A true and worthy ideal frees and uplifts a people; a false ideal imprisons and lowers. Say to men, earnestly and repeatedly: "Honesty is best, knowledge is power; do unto others as you would be done by." Say this and act it and the nation must move toward it, if not to it. But say to a people: "The one virtue is to be white," and the people rush to the inevitable conclusion, "Kill the 'nigger'!"….

Is not this the record of present America? Is not this its headlong progress? Are we not coming more and more, day by day, to making the statement "I am white," the one fundamental tenet of our practical morality? Only when this basic, iron rule is involved is our defense of right nation-wide and prompt. Murder may swag-

ger, theft may rule and prostitution may flourish and the nation gives but spasmodic, intermittent and lukewarm attention. But let the murderer be black or the thief brown or the violator of womanhood have a drop of Negro blood, and the righteousness of the indignation sweeps the world. Nor would this fact make the indignation less justifiable did not we all know that it was blackness that was condemned and not crime….

This theory of human culture and its aims has worked itself through warp and woof of our daily thought with a thoroughness that few realize. Everything great, good, efficient, fair, and honorable is "white"; everything mean, bad, blundering, cheating, and dishonorable is "yellow"; a bad taste is "brown"; and the devil is "black." The changes of this theme are continually rung in picture and story, in newspaper heading and moving-picture, in sermon and school book, until, of course, the King can do no wrong,—a White Man is always right and a Black Man has no rights which a white man is bound to respect….

All this I see and hear up in my tower, above the thunder of the seven seas. From my narrowed windows I stare into the night that looms beneath the cloud-swept stars. Eastward and westward storms are breaking,—great, ugly whirlwinds of hatred and blood and cruelty. I will not believe them inevitable. I will not believe that all that was must be, that all the shameful drama of the past must be done again today before the sunlight sweeps the silver seas.

If I cry amid this roar of elemental forces, must my cry be in vain, because it is but a cry,—a small and human cry amid Promethean gloom?

Back beyond the world and swept by these wild, white faces of the awful dead, why will this Soul of White Folk,—this modern Prometheus,—hang bound by his own binding, tethered by a fable of the past? I hear his mighty cry reverberating through the world, "I am white!" Well and good, O Prometheus, divine thief! Is not the world wide enough for two colors, for many little shinings of the sun? Why, then, devour your own vitals if I answer even as proudly, "I am black!"….

Chapter Ten: Race and Perception

Race in the Unconscious Mind

In the 1950s researchers grew increasingly suspicious that the opinion surveys they used to measure racism were unreliable. Experimenters sought to find out if a person's opinions about race might in fact conflict with their unconscious cognitive processes. In one of the first controlled laboratory studies of this question, researchers at the Ohio State University recruited white male students to perform a word association exercise while measuring their skin conductance. Skin conductance (or electrodermal or galvanic skin response (GSR)) reflects a person's stress or anxiety and can be easily measured with the same equipment used in classic "lie detector" tests. The great advantage of recording skin conductance is that it is a physiological response that is not consciously controlled, but is an automatic response to stimuli. The word association tests were irrelevant to the experiment, just something to distract the subject from the real variable which was that occasionally during the test an assistant would enter the room and readjust a dummy set of wires taped to the subjects' hand. On one occasion the assistant who touched the subject to readjust the wires was white and on another he was black. Skin conductance data later revealed "a highly significant difference in GSR response" between the white and black assistants when they touched the subjects. Such skin conductance experiments were widely replicated, showing that no matter how white subjects claimed to have non-racist attitudes, they displayed automatic stress even just being shown pictures of black people.

By the 1970s, the galvanic machines were replaced by electronic instruments that could infer stress in a person's voice by examining recorded audio wave patterns. Such a device allowed for asking direct questions of subjects and comparing their level of autonomic (unconsciously controlled) stress to their answers. Black, white, and Puerto Rican subjects were then asked, "Would you be comfortable sitting next to a (black, Puerto Rican, white) person you did not know in the cafeteria?" "Would you be comfortable having a (black, Puerto Rican, white) roommate?" "Would you be comfortable if a member of your family married a (black, Puerto Rican, white) person?" "Would you be comfortable if you had a blind date with a (black, Puerto Rican, white) person?" and so on. All three groups of subjects displayed significantly higher stress levels when considering sitting next to, dating, marrying, or in any way interacting with a person from the other group, regardless of how they answered the questions.

Further techniques to detect unconscious bias were innovated in the 1980s, as devices (facial electromyographic sensors) that could measure tiny movements of facial muscles that indicated positive or negative emotion were developed. These experiments confirmed the earlier ones as well—subjects may have claimed unbiased willingness to interact with partners of different races but their physiological responses indicated the opposite reaction. Similar research has also been done with electroencephalography, the measurement of electrical activity in the brain. Clearly, much of the categorizing of race happens before and beneath a person's conscious thinking about it.

The Cognitive Economy

Philosophers going back to Plato have pondered the difficulties of perceiving the world and reality directly. For a time in the Victorian era of the 19th century it was popularly thought that any distortions or errors in grasping reality were the result of faulty structures of some people's brains and that normal individuals with healthy brains had no such difficulty. But by the end of that century a number of thinkers began to conceive of the brain not as an organ that primarily senses the world, but as one that interprets it. This troubling thought erased the belief that the difference between grasping reality correctly, or in error, was the same as that between health and disease. Rather, everyone suffered from a gap between reality and understanding and that break was an unavoidable part of being a social animal.

Modern philosophers like William James distinguished between two separate but intertwined processes of the mind. One was gathering all the signals from the senses and registering them as perceptions, and the other was taking this raw stream of impulses and making coherent ideas out of it. In order to turn a constant stream of sense signals into concepts that we can think about, the mind has to group signals into categories. Categorization is a mental process fundamental to the way humans think and understand their world. (We call these inherent functions of the mind 'cognitive processes' and the act of such processing 'cognition.')

Such categories are not the same for all people

because they are largely a product of language (which varies from culture to culture) and of our own direct experiences (which vary from person to person). Once our mind puts a sensory impulse into a category, it defines and limits it. It makes assumptions about its character beyond what is actually sensed. As William James put it, "When we conceptualize we cut and fix, and exclude anything but what we have fixed, whereas in the real concrete sensible flux of life experiences compenetrate each other." In other words, through language and the habits of our society, our ability to accurately perceive reality is limited and distorted.

Our experience of reality begins with our senses receiving stimuli and sending messages to the brain. At any given moment our brains are more or less flooded with these sensory messages and without some way of organizing and sorting this information, our experience of being in the world would be just a confusing and unending stream of sensations. The amount of information our brains routinely process in a moment is astonishing; the fastest supercomputers today take forty minutes to process the equivalent of what the human brain does in a second.

Being able to weed out the ordinary and routine from the truly noteworthy and unusual helped our ancestors survive and provided a strong evolutionary pressure to embed this ability deeply in all of our brains.

Psychologists call this mechanism the "Cognitive Economy" because it automatically conserves our mental energy by organizing a never-ending rush of sensation into categories before we are even conscious of them. Researchers have shown that even very young children do this and therefore it seems to be a universal adaptation to the need to quickly decide if an object or thing is a threat or not. As attention and perception is limited, a snap judgement allows the mind to focus all its energies on those things that seem out of the ordinary and unusual, rather than those frequently encountered and therefore dismissed as familiar. As the mind automatically recognizes and sorts things into kinds that share similar qualities, it filters and limits the sensations we are consciously aware of, simplifying our perceptions so we can devote more attention to the unknown shadow in the tall grass that might be a lion. (All the senses related to "shadows" "grass" and "tall" are already sorted and

Figure 10.1 Woman taking polygraph test.

categorized for us before we are conscious of them so we can consider the possibility of that more important type, the lion.)

The filtering and sorting that goes on beneath our awareness is what allows us to think and be rational beings. But it comes at a cost. By the time humans grow into adulthood they are very practiced and skilled categorizers, often overlooking the details and specificity of things as soon as their mind puts them into a familiar category. Much of what we perceive is unavoidably shaped and distorted by the way our minds define the categories used to represent the world. Because reality is far more varied and complex than the categories we develop to represent it, something is always added or lost in this translation.

race are not even apparent until continental distances are traversed. Rather, some scientists propose that racial identification is a late byproduct of mental mechanisms that evolved to quickly recognize natural categories. Others argue it piggybacks on systems that evolved to understand and navigate the coalitions and factions that probably bedeviled most human communities. The evidence is scanty in favor of any of these theories.

Regardless of the evolutionary origins of this phenomenon, the effect is real and has a deep and significant impact on modern life. Its existence means that racism is not merely a matter of choice, or experience, or environment, or even upbringing, but that part of what contributes to racism is a deep mental machinery that compels people

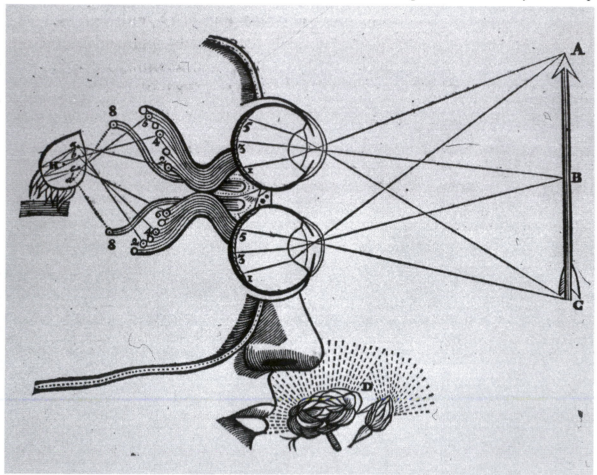

Figure 10.2 René Descartes, *L'Homme...* (Paris: Charles Angot, 1664), p. 79.

Behavioral experiments have shown that the recognition of race is nearly automatic in modern American populations. Like gender and age, race appears to be subject to some sort of automatic category processing in the brain. The origins of this mechanism of racial recognition are still disputed, though anthropologists generally agree that human evolution could not have evolved around the need to distinguish race, as for all of human history, until the last moment, few people traveled more than a handful of miles from their home and the sorts of differences that we call

to automatically think in racial patterns.

What is lost or added when the mind automatically sorts sensory stimuli into categories is particularly important to the study of race and ethnicity. The mind's sorting mechanism has the tendency to exaggerate the differences between objects that it puts into different categories and to soften differences between those things it lumps together as the same type. Psychologists call these "accentuation effects" and they tend to sensitize people to physical differences or other markers of racial and ethnic difference. By stretching perception so as to place people into separate categories, accentuation effects contribute to making race seem real, reliable and stable, when, in fact, such physical differences are not categorical but a continuum of subtle differences that are often ambiguous and uncertain. Among the categories produced by these influences are ones that we call "stereotypes," which are merely a type of cognitive category whose shared social origins and connections are more visible and obvious to us.

Complicating things further, the categories that our mind uses to sort the world are an outgrowth of our in-born tendencies, personal experiences, social influences, language, as well as more formal knowledge that we call ideologies. All our experiences, our memories, our values, our myths, our beliefs, and our yearnings all contribute to shaping these cognitive categories. As humans mature they become increasingly susceptible to a particular social-ly-produced construct of ideas, values, and beliefs that can structure the arrangement and operation of cognitive categories. Such a construct is called a schema.

Schemas are more than just ideas or beliefs, as they are not just collections of information but are particular habitual and automatic routines that organize cognition along certain paths. In other words, they aren't just information or data but a complex of presumptions about the world that then influence and modify how sensation is processed into perception. For example, a magician's tricks are entertaining because they upend our presumptions and working principles, our schema, of how the world works—we thought the hat was empty before the magician pulled a rabbit out it. Our surprise is a result not of our perceptions being fooled (we accurately perceived both the rabbit and the hat) but of the violation of our schema that empty hats don't contain rabbits. Schemas, then, are theories of how the world works, particularly knowledge about the caus-es and consequences of things, not just knowledge of the things themselves.

While people might be automatically classified into ethnic groups or races as a result of the cognitive econo-my of the mind, schemas predispose people to understand sequences of experience—interactions and situations—in particular ways. It is through a racial schema that white southerners a century ago might have read a black person meeting their gaze and not averting their eyes as a rebel-lious and rude act. Or it is through a particular schema that a black person today might read a clerk's attention to them in a clothing shop as unwarranted suspicion and racial pro-filing. Schemas, then, make sense of events and happenings in the world but, like cognitive categorization, may do so at the cost of exaggerating differences and simplifying sim-ilarities, thus contributing to the sense that race is "real."

Racial categorization involves not just the body, but enlists all the social markers that surround a person. The schemas that define race operate on a wide range of so-cial beliefs, observations, and theories including class. Re-flecting the social fact that black Americans on average earn two-thirds of what American whites do and possess one-twentieth the wealth, Americans have come to closely associate blackness with poverty and whiteness with afflu-ence.

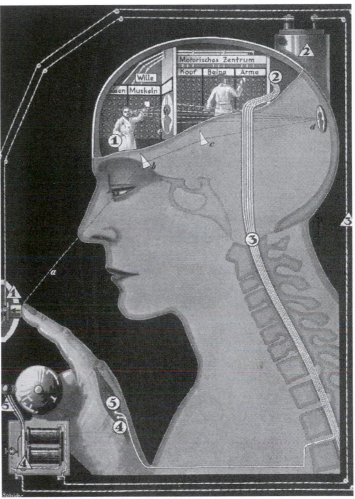

Figure 10.3 Fritz Kahn, *Das Leben des Menschen...* (Stuttgart, 1926).

Schemas begin as assumptions and ideas adopted from one's social environment and as such they are just as prone to be faulty and wrong-headed as most commonly held but rarely examined beliefs. Humans have a tendency to more readily perceive and retain information that aligns with their presumptions than with that which contradicts them. This is called "Confirmation Bias." Schemas, be-ing unconscious systems of assumption about the world, strongly contribute to confirmation bias as they render less visible disconfirming experiences thereby making isolated examples that seem to confirm our presumptions appear more common than they really are.

Like feedback between a microphone and a hum-ming speaker, schemas both contribute to confirmation bias and are strengthened by it. A schema mutes our ability to see exceptions to its rule, and, as it does, it is reinforced by a succession of experiences that seem to confirm it. Such natural and common habits of mind have been shown to powerfully bend our views of the world.

Race as Schema

In general, schemas can be thought of as beliefs or theories of the world that fundamentally shape perception. A racial schema operates on the assumption of a tight connection between physical appearance and behavior. It derives this idea both from social stereotypes but also by accentuation effects that exaggerate experiences that confirm them. In this, the racial schema shares the same logic of causation as does astrology. There is great similarity in the idea that the movements of the planets influence human character with the idea that superficial physical features also determine such essential qualities. When someone accepts this idea it becomes a mental structure, a schema, that is used to understand and make meaning of one's experiences.

Almost any idea can become a schema. What elevates

Figure 10.4 Generating ideas, digital artwork by Bill McConkey.

a simple idea to this level is the way people in society employ this idea in their perception of their everyday lives. Take for example three different ideas: believing in unicorns, that baseball is the greatest sport, or that Friday the 13th is an unlucky day. All of these beliefs can be easily embraced or discarded because they are not strongly reinforced by the daily actions of most people. But, were most people to stay in their homes and avoid bathing or using sharp objects on Friday the 13ths because of the extreme hazard of tempting fate on an unlucky day, suddenly the idea of Friday the 13th would become a reality that would be hard to avoid whether one believed in it or not. Suddenly, every bad thing that happens on that particular day would have an explanation and every freak accident becomes evidence for the truth of the idea of unluckiness. At bottom, this is how race operates—it is a belief that gains substance through patterns of mass behaviour that provide its circular validation.

One of the most unique features of a racial schema is that it is resistant to disproof because certain of its qualities are magical or beyond perception. Ghost hunters rush to claim that the sudden chill in the air or the distant creaks and groans heard in an old house are evidence for their belief. But what sort of evidence would prove that ghosts don't exist? To open a door on a room and point out that there is no ghost inside to be seen doesn't disprove the existence of ghosts since they are believed to move in and out of the material world at their whim. Even when a ghost hunter is caught doctoring a photograph or having an accomplice rattling chains in the basement, the gullible may admit the hunters might be frauds, but insist ghosts are real.

Ghost belief is quite common because its principles allow common, everyday experiences to seemingly confirm it. Any puzzling sound, the window that seems to open or close on its own, an unidentified knock on the door, all these real phenomena are strong evidence for ghosts because they themselves are physical. In other words, ghost belief is a strengthened because it involves a process of attaching meaning to actual, tangible things, in this case sounds, windows and doors.

Race schema operates in the same way. Race schemas are confirmed in everyday experience as people with different appearances are encountered and they are real and their physical differences are there to be perceived. Just as interpreting the sound of a door slamming shut in the attic with the action of a spirit is associating something physical with something imaginary and non-provable or disprovable, so is interpreting a person's appearance with a set of ancestral characteristics and relationships.

This is especially true of race because race is not only a myth about the characteristics and qualities of any individual who is considered a member of a certain race, it is also a myth that humanity can be divided into the essential groups called races. Thus race is a myth about a mythical group, a myth within a myth, and these two categories of myth reinforce each other against actual facts or experience. For example, someone meets another person they consider a different race but doesn't act in the ways a person of that race is supposed to act. Does this situation disprove the concept of race? But the racial schema is elastic and allows for at least two possibilities that allow the myth of race to be sustained: the individual could be wrongly placed as a member of that racial group or some aspects of the assumed qualities of the racial group could be wrong. Either way, the experience of meeting a person who does not fit the racial schema ends up reinforcing the idea of races rather than leading to the conclusion that races are not real.

Language and Perception

Language is not just something we use to speak, it is also the means by which we think. Language provides us with a set of fixed concepts that we do not weigh and decide to adopt. Rather, because many of language's most basic structures are the machinery which allows us to think at all, these ideas are not ones that we normally think of as choices. To us they just appear as fundamental reality.

For example, the English language divides time into three categories: past, present, and future. But time is not really three different things, it is actually one thing and our choice of thinking about it as three different things is arbitrary. We could just as easily divide time into any number of discrete units: we could have a different tense for the past that existed before we were born, or a different concept of time for the future that exists in the lifetime of our grandchildren. The language of the Asmat peoples of New Guinea is divided into seventeen different tenses, reflecting their extraordinarily rich and deep understanding of time. Like time, most things in the natural world do not divide neatly into distinct categories with clear boundaries between them. Reality seems to prefer fuzzy differences, a world where things are different but these differences shade gradually one to the other. Light can be broken into a spectrum of colors but these colors exist on a rainbow continuum from deepest red to deepest violet. Every musician knows that while the 88 keys of the piano represent different distinct notes, an endless range of tones exists between them. Language is like a screen through which this unruly world is sieved into different things; language tends to separate what is a continuum of reality into distinct categories.

Many of the concepts that language provides are interpretations of the natural world. Different cultures have greater or lesser varieties of words for color and the number of words available for colors determines and limits the way we view them. We generally don't think of colors by their abstract quality, but rather by example. How would you think of "red" or "blue" without referring to some object? We might say, "blue" is the color of the sky and "red" is the color of blood. But while English has only one category for "blue", Turkish has separate categories for light blue and dark blue. The Welsh language combines both "green" and "blue" into a single category.

Language is a powerful force shaping perception because it shapes the structure of the cognitive categories used to make sense of the world. This relationship between the structure of language and the arrangement of cognitive categories is not a simple one-to-one relationship between a word, an idea, and a category. Rather, language operates through a dynamic and floating association between multiple words and concepts. Any word points to a concept not

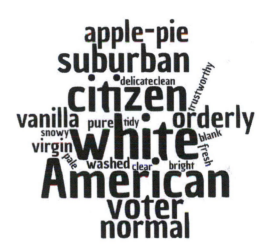

only directly but by its association with other words and kindred ideas. Instead of thinking of words linking tightly to ideas, it is more accurate to think of clouds of word associations that connect to each other in fluid ways.

Studies have shown on a simple level that white and black Americans have different clouds of word associations about each other. Simple word association studies that ask people to select adjectives that describe various groups have shown that people of all races tend to associate whites with being "inventive, educated, smart, rich, and greedy" and black Americans as "corrupt, funny, friendly, independent, and poor." However, black and white subjects diverged somewhat, black subjects adding "corrupt and prejudiced" to their list of adjectives about whites, and white subjects adding "athletic, humorous, loud, and lazy" to their description of blacks. Such studies reveal both conscious bias but also provide a glimpse into the elements of the mental schema that steer perceptions at a deeper level.

Priming Stereotypes

Research into cognition has shown that, over time, people accumulate a thick tangle of mental associations to any social category. These associations can be stereotypes, like Norwegians are stoic, or they can be emotions linking a group to fear, joy, disgust, or comfort. Such associations and biases can lie dormant, not thought about, until they are activated by some trigger. Finding ways of activating these associations is called "priming" the response and often it takes as little as showing a vague image or describing a situation in a particular way.

One classic experiment demonstrated how stereotypes powerfully and unconsciously guide behavior. Researchers had two groups of subjects complete word puzzles while being timed. Subjects were told that the point of the experiment was to see how quickly they could unscramble jumbles of letters into words, though this was actually unimportant. Instead, what was going on was that one group was unscrambling words that were all associated with stereotypes of the elderly, words like "grey," "wrinkled," and "Miami." The other group, the control, unscrambled random unrelated words. When the subjects had finished their task they were dismissed and assumed the experiment was over, but it was at this point that the actual data gathering began. Participants were carefully timed to see how quickly they walked from the testing room, down a corridor, and onto an elevator. Consistently, those participants who had been 'primed' with words associated with aging walked more slowly than those who had not been exposed to them.

Other experiments have documented how the priming of stereotypes works particularly powerfully when it comes to stereotypes of race. In one such experiment when subjects were first told they going to participate in a study about "crime," and shown pictures on a screen in which their eye movements were tracked, they looked more frequently at the faces of black men in a grid of various faces. The effect vanished when subjects weren't primed with the word "crime." Numerous other studies have shown that racial biases can be triggered among whites by all manner of primers, such as showing them photographs of President Obama, listening to black voices, watching angry conservative political advertisements or news stories about black criminals, playing black game avatars, or listening to jury instructions about the presumption of innocence.

Researchers have documented that people don't just judge race by a person's face, but also by other assumptions about a person, such as where they are or the clothes they wear. For example, one team of researchers showed research participants pictures of men's faces and asked them to label them either "white" or "black." Some of the men in the pictures wore suits and ties while others wore work shirts.

Study participants were more likely to label a person white if they wore business attire and more likely to label them black if they wore work clothes. This tendency increased in proportion to the ambiguity of the color and other features of the faces. Similar effects have been found when faces are associated with stereotypical words, such as "welfare," "inner-city," "poverty," or "criminal." Faces were more likely to be identified as Indian when subjects were told the person died of cirrhosis of the liver.

One powerful proof of the fact that many words have complicated racial associations is that language can be manipulated to activate racist stereotypes without using explicit racial terms. This phenomenon, known as "dog whistle" campaigning, has been exploited by politicians and political parties to appeal to the baser racist feelings of their constituency without exposing themselves to charges of racism. The effect has also been demonstrated in controlled experimental settings. For example, one group of researchers explored this effect by conducting a national survey of attitudes about crime and altering just one or two words to the questionnaire. Half of their respondents were asked if they supported spending tax dollars to lock up "violent criminals" while the other half were asked if they supported spending tax dollars to lock up "violent inner city criminals." Other questions on the survey assessed subjects' level of stereotypical attitudes towards blacks. The results were surprising in how consistent they were. Those respondents who had higher levels of stereotypical bias responded to the trigger words "inner city" at rates up to fifty percent higher than the control group.

Developmental Theories of Race

Even a young child's ability to categorize objects, especially to distinguish people into types, probably draws upon an evolutionary mechanism that is universal and developed over a long period of time. It is easily imagined how being able to identify people who seem similar to those who are familiar and trusted might help an infant thrive, or even survive, in a complex social situation. However, if this was the case, it is also likely that such an ability to group people into categories did not evolve on the basis of race, as for the bulk of human history, prior to the rise of long distance migrations and long distance trading, there would have been few opportunities to interact with anyone but relatively close kin. Rather, this innate ability probably grew up on the basis of discriminating differences of gender, age, and status.

Various studies have measured this early ability to distinguish those like and different from one's own intimate circle. Young infants shown various faces reliably give more attention to those faces like the ones they are most familiar with. This doesn't mean like their own faces, but like those that predominate around them. For example, one study showed that Ethiopian infants gave more attention to black faces if they lived in Africa, but showed no greater attention for either white or black faces if they lived in Israel. Other studies showed babies as young as five months old gave more attention to people speaking in familiar accents than those speaking in different ones.

Attention should not be confused with preference. The fact that infants devote more attention to those in familiar categories does not necessarily mean that they prefer people in such categories or that they dislike others. Psychologists generally agree that actual preferences and discriminations appear later; gender first, as children begin displaying a preference for others of their own gender around two years of age, and race only later, somewhere around four or five. Interestingly, one study showed five year olds observed racial differences but, unlike gender, they didn't believe they were biological or even permanent. Another study showed that white children did not express any preference toward white or black strangers at 10 months or 2.5 years old, but did exhibit strong preferences by age five.

The upshot of all this is that humans have an innate tendency to categorize and pigeon-hole new information (especially gender and age), but the content of such categorizing, its meaning and direction, is learned and absorbed from society. This appears to be especially true of the category we call race. Studies of the mental development of young children have shown that children as young as the preschool age of four or five become aware that people are grouped into racial categories. But unlike adults whose racial view of the world combines both the perception of superficial bodily differences with assumptions about unseen qualities and characters of a person, children in early childhood may be aware of racial categories but do not yet invest those categories with additional meanings beyond the physical. Young children do not necessarily see race as something inherent, biological or even fixed. They see it only as a means of grouping similar objects, like short and tall, round and square. It is not until they reach school-age that they begin to attach larger meanings to physical appearance.

American children develop an understanding of racial categories before they are able to reliably sort people into races. While this seems backwards, it makes sense if one does not assume that racial perception is a natural observation of the world but actually is a learned behavior. As psychologist Lawrence Hirschfeld put it, "children

Figure 10.5 First grade class, Albemarle Road Elementary School, Charlotte, North Carolina, Feb. 21, 1973.

develop racial categories in response to an impulse to discover the sorts of humans there are rather than as an attempt to catalog physical differences among the humans they encounter."

So where do children learn about race before they see it? Most people would suspect that this must begin in the family and that children would be most likely to acquire such ideas from their parents. But studies that correlated parental and their young children's attitudes have failed to find a close link between them. As it turns out, parent's beliefs about race are a poor predictor of their young child's attitudes. However, as children mature their attitudes do tend to align with their parents. Another likely suspect for influencing children would be other children, but careful studies have likewise shown that peers have significantly less impact than expected and cannot account for childhood development of racial attitudes.

Studies of racial attitudes in children show that, somehow, even very young children absorb the larger racial categories and messages of their society. This is true even when those messages are opposite what parents attempt to teach their children, as when well-meaning parents attempt to raise their children to be color-blind. Young American children display highly pro-white biases and do so across all racial groups. White children exhibit the most pro-white beliefs. A significant number of young children of color also express pro-white feelings, though not a majority. Interestingly, all children, regardless of their own color, exhibit the most pro-white feelings at younger ages and as they mature hold those pro-white attitudes less tightly. Non-white children develop more positive feelings about their own racial group as they grow older and white children display more positive attitudes towards other groups. This all makes sense if one considers that it is the youngest children who are most susceptible to the messages imparted by media and other cultural communications.

Evidence suggests that such susceptibility to social messages is a product of the course of brain development in young children. At an early age when the brain begins processing language the categories it uses are more exclusive and rigid than they eventually become. Young children naturally process their understanding of the world into sharply defined distinctions of 'this and not that' and only later, as they mature, gain the ability to consider objects that lie between categories, or share properties of several categories. This insight helps us to understand why it is that younger children so readily absorb the social messages about races they encounter.

While young children readily develop an understanding of racial differences in American society, mostly as they absorb social messages about race, they don't necessarily also develop an understanding of racism, or the existence

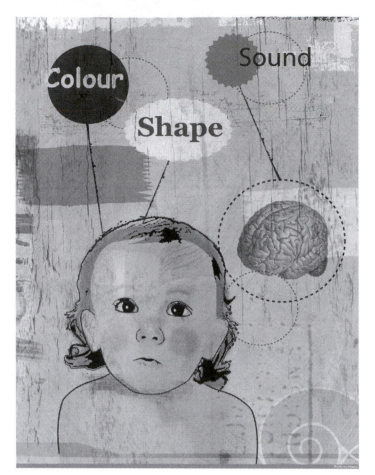

Figure 10.6 Learning and Memory, illustration by Bill McConkey.

of prejudices about a specific racial group. Research has shown that children tend to develop this awareness in middle childhood and that children in different racial groups develop this knowledge at different rates. Significantly, black and Latino/a children acquire an awareness of racism earlier than white children do. By age 10, according to one study, four out of five black and Latino/a children were aware of racism but only three out of five white kids were as knowledgeable. One explanation for this is that in a racist society, there are greater consequences to not knowing about racism for those subject to its discriminations than there are for those who benefit from them.

Close studies of the way children and adults perceive and recognize human faces clearly show that the manner in which faces are recognized changes as children mature. Young children recognize only particular individual features of the face and in later years gain the ability to perceive the relationship between features (symmetry of eyes, for example) or to process the whole face as a unit at once which apparently does not happen until around seven years of age. More strikingly, research appears to show that even before they reach school-age, children use different methods to evaluate faces they deem to be of their own race and those that they view as of other races. In general, children apply their more sophisticated facial recognition abilities on faces they consider racially like their own, and cruder methods for those seemingly unlike themselves. What this means is that from a young age children have acquired the habit of literally not seeing racial others as they do themselves and those they consider within their own race. The sad old racist excuse that "they all look alike to me" may be rooted in the psychological development of children.

However, this effect is stronger the less diversity a child has in her or his social environment. In other words, children learn to tune or adjust their sensitivity to perceiving others depending on what those in their immediate social environment look like. Children who live among those having a wide variety of facial types and colors tend to apply more of their recognition skills to distinguishing faces of all hues. But for children who come to only associate one skin color with those in their social group, they rely more on cruder tools, such as color alone, to distinguish the faces of those deemed 'them'.

'Own Race Bias' Effect

Criminologists first began studying the connection between races and perceptions over a century ago as they investigated the troubling problem of witnesses misidentifying suspected criminals. In 1914, Harvard psychologist Gustave A. Feingold published a paper in a legal journal in which he observed that witnesses had more difficulty identifying the faces of people of other races than those of individuals who shared their own race. As Feingold put it in the racist language of his day, "it is well known that... to the uninitiated American, all Asiatics look alike, while to the Asiatic all white men look alike." While few studies actually documented this "own race bias" effect, for decades scholars presumed it was a real and powerful phenomenon and bothered more with theorizing its causes than proving its existence.

Two theories dominated explanations for the "own race bias" effect. One simply presumed that people's ability to distinguish the faces of other races was varied by the degree of their own racial prejudices. More bigoted people perceived the faces of people of other races to be more similar while less prejudiced people were better able to see facial differences across races. The other leading theory held that some racial groups actually had more similar appearances and therefore the difficulty in distinguishing their faces was not the fault of the observer but the observed.

By the 1980s, both of these theories had been thoroughly discredited. Early experiments that seemed to show that inherent prejudices accounted for differences in the ability to distinguish faces were shown to be confusing the tendency of bigoted individuals to label all differences as racial for a lack of perceptual accuracy. Additional experiments showed no particular relationship between racial attitudes and the ability to perceive faces within or across racial groups. Theories that racial groups varied in the degree of similarity of their facial features were discredited by a studies that conducted detailed measurements of facial physiognomies and found no race was significantly more homogenous than another.

Since then the "own race bias" effect has been better documented, dozens of studies cumulatively estimating that most people are about one and a half times better able to distinguish faces of those from their own race than those of other races. Modern theories of this effect have focused on the possibility that perception is not inherent but is shaped, molded, trained, and constrained by one's environment and experiences. This theory of perceptual learning holds that individuals exposed to greater interracial contact at an early age grow to become better at distinguishing faces and appearances across races. Conversely, those whose formative childhood has limited interracial interactions are less able to perceive interracial facial differences later in life. A number of comparative studies of children who grew up in integrated and segregated neighborhoods, in both the U.S., Great Britain, and South Africa, found evidence to support this developmental theory, though other studies comparing individuals in Canada and South Asia did not.

As it turns out, perceptual learning may not be limited to the formative years of childhood. More recent studies have correlated the "own race bias" effect to indirect interracial contact. One study found that a sample of whites who were avid basketball fans were significantly better at distinguishing the faces of black people than were whites who weren't basketball fans, a difference the researchers theorized was the result of white basketball fans having learned more accurate interracial perception by watching a sport dominated by black athletes. Other psychologists have demonstrated that more accurate perception of other race faces can be trained through practice, though these improvements are temporary.

Implicit Bias

When the brain's penchant for automatically sorting sensory images into categories is combined with schemas built on assumptions of racial differences, the result can be racist perceptions and behaviors that lurk just beneath consciousness. Scientists refer to such forms of unconscious prejudice as "implicit bias" and they have developed many tools to measure how widespread and how powerful a phenomenon it is.

Because the automatic cognitive processes of the brain developed as means of economy--as ways of rationing its processing abilities and focusing its greatest effort on things are surprising, different, unusual, and therefore possibly dangerous to us--scientists discovered that these automatic processes become more active when we are must react to something quickly. Just as the muscles in the knee can be tweaked into contracting by a slight tap with a rubber hammer, the automatic cognitive systems of the brain can be engaged when subjects are asked to do complicated tasks quickly or shown images that flash for a split-second.

Psychologists have documented many aspects of perception and cognition (the act of thinking), general features of the mind, that contribute to thinking and behaving in terms of social categories. In order to think of race we first have to perceive it; to identify it through our senses and this process of perception is highly subject to the particular social environment and experiences a person is subject to over the course of her life. Once perceived, race has to be made meaningful by our associating it with values and beliefs that also are absorbed from the culture around us.

In 1998 a team of researchers developed the Implicit Association Test (IAT), a tool that could measure the associations a person makes between different words and concepts. Subjects are shown combinations of images and words and must group them together at a pace that does not allow for much reflection. By measuring the speed with which different images and words are grouped together, the program can estimate which images and words have associations that are more automatic than consciously chosen.

IAT tests produce results that indicate if one has a low, moderate, or high preference for one group or another, or no preference at all. Such results often surprise the test takers as they often conflict with conscious beliefs and attitudes. Hundreds of papers based on the IAT have been published since it was first introduced and the vast majority of these studies have shown that white Americans have implicit attitudes that favor whites and have negative associations with non-white people. IAT tests have been used to demonstrate hidden bias in policing, in health care, in education, and in employment.

While the IAT test has been criticized by some social scientists, its predictive effects have been larger than the legal standards set by courts in racial discrimination case law. Federal courts use the "four-fifths" rule standard, meaning a member of a group can claim evidence of discrimination if members of that group have only 80% of some good (jobs, housing, education) as a more privileged group. Meta analysis of hundreds of IAT studies show that on average, the IAT results are predictive to better than the four-fifths standard (r = .236).

Implicit bias has real-world impacts as one comprehensive review of ten year's worth of clinical research revealed. Of 37 studies of implicit racial bias done on health care providers, all but six found evidence of systematic pro-white and anti-black (or Hispanic, Indian and dark-skinned) attitudes. Six studies found that higher implicit bias led to racial disparities in treatments and therapies. A rival meta-study of 27 research projects that examined the implicit biases of health professionals concluded that "The evidence indicates that healthcare professionals exhibit the same levels of implicit bias as the wider population." As a result, "Correlational evidence indicates that biases are likely to influence diagnosis and treatment decisions and levels of care in some circumstances..."

Likewise, implicit biases have been shown to play a role in performance evaluations in the workplace, one controlled study revealing that "strong correlations between performance evaluations and implicit but not explicit racial attitudes and prejudices..." Implicit racial attitudes have been shown to exert a powerful role in how people make decisions about allocating resources, one study showing that implicit biases strongly predicted which students

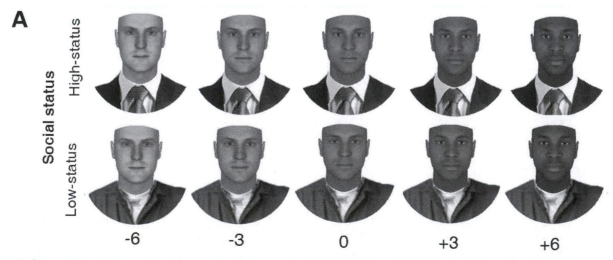

Figure 10.7 'Figure 1: The influence of status cues on race categorization,' in J.B. Freeman, A.M. Penner, A. Saperstein, M. Scheutz, N. Ambady, "Looking the Part: Social Status Cues Shape Race Perception," PLoS ONE 6:9 (2011).

would most heavily cut minority groups when asked to distribute a 20% budget reduction between different student organizations.

Implicit bias shapes people's perceptions of the world around them in many observable ways. Researchers have documented that whites consistently overestimate the size of racial minority groups at almost every level from the smallest of a school or neighborhood to the largest of a city, region, or even the entire nation. An analysis of a broad national survey (the General Social Survey) in 2000 found that roughly half of Americans believe that whites were a numerical minority in the American population (in 2000 whites were approximately 75% of the U.S. population). More than two-thirds underestimated the white population significantly and 80% overestimated the black population, on average more than doubling its size (the average belief was that the black population was 31% when it was closer to 12%) Looking more deeply into the data, surprisingly, these misperceptions were not shaken by direct experience: rural Americans, who presumably lived in less diverse communities, were just as likely to misperceive minority numbers as were urbanites. Likewise, whites who lived in states where African Americans were 1% of the population were just as likely to double their estimates of the black population as whites who lived in states where blacks were 20% of the population.

By now generations of research have revealed and documented how prejudice is not just a quality of diseased or abnormal personalities, but is a product of some of the inescapable processes of cognition. In one sense this makes the problem of discrimination more difficult as it is not possible to simply chalk up the problem to a group of bigots. Unfortunately, bias of various kinds is a deep tendency of the way humans think and is a problem all people need to confront for themselves. But in another sense, the fact that our brains' categorical way of understanding the world along with the more important fact that these categories are not fixed but are themselves in constant interplay with society, experience, and language suggests that we all have the capacity to change our patterns of thought.

Categorical thinking may be inescapable, but our existing cognitive categories are not. Evidence shows that we can influence even the hidden, implicit biases we all have as a result of our mental makeup by consciously exposing ourselves to new situations, by altering our behaviors, and by expanding our sphere of social interactions.

Cognitive categories are closely related to another type of thinking that will be examined more closely in the next section on stereotypes. But they should not be confused as being the same thing. While categories are flexible and subject to modification, the key quality of stereotypes are that they are fixed, unchanging ideas in an otherwise dynamic world of images and ideas.

Justification-Suppression Model of Bias

In today's officially "color-blind" society, where racism is viewed more as an individual fault and or even a form of mental illness, most white people avoid behaving in ways that could be interpreted as being racially biased. They do so even though racist thoughts and implicit preferences toward their own race and against others have been shown experimentally to be very common. This means that many people consciously suppress their inner biases in daily life.

Psychologists have noted that this stress between a public standard of non-racist behavior and private implicit bias leads to a particular pattern of discriminatory treatment. In most situations, most people successfully suppress their biases. However, when a situation arises in which a racial other can be treated negatively but in a way that a person's behavior can be justified by unbiased explanations, the latent racial prejudice is not suppressed and bias is expressed. This "Justification-Suppression" model of contemporary racism has been charted experimentally in many studies.

In one of the first such studies, conducted in 1971, Donald A. Saucier and Leonard Bickman had assistants with identifiable black or white voices cold call New York City phone numbers belonging to white or black residents. The caller pretended to have called the wrong number and explained that their automobile had broken down. They said they were using their last quarter for the pay phone call, and asked the person they had reached do them a favor and call the towing company on their behalf. Carefully tabulating the percentage of times a listener actually performed the favor against the racial identities of the two parties, revealed that whites were far more willing to do the favor when they presumed the caller was also white. Researchers hypothesized that whites were more willing to turn down the requests of black callers because they could tell themselves that the reason they were doing so was unrelated to race; that they did so because they didn't trust strangers, or it was too much bother, or they would turn down such a request from anyone.

Similar experiments has been replicated dozens of times since, one meta-analysis of 31 studies that tested the Justification-Suppression hypothesis concluded that:

> ...as helping scenarios contained higher levels of various attributional cues that would justify one's failure to help a target of any race, help was given less often to Black targets than to White targets. It appears that the ability to rationalize not helping with nonracist explanations allowed individuals to express prejudice without fear of either themselves or others attributing their

Figure 10.8 Photo by Darryl Leja, NHGRI.

behavior to any prejudicial attitudes that they may harbor toward Blacks.

One of the most prevalent areas where this Justification-Suppression effect is common is in the service industries of transportation and dining, where service workers earn tips. Where workers labor in exchange for a gratuity, there exists a ready alternative justification for discriminatory treatment and that is the expectation of a poor tip. Servers and cabbies have been shown across many studies to predictably deliver worse service to customers of color. But because of widespread folk belief that white customers tip better than non-white customers, such workers often don't see themselves as acting with racial prejudice, but simply giving better service to better tippers.

The harm of such slights as being last to be seated in a crowded dining room, or being passed on the street by a cab, is greater than the actual loss of service because of the psychological toll such experiences have. Often the more subtle the discrimination the more frustrating the situation as the victim of the ill-treatment cannot be entirely sure that race was truly operative. Being unable to "know for sure" amplifies the event's impact because the targeted person questions both the situation and him or herself. Such prejudice has a cloudy nature, both present but deniable, and therefore more frustrating in its indeterminacy.

Perceptual Segregation

Implicit bias and perceptual schemas reinforce each other and influence patterns of belief and behavior that dif-

fer by racial identity. Co-workers, neighbors, or friends of different races may perceive the same situation in dramatically different fashions based on this mixture of implicit assumptions and frames of understanding about the world. This effect, called Perceptual Segregation, often underlies those common situations when people of color perceive an instance of racial discrimination and whites nearby do not.

Perceptual segregation arises from opposing frameworks for interpreting reality. White people, due to not having been the target of racial bias, strongly believing that their society is equitable, and that racism was a minor part of American history, tend toward the presumption that other causes besides racism are more likely to be responsible for situations where racism is charged. When faced with instances of racism, white people tend to view them as exceptions to the general rule of a colorblind society. People of color, having likely directly experienced discrimination in their own experience, and learning much more about the inequalities and injustices of American society (as such information, deemed essential to survival, was passed intergenerationally within the minority communities) are more willing to presume that their differential treatment was due to racism and not some other explanation. Black and brown folks tend to depend more heavily on discussions with others of their own social groups for information, as it has long been true that sharing such knowledge within their community was vital. However, people of color tend not to be eager to share this knowledge with whites, who are assumed, rightly or wrongly, to be operating from a colorblind schema and therefore would respond unfavorably to "race talk."

In a situation where black people perceive mistreatment on the basis of their race, white folks often search for other explanations than race, saying, "maybe he treats everyone that way," or "maybe she didn't mean it like it sounded." Whereas people of color, accustomed to such slights, have no need to question what appeared plain to them. The effects of perceptual segregation go well beyond direct experiences to matters of national importance. Such perceptual divides help explain the dramatic differences in opinion between blacks and whites regarding many issues, such as the O.J. Simpson trial, or the Black Lives Movement that is supported by two-thirds of blacks but only 40% of whites.

Western culture has since the Enlightenment celebrated universal values and universal principles while assuming that white people embody and represent such universalism. As such, western culture has worked to highlight the differences of all other people, thereby deepening the racialization of non-Europeans while lessening the idea that Europeans belong to a racial group at all. One result of western humanism is to encourage white people to view themselves as individuals and not members of a racial group at all. The combination of western universalism tied to white individualism has fueled a tendency of whites to assume their experiences are most representative of reality and to disregard the perspectives of those who cannot escape their racialization. In this way the ongoing power of racism is denied thereby closing this logical loop and reinforcing the belief in white universalism and individualism.

Compounding this outlook, is the extensive segregation of American communities and workplaces that allow white people to enjoy living in a society in which the power of racism is denied or forgotten. Personal race does not intrude upon the daily lives of most white people. Not only is it uncommon to experience anxiety or fear that they will be judged negatively because of their race, white people are rarely made aware of their whiteness at all. Race, after all, white people tend to think, is something "they" have, not "us." Submerged in a social environment that denies race has any consequences and in which whiteness is normal and unnoted, white people are insulated from the sorts of racial stresses that are frequent experiences for people of color.

White insulation from race in America is also cushioned by the unexamined normality and seeming naturalness of segregation. White people inhabit a conscious geography in which white neighborhoods are defined as good and diverse ones are suspect or bad neighborhoods, but this belief system is then denied by the avoidance of racial terms altogether. A white person will say, don't buy a house in that area, that is a bad neighborhood, rather than calling it a black or Hispanic neighborhood. In fact, within the logic of whiteness, the fact that most white communities lack racial and ethnic diversity is not a problem or a loss, but a benefit.

As a result of this racial insulation, white people live in a state of racial fragility, a psychological condition in which they are overly sensitive to any situation in which race becomes relevant. This does not require an experience of racial discrimination, which given the historic power and privileges of whiteness is uncommon for whites, but merely any meaningful discussion of race or even a suggestion that race has consequences in America. For many white people, who have long lived in the expectation that their whiteness, if it is perceived at all, is normative and beneficial, the sudden experience of race being important and relevant is painful and such situations are actively avoided.

When the denial of race breaks down and when faced with such racial stresses, white people's racial fragility commonly results in argumentative behavior and oftentimes emotional displays of anger or its related reaction, stubborn silence. This is because not being accustomed to navigating life in a racist environment, whites have not learned the skills of managing the awareness of race that people of color have been forced to acquire.

Race as Action

Many ideas are communicated through gestures and actions rather than with language, especially ideas relating to social status. The simple act of walking can communicate powerful meanings and judgments about one person's perceptions of another. Take, for example, two people who approach each other on the same sidewalk. There are many subtle meanings conveyed by the different ways one person responds to another. One person may slightly step aside to give the other a clear path, or he might square up and forge ahead forcing the other to make room, or she could ignore the other person as if they didn't exist, or he could cross the street to avoid the other person entirely; in each case a different message about the meaning of the other is expressed.

A century ago, W.E.B. Du Bois wrote about how he first became conscious that he was Black not by anything said to him or about him, but by a gesture:

> I remember well when the shadow swept across me. I was a little thing, away up in the hills of New England... In a wee wooden schoolhouse, something put it into the boys' and girls' heads to buy gorgeous visiting cards—ten cents a package—and exchange. The exchange was merry, till one girl, a tall newcomer, refused my card,—refused it peremptorily, with a glance. Then it dawned upon me with a certain suddenness that I was different from the others; or like,

mayhap [perhaps], in heart and life and longing, but shut out from their world by a vast veil.

While race becomes seemingly real because of the actions of people in their everyday lives, race gains power from the stakes involved in these interactions. In America, wealth, power, rights, and privileges have for centuries been distributed along racial lines. Because social behaviours based on race have carried such great importance, the impact of even small actions built on racial meaning can be profound. Society and history charges the line between one race and another with real consequences and by doing so makes the line itself seem real.

The tendency of people's daily behavior to be influenced by racial beliefs is heightened by the great social advantages that could come with having some means of immediately discerning a person's character, intentions, or purpose. Storekeepers could profit if they could accurately size up their customers to decide who is most likely to make a big purchase and who may be tempted to slip some goods into their pocket. Police officers' work would be much easier if they could read people and decide who was suspicious and who was dangerous. Meeting a stranger alone on a lonely street would be less tense an interaction if you could determine at a glance what sort of person they were. Such situations tempt people into believing that they can do the impossible, reading character through appearance.

Over time such practices become circular and self-fulfilling. A store clerk only challenges people who fit a certain racial profile and as a result finds shoplifters fit this description. A cop watches certain groups more than others and she finds most of her arrests come from those races. The nervous person who avoided interacting with someone on the street who appeared to be of a different race might credit himself with having avoided an incident. In all of these examples the person utilizing race as a short-cut to knowledge about another person could feel that their actions were confirmed by reality. Of course what reality confirmed is that discriminatory actions create discriminatory effects.

Each of these individuals behaved as if race were real and through such behavior made it real. Race, while a mythic quality, becomes unavoidable as the store clerk, or the cop, or the stranger down the street, looks suspiciously at the dark-skinned other and this other person is thrust into the position of wondering if they are truly being singled out. In such a situation race is a product of the social context, it is produced not by the jagged emotions of hatred or disgust, but by what those involved in the interaction considered natural and commonsensical.

Keep in mind that society is governed by more than its laws and physical arrangements. Society is also governed by widely held expectations and values that set the boundaries and standards for individual behavior. Many things that people can do are not against the law but are considered inappropriate, distasteful, or shameful. Most people's daily lives are far more limited and confined by their concern for others' views of them than by the official rules of the law.

Who then sets these informal expectations and values? Partly they are the product of history, a legacy of the accumulation of past values and viewpoints, but the past cannot carry forward in time, through such informal means, as it can through formal structures, such as laws and architecture, that stand apart from living people. Informal social values and expectations are either taught, that is communicated from one person to another, or learned through direct experience interacting with others and modelling one's behavior on what seems successful in others or that proves successful through trial and error.

White supremacy was a system that extended far beyond the formal codes and clauses of law books. Rather, its true force was felt as a social system of everyday expectations and unstated rules of etiquette. Such unwritten rules were reinforced by the economic and political power white communities monopolized.

For example, after the Civil War middle class and elite white families across the nation employed black domestic servants. By 1920, domestic service was the leading category of non-farm employment among black Americans. Part of the expectation of service was that black servants make themselves as invisible as possible and, more importantly, avoid seeming to scrutinize or observe their employers. As one white socialite recalled, "Blacks, I realized, were simply invisible to most white people, except as a pair of hands offering a drink on a silver tray."

Likewise, southern whites for generations expected all black people to cast their eyes downward when speaking to them; making direct eye contact was considered impudent and disrespectful. In this way white expectations served to make black people invisible, neither seen or seeing.

Our roles and identities don't just exist, they exist because we act them out, we behave according to the expectations others have of those roles and identities. Shakespeare understood this four hundred years ago when he famously wrote the line, "All the world's a stage, And all the men and women merely players; They have their exits and their entrances, And one man in his time plays many parts…" We are not just who we are, we are who we perform we are. This does not mean that we all simply fall into playing the customary roles and relationships we find ourselves in, but it does influence our behavior as the degree to which we fulfill the expectations of others in any situation then becomes a conscious choice of conformity or acting against type.

ADDRESSING IMPLICIT BIAS IN THE EARLY CHILDHOOD SYSTEM

By Linda K. Smith, Deputy Assistant Secretary for Early Childhood Development and Shantel Meek, PhD, Senior Advisor for Early Childhood Development, U.S. Department of Health and Human Services

The early childhood field has its roots in social justice. Whether it's fighting for more resources and access to services for our most vulnerable children and their families, or advocating for fair compensation and better workplace conditions for child care providers, our field has always acted on doing what's right. Last month, at our annual State and Territory Child Care Administrator Meeting, Dr. Walter Gilliam from Yale, presented a new set of research findings that have given our field a new cause to take on: implicit bias.

In his experimental study, Dr. Gilliam asked early educators to watch a video of children in a classroom and press a button each time they saw a "behavior that may become a potential challenge". The video included four children- a black boy and girl and a white boy and girl engaged in a small group activity. In reality, the video had no challenging behaviors in it. Using an eye tracking device, the research team measured where teachers were looking on the screen. Findings revealed that teachers spent significantly more time looking at the black boy in the video, than any other child.

This research may shed some light on the stubborn disparities we see in expulsion and suspension practices. If early educators are scrutinizing black boys more- looking at them more, expecting more challenging behavior from them- we may expect they may find it, or in some cases think they've found it, even if objectively it is not there. So, while this study is only one study, we interpret it in the context expulsion and suspension data, and in the context of the research that has studied implicit bias in K12 settings.

More than 10 years ago, Dr. Gilliam's research found that expulsions happens at high rates in our world, and

that the early childhood system isn't immune to the racial disparities that plague exclusionary discipline in K12 settings. Indeed, he found that black preschool-aged boys were much more likely to suffer from these harsh disciplinary practices. A couple years ago, the Federal government published its own data on preschool suspensions for the first time. The results were remarkably similar. Though black boys made up 18% of preschool enrollment, they made up 48% of preschoolers who had been suspended. New Federal data released just this year, again, show that the numbers haven't moved. While black children make up 19% of enrollment, they make up 47% of suspensions. This year's data also reveal that black girls make up 20% of the female preschool population, but 54% of all preschool girls suspended.

Of course, when we see such pervasive and long lasting disparities, many of us consider the possibility of bias in the system. Dr. Gilliam's research is important because it provides us with the first set of data that explicitly finds implicit bias in the educators and directors who work in our early childhood programs. While it is exceedingly disturbing that bias, which is pervasive across all systems, is also present in our early childhood programs, it is not surprising.

All of us have biases- no matter what our profession, no matter where we live, or where we're from. We are all exposed to a society that is full of implicit biases—biases of all kinds. In fact, research shows that while explicit bias has decreased in our country over time, implicit bias has remained stable. And it is instilled in us at very early ages. For example, research shows that children as young as 7 begin to show implicit racial biases. One study found that when 5- 7- and 10- year-olds were asked to rate their own pain and the pain of others, 7- and 10- year-olds rated black children as feeling less pain than others.

So, at the end of the day, the question is not whether or not we have bias. The question is how we can address it. During his presentation Dr. Gilliam said there are two types of people-- people with implicit biases who are willing to acknowledge them and address them, and people with implicit biases who turn away and are unwilling to acknowledge them. I'm confident that the people who make up our field- us included- are the former. I know that for the vast majority of our field, the implicit biases we have are not consistent with the principles or world views we ascribe to. They are not consistent with who we aspire to be as individuals, or as a field. Addressing this difficult issue head on is at the very foundation of who we are as a field. This is a challenge that we must work through together....

https://www.acf.hhs.gov/ecd/resource/addressing-implicit-bias-in-the-early-childhood-system

INTERIM REPORT OF THE PRESIDENT'S TASKFORCE ON 21ST CENTURY POLICING

U.S. Department of Justice, 2015

[Note: This report was removed from the U.S. Department of Justice website sometime in 2017.]

...In light of the recent events that have exposed rifts in the relationships between local police and the communities they protect and serve, on December 18, 2014, President Barack Obama signed an Executive Order establishing the Task Force on 21st Century Policing.

In establishing the task force, the President spoke of the distrust that exists between too many police departments and too many communities—the sense that in a country where our basic principle is equality under the law, too many individuals, particularly young people of color, do not feel as if they are being treated fairly.

"When any part of the American family does not feel like it is being treated fairly, that's a problem for all of us," said the President. "It's not just a problem for some. It's not just a problem for a particular community or a particular demographic. It means that we are not as strong as a country as we can be. And when applied to the criminal justice system, it means we're not as effective in fighting crime as we could be."....

Building trust and nurturing legitimacy on both sides of the police/citizen divide is not only the first pillar of this task force's report but also the foundational principle underlying this inquiry into the nature of relations between law enforcement and the communities they serve. For the last two decades, policing has become more effective, better equipped, and better organized to tackle crime. Despite this, Gallup polls show the public's confidence in police work has remained flat, and among some populations of color, confidence has declined. This decline is in addition to the fact that nonwhites have always had less confidence in law enforcement than whites, likely because "the poor and people of color have felt the greatest impact of mass incarceration," such that for "too many poor citizens and people of color, arrest and imprisonment have become an inevitable and seemingly unavoidable part of the American experience." Decades of research and practice support the premise that people are more likely to obey the law when they believe that those who are enforcing it have the legitimate authority to tell them what to do. But the public confers legitimacy only on those whom they believe are acting in procedurally just ways....

There are both internal and external aspects to procedural justice in policing agencies. Internal procedural justice refers to practices within an agency and the relationships officers have with their colleagues and leaders... External procedural justice focuses on the ways officers and other legal authorities interact with the public and how the characteristics of those interactions shape the public's trust of the police. It is important to understand that a key component of external procedural justice—the practice of fair and impartial policing—is built on understanding and acknowledging human biases, both explicit and implicit.

All human beings have biases or prejudices as a result of their experiences, and these biases influence how they might react when dealing with unfamiliar people or situations. An explicit bias is a conscious bias about certain populations based upon race, gender, socioeconomic status, sexual orientation, or other attributes. Common sense shows that explicit bias is incredibly damaging to police-community relations, and there is a growing body of research evidence that shows that implicit bias—the biases people are not even aware they have—is harmful as well.

Witness Jennifer Eberhardt said,

> Bias is not limited to so-called "bad people." And it certainly is not limited to police officers. The problem is a widespread one that arises from history, from culture, and from racial inequalities that still pervade our society and are especially salient in the context of criminal justice.

To achieve legitimacy, mitigating implicit bias should be a part of training at all levels of a law enforcement organization to increase awareness and ensure respectful encounters both inside the organization and with communities....

The first witnesses...also directly addressed the need for a change in the culture in which police do their work: the use of disrespectful language and the implicit biases that lead officers to rely upon race in the context of stop and frisk. They addressed the need for police officers to find how much they have in common with the people they serve—not the lines of authority they may perceive to separate them—and to continue with enduring programs proven successful over many years.

Several speakers stressed the continuing need for civilian oversight and urged more research into proving ways it can be most effective. And many spoke to the complicated issue of diversity in recruiting, especially Sherrilyn Ifill, who said of youth in poor communities,

> By the time you are 17, you have been stopped and frisked a dozen times. That does not make that 17-year-old want to become a police officer ....The challenge is to transform the idea of policing in communities among young people into something they see as honorable. They have to see people at local events, as the person who lives across the street, not someone who comes in and knows nothing about my community...

The task force heard many different ways of describing a positive culture of policing. David Kennedy suggested there could be a Hippocratic Oath for Policing: First, Do No Harm. Law enforcement officers' goal should be to avoid use of force if at all possible, even when it is allowed by law and by policy. Terms such as fair and impartial policing, rightful policing, Constitutional policing, neighborhood policing, procedural justice, and implicit bias training all address changing the culture of policing. Respectful language; thoughtful and intentional dialogue about the perception and reality of profiling and the mass incarceration of minorities; and consistent involvement, both formal and informal, in community events all help ensure that relationships of trust between police and community will be built. The vision of policing in the 21st century should be that of officers as guardians of human and constitutional rights....

Part Five: Structures of Racism

Part 5: Structures of Racism - Introduction

Our next unit examines aspects of racism and discrimination that are built into the organization and arrangements of our society. We call these features "structures." Just as a building shapes the spaces, functions and movements of the people who inhabit it—you wouldn't normally cook in a bathroom or exit through a window—a social structure also directs how people interact and behave. Society is composed of many structure that shape behavior, some, like laws, police, and courts are an obvious force bounding and influencing behavior, while others, like the lending policies of banks or the admissions standards of universities may exert powers few fully perceive.

Like buildings, social structures can be quite old and even rundown and neglected but still exert their power to control how people use the spaces they occupy. Many social structures were created long ago and some have even been publicly rejected in modern times. But few social structures are ever completely dismantled—even slavery, an institution no longer sanctioned in law or morality, still exists in the form of human trafficking. Old social structures don't die or become obsolete unless they are actively fought by large segments of the population or are replaced by different and more powerful structures.

We will begin by examining the most visible structures of society, the structures that formally govern us, the laws, the government that enacts and enforces them, and the political system that chooses our policymakers. Some scholars have viewed racism as a sort of psychological

Figure 11.1 Scene at Smithland, Kentucky, 1935.

disorder whose roots lie in deep in childhood or in the brain. Such theories are interesting but fail in their ability to explain why racism is more prevalent or vicious at some times and places than others. By focusing on the individual as the primary factor in racial discrimination, such theories miss the larger patterns of interactions among individuals. Such patterns of interaction are called "social" interactions and we generally refer to the sum total of such interactions as "society."

Most people when they try to define 'society' think of it as being synonymous with their nation. They might say that "American Society" consists of a system of democracy, liberty, and a free market. While these elements are important, they are all part of only one of the two primary categories that defines a society. They are all social structures and social structures are only part of the story.

A social structure can take many forms. It can be a set of formal rules of behavior that are enforced by the government that are called laws. It can be a system for establishing or changing those rules, a system we commonly call "government." Or it can be something even more fixed and built into the environment, such as the architecture of an American city that is designed to accommodate people who live in small separate family units rather than large extended families. (Of course the question that follows this observation is which comes first, the nuclear family or the architecture structuring it?) Technology is a powerful social structure that shapes many of the ways people interact—a society that primarily walks from place to place has different social interactions than one that relies on personal automobiles or one that groups people together on trains and buses.

Social structures are all around us. They are built into and expressed through every brick, beam, and tool of our society. Complicating things, they accumulate over time with the succession of ages and their particular technologies and ways of living. We live in both the structures of our own time and the residue of the structures of the past that become imperfectly adapted to the present. In this way the past constantly exerts pressure on the present, mixing the old with the new and resisting change. For example, most American schools close in the summer months, a legacy of the time over a century ago when the majority of Americans were farmers and needed their children's labor during the busiest part of the growing season.

Structures are important to understanding how society works but they aren't the whole story. Structures depend on how they are used and how they are viewed. People can and do use structures in different ways and they can attribute different meanings to them. For example, Labor Day is a social structure in the sense that it is both a custom and a law that mandates that government offices, schools, and many businesses close on the first Monday in September. Originally, Labor Day was generally a day when unions held picnics and grand parades and politicians gave speeches. Today, most Americans use Labor Day as an opportunity to take one last vacation at the end of summer, to enjoy time with their family, or to just relax—the public and political purpose of the holiday is largely forgotten.

Social structures are only as real as their ability to influence human behaviour. In one sense, social structures only exist because people behave as if they do. Laws might seem to exist on paper but those are only words; laws really only exist in the fact that most people observe them. A manager of a business has power because everyone involved plays their appropriate roles as either boss or employee and the public generally observes this arrangement of things as legitimate. Such roles and ways of behaving within them are called "social relations."

While social structures tend to have physical substance—the iron bars of a jail cell, the cement of a highway, the print on a dollar bill—social relations only exist in the moment, the moment when two or more humans interact with each other. Otherwise they live only as ideas in people's minds. Of course, most ideas that underlay social relationships are very powerful and deeply held, so much so that most people think of these relationships as "natural" rather than being something that varies from society to society and from one historical time to another.

By distinguishing social structures from social relations, a peculiar characteristic of social structures becomes evident. Social structures are formed by the social relations that were customary and influential at the time of their creation. But once created, social structures also influence and define future social relations. In other words, they have a two-sided nature: they are both the product of one moment in time and a force in another. Social structures always bear the imprint of their making and generally act as force perpetuating that stamp upon society. Sometimes very old or powerful structures continue to exert force upon society even after they are replaced or destroyed by other social structures.

This is particularly true in considering the social structures that have upheld racism in America. Both slavery and government-mandated racial segregation were long-lived social structures that were eventually destroyed, the one by war and the other by a broad social reform movement. But because each of these social structures served to limit the scope of opportunities for black Americans and expand those for whites over many generations, even after these structures were toppled they left a society arranged in terms of white and black.

Chapter Eleven: Economics of Inequality

The Meritocratic Principle

In 1776, Thomas Jefferson wrote the words that seemed to expressed the core principles of the new American republic. "We hold these truths to be self-evident, that all men are created equal, that they are endowed by their Creator with certain unalienable Rights, that among these are Life, Liberty and the pursuit of Happiness." Jefferson wrote these words in a Philadelphia boarding house, perhaps while being served tea by one of his many slaves.

Jefferson said that "all men are created equal," in other words that they possessed equal rights—an equal chance to make the most of their lives, not that all people should in fact be equal. Most Americans still believe this. Many believe that inequality is acceptable to most people because they believe that in this country everyone, no matter what their inherited circumstances, has the opportunity to rise and be successful. Sure, some people get a better start because of their wealth or family connections, but no one is held back arbitrarily like in the past. Those who linger in poverty do so because they lack the ambition, energy, and intelligence to make a better life for themselves. Some children may live in squalor out of no fault of their own—their deadbeat parents are to blame for that—and these deserving poor should be helped out with public benefits and private charity. But the rest have only themselves to blame.

This common way of thinking about poverty and opportunity would be even more prevalent if it weren't for a number of troubling facts that don't fit well with these ideals. As a theory of individual behavior this "meritocratic" argument is quite consistent. If you look hard enough you can usually find some fault in the character of a poor person that can be used to explain the source of their hardship. (Of course, rich people have faults too, though these seem not to be as costly to them.) But the problem is that it is not just individuals who are poor, sick, uneducated, drug-addicted, criminal, or unemployed in America. Some neighborhoods are more plagued by these problems than others. Some groups of people that we identify as races seem more prone to these problems than others.

Here is the problem: Americans also like to believe that they live in a color-blind, multicultural society. In our enlightened age we reject the racist notions of the past, such as the idea that some races are inferior to others. We are repelled at racist stereotypes that some races are more criminal than others, or lazier than others, or dumber than others. We don't like to admit to ourselves that we believe that the color of someone's skin has any more meaning than the color of their eyes. So how then do we explain the fact that black and brown people are many times more likely to live in poverty than whites? Are many times more likely to serve time in jail than whites? Are many times more likely to be unemployed than whites? Score well below whites on virtually all academic achievement tests? Black and brown people in America even have significantly shorter lifespans than whites.

Americans can't have it both ways. They can't believe that they live in both a "meritocracy" where individual talent and effort determine success and a "color-blind" society where race doesn't matter. As a result, most people shy away from even thinking about these racial differences and

Figure 11.2 Man posing as Uncle Sam stands near the White House

disparities. One way to avoid these ideas clashing in the mind is not to think too long or hard about either one. But the fact remains, either race explains these differences by allowing whites to rise above other racial groups according to their different natural abilities, or America is not the land of color-blind equal opportunity that most people believe it to be. In other words, either race or racism explains the world we see around us.

Because today racism is unpopular, uncool, and impolite, few people would openly embrace the explanation that poverty, crime, and many other social problems are the result of racial differences. But it is difficult to see how America could systematically hold back a vast group of people when there are no racial laws, private racial discrimination is outlawed, and compared with the hateful racist attitudes of the past, people today seem quite tolerant and mostly free of prejudice. So how do we explain why race continues to be a very strong predictor of success or failure in America?

How can we decide which factor, race or racism, is the root cause of American inequality? Most Americans would agree that the nation failed to live up to its principles of equality while it grew rich upon slavery and the dispossession of native peoples. But when did the United States of America fulfill its promise of "liberty for all"? When slavery was abolished with the Thirteenth Amendment to the Constitution in 1865? When racist Jim Crow laws were declared unconstitutional by the Supreme Court in 1954? When Congress finally outlawed housing discrimination in 1968? When a black man was elected president in 2008? Or not yet?

While the majority of the poor in America are white, black people are twice as likely to be poor than whites. Roughly a quarter of black Americans live under the poverty line compared with ten percent of whites. There are two factors that drive this wedge between the lives of people who are divided by their skin and features. The first is income, the amount of money someone earns in a given period of time. Alongside but distinct from income is wealth, the sum of all things of value a person possesses such as a house, a car, or a bank account, minus any debts one owes. While both of these factors reflect both current practices and structures of discrimination, wealth is, to a far greater extent, a legacy of the past.

Income data for 2015 shows that black workers earn on average 75% of the wages of white workers. White men's median hourly wage was $21, compared to just $15 for black men and $14 for Latinos. The income gap is smaller among women: white women make an average of $17 compared to the $13 an hour black women earn, and $12 an hour that Latinas do. This large gap in income between racial groups has been stubbornly consistent for more than 40 years. In the early 1970s that gap between whites and blacks, or Latinos, was nearly identical to today in percentage terms. As the U.S. Census Bureau put it in the driest of prose: "Between 1972 and 2015, the changes in the Black to non-Hispanic White income ratio and the Hispanic to non-Hispanic White income ratio were not statistically significant." Then black men earned 73% of what white men earned, the same figure as that for 2015, and Latinos earned 71%, two points higher than the 69% mark of 2015.

Among those who do have a job, the gap between the quality and pay of jobs held by whites and black is very wide. In 2012, 88% of all "Executive/Senior Level Officials & Managers" jobs were held by whites compared with less than 3% (2.93) for blacks and 3.65% of hispanics. Nearly three-quarters (74.2%) of all "Professional" jobs were held by whites, while only 7.5% of blacks and 5.4% of Hispanics. Looking at these numbers differently, one-third of all white jobs are either "Executive" or "Professional" while only one-quarter are "Operatives," "Laborers," or "Service Workers." In contrast, nearly half of all blacks (48.3%) and Hispanics (53%) work in these low paid occupations while only one-in-ten (11%) blacks and one-in-twelve Hispanics (8.6%) possess the power executive and professional jobs.

Governments are generally considered to be the fairest employers due to their generally stricter policies against employment discrimination and generally tougher enforcement of them. Nevertheless, employment disparities are wide and obvious among government employees as well. In a 2011 survey, the median salary all black government employees was 15% lower than the median salary of all white government employees ($49,118 vs. $41,739).

The question of why income continues to be so widely differentiated by race is a very important one. Scholars have looked at various factors but most appear to be related to the legacies of past discrimination and white privileges. Families that have resources to begin with have a much better chance of accumulating more than those without. No group in America has historically been blocked from accumulating wealth more than African Americans and these historical legacies continue to have effects. Secondly, income at the highest levels is built on social networks—who do you know often determines who gets in the door. Country clubs, ivy league colleges, board rooms, etc., continue to be largely white social networks.

One of the most common myths about the origins of economic inequality is that economic discrimination is only a system of exclusion. Most everyone, at least in public, now agrees that outright racial discrimination in hiring, promoting, or compensating individuals is wrong and should be prohibited. Few people, however, recognize that this is only one side of inequality. In America, where most businesses are privately owned and most of these important decisions come to down the decision of a single individual, there is also the inequality that is produced by unfairly positive judgements. As one researcher put it, "All that is necessary to maintain, if not create, disparities in any number of outcomes is for members of the dominant, high-status group to trust, cooperate, and work for the betterment of their ingroup more than for outgroups."

A survey of nearly 1000 human resource managers across the United States found that the most common "ethical" problem in their organizations was employment on the basis of favoritism. Best estimates are that about half of all job openings in the United States are filled without ever being advertised.

This form of discrimination, called, "In-group Favoritism," is a more insidious force maintaining racial (and sexual and other) inequities because it is less public than formal exclusion, often working through private social networks that lend their in-group members social advantages. Moreover, because many people historically privileged by racial inequality have come to expect these advantages, they appear to them normal, even invisible and are often not even perceived as anything other than deserved. Language, and the thought patterns that language breeds, encourages such perception because most common definitions of the words 'discrimination' and 'prejudice' point to negative bias and exclusion against others, not positive bias or excessive inclusion of others, though both are equally discriminations and prejudices. Similarly, essayist Tim Wise points out that the English language has words for being "underprivileged" but not for being "overprivileged" though one condition cannot exist without the other (note: my spell checker just flagged my use of the word 'overprivileged' as an error).

It is in the area of wealth where the racial differences in America are most striking. Today, on average, white families possess nearly twenty times the wealth of black families in America. A 2013 survey of household wealth found that white families possessed average wealth of $144,200 compared with $11,200 for black families. This extreme gap between white and black wealth has been a pattern throughout American history and because wealth has a tendency to accumulate and persist across generations, the longevity of this gap has worsened it.

Disparities in wealth are only partially a result of the differing employment profiles of white and black Americans. The unemployment rate for blacks has consistently been two times or more the rate for whites over the last fifty years. Since 2008, the black unemployment rate has exceeded the average national unemployment rate during the Great Depression of the 1930s. But these trends are relatively new. In 1948, the unemployment rate for black teens was lower than that for white teens. Sixty years later, black teens were unemployed at a rate double that of white teens.

Much, if not most, of the wealth disparity that can be seen today was not the result of impersonal forces like the labor market or the ups and downs of the overall economy, nor was it mostly the result of individual acts of prejudice and discrimination. Rather, the great gulf between the wealth of whites and people of color in America is the direct result of conscious and deliberate public policies intended to increase the wealth of white families and to bypass all others. America's racial class structure in the twenty-first century is the result of more than a century of government welfare and public subsidies for whites that excluded black and brown citizens, though they had to pay for them through their taxes like everyone else.

In order to fully understand the origins and reasons for these vast disparities in income and wealth, two prongs of explanation need to be pursued. One fork follows the bitter history of employment and educational discrimination that has drawn a color bar across the labor market, placing the highest paid and most stable jobs beyond the reach of people of color. The other fork leads to public policies that have disproportionately funnelled government benefits to whites turning the state into an engine of unequal wealth creation. We will begin at the point that 90% of black Americans entered the free labor market, with the destruction of slavery.

PART ONE: DRAWING THE COLOR BAR

There can be no doubt that experiencing slavery left people with few resources with which to survive, let alone build wealth, in a competitive market economy. While all black people in America experienced intense discrimination, those who had lived in freedom were better suited than those bound by chains after the war. In 1870, nearly two-thirds of the black adult men born in freedom could read and write. Of those born in slavery, the rate was 13%. The average freeborn black man owned $436 in property while his counterpart who suffered slavery could claim only $116.

Such statistics are not surprising given what is known about the brutal poverty of slavery. What is surprising is the fact that in the face of overwhelming oppression, both on the part of their own state and local governments and from their white neighbors, black workers somehow managed to rise over the next generation. Nationally, black income was less than a quarter that of white income when the Civil War ended. By 1900, this gap had closed significantly, with black income more than a third of white income. In fact, by virtually every measure, literacy, land ownership, and wealth, this was a generation that advanced against all odds.

Convict Leasing and Forced Labor

As soon as political power was retaken by traditional white leaders, the entire machinery of the state was oriented to serve their needs. What Southern elites most desired was a cheap, pliant labor force, just the opposite of the trends at work since emancipation. Most freedmen and freedwomen were struggling to gain independence by leasing land rather than working for wages on another's farm. Many southern states made tenants easily exploited by landlords by passing laws granting landlords the right to take possession of a tenant's entire crop, sell it on whatever terms he wished, and pay back only the remainder after keeping the rent.

Most significantly, the criminal justice system was converted from incarcerating criminals in the interest of public safety to creating them in the service of private gain. Within months of the reestablishment of white rule in South Carolina, the state assembly passed a bill authorizing the leasing of convicts to private bidders. Florida went a step further and simply closed its state prisons to force convicts to be leased out.

Local sheriffs began rounding up black men and charging them with vagrancy, a crime whose penalties were increased so they could be then be leased to local farmers and contractors. States made it a crime to leave one's employment before the stated term of service was complete—usually a year in most cases. State governments moved to make this more difficult by passing laws criminalizing not being able to pay back loans or keep up leases. Most southern states began revising their criminal codes to increase the penalties for minor crimes so as to fill the chain gangs and leased labor crews their economies increasingly relied upon. Many went so far as to expand the definition of grand larceny to include the theft of anything worth more than $10 and imposing a sentence of five years at hard labor. Mississippi's Leasing Act of 1875 specified that only those facing a sentence of ten years or more were to be sent to the state prison in Jackson and all others were to be leased locally.

In Virginia, many of the convicts in the state prison were leased out to build the Chesapeake and Ohio Railroad in 1871, a line that was then digging and blasting its way through the Blue Ridge mountains. According to one careful study of burial records at the prison, over less than a two year span, of 380 mostly black convicts leased to the railroad, one-third were killed on the job. Many convicts were leased to mining companies and forced to dig coal

Figure 11.3 Georgia convicts working on a road in Oglethorpe County, May 1941.

and ore. Convict workers were treated as slaves had been: frequently beaten for falling behind in their work or failing to meet their daily quotas. One mine used a leather strap for this purpose that was called the "negro regulator."

Southern states usually didn't lease white men to private interests but kept them in penitentiaries where they could be "rehabilitated," often trained to learn new skills in prison woodworking and carpentry shops. Black men were usually designated for leasing outside the prison.

For five years after the war, the state of Tennessee contracted to lease convicts in a Nashville factory that manufactured an array of farming hardware including plows, mowers, wagons, and saddles. While it lasted this deal was a boon for the employer who paid only 43 cents per day per worker and the state paid all the convicts' meager costs for food, shelter, and guarding. Prison officials developed a lower cost system by 1871 that sold convicts to brokers for a yearly fee. Brokers found jobs for the men they purchased and profited in the margin between the wages they earned and the least possible expenses they could incur to keep them alive and productive. By 1886, sales of convicts brought the leading states of Tennessee and Alabama over $100,000 in profit each year while saving their treasuries the expense of imprisonment that would have cost $250,000 per year.

In Tennessee, black convicts helped construct many miles of railroads and were put to work in the many coal mines that spread across the eastern mountains. Mining companies found that black convicts were not only a particularly cheap labor supply, but they drove down free miners wages by making it harder for unions to threaten to strike. By mixing black convicts and free miners in the same mine, coal companies were able to constantly threaten unions that if they struck the mine had a ready backup source of labor in men who had no freedom to leave their jobs. The president of the Tennessee Coal, Iron, and Railroad Company, Arthur St. Clair Colyar, who had run coal companies with enslaved workers before the war, celebrated the use of convicts, "...we found that we were right in calculating that the free laborers would be loath to enter upon strikes when they saw that the company was amply provided with convict labor."

Few detailed descriptions of the day-to-day conditions that convict workers faced have been left to history. It is generally known that food was meager and convicts were forced to sleep two to a bunk. In 1877 Tennessee's legislature passed a law to limit the brutality of guards by requiring each camp to designate a single guard as the "whipping boss" who would be responsible for all beatings. The overall statistics paint a grim picture of their lives. Alabama's prison inspector reported a death rate of greater than 10% per year in that state's labor camps.

Convict leasing was particularly important to southern states as their main function as governments was policing and repressing their black populations. By the 1880s and 1890s, policing and punishment were the main expenses of southern states, consuming 20% of all state funds, more than the combined cost of education, healthcare, pensions, and the expenses of maintaining state facilities. While only 5% of Tennessee's state prisoners were black before the Civil War, by 1891 three-quarters were. Most of these prisoners had been convicted for petty theft, such as stealing a chicken, a pig, or a wood rail; a crime that carried up to a five year prison term.

Still, though convict leasing proved lucrative for both states and private employers, it victimized a comparatively small proportion of the population. Far more extensive was the system of peonage, a type of debt slavery, whereby individuals were trapped into a continuous cycle of debt followed by servitude to pay off the debt, that rarely ended.

Peonage

When white landed interests retook control of state governments in the South in the 1870s, they pushed for measures that would limit the freedom of workers to bargain for higher wages. Southern states passed laws criminalizing "enticement," which was when an employer offered the employee of another firm a higher wage. Combined with laws that made it a criminal act to leave one's employer if a worker owed that boss money, such measures took away the simplest and most direct right a worker has, to quit and leave.

Information is power, just as knowledge is power and white southerners took great care to restrict it. Northern black newspapers were routinely intercepted and discarded by local postmasters, a practice that dated back to state laws passed in the 1830s and 1840s making it a crime to distribute abolitionist literature and empowering postal officials to confiscate subversive literature. Black workers largely depended on word of mouth to find about job opportunities, especially when those prospects were in other states.

For the most part, most workers seeking a better job depended on labor recruiters who were paid commissions to find hands for large farming operations or industrial concerns, like timber and mining companies. These recruiters would travel throughout the South, often providing not only information but train tickets and cash advances. In 1873, after labor recruiters helped over 20,000 poor laborers in Georgia to secure work in other states, Georgia's planters and bosses feared they may have to raise their wages to compete, so they instead used their control over the government to pass a law that they hoped would effectively prohibit recruiters from operating in their state. Georgia's

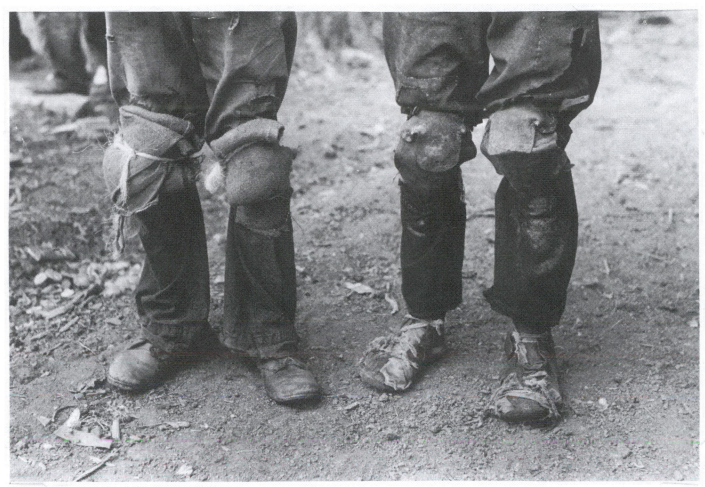

Figure 11.4 Cotton Pickers with Knee Pads, Lehi, Arkansas, 1938.

"anti-emigrant agent law" simply required all agents to register with the state and pay an annual license fee. However, the fee was set at $100 per county. With 159 counties Georgia required a fee that most agents couldn't pay. When one intrepid agent actually paid the fee and boldly continued to recruit in the face of death threats, Georgia raised the fee to $500 per county. North Carolina didn't make the same mistake and just set its initial emigrant agent license fee at $1000 per county.

Collusion between corrupt local officials and wealthy farmers produced a system in many areas where black men and women would be arrested on trumped up charges, then bailed out of jail by farmers who would force them to labor to work off the bail debt. As leaving a place of employment if a debt was owed was also a crime in many southern states, if these workers left their labor camps they would be hunted down by local police and returned at gunpoint. In 1901, Samuel M. Clyatt was making his usual run back to his turpentine operation after purchasing a number of men from a Florida sheriff when one of the men escaped from the back of his locked truck. Clyatt was later prosecuted in federal court, but with a well-financed legal team supported by contributions from timber and farm trade as-

sociations, he successfully appealed his case all the way to the Supreme Court.

Clyatt and his wealthy backers hoped to win a ruling that would declare Congress' 1867 Anti-Peonage law unconstitutional, thereby allowing them to continue or even expand their human trafficking. In *Clyatt v. U.S.* (1905), the high court upheld the power of Congress to pass such a law on the strength of section two of the 13th Amendment, but it ruled that Clyatt was wrongfully convicted because the man he purchased escaped before he actually performed any labor, therefore, he hadn't actually been subjected to peonage.

Federal investigators were surprised at the extent of such peonage rings. Upon looking into reports of a few men being held against their will in southern Alabama, investigators found evidence that thousands of sharecroppers and laborers were held against their will by dozens of large landowners in virtual slavery. One Georgia lawyer, retained to locate some missing boys, found one on a farm in Dadeville, Alabama and purchased him for $25 cash and another working at a sawmill in Jackson's Gap. The latter boy's freedom cost $48.

Courts had declared the practice illegal but refused to

Figure 11.5 Labor protesters, Jan. or Feb. 1930.

impose penalties harsh enough to deter wealthy business-men from engaging in the practice. As long as large southern farming operations depended upon large amounts of labor that they did not care to pay market wages for, peonage continued to flourish. Understaffed U.S. Attorney's offices could do little more than document the extent of the problem while political leaders in Washington turned a blind eye to the issue entirely. In 1907 the Justice Department reported 83 pending peonage cases on its case list.

Sharecroppers, farmers who rented their land and received advances of seeds, fertilizer and other goods prior to planting in exchange for giving the bulk of their crops to the landlord at harvest time, were typically caught in a cycle of dependence and poverty due to southern states laws criminalizing unpaid debts. Account ledgers were kept by landlords who also marketed the crops providing great financial incentives to lie and cheat their tenants. Landlords would carefully calculate how much money they needed to advance to make sure their tenants would still owe a debt at the end of the year.

Not until 1911, would a case testing state 'false pretenses laws,' laws that criminalized not having the ability to pay back a loan, reach the Supreme Court. In *Bailey v. Alabama*, the question turned on whether Alabama's debt peonage law was a violation of the Thirteenth Amendment's prohibition of "involuntary servitude." In that state, sheriffs would take black debtors, rivet iron manacles and chains on their legs, and lease them out to the highest bidder to pay back the debt. They were forced to work under the threat of beatings from a "whipping boss" who wielded a three-foot leather strap.

Lonzo Bailey was a farm worker who agreed to work on the Scott's Bend plantation for a year for the sum of about 35 cents a day. As a bonus, the labor contractor for the plantation paid Bailey his first month's wages in advance. Bailey worked for a month and a few days and quit, leaving about five dollars of his advance unearned. Bailey was arrested and sentenced to forced labor for 136 days.

Word of Bailey's arrest reached Booker T. Washington who quietly hired an attorney and bankrolled Bailey's legal appeals all the way to the Supreme Court.

Seven of the nine justices voted to overturn this system of forced labor, the two dissenters included Oliver Wendell Holmes, Jr., who notoriously seemed to always take the side of the powerful against the oppressed. Holmes fumed against the majority for weakening the protections given to employers, "it certainly would affect the terms of the bargain unfavorably for the laboring man if it were understood that the employer could do nothing in case the laborer saw fit to break his word." Most southern states responded to the court ruling by scrubbing such "false pretenses" laws from their books, Florida and Georgia clung to their antiquated laws until the 1940s when subsequent appeals court cases forced them to abandon them.

Though such systems of forced labor were weakened by federal courts, the exploitation of sharecroppers by white planters continued as usual. Black sharecroppers were regularly cheated by landlords who manipulated the cost of the seeds, fertilizer, and tools they loaned at planting and the prices they received for crops at harvest. In the Jim Crow South, black sharecroppers had little ability to take their grievances to civil courts and had few options but to take whatever terms were offered.

Black farmers who challenged the system of debt servitude were met with overwhelming violence. When World War One caused a spike in the price of the cotton they were growing, the sharecroppers of Phillips County, Arkansas, organized a union and demanded higher credits for their crops from their landlords. Some of the union's leaders had just returned home from Europe's battlefields and having fought German armies and were not afraid to challenge white planters. In late September, 1919, the sharecroppers union, the Progressive Farmers and Household Union of America, met in a local church and were fired upon during their meeting. Union members returned fire and killed one of the whites who ambushed them.

Alarmed at this act of armed self-defense, local authorities deputized hundreds of men from surrounding counties, local planters formed their own posses, and the all-white veteran's organization, the American Legion, called its membership to arms. These forces ransacked through the countryside, torturing and killing any African Americans they could lay their hands on. More cowardly attackers sniped at blacks from the windows of automobiles. White vigilantes dragged the bodies of their victims through the streets of the town Elaine, Arkansas. No official count was made of the number of black men and women killed that week, but historians estimate that as many as two hundred people were murdered. No whites were charged with any crimes but hundreds of black men were thrown into jail and tortured until they signed confessions. These confessions were used to indict 73 black men for the murders of the five white men who were shot and killed, mostly in self-defense. All-white juries deliberated for just a few minutes before condemning twelve men to death and sentencing the others to long prison terms.

Though white journalists showed little interest in questioning the condemnation of twelve black farmers in Phillips County, Arkansas, the brilliant journalist and investigator, Ida B. Wells, courageously exposed the story and with Walter White of the NAACP, organized a legal defense of the "Elaine 12." NAACP attorneys secured affidavits proving that the convicted men's confessions had been obtained while being beaten, strangled, and tortured with electric shocks. In 1923, the U.S. Supreme Court, for the first time, ruled that their trial was unfair because it was conducted in a mob atmosphere, or as the chief justice described it, "counsel, jury and judge were swept to the fatal end by an irresistible tide of public passion..."

The fearful exploitation of black sharecroppers was exposed again during the great flood of 1927. In that year unusually heavy rains combined with an early snow melt pushed the Mississippi river over its banks for miles inland, from Missouri to the delta, in what was the worst flood disaster in United States history. Besides sweeping away thousands of homes and other structures, the flood momentarily disrupted the unfree labor system that characterized farming across a half-dozen states.

Black farmers and sharecroppers were at first largely left to their own devices by rescuers who selectively plucked whites and mules from the rising waters before saving black families. River waters remained above flood stage for four months and during that time tens of thousands of homeless black farm families were forcibly gathered into Red Cross camps in Arkansas and Mississippi. Pressured by wealthy white farmers, who worried that the flood would provide an opportunity for their tenants to flee their customary debt bondage, state officials turned the Red Cross camps into prison camps. Armed guards patrolled the camp perimeters, protesters and those refusing to labor were beaten. Camp inmates were forced to wear tags that included both their name, and the name of the landlord who owned their debts. Refugees were only permitted to leave if they were returning to the plantation or property of their landlord.

A few determined men and women managed to escape and one man who had fled to Memphis told an investigator:

> Year after year I have raised the best crops I could and spent as little for supplies as I could. I have never complained though I knowed he wasn't treating me right. But when the flood came and I had to wade in water up to my neck holding my grandchildren high over my head to save them, I appeald to this white man to help me save my family and he said to me "don't bring your troubles to me." I will never go back to Arkansas again.

Classical Economics and Racism

According to classical economic theory, the nature of the competitive market should work against racial discrimination in employment. Generally speaking, employers have two, usually contradictory, interests. They want to pay the lowest rate of wages they can to recruit and retain their workforce, but they also want to hire the most productive workers for a given job. These two goals often sit on opposite sides of the teeter-totter; low wages usually means less committed, less productive workers, while more productive workers generally cost more to hire, retain, or to make productive in the first place.

For any particular wage an employer is willing to offer, their chance of hiring the most productive and skilled worker is a function of the size of the pool of workers available. Just like picking sides for a pickup game of soccer, choosing players from a group of 100 will probably field a more talented team than choosing eleven from a group of 15. In economic terms, as the labor market increases (the size of the group the employer can choose from), the lower the cost of labor and/or the higher the average productivity. This means that anything an employer does to arbitrarily reduce and limit the labor market will cost them money in the end. Drawing a bar of color or sex across the door to the employment office simply doesn't make economic sense.

However, there are special circumstances that can limit these additional costs to an employer. For example, if all employers in a particular market behave in this way, all of them will suffer the same additional costs and none will gain a competitive advantage over the others, and this inefficient arrangement can continue indefinitely. Racial exclusivity also allowed employers to use the excluded group as a strategic reserve; the existence of a group that could be recruited at any moment gave employers leverage over their workers and gave them the edge in fighting off unions. One manager of a southern iron foundry, who employed a token number of black molders in his shop in 1901, when asked why he hired any black men, responded, "If a white man gets 'cocky,' it does seem good to ask how he would like to see a nigger get his job." One of the more astute observers of labor economics in the early twentieth century, John R. Commons, noted about the same time, "almost the only device and symptom of originality displayed by American employers in disciplining their labor force has been that of playing one race against another."

Workers have the opposite economic interests. Wages generally go up as the labor market shrinks and because of this logic, trade unions have a greater interest in limiting access to jobs than expanding it. As a result, most trade unions, for much of the history of the labor movement, have struggled to keep women and people of color out of their industries.

Economists refer to this situation as a "split labor market." A "split labor market," as defined by labor economist Edna Bonacich, is one in which two or more groups of workers command different rates of wages for the same work. Applying this theory to the generally lower pay of immigrants at the turn of the century, Bonacich explained that the cause of immigrant workers "cheapness" was not intrinsic to their cultural or genetic character (as labor unions charged), but was a function of the relative level of wages in their country of origin. As she pointed out, workers can be induced to immigrate when the marginal return on their labor merely exceeds that of their homeland. Therefore, the poorer the home economy of the immigrant, the lower the wages that were necessary to recruit their labor.

For American workers, differences in wages by race and ethnicity were a reflection of the varying opportunities and power each group had in society. In addition to being influenced by the size of the labor market, wages were also affected by how much it costs to attract workers away from alternative employments. Workers who had a variety of options and opportunities to pursue required a wage higher than those alternatives to lure them into the job. Thus, wages were not only set by supply and demand, but they were pushed down or lifted up by the relative social power and freedom a group enjoyed. The existence of vast rural poverty, racist criminal codes, Jim Crow segregation, political disenfranchisement, and lynch law terrorism, drove down wages for black Americans throughout the South, as these oppressions swallowed up most opportunities and left few alternatives to any job at any wage.

Economic theory does not take into account the fact that employers need not actually understand the true nature of their own situation. Like the workers they hire, they were just human, subject to all the follies and misunderstandings that humans can fall prey to. White factory owners and businessmen were subject to the same stereotypes and prejudices that all white Americans were and viewed their workers through the lens of race. Mislead by their bigotry, they usually failed to appreciate the potential of the men and women they excluded from employment, unable to see beyond the fictional image of Sambo, Mammy, the Chinaman, the Mexican, or the Indian savage.

In an often cited 1991 study of Chicago employers, researchers found that employers commonly made hiring decisions on the basis of racist stereotypes of young black men as being lazy, unreliable, and difficult to manage. So surprisingly open were the dozens of employers researchers interviewed about their racial preferences, that they wrote, "we were overwhelmed by the degree to which Chicago employers felt comfortable talking with us—in a situation where the temptation would be to conceal rather than reveal—in a negative manner about blacks."

As already noted, in spite of the black community's steady loss of political power in the last third of the nineteenth century, and in the face of a growing movement towards racial segregation, it did just what Booker T. Washington had long urged them to do, it pulled itself up by its own bootstraps. By the 1890s, black workers had made inroads in the textile, steel, and railroad industries, the three most technologically advanced and growing areas of the New South economy. One in five textile workers were black in the 1890s. A growing proportion of the labor force in Birmingham, Alabama's steel furnaces were black. Black firemen and trainmen were a common sight on southern railroads. Rates of business ownership in the black community reached parity with those in the white community by the end of the century. Booker T. Washington commemorated this achievement by founding the National Negro Business League in 1900.

It took both a massive campaign of government repression that was coordinated with the private action of labor unions to interrupt this economic progress. While labor unions and governments were typically enemies, they somehow found common cause in working to exclude black workers from good jobs. The Amalgamated Association of Iron and Steel Workers made no progress in organizing Birmingham's mills until its chief demand was drawing a color bar between low-paying menial jobs and better-paying skilled ones reserved for whites alone. Textile unions did not protest the passage of state laws requiring the segregation of factories, but used them to drive black workers out of higher-paying, more secure jobs. Even when the nation's largest union, the American Federation of Labor (AFL), hired two black organizers to work in the South, they were instructed not to challenge segregation or "local customs."

With the exception of factories in New Orleans, most all of the region's growing garment factories employed only white women for the better paid sewing jobs and only hired a small number of black workers for cleaning or work in the hot and disagreeable pressing department. For the rural white women who made up the bulk of the factory workforce, the steady wages they earned gave them an economic independence few of them had experienced before and, for many, lifted their families out of rural poverty. When the International Ladies Garment Workers Union (ILGWU)

Figure 11.6 AFL Labor Leaders, Timothy Healy, William B. Fitzgerald, William D. Mahon, Hugh Frayne and Louis Fridiger, ca. 1916.

began organizing apparel factories in the South, it did so without challenging the established racist caste system.

As the AFL grew, the number of black skilled workers fell and the gap between the wages paid menial workers and skilled workers increased. By the 1920s, the AFL had succeeded in winning government protections for its members for the first time, most notably with passage of the Railway Labor Act that gave the union government-protected negotiating rights with railroad companies. Railway unions quickly took advantage of this power to push contracts that forced the railroads to preferentially hire and promote white workers. As one union leader publicly stated, "the Negro is an undesirable in our particular vocation [and]...therefore should be supplanted by a white man in all instances." By the time the Supreme Court intervened in 1944 and in *Steele v. Louisville & Nashville Railroad* unanimously ordered unions to represent fairly all their members regardless of their race, the damage had been done. In little more than a decade two-thirds of all black firemen and brakemen had already lost their union jobs.

Outside of the South, where only 10% of black people lived at the dawn of the twentieth century, the situation was not much better in spite of the absence of legally-mandated segregation. In the rapidly growing steel mills of the midwest black workers were limited to low-paying menial jobs. One survey in Pittsburgh done in 1910 found fewer than 500 black workers in mills that employed over 47,000 workers. When the AFL began organizing in that area around World War One, it avoided recruiting black members. Little wonder when the unions launched a coordinated "Great Steel Strike" in 1919, black workers rushed to take the jobs of the very men who had kept them out of the industry.

The strike broke the unions and in the nonunion climate of the 1920s, some black steel workers managed to struggle into skilled positions. But the numbers remained low as management organized its workforce according to racist presumptions. In 1920, nearly three-quarters of all

Figure 11.7 Workers at the Stockham Pipe & Fittings Company, Birmingham, Alabama, ca. 1950.

black steel workers were laborers and only one in twenty-five worked in a skilled trade.

When new, more radical unions were organized in the 1930s, more rhetorical support was given to civil rights and the equality of union brothers and sisters of all colors, but these leadership efforts usually failed to change customs on the ground. The United Steel Workers union (USW) supported national civil rights campaigns while its local unions agreed to contracts that established different and discriminatory promotion ladders and seniority systems for its white and black workers. Occasionally, the union leadership would intervene to squash the most embarrassing displays of racism, as when white steel workers in Lorain, Ohio, struck in 1947 to protest the hiring of three black bricklayer apprentices and the national office forced them back to work. In the end, even progressive unions like the USW only began to seriously address its racist employment and union structures under federal court orders in the 1960s.

Besides simply not accepting them as members, trade unions used a variety of other methods to restrict the ability of black workers to enter better-paying trades and occupations. Trades unions, such as plumbers, masons, electricians, and even barbers, lobbied successfully to have states license their trades. While it might seem odd that unions would demand government regulation of their own trades, it makes sense when the fact that politically well-connected unions could count on having their own leaders appointed to their own governing boards. By requiring anyone who wished to work in a trade to obtain a license, states essentially handed to unions a tremendous power to limit entry into their trades and control their own labor markets.

One of the ways licensing excluded black workers was through the common requirement that a person had to complete a certified apprenticeship before being eligible to work in the trade. As most trade schools excluded black students, and unions that ran their own apprenticeship programs would also refuse to admit blacks, apprenticeships worked to prohibit black workers. Such laws became common in the 1890s but it was not until 1950 that a state supreme court, in this case in Illinois, struck such provisions down for their discriminatory effect.

The impact of these laws was dramatic. By the early twentieth century the skilled building trades unions were nearly all white, though many blacks had worked as carpenters and masons in the nineteenth century. After passage of Ohio's plumber licensing law, unions used the law to drive black plumbers from the industry. By 1910, Cleveland, a city that once had a large number of black tradesmen, counted only five licensed black plumbers.

In 1890, one in five of all the barbers in America were black and it was common for white men to have their hair cut and beards shaved by black barbers. At that time, the AFL Journeymen Barbers Union included 1,000 black members. By 1928, that union had grown overall but its number of black barbers had dwindled to 239 and black barbers, unable to get state licenses, lost their white clientele.

Labor unions' racism forced black workers into an uncomfortable relationship with the labor movement. As workers who had long suffered from the tyranny of their bosses, low pay, and insecure employment, they understood the importance of collective action and worker solidarity. But being systematically excluded or pushed into second class status by most labor organizations, their better interests were served when federal and state courts restricted the power of unions. Unions that became powerful enough to force employers to hire only union members, what is known as the "closed shop," were a dangerous threat to black workers as such power was often used to exclude them entirely. Civil rights organizations walked a fine line, needing the support of labor unions as natural allies but having to lobby against them when the Democratic party moved to enhance their power without also requiring that they treat all their members equally without regard to race or color.

When President Franklin Roosevelt pushed for a federal law that would strengthen the rights of workers to unionize in 1935, Congress passed the Wagner Act, a law that placed unions on a firm legal footing for the first time. The Wagner Act established mechanisms for governmental certification of unions and protection for their right to be the exclusive bargaining agents of their members. With this law, American labor unions suddenly held a degree of power and legal standing they had never enjoyed before. The Wagner Act tripled the proportion of manufacturing workers in unions in just five years.

However, in spite of black leaders mounting a nationwide campaign demanding a nondiscrimination clause be added to the bill, Congress refused to include such a requirement. One of the forces working behind the scenes to kill this amendment was none other than the AFL. Once passed the Wagner Act greatly increased labor unions' power to exclude or discriminate against black and other nonwhite workers.

Armed with this power, white-dominated unions could freely bargain contracts with employers, and in some cases with entire industries, that harmed their own minority members by locking them into lowest rungs of their occupational ladders, segregating them into the dirtiest, lowest-paying, jobs, or simply eliminating them altogether. In Long Island City, New York, armed with these new labor laws, the Brotherhood of Electrical Workers, Local 3, organized a number of electrical supply firms, contracted for a closed shop, and refused to admit the black workers who already worked for those companies to become

Figure 11.8 A. Philip Randolph, 1964.

members. Several dozen black electricians were forced into unemployment. Across the river in Manhattan the Building Services Employees Union forced many hotels, restaurants, and commercial buildings to fire their black service staffs and hire only whites. With NAACP protesters at the doors of the 1934 AFL convention, carrying signs reading "White Unions Make Black Scabs," the national union federation voted down a measure to expel any affiliated "union maintaining a color bar."

World War Two Expands Opportunities

World War Two had a profound impact on the nation's racial employment patterns. As factories strained to fulfill lucrative government contracts for war supplies and millions of young men entered the military, a severe labor shortage temporarily opened some industries to minorities, and to women, long excluded from them. Nevertheless, the old patterns of discrimination remained strong in many sectors of the economy.

Even under the pressure of fulfilling open-ended "cost-plus" guaranteed profit government contracts, many companies refused to employ people of color in any but broom-pushing positions. A. Philip Randolph, a labor organizer who had successfully built up the Brotherhood of Sleeping Car Porters into the largest black led union in America and won a landmark contract from the Pullman Company in 1937, demanded that President Roosevelt take action to establish equal employment opportunities in the war industries. Randolph noted that at that moment the federal government had a unique power to influence the business world, the power of government contracts. All Roosevelt had to do was insert in federal contracts the requirement that they be fulfilled without racial discrimination and the government would hold a lever that could shift practices throughout the economy. Roosevelt, fearing losing the support of the powerful southern wing of his party, refused until Randolph threatened to lead one hundred thousand black protestors in a march on Washington.

President Roosevelt headed off the threatened march

by signing Executive Order 8802 prohibiting discrimination in the fulfilment of any federal contract on the basis of "race, creed, color, or national origin." Randolph knew the order was only a halfway measure as it had no teeth, but also knew his campaign needed to be perceived as having winning momentum so he hailed it as the "second emancipation proclamation." The president avoided putting any specific penalties for discrimination in the order and Congress refused to adequately fund the toothless agency charged with monitoring its progress, the Fair Employment Practices Commission (FEPC). Nevertheless, with a small but dedicated staff, the FEPC conducted extensive investigations and held open hearings in which they publicly exposed the rampant racial discrimination in some of the largest American corporations, in some cases shaming these companies into opening more opportunities to people of color.

The FEPC's work was aided by a Supreme Court ruling in 1944, *Steele v. Louisville & Nashville Railroad*, that for the first time declared that labor unions, since their power was derived from the authority given to them by Congress, had an obligation to represent all their members, and even nonmember workers, in the industry fairly when negotiating a contract with their employers. This "doctrine of fair representation," while not nearly as effective or useful as a nondiscrimination clause in labor law would have been, did mark a legal path for black workers to sue labor unions that completely disregarded their interests.

Between the pressures of the war and the success of activist movements, like that led by A. Philip Randolph, doors were opened and those long held back rushed through. Over a million black men and women entered industrial occupations for the first time during the war and by 1945 there were twice as many blacks in skilled industrial jobs than there had been before the war began.

One side effect of the rapid increase in the number of black and brown people in the skilled industrial jobs previously protected as being for whites only, was that it put pressure on the leading labor unions to begin accepting and even recruiting black members. The big two labor unions in America, the AFL and the CIO, both launched organizing drives targeting southern workers in 1946. By that year, only ten percent of the AFL's membership was African American, the majority of whom were southerners. The CIO committed 200 full-time organizers to their effort that they dubbed, "Operation Dixie."

Both unions focused their efforts on factory workers, particularly the half million textile workers. This proved a strategic blunder as these workforces that were overwhelming white and politically conservative proved more interested in maintaining their racial privileges than building a powerful interracial labor movement.

With the failure of southern organizing drives, union leaders lost their determination to take any meaningful steps to end discrimination in their organizations. In 1967, only 2% of unionized building trades workers were nonwhite. Even in the most liberal of unions, the United Automobile Workers, black workers were segregated into menial, lower-paying jobs while the well-paid and secure skilled trades were reserved for whites. A survey in 1960 found only 2% of the United Auto Workers (UAW)'s skilled trades members were black.

Figure 11.9 "United We Win," World War Two Poster,

Unionization in the black community went furthest in the auto industry. In 1940, only 4% of auto workers were black but by 1960 one-in-five were. In Detroit where the auto industry was centered, a remarkable coalition between the UAW and traditional civil rights organizations such as the NAACP and the Urban League led to the mass unionization of 100,000 of the industry's black workers in the area. Tragically, this success was resisted by white workers who staged "hate strikes" whose demands were to uphold the traditional color bars in factories.

Just at the moment when some industries first felt legal pressure to end their longstanding discriminatory practices and integrate their workforces, technological innovation and globalization trimmed the need for manual labor. Between World War Two and 1965, twenty-five states passed anti-discrimination employment laws. These laws had barely begun to make inroads when automation and outsourcing began to have the greatest impact in those industries, and those job classes within industries, that employed the highest proportions of nonwhite workers. Railroads, mining operations, and meat-packing industries were quick to automate in the 1950s and 1960s, eliminating tens of thousands of jobs primarily filled by black and brown workers. By the 1970s steel factories across the nation shut down as cheaper steel from overseas became available.

While all manufacturing workers felt the pressure of automation and globalization, minority workers faced an additional burden. The jobs that black workers succeeded in prying open began to relocate to all-white suburbs. Manufacturing facilities had once been forced to locate in cities because cities were where their labor supply and the infrastructure of transportation were centered. Factories needed railroad junctions, most of which were located in major metropolitan areas, so as to have access to their raw materials and international markets. But with the development of a vast highway network, railroads were replaced with trucks that could rumble anywhere. In Chicago, where a spine of factories paralleled the main railroad trunk that ran north to south deep into the black neighborhoods south of the loop, nearly 100,000 jobs left the city for the far-flung suburbs between 1957 and 1963. By 1966, half of all industrial jobs were located in suburban communities.

As the jobs left the city, black unemployment began to climb. In 1953 unemployment in the black community was less than 5%. A decade later it had more than doubled and continued to climb steadily from there.

Color Bars to the Medical Professions

A similar pattern of restriction of job opportunities, occurred with the licensing of various medical professionals, such as doctors, pharmacists, and dentists. Beginning in the early part of the twentieth century, state legislatures began passed laws specifying minimum standards for professional training programs. Ignoring the fact that most southern colleges and universities did not admit black students at all, and few universities in the North admitted students of color in anything more than token numbers, these laws had the immediate effect of closing many college and programs that had once trained most black doctors and other professionals. Five of the seven black medical colleges in the United States were closed because they did not meet the accreditation standards of the American Medical Association (AMA).

One of these standards seemingly designed to close specialized medical schools that served the black community was a requirement that medical schools offer full baccalaureate programs as preparation for medical studies.

Figure 11.10 Dr. W. G. Anderson, Albany, Georgia, Aug. 18, 1962.

At the time, an undergraduate degree was not commonly required to be admitted to medical school. Only one in six physicians, white or black, in 1911, held bachelor's degrees.

Those few dedicated and persistent black students who managed to earn medical degrees had only leaped the first of many hurdles the white medical establishment put in their way. Most banks refused to extend credit to black physicians to set up their medical offices that required large outlays for equipment and instruments. Most insurance companies refused to underwrite liability insurance for black doctors. The AMA made sure banks and insurance companies knew who to discriminate against by publishing annual directories of physicians that listed all black practitioners with the designation "col." (for "colored") appended to their names.

All southern affiliates (and many northern ones as well) of the American Medical Association refused to admit blacks as members. In 1938, only 0.3% of the membership of the AMA were black. Most hospitals required membership in the AMA as a condition of granting hospital privileges. Without the ability to admit and treat patients at comprehensive hospitals, black physicians were forced to refer any patients that required specialty treatments or procedures to their white colleagues.

White physicians benefited from these color bars by accepting wealthier black people as patients and leaving for the black doctors those whose ability to their bills seemed uncertain. White interns and medical students benefited from a nearly endless supply of black patients to practice on. Larger research oriented hospitals, like Johns Hopkins in Baltimore, Maryland, refused black physicians access while using black patients as subjects for medical experiments and untested treatments. Most of these hospitals were segregated and reserved only a small proportion of their facilities, usually basements and poorly maintained "annexes" for black patients. As these institutions were subsidized by public funds, segregation amounted to transfer of wealth from the black community to the white.

Compounding these obstacles was the fact that training in specialized areas of medicine, such as required before a physician could be certified as a surgeon, was dependent on both membership in the medical society and having admitting privileges in a comprehensive hospital. This double bar effectively prevented black doctors from being trained in medical specialities for much of the twentieth century. In 1931 there were over 25,000 medical specialists in the United States. Two of them, Dr. Daniel Hale Williams of Chicago, and Dr. William Harry Barnes, of Philadelphia, were black. More than a quarter century later the number of medical specialists had nearly tripled to 73,121 but the number of black surgeons and other specialists had grown to just 350, or 0.005% of the total.

As a result most black communities suffered a shortage of doctors, dentists and other professionals for generations. By 1940 the national standard was to have one doctor for every 800-1000 people in a community. There was one black doctor for every 3,100 black Americans. In Georgia the ratio was 1 to 7,100. In Mississippi it was 1 to 18,000. Life expectancy for blacks was ten years shorter than whites by 1941. Six years later it had widened to eleven years.

The legacy of exclusion from these vital professions continued to be felt long after these color bars were smashed by the Civil Rights Act of 1964 and the Medicare Act of 1965 (which the AMA vigorously opposed). In 2006, blacks were 12.3% of the national population but only 2.2% of physicians. This was a lower proportion of black physicians than in 1910, before the majority of black medical colleges were destroyed, when 2.5% of doctors were black.

Education

In order to understand the reasons for the deep and long-term differences in income between whites and blacks, it is also necessary to look beyond the economic world altogether. While we have seen that unfair employment laws, union exclusion, and employer discrimination all played a role in closing off the best jobs and highest paying careers to blacks, Latinos, and other people of color, they do not explain all of it. This is because by the twentieth century, as the economy was rapidly moving from agriculture to manufacturing, whites enjoyed far greater access to the technical training required in the fastest growing and best paying segments of the economy. By one recent estimate, half of the wage differences between white and black workers by 1940 was directly attributable to racist inequalities in educational opportunities.

The roots of educational inequality extend back into slavery. Though not all southern states made it a criminal offense to teach an enslaved person to read or write, even in states where education was legal, unwritten codes and community custom made both teaching and learning an extremely dangerous act. Illiteracy was promoted not only as a means of social control (whites could communicate secretly through notes and letters) but also because ignorance fed into the racial stereotypes by which the system of oppression was justified. The best estimates are that by Emancipation Day not even ten percent of former slaves could read.

Freed people immediately understood the value of education as a means of power, as it was one of the links of the chains holding them down for generations. For them, the association of learning and freedom was obvious and the lengths freed men and women would go to obtain it after the war were legendary. One former slave owner and Confederate Army veteran observed the mania for education that accompanied emancipation and wrote, "I never saw people more anxious nor Schollars (sic) labor harder to learn."

Though philanthropists and reform-minded whites, mostly from the North, aided efforts to establish schools and train teachers, the great bulk of the education that occurred through the remainder of the nineteenth century was entirely an effort organized, funded, and staffed by the black community itself. At first any church, barn or shed could serve as a school and because of the lack of teachers the typical school had over one hundred pupils. Even after white charity and a limited federal government effort was withdrawn at by 1870, and in the face of unrelenting hostility and violent attacks, black schools continued to be built entirely from the labor and meager cash of black communities. School enrollments continued to climb, reaching one-third of all black children by 1880.

Black schools were commonly the targets of white supremacist groups. "Yankee" teachers were threatened and driven off, their schools and homes sometimes attacked and burned. Klansmen burned down a Franklin county, Tennessee, schoolhouse eight days after it was finished by donations of labor from black carpenters. Though records are scattered and spotty at best, it is known that in 1866 alone at least a dozen schools were burned in Maryland, while in 1869 forty were torched in Tennessee. As late as 1872, schools were still being set afire in Virginia while white Alabamians that year burned down the main building of the newly founded black teacher's college, Talladega College.

A few teachers paid for their dedication with their lives: Rev. Richard Burke, who organized a school in Sumter County, Alabama, was murdered by night-riders as was Benjamin Randolph, a graduate of Ohio's Oberlin College

Figure 11.11 Children and teacher, Annie Davis School, near Tuskegee, Alabama, 1902.

who taught school in South Carolina. Charles St. Clair, a war veteran, and Franklin Sinclair, who both established schools for black children in Louisiana, were murdered soon after commencing classes. William H. Adams was killed for teaching in Rock Dam, Texas. Teacher Richard Burke was killed by the KKK in Sumter County, Alabama. William and Alzina Haffa, a couple from Philadelphia, were the first teachers in two schools in Auburn, Mississippi. They were dragged from their bed in 1875 by a crowd of as many as 75 white men who shot William, then forced Alzina to watch him slowly die over the course of the night and then to dig his grave.

It was not just hate fueling attacks on the education of black children, it was also the awareness on the part of whites that education was empowering. Schooling made it possible for black children to grow up and compete with whites for jobs, political gains, and status. It didn't take a trained theorist to understand the relationship between knowledge and power. In 1867, when teacher Thomas Barton was seized from his home in New Hanover county, North Carolina, and beaten, one of his abductors said to

him, "the niggers were bad enough before you came but since you have been teaching them, they know too much and are a damn sight worse."

Even after vigilantism and violent attacks against black schools became less frequent, southern school boards discouraged white teachers from teaching in black schools. Many southerners long after the Civil War considered teaching black children an act of racial treason and shunned white women who did so. In some areas, school boards followed an unwritten policy of not hiring white teachers to work in white schools once they had worked in a black one.

Southern state governments gave little thought or effort to black schooling. Many states, like Kentucky, immediately after the war, included in their new constitutions provisions prohibiting the mixing of white and black students. In some states segregated education was actually a system whereby black citizens paid taxes in support of white children's education and received little funding for black pupils in return. For nearly two decades after the war, Kentucky only appropriated to black schools the "excess" funds remaining after the budgets of white schools were met. The poorest southern states, like Mississippi, didn't establish public school systems until the turn of the twentieth century, well after Plessy v. Ferguson granted them the permission to create separate facilities by race.

Republican Senators repeatedly introduced legislation in the 1880s that would create a federal educational system. Schools would be funded and regulated from Washington, a step that would have revolutionized black education in the South. Three times the Blair Education bill passed the Senate in 1884, 1886, and 1888, but it was blocked from being considered in the House by the Democratic Speaker, John Carlisle, of Kentucky. When it came up for consideration a fourth and last time in 1890 it had the nearly unanimous support of the black press and black spokesmen including both Booker T. Washington and Frederick Douglass. But though Republicans controlled the Senate the measure received less support than it had in its previous three votes and was tabled without a vote.

When Congress expanded its support of higher education by passing a second Morrill Act in 1890 that provided land-grants to found colleges, it encouraged the creation of a two-tier segregated system of colleges and universities. Though the Morrill bill began as an attempt on the part of liberal Republicans to ensure that federal resources were not given to colleges that used "a distinction of race or color" to admit students, by the time the bill passed into law its purpose had been reversed. States were given the option of instituting either one large land-grant college that was barred from discriminating on the basis of race or color, or two racially segregated colleges, a policy that only served to aid the spread of segregated colleges. All seventeen southern states seized on the second option and created black colleges that were never funded anywhere near the levels of support given to their all-white institutions.

By the 1950s, most states outside the South (except for Arizona, Iowa, Maine, Michigan, Minnesota, New Hampshire, North Dakota, Ohio, Rhode Island, South Dakota, and Vermont) passed laws prohibiting discrimination in state-supported colleges and universities. But these laws were weakly observed. As early as 1951, the American Council on Education, the chief standards and policy-making body for university procedures, declared that colleges and universities should not request racial information from applicants, because such information was commonly used to discriminate against minority students. Nevertheless, most colleges and universities asked students to identify themselves by race, national origin, and religion, or required that applicants submit a photo with their application or required a personal interview with an admissions officer as before being admitted.

Later in the 1950s, when all-white southern universities were ordered by federal courts to desegregate, many simply scrubbed their admissions forms and policies of references to "white" and "negro" students and instead adopted rules that all applicants had to submit two letters of reference from alumni of that college to be considered for admission.

Southern state legislators never took seriously the court's principle that segregation required 'separate but equal' facilities for all. Discarding the qualification of equality, they allocated public funding for all services as much as possible to benefit whites alone. Only one in seven of all the libraries in the South allowed blacks to enter their reading rooms or check out books. One 1930 survey of school funding in the South found that states spent an average of $61 per year on their white pupils but only $9 on black students. This level of funding was so low that black schools were forced to limit the length of their terms so as to preserve their budgets.

Black schools provided an average of 123 days of schooling, one-fifth shorter than the typical white school year of 156 days, though this was done partly to accommodate the needs of planters who relied on cheap child labor to plant, weed and harvest their crops. Children were excluded from child labor laws, including the national Fair Labor Standard Act of 1936. In the 1930s, five times more black children worked outside the home than white ones.

Perhaps the most well-known landmark of the Civil Rights movement was the 1954 Supreme Court ruling in *Brown v. Board of Education of Topeka, Kansas,* that struck down public school segregation and the legal precedent upholding Jim Crow segregation in general, *Plessy v. Ferguson.* But this decision was not as transformative as most people wish to believe it was. The followup decision of the next year called for school districts to desegregate with "all deliberate speed," a misleading lawyerly phrase that means little. Because it contains the word "speed" it seems to imply vigor and quick action, but slow is also a "deliberate speed" as is, in fact, any chosen speed at all.

It wasn't until 1971, in *Swann v. Charlotte-Mecklenburg Board of Education,* that the Supreme Court specifically supported school desegregation plans that assigned students to schools based on their race. Almost immediately following this step, the court retreated, ruling in 1973 in *Keys v. School District No. 1* that lower courts could only order school districts to desegregate if they had been formerly segregated by law, not by circumstance (what lawyers call de jure rather than de facto segregation). Then the following year, the high court, in *Milliken v. Bradley,* refused to authorize a desegregation plan that covered Detroit and its lily-white suburbs on the grounds that suburban segregation had not been the product of law or design. Milliken effectively meant that most northern cities could not draft effective desegregation plans even if they had wanted to because, without reaching into the suburbs where the white kids went to school, there were not enough white schools or white pupils to integrate urban black children.

One of the only effective tools for desegregating schools, the humble school bus, was the subject of an increasingly vicious white backlash in the 1970s. Though used effectively to desegregate school districts in New Jersey and elsewhere, the start of busing plans (referred to as derisively as "forced busing" by its opponents) in Boston sparked demonstrations and riots. Nixon made opposition to busing an effective political campaign promise in 1972 and Congress passed legislation restricting the practice in both 1972 and in 1974, though an effort to add an anti-busing amendment to the constitution failed.

Though *Brown v. Board of Education* demanded the abandonment of racially segregated school systems in 1954, a class action lawsuit brought on behalf of California school children in the year 2000 revealed that even in that most progressive of states, education remained divided by race. 98% of the students in that state who attend schools in which at least half of the teachers do not have proper teaching credentials were nonwhite.

Educational discrimination took many forms. In several states legislators intentionally disadvantaged Latino children by restricting the use of Spanish in schools.

For the better part of fifty years, Spanish coexisted

along with English in the territory that would eventually become New Mexico, Arizona, and part of Nevada. Legal and court records, and all official communications were printed in both languages. Many of the schools in the region were bilingual. Spanish was not eclipsed by English until just before statehood was declared in 1912 when the number of English speakers finally outnumbered those who primarily spoke Spanish. Even though New Mexico's constitution guaranteed the continuation of the state's recognition and use of Spanish, officials gradually began to discriminate against Spanish-speakers.

During World War One, a federal propaganda campaign urged "100 Percent Americanism" and "One Language, One Country, One Flag." Though aimed primarily at European immigrants, this campaign framed Spanish-speakers as being less American. This continued in the 1950s as popular media drew a clear line between behaviors and qualities that were "American" and those that weren't.

In the wake of the popular movements for expanding social and civil rights in the 1960s, a movement for greater acceptance and public support for bilingualism gained grown. In 1968, Congress passed the Bilingual Education Act providing federal funding for bilingual schooling for

Figure 11-12 Texas School, Nov. 1965.

the first time. Though chronically underfunded, this legislation was supported by a Supreme Court ruling in *Lau v. Nichols* (1974) that held that bilingual education was mandatory whenever a public school district had more than 20 students who did not speak English. At the same time most states passed laws mandating and expanding their funding for bilingual education.

Like so many other liberal reforms that experienced rapid success in the 1960s and 1970s, the quickness of these changes provoked an equally powerful cultural backlash. By the 1980s an "English-only" movement gained power. Eventually, nearly half the states passed laws making English their "official language" and many others, including California, moved to end funding for bilingual schooling. In Arizona where that state's English-only law passed narrowly by popular referendum, state employees were prohibited from conducting their business in any language but English. Arizona's law was so extreme that its own state supreme court struck it down.

Congress came close several times to passing a similar measure on the national level. Speaker of the House Newt Gingrich sounded more like he was debating the Treaty of Guadalupe Hidalgo from a century earlier than such a law when he declared during one impassioned speech that "... English is the common language at the heart of our civilization." Though this measure failed in 1996, it has been reintroduced into every congressional session since.

PART TWO: WHITE WELFARE

As seen in the previous section, racial discrimination has two sides. The more commonly recognized side is the one that limits, prohibits, and segregates people of color into narrow spaces and opportunities. This is the face of racism that white Americans have reluctantly admitted since the triumph of the civil rights movement. Officially, America now accepts that its longstanding practices of barring black and brown from schools, factories, hospitals, union halls, and legislative chambers was wrong. Some of this history is even taught to children in schools. But such willingness to face the past does not extend to the other side of this coin: that exclusion and discrimination was also a vast and efficient system for funnelling the benefits of economic progress and growth unequally into the hands of the white community. By limiting the ability of people of color to work in certain jobs or pursue certain professions, whites had an easier time obtaining such positions. Segregating schools allowed states to use the taxes they raised from minority communities to subsidize white's education. Racial discrimination was not just an individual expression of bigotry, but was a largely official public policy of subsidizing white opportunity and wealth.

The governmental system of allocating much of its tax revenues to providing welfare to whites began while the North was still fighting the Civil War and continued without pause to the present day. While virtually none of these programs were expressly designated as being for the benefit of whites alone (and because of their seemingly neutral language their racist character has remained hidden) they were carefully designed, implemented, and defended to do just that.

Civil War Pensions

Figure 11.13 "The Veteran," by Thomas Waterman Wood, 1866.

At the conclusion of the Civil War, a grateful Congress voted repeatedly to distribute pensions and bounties to veterans, their widows, children, and their survivors. Eventually, the Civil War pension system would balloon into the world's largest and most generous social welfare system at that time. At their peak, pensions consumed 42% of the entire federal budget for many years. Over a million veterans and their dependents and heirs received cash payments totalling 140 million dollars per year. On average, pensioners received a cash payment of $139, which was equivalent to 37% of the average annual wage.

By the end of the war over 200,000 black soldiers and sailors had served and played a key role in defeating the rebellion and overturning slavery. Of these, only 79% survived the war, a rate far worse than the 85% of white soldiers who lived to tell their tales. Many of these survivors were injured and suffered chronic maladies as a result of their service and they applied for pensions just as white veterans did.

While policymakers in Washington claimed that they intended veterans' funds to be allocated without regard to race and color, the local officials in charge of actually distributing pensions had different ideas. Pension bureaucrats were openly suspicious of black applicants and unashamed of describing them as "dishonest," or to dismiss them as the tools of frauds and "sharpers" who would take a cut of their pension. They rejected black applicants in far higher numbers than white ones.

In 1890, Congress expanded this welfare program by granting pensions to war veterans who became disabled after their duty ended and, later, in 1907, Congress voted to provide all Civil War veterans with old-age pensions when they reached the age of 62. However, to obtain benefits, applicants had to document their service through both obtaining certified War Department records and by obtaining letters of support from former commanders. This was far more difficult for black veterans than white ones as many black soldiers were men who had escaped servitude in the South and so had few written records, no permanent address at the time of their enlistment, and often had changed their names from those they had been given by their enslavers. Black men from the North who volunteered were also likely to have less documentation of their lives as most weren't ever eligible to vote, obtain licenses, or have other official interactions with their state governments. Given that the War Department kept very shoddy records to begin with, applications from black veterans who had few official certificates of their identity faced an uphill battle to prove their identity and their service.

In addition, all pension applicants had to submit to a physical examination by a panel of physicians who had the power to deny the claim. Even with a favorable medical panel opinion, the claim had to survive a second level of approval, from a local Pension Review Board. Such a system provided for individual and group prejudices to intrude at many points. Black veterans were rejected at far higher levels than whites and those that were approved for pensions received smaller awards than white veterans did. According to a survey of over 8,000 pension applications, white applicants were approved 78% of the time and black applicants were approved 39% of the time.

So rigorous were these requirements, and so low the rate of approvals of black veterans, that most black veterans did not even bother. Twice as many white veterans applied for pensions than black veterans. According to one careful estimate, overall, fewer than one out of five of all black veterans applied for pensions under this system. The least likely group to apply for pensions were black veterans who had been born in slavery.

Confederate veterans were ineligible for federal pensions and bonuses, but many southern states established their own pension systems, none of which offered to include the millions of enslaved men and women who served the Confederate forces, performing all the hard dirty labor an army requires.

Aid for Mothers

In the first decades of the twentieth century, progressive reformers succeeded in pressuring states to take more responsibility for their poorest citizens. A majority of states moved away from the old system of orphanages and poor farms and began granting cash allowances to widowed and abandoned mothers with dependent children. Illinois led the way when it passed the first aid program to children that kept them in their own homes in 1911. Within two years, eighteen states followed suit and by 1920 forty states launched programs of direct aid to mothers. By the 1930s, only Georgia and South Carolina refused to use state funds for this purpose.

At the time, it was believed that such programs were best administered at the local level and individual counties were given extensive authority over how they thought they should operate. Counties were even allowed to opt out of welfare systems altogether in most states. Only about a third of states required some form of state oversight of local welfare administrations. Whether purposely or inadvertently, such a degree of local autonomy and a lack of consistent standards ensured that local prejudices would influence how funds were allocated.

In most places, women who applied for aid were required to have themselves and their homes examined periodically by inspectors who had final authority to recommend or deny inclusion in the programs. Inspectors also had the authority to advise on the amount of cash assistance, and to change or suspend that amount whenever they felt necessary. Because most state laws mandated that only married women of good character and "suitable homes" were eligible for assistance, inspectors had vast latitude to pry into women's relationships and to apply racist presumptions to nonwhite applicants.

African American mothers were rejected from such programs in disproportionate numbers, as were Latinas and some recent European immigrants (one Italian mother was found unsuitable because she used garlic in her cooking which the inspector condemned as an aphrodisiac).

Figure 11.14 Porter with her gear, 1917.

Black and Latina women were rejected for not attending the "right" church, not having "good books" in the home, and having "unruly" neighbors. As one scholar of this era of social welfare put it, local administrators "tended to restrict the programs to nice Anglo-Saxon widows and to... protect their young programs from Negro and unmarried mothers…" Across the South, where four in five of all black families lived in 1930, and where they represented nearly a third of the overall population, only 3.5% of those families that received mother's pensions were black. In Chicago, in 1917, the proportion of the population that was Irish or black was about the same, around three percent, but Irish-American mothers received 22% of the pensions and black mothers were awarded 2.7%. A total of one black woman in all of St. Louis in 1923 received a benefit check. Likewise, in all of North Carolina in 1931, only one black family qualified for aid.

In 1935, all the mothers' pension programs were swept into the New Deal's expanding welfare state. Title IV of the Social Security Act incorporated the existing programs into the Aid for Dependent Children program that retained many of the older programs' local control and moralistic judgments of an applicant's "worthiness" for aid. While the rest of the Social Security Act accepted applicants as long as they fit the criteria of being in a certain class, based on age or disability, the ADC continued to investigate and decide if its candidates were "worthy."

Southern Democrats and some New Deal bureaucrats, who feared that such programs would empower black workers and communities (and create administrative challenges to include them), forced the exclusion of agricultural workers and domestic laborers from the historic program of social insurance. At the time, the two largest categories of black employment were agriculture and domestic service. In effect, the Social Security program represented two different systems of welfare—one that granted benefits automatically to whites and another that begrudgingly allocated payments to "needy" and "worthy" black families only after they had been subjected to investigation.

By excluding from its coverage people who labored in the jobs most commonly held by people of color, agricultural laborers and domestic workers, more than three-fifths of black workers worked in these sectors and were denied social security benefits. Likewise, in 1938, when the Fair Labor Standards Act established minimum wage and overtime standards, these same groups were left out from its protections. As late as 1945, one-third of all black men and two-thirds of all black women remained excluded from the Social Security program. (In 1954, a Republican Congress voted to end these occupational exclusions but as it required five years of participation in the system before a person qualified for benefits, racial exclusions lasted until at least 1959.)

In fairness, it should be noted that both northern and southern lawmakers were equally responsible for dropping domestic workers from the benefits of Social Security and unemployment insurance. The legislative record on their motives is sparse and inconclusive, but it does not stretch the imagination to consider that a Congress that had no female Senators and eight female Congress members thought little of an occupation in which nine of ten workers were women, and of these nearly half were black. More cynically, it might be considered that nearly all members of Congress employed domestic workers themselves and therefore had an employer's perspective on the issue. Senator Pat Harrison was noted asking a staffer, "Suppose my wife had trouble with the cook and had to fire her…would I come under the provisions of the act?"

During the Great Depression when the New Deal steered the government to provide employment and relief to millions of Americans, these jobs were largely reserved for whites. Roosevelt's Works Progress Administration that directly employed workers had a checkered record of discrimination. While nationally black workers were employed in numbers greater than their proportion of the population, black unemployment was far higher than white. In several states in the southwest Indians and Mexican-

Americans were simply excluded from the program. In New England jobless whites were given WPA jobs while jobless blacks were put on 'cash relief' rather than given work.

Aid to Farmers

Americans romanticize their farmers as the backbone of the nation, sturdy in their independence and self-reliance. This image of the hard-working and therefore virtuous farmer has itself been cultivated since Jefferson first celebrated "yeomen" farmers as the security and soul of a democratic republic, because, being self-made, and living on their own labor, they bent their knee to no ruler. Such myths survived slavery, when successful planters required tremendous government help in keeping their "property" from revolting or running away. They later survived mechanization and the rise of the corporate farming.

These myths continue today even though the average farm operation is 430 acres and the average farm family income is half again as large as the median national income. Half of all the products raised on farms in America comes from farms that earn more than a million dollars in gross income each year and half of these earned more than five million. The median wealth of American farmers in 2015 was a whopping $827,300, a figure not significantly skewed by the 4.2% of farms categorized as "large-scale." Even the average wealth of those farmers classified as "small family farms" averaged just below $800,000. Farmers receive a lavish assortment of government subsidies each year amounting to 10.8 billion dollars in direct payments and underwritten services, or an average of $13,546 per "primary" farmer.

Farming in the United States has become one of the whitest of all occupations. In 2012, there were 2,109,303 "principal" operators of farms in the nation. Of these, only 7% are black, Asian, Indian, or Hispanic. Only 33,371, or 1.6% of the total, were black.

This last figure is especially striking as one century ago black farmers were overrepresented in farming. In 1910, there were 803,801 black farm operators constituting 16% of all farm operators in the nation. Counting all those who worked in agriculture and not just operated their own farms, in 1910 nearly a quarter of all farmers were black. Somehow, in the course of the last one hundred years, farming went from being one of the most integrated of occupations to being one of the least diverse. This didn't happen by accident, nor by choice, but by a sustained and coordinated government effort to subsidize and promote white farmers and drive black farmers off their land.

Black farms were mostly southern farms at the turn of the century. Ninety-eight percent of black farming

Figure 11.15 Farmer and child, 1939.

operations were south of the Mason-Dixon line where 90% of the black population lived in 1910.

Farming's most important and most expensive resource is land and providing land to white farmers was the government's first form of social welfare. From the inception of the American republic, one of the central activities of federal and state governments was violently moving native peoples off of desirable land. Government agents then mapped and surveyed the "frontier" so as to render it a commodity that could be sold and whose ownership could be recorded and transferred. Government land offices sold both large tracts of land to speculators and smaller plots to individual farmers.

As government land sales (and in some states land ownership generally) were generally reserved for "citizens," nonwhites faced greater obstacles in obtaining the subsidized cheap land the government provided. For example, in 1844, the provisional government of Oregon territory passed a law requiring all blacks to leave the state and prohibiting all others from migrating there or risk the punishment of being auctioned off to the highest bidder. A shift in legislative control led to the laws repeal and then its repassage in 1849. Finally in 1857, Oregonians had their chance to vote on their state's new constitution and a number of provisions and affirmed their constitution by a margin of 4,582 votes. Oregonians also voted to exclude all black people from their new state by a much larger margin of 7,559. Though the law was never actively enforced, it sent a strong message and clearly warned black people away. By 1880 there were fewer than 500 black people in the whole state compared with California that had no such law and attracted over 6000.

Black people were not yet declared citizens by right of birth when Congress passed the first of several great "Homestead" laws, providing virtually free farmsteads to those who could move to the west and occupy their claim for a five year period. This would not happen until four years later. In 1872, Congress revised the law adding a specific provision that grants were not to be made with "distinction on account of race or color," though such language appears to have had little impact on local discrimintaory practices.

At least 30,000 black homesteaders did manage to leave the South and journey into Kansas where they founded a string of towns. This was the largest movement of black homesteaders westward and it was dwarfed by the number of whites who benefited from the law. Unfortunately, there exists virtually no demographic data broken down by race to estimate how often black pioneers were successful in obtaining homestead grants, though anecdotal evidence from the operation of the homestead law in the South indicates discrimination and fraud against black applicants was rife.

Between 1862 and 1913, 2.4 million people filed claims for western lands under the act, a disproportionate number of them white. It is estimated that today, the accumulated family wealth of 46 million white families, about one in four, began with the government land grants given by the Homestead Act of 1862.

In 1866, President Andrew Johnson signed the Southern Homestead Act, a law modeled on the previous 1862 measure that opened up millions of acres in the west (much of it still possessed and occupied by native peoples) to American farmers. However, unliked the original Homestead law, the Southern Homestead Act was intended to help emancipated black families become self-sufficient by making them landowners rather than tenants. Its key feature was the nation's first racial anti-discrimination measure, stating that "no distinction or discrimination shall be made in the construction or execution of this act on account of race or color."

In spite of this provision, most of the 46 million allocated acres were claimed by whites. In Louisiana, where only half the population was white, 79% of homestead lands were claimed by whites. In other states where much of the land available under the Homestead law was wooded, lumber interests used their influence to fraudulently file vast numbers of claims. These companies would then strip off the timber and abandon the claims. One Florida official estimated that half the timbering done in that state was accomplished by timber companies making fake homestead claims. In 1876, Congress repealed the Southern Homestead Act, opening up public lands to simple purchase by corporations.

Although black farmers had difficulty securing land from the government, they also faced hostility from the white community that generally criticized any whites who sold land to black families, as it was well known that landownership was a large step towards independence. The reluctance of whites to sell land to black farmers significantly raised their cost of obtaining land. While for some white sellers the only color that mattered was green, there were enough white sellers who factored race into their calculations that the overall price of land was much higher for black purchasers. One careful survey of land sales in 1880 Tennessee found that on average, black purchasers paid $24.13 per acre compared to white buyers who paid just $15.28. So intense was this white jealousy of even the smallest suggestion of black farmers' prosperity that many black families intentionally left their homes unpainted.

Figure 1.16 Poster advertising lands, 1872.

Nevertheless, black families and communities found ways of supporting and lifting each other up into land ownership. Incredibly, rates of black land ownership grew throughout the fifty years after the Civil War in spite of white resistance. Even during the period around the turn of the century when Jim Crow and political disenfranchisement extended their reach throughout the South, a steadily growing of proportion of farmers managed to buy their own land. In 1890 fewer than 9% of black farmers owned their own land. Twenty years later this proportion had increased by a fifth. Similarly, overall rates of black homeownership in the South rose in this period from less than 18% in 1890 to over 23% in 1910. (Reflecting the fact that the South had no monopoly on racism, northern black communities experienced declining rates of homeownership at this same time.)

What would seem to be a great puzzle is that as the federal government expanded its aid programs to farmers in the twentieth century, the number of black farmers fell far more sharply than that of white farmers. Somehow, as the government more forcefully intervened to "save" the farm economy, this intervention further drove black farmers off the land. This "puzzle," however, is not so mysterious if one considers that most government subsidies were funneled into the hands of white farmers who were able to use those funds to modernize and then outcompete the black

farmers who had been passed by.

The U.S. Department of Agriculture (USDA) was also established in 1862 as an agency that could assist farmers with implementing new farming techniques, granting low interest loans, and other direct aid. Because the USDA was organized to be locally controlled, black farmers were marginalized in areas where Jim Crow segregation prevailed, which was in those areas where nine in ten black farmers lived. No black man or woman served on a USDA county committee anywhere in the United States until 1964.

The Great Depression devastated farming around the country but no group felt its effects more severely than black farmers. From 1935 to 1959, 28% of white farmers who farmed their own land were forced out of business, while 40% of black farm-owners went bust. Much of this disparity was related to the technical assistance white farmers received that helped them diversify their crops and implement procedures that restored and preserved soils better than traditional methods. As noted in a government study done in 1965:

Aided by Federal loans and technical advice, a large percentage of the South's white farmers have increasingly diversified their crops and applied modern farming practices, so that in 1959 slightly less than half were dependent upon the

Figure 11.17 Wife of Sharecropper, Lee County, Mississippi, 1935.

Figure 11.18 Agricultural Adjustment Administration meeting at courthouse to discuss allocations. Eufaula, Oklahoma, 1940.

traditional row crops—cotton, tobacco, and peanuts. Concomitant gains have been made in arresting soil exhaustion and erosion. Southern white farmers have raised their incomes, increased the size of their farms, improved their housing, and advanced their education.

Black farm families were left out of this shower of government benefits. Such benefits reach individual farmers through the agents of the Rural Extension Service, a federal program that employs agents to inform rural families of the various benefits the government provides, and to provide technical assistance to farmers. While federal rules required states to employ black county agents, their budgets were controlled by the white heads of the state agencies. A government audit of county agents in 1939 found that black county agents were so poorly funded, few even had offices and were forced to work out of their homes. Meanwhile, white county agents were usually housed in downtown office buildings with secretarial assistance, typewriters, phones, printing facilities, and air conditioning. One black farm agent in Alabama used his own money to purchase a mimeograph machine. This in spite of the fact that black rural agents were given caseloads at least double those of white agents.

White farmers benefited from the well-funded experimental farms of white land-grant universities that received millions in federal grants for agricultural research. In the 1950s Texas employed 43 agricultural specialists whose job it was to disseminate this information with its white county agents. The state employed no specialists to work with its black county agents. Moreover, black county agents were usually not invited to the periodic conferences where the latest news and discoveries were discussed. Most black agents were excluded even from routine weekly staff meetings. This was not merely a matter of bigotry;

rather, by limiting the information given to black farm agents southern states were able to further reduce black participation in government programs. Of course, these disparities were evident in counties that even had black rural agents. A study done in the early 1960s found that of 125 southern counties surveyed, 42 had no black agents at all.

Here was a system of racial preferences and privileges for whites that rested partly on a monopoly of information. Surveys undertaken in the years of Jim Crow found that most black farmers and rural families had no idea of the government assistance that was theoretically available to them. 72% of farmers had no idea that there were government loan programs for soil improvement or water projects. 57% did not know there were low interest loans available to repair and upgrade rural homes and buildings. 68% had never heard that the government offered operating loans. During the 1940s and 1950s, only one-fifth of black farmers managed to benefit from Farmers' Home Administration loans.

Along with limiting access to information about government loans, though the money and program was federal, it was largely controlled by local appointed and elected boards. (This was one of the grand compromises President Roosevelt had to make with the 'Dixiecrat' wing of his party in order to get his New Deal programs through Congress.) By the early 1960s, the Farmer's Home Administration ran through 3,000 county delegates, none of whom was black. The even larger Agricultural Stabilization and Conservation Service (ASCS), that ran the crop subsidy programs, had 37,000 members of its county committees and until 1964, not one was black. While theoretically the vast federal bureaucracies within these departments could have pushed for a more equitable distribution of loans and subsidies within the terms of federal law, these administrations were just as lilly-white. The Farmers Home Administration (FHA) had over 5,000 full time employees and a total of 40 were black. The Soil Conservation Service (SCS) employed over 6,000 professionals and a similar number, about 40 were black. The ASCS had no black professionals though it employed one full time black custodian for a time.

By 1959, over ninety percent of black farmers derived more than half of their income from one of three staple crops, cotton, tobacco, and peanuts, making them subject to crippling market swings in the price of their sole crop. Black farmers without access to government subsidized loans, subsidized crop insurance, technical assistance, and other benefits, earned far less than white farmers. In 1964 the amount of federal agricultural aid annually distributed in the South topped two billion dollars, a massive subsidy that was divided and allocated secretly by all-white county agricultural boards.

Worse, from the 1940s and into the 1960s, many southern USDA offices punished black farmers who had attempted to vote, run for office, send their kids to a white school, or even protest their own unfair treatment. When complaints were lodged in Washington about the abusive and discriminatory action of local USDA offices, USDA bureaucrats simply referred these complaints back to the very same offices complained about.

As late as 1997, a government inspector's report noted that the USDA had no written guidelines or procedures in place for handling discrimination complaints. That same year a group of three black farmers filed a class-action lawsuit against the USDA charging systematic and long-term racial discrimination. Eventually 15,000 plaintiffs joined the suit, *Pigford et al. v. Dan Glickman, Sec., U.S. Department of Agriculture*. In the largest settlement of its kind, the government agreed to pay each plaintiff $50,000 and to cancel their outstanding debts. Tens of thousands of other farmers who missed the initial filing deadline still have suits and claims outstanding.

Rural Electrification

A twenty block stretch of New York City's Broadway Avenue, encompassing the theatre district from 42nd street north, was the first street in America to be lit by electric street lights in the 1880s. This glowing avenue lined with brilliant marquees and signs was dubbed "the Great White Way." As other cities electrified in this era, even small towns, they too proudly referred to their best lit commercial corridors as their "Great White Way."

Such a name had additional meaning to black citizens for whom in many of these cities such downtown areas were some of the most segregated spaces, where both public officials and private security more aggressively policed racial boundaries. Atlanta coordinated the lighting of its main artery, Peachtree Street, with a renewed push to segregate the area in 1909. Naming their most important business streets, the "Great White Way," was just another way that whites claimed their racial control of urban spaces.

This glorification of electric light was just one indication of the great importance that the spread of electric power had to the economic growth of the early twentieth century. Electricity revolutionized both production, by allowing for more productive arrangements of machines and labor, and consumption, by mechanizing many time-consuming household tasks. Electrification was particularly advantageous to those farmers who could link their farms to the electric grid, as a variety of powered implements made their operations more efficient and competitive at a time of falling prices for the goods they produced.

Figure 11.19 Rural Electrification Administration Poster, ca. 1930s.

Like so many other vital goods and services at this time, the ability of people to access electricity was partly determined by their race. Because many towns and smaller cities ran their own municipal power systems, decisions as to what streets were to be lit, and what neighborhoods were to be prioritized in the extension of their services, were made by white officials with typically racist presumptions. Such officials, viewing black neighborhoods as naturally crime-ridden and dangerous, and white neighborhoods as requiring protection from criminals, located more street lights in white neighborhoods and business districts so unwelcome strangers could be seen at night. Black homeowners were less likely to be connected to electrical services as they were presumed to be higher risks for nonpayment of their bills.

Federal funding for rural electrification began flowing as part of the New Deal in the late 1930s and in many places it too operated to overly benefit whites and disadvantage blacks. The need was great: in 1930 only 10% of rural residents were electrified. In order to plan the routes and the phasing of their utility projects, states conducted surveys to estimate the needs and potential consumption of electricity. In the case of North Carolina, state statisticians added a "correction factor" to these estimates that artificially discounted the electrical usage of black residents compared to whites. (Statisticians justified this fudge factor by claiming that surveys of black households were less reliable than those of white households because black people were less honest.) In this way, the system was built supposedly according to the logic of capturing the highest consumption rates, but these rates were based on data that had been prejudiced from the start. In this way, a federal program that on its face appears to be racially neutral and of benefit to all Americans, ended up giving white rural residents and farmers a competitive boost over black families and farmers. Likewise, in the West native communities were usually last to be connected to the power grid.

The G.I. Bill

Just as the patchwork system of Civil War veteran's pensions quickly became the largest social welfare program of the nineteenth century, primarily benefitting whites, Congress opened the treasury in grateful recognition of its millions of veterans who had fought in World War Two. And just as the earlier veterans' program highlighted how the shadow of discrimination can extend over time, even generations, so did the veterans programs of the 1940s to the 1970s reveal how the denial of opportunity in the past can compound over time. Black men who fought in the Civil War were often denied the benefits readily given to whites because of local prejudices and because black vets had difficulty proving their identities—identities uncertain because many had been born into slavery. World War Two black vets, like whites who were honorably discharged, were eligible for the largest collection of social welfare benefits ever offered to a group of Americans, but they couldn't take advantage of them because veterans programs were administered by local authorities who were legally permitted to racially discriminate.

Over the course of the war, nearly sixteen million men (and some women) were drawn into the armed forces. Of these slightly more than 1.3 million were black, between 340,000 and 380,000 were Latino/a, 44,000 were Native American, 11,000 were Chinese American, and 25,000 Japanese American. All served in a military that was strictly segregated by race, which meant not just that soldiers were separated into different units, but that the opportunities to learn advanced skills or gain the leadership experience that could translate into business success after the war were reserved for whites. Most nonwhite soldiers

Figure 11.20 Tuskegee airmen attending a briefing at Ramitelli, Italy, Mar. 1945.

were placed in service units where few skills were taught or acquired beyond the discipline of soldiering. Every black man who entered the Navy until late in 1944 was designated a "steward," a nautical term for servant.

Armed forces service was an opportunity for many men and women to learn new skills and gain advanced education. In a war that was ultimately won by technological advances, specialized technical education was vital. The Army placed over one hundred thousand of its soldiers in civilian colleges and of these 789 were black. Most advanced specialties, communications, engineering, and intelligence, were reserved for whites only. Only one percent of black soldiers were made officers while eleven percent of all white soldiers were promoted or trained to this level.

As the war neared its victory, Congress passed the Selective Service Readjustment Act, popularly known as the "G.I. Bill." Congress continually added to its overflowing basket of benefits over the next decade, often voting funds unanimously. From 1944 to 1971, the G.I. Bill would consume over 95 billion dollars, in some years reaching 15% of the total federal budget. More than any other government initiative, the G.I. Bill raised millions of Americans into the middle class by granting them college grants, job training and placement, unemployment insurance, mortgage subsidies, small business and farm loans, and medical and dental services, administered by a federal army of bureaucrats numbering 225,000.

Like so many other federal programs established prior to the victories of the Civil Rights Movement, the G.I. Bill was deliberately structured so as to funnel a disproportionate share of these benefits to white families and greatly restrict the ability of nonwhites to access them. This was done in the usual manner of decentralizing the vital decisions about eligibility and benefits to local officials (invariably all white), funnelling funds through private hands such as commercial banks and private colleges who could legally discriminate against anyone they wished, and prohibiting federal agencies from having oversight and regulatory powers over these local and private entities.

The most lucrative benefits of the G.I. Bill, those heavily subsidizing home mortgages, went to white vets. Very few home loans went to people of color. For example, in Virginia's largest 13 cities, of 3,229 home, business and farm loans provided to veterans, 2 went to blacks. In New York and New Jersey, of 67,000 mortgages provided by the G.I. Home Loan Corp., fewer than 100 went to non-whites.

Educational benefits were only useful if a veteran could enroll in certified training program or, better yet, a college. But all colleges and universities, except for historically black colleges, discriminated, most in the South did not accepting black applicants at all and most in the North admitting only a token number. Of 647 colleges

and universities in the South, only 102 admitted black students and these segregated black institutions were small and poorly funded and none had a doctoral program or an engineering school. Half of all black colleges had fewer than 250 students and only one in ten had enrollments greater than 1,000. Southern white colleges enrolled five times the number of students black colleges did and were far better funded by their state governments. Because white schools excluded them and black colleges didn't have the capacity, 20,000 eligible black veterans were denied admission (and therefore their benefits) in 1947 alone. Uncounted thousands of others simply didn't bother to apply, knowing the odds against them. Meanwhile, more than a quarter of all white veterans took advantage of their government funded college programs. As a result the educational gap between whites and blacks in America widened in the decades following 1945.

The ability of black veterans to access government benefits was even worse when it came to vocational training and on-the-job programs that simply refused to include nonwhites. In the first two years of government funded training programs, 102,000 white southerners but only 7,700 black vets enjoyed the benefits of learning better-paying, higher-skilled jobs. (Keep in mind that blacks were more than a quarter of the southern population at the time.) Similar stories can be told about job placement programs, low-interest small business and farm loan programs, and, most importantly, the veterans housing programs that helped millions of working class white families move into the new middle class suburbs built in rings around American cities.

Mortgage Subsidies

The most common American asset, a house, was most heavily subsidized by the U.S. government at the very time that racial discrimination was legal and widely practiced. The famed "New Deal" that helped end the Great Depression was followed after World Two by federal government policies that for the first time gave prospective homeowners low cost government loans to purchase their homes. These housing programs, which were at the time among the largest government subsidies ever given to American citizens, largely excluded nonwhites. The 1934 and 1949 Housing Acts that subsidized mortgages for white families, helped 35 million white families purchase a home between 1934 and 1978. For reasons explored in detail in chapter 13, people of color were systematically excluded from this huge federal subsidy and were kept from home ownership.

The timing of these exclusions are even more important as the great boom in suburban home building between the 1940s and the 1970s took place in an environment with few regulatory or zoning restrictions that have since raised home prices. Whites who were assisted by the federal government to purchase homes in those decades obtained real estate that has since soared in value, building an immense amount of equity and wealth that has been passed down to succeeding generations. This is why by 2015, 72% of white households owned their own home compared with 43% of black families and why white families held 13 times the wealth of black households.

Whiteness as Property

Given all the wonderful government benefits bestowed on whites and denied to blacks it is no wonder that whiteness came to be protected and policed as a form of property. Legally, whiteness has been ruled to be something of material and measurable value. Whiteness and property share an essential attribute—they both are based on the right to exclude others from certain benefits and privileges. To own property in land boils down to the right to exclude others from using or occupying that piece of the earth. To own whiteness, likewise, in America has consisted of the right to exclude nonwhite people from various spaces and opportunities of public and private life.

Whiteness was central to the definition of American citizenship, a status that determined more than just voting, but also the right to hold property or obtain a license to operate a business. For much of American history, a Native American had no individual property rights but instead only had the collective rights secured (or more commonly surrendered) by treaty with the federal government. In that context, whiteness was an aspect of land ownership. During the high point of slavery in the early nineteenth century, courts used whiteness a crucial means of determining whether someone was eligible to be enslaved. As only nonwhite persons could legally be enslaved in many states, whiteness was used as a legal defense against being enslaved.

As late as 1957, the Supreme Court of South Carolina recognized that to wrongfully call a white person "black" was libel but not the reverse. A black person had no grounds to sue for being called "white" as there was no value in being black the same way there was in being white.

In 1896, Homer A. Plessy, a New Orleans shoemaker who was, as the Supreme Court noted, "of mixed descent... one eighth African blood; that the mixture of colored

Figure 11.21 Woman and man looking at a house under construction in Arlington, Virginia, Aug. 1966.

blood was not discernible in him," took a seat in a white railroad car and announced to the conductor, "I have to tell you that, according to Louisiana law, I am a colored man." The conductor summoned an officer who arrested Plessy.

When the case reached the Supreme Court all but one of the justices were unpersuaded that segregation was inherently unequal and therefore in violation of the Fourteenth Amendment. In typical fashion, the court blamed black people for their own victimization, writing: "[T]he underlying fallacy of the plaintiff's argument consists in the assumption that the enforced separation of the two races stamps the colored race with a badge of inferiority. If this be so, it is not by reason of anything found in the act but solely because the colored race chooses to put that construction on it." That left Plessy and his lawyers only one argument: that by forcing him to ride in the black railcar the state took his property, his property in whiteness, without due process (in other words, legally determining what his race actually was first). As Plessy's lawyers put it, "the reputation of belonging to the dominant race . . . is property, in the same sense that a right of action or inheritance is property." Lead counsel, Albion W. Tourgée, explained further:

> How much would it be worth to a young man entering upon the practice of law, to be regarded as a white man rather than a colored one? Six-sevenths of the population are white. Nineteen-twentieths of the property of the country is owned by white people. Ninety-nine hundredths of the business opportunities are in the control of white people. . . . Probably most white persons if given a choice, would prefer death to life in the United States as colored persons. Under these conditions, is it possible to conclude that the reputation of being white is not property? Indeed, is it not the most valuable sort of property, being the master-key that unlocks the golden door of opportunity.

The same justices who ruled that segregation was constitutional were sympathetic to Plessy's loss of ownership over his whiteness. They granted that Plessy had the right to sue the railroad company for damages if they had incorrectly seated him in the wrong section:

> If he be a white man and assigned to a colored coach, he may have his action for damages against the company for being deprived of his so-called property. Upon the other hand, if he be a colored man and be so assigned, he has been deprived of no property, since he is not

lawfully entitled to the reputation of being a white man.

The U.S. Supreme Court was able to twist itself around squaring a law that treated people unequally with another that required "equal protection of the laws." The jurists famously did so by arguing that segregation could be "separate but equal." But they also upheld whiteness by agreeing with Plessy that whiteness was something of actual value like any other property.

In an odd and twisted way they were right. Whiteness has conferred great material benefits to generations of white Americans who quickly forgot that they were the privileged recipients of benefits derived from their skin color.

Figure 11.22 Man at the Jekyll Island Club Hotel, 1990.

COUNTY CONVICT CAMPS.

There are forty-four camps in thirty-seven counties, the prison population being augmented by prisoners from neighboring counties. Thirty-one have reported, but only twenty-seven give the number confined, as follows:

White males	177
Colored males	796
Color not given	100
Colored females	3
Total	1,076

Twelve of these were boys under sixteen. The three women are employed as cooks in the Guilford camps; Anson, Buncombe, Nash, Randolph, Sampson and Mecklenburg No. 2 not reporting. Bertie reports prisoners quartered at the County Home and working the farm there, not giving data.

There are over twelve hundred prisoners in the camps, and attention has been called by some of the visitors to the apparent youth of these men. Nine deaths during the year. Comparatively little tuberculosis; one prisoner with the disease was pardoned, another occupies a separate tent at night, and one died. Four counties reported that blacks and whites occupied the same room or tent at night. These were advised of its illegality. Four others reported as follows: "Separate divisions" of the same room; "curtains between"; "same room, different ends"; "yes, with divisions." We do not think that this meets the requirement of the law, which is absolute separation of the races in their sleeping quarters.

Six counties report no whipping, punishment for infraction of rules, confinement in steel cell and deprivation of tobacco or other privilege. The other camps punish by flogging with the leather strap. No religious services in eight; in others occasional. Guards receive from $20 to $40 per month; supervisors, from $30 to $100. There is no classification of prisoners. Felons, misdemeanors and men working out fines wear the stripes and receive like treatment.

GRANVILLE.

The camp has two frame buildings, 14 x 15 feet, and one steel cage, 9 x 18 x 7 feet. Whites and blacks separated at night. Spring water. Heaters. Ventilation by windows. No suffering from cold. A mattress and four double blankets to four men. No women. All the food they want. Three meals; no warm drink. Required to bathe. Blankets washed about once a month. Camp is scoured and lime used. Excreta carried off. Free of vermin. New mattresses once in three months. Punished by whipping. Small whip used. The sick are well cared for. No deaths. No tuberculosis. Hours of work, from sun to sun. Three employees. Superintendent receives $60 per month, two guards $32.50. No religious services. Locked in cage on Sunday. Prisoners are not chained together at night. Some wear chains all the time. Boys confined with the men. Now confined: 10 colored males, 2 under sixteen, and 4 white males; total, 14.

Remarks.—We have ordered another steel cage and will soon have more room for prisoners.   D. N. HUNT.

Received September 23, 1908.

Excerpts from *EMPLOYMENT: 1961 U.S. COMMISSION ON CIVIL RIGHTS REPORT*
(Washington, D.C.: Government Printing Office, 1961)

STATE EMPLOYMENT OFFICE ADMINISTRATION

... To the extent that [Federal] policy permits discrimination in the use of the services rendered by local employment offices, it contributes to discrimination in employment. The manner in which State employment offices are administered can determine the degree to which the Federal nondiscrimination policy is effective...

Under existing Federal regulations the States are free to maintain racially segregated employment offices. In 1958 there were 15 cities in 4 States with physically segregated employment offices; 25 cities had offices with separate entrances and separate personnel to process white and Negro applicants; and in over 70 other cities the offices had either separate waiting rooms or separate service points for the different races. In some areas of the South, where the office is too small to support more than one employee, Negro and white applicants sit on different sides of the interviewer's desk....

Since segregated offices cannot be maintained without racial records, the USES [United States Employment Service] policy prohibiting the recording of racial information becomes meaningless. Moreover, if job orders are submitted only to the "white" office, they need not contain discriminatory specifications; this makes it difficult, if not impossible, to enforce the Federal proscription against processing discriminatory job orders placed by Federal agencies or Government contractors. In an effort to cure this problem, USES requires that where such orders are received by one segregated office, they must be transmitted to its counterpart. But even this requirement raises practical difficulties. Unless job orders are referred simultaneously, the job may already have been filled by the time the order is referred to the second office. And job orders are rarely, if ever, referred simultaneously...

The day-to-day operations of segregated offices illustrate some of the administrative problems. When the District of Columbia maintained segregated offices, switchboard operators felt it necessary to ask prospective employers who had not requested a particular office whether they wanted white or Negro workers. The very nature of the question invites discriminatory job requests. Duplicate job orders were referred to the segregated offices, but sometimes one office had already filled the job before applicants from the other office could possibly appear at the employer's place of business.

In North Carolina, the local offices may request a private employer submitting a job order to indicate a racial preference. "This is done 'only in cases where there is doubt about the employer's requirements.' " Where no such doubt exists, employment service personnel themselves determine whether to refer whites or Negroes according to their view of the " 'social and economic characteristics of the community' " and knowledge of " 'customary hiring requirements.' "....

In Atlanta the director of the employment service stated that all phone calls go directly to an order-taking unit which sends duplicate order forms to each of the segregated offices.

There have been allegations that, although all orders are made in duplicate, orders for "traditional white jobs" are not sent to the Negro unit until after the jobs have been filled.

As this Commission has found in other situations, the mere existence of segregation leads to discrimination. In Georgia, the State employment service facilities are segregated and there are no Negro employees of the employment service outside Atlanta. Employment by the employment service, and facilities available to Negro applicants in Atlanta are "separate" but a long way from equal. Over half of the people using the facilities of the Atlanta office are Negro. Yet the Negro staff consists of 17 people while the staff servicing white job seekers numbers 53 (a few of the white personnel perform jobs necessary for both sections), and the space assigned to the Negro section, handling over half the business, is no greater than one-quarter of the space provided for whites....

THE CONSTRUCTION CRAFT UNIONS

Because union membership or referral by the union is a virtual necessity for obtaining employment on unionized projects (the bulk of commercial construction), the extent of Negro membership in construction craft unions determines the extent of Negro employment in this industry. Indeed the Negro has made little progress beyond his base of traditional strength in the "trowel" trades (plastering, lathing, bricklaying, and cement finishing) and unskilled and semiskilled construction labor. Census and Bureau of Labor Statistics figures show that between 1910 and 1960, in the carpentry trade, the Negro has actually lost ground. On the other hand, the number of Negroes employed as construction laborers has increased by 50 percent during the past decade. In the plumbing, metalworking, and electrical trades, both 1950 census figures... show that Negro employment is minimal.

A 1957 Urban League study of Negro membership in construction unions in 32 cities showed a uniform pattern of exclusion from certain craft unions. Commission field investigations revealed the same pattern. In Baltimore there are no Negro members of the ironworkers, steamfitters, plumbers, electrical workers, or sheetmetal workers unions. The cement masons, painters, plasterers, lathers, bricklayers, construction laborers, operating engineers, and riggers unions do have Negro members....

Some [unions] openly practice racial discrimination in their membership policies. Local union officers have been known to explain the absence of Negro members in the following terms: " 'Nigras' are all afraid of electricity"—"Jews and colored folks don't want to do plumbing work because it is too hard."...

When discrimination exists, it is apparently by tacit agreement of the local union membership. None of the construction unions surveyed have racially restrictive provisions in their constitutions or bylaws. Most, however, require that an applicant for membership be approved by the local before ac-

ceptance. It is clear that the absence of Negro members in the "lily-white" construction locals means that few, if any, Negroes will be employed in these highly paid craft jobs on union construction projects. Obviously, then, to the extent that union membership practices are discriminatory, they deny employment opportunities to Negroes on racial grounds....

Even those unions which admit Negroes to membership, however, may discriminate against them with respect to job opportunities. Examples of such discrimination may be found in both the segregated union situation and in integrated unions where Negro membership is minimal....

Negro locals in Atlanta may be called upon to provide token Negro participation on some Government projects. Frequently, however, they find themselves completely excluded from jobs as most contractors hire through the white locals. It was reported in Atlanta that members of one of the white locals recently walked off the job in protest against the contractor's hiring workmen from the sister Negro local. Allegedly on other occasions white unions members were brought in from other cities to avoid placing Negroes on jobs. The competition between Atlanta's white and Negro locals has hit the Negro locals so hard that one has become virtually extinct; members of the other have been forced 131 to seek work below union rates, because of their inability to find jobs on union construction."...

INDUSTRIAL UNIONS

Industrial unions bring together both the skilled and unskilled into the same organizations and rely upon numerical strength—rather than control of a special skill—to provide bargaining power. This more egalitarian approach usually results in Negroes and whites becoming members of the same union, a situation more conducive to equality of treatment....

In industrial plants union membership appears readily available to Negroes. Of 17 unions studied by the Commission in Atlanta and Baltimore, all have Negro members (as do all those studied in Detroit). The one international in Atlanta that maintained a separate Negro local has recently merged it with the white locals. Ten of these unions have Negro members on their executive boards, and Negroes are serving as minor officers or job stewards in all. In one Atlanta union, a Negro was recently chosen to head the union election committee by his fellow white committee members. Another Atlanta local has had a Negro organizer on its payroll for a number of years. All of these unions hold integrated meetings, although there appears to be seating segregation in some of the Atlanta meetings. But even Atlanta's union halls do not usually have separate drinking fountains or restroom facilities. In Baltimore, some locals sponsor integrated recreational and social activities, something which rarely occurs in Atlanta. In Atlanta, however, many union members may have their first experience in integration within their unions.

But the fact that these unions accept Negroes as apparent equals does not mean that Negroes enjoy similar status on the job. In Atlanta Negro union members may work in a plant that is entirely segregated; separate drinking fountains, restrooms, eating facilities, and even timeclocks are customary. There is no indication that the unions are attempting to change this in-plant segregation. On the other hand, in Baltimore few vestiges of the segregated system are visible. One Baltimore union was reported to have prevailed upon an employer to eliminate its practice of segregated employee picnics.

The most important manifestation of unequal job opportunity, however, is the frequently inferior job status of Negro employees in the industrial plants. Most of the firms interviewed in Atlanta, Baltimore, and Detroit employed substantial numbers of Negroes. Often, however, Negro employees were found only in unskilled and semiskilled jobs....

The Commission's investigation in the Baltimore and Detroit areas revealed no instances of disparity of wage rates between Negroes and whites performing similar work, nor any evidence of union unwillingness to enforce bargaining contracts on behalf of Negro employees. Atlanta, where the idea of distinct Negro and white jobs still prevails, presents a different picture. With only limited exceptions, Negro employees are confined to unskilled classifications, principally janitorial and common labor jobs. Unions apparently are unwilling to try to improve job opportunities for Negroes. For the most part these unions were confronted with company restrictions on Negro employment at the time collective bargaining was established. The departmental or occupational seniority provisions subsequently written into the collective-bargaining agreements have merely served to freeze preexisting discriminatory employment patterns. Clearly, if Negroes traditionally have been assigned to unskilled jobs in nonproduction departments, their chances of advancement to better work are hampered by such seniority systems....

An Atlanta representative of an international noted for its enlightened attitude on race relations provided some insight into union attitudes. When his union organized the plants in question, production jobs were exclusively white. He explained that, although the union had never urged an employer to discriminate in job assignments, officers of the union—having a predominantly white membership—were unwilling to jeopardize their positions by trying to persuade an employer to give production jobs to Negroes. So the stalemate continues, the company acceding to supposed community attitudes and the union acquiescing for fear of antagonizing a membership sharing these attitudes. The Negro is the victim.

Chapter Twelve: The Color of Politics

"A man with a ballot is his hand is the master of the situation. He defines all his other rights. What is not already given him, he takes." - Wendell Phillips

Throughout American history voting has been both a powerful instrument of allocating resources and privileges as well as a means by which Americans have defined and expressed their identities. Voting is the fundamental force that directs how public resources are distributed. Those groups who have dominated the ballot box have received a disproportionate share of the government's protection and it's bounty. In the first decades of American government the wealthiest landowners controlled most state and local governments and they made sure that government resources were expended to construct roads near their farms, or to levy taxes that weighed most heavily on the poor. Slave-owners controlled the federal government for seventy years and ensured that federal power was used to recapture runaway slaves and make cheap land available to expand the frontiers of slavery by conquering and expelling Indian tribes.

Today, Americans view voting as a right, though this is a thoroughly modern view of the institution and one not shared by the founding generation. The revolutionaries who built the American republic in the last third of the 1700s viewed voting not as a right but as a privilege; a privilege to which only a few wealthy white men were qualified to claim.

Figure 12-1 Congress voting the Declaration of Independence, from unfinished painting by Robert Edge Pine and Edward Savage, early 19c.

To understand the political beliefs of the founders, so different and distant from our own, it is essential to appreciate how rare and fragile an experiment a republic, a government ruled by its people rather than a hereditary ruler, a church, or a group of aristocrats was. It was commonly understood that the great empire of Rome fell after a disastrous excess of popular participation in government. The very word "democracy" was at the time a disreputable one with a strong connotation of mob rule that inevitably devolved into either anarchy or popular dictatorship, otherwise known as rule by a demagogue (a word sharing the same root as democracy).

The problem, it seemed to people like Jefferson, Adams, Washington, and Madison, was that democracy, if not carefully confined, had a tendency to allow the self interest of a particular group to overwhelm the best interests of the nation. Even worse, various groups, defined by their selfish interests, could become permanent competitors for the wealth and power of the government. Madison called such groups "factions." A representative government, they believed, should be a body in which differing ideas, opinions, and interests could meet and arrive at a consensus through healthy debate and compromise. However, were a faction to gain control of all of the levers of government, they would have no need to compromise and would just direct all its wealth and power toward themselves.

Even worse was the possibility that a faction could gain power through corrupt means. They feared that powerful men could control the votes of those dependent on them. The founders feared that wealthy men could buy votes from those poor enough to part with them. They feared that the weak-minded, criminal, or the unprincipled might constitute a sizeable voting bloc.

In order to avoid such "corruptions" of their republic, the founders believed it was necessary to restrict voting to those who were independent and who had a stake in society. Independence, in this sense, meant someone who was free from dependence on another, as servants, slaves, and most women were not (we still hold to a vestige of this idea in not allowing adolescents under 18 to vote). A stake was thought of as ownership of sufficient land or property to allow someone not to be tempted to sell their vote cheaply and to consider issues and problems from a longer term perspective (requirements that someone have lived for a certain time in one community also served this purpose). It is important to note that while this philosophy had the effect of barring a large number of people of color from voting, race was not the issue at the time. Such classes of people were kept from political participation not principally because of their color or sex, but because of their status and seeming lack of proper independence. This is important to note as, within a generation, white Americans will move to base their political systems on race, on white supremacy, and this shift is obscured if the earlier voting rights prohibitions are seen as simply racist or sexist acts.

At the time of the drafting of the U.S. Constitution in 1787, different states had different qualifications for voting and as the drafters did not view voting as a right they needed to protect, they left it to individual states to determine who could and could not cast a ballot. Neither the U.S. Constitution or its Bill of Rights say much about voting. Article 1, establishing Congress, specifically allows states to set "The Times, Places and Manner of holding Elections for Senators and Representatives…" Only one rule for voting was specified: states must set the same voter qualification standards for the U.S. House of Representatives as they set for their own "most numerous branch" of their legislature. Voters, however qualified, were denied a direct role in choosing the nation's higher chamber, that was to be "composed of two Senators from each State, chosen by the Legislature thereof…"

When America first became a republic it was a patchwork quilt of voting laws. All but one state, Vermont, limited voting to its wealthier citizens. Ten states required ownership of a certain minimum amount of property to vote while three others enfranchised only those who paid a certain minimum amount of taxes. Twelve states limited voting to men, New Jersey being the outlier that allowed women to vote until taking it away in 1807. Only the three largest slave-holding states (South Carolina, Georgia, and Virginia) limited voting to white men while four others in New England specifically allowed black men who had won their freedom to vote.

Thus, in the first decade of the nation's existence, in most states it was possible for free black men (and black women in New Jersey) to vote. But this situation did not last long as most states moved to specifically ban black voting in the first decades of the 1800s. By 1855 only five states in New England (Massachusetts, Vermont, New Hampshire, Rhode Island, and Maine) still allowed black men to vote.

The reasons for this drive to exclude voters on the basis of their race were rooted in fear and a rising tide of racism. Factional politics were not much of a factor as northern states had small black populations. So powerful was the specter of the black voter "corrupting" the political process that states with miniscule black populations devoted an extraordinary amount of effort in amending their constitutions and holding popular referendums to exclude them. Ohio, Indiana, and Wisconsin had fewer than one percent black residents but all held special constitutional conventions to ban black voting. With but one exception (Rhode Island) everywhere the question of prohibiting black voting was put to the voters it passed overwhelmingly.

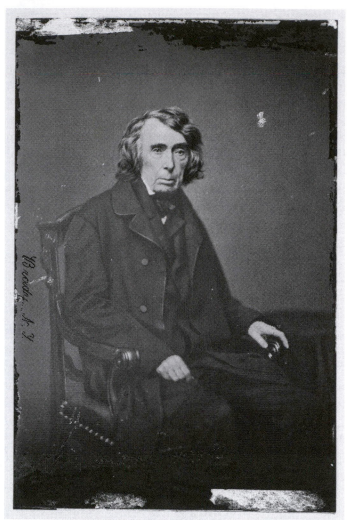

Figure 12.2 Roger B. Taney, ca. 1855-1865.

not, and could not be, citizens under the U.S. Constitution which was specifically written to establish the political rights of whites. This declaration was not a mere technicality, but a sweeping overview of the nature and character of American government, a government constructed by and for white men only. As Chief Justice Roger Taney explained, even that much misunderstood phrase, "we the people," referred only to white men:

> In the opinion of the court, the legislation and histories of the times, and the language used in the Declaration of Independence, show, that neither the class of persons who had been imported as slaves, nor their descendants, whether they had become free or not, were then acknowledged as a part of the people, nor intended to be included in the general words used in that memorable instrument.

Taney continued his review of history by observing that there was no ambiguity, no indecision or hesitation in the founder's belief in complete white supremacy:

> ...a perpetual and impassable barrier was intended to be erected between the white race and the one which they had reduced to slavery, and governed as subjects with absolute and despotic power, and which they then looked upon as so far below them in the scale of created beings, that intermarriages between white persons and negroes or mulattoes were regarded as unnatural and immoral, and punished as crimes, not only in the parties, but in the person who joined them in marriage. And no distinction in this respect was made between the free negro or mulatto and the slave, but this stigma, of the deepest degradation, was fixed upon the whole race.

In an odd, but revealing way, Taney exposes the towering hypocrisy of the founders but renders them consistent and honest by reading into their words the implicit exceptions the founders themselves chose not to write:

> We hold these truths to be self-evident: that all men are created equal; that they are endowed by their Creator with certain unalienable rights; that among them is life, liberty, and the pursuit of happiness; that to secure these rights, Governments are instituted, deriving their just powers from the consent of the governed."
>
> The general words above quoted would seem to embrace the whole human family, and if they were used in a similar instrument at this day

In states with relatively large populations of urban laborers, like New York and Pennsylvania, working class activists demanded both the elimination of property requirements for voting and the exclusion of black voters. In this way, by stressing their differences from the idle wealthy at the top and what they viewed as the dangerous and undeserving poor at the bottom, workers defined a distinct working class identity, one that was both a vital contributor to the nation through its production and was white. As one Jeffersonian party official who campaigned for a high property requirement for blacks only declared in 1821:

> The minds of blacks are not competent to vote. They are too degraded to estimate the value, or exercise with fidelity and discretion this important right...Look to your jails and penitentiaries. By whom are they filled? By the very race it is now proposed to clothe with the power of deciding upon your political rights.

In 1857, in the famed case of Dred Scott v. Sandford, the Supreme Court declared that black Americans were would be so understood. But it is too clear for dispute, that the enslaved African race were not intended to be included, and formed no part of the people who framed and adopted this declaration; for if the language, as understood in that day, would embrace them, the conduct of the distinguished men who framed the Declaration of Independence would have been utterly and flagrantly inconsistent with the principles they asserted; and instead of the sympathy of mankind, to which they so confidently appealed, they would have deserved and received universal rebuke and reprobation.

The chief justice found numerous legal examples to support his view that black people were never intended to be citizens of the American republic: the Naturalization Act of 1790 that limited citizenship to whites, the Militia Act of 1792 that required all "free able-bodied white male citizen[s]" to serve in the militia, the Maritime Act of 1813 that prohibited the hiring of sailors except "citizens of the United States, or persons of color, natives of the United States…" In the end, Taney had no difficulty finding abundant evidence in support of his conclusion that "the African race were not included under the name of citizens of a State, and were not in the contemplation of the framers of the Constitution when these privileges and immunities were provided for the protection of the citizen in other States."

Dred Scott was the definitive statement of American's predominant view of black people's rights on the eve of the Civil War. Though the decision was written by a southern slave owner and upheld by all six of the southerners on the Supreme Court, it expressed the sentiments of most white Americans. This was made abundantly evident after the war when ten states and one territory (Colorado) held statewide referenda on the question of allowing blacks to vote. Only twice, in Minnesota and Iowa, did such proposals pass.

Hypocritically, while northern states refused to open their elections to black male citizens, congressmen from those same states voted to require the defeated southern states to allow black voting as a condition of their being allowed back into the Union. The Reconstruction Act of 1867, passed over President Andrew Johnson's veto, placed the rebellious states under military rule until they approved new state constitutions that elected new state legislatures without regard to color, and also ratified the 14th Amendment to the U.S. Constitution. Within a year, seven southern states had met these conditions and allowed masses of black voters to participate in governing for the first time.

The continued unpopularity of the idea of black voting rights among northern whites was again evident as Democrats seized upon Republican support for black voting to make huge gains in the first election following passage of the Reconstruction Act. Republican politicians tried to walk a fine line thereafter, moderating their talk of equality but continuing to legislate in support of black rights in the South. This shift proved enough to hold onto the presidency in 1868, electing the hero General Ulysses S. Grant to the highest office, but losing more seats in Congress and state legislatures in the process.

Sensing that the tide was against them, radical Republicans decided they had to act quickly before losing more electoral strength and plunged ahead by proposing an amendment to the Constitution that would prohibit all states and territories from restricting voting on the basis of "race, color, or previous condition of servitude." Another more radical version of the amendment that would have positively asserted the right of all men "of sound mind" to cast ballots was defeated. In the Senate, versions of the amendment that would have struck down all sorts of property and literacy requirements, poll taxes, and other creative ways of denying people the right to vote, were voted down, revealing that the politicians who debated the Fifteenth Amendment were aware that it was a limited measure that could be effectively negated by states that were bent on doing so.

Nevertheless, the proposed Fifteenth Amendment was a revolutionary shift in federalism, shifting the authority to establish the basis of elections from the states to the federal government for the first time. While not conferring the right to vote on anyone and, for the first time, and specifically excluding women from the rights granted in the Constitution, the act did grant to Congress the "power to enforce this article," a much overlooked phrase that was the foundation stone for the civil rights revolution that had to wait another century to succeed.

The Constitution vs. Force

One of the greatest misunderstandings of American history, a myth long perpetuated by historians and public leaders uninterested in the mechanics of racial oppression, was that the passage of the three constitutional amendments after the Civil War ended slavery and established racial equality under the law. The misunderstanding here is the false idea that constitutional amendments change the way governments act or direct how society is organized. Constitutional provisions merely establish the scope and limits of legislation and governmental action, but, crucially, they lack the most essential element in actually changing institutions and behaviors, the power to enforce their principles.

The Thirteenth (1865), Fourteenth (1868), and

Fifteenth Amendments (1870) to the U.S. Constitution, that abolished slavery, established equality before the law and birthright citizenship, and allowed for black men to vote, all contain a similar last section that is usually overlooked because it reads like simple legal boilerplate: "Congress shall have power to enforce this article by appropriate legislation." Without this humble little clause, these amendments would have been little more than wishful suggestions, because it is not the Constitution that governs, but Congress. In order to realize the principles of these revolutionary reconfigurations of the Constitution, Congress had to pass laws directing how states and individuals may act and prohibiting and punishing violations of these principles.

In 1866, to fulfill these new constitutional principles, Congress passed a civil rights bill over President Andrew Johnson's veto (it was only the eighth time Congress had passed a bill without a president's signature). The Civil Rights Act of 1866 contained a both a clearer definition of what equality before the law meant than the constitutional amendments, but, more critically, contained actual means of enforcement, the usual means of governmental coercion, police, courts, jails, and armies. The law defined equality in as air-tight a manner as one could imagine at the time:

...citizens, of every race and color, without regard to any previous condition of slavery or involuntary servitude...shall have the same right, in every State and Territory in the United States, to make and enforce contracts, to sue, be parties, and give evidence, to inherit, purchase, lease, sell, hold, and convey real and personal property, and to full and equal benefit of all laws and proceedings for the security of person and

Figure 12.3 The Fifteenth Amendment and its results, drawn by G.F. Kahl (Baltimore: Schneider & Fuchs, 1870).

property, as is enjoyed by white citizens, and shall be subject to like punishment, pains, and penalties, and to none other, any law, statute, ordinance, regulation, or custom, to the contrary notwithstanding.

That first section established the principle of the matter, just as the constitutional amendments did, but it was the second and subsequent sections that gave the federal government a club with which to threaten and beat violators:

...any person who, under color of any law, statute, ordinance, regulation, or custom, shall subject, or cause to be subjected, any inhabitant of any State or Territory to the deprivation of any right secured or protected by this act, or to different punishment, pains, or penalties ...by reason of his color or race, than is prescribed for the punishment of white persons, ...shall be punished by fine not exceeding one thousand dollars, or imprisonment not exceeding one year, or both, in the discretion of the court.

Finally, knowing that local and state courts could not be relied upon to protect the rights of the people who those same officials had tortured and kept in chains, the law gave federal courts and federal marshals and federal officials the sole power to enforce the civil rights law. "...district courts of the United States...shall have, exclusively of the courts of the several States, cognizance of all crimes and offences committed against the provisions of this act..." So sweeping was the grant of power to federal courts and federal officials, that provision was made for the president to dispatch federal judges and marshals wherever he felt they were needed to enforce the law and even to use the military if he wished: "it shall be lawful for the President of the United States...to employ such part of the land or naval forces of the United States, or of the militia, as shall be necessary to prevent the violation and enforce the due execution of this act."

Southern states defied both the Constitution and these federal laws. In areas where simple fraud was not sufficient to suppress the black vote, a hostile white population supported acts of violence and terrorism against black politicians and black voters. Though often portrayed as isolated bands of "night riders" or "Ku Klux Klan" members, the scope of violence throughout the South was greater than any single organization or vigilante group could have wrought. In the election season of 1868 for example, in Louisiana alone, 1,081 people, most of them black, were murdered.

Figure 12.4 Ku Klux Klan, Watertown, N.Y., Division 289, 1870.

To counter such wholesale disregard of the law, in 1870, 1871, and 1875, Congress passed "Force Acts," laws that provided clear penalties and specific means of enforcing the constitutional amendments. Such Force Acts specified that individual violators, not just state officials, were subject to arrest, conviction, and punishment by federal officers and federal courts. Judges, prosecutors, marshals, jailers, and soldiers are what make laws effective, not words on a constitutional page.

By the time President Ulysses S. Grant finished his first term in office, he had abundant and extensive powers to enforce civil rights. The fact that such rights would be routinely denied and ruthlessly violated for another century was not for lack of legal authorization, but for lack of political will. Only for a brief period immediately following passage of the Civil Rights Act of 1866, was there any federal effort to protect the rights of black people in the South. During these few years, 1870-1877, the U.S. army suppressed white vigilantes, federal judges oversaw elections and heard civil rights complaints, and black voters proved their power by electing two U.S. senators, fourteen U.S. congressmen, and over a thousand local officials. But with the election of 1876, the incoming president, Rutherford B. Hayes, withdrew the army and other federal officials from the South and no subsequent president would attempt to enforce federal civil rights laws until President Dwight Eisenhower would deploy the army to Little Rock, Arkansas, in 1957 to enforce a federal court's order to desegregate Central High School.

Creeping Disenfranchisement

As predicted by congressmen who had pushed for a broader version of the Fifteenth amendment that would have prohibited poll taxes and other tricks, the right of southern black men to vote was steadily undermined. Legally, state governments imposed property requirements and poll taxes to depress the vote. Polling locations were limited to disadvantage areas with large black populations. Voting districts were gerrymandered to pack black voters into disproportionately few districts. Some states, like North Carolina, switched from electing county commissioners and other key officials to having the governor appoint them, thus removing the ability of even black majority districts to elect their own local officials. As these local officials were the ones who counted and certified ballots, black votes were routinely discarded and ridiculous undercounts in large black districts reported.

Northern disinterest in black people's right to vote was again demonstrated in 1878 when the Democrats, who ran racist campaigns against the extension of rights to black citizens, won majorities in both houses of Congress. For the next decade the ability of black southerners to vote and hold office deteriorated, though it was not stolen completely. In the presidential election of 1880, an estimated two-thirds of adult black men successfully defied the heavy climate of threat and intimidation and voted. Likewise, as many as sixty percent of eligible black voters cast ballots in state elections for most of that decade. But by the late 1880s, violence, fraud, and changes to local registration requirements whittled away at the black vote.

By 1888, white racists controlled all of the South's legislatures, governor's mansions, and congressional delegations, exposing previous Republican efforts at establishing political equality in the South as a half-hearted failure. But that year Republicans won back both houses of Congress and installed a Republican in the White House (though a weak Benjamin Harrison who had lost the popular vote). For the first time in fourteen years, Republicans had the chance to solve what they had come to call the "Negro Problem," though of course what they meant was the problem of white Democrats using fraud and terror to deprive black men of their right to vote. Key Republican Senators focused their efforts on passing a new improved Federal Elections Bill that would empower federal officials to register voters, supervise polls, and certify elections.

But in the twenty years since the passage of the Fourteenth Amendment, white public opinion had swung away from seeing the plight of freed men and women in the South as a political problem and toward seeing it as a matter of simple charity. Northern businessmen and philanthropists were happy to fund the Tuskegee Institute

Figure 12.5 'This is a white man's government,' The Democratic Platform, by Thomas Nast, 1868.

in Alabama that they saw as a showcase of black self-uplift through vocational training. But support for using political or military power to enforce federal laws had waned within the Republican party establishment.

President Harrison himself was a perfect example of the dimming concern with black rights in the Republican party. Though a former brigadier general in the Union army, by the time of his presidency Harrison gave little priority to the needs or struggles of black Americans. Soon after moving into the White House his own friendly Republican newspapers reported that he had fired all the mansion's black staff and replaced them with white servants. Later, many of his northern black supporters were frustrated that he appointed fewer black civil servants, a total of just ten men, during the course of his term.

Congress at this time actually considered three revealing major pieces of legislation to address the "Negro Problem" during this Congressional session. The previously mentioned Federal Elections Bill, a bill that would provide federal funding for the establishment and improvement of education for southern blacks, and a Democratic bill that would provide federal funds to assist black Americans to emigrate, preferably out of the country but funding would also be provided to relocate them to colonies in the West. But, in the end, none of these measures passed even though Republicans invested much of their political capital in pushing for the Federal Elections Bill. The bishop of the A.M.E. church in Atlanta, Henry McNeal Turner, had just cause to remark, "I have not deserted the Republican party, the Republican party has deserted me and seven millions of my race."

What this episode revealed was that northern voters had soured on any attempt to pass "special" legislation for blacks, even in the face of shockingly obvious disregard of the existing laws on the part of white southern politicians. Northern Democrats jumped on the Republican's championing of black voting rights to once again appeal to the racist emotions of the white electorate and sailed to victory in the 1892 elections, gaining control of both Congress and the Presidency for the first time since the war.

In its defense of white supremacy, the Democratic party was disciplined and consistent. When four Democrats were pressured into voting for the Thirteenth Amendment abolishing slavery in 1865, they were the last of their party to vote for a civil rights measure in that century. From 1866 to 1900, not one Democrat in either the House or the Senate voted in favor of any of the dozen or so civil rights measures considered during that time.

Democrats took advantage of their newfound power and repealed the last remaining enforcement acts passed during Reconstruction and still on the books. These laws, passed in the 1870s, empowered the federal government to intervene to protect voters whose civil rights were violated. It was these laws that were the basis for the brief period of federal military intervention when black voting rights were protected and hundreds of black officials were elected throughout the South to every position from town clerk to state governor. Though these measures had not been invoked in decades, southerners feared their latent power and northern Democrats supported their repeal as a symbol of their white national unity and their opposition to black equality. In February, 1894, the Senate followed the example of the House and passed repeal of all enforcement measures with every Democrat voting in favor and all but two Republicans voting against (with nine Republican running from the issue by choosing not to vote at all).

The failure of the Federal Elections Bill and then the repeal of the enforcement acts sent a clear signal to southern states that they had nothing to fear from northern Republicans or the federal government. That Republicans now had no interest in interfering with white control of elections in the South was made abundantly clear when the G.O.P. won back control of Congress and elected their candidate president in 1897 and yet shied away from introducing any new federal election laws.

Ironically it was Republican political success that caused their leaders to lose interest in the cause of civil rights. From the 1860s to the beginning of the 1890s, neither party was able to gain more than a slight edge on the other and throughout this period the Republicans needed the support of a minority of black voters in southern states to hold onto Congress. Civil rights for Republicans, though proclaimed as a moral issue, was, at bottom, driven by their partisan interests. As soon as it became clear that their increasing support in the West, combined with the burgeoning population of their bastions in the Midwest and the East, had tipped the map in their favor to the point where they no longer needed minorities in the South to win, the G.O.P. stopped making any serious effort to uphold civil rights.

In what proved a fitting symbol of the party's abandonment of its black constituents, for the first time the Republicans held their 1896 national convention in a segregated city in a border state, Missouri. Black delegates arriving in St. Louis found they weren't welcome in the city's hotels and had to sleep in a chartered train car.

Though Republicans controlled the federal lawmaking power and the Presidency for the next fourteen years, they did nothing to protect the right of black or Mexican-American citizens to vote. They even failed in their half-hearted attempts to make lynching a federal crime. This inaction had deadly consequences for some of the federal officials they appointed to office.

In 1897 and 1898, President McKinley appointed the usual handful of southern black party leaders to minor offices. Isaiah H. Loftin, a college graduate and a local school teacher, was appointed postmaster of Hogansville, Georgia. Loftin was brave to have accepted the job, as the last black man to have held the office, just a few years earlier, had been shot at repeatedly and his post office burned down. Loftin's immediate white predecessor refused to vacate the position and after Loftin negotiated a settlement whereby he could stay on to deliver the mail to white households, Loftin too was shot down in the street but survived. Though McKinley promised to investigate and prosecute those responsible, the culprits were not identified.

Frazier B. Baker, who McKinley made postmaster of the small town of Lake City, South Carolina, had his post office burned down within months of assuming the job. Baker persevered in spite of the warning and one night a mob of hundreds of whites stormed his home, fatally shooting Baker and his baby daughter. Under pressure from a campaign conducted by civil rights leader Ida Wells-Barnett, McKinley sent federal agents to investigate and they succeeded in having thirteen men charged with

Figure 12.6 Cartoon used in the campaign for the ratification of the North Carolina disfranchising constitution that shows Negro vampire bat rising from a 3rd party ballot box, 1900.

the murders. Though faced with overwhelming evidence, all thirteen were released by a local jury of their white peers. McKinley quietly let the matter drop.

Between the Republican party's retreat from enforcement of its own constitutional amendments and its abandonment of its own black voters, southern whites realized little now stood in the way of their completing the full disenfranchisement of their state's black citizens.

Complete Disenfranchisement

Mississippi led the way to the complete disenfranchisement of its black voters when it called a constitutional convention in the summer of 1890 and drafted a new state constitution. The magnolia state's new charter contained a number of novel regulations governing elections. Voters were required to prove their literacy to the satisfaction of the state registrar. All voters had to have been resident in their district for a full year before voting, and all voters were charged a $2 poll tax to vote (which doubled to $4 if the voter failed to pay in the previous year). More generally, the new constitution included a dizzying number of vague powers that were handed to county clerks and registrars that allowed them nearly complete authority to decide who could be registered to vote or not. While Mississippi's laws effectively reduced black voter participation from around 30% to near zero, they also suppressed the turn-out of poor whites.

Louisiana solved this problem in drafting its new constitution in 1898 by exempting anyone whose grandfather could vote in the election of 1860 from its voting restrictions. Within a few years poor whites were voting in the usual numbers while the black vote plummeted from around 130,000 in 1896 to just 5,320 in the following election. Alabama followed suit and

incorporated similar provisions in its new constitution of 1901. Virginia patterned its revised constitution of 1902 on the same plan. When Georgia copied them all in 1908, its black electoral participation rate fell from 28% to 4%.

All of these new state constitutions and voting laws that were meant to completely disenfranchise blacks were given their first major test in 1903 when the case of *Giles v. Harris* was heard by the Supreme Court. The plaintiff, Jackson W. Giles, represented more than five thousand Alabama black voters who had been excluded from registering by Alabama's revamped constitution of 1901. There was no doubt that the intention behind Alabama's voting laws was to exclude black voters as the president of the constitutional convention proclaimed publicly that the body had met "to establish white supremacy in this State." Chief Justice Oliver Wendell Holmes, Jr., ruled against Giles and the black citizens of Alabama, saying that he could not understand how adding more voters to a fraudulent system would make it less corrupt. Holmes refused to put the court in the position of having to "supervise the voting in that state" and, instead, denied the only legal or political recourse Giles had. With the high court's approval of southern states racist disenfranchisement schemes, the exclusion of blacks from the political system was nearly total.

George Henry White, son of a farmer whose land was so poor turpentine was his primary crop, grew up to become a graduate of Howard University, school principle, lawyer, and Congressman from North Carolina's gerrymandered "Black Second" District. After serving two terms, George Henry White realized that due to the disenfranchisement of his district's black voters he could not win a third. On Jan. 29, 1901, his last day in the House, Congressman White delivered his farewell speech, knowing that it was not only his personal farewell, but the end of black representation in Congress. When he stood to deliver his final remarks, George Henry White was the last black representative in Congress, one of twenty who had won seats in that body since 1869. Congressman White concluded with these lines to a burst of applause from his white colleagues in the chamber:

> This, Mr. Chairman, is perhaps the negroes' temporary farewell to the American Congress; but let me say, Phoenix-like he will rise up some day and come again. These parting words are on behalf of an outraged, heart-broken, bruised, and bleeding, but God-fearing people, faithful, industrious, loyal people - rising people, full of potential force....The only apology I have to make for the earnestness with which I have spoken is that I am pleading for the life, the liberty, the future happiness, and manhood suffrage for

one-eighth of the entire population of the United States.

After Congressman White went home that night, another black representative from a southern state would not

Figure 12.7 Hon. George H. White, 1902.

be seated in that chamber for another seventy-two years.

It is important to bear in mind that the right to vote is not an empty or symbolic right. Without representation in a republic a group can exert very little pressure upon the government to protect their interests, their property, and even their lives. In the South under disenfranchisement and Jim Crow, people of color were not even afforded the most basic functions of government—the protection of the state from criminal attacks. From the end of the Civil War to 1959, no southern white man was ever convicted of raping a black woman. In 1959 when four white men in Tallahassee, abducted Florida A&M University student Betty Jean Owens at gunpoint in front of three witnesses and raped her, they never expected to face any consequences for their crime. Only the pressure of a rapidly growing and well organized civil rights movement forced the grand

jury indictment that eventually led to the men's unusual conviction.

Republicans, once the champions of civil rights, accommodated themselves to this new, more complete, white political supremacy. President Theodore Roosevelt broke with his party's long tradition and made no political appointments of black officials in the South and began segregating federal offices, a process that would later be taken up with a renewed zeal by President Wilson. When Senator Platt of New York introduced a measure to invoke the terms of the Fourteenth Amendment and reduce the apportionment in Congress of southern states in proportion to their disenfranchisement of black voters in 1904, he received little support from his party and none from the president. President William Taft followed Roosevelt's policy of not appointing black officials in the South but unlike his predecessor who quietly did so, Taft publicly stated this as policy: "I am not going to put in places of such prominence in the South, where the race feeling is strong, Negroes whose appointment will only tend to increase that race feeling…"

By 1912, the Republican party's embrace of white supremacy was complete as all references to voting rights were scrubbed out of its party platform. By 1920, the Republican party in several southern states, including Virginia and Alabama, began refusing to allow black representatives into its party conventions or become members of the party.

Racial Discrimination and the Courts

Black folks did not simply accept this steady erosion of their rights as citizens, but the options for legal redress were closed off one by one. Black leaders and activists turned to the federal courts which, after their abandonment by the Republican party, stood as one of the last institutions still open to even hearing their appeals. Booker T. Washington secretly funded a string of legal challenges to the Grandfather Clause and the other deceitful ways southern states had stolen the ballot from the black community. In the decade between the middle 1890s and the middle 1900s, a dozen of these cases wound through the federal appellate system and posed the question of how far states could discriminate in voting. Out of a dozen cases involving various disenfranchisement provisions of several states, the U.S. Supreme Court ruled against the rights of voters all twelve times.

Following a white mob attack on the black community of Springfield, Illinois, that murdered two black men, burned the black business district and numerous blocks of black-owned homes, and forced two-thirds of the city's 3,100 black residents to flee, activists organized a national conference to discuss the ongoing problem of civil rights

White Primaries

For Democratic politicians, disenfranchising black voters down to a handful of voters was not enough. In the early 20th century white Democrats began moving to totally purge all black participation in the electoral process. They had one important tool with which to accomplish this task, the political primary, a feature of the American political system that was neither quite public or wholly private, but somewhere in-between.

In 1921, in a case unrelated to civil rights, *Newberry v. U.S.*, the Supreme Court declared that political parties, and the primaries by which they selected their candidates, were completely private undertakings, beyond the reach of the Constitution or Congress' power to regulate elections. A number of states jumped at this opportunity and passed laws restricting participation in political primaries to white voters. In 1927, in *Nixon v. Herndon*, the NAACP successfully challenged a particularly obvious Texas statute that read: In "no event shall a negro be eligible to participate in a Democratic primary election held in the state of Texas…"

But this was a short-lived victory as states simply replaced such laws with new ones that did not mention race, but merely gave full authority to political parties to set their own rules and requirements. Once again the NAACP tested the new laws and once again the high court ruled in *Smith v. Allwright* (1944) that because primaries were part of the state's election machinery and regulated by state law, they were covered by the nondiscrimination requirements of the Fourteenth Amendment. Attempting to skirt this ruling, a number of states began scrubbing all primary election regulations from their state codes. In one marathon session of the South Carolina legislature, in one day in 1944, it passed 150 laws eliminating all references to primaries from its law books.

Finally, in 1947, a federal court issued a sweeping ruling (later upheld by the refusal of the Supreme Court to review it) that smashed all such schemes to smuggle the white primary around the Constitution.

When the Supreme Court struck down white-only primary elections in 1944, some farsighted observers could see that the political power of minority communities would inevitably begin to grow. As two million black men and women moved out of the South towards the booming cities and industries of the North and West during the war, the number of black voters in the country more than doubled in less than a decade. By the 1950s the trends were clear: the number of black voters would grow both through victorious legal and social struggles in the South and migration to the North and West and with this growing political power the days of legally mandated segregation and white supremacy were numbered.

Figure 12.8 Founding members of the Niagara Movement, 1905.

in 1909. At this conference it was agreed that the denial of political rights was at the heart of the black community's oppression and powerlessness and a new organization, the National Association for the Advancement of Colored People (NAACP) was formed.

The NAACP took the lead in organizing litigation to challenge discriminatory voting laws and narrowed its sights on one in particular, the Grandfather Clause that had been recently been copied from Louisiana's model in Oklahoma. In 1915, reversing a decade of support for disenfranchisement laws, the U.S. Supreme Court, in *Guinn and Beal v. United States*, struck down Oklahoma's Grandfather Clause because it "had the purpose to disregard the prohibitions of the Fifteenth Amendment…" Oklahoma responded by passing a new more deceitful law that wrapped the same Grandfather Clause in a new disguise, permanently registering all voters who had been qualified to vote before the court's action and giving anyone who did not vote in a prior election ten days to register or be forever banned from voting in the state. Oklahoma successfully used this new law to keep blacks from voting for twenty-three more years until the NAACP challenged it and the Supreme Court struck this law down in 1939.

Gerrymandering

There are more ways to keep minority voters from expressing their political will than just blocking their right to vote. One of the oldest political tricks, drawing the lines that define a district in such a way as to minimize the votes of opposing parties and maximizing the power of one's own, proved particularly effective in limiting the ability of black communities to have a voice in government. Gerrymandering, as this tactic is called, can work in two ways, either "packing" or "cracking." Undesired voters can either be packed together into as few districts as possible, thereby limiting the number of seats they can control in a governing body, or they can be carefully divided and "cracked" into different districts so that they cannot muster a majority in any election.

When white Democrats took control of the legislature in North Carolina as a result of a violent campaign in the 1870s, they used both these tactics to limit the number of black elected congressmen. They redrew the state's district map (a process technically called "apportionment") so as to pack a majority of potential black voters into a single district that eventually came to be known as the "Black Second." At the same time they divided the remaining black communities among the remaining districts so they would not have a majority in any of them. At the end of their apportionment, even though one-third of the adult population were black, black voters could at most elect one congressman out of eight. Later, in 1900, when North Carolina followed the lead of other southern states and revised their voting laws to exclude most black voters entirely, they dismantled the "Black Second" so as to equalize the state's districts as this particular trick was no longer needed.

Similar apportionment schemes were common not only through the South, but through the nation. Until its districting system was struck down by the Supreme Court in 1964, Alabama elected a majority of the members of its state house from counties that together held but a quarter of the state's population. Los Angeles County supervisors systematically adjusted their five districts through the 1960s and 1970s to deny the fast-growing Latino population a representative on their board. Apache County, Arizona, packed 88% of its Native American population into one district that was fifteen times the population of its smallest district.

When a significant number of black voters entered the voting rolls in cities, many cities revised their electoral systems to deny them representation in governing councils. Many cities switched from electing their councilmen by district to systems where all councilmen were elected in at-large elections. An at-large system is one in which a certain number of the highest vote-getters across the city win offices. Atlanta adopted the at-large voting system in 1868 to prevent black voters from electing a black alderman. Atlanta had one election in the 1860s in which black voters elected their officials by ward system and black candidates won two of ten seats in the city's council. After adoption of the at-large system, no black official was elected to Atlanta's government again until 1953. Mobile, Alabama, was roughly one-third black but that city's at-large system kept black officeholders out of city government until 1982. Most large cities in the South and quite a few in the North had similar systems for some period of their history. Fremont county, Wyoming, a county that is one-fifth Native American, operated on an at-large voting system that denied any Indians seats on the five-member county board until 2010.

Immigrant Voting Rights

The right to vote has not always been based on citizenship. For a decade or more after the founding of the American republic many states had no citizenship requirement to vote. However, as the right to vote was expanded by lowering or abolishing property requirements and adding poll taxes, new more nationalistic legislators added prohibitions on foreign residents' ability to vote. By the time Andrew Jackson left office, foreign residents were no longer able to vote in nearly every state and territory.

But just as quickly as Jacksonian nationalism swept voting rights away from foreigners (and most free blacks) the pressure of continued immigration pushed to restore them. As Germans flooded into the midwest and the Irish crowded into eastern cities, politicians began to court these growing voter bases by relaxing the requirements for voting. Wisconsin, with more than a quarter of its population foreign-born, led the way in 1848 by allowing anyone who had resided in the state for two years, and signed a form declaring their intent to become a citizen, to vote. By the 1890s, sixteen states allowed immigrants who had not yet become citizens to vote.

At the time these laws were passed the majority of immigrants to America came from Germany, Ireland, and England. As the stream of immigrants moved from northern and western Europe to southern and eastern Europe and from mostly Protestant immigrants to mostly Catholic, Orthodox, and Jewish ones, states moved to abolish their laws that permitted noncitizens to vote. All did so by 1926, Arkansas being the last state to permit immigrant voting.

In their place, states moved to make it more difficult for new citizens to exercise their franchise. New Jersey passed a law in 1888 requiring naturalized citizens to present their naturalization documents to officers at polling stations before they were given a ballot. Several states instituted long waiting periods after an immigrant was legally naturalized before he was allowed to vote.

Native Voting Rights

Indians were long excluded from all forms of political participation. The U.S. Constitution placed native peoples in a separate legal status, referring to "Indians not taxed" and excluded them from calculations for seats in the House of Representatives, thereby implying that they were not to be part of the voting public. Rather, indigenous peoples were covered by the legal fiction that they were sovereign nations who had the right to make treaties only with the federal government and not the states. This was a legal fiction because that sovereignty was only respected when it benefited whites, such as when tribes were forced to cede lands or agree to become refugees and abandon their communities. In 1871, the building of transcontinental railroads and a rush of new settlers into western territories pushed Congress to abandon the notion that treaties were agreements between two sovereign nations and declared that the United States did not consider Indian nations sovereign nations but as dependencies that they could do with as the federal government pleased. A dozen years later, Congress did just that by passing a law that subjected all native peoples, even those living on tribal lands, to prosecution in federal courts for major crimes.

Until the Civil War, states largely determined who could or could not be considered citizens and they excluded indigenous peoples from citizenship and all that went with it, such as the right to vote, to serve on juries,or to enjoy the full protection of the law. By the 1830s, after a series of Supreme Court decisions clarified the constitutional status of Indians, the federal government officially considered Indians foreigners because they were members of tribes legally defined as "domestic, dependent nations," a status that rendered them neither fully in or out of the United States. Such ambiguity was exploited in the interests of exclusion as when on the eve of the Civil War, the U.S. Attorney General ruled that Indians were not foreigners under the terms of the nation's naturalization laws, meaning that though they were not U.S. citizens they had no right to apply to become citizens through the usual procedures.

Even after that war when Congress passed the 14th Amendment to the Constitution to confer citizenship on the millions of people freed from the bondage of slavery, this provision excluded native peoples. The wording of the amendment included a subtle but powerful clause that excluded Indian people: "all persons born or naturalized in the United States, and subject to the jurisdiction thereof, are citizens of the United States and of the state wherein they reside." The clause, "and subject to the jurisdiction thereof," was the anchor upon which federal and state courts denied native peoples, even those living in American towns and cities far from reservations, rights for the next fifty years.

In 1887, as mining and ranching interests demanded greater access to Indian lands, Congress offered citizenship to any native person who left their tribal territories, or who were willing to claim private ownership of communally held tribal lands. Sold by its promoters as a means of "civilizing" and "Christianizing" the "heathen savages," the so-called Dawes Act made citizens of a majority of native people at a steep price. The Dawes Act was a machine that effectively transferred millions of acres of land from native to white hands.

Thousands of native people volunteered and fought in World War One and their service persuaded Congress after the war to pass a bill granting Indian veterans citizenship. By 1924, two-thirds of native peoples had become U.S. citizens and as by that date it would have little practical effect, Congress passed the Indian Citizenship Act that naturalized all native peoples who lived within the borders of the United States. It should be noted that the law proclaiming all native peoples citizens of the United States

Figure 12.9 Warren G. Harding, Aug. 31, 1920.

was yet another denial of Indian sovereignty as tribes were not asked if they wished to accept such a modification of their status, it was simply imposed upon them.

The Era of Avoidance

For nearly half of the twentieth century both major political parties attempted to keep civil rights issues out of their national campaigns while quietly courting a growing block of black voters in the swing states of Illinois, Ohio, and New York. Publicly both parties expressed little but contempt and hostility to America's people of color and even refused to showcase the few positive actions they had taken in the direction of equality.

Black leaders faced an impossible situation at the beginning of the twentieth century. The Democratic party had been successful at nearly completely disenfranchising black voters in the South, where three-quarters of black people lived, and the Republican party had abandoned any serious attempts to defend their civil rights. When the National Association for the Advancement of Colored People (NAACP) organized in 1909 and the National Urban League formed two years later, these allied civil rights organizations focused their political campaigns on the one issue whose horror and flagrant violation of the nation's bedrock principle of rule-of-law they thought might have a chance of success. In 1919, both organizations lobbied hard for passage of a bill introduced in congress by representative Leonidas Dyer of Kansas that would make "leading, aiding or abetting" a lynch mob a federal crime. The Dyer Bill also fined counties where such outrages occurred $10,000. That year the NAACP released a well-documented report that totaled the horrific sum of 3,224 lynchings since the 1880s.

It seemed for a moment as though the Republican party might unite behind the Dyer bill, especially as their 1920 standard-bearer, Warren G. Harding, declared during the campaign that "I believe the Federal government should stamp out lynching and remove that stain from the fair name of America...I believe the Negro citizens of America should be guaranteed the enjoyment of all their rights." Democrats pounced on Harding's statement and warned voters that if Harding were to be elected whites would be forced to allow their daughters to marry black men and armed black militias would guard polling places. Professor William E. Chancellor, a professor at the College of Wooster, a school not far from Harding's Ohio home, published an article purporting to prove by Harding's genealogy that the presidential candidate was legally a black man. Chancellor was fired and the Republicans hurriedly released Harding's family tree that "proved" he was, in fact, a white man. (Harding himself was less concerned, telling one Cincinnati reporter, "How do I know, Jim? One of my

Figure 12.10 Flyer, "The Ku Kliux Klan Invites You to the Portals," ca. 1904-1937.

ancestors may have jumped the fence.")

Civil rights campaigners' hopes were lifted in April of 1921 when President Harding addressed a joint session of Congress and urged it to "rid the stain of barbaric lynching from the banner of a free and orderly representative democracy." With majorities in both chambers of congress, the Dyer bill was passed by the House but ran into a Democratic filibuster in the Senate and Harding softened his support leaving the bill to die.

In the end, Harding was no racial progressive and only hoped to find a way of setting racial issues aside and competing with Democrats on other issues. Harding privately wrote that "my great hope is to see the matter so justly handled that we can get away from the bugaboo of the black race and establish a Republican party in the South." This is pretty much what followed as both parties increasingly avoided civil rights issues until after World War Two.

The rise of the Ku Klux Klan as a political power in the 1920s added to the subtle wedge that defeat of the Dyer anti-lynching bill opened between the Republicans and the black voters who had long been loyal to the party of Lincoln. The Klan was a defunct organization when it was revived in 1915 by William J. Simmons, a salesman who was both inspired by D.W. Griffith's movie *Birth of a Nation* and by the potential profits to be made through sales of memberships. By 1924 the Klan's message of "100 percent Americanism," its campaigns against Jews, Catholics, and people of color, and its claims of protecting the moral values of white America, brought it to national prominence. Most importantly, the Klan's influence reached far outside the South and into areas that were politically sensitive to both parties, such as the Midwest. A Klan-endorsed independent candidate won the governor's seat in Indiana. Politicians in Ohio, Maine, Colorado, and other states feared that crossing the Klan was political suicide. When the Republicans held their national convention in Cleveland in 1924, the Klan set up a prominent headquarters near the convention hall. Republican leaders then squashed an attempt to vote on a resolution condemning the KKK. Meanwhile at the Democratic national convention, an anti-Klan resolution came to a floor vote and was narrowly voted down, indicating a sort of tacit Democratic Party endorsement of the organization.

Figure 12.11 John Collier, U.S. Indian commissioner, appears before Senate Indian Affairs Committee. Washington, D.C., June 10, 1940.

To his credit, during the 1924 campaign, Democratic presidential candidate, John W. Davis, spoke out against the Klan. During one New Jersey speech, Davis stated, "if any organization...whether Ku Klux Klan or by any other name, raises the standard of racial and religious prejudice... it does violence to the spirit of American institutions and must be condemned." Davis dared Coolidge to make a similar denouncement and Coolidge declined, remaining characteristically silent on the issue. After Coolidge's ticket-mate, Charles G. Dawes, gave a speech in Maine that excused Klan actions, some magazines began referring to Coolidge as the "Ku Klux Kandidate." Coolidge spent his

first years in the White House avoiding civil rights issues and courting white southern votes.

Herbert Hoover, continued his predecessor's attempt to peel southern whites away from the Democratic party by further distancing himself from any taint of interest in civil rights. In the campaign of 1928, Hoover never mentioned that while he was Secretary of Commerce he had ordered his department to desegregate. Likewise his Democratic opponent, Al Smith, chose not to discuss his championing a law to outlaw the Ku Klux Klan while he was governor of New York. But Hoover made a huge impression with white southerners when he led a charge to purge all his party's black delegates from the Republican convention and succeeded in holding the first all-white Republican National Convention since the Civil War. Al Smith, fearing that his record as a Yankee governor might cost him votes in the South, arranged for the few black delegates to the Democratic convention to be segregated behind wire fences and supported the nomination of Senator Joseph Robinson of Alabama, a fierce segregationist, as his running mate. Just to be sure the message was clear, Smith told reporters that he believed in hiring blacks in his administration only to "fill such jobs as they are given in the South, to wit: porters, janitors, charwomen, etc." W.E.B. Du Bois expressed the sentiment of most black voters: "it does not matter a tinker's damn which of these gentlemen succeed."

Such a contest between two candidates each portraying himself as the more able defender of white supremacy was only possible because of the legal and extralegal forces that kept people of color from voting. Black voters, the largest minority group, amounted to less than 5% of eligible voters in the nation. Hoover's racism proved more effective than Smith's and he showed surprising strength in the South, winning Texas, Florida, North Carolina, Tennessee, and Virginia, and the Presidency.

By the time of the 1929 stock market crash and the start of the Great Depression, neither party had made any particular gesture to win the support of a steadily growing black electorate. But because Republicans had long been the unjustified beneficiaries of black votes, they had more to lose by neglecting this block of voters. Democrats at this time were dependent on their southern wing that was essentially a one-party, white supremacist state in the South, while Republicans privately made promises to black leaders they had no intention of keeping. In the end, black voters faced two parties hostile and indifferent to their interests, a situation that loosened their loyalty to the party of Lincoln and laid the groundwork for a dramatic partisan shift.

Franklin Delano Roosevelt was elected president in 1932 in the usual manner for Democrats, by selecting a southern segregationist, John Nance Garner of Texas, as his running mate and appealing to the "solid South" of white voters. FDR's margin of victory was similar to Hoover's

Figure 12.11 Marian Anderson at the dedication of a mural commemorating her free public concert on the steps of the Lincoln Memorial in 1939, in the Department of Interior Auditorium on January 6, 1943.

four years earlier, an outcome not unexpected as the incumbent had to run on a record that included leading the country into an economic depression with a 20% unemployment rate. Black voters split nearly evenly between the Democrats and Republicans, a fitting judgement on two parties that had both abandoned them.

Nevertheless, over the next four years, Roosevelt's New Deal, though designed to deliver most of its benefits exclusively to whites, provided much needed relief to black communities. When Roosevelt ran for reelection in 1936, he did so with an unprecedented degree of support from black leaders and the black press and pulled a record three out of five black voters into the Democratic column.

Recognizing the growing importance of the black Democratic vote, FDR sent clear signals to the black community that he was their best bet, though publicly he refused to support legislation to make lynching a federal crime or to outlaw poll taxes that remained a racist tool to keep nonwhite voters from casting ballots. Roosevelt appointed a record number of black experts to work in his administration, though always below the cabinet level. (It wouldn't be until 1966, when Lyndon Johnson appointed Robert Weaver as secretary of the newly created Department of Housing and Urban Development, that a black official would join a president's cabinet.)

Roosevelt's record in regard to other racial minorities was even more mixed. He appointed a well-known reformer, John Collier, to be Commissioner of Indian Affairs and supported Collier's dismantling of the policy of "allotment" that had broken up reservation lands and made them available to private speculators and corporate interests. But Roosevelt did not lift a finger to oppose the actions of various western states that were rounding up and summarily deporting hundreds of thousands of Mexicans. FDR signed the Tydings-McDuffie Act (1934) that reclassified Filipinos from being residents of a U.S. territory to being "aliens" ineligible for federal aid and subject to deportation. First lady Eleanor Roosevelt established herself as a civil rights advocate even as her husband struggled to hold the southern wing of his party by not supporting measures that would combat segregation. Most famously, Eleanor resigned her membership in the Daughters of the American Revolution Society when that organization refused to allow the world-famous black contralto, Marian Anderson, to sing in Washington's Constitution Hall and arranged for her to sing at the Lincoln Memorial instead.

The simple fact was that until the Civil Rights movement began achieving judicial victories in the 1950s and 1960s, both major parties were content to ignore issues of systematic and institutional racism. Democrats were a party tied to its historic commitment to white supremacy and its southern wing that held sway over a third of the nation's states and which, because of their one-party longevity in office, controlled virtually all the committee chairmanships in congress. Republicans depended on the loyalty of its black voters without actually delivering any meaningful measures for fear of angering their white constituency. In the postwar period, the black vote was almost evenly split between the two parties and both parties made similar empty rhetorical appeals to them.

For a brief moment it looked as though President Harry Truman might push the Democratic party into a stronger civil rights stand. In 1946, Truman issued an executive order establishing a commission on civil rights to investigate the issue, and when its report, entitled, "To Secure These Rights," was released the following year, Truman endorsed its proposals to end segregation and discrimination in the federal government, to abolish poll taxes, and to make lynching a federal crime. As he campaigned for his first election as president (he had assumed the office upon the death of Roosevelt in 1945), Truman issued executive orders desegregating the armed forces and creating a permanent commission to root out discrimination in federal employment.

Truman's own party rebelled against his civil right initiatives. At the 1948 Democratic convention in Philadelphia, the Mississippi and Alabama delegations staged

Figure 12.12 1964 Democratic National Convention, Atlantic City, New Jersey.

dramatic walkouts in protest of passage of a party platform that endorsed the president's civil rights agenda. Truman waited until after the convention to issue his order desegregating the armed forces, but when he released it the disgruntled southern wing of his party broke away and supported Senator Strom Thurmond of South Carolina who ran for president on the ticket of their newly founded "States Rights Democratic Party." Thurmond carried four crucial southern states and came within a whisker of denying Truman an electoral college victory.

Truman's near defeat because of southern defections frightened Democrats into retreat from his civil rights agenda. The party's nominee for president in 1952 and 1956, Adlai Stevenson of Illinois, remained so cold to black voters that many returned to the Republican fold. Dwight D. Eisenhower attracted the highest proportion of black votes for a Republican candidate since 1932 and the most any Republican presidential candidate would earn since.

As late as the campaign of 1960, both political parties equally ignored and equally attracted the votes of people of color. Neither party in that campaign had clear stands on the major civil rights issues of the day, school integration and voting rights. John Fitzgerald Kennedy

had a poor civil rights voting record in the Senate where he had cast a decisive vote against a provision in a 1957 civil rights bill that essentially made it unenforceable. Even though Kennedy was a thorough Yankee from the most Yankee state of Massachusetts, he was favored for a place on the 1956 ticket as vice-president by the party's southern "Dixiecrat" wing.

Kennedy's Republican opponent, Richard Milhous Nixon, was one of the more outspoken proponents of civil rights and had taken the opposite position from JFK on the 1957 bill. Unlike JFK's running mate, Texan Lyndon Baines Johnson, who had been put on the ticket to appeal to the segregationist south, Nixon's running mate, Henry Cabot Lodge, had spent much of his career pushing for federal civil rights enforcement. Nixon assumed he would easily win the majority of black votes just as Eisenhower had done, especially since it was Eisenhower who had stuck his neck out and ordered federal troops into Little Rock, Arkansas, in 1957 to enforce the court order desegregating schools. Neither candidate made any special appeals or campaigns for the black vote, except for one magnificently important phone call.

Fewer than three weeks prior to the election, fifty-two activists, including Dr. Martin Luther King, Jr., walked into Rich's department store in downtown Atlanta and took seats at the lunch counter in the 'Magnolia room.' They were the first to defy custom and law and attempt to integrate this Atlanta institution and city police quickly arrived and arrested the entire group. A hostile judge freed all the protesters when they plead guilty and paid small fines except for Dr. King, who, the judge noted, was still in the probationary period of an earlier infraction, a trumped up charge for driving without a license. King was denied bail and sentenced to four months in Reidsville State Prison, a punishment his supporters feared could easily lead to his being killed by a racist guard or inmate. On the day he was transferred from the Atlanta jail to the state prison, JFK called Coretta Scott King and assured her that

Figure 12.13 Fannie Lou Hamer, Mississippi Freedom Democratic Party delegate, at the Democratic National Convention, Atlantic City, New Jersey, August 1964.

he would do what he could to aid her husband. At the same time, Kennedy's brother Robert, called the Atlanta judge and pressured him into releasing King on bond.

News of JFK's phone call was front page news in the black press but was buried deep in the back pages of national papers. For many in the black community it meant much more than party platforms, staged votes, and promises that were never kept anyway. Here was a candidate who, despite appearances and his own sorry record, seemed to be on their side and, more importantly, took action. Kennedy won a squeaky close election by just 9,000 votes in the state of Illinois. Bitter Republicans blamed Kennedy's narrow victory on the enthusiasm of dead voters in Chicago graveyards for Kennedy, but astute political observers recognized a new phenomenon. The northern black vote had swung the election. Kennedy owed his office to the 15% of black voters that had swung from the Republican to the Democratic column.

Little could anyone know then, but this was the last election in which the two parties could both assume some measure of black support. Increasingly from that year on, the two parties would begin to polarize along lines of race as the Republican party would increasingly brand itself as the party of white voters and the Democratic party would more openly embrace the hopes and ambitions of African Americans.

This growing power of the Republican Right was proven when Barry Goldwater won the party's nomination for President in 1964. Goldwater was one of only eight Senators, not from southern states, to vote against the Civil Rights Act of 1964 and he understood the deep white resentment and anxiety that the easing of Jim Crow had caused. Speaking privately to a Georgia politician, Goldwater reportedly said at the time, "We ought to forget the big cities. We can't out-promise the Democrats….I would like to see our party back up on school integration. The Supreme Court decision is not the supreme law of the land." Goldwater avoided using the explicit racism of the past but instead hammered away with euphemisms that communicated to whites his identification with their racial interests (what political scientists call "dog whistles"). Goldwater denounced "urban crime" (meaning dangerous minorities) and "disorder" (civil rights campaigners) that threatened all "good citizens" (white people) and championed "states rights" (disenfranchisement) and "freedom of association" (segregation). Embracing whiteness both symbolically as well as rhetorically, Goldwater's advance team filled the southern auditoriums where he campaigned with overflowing arrangements of white lily flowers and arrayed scores of girls in white gowns on stage.

On the other side, Lyndon Baines Johnson was the first southern nominee for president on the Democratic ticket since the days of Reconstruction. In spite of his southern bonafides, he faced a segregationist primary challenge from Alabama governor George Wallace. Wallace knew that under his party's rules he had no chance of winning the nomination from an incumbent president, but he hoped a strong showing in the primaries would send

Figure 12.14 Barry Goldwater, Sept. 1962.

Hubert Humphrey as vice president, a Minnesota senator long recognized as the most liberal advocate of civil rights in the party.

In the election, Goldwater won only six states, his home state of Arizona and five deep south states: Louisiana, Alabama, Mississippi, Georgia, and South Carolina. But these were the most southern states any Republican had won since 1872 when military forces watched over the polls. Goldwater's southern supporters were virtually all white, while nationally Goldwater attracted only 6% of nonwhite voters.

In spite of the Wallace insurgency and the political alarm bells it set off in the party, Johnson plunged ahead, twisting arms and pushing a landmark voting rights bill through Congress in 1965. The Voting Rights Act prohibited many of the tricks southern states had used to prevent black voters from registering or casting their ballots, even allowing for the federal Justice Department to send federal registrars to historically racist counties to register voters directly. Most importantly, one provision, Section 5, required states with a history of racist voter suppression to submit any changes to their election systems to the Justice Department for approval before becoming law. This law finally broke the back of racist voter discrimination in the heart of the deep South. Mississippi, where only one in twenty of possible black voters managed to register in 1960, by the nation's bicentennial had raised this to two out of three. Across the South in this period the number of registered voters rose from 1.5 million to over 4 million.

Less famously, but no less importantly, alongside passage of the Voting Rights Act, a proposal to add a constitutional amendment abolishing poll taxes advanced quietly through enough state legislatures to become the Twenty-Fourth Amendment in August of 1964. Ironically, the United States, a nation born in a rebellion against class privileges of voting and officeholding, was one of the last countries in the world to abolish fees intended to keep the poor from voting.

Goldwater lost the election of 1964 but proved that Republicans with an anti-civil rights message could do well among white voters. That is why the advent of the "Republican Right" in the 1960s was such a seachange in the modern political system. For the first time in the twentieth century, the two major political parties were becoming increasingly polarized by race. Democrats were becoming a multiracial party in the North and the party of blacks in the South. Republicans were becoming a white party in the North and the exclusive representative of whites in the South. After passage of the civil rights laws, many formerly Democratic white congressmen flipped parties and became Republicans, including such fixtures of the Senate as Strom Thurmond, Jesse Helms, Trent Lott, and Phil Gramm. In reaction to the Democratic Party's embrace of civil rights

a message to Johnson and restrain him from further pursuing a civil rights agenda. Wallace discovered a well of white resentment in the North, winning nearly a third of the votes in Indiana and more than that in Wisconsin.

White resentment at Johnson's steps to further integration collided with the increasingly visible and vocal civil rights movement at the Democratic national convention. Two states, Alabama and Mississippi still sent delegates selected from all-white primary elections to the convention. They were met by representatives of the Mississippi Freedom Democratic Party, a grassroots organization bravely fighting for the right to vote. In a live broadcast on national television, MFDP leader Fannie Lou Hamer gave an impassioned testimonial to the convention's credentials committee and forced Johnson's team to negotiate. Democratic leaders said they couldn't agree to seat the MFDP delegates in place of the Mississippi regulars or risk a total walkout of southern states. Instead they offered the MFDP two seats in the convention and a promise that in 1968 the party would have no all-white primaries and an integrated convention. To seal the deal, Johnson added

Figure 12.15 Pres. Nixon with Sammy Davis, Jr., new member of National Advisory Council on Economic Opportunity, July 1971.

and new government initiatives to end poverty by spending it out of existence, a new more socially and fiscally conservative wing of the party gained strength.

When Richard Nixon plotted his second run for the White House in 1968, he adopted the lessons of Goldwater's campaign and followed what his strategists called the "Southern Strategy" to appeal to disaffected southern white voters and to realign the formerly all-Democratic "solid south" into a Republican bastion. Nixon pitched his campaign to appeal to white Democrats, including white ethnics, especially Catholics in the North, who felt abandoned by their party's support for civil rights measures like school busing. Nixon really had little to lose politically by appealing primarily to whites as by then only three percent of black voters registered as Republicans. Doubling down on dog-whistle racial rhetoric in anticipation of his reelection run in 1972, Nixon swept every southern state.

Nixon's defeat in Vietnam, and his many scandals leading to his impeachment and resignation, destroyed his reputation and the prospects for his party in 1976. On the other side, the nomination of Jimmy Carter revealed the identity crisis of the Democrats.

The plain truth of the candidate from Plains, Georgia, was that the Democratic party had become more reliant than ever on the black vote and could not simultaneously hold its white southern base and appeal to black voters at the same time. However, Democrats were not ready to accept this and tried to navigate an impossible line between the two constituencies.

Carter himself embodied these contradictions. A liberal from the deep south, as a young man he had been raised with black servants and field hands who called him "massa." As he came of age, Carter chose to not embrace the racism of his class, refusing to join the local chapter of the White Citizens Council, an organization coordinating protests against integration, and instead advocated the integration of his Baptist church. But when elected to his first public position, as a member of his local school board, he approved unequal funding for black schools and a shorter school year for black children so they could spend more time picking cotton.

When he made his bid for the governor's mansion in 1970, he ran a racist campaign that was victorious due to his support from segregationists and white rural voters. But immediately after taking the oath of office, Carter gave a speech in which he declared, "...I say to you quite frankly that the time for racial discrimination is over...no poor, rural, weak, or black person should ever have to bear the additional burden of being deprived of the opportunity of an education, a job or simple justice." Many of his supporters standing around him were stunned, including segregationist Lieutenant Governor Lester Maddox, about whom one reporter quipped, "The sound of Lester Maddox's jaw dropping still echoes in the Statehouse." Carter substantially increased the number of black appointees working in state government and in contrast to his predecessor, who refused to allow the slain body of Dr. Martin Luther King, Jr., to lie in state at the capitol, Carter declared King's birthday a state holiday and hung his portrait prominently in the statehouse.

Just as he had in running for the governor, in running for president Carter subtly appealed to angry white voters by seeming to denounce welfare spending, public housing, and forced busing, while leaving the door open to supporting such measures later. Hard pressed in the primaries by George Wallace, who represented a somewhat reformed version of the old Dixiecrat wing of the party, Carter at times sounded like a racist, telling a reporter at one point that neighborhoods had a right to maintain their "ethnic purity" and oppose "black intrusions." But behind the scenes Carter assembled an integrated campaign staff that made inroads with the broader black community by pointing to his record and not his words in Georgia. Carter ultimately won the Democratic nomination by splitting the white vote and enjoying the solid support of black voters.

Carter's election was in many ways a fluke, a result of a nation scarred by war, the Watergate scandal, and a creeping economic stagnation rather than the competition of issues or personalities that often take center stage. Waiting in the Republican wings for his chance was Ronald Reagan, former governor of California who in 1976 had narrowly lost a bruising primary battle with Gerald Ford. While Reagan chose to avoid most hot-button racial issues in his campaign, he had mastered the exploitation of symbolic moments to send a message to his supporters. Reagan's handful of small attempts to reach out to black voters fell flat, but they succeeded in telegraphing a tone of hostility to black concerns. While giving a speech in the South Bronx, he was heckled by a resident and he turned to the black woman and yelled, "I can't do a damn thing for you if I don't get elected!" As one political analyst of Reagan's campaign noted, "Perhaps part of Reagan's appeal to the white backlash was that he was the rare white politician who would show public anger at blacks without apology or hesitation."

Once in office, Reagan hired onto his campaign staff a young strategist named Lee Atwater who had previously worked on arch segregationist Strom Thurmond's senatorial campaign. Atwater's genius was manipulating racial symbols in a way that stirred white voters to flee the Democratic party. His signature moment came in 1988 when Reagan's vice president, George Herbert Walker Bush, running for his own term as president, faced a strong challenge from the governor of Massachusetts, Michael Dukakis. Rarely do political parties win third presidential terms and Dukakis, though not a particularly charismatic or effective campaigner, was rising in the polls when Atwater convinced Bush to make a local Massachusetts criminal case the centerpiece of his campaign.

Massachusetts, like several other states, had programs intended to help inmates who were close to parole or their release dates reintegrate back into their communities, rather than just pushing them out the gates holding a box with their possessions. William "Willie" Horton was serving a life sentence for a murder he had committed as a teenager in 1974 and was close to being paroled. Prison officials recommended him for "furloughs," or weekend passes, to visit his family and during one of these releases Horton left the state and beat a man and raped a woman. To Atwater, the image of "Willie" Horton, a large black man with a bushy hairdo, was the symbol he had been searching for to associate Dukakis with liberal coddling of dangerous black criminals. Atwater was famously quoted saying of Dukakis, that he was going to make "Willie Horton his running mate." The Bush campaign put out an advertisement showing white and black inmates walking through a revolving prison door that in combination with private political action committee advertisements that prominently featured Willie Horton's mug shot, probably won the election. Later, Atwater explained confidentially to a biographer how he thought politics had evolved in the post-civil rights period:

> You start out in 1954 by saying, "Nigger, nigger, nigger." By 1968 you can't say "nigger"—that hurts you, backfires. So you say stuff like, uh, forced busing, states' rights, and all that stuff, and you're getting so abstract. Now, you're talking about cutting taxes, and all these things you're talking about are totally economic things and a byproduct of them is, blacks get hurt worse than whites.... "We want to cut this," is much more abstract than even the busing thing, uh, and a hell of a lot more abstract than "Nigger, nigger."

It was only in the 1990s with Bill Clinton's success at winning back some of the party's lost "Reagan Democrats" that Republican strategists began raising the issue of racial diversity within the party. These pundits understood that given demographic trends the racially divisive politics that had proven so successful for the GOP were losing their effectiveness. Republican party leaders attempted to broaden their appeal and made gestures of support for black concerns, such as George H.W. Bush's nomination of Clarence Thomas to the Supreme Court, George W. Bush's selection of Colin Powell to be the first black Secretary of State, and of Condoleezza Rice to be the first black woman to hold that office.

For a time, these efforts seemed to pay off as the number of black delegates to the GOP convention tripled between the election of Reagan and the reelection of George W. Bush (from 55 out of the more than 2,000 delegates in 1980 to 164 by 2004). But with the candidacy of Barack Obama attracting a record number of black votes, and the steadily increasing power of extremely conservative elements within the Republican party, most notably the so-called Tea Party faction whose membership overlapped with openly white supremacist fringe elements, black participation in the GOP collapsed again.

Barack Obama rose to the top of the Democratic Party ticket in 2008 by appealing to young voters and many people who increasingly felt that the Washington power structure no longer understood or cared about their problems. Promising "hope" and "change," the junior senator from Illinois was able to successfully position himself as a Washington outsider, an identity only enhanced by the fact that Obama was a black man. His opponent was Arizona senator John McCain, a man who had held his seat for more than two decades by the time of the election. To balance McCain's image as a beltway insider, the GOP

Figure 12-16 Official portrait of President-elect Barack Obama on Jan. 13, 2009.

picked Sarah Palin, the one-term governor of America's third-least populous state, as his running mate. While Palin appealed to the growing hard right wing of the party, she alienated many moderates and voters of color with her shoot-from-the-hip comments. Black voters were reminded that, while governor, Palin refused to issue a proclamation commemorating Juneteenth, the holiday celebrating emancipation from slavery.

Obama's historic election as president marked a special moment in American history, though it proved not to be the turning point toward an inclusive, post-racial political era that many pundits hailed it to be at the time.

On the one hand, Obama's victory reflected more of a generational shift than a racial one. Demographers noted that the election of 2008 was one of the first in which the so-called "Millennial Generation" was able to vote. This generation, those born in the 1980s and 1990s, is by far the largest generational cohort to be born in America since the famous Baby Boom of the 1950s and early 1960s, and, more importantly, a much more diverse one. Where previous generations born in the twentieth century were roughly one-quarter people of color, the Millennial Generation is four-tenths African American, Latino, Asian, Native, or

others who identify themselves as "mixed." One-in-five has a parent who immigrated to America. Where it not for the votes of Millennials, two-thirds of whom cast their ballots for Barack Obama, America would not have elected its first African American president.

On the other hand, careful sociological analysis of county by county voting patterns later revealed that Obama's candidacy uncovered a deep racial resentment that continued to divide Americans. Fewer than a third of whites who lived in the states of the old Confederacy voted for Obama. Only 43% of white voters overall chose Obama. There is also some evidence that whites who perceived themselves as losing demographic ground to minorities were more likely to vote for McCain. Those counties that went more Republican in 2008 than they had in 2004 were those that were predominantly white in states with high black populations.

A team of social psychologists examined data from over a thousand people who took tests to evaluate their unconscious (or "implicit") racial bias and discovered that implicit preferences for whites and discomfort with blacks was a strong predictor of voting patterns in the 2008 election. Another group of political scientists found that though few whites would publicly state any hesistation in voting for a black candidate, nearly one-in-three whites expressed such concerns when they believed their opinions were anonymous and private.

Four years later, facing a black incumbent president, rather than reaching out to voters of color, the Republican party intensified its appeal to white voters by provoking their fears that America would soon be governed by a non-white majority. In the final days of the campaign between President Obama and challenger Mitt Romney in 2012, Republican vice presidential candidate Paul Ryan told voters that President Obama was a leading the country down a road that threatened the "Judeo-Christian" values upon which the country was founded. "It's a dangerous path, it's a path that grows government, restricts freedom and liberty, and compromises those values, those Judeo-Christian, Western civilization values that made us such a great and exceptional nation in the first place..." Such mention of "western civilization" as being threatened by a black president and his multiracial coalition of supporters was a dog whistle of unmistakable volume.

As the election returns were tabulated the night of the President Obama's reelection, conservative pundit Bill O'Reilly bitterly described the results as representing the end of "traditional" white America:

> [It's] a changing country, the demographics are changing, it's not a traditional America anymore. And there are 50 percent of the voting public who want stuff. They want things. And

who is going to give them things? President Obama. He knows it and he ran on it.

And, whereby, 20 years ago President Obama would have been roundly defeated by an establishment candidate like Mitt Romney. The white establishment is now the minority. And the voters, many of them, feel that this economic system is stacked against them and they want stuff.

When Donald Trump stampeded to win the Republican nomination in 2016 with a campaign that openly catered to white fears of racial equality and the increasing cultural diversity of America, the Republican party became a nearly all-white party. At the Republican convention in Cleveland that embraced Trump as the party's leader, out of 2,742 party delegates only 16 were black.

According to the definitive review of the 2016 election, the American National Election Study (ANES), a series of surveys and data analyses that has been conducted since Truman was elected President in 1948, Trump rode to victory on a wave of white prejudice. Comparing party choice to racial attitudes, the ANES found the largest

partisan division in racial attitudes since it began tracking the issue in 1988. Donald Trump's pledge to "Make America Great Again" and his open gestures of nationalism and intolerance towards religious and racial minorities, such as Muslims and Mexican-Americans, attracted the votes of most white people. According to exit polls on election day, Trump beat Hillary Clinton by 21 percent among white voters (58% to 37%). This was a larger white margin than Romney polled in 2012.

These patterns had deeper roots than just the backlash against Obama. In 2016, a group of political demographers compared data from the era of slavery with a large survey of Americans' contemporary political attitudes. Startlingly, they discovered that slavery, though now formally abolished for more than 150 years, continued to exert a powerful influence over white people's political views and party affiliations. They found that "whites who currently live in counties that had high concentrations of slaves in 1860 are today on average more conservative and express colder feelings toward African Americans than whites who live elsewhere in the South." This effect was not related to the overall present-day proportion of blacks in that particular community, but rather to the historical importance of slavery in that locality.

Structural Disenfranchisement

Civil rights laws revolutionized American politics and eradicated the worst forms of racial disenfranchisement, racist registration systems, white-only primaries, poll taxes, racial gerrymandering, and literacy tests. But in sweeping away these supports of the old Jim Crow political system, the federal civil rights laws were not able to actually implement the principle that each person's vote should count equally, regardless of their color. The problem is that a number of the structural features of the Constitution enhance the power of white voters and diminish that of people of color. As these effects are a consequence of the deeper architecture of American government, they are beyond the reach of the Voting Rights Act and similar legislation.

Two constitutional structures, the U.S. Senate and the Electoral College, are particularly effective in diminishing the value of the votes of people of color. Both of these institutions were originally established to balance the power of voters against the power of the states that made up the federal union. In the words of the founders these bodies were designed to protect minorities, such as the interests of small states, against the "tyranny of the majority." As such, states, no matter how large or small, have equal representation in the Senate and an outsized role in the Electoral College.

At the time of the drafting of the U.S. Constitution

Figure 12.17 Trump Taj Mahal, 2000.

in 1787, the largest state, Virginia, contained 110,936 potential voters, that is free white men above the age of 16. The smallest state, Delaware, had 11,783 such persons for a difference of nearly ten to one. Today, the smallest state, Wyoming, has around a half million citizens, while the largest, California, has 35 million, a difference of 70 to 1, or seven times that of the largest size disparity at the nation's founding.

Moreover, out of the original thirteen states, four were large and four were small, the majority falling in the middle. Today a dozen states have so few residents that they qualify for just one or two congressional seats. Of these, only Rhode Island, Hawaii, Alaska and Delaware have a significant nonwhite population. The rest average just two percent nonwhite voters. But these small, overwhelmingly white states, that collectively hold nearly one-quarter of the seats in the Senate, have just 3.8% of the nation's total population. These population disparities also skew the Electoral College vote for president.

The situation is even worse when it comes to Latino representation. Because of historic patterns of residency, California, Texas, New York and Florida, have the bulk of Latino Americans. As a result of not being more spread across the fifty states, Latinos have fewer senators and less pull in choosing the president and are among the most underrepresented groups in American politics.

Political scientists have calculated that because of systematic underrepresentation in the Senate, black voters are missing 2.4 seats in that body and Latino voters are lacking 5.3. Or, to put it another way, whites benefit from this malapportionment by gaining nearly seven seats in the Senate their numbers alone would not merit.

While the Supreme Court did away with white-only primary elections in 1944, both political parties sequence their primaries so as to give the greatest national spotlight to two of the whitest states in the union, Iowa (91.3% white) and New Hampshire (93.9% white). Though New Hampshire residents are quick to tell others that their state has been "first in the nation" since 1920, this is a misleading statistic as presidential primaries were not important contests until the 1960s when both parties shifted power away from insiders and party officials to citizens, by allowing more delegates of their nominating conventions to be chosen by popular ballot. In effect, as voting rights legislation allowed for greater minority participation in elections, both parties established nominating calendars that artificially increased the political importance of a handful of nearly all-white states.

The diminishing of nonwhite voters' power is made even worse by the fact that citizens living in the District of Columbia do not have any representation in the Senate, even though the population of D.C. is larger than the states of Vermont or Wyoming. The black population of the district is quite large, amounting to 0.9% of all black Americans. D.C.'s white population amounts to one-tenth of that proportion of the overall white population, 0.09%. While the citizens of the district were finally granted the right to vote by the Twenty-third Amendment passed in 1961, a proposal to establish the district as a state, thereby allowing it congressional representation, failed by a wide margin in 1993. In the spring of 2016, a district-wide nonbinding referendum on whether the capital should become the nation's 51st state received 86% of votes in favor of statehood.

In addition to people of color being structurally disenfranchised because they happen to live within a few miles of the nation's Capitol, another four million citizens are disenfranchised because they happen to live in territories that were captured more than a century ago. The people of Puerto Rico, Guam, the U.S. Virgin Islands, and American Samoa do not have any representatives in Congress and are not allowed to vote in presidential elections. Collectively, these territories would constitute the nation's 27th largest state.

Felon Disenfranchisement

Since the 1970s, on the strength of the Voting Rights Act, such apportionment schemes that blatantly worked to diminish the ability of minority voters to elect representatives of their choosing have largely been struck down by the courts. But just as the political system seemed on the verge of a historic overcoming of its racist past, a new system of disenfranchisement began spreading and shaping American politics.

One of the most effective dog-whistle appeals to white voters, part of Nixon's "Southern Strategy" campaign, was to repeatedly and strongly denounce "disorder and crime in the streets" and to pledge to make criminal laws tougher so as to create more respect for "law and order." During a decade in which a number of dramatic urban rebellions, including the Watts, Los Angeles, riot of 1964, the Detroit riot of 1967, and the numerous city rebellions sparked by the assassination of Dr. Martin Luther King, Jr. in 1968, such campaign themes needed little embellishing to take on a racist cast. News broadcasters fed the association of race and criminality by disproportionately focusing their news coverage on crimes committed by black offenders while downplaying the much larger number committed by whites.

Conservative politicians discovered that being "tough on crime" was good politics and initiated a cycle of steadily rising penalties for even nonviolent crimes. They would campaign for tougher sentencing and parole laws, fulfill these pledges as lawmakers, and then use the same formula to campaign for even stricter standards at the next election. With the advent of Ronald Reagan's "War on Drugs," America jumped ahead of Russia as the world's leading jailer of its own citizens. In the thirty years following Nixon's 1972 presidential campaign, the number of jail and penitentiary prisoners increased by a factor of ten, from 200,000 to over 2 million, the vast majority disproportionately people of color. By 2010, the United States was locking up black men at ten times the rate that South Africa was during the height of apartheid in 1984.

While legal and philosophical precedents for taking away the right of criminals to vote date back to ancient Greece, in America it wasn't until passage of the Fifteenth Amendment to the Constitution establishing the right of black men to vote, that it became common. Only eleven states adopted laws restricting the voting rights of felons prior to Reconstruction, but seventeen states followed suit by the end of the nineteenth century. Nine former Confederate states passed such felon disenfranchisement laws between 1867 and 1876. Many of these states expanded the list of crimes that would customarily merit disenfranchisement to include minor crimes that were being used to catch as many black citizens in its dragnet as possible. South Carolina added "thievery, adultery, arson, wife-beating, housebreaking, and attempted rape" to its list of felonies that would merit disenfranchisement, but dropped murder from the list, as that was one crime that white people would stand a good chance of facing conviction. In 1875, Alabama added the crime of "larceny," even if a misdemeanor, to crimes that warranted disenfranchisement, meaning that shoplifting or cutting timber without permission would suffice. At its constitutional convention of 1901, Alabama added the vague crime of "moral turpitude" to its list and the sponsor of the amendment boasted that his measure would help "establish white supremacy" in the state.

During the period of civil rights advancement in the 1950s and 1960s, 23 states did away with, or reduced the scope of, their felony disenfranchisement laws. Many states moved to allow those on probation to vote and to automatically restore voting rights once a prisoner had completed their sentence. But due to the severity of criminal statutes already on the books, including mandatory minimums and harsh penalties for drug crimes, the number of people whose criminal records disqualified them from voting continued to increase. By 2000, at least 4.7 million Americans were prohibited from voting because of their criminal records. Less than a decade later this number had climbed to 5.3 million, a number that included one out of every fifteen adult black men.

That millennial year's presidential election highlighted the problem of disenfranchisement. In one of the closest elections in history up to that time, the contest between

Figure 12.18 Bunk and toilet at the West Virginia State Penitentiary, Moundsville, West Virginia, that operated from 1876 to 1995.

Albert Gore and George W. Bush was decided in Florida in the Republican's favor by a total of a few hundred votes. Florida was one of the states that disenfranchised felons for life and had an estimated population of 827,000 disenfranchised citizens, a disproportionate number of them people of color. Political scientists agree that had Florida not had such restrictive felony disenfranchisement laws, the Democrat Gore would have won easily.

Racial inequalities are built into the criminal justice system, especially as it has been intensified by the drug war. Criminological studies have shown that rates of illicit drug use are consistent across most racial and ethnic communities. Some studies have indicated that rates of illegal drug use may actually be higher in the white community. But at every step of the criminal justice system, there are institutional biases in favor of whites and against people of color. Police are more likely to make arrests in poor neighborhoods where drug dealing occurs in public places and where suspects are more easily swept up. Once arrested, black defendants are pressured to take plea deals while whites are often offered special diversion programs to purge their records of convictions. Sentencing laws are designed to give harsher sentences to drugs more common in minority neighborhoods—the federal penalty for possession of "crack" is one hundred times more severe than that for possession of powder cocaine, though chemically they are the same active substance. The difference, of course, is that powder cocaine is culturally more popular with white users.

Mass incarceration has had an impact far broader than just the political. The total output of the American economy more than doubled between 1980 and 2004. But during that same quarter century, the poverty rate hardly budged, falling just 0.3% during that period of robust growth. While many factors, both domestic and global figure into the story of why poverty remained so widespread in the midst of expanding prosperity, one important and much overlooked factor was the impact of new federal policies that resulted in a vast expansion of the number of people imprisoned for minor (and mostly nonviolent) crimes. From 1975 to 2005, the rate of people imprisoned in America more than tripled, from 111 inmates per 100,000 population to 491. Because it is perfectly legal to discriminate against someone on the basis of their criminal record, imprisonment greatly narrows a person's job opportunities upon release and increases the likelihood that they, and their family, will live in poverty. Experts estimate that had mass incarceration not occurred, the poverty rate would have fallen by 10% over this same period.

The long-term denial of the rights of citizenship and especially the right to vote has been the foundation upon which the economic and social subjugation of African Americans has been built. Without political rights governments have been free to ignore the needs of the black community and to structure their laws and programs to funnel privileges and resources only to whites. At the very moment that black Americans successfully struggled to claim their share of the governmental pie, whites began voting overwhelmingly to shrink the very governments and programs that had successfully pushed them and their families into the middle class. This new conservatism could claim to be color-blind in its hostility to social programs and entitlements, but only when that blindness refuses to recognize the past.

Figure 12.19 The Confrontation, Selma, 1965. Artist Franklin McMahon.

Fannie Lou Hamer, Testimony Before the Credentials Committee, Democratic National Convention
Atlantic City, New Jersey - August 22, 1964

Mr. Chairman, and to the Credentials Committee, my name is Mrs. Fannie Lou Hamer, and I live at 626 East Lafayette Street, Ruleville, Mississippi, Sunflower County, the home of Senator James O. Eastland, and Senator Stennis.

It was the 31st of August in 1962 that eighteen of us traveled twenty-six miles to the county courthouse in Indianola to try to register to become first-class citizens.

We was met in Indianola by policemen, Highway Patrolmen, and they only allowed two of us in to take the literacy test at the time. After we had taken this test and started back to Ruleville, we was held up by the City Police and the State Highway Patrolmen and carried back to Indianola where the bus driver was charged that day with driving a bus the wrong color.

After we paid the fine among us, we continued on to Ruleville, and Reverend Jeff Sunny carried me four miles in the rural area where I had worked as a timekeeper and sharecropper for eighteen years. I was met there by my children, who told me that the plantation owner was angry because I had gone down to try to register.

After they told me, my husband came, and said the plantation owner was raising Cain because I had tried to register. Before he quit talking the plantation owner came and said, "Fannie Lou, do you know - did Pap tell you what I said?"

And I said, "Yes, sir."

He said, "Well I mean that." He said, "If you don't go down and withdraw your registration, you will have to leave." Said, "Then if you go down and withdraw," said, "you still might have to go because we are not ready for that in Mississippi."

And I addressed him and told him and said, "I didn't try to register for you. I tried to register for myself."

I had to leave that same night.

On the 10th of September 1962, sixteen bullets was fired into the home of Mr. and Mrs. Robert Tucker for me. That same night two girls were shot in Ruleville, Mississippi. Also Mr. Joe McDonald's house was shot in.

And June the 9th, 1963, I had attended a voter registration workshop; was returning back to Mississippi. Ten of us was traveling by the Continental Trailway bus. When we got to Winona, Mississippi, which is Montgomery County, four of the people got off to use the washroom, and two of the people - to use the restaurant - two of the people wanted to use the washroom.

The four people that had gone in to use the restaurant was ordered out. During this time I was on the bus. But when I looked through the window and saw they had rushed out I got off of the bus to see what had happened. And one of the ladies said, "It was a State Highway Patrolman and a Chief of Police ordered us out."

I got back on the bus and one of the persons had used the washroom got back on the bus, too.

As soon as I was seated on the bus, I saw when they began to get the five people in a highway patrolman's car. I stepped off of the bus to see what was happening and somebody screamed from the car that the five workers was in and said, "Get that one there."

When I went to get in the car, when the man told me I was under arrest, he kicked me.

I was carried to the county jail and put in the booking room. They left some of the people in the booking room and began to place us in cells. I was placed in a cell with a young woman called Miss Ivesta Simpson. After I was placed in the cell I began to hear sounds of licks and screams, I could hear the sounds of licks and horrible screams. And I could hear somebody say, "Can you say, 'yes, sir,' nigger? Can you say 'yes, sir'?"

And they would say other horrible names.

She would say, "Yes, I can say 'yes, sir.'"

"So, well, say it."

She said, "I don't know you well enough."

They beat her, I don't know how long. And after a while she began to pray, and asked God to have mercy on those people.

And it wasn't too long before three white men came to my cell. One of these men was a State Highway Patrolman and he asked me where I was from. I told him Ruleville and he said, "We are going to check this."

They left my cell and it wasn't too long before they came back. He said, "You are from Ruleville all right," and he used a curse word. And he said, "We are going to make you wish you was dead."

I was carried out of that cell into another cell where they had two Negro prisoners. The State Highway Patrolmen ordered the first Negro to take the blackjack.

The first Negro prisoner ordered me, by orders from the State Highway Patrolman, for me to lay down on a bunk bed on my face.

I laid on my face and the first Negro began to beat. I was beat by the first Negro until he was exhausted. I was holding my hands behind me at that time on my left side, because I suffered from polio when I was six years old.

After the first Negro had beat until he was exhausted, the State Highway Patrolman ordered the second Negro to take the blackjack.

The second Negro began to beat and I began to work my feet, and the State Highway Patrolman ordered the first Negro who had beat me to sit on my feet - to keep me from working my feet. I began to scream and one white man got up and began to beat me in my head and tell me to hush.

One white man - my dress had worked up high - he walked over and pulled my dress - I pulled my dress down and he pulled my dress back up.

I was in jail when Medgar Evers was murdered.

All of this is on account of we want to register, to become first-class citizens. And if the Freedom Democratic Party is not seated now, I question America. Is this America, the land of the free and the home of the brave, where we have to sleep with our telephones off the hooks because our lives be threatened daily, because we want to live as decent human beings, in America? Thank you.

Telephone
MUrray Hill 2-0500

425 LEXINGTON AVENUE
New York 17, N. Y.

THE WHITE HOUSE
MAY 14 11 36 AM '58
RECEIVED

May 13, 1958

The President
The White House
Washington, D. C.

My dear Mr. President:

I was sitting in the audience at the Summit Meeting of Negro
Leaders yesterday when you said we must have patience. On
hearing you say this, I felt like standing up and saying, "Oh
no! Not again."

I respectfully remind you sir, that we have been the most
patient of all people. When you said we must have self-
respect, I wondered how we could have self-respect and remain patient considering the treatment accorded us through
the years.

17 million Negroes cannot do as you suggest and wait for the
hearts of men to change. We want to enjoy now the rights
that we feel we are entitled to as Americans. This we cannot do unless we pursue aggressively goals which all other
Americans achieved over 150 years ago.

As the chief executive of our nation, I respectfully suggest
that you unwittingly crush the spirit of freedom in Negroes
by constantly urging forbearance and give hope to those pro-
segregation leaders like Governor Faubus who would take
from us even those freedoms we now enjoy. Your own experience with Governor Faubus is proof enough that forbearance and not eventual integration is the goal the pro-
segregation leaders seek.

In my view, an unequivocal statement backed up by action
such as you demonstrated you could take last fall in deal-

MAY 26 1958

The President   Page 2   May 13, 1958

ing with Governor Faubus if it became necessary, would let
it be known that America is determined to provide -- in the
near future -- for Negroes -- the freedoms we are entitled to under the constitution.

Respectfully yours,

Jackie Robinson

Jackie Robinson

JR:cc

[George W. Bush won the presidential election of 2000 though he received fewer 543,895 fewer votes than his opponent, Al Gore. Florida was the pivotal state in that election. Bush was declared the winner of that state by a margin of 537 votes out of nearly six million ballots. Prior to the election more than 100,000 citizens were improperly removed from the voting rolls and prevented from voting, most of them people of color.]

Excerpts from *Voting Irregularities in Florida During the 2000 Presidential Election,* U.S. Commission on Civil Rights, June 2001.

Rigid sentencing guidelines and voter removal requirements for reformed offenders have been linked to the "War on Crime" in America. The result, however, of implementing these initiatives make convicted criminal offenders the only class of mentally competent Americans disenfranchised or separated from the right to vote. Advocates of stricter punishment of particular crimes, however, seldom acknowledge the diverse manner in which people of color receive more frequent convictions and harsher sentences than their white counterparts. Thus, the disenfranchisement of this class of citizens is sometimes overlooked in debates about the electoral process.

Since the Reconstruction Era following the Civil War, conviction of certain types of crimes supposedly committed more often by African Americans than other ethnic groups, resulted in their disenfranchisement. During the Reconstruction Era, South Carolina, for example, cited the following as crimes "to which [the Negro] was especially prone": theft, arson, attempted rape, adultery, "wife beating," and "housebreaking." Crimes equally or more likely to be committed by whites, such as murder and fighting, generally did not result in disenfranchisement. The long-term effects of the disparity in consequences for alleged criminal behavior between races of people still ripples throughout the United States. Around 3.9 million Americans are disenfranchised. Thirteen percent of African American men are disenfranchised and account for over 36 percent of the total disenfranchised population.

The state of Florida is one of eight states that permanently disenfranchises former felons or felons who have satisfied all sentencing requirements. Florida Justice Institute Staff Attorney Jonel Newman testified that Florida leads the nation in disenfranchising felons and in prosecuting children as felons. Over 31 percent of the disenfranchised population in Florida are African American men. Of all the disenfranchised former felons in the U.S., one-third are found within the borders of the state of Florida...people of color, particularly African Americans, have a greater likelihood of appearing on the Florida felon exclusion list. Moreover, African Americans have a better chance of erroneously appearing on the Florida felon exclusion list. For example, in Miami-Dade County, over half of the African Americans who appealed from the Florida felon exclusion list were successfully reinstated to the voter rolls.

One commentator calls the disenfranchisement of voters a "stark reality" that:

necessarily depletes a minority community's voting strength over time by consistently placing a greater proportion of minority than majority voters under a voting disability at any given time. For this reason, the effects of the intentional discrimination that

originally motivated felon disenfranchisement still linger.

Former U.S. Supreme Court Justice Thurgood Marshall, opined that disenfranchisement doubtless has been brought forward into modern statutes without fully realizing the effect of its literal significance or the extent of its infringement upon the spirit of our system of government:

The "[d]enial of voting rights creates permanent outcasts from society, persons internally exiled who are left without any opportunity ever to regain their full status as citizens." As the statistics indicate, African Americans and other racial minority groups are overrepresented among the disenfranchised, and the denial of voting rights based on felony conviction has a racial discriminatory impact on these groups....

Historically, individuals convicted of certain types of crimes, alleged to be committed more by African Americans, are affected by felon disenfranchisement. The ripples of the practice of felon disenfranchisement resulted in the greater likelihood of people of color, African Americans in particular, having a greater likelihood of appearing erroneously on the Florida felon exclusion list.

In claiming to address the same types of fraud found during the 1997 Miami mayoral election, the Florida legislature enacted chapter 98.0975 of the Florida statutes, which required the Division of Elections to contract with a private entity to purge its voter file of any deceased persons, duplicate registrants, individuals declared mentally incompetent, and convicted felons without civil rights restoration. As a result, DBT Online was eventually approved to assist the Division of Elections in the removal of ineligible voter registrants from the voter file.

Through a matching logic prescribed by the Division of Elections, DBT Online performed an automated matching process against databases provided by the state of Florida and its own databases. Ultimately 173,127 Floridians were identified as potentially ineligible to vote in the November 7, 2000, election. Of those on the list, 57,746 were identified as convicted felons. Based on DBT Online's statistical verification, the list it provided to the Division of Elections was 99.9 percent accurate. The Division of Elections distributed the appropriate portions of the list to the 67 supervisors of elections....

DBT Online was not required to provide a list of exact name matches. Rather, the matching logic only required a 90 percent name match, which produced "false positives" or partial matches of the data. Moreover, the Division of Elections

required that DBT Online perform "nickname matches" for first names and to "make it go both ways." Thus, the name Deborah Ann would also match the name Ann Deborah.

At a meeting in early 1999, the supervisors of elections expressed a preference for exact matches on the list as opposed to a "fairly broad and encompassing" collection of names. DBT Online advised the Division of Elections that it could produce a list with exact matches. The Division of Elections, however, opted to cast a wide net for the exclusion lists.... The evidence does show that some election officials decided that it further served the state's interests to capture as many names as possible on these exclusion lists....

The Florida legislature's decision to privatize its list maintenance procedures without establishing effective clear guidance for these private efforts from the highest levels, coupled with the absence of uniform and reliable verification procedure, resulted in countless voters being deprived of their right to vote.

Human Consequences of Felon Exclusion List

The use of the parameters dictated by Florida's state officials and the lack of any meaningful verification process left many county supervisors confused, and as a result, many Floridians were erroneously removed from the voting lists. One such Floridian was Willie D. Whiting, Jr., a member of the clergy and registered voter in Tallahassee, who went with his family to vote at his assigned Precinct 42 in Leon County. When Apostle Whiting presented his driver's license for identification purposes, the poll worker stated that his name was not on the registration list and called the supervisor of elections in Leon County to verify his registration status. Apostle Whiting asked to speak with a supervisor at that office, and he was told that an individual named Willie J. Whiting, born two days after Apostle Whiting, had been convicted of a felony in the state of Florida. Consequently, Apostle Willie D. Whiting, Jr. learned that he had been wrongfully removed from the registration list. After Apostle Whiting threatened to contact an attorney, he was allowed to vote.

The Commission received testimony from William J. Snow, Jr., a Miami-Dade resident. Mr. Snow testified that he received notice that he would be ineligible to vote in the November 7, 2000, election because of a felony conviction. Receiving the notice "caused a great stress" upon Mr. Snow's heart as he has never been convicted of a felony. Mr. Snow testified that the problem has been corrected. Mr. Snow has been a Miami-Dade County resident for more than 33 years and voted in the 1996 election without incident.

Marilyn Nelson, a poll worker with 15 years of experience in precinct 232 for Miami-Dade County, encountered "quite a few" people whose names did not appear on the roll at her precinct, and when she called the supervisor's office, she was told that their rights had been taken away from them due to an alleged felony conviction. She was further instructed by the supervisor's office that she could not inform those voters of the reason for their removal from the roll, but she was instructed to "tell them to call downtown at a later date."

Dr. Daryl Paulson testified that the Hillsborough County supervisor of elections estimated that 15 percent of those purged were purged in error, disproportionately African American. Another source estimated that 7,000 voters, mostly African Americans registered as Democrats, were removed from the list.

According to news reports, even those who had received a full pardon for their offenses were listed on DBT's exclusion list. Reverend Willie Dixon, a Tampa resident, received a full pardon for drug offenses in 1985, and has since become a youth leader, a bible preacher, and a "pillar of the Tampa African American community who has voted in every presidential election." But despite his 15 years of voting history status, Pam Iorio, the supervisor of elections for Hillsborough County, sent Rev. Dixon a letter informing him that he had been removed from the rolls because of his prior conviction. Eventually, Rev. Dixon was able to verify his status as a registered voter.

Media accounts also captured the impact of list maintenance activities and the frustration it caused for Florida voters. In 1959, Wallace McDonald was convicted of a misdemeanor, vagrancy, for falling asleep on a bench in Tampa while he waited for a bus. In 2000, Mr. McDonald received a letter from Pam Iorio, the Hillsborough County supervisor of elections, informing him that as an ex-felon, his name had been removed from the rolls. Despite the efforts of his attorney to correct the problem, Mr. Wallace was not allowed to vote. Mr. McDonald stated:

> I could not believe it, after voting all these years since the 50s, without a problem . . . I knew something was unfair about that. To be able to vote all your life then to have somebody reach in a bag and take some technicality that you can't vote. Why now? Something's wrong...

Voting Irregularities in Florida During the 2000 Presidential Election, U.S. Commission on Civil Rights, June 2001. http://www.usccr.gov/pubs/vote2000/report/main.htm

Chapter Thirteen: Engineering Segregation

As the twenty-fifth anniversary of the *Brown v. Board of Education of Topeka, Kansas,* Supreme Court decision approached, the U.S. Civil Rights Commission, warned that schools were more segregated in 1977 than they had been in 1954. When the fiftieth anniversary arrived in 2004, commentators again noted that on average, black and white students were less likely to attend school together than they were before Brown. At sixty, editorial writers rolled out the same script once more, in spite of ending government-mandated racial segregation, America had become an even more racially divided society.

Most Americans assume that the extreme separation of neighborhoods by race in America is the product of individual decisions, a result of the natural desire of people to live among others like themselves. The old saying, "birds of a feather flock together," is repeated as if it were some sort of proof of this phenomenon. To those who have never faced housing or financial discrimination, America seems like a place where the patterns of where people live is a product of millions of free decisions in an open marketplace. If these free choices add up to racial separation, then that is no one's fault and it does not need remedying, as it is the fulfillment of what America stands for, the freedom to do or live where you want.

What most Americans don't recognize is that the racial geography they live in is the result of a vast effort at engineering the separation of people by their race. Though not as visible as school segregation, the division of American society into racially defined neighborhoods was just as much a conscious policy implemented by the nation's most powerful institutions over many decades of time. Though these policies were defeated and abandoned by the 1970s, because they involve physical structures and property they are deeply resistant to change.

One of the reasons why the intentional segregation of American neighborhoods has been hidden from view is that these policies were the result of the interaction of private and public actions. Unlike the segregation of schools, or public accommodations like drinking fountains and bathrooms, neighborhood segregation was not simply the result of states passing laws requiring the separation of races. Though such laws were attempted early in the twentieth century and in force for a decade or more in some cities, they proved less effective than private systems of racial discrimination that were then upheld by the courts. For the most part, the geographic segregation of people by race

was a complex partnership between private financial institutions (banks, mortgage companies, and insurers), developers and builders, private neighborhood associations, realtors and brokers, local city planners, white vigilantees, federal agencies, and a judicial system that protected them all.

Before Housing Segregation

American cities and towns were not always segregated. In fact, prior to the 1890s, with the exception of a few well-defined Chinese enclaves, most urban areas were quite integrated, with whites, African Americans, and recent European immigrants, living on the same blocks. Early to mid-nineteenth century cities tended to be concentrated, with total areas not much greater than a few miles, or about as far as a person could walk in an hour. Though these "walking cities" had people of all races and classes interspersed throughout, this does not mean that they were somehow models of equality and tolerance. Great disparities of wealth existed on the same city blocks as large townhouses fronted shaded boulevards while to their rear alleyways were dense with tenements and the people who did the cooking, cleaning, and laundering in an age before there were any labor-saving machines.

The first attempts to segregate urban spaces were undertaken not by governments but by white mobs who employed targeted acts of violence in an attempt to ethnically cleanse their neighborhoods of those they deemed racially other. Rioters attempting to drive out their black neighbors unleashed their fury dozens of times in northern cities prior to the Civil War.

Prior to the early 1800s, rioting was not seen as an explosion of lawless disorder, but as a customary part of the political system. This idea grew out of the old aristocratic order and was a reaction to the concentration of all formal institutions of government in the hands of a few lords and rulers. In a society in which common people had very little formal voice in government, the occasional riotous demonstration was looked upon as legitimate means of expressing grievances. As socially-approved expressions, riots were highly scripted and bounded by custom. Though they could often be violent, it was expected that such violence would be carefully targeted and proportionate to the complaint. Riots developed ritual actions, like "tarring and feathering" during the American Revolution, that were designed to humiliate as much as to injure.

But this system of ritualized rioting and violence broke down in the early 1800s as the targets of rioters expanded from symbols of wealth and power to target groups of people deemed racially "other." Many demonstrations that began against a political party or a particular perceived harm, like an abolitionist newspaper, a banker whose bank failed, or a neighborhood blight like a brothel, quickly expanded into a general assault on a racialized group. Protestants engaged in numerous attacks on Catholic, particularly Irish, communities. Californians assaulted Chinese mining camps and, most commonly, white mobs burned and rampaged through black neighborhoods in eastern cities.

Because they did not consider racial minorities to be a part of their society, the violence these mobs unleashed was not bounded by the traditional and customary restraints that ancient rioting was expected to respect. Though called "race riots" these explosions of violence are more accurately termed "ethnic cleansing" as they really weren't riots in the traditional sense and they weren't fights that erupted along the boundary of race but were instead organized white attacks upon minority communities.

Between 1824 and 1849, there were at least forty-one "race riots," or more properly, attacks on black communities, many of them clearly aimed at not just intimidating or punishing for some perceived wrong, but directed for the purpose of forcing black people to completely abandon an area. In this span of time the city of Cincinnati, the largest city west of the seaboard states, exploded in five murderous riots that collectively were aimed at purging the city of its growing number of black residents (still less than ten percent of the city's 24,000 residents in 1829) and remaking it into an all-white space.

On August 15, 1829, a mob of whites attacked African Americans throughout Cincinnati with the aim of forcing all them all to leave the city. A local newspaper's terse account reads:

Riot in Cincinnati - We learn by a letter from that place, that on the 15th instant, a large number of the inhabitants turned out and collected together, with the determination of forcing out of the city the free negroes, who had not complied with the law of the state with reference to

THE RIOTS IN NEW YORK : DESTRUCTION OF THE COLOURED ORPHAN ASYLUM.

Figure 13.1 The Burning of the Coloured Orphan Asylum, Aug. 15, 1863.

citizenship. The houses of the blacks were attacked and demolished, and the inmates beaten and driven through the streets till beyond the limits of the corporation. During the affray, one of the assailants, a young man of respectable character, was killed.

Another paper estimated that three hundred or more of the city's black residents were forced to flee but the population figures for the area suggest that this was a low estimate. According to the annual city directory, prior to the riot there were 2,258 black residents and a year later this community had dwindled to just 1,090.

Seven years later, in April of 1836, white mobs attacked again in Cincinnati. Black-owned homes and shops were torched and many in the black community had to flee to the woods and swamps of the Ohio river to escape the mob.

In January of 1841, white crowds in Dayton, Ohio, attacked, burned, and looted the homes and business of black residents for two consecutive days before authorities decided to intervene and put down the riot. In the smoking aftermath of the violence, city police arrested only those black Daytonians who had armed themselves and attempted to defend their property. Later that summer, a smoldering level of attacks on random blacks in Cincinnati built up into an effort to force all African Americans to flee the First Ward, where nearly half of all black Cincinnatians lived. A twenty-seven year old man who had purchased his own freedom and fled to the city some years before, Major James Wilkerson, organized the residents of the neighborhood into squads and deployed defensive positions at key rooftops and street corners to fight the onslaught that was expected at any time. When the mob attacked, it did so, according to the *Cincinnati Gazette*, "with the avowed purpose of attacking the negro houses and driving that class of people from the city." Neighborhood defenders repulsed the first wave of the attack, but the white rioters regrouped and assaulted again, this time with a six-pounder cannon they rolled up Sixth street.

Mayor Davies called out two companies of the city militia who promptly joined the white attackers and apprehended only armed black men. City officials improvised an outdoor stockade to contain the five hundred black men who had been arrested. They then announced that their release was dependent on their complying with Ohio's old "black laws" that required all black people in the state to register and supply a $500 bond to guarantee their "good behavior." Cincinnati officials required all the men to produce papers proving their freedom, their birth in the state, the affidavits of two character witnesses, and proof of bond, or be "deported" across the river into slave Kentucky. After a day in the temporary pen, the men were marched off to

be crowded into the city jail.

While the black neighborhood's defenders were disarmed and jailed, the city did nothing to prevent white gangs from looting their homes and businesses. Police and city officials warned looters not to start fires that would threaten white structures and stood by as crowds literally reduced black businesses to rubble with heavy tools. Through the night the men who had been herded into jail heard reports of their families being attacked, women raped, and an elderly man beaten to death. A group of refugees from the city fled north twenty miles to Lane Seminary, an abolitionist college where students armed themselves and took up defensive positions in case the mob might follow.

After three nights of rioting, white anger was spent and the riot ended. The violence had achieved much of its purpose and dramatically reduced the growth of Cincinnati's black population. Where in 1840 African Americans represented nearly 5% of the city's population, by 1850 it dropped to 2.8%. Outside of the city, the horrors of the event elicited some sympathy as the Ohio legislature moved to repeal a ban on accepting any petitions from nonwhites. Naturally, none of the rioters were ever prosecuted, as both authorities had no interest in doing so and state laws prohibited African Americans from giving testimony in court.

Cincinnati's violent attempt to dispossess the black community was frighteningly common in both the North and the South in the decades leading up to the Civil War. In at least ten of the worst riots in northern cities between 1829 and 1841, total expulsion of all black people from town was the goal of the rioters. Philadelphia, the City of Brotherly Love, exploded in five large attacks upon the African American community between 1832 and 1849. New York's white mobs attacked black neighborhoods repeatedly, most famously and most bloodily in 1863 in the midst of the Civil War. Most of these resulted in the same consequences as in Cincinnati: black neighborhoods looted and destroyed, especially centers of black life like churches and businesses, and hundreds forced to flee as refugees.

What is most amazing about these repeated, almost predictably periodic outbreaks of white violence, was the resilience of the African American community that patiently rebuilt and reorganized with what little resources they had. While a number of smaller towns were successful in completely expelling all African Americans from their borders, in larger cities property and lives may have been lost but the social fabric remained strong.

White attacks on communities of color were more successful in shaping demographic patterns elsewhere in America. In the West, white violence eventually forced thousands of Chinese placer miners from their claims along California's rivers. As the state effectively banned them from agriculture by restricting land sales to "those eligible for citizenship," Chinese people had few other options but to work in the railroad and mining industries where temporary labor camps were segregated, or to pack into already overcrowded "Chinatowns" in a few prominent cities. But even these enclaves were not secure.

In Eureka, California, in 1885, after a councilman was killed by a stray shot that came from the city's Chinese district, city officials held a mass meeting that agreed on the following resolutions:

1) That all Chinamen be expelled from the city and none be allowed to return.
2) That a committee be appointed to act for one year, whose duty shall be to warn all Chinamen who may attempt to come to this place to live, and to use all reasonable means to prevent their remaining. If the warning is disregarded, to call mass meetings of citizens to whom the case will be referred for proper action.
3) That a notice be issued to all property owners through the daily papers, requesting them not to lease or rent property to Chinese.

City leaders then informed Eureka's Chinese residents that they had twenty-four hours to leave or be killed. A white mob encircled the district and built a gallows to emphasize their point. Eureka's entire Chinese population fled onto two steamships that ferried them and whatever possessions they could carry to San Francisco.

Later that same year, another white mob, this time of union miners, attacked the Chinese settlement in Rock Springs, Wyoming, forcing the entire population to flee and leaving twenty-eight murdered men in the street amidst their burning homes. Sixteen white union miners were arrested but a grand jury refused to indict any of them.

City officials in Tacoma, Washington, followed the example of those in Eureka and drove the city's several hundred Chinese residents out and seized their property. Seattle was on the verge of following suit; its public officials led a mob that ransacked Chinese homes and businesses and marched hundreds of Chinese families to the city's port and forced half onto an overcrowded ship before the governor intervened and foiled the total ethnic cleansing of the city.

Nevertheless, more than a dozen west coast communities followed suit in the coming years and forcibly expelled their Chinese residents. One historian counted expulsions in 35 California communities in the first four months of 1886 alone. The Chinese ambassador issued a formal protest in Washington, saying there was "a concerted movement in progress to drive out the Chinese from all the cities and towns of California except San Francisco, and that the Governor of the State and the Sheriffs of the various counties evinced no disposition to protect

Figure 13.2 The Anti-Chinese Riot in Denver, Oct. 31, 1880.

the Chinese in their rights." Effects of this widespread expulsion movement were evident in the decadal population statistics: Chinese compromised nearly 10% of California's population in 1880 and only 6.5% a decade later. The only areas where Chinese population remained stable were San Francisco and the Central Valley area where growers were dependent on Chinese farm labor.

By 1880, the population of Chinese immigrants in America reached 105,000, a total that would remain fixed for the next sixty years due to a near total ban on Chinese immigrants. Increasing attacks from whites and hostile government actions forced Chinese Americans to segregate themselves for their own protection. In 1880 half of all the Chinese people in America lived in rural California, but this number steadily dropped in the face of continuing white attacks and discrimination and many were forced to squeeze into San Francisco's Chinatown for protection. By 1890 nearly one quarter of all Chinese people living in America had crowded into San Francisco, which Chinese Americans called "Dai Fou," or "Big City."

As they retreated into ethnic enclaves these

"chinatowns" became the target of white Americans fears and racist projections. Failing to see that these enclaves were largely of their own making, whites instead believed that these dense communities reflected the natural "clannish" tendency of Chinese people. Whites having little genuine contact with Chinese Americans began to imagine chinatowns as mysterious and dangerous districts filled with vice, disease, and organized criminal networks. By the 1990s, Chinese Americans had the lowest rates of residential segregation compared with non-hispanic whites. Nevertheless, they continued to be widely viewed in popular culture as being clannish, living in "Chinatowns," and being foreigners to America.

Racial Cleansing in the North

White violence played a role in ethnically cleansing neighborhoods in the midwest and north in the early twentieth century as well. Though in small numbers prior to the twentieth century, African Americans had made homes in most towns of any size in a broad arc of states bordering the South. The census of 1890 found only 119 counties in the U.S. where African Americans were absent. Towns that had no black residents were remarked upon as being unusual. Even Michigan's remote upper peninsula, had hundreds of black residents.

But in the first decades of the twentieth century, just as white mob violence drove Chinese residents out of dozens of western towns, white mob violence forced African Americans to abandon their homes and flee from at least fifty towns and cities. Many more cities and towns used the threat of violence and police intimidation to prevent the growth of their black populations. Between 1890 and 1930, the number of counties with no black residents more than doubled. Illinois had African American residents in all of its counties in 1890 and six that had zero by 1930. Missouri went from no counties without black residents in 1890 to a dozen by 1930. This retreat in the area of black residency occurred during a period in which the black population increased by more than half and when more than a million African Americans moved out of the South.

Many towns used their local police and courts to harrass black residents and force them live outside of town, though they could work there during the day. Some towns even placed signs at their borders warning black visitors that blacks were not allowed after dark. These places were dubbed "sundown towns" and historian James M. Loewen has identified thousands of them scattered throughout America. Some towns in Nevada sounded a whistle a dusk to remind Indians to leave before dark.

Sundown towns were common everywhere in America except in the deep South where the legal structures of Jim Crow and a rigid caste system of labor most divided black and white populations. Parts of the South that had large white majority populations, such as much of the Appalachians, the Ozarks of Missouri and Arkansas, and parts of central and southern Florida, were the exception to this rule and enthusiastically murdered, beat, and burned many of their black neighbors out of their communities around the turn of the twentieth century.

The racial cleansing of entire towns was usually sparked by accusations of a criminal act on the part of a black man that quickly led to his lynching and then a general assault on the entire black community. Half of the black population of Joplin, Missouri, was forced to flee in a single night of white rage in 1903. Eerily similar events unfolded in Springfield, Illinois, Abraham Lincoln's hometown, where over two days of violence white rioters attempted to burn out the entire black population, succeeding in forcing over two thousand people to flee. As was typical in the aftermath of these outbursts, though two men were murdered in public and hundreds of arsons committed, no person was convicted for actions taken against black citizens. Dozens of towns and cities suffered similar outbreaks of white racial cleansing in the two decades leading up to World War One.

The vast majority of these white riots took place in small and mid-sized cities. White mobs were less eager to start trouble in bigger urban areas because larger African American communities were better prepared to defend themselves from attack and urban police forces were more professional and, though deeply biased against their black residents, were charged with maintaining "order." But even large cities eventually burst into the flames of racist attack.

During the summers of 1919-1921, some of the worst urban rioting in the nation's history took place, all following the pattern of white mobs attempting to more firmly mark the boundaries between white and black neighborhoods and to restrict the latter as much as they were able. White attacks on black neighborhoods erupted in at least two dozen cities in this period.

One of the worst riots of the summer of 1919 occurred in Chicago. Though the racist violence that broke out that July had many causes, the collective belief on the part of white homeowners that the presence of blacks threatened their property was at its heart. The so-called "riot" was centered in the Chicago neighborhood of Lake, once a separate town that had been absorbed into the growing metropolis and was one of the communities bordering the vast stockyards that were the economic engine of the region.

As late as the 1890s, Chicago's African American population was less than 15,000 out of a city of a million. Though dispersed around the city at first, as their numbers increased they were increasingly forced and crowded into a narrow strip of land extending south from the downtown, the famed South Side that contained half of all black Chicagoans in 1900, three-quarters by 1910, and nine out of ten by 1930. By 1919, half of all the black men who worked in Chicago's manufacturing sector worked in one industry, the meat-packing industry, primarily segregated into the hardest and most disagreeable jobs on the killing floors. But these workers could not live near where they worked because the neighborhoods surrounding the stockyards, like Lake, were all-white.

When the War to End All Wars temporarily suspended immigration from Europe, the primary supply of laborers for Chicago's factories was disrupted and employers reluctantly turned to the black population for recruits. Lured by the prospect of factory jobs, and pushed out of the South by mechanization and low cotton prices that encouraged large farmers to convert their fields to less labor intensive crops, 70,000 southern migrants crowded into Chicago's South Side. Though apartments went vacant in the white neighborhoods west of Wentworth Avenue (today's north-south Dan Ryan expressway), in the black ghetto families doubled and tripled up in the same rooms.

A few brave black pioneers attempted to move into white neighborhoods and were met with threats and violence. In the first six months of 1919, there were two dozen bombings of black homes, killing one six-year old girl. Police refused to investigate. The neighborhood of Chicago Heights saw so many repeated attacks upon blacks who attempted to rent or buy in the area, that the sheriff prohibited gun sales.

It was in this simmering environment of white attempts to repress and contain the growing black community that the city descended into chaos on July 27, 1919. Eugene Williams, black and seventeen years old, was stoned by a white crowd when he drifted too far across an imaginary line dividing the black and white sides of a lakefront beach and drowned. Matters quickly escalated when police officers refused to arrest a rock-thrower and someone, likely James Crawford, fired at police and they responded by shooting him dead. Within hours neighborhoods in the area were bedlam, though most of the violence was perpetrated by whites taking advantage of the riot to ethnically cleanse their neighborhoods of the black families who had dared to move into them. According to one investigation, forty percent of violent incidents occurred in the nearly all-white neighborhoods adjoining the stockyards, not the black South Side, itself. While most of the victims of the riot were black, few whites were arrested. So few, in fact, that a local judge was so exasperated at the many black victims being arrested and brought to his bench by the police that he exclaimed, "I want to explain to you officers that these colored people could not have been rioting against themselves... Bring me some white prisoners."

The riot began on a Sunday and the following day, Monday, after work, black stockyard workers had to crowd onto streetcars to commute through the white neighborhoods they were prevented from living in to get home. White mobs threw up barricades and ambushed them. Five black workers were murdered and thirty others seriously wounded by crowds that pulled them from the streetcars. Hundreds others ran for their lives through a gauntlet of howling rioters. That night, white caravans of automobiles drove through black neighborhoods shooting from their windows. A white sniper who was shooting from an upper window of the Angelus apartment building on the fringe of the South Side, was protected by a line of police who denied hearing any shots and eventually themselves shot into a gathering black crowd, killing four.

In the wake of the nearly week-long riot, white Chicagoans' determination not to have any black neighbors hardened. Whereas some neighborhoods were willing before to tolerate a small number of black residents, especially renters rather than homeowners, after the 1919 riot they organized to draw the color line absolutely. New white neighborhood associations formed whose main purpose was to maintain segregation. Those areas bordering the black belt of the South side, Kenwood and Hyde Park, were especially active. These two neighborhood associations' newsletter declared:

DAMAGE DONE BY A BOMB
This bomb was thrown into a building at 3365 Indiana Avenue, occupied by Negroes. A six-year-old Negro child was killed.

Figure 13.3 Chicago police inspect damage done by a bomb that killed a 6-year old African American girl in 1919.

Keep the Negro in his place, amongst his people and he is healthy and loyal, [but] remove him, or allow his newly discovered importance to remove him from his proper environment, and the Negro becomes a nuisance. He develops into an overbearing, inflated, irascible individual, overburdening his brain to such an extent about social equality that he becomes dangerous to all with whom he comes in contact.

Racial cleansings continued in the years after the bloody summer of 1919. Over the course of a week in 1923, white mobs, led by the county sheriff, lynched at least six men and women and burned the all-black town of Rosewood, Florida, to the ground, scattering its several hundred residents who never returned. Not only was this crime not prosecuted at the time, it wasn't until 1994 that the state of Florida recognized what caused the once thriving town, with three churches, a school, a Masonic hall, and a train station, to become a ghost town.

The Tulsa neighborhood of Greenwood was by 1920 one of the most prosperous African American communities in America. Tulsa, a city boomed by oil money, had long had a sizeable black presence with many black doctors, lawyers, and businesses concentrated along Detroit and Greenwood Avenues. Greenwood was home to two important black-owned newspapers that reached readers throughout the South. On May 31, Dick Rowland, a young black man who worked in the lobby of the downtown Drexel building, tripped while stepping into an elevator and fell against Sarah Page, the young white elevator operator who yelled out "rape!" in surprise. Rowland was swiftly arrested and jailed in the courthouse.

When the usual lynch mob formed around the courthouse demanding the sheriff hand over Rowland, some of the leaders of Greenwood decided to take a stand and defend the rule of law. A group of black men, led by war veteran O.B. Mann, armed themselves and stationed themselves at the door to the jail. A white man grappled with Mann, attempting to take his pistol, and Mann shot him dead sparking a gunfight around the courthouse.

Though the armed men withdrew, city officials determined to meet such a display of black resistance with overwhelming force. City police and units of the state national guard aided white mobs in ransacking and burning the Greenwood neighborhood that was home to nearly ten thousand people. Black men and women were shot on sight. Police cars dragged men to their deaths. Guardsmen used airplanes to drop bombs in what was the first aerial assault on an American city in history. Mobs looted valuables from black businesses and homes by the truckload before burning the districts thirty-five square blocks to the ground. Firefighters only intervened to keep the flames from spreading to white neighborhoods. Thousands of Tulsa's black citizens were arrested, paraded through the streets, and penned in the city's ball park.

According to a state commission established in 1997 to investigate the details of the massacre, the deaths of thirty-nine black Tulsans were well documented and there is some evidence that hundreds of other victims were buried without documentation. (Though the head of the Red Cross in the area at the time claimed to have interned hundreds of bodies in mass graves, archaeologists have so far failed to locate mass graves using ground penetrating radar.)

Tulsa's African American community disappointed

Figure 13.4 Greenwood after attack on June 1st, 1921, Tulsa, Okla.

the racial cleansing hopes of their white neighbors by rebuilding Greenwood and not leaving town. But, as was the usual effect of such violence throughout America, the boundaries marking the limits of black settlement were more brightly drawn in the aftermath of the attack.

20th Century Housing Segregation

The segregation of American cities by both race and class was a long process, partly driven by new transportation technologies, such as the railroad and trolley, that allowed the wealthy to move away from the commercial center of the city. Early suburbanization created scattered colonies of small upper class white neighborhoods on the edges of cities, but left the bulk of the population intermixed and living in increasingly dense urban cores. Beginning in the 1890s, the black urban population began to grow, though not out of proportion with the explosive growth of cities overall in this decade. Nevertheless, the African American population of many cities and towns doubled in the last decade of the nineteenth century and was poised to continue this level of growth into the next when white resistance interrupted.

Several southern cities responding to their swelling African American populations by enacting laws that restricted people of color from living in any neighborhoods in which white people were a majority of the residents. Baltimore pioneered this sort of legislation in 1911 when it passed an ordinance designating certain city blocks "white" or "black" and prohibiting anyone from living on a block that wasn't designated for their race. The purpose of the law was detailed in its own description, that said it was an: "ordinance for preserving peace, preventing conflict and ill feeling between the white and colored races in Baltimore city, and promoting the general welfare of the city by providing, so far as practicable, for the use of separate blocks by white and colored people for residences, churches and schools." Hailed as the "Baltimore Idea," this ordinance was adopted as a model by other southern cities including Richmond, Norfolk, Greenville, Winston-Salem, Atlanta, and Louisville, among others. St. Louis came close to passing such an ordinance but it was narrowly defeated.

Where such laws were enacted they were vigorously enforced and caused swift changes in the social geography of the cities and the lives of the people targeted by them. To take one typical example, on the eve of the passage of the racial residency ordinance in Louisville, a growing black middle class of entrepreneurs and professionals had spread across the city. Known locally as "the 400," these leading families were suddenly forced to sell the homes they had struggled to build and were forced to move to the only neighborhood open to them, the so-called "Smoketown," a

A NEGRO FAMILY JUST ARRIVED IN CHICAGO FROM THE RURAL SOUTH

Figure 13.5 Family arriving in Chicago from the Deep South, 1922.

district where the city officials also pushed most of the bars, gambling dens, and brothels.

These residential segregation ordinances were successfully challenged in court because they impacted upon the property rights of white businessmen. While the Supreme Court of Virginia upheld Richmond's racist residency restrictions, high courts in three states struck them down. In 1917, in the case of *Buchanan v. Warley*, the U.S. Supreme Court swept all such laws into history's dustbin by unanimously ruling that they violated the constitution, not because they treated citizens unequally or unfairly, but because by preventing the white plaintiff from selling his property to a black person, the state had deprived this white man of his constitutional right to due process. Though most of these laws were in force for fewer than six years, the damage had been done and the racial segregation of these cities were deepened at a critical moment of black population growth.

In the wake of *Buchanan v. Warley*, city governments did not abandon their efforts to engineer racially divided neighborhoods but instead turned to the young profession of urban planning to formulate ways of achieving racial separation within the Supreme Court's ruling. Atlanta attempted to use newly acquired zoning powers to separate and limit black neighborhoods, developing a system of zoning based on race: "R1-White district; R2-colored district; and R-3-undetermined." Real estate interests sued and won, forcing the city to abandon these specifically racially named districts, but continued to steer development according to the same plan successfully over the next half century. Birmingham, Alabama, switched from simply prohibiting black residents from living in white areas to

Figure 13.6 Picket line at Mid-City Realty Company, South Chicago, Illinois, July 1941.

denying building permits to developers who attempted to construct housing for African Americans in areas zoned as white neighborhoods. Birmingham continued this practice through at least the 1940s. In the 1920s New Orleans adopted a system whereby black residents had to obtain the permission of all the homeowners on their block before moving in, though it too was struck down by the Supreme Court in 1927. Charleston, South Carolina, adopted a city plan to preserve its historic downtown from modern development in 1931 and the plan specified that such "preservation" required making this area exclusively white, failing to note that several thousand African American residents lived there.

In most cities throughout the country, zoning did not have to be explicitly racial to serve the purpose of promoting segregation. Because of the private discrimination of banks, insurance companies, land developers, real estate agents, and homeowner associations, American cities were becoming progressively more segregated in the early twentieth century and city governments did not have to plan or create black and white neighborhoods. Instead, they could use their extensive powers to determine the location of industries, roads, parks, schools, and city services to more

powerfully define and separate neighborhoods by race. Industrial corridors, the location of railroad tracks, and the designation of certain neighborhoods as single-family or multifamily buildings were highly effective in fostering segregation.

While courts had ruled that the constitution prohibited taking property without due process and therefore rendered specific racial residency ordinances illegal, the same courts found no such property interest in schooling and upheld Jim Crow schools. Cities found they could use the power to locate segregated services, such as schools and parks, to engineer the segregation of neighborhoods. Schools and parks designated for black residents would be sited only in existing black neighborhoods, while white-designated schools and parks were built to encourage the expansion of white development.

Racial Covenants

Perhaps no legal instrument played as large a role in dividing American cities along racial lines than the simple property contract. Beginning soon after the Supreme

Court struck down explicit racial zoning laws in *Buchanan v. Warley*, private real estate developers began drafting racially restrictive clauses that they put into the contracts they used to sell the lots and homes they built. In one sense these were private agreements (technically they are legally termed "covenants" because they continue in force after the property is transferred from one party to another) to not sell or rent the property to a person of a specified race or religion. But because courts quickly ruled that they were legal and enforceable (the Supreme Court upheld them in the 1926 case of *Corrigan v. Buckley*), they became an instrument of public policy as well. For example, states passed laws giving neighbors who were not parties to such contracts the legal standing to sue those who violated them. In this way a seemingly private act of discrimination was converted into a tool of government social engineering.

Racial covenants spread rapidly across America at the very moment that African American families began to move in large numbers out of the old South and into northern and western cities, and at a time when home building boomed and cities across the nation multiplied in size. This confluence of factors meant that these legal instruments of racial discrimination appeared at the most critical juncture that heightened their ability to score a deep and lasting scar across the social landscape. Though home and apartment construction stalled during the war years of 1917-1918, by the early 1920s home building boomed and developers laid out thousands of new neighborhood developments.

Developers became very adept at both marketing their new subdivisions and finding ways of building their value. Perhaps the greatest selling point of a subdivision, and one the lent the most to its value, was its exclusivity. Each subdivision was organized to attract a specific class of homebuyer. Working class subdivisions were constructed near manufacturing centers with tidy bungalows and cottages on small lots in a grid pattern. At the other end of the spectrum, estate subdivisions featured large homes on acre lots situated on curvilinear streets. To ensure the distinctive neighborhood aesthetic appropriate to each class, restrictions were written into the deeds as covenants. The number of restrictions varied also with the wealth of the neighborhood. In lower income subdivisions, homeowners were not allowed to keep farm animals on their property, to build houses with more than two units, or to sell alcohol. Upscale developments had lists of restrictions that ran for pages, governing everything from house styles, building setbacks, fencing, landscaping, and property uses. All of these restrictions were vigorously policed and and enforced by the realty companies, the homeowner associations that were organized in this era, and city governments.

Of all these covenants, the most common restriction was not aimed at chicken or moonshiners, but people of color. A typical example is found in section 6 of the list of

Figure 13.7 Poster by Record Section, Suburban Resettlement Administration, Dec. 1935.

restrictions for the Westmoreland neighborhood in Toledo, Ohio. Entitled, "NUISANCES", this section prohibited building "stables, cattle yard, hog pen, fowl yard or house, cesspool, privy vault" and banned "poultry, hogs, cattle or other livestock or any noxious, dangerous or offensive thing..." Section 6 concluded with this paragraph:

> At no time shall any lot in Westmoreland or any building erected thereon be occupied by any negro, or any person of negro extraction, or any Chinese, or any person of the Mongolian race, but this prohibition is not intended to include or prevent occupancy by said persons as domestic servants or while employed in and about the premises by the owner...

The language of these racist clauses varied slightly but the effect was always the same. The line permitting residence of black servants was dropped in lower income areas. Sometimes the restriction permitted only those of the "Caucasian race" to live in the neighborhood. Occasionally, the term "Ethiopian extraction" was substituted for "Negro." Either way, a city's growing African-American population was systematically excluded from new housing developments and entire sections of cities. In Toledo, for example, by the 1930s, most of the city's fast-growing black population was crowded into just four census tracts, including the two deemed to be the most substandard with the greatest number of houses in need of repair.

Realtor associations played a large role in promoting racially restrictive covenants and spreading them throughout the country. The National Association of Real Estate Brokers in 1924 included among its code of ethics that bound its members, that "a realtor should never be instrumental in introducing into a neighborhood...members of one race or nationality...whose presence will clearly be detrimental to property values..." In 1927 the Chicago Real Estate Board drafted a model racial covenant and launched a campaign among its members to have it adopted throughout the city. Eventually 80% of the housing in the city of Chicago was covered by racially restrictive covenants. But not only private entities promoted racially restrictive housing covenants. In 1931, a federal committee organized under President Hoover, recommended that all new neighborhoods adopt such restrictions.

A majority of developments built around suburban New York in the 1930s and 1940s were found to have racially restrictive covenants. From the 1940s to the 1960s, Detroit had 192 homeowner associations enforcing racial restrictions. Los Angeles courts heard over one hundred lawsuits enforcing racial restrictions in a single decade.

Racially restrictive covenants were struck down in 1948 in a case, *Shelley v. Kraemer*, that foreshadowed the much more famous blow against Jim Crow that came six years later in *Brown v. Board of Education*. In *Shelley v. Kraemer*, the court reversed its earlier endorsement of such covenants finding that because they were only effective because courts and police enforced them, they were indeed matters of state and therefore the Fourteenth Amendment to the Constitution did require "equal protection of the law." But, as was the longstanding pattern of the history of housing segregation, the abandonment of one system of discrimination seemed to come only when it had already been replaced by other, more effective means of achieving the same end. In this case, by the time of this decision in 1948, the center of power and the source of discrimination had moved from developers and homeowner associations to the new federal government agencies that provided financing for America's greatest housing boom—a boom that completely, and intentionally, left people of color behind.

Though racially restrictive covenants became unenforceable after 1948, the attitudes supporting them did not quickly change. In 1972, over half of southern whites (53%) and a third of northern whites (35%) were willing to admit to survey-takers that they believed whites had a right to keep blacks out of their neighborhoods. Nearly three-quarters of southern whites (73%) and almost two-thirds of northern ones (60%) said home-owners had a right to racially discriminate in selling their home. All whites, whether northern or southern, old or young, educated or not, overwhelmingly opposed school busing to integrate schools (80-94%) and thought that blacks were wrong to "push" into where they weren't wanted (58-84%). Even scholars referred to the movement of black citizens into white neighborhoods as "infiltration."

Federal Public Housing Policy

Federal government involvement in public housing began during World War One, when the rapid expansion of some key war industries outstripped the available housing for their new workers in many communities. Beginning in 1917, the federal government constructed eighty-three public housing projects spread across half the states to house 170,000 war workers and their families. Only white workers were eligible to live in these publicly-financed apartment buildings. When the war ended, these buildings were sold off, but the all-white neighborhoods they created continued long after peace was declared.

When the federal government again launched a program to assist its citizens secure decent and affordable housing during the Great Depression of the 1930s, it continued the same policies of segregation. The first of these efforts was the Tennessee Valley Authority (TVA), a mas-

Figure 13.8 Techwood Homes, Building No. 16, 488-514 Techwood Drive, Atlanta, Fulton County, GA, ca. 1930s.

ment resources to both provide modern safe housing and to redevelop slums. More significantly, the people displaced by these redevelopments were usually a far more diverse group of people than those that took their places, as no mixing of racial groups was allowed in PWA properties. In this way government housing policy effectively increased the overall segregation of American cities.

For example, in order to construct the Techwood Homes project in Atlanta, the PWA condemned and demolished buildings that housed 1,600 families in a part of the city known as the "Flats." The Flats was one of the more integrated neighborhoods in the city, one-third of whom were African American and the rest of a mix of whites and various European immigrants. Techwood Homes, when it was completed, provided accommodations for 604 families, all of them white. In St. Louis, the 1934 DeSoto-Carr project was the mirror image of Techwood Homes. The PWA demolished a neighborhood that had an even proportion of blacks and whites and built in its place a blacks-only housing project. Cleveland's Lakeview Terrace project replaced an integrated Italian, black, and Polish neighborhood with a whites-only housing development.

Of the 26 PWA projects built before the Supreme Court ruled that the federal government did not have the right to condemn property through eminent domain for the purpose of building housing in 1935, all but two were strictly segregated, and the two that were not for whites or blacks only, were segregated by building within the grounds of the development.

As it had twenty years before during the last great world war, when war clouds gathered in 1940 and the federal government began tooling up for another global conflict it found it necessary to construct housing for the

Figure 13.9 "First Negro family moving into Sojourner Truth homes, Feb. 1942."

sive project to harness the untapped power of the South's major rivers and electrify the least industrialized region of the nation. As dams and other infrastructure were built in remote areas, the TVA had to first construct housing for its workers. At its headquarters in Norris, Tennessee, the TVA constructed 500 model houses that were made available to its white employees. Black workers were offered flimsy and overcrowded barracks in a separate camp.

As the depression worsened, President Roosevelt launched the Public Works Administration (PWA), an agency charged with stimulating employment by constructing post offices, libraries, and other public buildings, including various types of housing. As was true of all New Deal projects, apartment buildings and other public housing were strictly segregated, with white and black developments usually located far from each other in neighborhoods that were deemed to be predominately black or white.

Such racial designations hid the fact that PWA projects were by law constructed in a manner that destroyed existing integrated communities. The 1937 legislation that funded public housing projects mandated that for every unit of housing built at least one unit of "substandard" existing housing had to be demolished. This provision was pushed by real estate interests who lobbied to keep public housing from flooding the real estate market with an adequate housing supply, thereby driving down rents and landlord profits.

PWA projects were intentionally sited not on vacant properties but upon neighborhoods declared "blighted." In this way, PWA planners thought they could use govern-

Figure 13.10 Sign with American flag "We want white tenants in our white community," directly opposite the Sojourner Truth housing project.

Figure 13.11 Youths Play Basketball at Stateway Gardens' Housing Project on Chicago's South Side, the Complex has Eight Buildings with 1,633 Apartments, May 1973.

rising numbers of war industry workers. Congress passed the Lanham Act (1940) that provided funds for a massive program of public housing intended to accommodate the influx of workers. Apartment buildings and single-family developments constructed at this time were strictly segregated, meaning in most cases that they were available only to white renters.

When the federal government decided to build the world's largest bomber plant outside Detroit in a field called Willow Run, far from any housing for the factory's thousands of workers, an entire community was rapidly built by government funds and all of its neat houses and apartment buildings excluded people of color. A development for black workers was proposed within the city limits of Detroit, far from where the new factories were being built. When the project, named the Sojourner Truth Homes, was completed, local white politicians pressured the federal government to exclude blacks from it as well. Only a last-minute intervention from First Lady Eleanor Roosevelt kept the project open to black renters, but soon after a few black families moved in, whites from surrounding neighborhoods rioted in an attempt to force

them out, sending thirty-three black Detroiters to the hospital.

Like Detroit, San Francisco experienced a boom in wartime employment as its bay and ports proved ideal for naval operations. Of the six large housing projects constructed during the war, four were for whites only and were located in white neighborhoods, one was open only to African Americans and was built in an already crowded black district (actually this neighborhood, Westside Courts, was only recently opened to black renters because the previous residents, mostly Americans of Japanese descent, had been taken to internment camps), and one was open to both groups but blacks and whites were housed in different sections of the development.

After the war many of these public housing developments were given over to local governments to manage and many cities kept them segregated until the 1960s. Boston's two largest housing projects constructed with Lanham Act money, the West Broadway and Mission Hill projects, excluded black renters until forced to integrate by federal courts in 1962. San Francisco's housing authority maintained the segregated patterns of its federally-built wartime projects until successfully sued by the NAACP in the 1950s. Similar examples can be found in every major city that built public housing in the 1940s.

For a few years after World War Two the housing shortage created by two decades of depression and war persisted. Truman succeeded in pushing through a new Housing Act in 1949, but majorities in both the House and the Senate stripped it of a non-discrimination clause, thereby giving the green light to racial discrimination. Real estate and landlord interests succeeded in requiring all public housing to be planned, sited, and administered by local agencies, not the federal government. As black voters remained gerrymandered, grandfathered, primaried, and poll-taxed, so that they had nothing near the voting power of their numbers, local control simply meant more segregation and exclusion. When the Los Angeles mayor supported expanding the city's public housing with the new federal money, local real estate interests ran an anti-housing candidate for mayor who won the subsequent election and cut the program in half. Detroit's city council followed the lead of mayor Albert Cobo who had campaigned on a pledge of stopping "Negro Invasions" of white neighborhoods and refused to locate any public housing intended for black residents in or even near white neighborhoods.

Local white resistance to public housing grew because whites no longer relied on federal housing programs as they had since the Great Depression. Instead, a far larger federal program of mortgage subsidies allowed white tenants to move to new suburbs and become homeowners. Just as it is said that generals tend to the fight battles of the past, not the present, it can be said that Truman pushed to expand the successful and popular public housing programs of his predecessor at a time when the white base of the Democratic party no longer wanted them. As a result, public housing increasingly became housing for the nation's racial minorities. Once this change became evident, Congress cut the program's funding per unit and imposed

Figure 13.12 Central Expressway Leading South into Dallas, May 1972.

even stronger mandates that the purpose of public housing was not to aid the poor, but to "revitalize" and "redevelop" the slums that "blighted" the cores of American cities.

The result was a dramatic contrast between the housing built largely for whites during the Great Depression and the housing constructed for blacks in the 1950s and 1960s. The more than fifty projects of public housing built by the PWA in the 1930s was in the words of one architectural historian, "With their low-rise profiles, careful landscape designs, and numerous amenities, PWA projects constitute some of the best government-backed housing ever built." Even when funds were cut back during the war, the resulting projects were popular with their residents and had far more space and amenities than most residents had experienced before.

St. Louis, Missouri, exemplifies this trend. During the Great Depression, the city's public housing authority built two projects, one for blacks and one for whites, both solidly constructed, red-brick town houses, spaciously laid out across the site (though the project for whites, Clinton-Peabody, was significantly more spacious than the one for blacks, Carr Square Village), with a public community center anchoring each neighborhood. By the time of the 1949 Housing Act, St. Louis civic leaders' concerns had shifted from providing housing for people to defending the valuable real estate of the downtown from a rapidly expanding black population (most of whom were streaming into the city escaping the intolerable conditions of the delta region to the south). Suddenly flush with a treasury of federal funds to construct housing and demolish "blighted slums," the city condemned scores of blocks of integrated neighborhoods where black populations were growing near the downtown and relocated their residents to a complex of thirty-three identical high-rise towers packed onto a fifty-seven acre lot on the north side of the city. Land cleared of black residences in the downtown core of the city was sold to developers to gentrify and whiten. St. Louis city planner, Harland Bartholomew was quite open about his intent to achieve "Negro deconcentration" from the areas near the downtown.

Architects who designed the first of these massive projects, the Pruitt-Igoe Towers, did the best they could within the constraints they were given: the city development agency specified their budget per unit and the small footprint of the project that was to house (or to use a more accurate term, warehouse) fifteen thousand people. The result was a brutal landscape of concrete and densely packed poverty. Unlike the public housing of a decade earlier, housing designed with white residents in mind, there were no community centers, children's playgrounds, or even a sprig of landscaping. Unlike the sturdily built depression public homes, many of which are still in demand today, only the poorest and cheapest materials were used, as one study found, "the quality of the hardware was so poor that doorknobs and locks were broken on initial use... Windowpanes were blown from inadequate frames by wind pressure. In the kitchens, cabinets were made of the thinnest plywood possible."

Across the nation, public housing funds were used in the 1950s and 1960s not to provide housing but to relocate and concentrate growing black populations into smaller and more undesirable sections of the city. Dallas used its public housing funds to condemn black neighborhoods encroaching on the downtown and relocate black families to a polluted site downwind from a lead smelter that emitted 289 tons of lead dust into the air each year. Chicago constructed its massive row of high-rise public housing buildings, the Robert Taylor Homes, in an attempt to keep its black residents concentrated in the existing south Chicago ghetto. Dozens of fourteen-story buildings containing 7,800 units were built along State street even though the federal Public Housing Authority had warned as early as 1950 in a major policy bulletin that such high-rises were "least desirable" and riddled with problems "too well known to warrant any comment."

It should be noted that until the mid-1960s, the tenants of these public housing projects were not the beneficiaries of government rent subsidies but were tenants who paid rent to the public housing authorities who managed the buildings. Once construction was completed, the federal government provided no additional subsidies or reserves for upkeep or renovation and the full cost of maintenance fell to the tenants themselves. Federal law squeezed the local housing agencies by capping the amount of reserves they could hold, all "excess funds" were required to be paid back to the government. Without any operating subsidies, public housing administrators deferred maintenance which, combined with the already shabby construction of these buildings, led to a swift deterioration in their condition. Most of the public housing authorities in the nation operated at a deficit by the mid-1960s. It wasn't until 1972 that federal housing and rent subsidies began to flow to local governments.

Black renters had little choice but to occupy whatever public housing was available as the amount of housing available to them was small and shrinking due to extensive discrimination and a black population of northern cities that swelled after the war. In the two decades after 1940, five million African Americans left the South for the North and West. As most small and medium sized towns had earlier violently purged themselves of their black populations and enforced "sundown" restrictions on black residency, most black migrants were forced into already crowded cities. The black populations of the two northern cities with the largest black communities, New York and Philadelphia, doubled in size. In other cities, like Chicago, Cleveland,

Detroit, and Newark, populations quintupled. Los Angeles' African American community grew by 425%.

At the same time public housing funds were used to concentrate black urbanites into ever more concentrated neighborhoods, a massive federal program to construct the interstate highway system was directed toward the same ends. In 1956 the National Interstate and Defense Highways Act allocated a record amount of federal dollars not only for the purpose of building roads, but for siting those roadways in a manner that would eliminate "slums." By the 1960s, federal highway dollars were demolishing as many as 37,000 housing units every year.

Many new interstate highways were routed so as to separate white and black neighborhoods or, as Miami's I-95 was located to do, separate black neighborhoods from the central business district. Los Angeles planned the route of its Santa Monica freeway to destroy Sugar Hill, a middle class African American neighborhood. Chicago's Dan Ryan expressway carved a clear line separating the black neighborhoods of Bronzeville and Washington Park from the white areas of Bridgeport, Back of the Yards, and Englewood, the same boundary fought over in the riots of 1919. In many cities the preferred straight routes of highway engineers were curved and twisted so as to maximize the demolition of black neighborhoods. Nashville's I-40 was twisted to bulldoze much of the city's black North Nashville neighborhood. New Orleans' I-10 was intentionally moved away from the riverfront due to the protests of white property owners and instead routed through the heart of the old middle class black neighborhood of Treme. I-75 was twisted from its line southward through Toledo to avoid the white neighborhood of the Old West End and to instead demolish a black neighborhood to its west, even though the snaking highway was later deemed one of the most dangerous in Ohio because of its drastic curves.

Officials in Montgomery, Alabama, chose to route I-85 through a neighborhood known to be the home of many of the city's black leaders rather than along vacant land that was actually closer to the highway's natural route. In the end President Kennedy quietly pressured Alabama officials to bend the route slightly to avoid demolishing the home and church of the Reverend Ralph Abernathy, an advisor to Dr. Martin Luther King, and one of the organizers of the 1956 Montgomery Bus Boycott, but the rest of the neighborhood was leveled. Birmingham's I-59 destroyed two black neighborhoods that contained 13 of the city's black churches and three of its black schools. Even in St. Paul, Minnesota, federal highway construction tore through the city's only black neighborhood, leading one scholar to write, "very few blacks live in Minnesota, but the road builders found them."

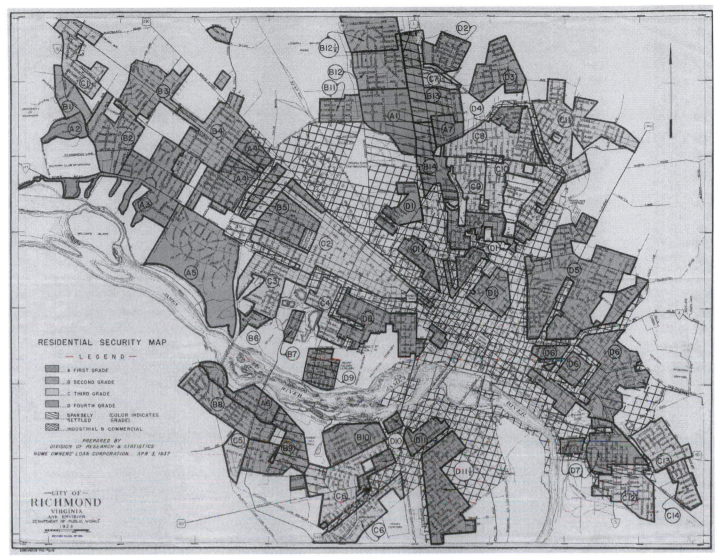

Figure 13.13 Redline Map for Richmond, Virginia, Home Owners' Loan Corporation, ca. 1935.

Redlining

Prior to President Roosevelt's New Deal, buying a home was a difficult undertaking. Most banks required a 50% down payment and offered loans whose terms expired after, at most, seven years. Back then loans were not amortized, meaning that the borrower paid only interest until the loan term ended whereupon the remaining debt was to be paid in one lump sum. Fewer than half of American families could save such a sum and consequently become homeowners.

When the economy fell into depression banks stopped lending money to homebuyers and the entire residential construction industry with its millions of workers crashed to a halt. New Deal economists knew that one way to kickstart this vital pillar of the economy, and to restore stability to the banking sector, was to have the federal government provide subsidies for private mortgages

and to insure the value of the mortgages banks sold. In exchange for their subsidies, banks were forced to accept strict regulations on what properties and which consumers they could loan money to.

One of the first regulations established as part of this federal mortgage insurance system, was issued in 1933 by the first federal housing agency, the Home Owners Loan Corporation (HOLC). The HOLC prepared maps that indicated what neighborhoods they would underwrite and which ones they deemed too risky. Some areas were excluded because they were at risk of flooding or the housing stock was too old and poor, but another criteria the HOLC included in its determinations was whether the neighborhood was mostly black, integrated, or nearly all-white. Invariably, black and integrated neighborhoods, no matter how prosperous, were excluded from the benefits of government mortgage backing.

The successor agency to the HOLC, the Federal

Housing Authority (FHA), continued the HOLC's policies and used its maps with their red lines plotted around neighborhoods that had a significant population of people of color. The FHA used these maps along with an underwriting manual produced in 1939 that stated, "if a neighborhood is to retain stability, it is necessary that properties should continue to be occupied by the same social and racial classes." Mortgages underwritten by the Veteran's Administration also were governed by the same racist "redline" maps.

FHA and VA policies encouraged the locating of new suburban developments in places that had "[n]atural or artificially established barriers" such as rivers, railroad tracks, or highways for the "prevention of the infiltration of....inharmonious racial groups." These federal agencies advocated that areas that had segregated schools be given higher priority for mortgage subsidies than those that were less so. The head of the FHA testified before Congress in the 1940s that his agency was under no legal obligation to not discriminate on the basis of race. In those few instances where whites who received FHA mortgages later rented to blacks, the FHA investigated and banned them from participation in the program.

FHA and VA funds built most of the vast suburbs that today ring American cities and they did so with the specific and legally-binding requirement that only whites be allowed to purchase homes in them. Massive developments like Levittown, outside of New York City, offered 17,500 two-bedroom homes available with no down payment and low interest terms, but was only open to white applicants. The dozens of suburbs on the scale of Levittown built around the country were entirely dependent on federal financing and all only accepted whites. The few builders who attempted to develop suburban communities for blacks were turned down for federal financing and mortgage subsidies, except for one development pushed vigorously by the mayor of New Orleans.

Mortgage subsidies were funneled into suburban construction rather than the renovation of existing urban neighborhoods. For example, by 1960, suburban areas in St. Louis county had received six times the FHA dollars that the city of St. Louis received in spite of the city's higher population. In New Jersey an audit conducted in 1966 could find no evidence of any FHA mortgages written in either of the predominately minority cities of Camden or Paterson. Racial discrimination in writing mortgages was formally allowed by the federal Home Loan Bank Board until 1961 and the practice continued unabated for long after that. It wasn't until 1974 that Congress passed the Equal Credit Opportunity Act that outlawed redlining.

The extremes of FHA and VA racial restrictions were seen in a suburban development on the northwest side of Detroit. FHA auditors determined that the planned

Figure 13.14 Sign advertising FHA subsidized suburban housing. 1940s.

development was too close to a black neighborhood and only approved the builder's application for a government loan after he built a half mile long, foot thick, six-foot high, concrete wall along Birwood avenue. Parts of this wall still stand as a monument to American apartheid today.

Royal Oak, a suburb north of Detroit, was delighted and proud of the segregation it had achieved by the 1950s. Its Chamber of Commerce chapter distributed a pamphlet in 1954, "Royal Oak: Michigan's Most Promising City," in which it boasted that its population "is virtually 100% white."

Suburbanization increased segregation not only by constructing white-only suburbs, but by drawing down the diverse populations of existing cities. The white people who flocked to the suburbs mostly left existing urban neighborhoods to do so, leaving the places they left behind less integrated than they had once been. Detroit, Michigan, is the most glaring example of this process in action. Michigan, being the center of the automobile industry, was also the nation's leader in building highways and suburban developments, at the cost of its mighty and proud city of Detroit. In 1950, Detroit had 1.5 million white people among its 1.86 million residents. Detroit had less than half this peak of population in 2010 and among its 711,088 residents, only 76,000 are white. All of the counties surrounding Detroit are majority white.

Housing Discrimination in the 21st Century

As a direct result of seven decades of federal subsidies to lenders and homeowners, by 2000 three-quarters of all white American owned their own homes. As a direct result of their long-term exclusion from these programs, especially at the critical early period of suburban building, African Americans remain mired in Depression-era levels of home ownership, with fewer than half of black families owning their own home.

Overall, American cities are actually more segregated today than they were a century ago. The degree of segregation is measured by the Index of Dissimilarity, a tool that computes the evenness of population distribution across a particular area. The Index of Dissimilarity is expressed as a number from 0 to 100, indicating the percentage of the minority population that would have to move from one place to another in order to achieve an even total distribution. One often cited study computed the average Index of Dissimilarity for a dozen northern cities to be 59.2 and for southern cities to be 38.3 in the year 1910. According to the U.S. Census Bureau, the same index in the year 2000 was 73.9 for the Northeast, 74.1 for the Midwest, 55.9 for the West, and 58.1 for the South.

The passage of anti-discrimination laws often gives a false sense that a particular problem of bias has been solved. But, as the history of the Reconstruction laws mandating "equal protection of the laws" demonstrates, legislation is only as effective as the will to enforce it. Perhaps this is nowhere more true in the modern era than in the case of housing discrimination. Congress passed the Fair Housing Act in 1968, but the Justice Department brought no major cases against any financial institution until it sued Decatur Federal Savings and Loan for systematic racial discrimination in the early 1990s. Though the Department of Housing and Urban Development was given additional prosecution powers by Congress in 1988, by 2003 HUD had prosecuted only four cases, though receiving thousands of complaints a year. Meanwhile housing experts estimate that the annual number of actual violations of housing anti-discrimination laws numbers in the millions.

A generation past the passage of the Fair Housing Act, strong evidence points to the fact that racial discrimination in housing remains common and pervasive. In the largest study of housing discrimination ever conducted, the Department of Housing and Urban Development (HUD) conducted 5,500 field tests between 2000 and 2002 in which they sent pairs of discrimination "testers," (men and women whose assumed identities were similar in all ways except for the variables of race, ethnicity, sex, and other protected categories) into thirty cities to see if they received different treatment. HUD researchers found that one in five of black testers received discriminatory treatment as did one in four Latinos. Renters were given little information about available apartments and shown fewer and inferior units. Prospective home buyers were steered

Figure 13.15 The sprawl of housing developments in McCordsville, a northern suburb of Indianapolis, Indiana, 2016.

away from wealthier and whiter neighborhoods and offered worse terms and financing. Other studies of large datasets on home purchasing have shown that black home buyers pay on average one-half percent higher rates of interest on their mortgages and were more than 80% more likely to be rejected for financing outright.

About the same time that federal and state housing laws began to prohibit racial discrimination, the number and intrusiveness of restrictions on building new homes and apartment buildings multiplied. Some of these regulations, like passage of the Clean Water Act in 1972, or new laws creating historical districts and landmarks, were not related to the racial tensions in the country, but nevertheless increased the cost of new houses by restricting the permissible areas where new developments could be built. Other regulations, especially local zoning ordinances, were often designed and tailored to preserve the racial exclusivity of white neighborhoods and suburbs by limiting new construction, prohibiting multi-family residences, and generally raising the cost of new houses by increasing the minimum size of lots, mandating certain architectural features, declaring large swaths of land "open" and "green spaces" exempt from development and even raising local property taxes. State and federal courts that had for a century frowned on and narrowly restricted local housing regulations of these sorts, suddenly seemed to be unable to find any regulation they didn't approve of.

A typical example of the use of zoning regulations in an attempt to price minorities out of the housing market and thereby preserve the white character of a suburban town was the efforts of Mount Laurel, New Jersey. Mount Laurel is a suburb of Philadelphia, just a few miles east of Camden, and in the early 1970s it passed new restrictions on multi-family buildings, of which Mount Laurel then had none. Mount Laurel's zoning law attempted to drive away apartment developers by limiting the number of children per unit to one per bedroom and charging landlords tuition surcharges for any building that had a total of more than one school-aged child per every three units. The NAACP sued and won a state court order that Mount Laurel had to allow for a fair number of low-income units within their town. But proving that winning in court does not mean winning in life, Mount Laurel allocated a total of 20 acres out of the town's 14,300 acres for multifamily developments, every acre of which was sited in a way so as to be unbuildable. On appeal, the NAACP lost when a the state supreme court refused to revisit the issue, saying it was impossible for courts to decide what was a "fair number" of

Figure 13.16 Cleveland, Ohio, May 1965.

affordable apartments.

Many scholars have studied the growth of local zoning and housing regulations since the 1970s and found a remarkable proliferation of their number and scope. Since the 1970s, the density of such regulations has increased dramatically, one index of such zoning laws rising 400% from 1970 to 2015. Housing prices have tracked fairly closely with such indexes, thus creating an effective economic barrier to those long barred from white towns and neighborhoods by racial covenants and mortgage redlining. Even urban areas are feeling the housing pinch. In 1960, Los Angeles was zoned for a population of ten million. Today, its zoning permits less than half that number. Nine of the eleven largest metropolitan areas in the United States today have rapidly rising housing and rental costs.

While it is illegal in all fifty states to discriminate in housing on the basis of "race, color, religion, national origin, sex, disability, and familial status," it is legal in all but thirteen states to refuse to rent to someone who receives a subsidy for their housing. As a disproportionate number of people in need of housing assistance because of historic patterns of discrimination are black, refusing to rent to "Section 8" tenants is an effective and mostly legal method of racial exclusion. Even those cities, such as Chicago, that have passed tougher fair housing ordinances, rarely enforce them, judging by the number of online apartment advertisements that clearly state "No Section 8."

Since the 1970s, many of America's predominantly white neighborhoods have steadily become more integrated at a slow but significant rate. In 1970, more than half of all census tracts (the Census Bureau divides the nation into approximately 66,000 tracts each containing between 2500 and 8000 people) had fewer than 1% black residents. By 1980, most white people lived in communities that were about 90% white. Thirty years later, in 2010, the proportion of white people in the average white neighborhood had fallen to just under 80%.

This small but significant decline in the level of segregation in most American cities is less the result of the enforcement of fair housing laws and civil rights laws, or even changes in white attitudes, than it is the result of other demographic trends. Partly it is a consequence of the declining proportion of whites in the U.S. population overall. It is also, most notably, due to the growth of a black middle class and the tendency of upwardly mobile black families to relocate to suburbs.

A significant trend of black migration to suburban areas began in the 1970s. Between 1980 and 2000, the rate of movement of black families into suburban areas outpaced all other groups. During this period, the black suburban population increased 42%. When changes in rates of segregation are broken down into those attributable to changes within the urban core, those attributable to

movement from the urban core to the suburban ring, and, finally, changes within the suburban area itself, it is evident that black suburbanization has been the leading demographic trend driving the decline in overall segregation across the nation. One study using data from the 2000 census found that only 41% of the change in the degree of segregation was explained by the movement of people within cities themselves.

What this suggests is that integration is primarily occurring by the movement of black families into predominantly white neighborhoods, not the other way around. Large-scale surveys of the attitudes revealed that most black people preferred to live in highly integrated neighborhoods, even where whites were a large majority. One

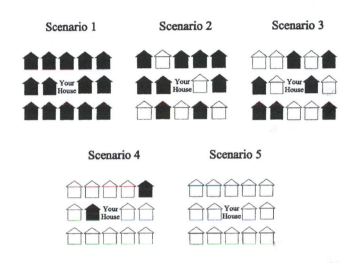

survey conducted interviews with over 2,000 black respondents who were shown five cards, each representing a different neighborhood's racial composition from all-white to all-black and three degrees inbetween.

All but one percent of those interviewed preferred to live in a community in which white and black were even numbers of residents. 89% were willing to live in a place with a white population six times larger than black. A significant number (35%) were even comfortable moving into a neighborhood that was all-white.

One bit of evidence for this is that the general trend toward residential integration is not evident in many nonwhite communities. Most nonwhite communities showed remarkable demographic stability, changing little in the twenty years from 1990 to 2010. Over 80% of the census tracts classified as black and highly segregated in 1990 remained highly segregated in 2010, while over 88% of those categorized as Latino and highly segregated were still classed that way two decades later. In fact, looking a bit further back, between 1970 and 2000, the proportion of census tracts that had a majority of black, Latino or Asian residents (or residents) actually increased slightly. Minority communities remain resistant to integration not because their residents are hostile to it, but because of the overwhelming reluctance of whites to move into these areas.

In 1990, only 0.3% of all U.S. Census tracts were classified as "highly diverse." Twenty years later this number had nudged up to 1.5% and the rate at which communities were graduating to this designation had noticeably slowed.

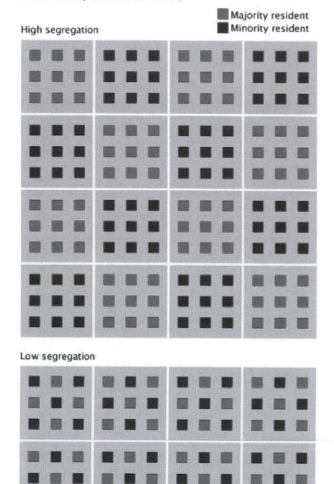

Distribution of Households Within One Hypothetical Metropolitan Area With High Segregation and One With Low Segregation: Dissimilarity Index (Evenness)

High segregation

■ Majority resident
■ Minority resident

Low segregation

Note: Neighborhoods within the metropolitan areas are delineated by the white lines.

Figure 13.17 Graphic model of the dissimilarity index

86% of the growth of these highly diverse communities took place in the decade after 1990 and only 14% since 2000.

Some scholars have suggested that whites have a particular threshold of comfort with neighbors of a different race; in other words, white communities accept a relatively small and token amount of integration but quickly reach a tipping point in which they act to police their neighborhood composition. Moreover, some data seems to suggest that in some cases white communities are becoming more, not less sensitive to increasing numbers of racial minorities in their communities.

Measures of the degree of isolation of one racial group from others shows that whites continue to experience a far higher level of racial isolation than all other groups, though it is gradually declining. By the 2000 Census, it appeared that white resistance to increasing numbers of blacks in their neighborhoods was measurable on the macro level. Even the cautious number-crunchers in the Census Bureau were moved to observe that those places that had the highest increases in black populations also saw increases in their various measures of segregation. Where the black population most increased so did the dissimilarity index (a measure of what proportion of a group would need to move to achieve an even distribution of people by race), as did the isolation index (the percentage of people of a similar race in a neighborhood), and the spatial proximity index (an estimate of how likely it is a person lives next door to another person of the same race).

Some demographers argue that segregation in America is not really easing, but is merely changing form and location and that the relative integration of some areas, such as suburbs closest to city centers, masks the increasing segregation occurring at a larger scale not within but between communities. This new "macro-segregation" is occurring as more far-flung suburbs are becoming whiter faster than cities and the older suburbs nearer to them slowly integrate. Analysis of census data confirms that as segregation within central cities has declined over the past twenty years, suburban segregation has increased, primarily as integrated suburbs become increasingly nonwhite and the number of suburbs with predominantly white populations has increased.

Macro-segregation may also be powerfully facilitated by governmental and legal structures that through zoning restrictions, aggressive policing, and cultural hostility discourage the settlement of nonwhites.

1901. TEN CENTS A WEEK

NEGROES

Driven From a Missouri City by an Infuriated Mob.

Several Lynched For Awful Crimes and all are Ordered Never to Return to the City.

By Associated Press.

Pierce City, Mo., Aug. 20—For nearly fifteen hours, ending about noon today, this town of 3000 people, has been in the hands of a mob of armed whites, determined to drive every negro from its precincts. In addition to the lynching last night of Will Godley, accused of the wanton murder of Miss Gazelle Wild, and the shooting to death of his grandfather, French Godley, the mob today cremated Pete Hampton, an aged negro, in his home, and set the torch to the houses of five blacks and with the state militia rifles, stolen from the local company's arsenal, drove dozens of negroes from town. After noon the excitement died down and the mob gradually dispersed, more from lack of negroes on which to wreak their hatred than from any other cause.

Many negroes who fled from the city are hiding in the surrounding woods, while others have gone distances in seeking safety.

Every negro has left town except a few railway porters known to be respectable, but who must also leave.

The citizens say that as the negroes have committed several such crimes in the last ten years, none shall live there in the future and the same feeling already exists at Monnett, four miles east of Pierce City and at the end of the Frisco passenger division.

It is now believed that Will Godley, who was lynched, is not the real culprit. A negro named Starks, under arrest at Tulsa, I. T., across the border from here, tallies exactly with the description of the murderer. He is held there awaiting identification. Unless the man is brought back here it is believed there will be no further trouble. If returned here he will surely be lynched.

Another suspect, Joe Lark, is under arrest at Springfield, Mo. Eugene Barrett, also known as Carter, in a confession with a rope around his neck today, accused Joe Lark, a Frisco railroad porter, of being implicated in the crime and Lark was arrested today at Springfield.

This afternoon Lark gave a detailed statement as to his whereabouts Sunday and he is not believed guilty. It is not likely that either suspect will be taken to Pierce City while the excitement runs high.

The funeral of Miss Wild took place today and was witnessed by several thousand people.

Pierce City is near the junction of four railroads and trains from all directions brought in a large number of armed men today, bent on bloodshed, if necessary. When the mob went to the section of the city occupied by negroes some one in the cabins opened fire, but no one was hurt. The mob then destroyed five houses, but the financial loss was small. Reckless firing broke several plate glass windows and a train was fired into. None of the passengers were hurt. The rifles were taken from the Pierce City military company and it is expected that all will be returned. Members of the company themselves are out hunting for the escaped negroes with rifles, and this suggested the idea of taking all the guns. The local hardware stores sold out their arms early, but several applications from negroes were refused. The mob was composed of a thousand or more. No masks were used and thirty negro families were driven from their houses.

THE NATURE OF HOUSING DISCRIMINATION
from *Housing: 1961 U.S. Commission on Civil Rights Report* (Washington, D.C., 1961)

A number of forces combine to prevent equality of opportunity in housing. They begin with the prejudice of private persons, but they involve large segments of the organized business world. In addition, Government on all levels bears a measure of responsibility—for it supports and indeed to a great extent it created the machinery through which housing discrimination operates.

The most obvious aspect of the problem involves the owner of a house who, from his own prejudice or by reason of outside pressure, refuses to sell or rent to members of particular minority groups. Frequently, such prejudice finds expression in restrictive covenants. These, the Supreme Court has held, are not judicially enforceable, but, being private arrangements, they are not constitutionally invalid. Their use is still widespread. In buying a home in the Nation's capital in February of 1961, Secretary of State Dean Rusk encountered and refused to sign a restrictive covenant barring occupancy of Spring Valley homes "by Negroes or 'any person of the Semitic race, blood or origin, including 'Jews, Hebrews, Persians, and Syrians.' "

Property owners' prejudices are reflected, magnified, and sometimes even induced by real estate brokers, through whom most housing changes hands. Organized brokers have, with few exceptions, followed the principle that only a "homogeneous" neighborhood assures economic soundness. Their views in some cases are so vigorously expressed as to discourage property owners who would otherwise be concerned only with the color of a purchaser's money, and not with that of his skin. Moreover, these views sometimes find elaborately systematic expression, as in the well-publicized program in Grosse Pointe, Mich. There, discrimination covered the full ambit of "race, color, religion, and national origin," and it was practiced with mathematical exactitude. Two groups, the Grosse Pointe Brokers Association and the Grosse Pointe Property Owners Association had established and maintained a screening system to winnow out would-be purchasers who were considered "undesirable":

> A passing grade was 50 points. However, those of Polish descent had to score 55 points; southern Europeans, including those of Italian, Greek, Spanish, or Lebanese origin had to score 65 points, and those of the Jewish faith had to score 85 points. Negroes and orientals were excluded entirely.

Similar exclusions are accomplished in other communities, though usually with less refinement than in Grosse Pointe. The financial community, upon which mortgage financing—and hence the bulk of home purchasing and home building—depends, also acts to a large extent on the premise that only a homogeneous neighborhood can offer an economically sound investment. For this reason, plus the fear of offending their other clients, many mortgage-lending institutions refuse to provide home financing for houses in a "mixed" neighborhood. The persistent stereotypes of certain minority groups as poor credit risks also block the flow of credit, although these stereotypes have often been proved unjustified.

Finally, private builders often adopt what they believe are the views of those to whom they expect to sell and of the banks upon whose credit their own operations depend. In short, as the Commission on Race and Housing has concluded, "it is the real estate brokers, builders, and mortgage finance institutions, which translate prejudice into discriminatory action." "Thus, at every level of the private housing market members of minority groups meet mutually reinforcing and often unbreakable barriers of rejection...

Since World War I, when Negroes first moved north in significant numbers, discrimination against them in residential areas had been fairly common in roughly its present form. By 1933, racial discrimination had become an operating practice of the private housing industry....

Federal policy in the housing field reflected and even magnified the attitudes of private industry. The FHA [Federal Housing Authority] indeed encouraged racial discrimination. Its explanation for doing so was the widespread belief that property values of a residential neighborhood suffered when the residents were not of the same social, economic, and racial group. Thus the FHA in its "Underwriting Manual" of 1938 declared: "If a neighborhood is to retain stability, it is necessary that properties shall continue to be occupied by the same social and racial groups." The Manual carried this principle a step further by recommending the use of restrictive covenants to insure against "inharmonious racial groups." It even contained a model covenant and thereby gave great impetus to the spread of racial discrimination in residential areas throughout the country—for the inclusion of the restrictive covenant in real estate sales contracts became almost a prerequisite of FHA mortgage insurance. When land was sold to Negroes or Mexican-Americans, under FHA policy, adjoining land generally would be classed as undesirable.

One housing expert has concluded that FHA's discriminatory policy widened the gap between the living conditions of whites and Negroes and increased the concentration of racial minorities in the older, more deteriorated neighborhoods. It did this, he has said, by aiding the increase of the total supply of new housing, particularly in the suburbs, while denying the minority groups access to it, thus forcing them into existing, substandard housing. Another observer has characterized the FHA policy as "separate for whites and nothing for blacks."

Other Federal agencies dealing with the private housing industry adopted similar attitudes. The FHLBB [Federal Home Loan Bank Board] and HOLC [Home Owners Loan Corporation] openly followed policies favoring the homogeneity of racial groups in residential neighborhoods. When HOLC acquired homes in white neighborhoods and offered them for sale, Negroes could not buy them. And when this agency made loans, its policy was to do so only if they were used to preserve racial segregation....

The Commission has found evidence of racially

discriminatory practices by mortgage lending institutions throughout the country. In Detroit the Commission heard of the "common policy of refusing to lend to Negroes who are the first purchasers in a white neighborhood." In Dayton the great majority of lending institutions are reported to want 30 or 40 percent Negro occupancy in a neighborhood before they will finance the purchase of a home for a Negro... In Los Angeles, the Commission was told, "if a white person buys a home and later wants to sell to a non-Caucasian, [and] the non-Caucasian tries to qualify for the loan, the lending institution will not approve of this successive non-Caucasian buyer. Now that necessitates refinancing which is expensive and burdensome and oftentimes impossible. So the lending institution tends to control certain areas in that manner."

Freedom of choice is often denied to whites as well as nonwhites. In San Francisco, the Commission was told, white persons desiring to purchase a home in an integrated neighborhood experience great difficulties in securing financing. The representative of a leading mortgage lending institution told one family that one such neighborhood in the Palo Alto area was "blacked out" and that no loans would be available....

The Federal Government has undertaken extensive programs of mortgage insurance (FHA), mortgage guarantees (VA) [Veteran's Adminstration],... to implement national housing policy. These programs have been a principal factor in the dynamic expansion of the homebuilding industry. William Levitt, one of the country's largest homebuilders, has said that "we are 100 percent dependent on the Government. Whether this is right or wrong, it is a fact." At the same time the programs have virtually eliminated the financial community's risk of loss from large numbers of mortgages. Thus Federal programs are a form of subsidy to the mortgage lending and homebuilding industries, yet the Federal Government has done little to see that the benefits from this subsidy—an increased housing supply—are available to all Americans on a basis of equal opportunity. In Detroit, a Commission witness pointed out that:

> The situation still persists where FHA- and VA-approved lending institutions are permitted to utilize the credit, the insurance, the guarantee of the Federal Government to practice discrimination and foster segregation in the private housing market.

In Los Angeles, a Commission witness referred to "the fact that the builders and developers refuse to sell FHA and VA homes to non-Caucasians." He added: "I think that public acceptance of residential segregation is kept at a maximum by the common knowledge that the Government through its housing agencies is a partner to the refusal of FHA and VA."

The resources of the Federal Government, then—its credit, its sponsorship, its very name—are involved in virtually all aspects of mortgage credit, and yet racial discrimination is a widespread practice among the enterprises which enjoy these Federal resources....

[F]our supervisory agencies—the Federal Home Loan Bank Board, Comptroller of the Currency, Board of Governors of the Federal Reserve System, and Federal Deposit Insurance Corporation—represent Federal authority over the community of mortgage lending institutions. The institutions which they regulate and supervise hold $363.3 billion in assets. Their home mortgage loan portfolios amount to $100 billion.

According to the evidence that the Commission has received throughout the country, the financial community in which these agencies play so large and vital a role is a major factor in the denial of equal housing opportunities to minority groups. In Cleveland, a real estate broker told the Commission's Ohio Advisory Committee of "the gentleman's agreement among the builder, the banker, and the real estate agent in which all have agreed to prevent an open market in housing as far as Negroes are concerned." He concluded: "in the final analysis it goes back to the bank."

Two of the four supervisory agencies acknowledge, at least implicitly, that discrimination in mortgage lending does occur. All four appear to agree that outright discrimination—the denial of credit on grounds of race, creed, or color alone—is improper. None, however, has conducted any inquiry into the extent to which the institutions under their supervision engage in such improper practices....

[Federal Reserve Bank] Board Chairman Martin implicitly recognized the discrimination problem when he said: "Ideally, decisions that member banks make as to whether or not to grant loan applications should rest upon financial considerations alone." He added: "considerations of race, creed, or color should not enter into business decisions."

The latter statement appears, in the Board's view, to be subject to an important qualification. In response to a question as to whether the race of the would-be borrower or the racial composition of the neighborhood might be legitimate considerations for a member bank to take into account in deciding whether to make a real estate loan, Chairman Martin had this to say:

> Since banks are primarily trustees of depositors' funds and must seek to protect those funds, it is entirely appropriate for them to take cognizance of historical patterns in real estate values. Both at the inception of any mortgage and during its life, a mortgagee must be concerned with the stability of the value of the underlying property and the trend of values in the neighborhood in which any particular property is located.

The reference to "historical patterns in real estate values" seems to be a gingerly allusion to what the Board believes is the likely result when a Negro moves into a white neighborhood. Thus, if a member bank felt that real estate values would become unstable, it could, for example, properly reject a loan application from a Negro who wished to buy a home in a predominantly white neighborhood. Therefore, Chairman Martin's first statement must be qualified to read: "considerations of race, creed, or color should not enter into business decisions except when the bank feels that they may affect real estate values."....

Chapter Fourteen: The Color-blind Era?

"What good is it to be allowed to eat in a restaurant if you can't afford a hamburger?" - Dr. Martin Luther King, Jr.

On Friday night, November 22, 1968, American families crowded around their televisions watched something that had never before been shown on television. Star Trek's communications officer, Lieutenant Nyota Uhura, (played by actress Nichelle Nichols) embraced Captain James T. Kirk (William Shatner) and they kissed passionately. This was the first time a white man and a black woman kissed on network television. (Actually, Sammy Davis Jr. aroused controversy for giving Nancy Sinatra a peck on the cheek during a variety show the year before, but this didn't count as a romantic kiss.) That script's scene had been hotly debated before it aired as producer Gene Roddenberry and director David Alexander were pressured by network executives to have Uhura kiss Spock (who was less risky being only half human) or have Kirk break off the embrace without showing their lips touching. Shatner insisted on the kiss being real and intentionally spoiled those takes that had him break off the kiss by crossing his eyes. Scriptwriters attempted to soften the impact of an interracial kiss by depicting Kirk and Uhura being forced by an alien's psychic power into the act. To everyone's surprise and relief, the expected flood of hate mail never materialized. Clearly white attitudes about race were shifting.

A national survey of racial attitudes begun before World War Two traced these changing attitudes. In 1942, fewer than half of all whites (42%) answered yes to the question, "Do you think Negroes are as intelligent as white people—that is, can they learn things just as well if they are given the same education and training?" By the 1960's, 80% of white people asked that same question agreed that blacks and whites were equally intelligent. An overwhelming number of Americans, when surveyed as to whether they favored one racial group over another in work, social life, or in the public sphere, claimed to judge and treat everyone equally, as they said they didn't "see race." In 1972, 97% of whites surveyed agreed that black people "should have as good a chance as white people to get a job."

While most of these opinions moderated over the next generation, with the percentage of those believing in a right to segregate neighborhoods or frowning on interracial marriage plummeting from near 40% nationally to just over 10% by 1996, some attitudes remained remarkably consistent. The proportion of whites who objected to sending their children to school with blacks was virtually the same in 1972 and 1996. Somewhere between 40 and 50% of whites would not send their children to a majority black school; another 20% would not send them to a school evenly divided between white and black; and around 5% wouldn't send their kids to a school with any black children. Likewise surveys have shown steady resistance on the part of most whites to living in a majority black neighborhood, though from 1976 to 2004 the number of whites who would consider such a neighborhood to live in rose from 16 to 34%. Meanwhile, surveys of black Americans have consistently indicated that their ideal neighborhood was an integrated one where half the residents were white.

Prior to 1970, fewer than one in one thousand whites married a black partner. Ten times more, one in a hundred, blacks married across racial divide. By 2000 the intermarriage rates for whites had risen to three in a thousand unions, and for blacks to four in a hundred marriages. (Of course, marriage is only one formal form of romantic relationships. A study of online dating ads found that nearly half of the ads posted by whites seeking partners said that race didn't matter to them. But their behavior didn't correspond to their stated beliefs. Nine out of ten of White romance seekers responded only to messages from other whites.)

Clearly social attitudes have undergone a major shift, but it remains unclear if that shift has actually reduced racism or merely caused it take different forms.

Color-blind Racism

In 2014 the television channel MTV interviewed 2,000 of their core viewers, those ages 14 to 24, about their views of race and racism in American society. The results revealed that the so-called millennial generation overwhelmingly rejects the racism of the past and has embraced the ideal of America as a color-blind nation where one's race should not block equality or opportunity. Nine out of ten of the young people surveyed said they believed in racial equality and that everyone should be treated equally.

Color-blindness was made a national aspiration as a result of the Civil Rights Movement of the 1950s and 1960s and Dr. Martin Luther King, Jr.'s powerful rhetoric, most memorably his "I Have A Dream Speech," of 1963 when he said that "I have a dream that my four little children will one day live in a nation where they will not be judged by the color of their skin but by the content of their character." As those openly advocating segregation and discrimination were largely silenced by the end of the 1960s and a national consensus emerged among politicians, the media, business interests, and popular culture that public expressions of racism were no longer tolerable, colorblindness became the national standard of behavior. By the 1990s when the Millennial generation was born, most white people had come to believe that this was not only a dream, a hope, or a goal, but had, in fact, become a reality.

MTV's viewers, particularly their white viewers, had been raised in a culture that disowned racism to such an extent that it no longer thought it appropriate to even discuss it. Only about a third of respondents said their families ever discussed race and nearly half said that they thought it was wrong to "draw attention" to a person's race even if doing so positively. The pollsters concluded that only one in five of young people "are comfortable having a conversation about bias."

Part of the reason for such discomfort in discussing race and racism is the widespread belief that it no longer exists, or at least not in a way that negatively impacts most people of color's opportunities. Two-thirds of white people interviewed said racial minorities had the same opportunities as anyone else in America (only one third of people of color thought so). Nearly half of the young white people interviewed thought that bias against white people was as big a problem as bias against people of color. Color-blindness as an ideal has morphed into something of a Catch-22, a problem that appears to have a solution, but whose answer circles back to the problem. In effect, the MTV'ers were saying that the evidence that America was a colorblind country was that racism was seldom discussed or seen and the solution to racism was not talking about it or seeing it.

Like those in the MTV survey, most white people today frequently claim that they "don't see color" or that they are "color-blind." They commonly say that the problem of racism would go away if people just stopped noticing or talking about race. Of course, only those people for whom their race does not carry the threat of discrimination, of ill-treatment, of suspicion, can say such a thing. People of color who live in a world divided by race cannot choose to be colorblind because the daily experience of being seen as black or brown is real. As one scholar put it when told by a colleague he "didn't see race," she said, "That's nice, for you… 'cos I see race every time I look in the mirror."

Scholars, such as Eduardo Bonilla-Silva, have noted how these "color-blind" ideals have morphed into a new racial ideology. This ideology identifies the source of continuing racism as the complaint against racism itself. Whatever inequalities exist, they do so because

Figure 14.1 Lyndon B. Johnson and Rev. Dr. Martin Luther King, Jr. in the cabinet room, White House, Mar. 18, 1966.

of deficiencies in minority communities and cultures themselves, not because of anything whites do. Rather, racism is perpetuated because people of color are too sensitive and pretend to see racism everywhere.

The Marley Hypothesis

Color-blind racism depends to a large degree on the systematic erasure and forgetting of the centrality that racism has played in the development and history of the United States. A growing body of research indicates that ignorance of America's racist past is much higher in the white population than among people of color. This is a curious phenomenon because overall, white people in America receive better educational opportunities and have more information resources, such as more access to high-speed internet and more and better-funded libraries in their schools and neighborhoods. Most puzzling of all, whites score much higher on standardized history tests in secondary schools than do blacks.

One group of researchers posed a theory to explain this phenomenon that they called the "Marley Hypothesis," after the refrain of Bob Marley's song, *Buffalo Soldier*, that includes the lines, "If you know your history, then you will know where you're comin' from, and you wouldn't have to ask me, who the heck do I think I am." They reasoned that:

> Accurate knowledge about documented incidents of past racism will be greater in subordinate-group communities than in dominant-group communities, and this difference in reality attunement will partly account for... group differences in perception of racism in current events.

It may be that more exposure to mainstream educational materials actually limits understanding of the reality of racism in America. This is because almost all elementary and secondary history textbooks are written from a patriotic and positivist perspective. They tend to presume the moral and institutional superiority of American institutions over others in the world and they portray history as a continual story of progress and advancement. Such themes combine to proclaim the legitimacy and justice of present national institutions, thereby reinforcing majority belief that racism has been overcome and eradicated.

American school books all mention slavery, but few discuss how the elements of slavery that maintained economic and legal oppression were not overcome until late in the 20th century. When Jim Crow segregation is discussed, it is usually only in the context of buses, drinking fountains, and schools, things that it is supposed all people had access to, though unfairly, when in reality Jim Crow was a system of denying access to the most vital things in modern life, jobs, housing, healthcare, and legal protection. This encourages many white Americans to minimize the actual harm of historic racism. For example, most white people will reluctantly admit that slavery did once exist, but they will frame this fact in a way that drains it of importance by saying that 'it happened a long time ago' or that 'my family never owned any slaves.'

Surveys of black understandings of the past and opinions about the equality and openness of the present show a vast disparity with white views of American institutions. People of color display higher rates of awareness of the details of America's racist history. There are many explanations for why such historical knowledge is more prevalent among communities of color, not least among them being the simple fact that for generations ignorance about the true state of America's racist society could have deadly consequences for nonwhites.

When faced with the facts of the stark difference in historical opinion by race in America, whites tend to assume that their own views about the fairness and equality of modern America are "normal" and obvious and therefore don't require explanation, while views counter to these beliefs must have extensive proof. Moreover, they tend to see those who frequently shout 'racism' as just being overly sensitive and less in touch with reality.

However, psychological studies into the different structures of belief underlying the vastly different attitudes of whites and blacks, point to white assumptions as being aberrant. One study quantified the belief structures of white and black subjects on a seven-point scale whose extremes were that a claim was "certainly true" or "certainly false," and the midpoint was the uncertainty of "might possibly be true." Consistently, when confronted with claims of government conspiracies against black people, such as the claim that "the government deliberately singles out and investigates Black elected officials to discredit them in a way it doesn't do with White officials," or "Black men are more likely to be put in jail than White men because the government wants to harm Black men," black people score near the middle of the scale (mean of 4.16) but whites score down near the extreme of negative certainty (mean of 1.67). Without even exploring how many of the thirteen conspiracy statements used in the study have strong evidence for or against their being true, the open-mindedness of African American subjects is far less needing of psychological explanation than the pervasive certainties of white ones.

In effect, studies such as this highlight that whiteness in the 21st century is an identity rooted in assumptions of societal fairness and equality. White people tend to assume that racism is individual, it exists because a few people are bigots. Being an individual fault or aberration, racism is not considered institutional or social thereby avoiding contradiction with a belief that the American story is one of uplift and progress. Vice-president Mike Pence, while campaigning about a month before the election publicly declared his opinion that there is "far too much of this talk of institutional bias or racism within law enforcement" and advised, "we ought to set aside this talk about institutional racism and institutional bias."

Another example of the Marley Hypothesis in action is the different responses of black and white people to those who have used the National Anthem as a means of political and social protest.

Protests against the national anthem first appeared in the 1960s amidst civil rights struggles and the deepening military quagmire in Vietnam. Popular poet and novelist Amiri Baraka (LeRoi Jones) criticized the anthem as "pompous, hypocritical, vapid, and sterile..." Baraka located these faults in white people's embrace of the idea of superiority, saying the anthem reflected "the kind of minds that

Figure 14.2 "Protest is Patriotic" overpass bannering, Sept. 2017

have canonized themselves into some kind of Chosen People. For me it's as fake as anything else in America." At the 1968 Olympics, Tommie Smith stepped up to the champions podium after winning gold in the 200 meter dash with his friend and teammate John Carlos who took bronze. Wearing black gloves to symbolize black power, Smith and Carlos raised their fists in the air when the Star-Spangled banner was played and were banned for life from Olympic competition in punishment for their silent protest against racism in America. American sprinters Wayne Collett and Vince Matthews, having seen the storm of condemnation that descended on Smith and Carlos, bravely accepted the consequences and turned their backs when the anthem was played in 1972 and were also permanently banned from the sport. Jimi Hendrix, an army veteran himself, famously took the stage at the 1969 Woodstock Art and Music Fair and mashed the anthem into a hard-edged wail of protest against the Vietnam War. All of these acts of conscience and political theater were widely and vigorously condemned by newspaper editors and television commentators across the country.

More recently, San Francisco 49ers quarterback Colin Kaepernick, took a knee rather than stand for the playing of the national anthem through the 2016 NFL season. Kaepernick explained:

People don't realize what's really going on in this country. There are a lot things that are going on that are unjust. People aren't being held accountable for. And that's something that needs to change. That's something that this country stands for freedom, liberty and justice for all. And it's not happening for all right now... These aren't new situations. This isn't new ground. There are things that have gone on in this country for years and years and have never been addressed, and they need to be. I'll continue to sit...I'm going to continue to stand with the people that are being oppressed. To me this is something that has to change. When there's significant change and I feel like that flag represents what it's supposed to represent, this country is representing people the way that it's supposed to, I'll stand.

Polling data reveals that Kaepernick's protest was

condemned by two-thirds of those who described themselves as white and approved of by three-quarters of those
identified as black.

American culture systematically whitewashes its racist past, both by forgetting what at one time seemed commonplace and by intentionally erasing those things that
now make white people feel guilty and conflicted. Leading
media corporations have locked up the most embarrassing
reminders of a pervasive racist culture in their vaults: Disney acts as if it never produced Song of the South while
Time Warner, the inheritor of the Looney Tunes series, has
banned the broadcasting of the eleven most offensive Tom
& Jerry, Bugs Bunny, and Speedy Gonzales cartoons since
the 1970s.

Even without active censoring, American culture
erodes the racist content of many of its cultural artifacts
by a process where they are abstracted from their origins
and then endlessly reproduced outside of their contexts.
Almost any common cultural product can serve as an example of this. Take perhaps the most popular Christmas
song, Jingle Bells, for instance.

The song originally titled, "Jingle Bells; or, The One
Horse Open Sleigh," was written in the 1850s by James
Pierpont, a composer who specialized in developing tunes
for the blackface minstrel theaters of New York and Boston. Jingle Bells debuted at Boston's Ordway Hall (a theater that advertised "Colored people not admitted") in
1857, sung by blackface performer Johnny Pell as part of
an act called the "Dandy Darkies."

While the song itself does not refer to either white
or black people, or blackness or whiteness (unlike the song
that directly preceded it that night: "Little White Cottage;
or, Nellie Moore") it was sung by a white man in black face
ridiculing the pretensions of some black men and women
who would dress in fancy clothes and ride in sleighs just
like rich whites did. The joke, as was the case with all racist
songs, was the idea that black people would always fail in
their attempts to act like whites. In the Jingle Bells verses
never sung today, the blackfaced singer recounts his failure
at sleighing:

A day or two ago
I tho't I'd take a ride
And soon miss Fanny Bright
Was seated by my side,
The horse was lean and lank
Misfortune seem'd his lot
He got into a drifted bank
And we—we got upsot.

A day or two ago,
The story I must tell
I went out on the snow,

A TEAM FAST TO THE POLE.

Figure 14.3 "Team fast to the pole," Currier & Ives, c1883.

And on my back I fell;
A gent was riding by
In a one horse open sleigh,
He laughed as there I sprawling lie,
But quickly drove away

In spite of his hardships, the black sleigh riders drove
on, "Laughing all the way," a cue for minstrel singers to
over-act the stereotype of the happy-go-lucky Sambo.

Similar echoes of a time when racism was open and
acceptable are all around American culture. Ice cream
trucks announce their arrival with a familiar tune, Turkey in
the Straw, that emerged from the blackface minstrel stage
to become the most popular song among white Americans
in the nineteenth century. Derived from a traditional English melody, the song was first performed and published
in America with the title "Zip Coon" and its lyrics featured
a black character comically failing at being a gentleman. Its
chorus of "O zip a duden duden duden zip a duden day"
was later adapted by Disney for the catchy feature tune
sung by Uncle Remus in Song of the South, "Zip-A-Dee-
Doo-Dah."

Figure 14.5 Good Humor Ice Cream Truck, 1942

A TEAM FAST ON THE SNOW.

Figure 14.4 "Team fast on the snow," Currier & Ives, c1883.

Generations of American school children were drilled through the motions of square dancing in gym classes largely because the auto tycoon Henry Ford made a crusade of reviving and promoting this dying folk dance in the 1920s. Ford did so not out of love for square dancing, but because of his belief that Jews and African Americans were conspiring to corrupt the morals of white Americans by spreading jazz music and jazz dances like the Charleston into white communities. Ford denounced "modern dances with their lesser demand for skill and spirit, their tuneless music, their tendency to jazz," or what he called the "moron music which they habitually hum and sing and shout day and night" that was produced by "Jews and their art-destroying commercialism." Ford believed that Jewish influences were destroying the moral foundation of America:

> The population could be turned into drug addicts if the same freedom was given to the illicit narcotic ring as is now given to the Yiddish popular song manufacturers...A dreadful narcotizing of moral modesty and the application of powerful aphrodisiacs have been involved in the present craze for crooning songs - a stimulated craze. The victims are everywhere. But too few of the opponents of this moral poison see the futility of scolding the young people thus diseased. Common sense dictates a cleaning out, and a clearing out, of the sources of the disease. The source is in the Yiddish group of song manufacturers who control the whole output...

Backed by his immense wealth, his political connections, and his fame, Ford quickly succeeded in enlisting many allies in his crusade to spread square dancing and stamp out jazz. Within a few years Ford succeeded in pushing dozens of universities to add square dancing to

Figure 14.6 Saturday night square dance, in Weslaco, Texas, 1942.

their theatre, dance, and music curricula. Ford required that all his thousands of dealerships hold folk music and square dancing events. When the first radio networks organized and broadcast coast to coast, Ford sponsored one of the earliest shows, the "Early American Dance Music" program. Ford also published square dancing manuals that he provided to schools for free. Today a majority of states (28 of them) have designated square dancing as their official state dance and in 1982 President Ronald Reagan signed a bill declaring square dancing America's official dance (though this status was not permanent).

Mixed-Race Identity

In 2000, for the first time, the U.S. Census Bureau began allowing individuals to select more than one racial category to describe themselves. Not only could individuals select from one or more of the five established racial categories, they could also check a box marked "Some Other Race." When these options were repeated in the 2010 Census, the rate of growth in the "mixed-race" population was officially quantified for the first time.

By 2010, the overwhelming majority (97%) of Americans reported that they belonged to a single race group. But the three percent of Americans who identified with more than one race surprised demographers by emerging as the fastest growing racial group over the previous decade. White people were the least likely of all groups to check off more than one racial box, a total of slightly more than three percent of white respondents, less than half the rate of black Americans and a quarter of the rate of Asian Americans. Nearly half of native Hawaiian, Pacific Islanders, and American Indians, identified with multiple races.

Such rapid growth in the number of people identifying as multiracial has been hailed in the popular media as evidence that American society is steadily progressing in a color-blind direction. Other scholars have questioned this rosy assumption and theorized that the groups most eager to identify as multiple races, Latinos and Asian-Americans, may not be challenging traditional notions of race but following the pattern of Catholic and Jewish European immigrants from a century before who began calling themselves "white" as a means of claiming a higher social status. Ultimately, the answer to this question lies not in what groups call themselves, but in what the white majority accepts as their standard.

Mixed race people have been part of American society since its colonial days and in America have always been subject to the law of hypodescent or the "one-drop rule." This rule assigns all people of mixed ancestry to the racial group with less social status and power. Usually this meant that people with both black and white parents, or grandparents, were legally and socially categorized as black. Most states defined precise proportions of racial ancestry that divided white and black, such as stating that one nonwhite grandparent or even one nonwhite great-grandparent placed a person in that nonwhite group. Seven states defined anyone with one-eighth or more African ancestry to be black. Some states, like Louisiana, went further and defined a black person as anyone with a "trace of black ancestry." Not to be outdone, Virginia narrowed its definition in 1930 from one-eighth black ancestry to the Louisiana standard that defined a black person as a person who has any black ancestors.

Louisiana's strict standard was tested as part of the famed Plessy v. Ferguson case that declared racial segregation to be compatible with the U.S. Constitution. Though a footnote in the case today, one of Homer Plessy's arguments as to why he should have been allowed to ride in the "white" railroad car, was that he was only one-eighth black and looked like a white man. The Supreme Court dispensed with this point by simply noting that it was "common knowledge" that a person with any black ancestry was indeed black and swiftly moved on to the main purpose of the decision, taking most civil rights away from black citizens.

In 1948, the state of Mississippi sentenced Davis Knight to the state penitentiary for five years for violating that state's laws against interracial marriage. Knight broke the law by marrying Junie Spradley, a white woman, and having a great-grandmother who was once the slave of his great-grandfather, making him one-eighth black. Appealed several times Knight's case arrived at the state supreme court whose justices feared ruling on the substance of Knight's appeal (that the miscegenation law was a violation of his civil rights) and instead ordered a new trial on a technicality. Local officials decided not to prosecute him a second time as their point, demonstrating the power of the state's race laws, had been made.

Nearly a century later, this question of who was white or black continued to percolate through the court system. In 1983, Susie Phipps, a Louisiana woman who had always assumed she was white, was denied a passport because the racial box she checked on her application form conflicted with the "colored" race the hospital had marked on her birth certificate. Five generations and 220 years removed from her black great-great-great-great grandmother, a Louisiana appeals court refused to alter Mrs. Phipps official state racial designation, a ruling upheld by the Louisiana Supreme Court. Under the glare of the national spotlight and the adverse publicity this case brought, the Louisiana legislature reluctantly repealed all its mandatory racial designation laws and allowed individuals to self-identify their race.

Figure 14.7 A New Jersey police chief, 1975.

Racial Policing

Though white and black perceptions of justice, equality, and the baseline level of racism that permeates society are deeply at odds, perhaps they are nowhere more dramatically opposed than in views of policing. Policing is the most direct point of interaction between the government and a citizen. While legislatures set policy, courts make rulings, and bureaucrats issue orders, it is the individual human in a uniform and wearing a badge of authority whose discretion and judgment counts on the street. While laws and policies may be entirely color-blind, the person enforcing those laws may not be.

According to national opinion surveys, white people have always generally assumed that police are fair and treat people respectfully regardless of their race. In the wake of the dozens of deadly urban uprisings that erupted across America between 1964 and 1967, at least half of them directly sparked by instances of police brutality, whites refused to believe that police could be racist. A national poll in 1968 asked what people thought caused the highly publicized outbreaks of violence and over half of African Americans said the cause was "police brutality" and only one-in-ten whites agreed with that explanation. In 1967, three times more black than white people believed that police brutality was a problem in their area. Two years later, in a Gallup poll, half of African Americans reported that

there was police brutality in their neighborhoods. Fast forward to 1991 and this wide gap in perceptions of policing remained: 59% of black people thought police brutality was a problem in their neighborhoods compared with just 37% of whites. Ten years later, in 2002, another poll showed that more than twice as many whites than blacks believed acts of police brutality against racial minorities "never happens," while five times as many African Americans than whites said it "often happens." By 2016, this racial chasm remained: three-quarters of whites but only one-third of blacks viewed the police as treating people of all races equally.

Calling these surveys "opinion polls" is actually misleading as, in the case of people of color, the questions being asked don't just solicit an opinion but draw on direct observation. One reason for the faultline between blacks and whites in their views of policing is that policing is experienced very differently by people of color. Statistical studies of extremely large datasets of search and arrest data have shown that people of color are far more likely to be stopped, searched, or arrested in America than whites are. A government study in 2005 found that, nationally, black motorists had their vehicles searched by police 9.5% of the time, while only 3.6% of white motorists underwent searches. One interesting study done in St. Louis in 2007 showed that both white and black police officers stopped black motorists disproportionately in that city. The racial gap in black officer behavior was actually larger than that of white officers, not because they stopped black drivers more, but because they stopped white drivers far less often.

Racial profiling is even more common in predominantly white neighborhoods and towns. Criminologists call this phenomenon "out-of-place" policing and it may be the most pernicious form of racial profiling as its effect is to maintain residential segregation by making life for people of color in white communities uncomfortable, inconvenient, and sometimes even dangerous. A treatise on policing published in 1967 advocated such "out-of-place" policing as sound policy, writing:

> A person of one race observed in an area which is largely inhabited by a different racial group may be stopped and questioned. A Negro in an area which is almost exclusively white is more suspect than a white in the same area, although a decision to stop for questioning may not be made on that basis alone. A white person in a Negro neighborhood late at night is very likely to be detained. But in the latter case the purpose of the detention is not usually to detect crime but to warn the person of the danger of being in that area, particularly if he is alone…

Policing has always involved a large degree of officer discretion, and prior to the civil rights era of the 1960s, police officers were openly encouraged to more heavily police minority communities. For a brief time this became more difficult as the Supreme Court in the 1950s under Chief Justice Earl Warren issued a stream of rulings limiting the use of illegally obtained evidence, forced confessions, and illegal searches. But in the wake of the urban uprisings in northern cities between 1964 and 1967, the court stepped back from its previous commitment to the Fourth Amendment and gave police broad authority to stop and search just about anybody they wished without cause.

In 1968, in the case of *Terry v. Ohio*, the Supreme Court ruled that police can stop, question, and search, anyone they suspect could be dangerous. Such searches need not have warrants or "probable cause," they only had to be "reasonable," the lowest possible legal standard. This ruling, which still governs today, granted enormous discretion to the police officer on the street and opened the floodgates to racial profiling. In 1996, the Supreme Court reaffirmed this low standard and applied it to traffic stops in the case of *Whren v. United States*.

The most extensive investigation of "stop and frisk" tactics was done in New York City where the city council required the police department to report the demographic data of every person stopped and questioned in 2006. That year police stopped 508,540 people, 85% of whom were African American or Latino/a in a city that was 44% white. Of these, only 50,346, or fewer than one-in-ten, were found to be wanted or to be engaged in a criminal activity.

Sociologist David Harris has documented that such racial profiling is not only racist, but is ineffective as a police tactic if the goal of policing is to stop crime. Harris' insight was that racial profiling was essentially a theory about how best to deploy limited police resources. Every city has a limited number of police officers and those officers have a limited amount of time. Sound policing depends on deploying those limited resources in the most effective way. Racial profiling is a theory of deployment that assumes that people of color commit more crimes on average than other people and therefore stopping them more frequently will result in more arrests and lower crime. Harris calculated the actual "hit rate" of arrests, the percentage of time a gun, some drugs, or other evidence of criminal activity is found during a police stop. Harris found:

> All of the studies in which the data collected allow for the calculation of hit rates have generated strikingly similar results. All of these studies show higher hit rates not for blacks and Latinos, but for whites. In other words, officers "hit" less often when they use race or ethnic appearance to decide which persons seem suspicious

enough to merit stops and searches than they do when they use suspicious behavior and not race as their way of selecting suspects. When stops and searches are not racialized, they are more productive.

Racial profiling and "stop and frisk" tactics are just the first step in the racialized criminal justice system in America. Once a person is searched or arrested, the operation of the court system then imposes many additional injustices. Numerous studies have shown that prosecutors tend to charge people of color with more serious offenses, juries tend to convict people of color at rates far higher than white defendants, and judges tend to sentence people of color to longer terms than similar white offenders.

One extensive review of nearly two years of conviction data from 185,275 cases in New York City, found that black and Latino defendants were more often detained, more often offered plea bargains, more often jailed, and given longer sentences for crimes against people, than whites or Asians. While only 17% of whites were detained in jail before their trials, 32% of black defendants and 24% of Latino/a defendants were put behind bars to await their day in court.

When faced with such statistics, many skeptics may presume that black defendants committed more serious crimes, had more extensive criminal histories, or maybe were just poorer. After controlling for all of these possibilities, this study found that blacks were still 47.8% more likely to be incarcerated than whites while Latinos were 14.4% more likely to be jailed. White New Yorkers arrested for misdemeanor drug crimes were significantly more likely to have their cases dismissed than blacks and Latinos.

A 2017 analysis of nearly 31,000 misdemeanor arrests in Wisconsin found that prosecutors were 74% more likely to drop or reduce these charges when the defendant was white than when the arrested person was black. Even when comparing only those charged who had no criminal histories, whites had their charges reduced more than 25% more often than blacks.

One of the most obvious and deadly cases of racial bias in America's criminal justice system is the fact that whites who shoot and kill blacks are frequently not prosecuted because their killing is ruled as being "justified." According to a study of over 400,000 killings from 1980 to 2014, just two percent of all killings are ruled justifiable homicides, but when the killer is white and the victim black, this number leaps eightfold to 17%. When the situation is reversed and blacks kills whites, such killings are judged to be justified just 0.8% of the time.

The general disinterest among whites in issues of racism in the criminal justice system is highlighted by the fact that few seem troubled that a large proportion of American

Figure 14.8 Banner outside the Minneapolis Police Department fourth precinct following the officer-involved shooting of Jamar Clark on Nov. 15, 2015. Photo by Tony Webster.

courts operate in routine defiance of a Supreme Court ruling. In 1983, in *Bearden v. Georgia*, the Supreme Court of the United States heard the case of a Georgia man whose probation was revoked and he was sent to jail because he could not pay his court fees and fines. The high court ruled that sending people to jail when they couldn't afford their fees and fines was a violation of the Constitution's guarantee of the equal protection of the laws. The majority of justices held that courts must hold hearings to determine a defendant's ability to pay and only jail those who actually refused to pay when they were otherwise able to do so:

> We hold...that in revocation proceedings for failure to pay a fine or restitution, a sentencing court must inquire into the reasons for the failure to pay. If the probationer willfully refused to pay...the court may revoke probation and sentence the defendant to imprisonment... If

the probationer could not pay despite sufficient bona fide efforts to acquire the resources to do so, the court must consider alternative measures of punishment other than imprisonment... To do otherwise would deprive the probationer of his conditional freedom simply...because, through no fault of his own, he cannot pay the fine. Such a deprivation would be contrary to the fundamental fairness required by the Fourteenth Amendment.

Around the same time as the highest court in the land ordered all lower courts to refrain from jailing Americans because they couldn't afford to pay their court costs, communities throughout the nation began expanding their reliance on court fees to pay for their local police and courts. Today, *Bearden v. Georgia* is largely ignored and millions of poor people, especially poor people of color, are trapped in a modern style debtor's prison by fines and court fees for minor infractions that snowball with interest and penalties. Were such a clear Supreme Court order dealing with, say, banks or churches, to be violated to such an extent, the outcry would be deafening and the entire machinery of government would rapidly move to resolve such a "constitutional crisis." But as the rights in question belong to the poor and especially poor people of color, nary a peep is heard.

Most states have compounded these problems by revoking the driver's licenses of those behind on their court-ordered fines and fees. Forty-two states and the District of Columbia have laws that suspend the driver's licenses of those who fail to pay debts to local courts (California only recently ended its driver license suspension system in June 2017). All but four of these states revoke licenses without any process for determining if the failure to pay was willful or simply the result of not having any ability to pay. Numerous studies of these license suspension systems have documented that they disproportionately impact communities of color. Surveys of suspensions in states as diverse as California, Virginia, and Wisconsin all found black drivers suffered suspensions out of proportion to their numbers.

States have also implemented laws requiring state issued I.D. to vote, a measure that when combined with state mandated license revocations for failure to pay court fees, creates a new form of poll tax and limits the right to vote.

No wonder then that there is a vast gap between white and black Americans in their confidence in the fairness of police. According to a Gallup poll in the summer of 2017, 61% of whites said they had "a great deal or quite a lot" of confidence in their police. This was twice the proportion of black Americans, only 30% of whom responded with as much enthusiasm (45% of Latinos expressed similar confidence in police).

While most whites claim to live in an equitable and color-blind society, the experience of most people of color is that race is an unavoidable force in their lives. While most whites polled say that whites and blacks are treated equally in today's society and 40% say too much attention is paid to race, 71% of African Americans report having experienced racial discrimination, and more than one-in-ten report dealing with it regularly. More than half believe that their race has limited their chances for success in life. Nearly half, 47% reported having been treated with suspicion because of their race in the past year. About the same number, 45%, said they had been talked down to as if they were not intelligent. Nearly one-in-five (18%) report having been stopped by police because of their race in the previous twelve months.

Racial profiling is also common in the private sector, particularly the retail industry. In 2005, the Macy's department store in New York City was successfully prosecuted by the state attorney general for systematically profiling, detaining and questioning black and Latino/a customers on suspicion of theft. Macy's competitor Barneys was caught in 2014. Even when not a corporate policy, clerks are far more likely to view people of color suspiciously than white customers. However, one careful year-long experiment, that actively watched every person who entered an Atlanta drug store, found that "that males of different races have comparable likelihoods of shoplifting..." Just as criminological studies of racial profiling in street policing have consistently found that policing behavior is far more effective than policing demographics, these researchers found strong statistical correlations between certain behaviors and shoplifting, such as looking for cameras, wearing clothes with large pockets, or leaving without purchasing goods, that make the individual as much as six times more likely to be a shoplifter.

Correlational Racism

In the Color-Blind Era race is viewed and practised in a less mechanical way than before. Whereas race used to be seen as determining a person's traits and behaviors, today these connections are not thought to be so tightly bound together. With over ten thousand African Americans elected to public office, prominent black scientists and business people, black actors representing a wide array of characters from all walks of life, the old white presumptions of black inferiority have lost their supports in American culture. But racist assumptions persist, disguised in a denial that race matters or that a person "sees" race. Instead of seeing race as destiny, as the underlying cause of everything else, many people today see race as a tendency, as a leaning toward one outcome or another. In other words, many people today conceive of race more as a likelihood that a person will display certain characteristics. Nevertheless, whether conceived as a theory of biology determining personality or as some vague idea of "culture" as doing so, the result is the same: race serves as the explanation for character.

In July 1965 a little known bureaucrat in the Department of Labor, who would later become a U.S. Senator, authored a study with the dull academic title, "The Negro Family: The Case for National Action." It caused a national sensation because it argued that the root of the black community's economic and social problems was not institutional discrimination or the legacy of centuries of racism, but African American culture itself. Moynihan located the fundamental engine of inequality not in wider society, but in the prevalence of single-parent households in the

Figure 14.9 Daniel Patrick Moynihan at a two-way television conference between business leaders and the Nixon administration sponsored by the Chamber of Commerce, Mar. 26, 1969.

black community and what he called the "scissors-effect," the contradictory increase in the number of black people on the welfare rolls even as the unemployment rate went down (though this correlation has since been thoroughly debunked). Moynihan identified a range of characteristics that he called the "tangle of pathology": unemployment, crime, absent fathers, teenage pregnancy, welfare dependency, and aversion to education, that he said was characteristic of black culture. The root cause of this "pathology" was the "Negro family" whose practices and character had been tragically corrupted by slavery.

Moynihan's work was part of an emerging trend in sociological studies that located the sources of racial inequality in the black family and black culture. Scholars such as Oscar Lewis, Nathan Glazer, Orlando Patterson, William Julius Wilson, have focused their work on what they have identified as various practices, behaviors, and beliefs that disadvantage the already disadvantaged. Their views have been challenged by scholars who charge that the focus on the black family and community just obscures the structural discrimination and injustices of American

institutions and society. It has been widely noted, for example, that rates of out-of-wedlock births in the white community are higher today than they were among blacks when Moynihan wrote his report.

The best evidence that such theories that hold that inequality is generated by the "pathologies" of black culture lead to excusing American institutions of responsibility for racial injustice, came from Moynihan himself. Moynihan, who was a member of Nixon's staff in 1970, recommended to the president that his policy on race should be one of "benign neglect": "The time may have come when the issue of race could benefit from a period of benign neglect. The subject has been too much talked about. The forum has been too much taken over to hysterics, paranoids, and boodlers on all sides." (Though, to be fair, it should also be noted that Moynihan, over the course of his long political career, was a dedicated supporter of increased federal spending on social programs to address poverty, especially among racial minorities.)

In many ways such theories of inequality as Moynihan's "tangle of pathology" have contributed to a new idea of race—what some scholars have dubbed "correlational racism"—that is more resilient than its predecessor. For one thing, unlike old-fashioned "biological racism" which had difficulty explaining the many exceptions that were observed to its rules, "correlational racism" comfortably allows for individuals who fail to conform to racist expectations. In the nineteenth century, an intellectual giant, like Frederick Douglass or Phillis Wheatley, directly threatened the racial explanations of the world by embodying the opposite of what racial science claimed. But in the twenty-first, races are viewed as groupings of diverse people, many of whom are exceptions to the qualities used to define the group. Everyone in the group is viewed as having a tendency towards embodying its definitions, but no one is required to. In this way, modern racism, unlike old-fashioned racism, is not open to disproof. There is no evidence that can be rallied to dispute the ideas that certain groups are more or less likely to display certain characters because every instance of a person not following the expectation can be disregarded because it is anticipated that every group will have many exceptions. Thus every instance in which the social expectation is fulfilled is proof of the existence of race and every instance in which it is not is also proof of the existence of race.

High economic inequality between whites and blacks skews perceptions and contributes to such racial/cultural stereotypes. For example, just comparing whites and blacks would lead to the conclusion that black teens are more likely to drop out of high school and less likely to complete a college degree. Such raw racial comparisons point to the black community having higher rates of out-of-wedlock births and greater reliance on government welfare.

But when white and black people with similar economic and demographic profiles are compared, these differences not only vanish, some of them even reverse. Blacks are more likely to have graduated from college compared with whites of equal economic background. A child's chances of ending up on welfare are no greater between those with black parents or white parents as long as those parents possess similar amounts of wealth.

Affirmative Action

Most white Americans share two wrong assumptions about affirmative action. They tend to believe that systems of affirmative action in which unearned preferences are given to people of color in employment, education, and government services are common today. They also believe such race-conscious systems intended to correct for past injustices are of recent invention. Both assumptions are false.

In one sense, all the legal, economic and social structures that excluded people of color from the full rights and privileges that white Americans enjoyed, everything from the whites-only Naturalization Act of 1790 to Jim Crow schools, neighborhoods, elections, and jobs, were a system of affirmative action, just affirmative action for white people. Most of the students who attended elite colleges before the 1960s only had to compete with about a third of the population to gain admittance, since women and most non-whites were excluded and even Jews were subject to a low cap on the number allowed in. But as these systems of preference benefitted whites, they apparently don't count as a race-conscious allocation of resources.

Even defining affirmative action as only those systems of racial preference that benefited racial minorities, the practice has a precedent that can be traced back more than a century. In the 1860s, Congress's leaders knew that it was not enough to simply proclaim that slavery was abolished and leave millions of people who had no property, no land, and no education, to scratch out a living on their own. Instead, Congress established the nation's first social service agency, the Freedmen's Bureau, whose mission was to aid emancipated families gain the land, tools, legal aid, and education they needed to become independent and thrive. Though it began with the best of intentions, the Freedmen's Bureau was quickly undercut by a hostile presidential administration and defunded once the Congressional majority was won by conservatives.

Figure 14.10 Graduates at Howard University listening to President Johnson deliver the commencement address, June 4, 1966.

The term "affirmative action" originated with the nation's first law prohibiting racial discrimination in employment, the Ives-Quinn Act, passed by the state of New York in 1945. That law established a state commission charged with remedying complaints of discrimination and among whose powers was the ability to "to take such affirmative action as hiring, reinstatement or upgrading of employees with or without back pay…" In other words, 'affirmative action' meant actions taken in direct response to instances of racial discrimination and for their direct remedy.

A similar limited sense of 'affirmative action' was evident in President Kennedy's Executive Order 10,925, issued in 1961, that prohibited all government agencies and government contractors from discriminating on the basis of "race, creed, color, or national origin," in hiring and promotion (it is noteworthy that at this point in time, sex was not a protected category). JFK's order further required that contractors "will take affirmative action to ensure that applicants are employed, and that employees are treated during employment, without regard to their race, creed, color, or national origin." Clearly, in the early days of civil rights legislation and protection, affirmative action simply meant vigorous efforts to undo and root out existing discrimination. (Kennedy opposed the idea of providing race-based benefits to compensate for past discrimination, saying "I don't think we can undo the past…In fact, the past is going to be with us for a good many years…We have to do the best we can do now…I don't think quotas are a good idea.")

However, after passage of the landmark federal civil rights laws of the mid-1960s, many activists and some political leaders questioned if prohibiting discrimination by itself was sufficient to create equal opportunity. Dr. Martin Luther King, Jr., was quite clear in advocating some sort of race-based system of preferences to overcome the entrenched discrimination of American society. King remarked, "It is impossible to create a formula for the future which does not take into account that our society has been doing something special against the Negro for hundreds of years. How then can he be absorbed into the mainstream of American life if we do not do something special for him now, in order to balance the equation and equip him to compete on a just and equal basis?"

In 1965, President Lyndon Johnson delivered the commencement address at Washington's Howard University, the most prestigious historically black university in the nation. Pushed by civil rights leaders, Johnson was then embroiled in the fight to pass a Voting Rights law. President Johnson surprised many by devoting much of his speech to the inadequacy of merely legislating against discrimination:

…freedom is not enough. You do not wipe away the scars of centuries by saying: Now you are free to go where you want, and do as you desire, and choose the leaders you please.

You do not take a person who, for years, has been hobbled by chains and liberate him, bring him up to the starting line of a race and then say, "you are free to compete with all the others," and still justly believe that you have been completely fair.

Thus it is not enough just to open the gates of opportunity. All our citizens must have the ability to walk through those gates.

This is the next and the more profound stage of the battle for civil rights. We seek not just freedom but opportunity. We seek not just legal equity but human ability, not just equality as a right and a theory but equality as a fact and equality as a result.

For the task is to give 20 million Negroes the same chance as every other American to learn and grow, to work and share in society, to develop their abilities—physical, mental and spiritual, and to pursue their individual happiness.

To this end equal opportunity is essential, but not enough, not enough. Men and women of all races are born with the same range of abilities. But ability is not just the product of birth. Ability is stretched or stunted by the family that you live with, and the neighborhood you live in—by the school you go to and the poverty or the richness of your surroundings. It is the product of a hundred unseen forces playing upon the little infant, the child, and finally the man.

The problem Johnson identified was a deep and profound one. To simply stop excluding people of color from jobs and other opportunities does not level the playing field. It does not make up for the fact that whites had received an unfair proportion of the education, public resources, and social advantages that allowed them to appear at a job interview or apply to a college with more credentials, experience, and social connections than those whose families had long been excluded from them.

Johnson's Secretary of Labor, W. Willard Wirtz, attempted to clarify and specify just what 'affirmative action' meant. He wrote that affirmative action was "an affirmative responsibility to counteract the effect of…previous [racist] policy…" Wirtz explained that affirmative action "does not mean hiring or admitting unqualified applicants" but rather taking three positive steps: "making it effectively clear that the old [racist] policy has been changed," "participating in the training and preparation of people who would have been ready if it had not been for the discrimination," and "accepting, when they are ready, those who would have been accepted earlier if there had not been a discriminatory policy." What Wirtz had in mind was probably the example of his predecessor, Arthur Goldberg, who implemented an 'affirmative action policy' for the Department of Labor that consisted of sending notices of openings to historically black colleges and sending recruiters and arranging for civil service examinations to be held at those campuses. Without changing any of the standards of his department's hiring policies, Goldberg was able to increase recruitment of black employees by nearly 20% in two years.

Likewise, most private government contractors that attempted to fulfill the mandate to increase "affirmative action" in these years, did so by simply getting information about openings to minority communities, recruiting people of color to work in personnel offices, and aiding training programs to expand the pipeline of qualified minority recruits. Such measures, when taken in coordination with efforts to prevent bias in hiring and promotion, proved effective in increasing minority employment without resorting to "quotas."

Towards the end of Johnson's term, his administration faced a situation that demanded more stringent measures to break down the barriers to equal opportunity in employment. But the law gave the government few powers to achieve this. The Civil Rights Act of 1964 was passed in the face of a filibuster by southern Senators that lasted 83 days and suceeded in stripping the powers of the proposed agency, the Equal Employment Opportunity Commission (EEOC). The bill originally envisioned an EEOC that would have the power to order private employers to stop discriminatory practices immediately, what are known legally as 'cease and desist' orders, and to have the power to take discriminators to court. Both the powers to issue cease and desist orders, and the power to sue offenders, were removed in a final compromise, leaving the EEOC with only the powers to investigate and to mediate.

Even with such limited powers, complaints immediately poured in, overwhelming the EEOC's tiny staff. Within its first two years the EEOC logged 15,000 complaints of which the EEOC was only able to resolve 110. By 1968 its backlog of cases reached 30,000 and by 1978 the files overflowed with 150,000 unaddressed complaints. While most large employers could see the economic benefits of opening their hiring to a larger pool of talent, many labor unions had the opposite interest. Especially in the construction trades, white-dominated labor unions had long upheld color-bars to membership, to their apprenticeship programs, and to jobs. In this regard, large northern cities had worse records of racial discrimination than

Figure 14.11 "Meany and big labor the enemies of workers everywhere." Wilfred Owen Brigade Poster, 1975,

southern ones.

In 1968, *Look* magazine featured the story of Vincent Whylie, a skilled construction worker in the trade of building wire forms that bind steel struts and beams together. Whylie had long worked in the industry in Daytona Beach, Florida, where he had been a member of his local trade union. Whylie, his wife, and five daughters, moved to Brooklyn where he was denied admission to New York's Local 46 Wood, Wire, and Metal Lathers Union and with it any prospects for work. When Whylie filed a complaint with the New York Human Rights Commission, it found that Local 46 had no active black members in a union of 6,000 white workers. *Look's* editor wrote, today "there are fewer union Negro plumbers or electricians than Negro Ph.D.'s…" Unemployed and with few prospects to work in his trade, Whylie wrote to President Nixon, saying all he "wanted was a chance to earn a decent living so that I will not have to rear my children on Welfare" and asked the President, "give me an opportunity of better working conditions by doing whatever may be possible to help me to get in Local 46."

In Philadelphia, massive government contracts employed thousands of construction workers building public buildings like the new federal mint, freeways, and public housing. But in a city that was one-third black, the city's trade unions remained nearly all-white. Philadelphia's Sheet Metal Workers Local 19 had 1,300 members, none of them African American. Out of 650 members of Elevator Constructors Local 5 not a single black worker was to be found. The electricians union had 1400 members, 14 of whom were African American.

Historians still debate whether appeals like that from Vincent Whylie softened Nixon's heart or whether the ever-calculating president hoped to drive a wedge between two Democratic constituencies, labor unions and civil rights organizations, but whatever the motivation, Nixon in his first term vigorously fought to impose tough hiring requirements on northern builders. Called the Philadelphia Plan after its model city, the program actually involved over fifty other cities. The Philadelphia Plan required government contractors to submit a minority hiring plan that included a target range of numbers of minority workers set according to the estimated proportion of qualified workers of color in the area. Failure to reach those goals would trigger a bureaucratic review of the contract and its possible forfeiture, though this rarely happened.

As some civil rights leaders warned, the imposition of numerical quotas as a means of battering down the doors barred by color backfired. Bayard Rustin, the organizer of the 1963 March on Washington for Jobs and Freedom where Dr. King delivered his famous "I Have a Dream" speech, opposed quota systems, warning "any preferential approach postulated on racial, ethnic, religious, or sexual lines will only disrupt a multicultural society and lead to a backlash." A coalition formed across traditional party lines opposing "quotas," and liberals were pressed to agree that Title VII of the Civil Rights Act of 1964 prohibited the preferential treatment of any racial group, even to remedy past wrongs. By the time Nixon began his campaign for reelection, he had reversed his position and gave speeches condemning "quotas" and appointed the former head of the New York City Building Trades Council as secretary of labor.

In the decade following Nixon's failed Philadephia Plan, legislatures and courts see-sawed back and forth over the question of what powers governments could wield to overcome historic patterns of inequality. Some federal courts approved legal remedies in private employment discrimination suits that included specific targets for the hiring and promoting of minority workers. Congress enacted, and the Supreme Court upheld, a minority business set-aside program in 1977 that required government contractors on public works projects to allocate at least 10% of government funds to minority businesses.

In the 1970s some universities and professional schools turned to quota systems to overcome longstanding biases in their admissions. When the University of California-Davis Medical School created a program in 1973 that set aside one-sixth of their slots for minority admissions, Allan Bakke, a white applicant who was denied admission, sued and successfully carried his suit to the U.S. Supreme Court. In a hodgepodge of opinions, the court effectively ruled that such set-aside programs violated Title VII of the Civil Rights Act of 1964, but that some less mechanical uses of racial preferences could be allowed in cases where there was clear and direct evidence of prior discrimination.

President Ronald Reagan rallied white support partly through his open hostility to all schemes intended to ensure that non-whites have equal chances to obtain public and private opportunities. By mischaracterizing all such measures as "quotas," Reagan pushed the public to consider affirmative action programs as being inherently unfair. The term affirmative action became widely seen as describing arbitrary policies of hiring, admitting, or advancing racial minorities regardless of their individual merits or talents. Consequently, any white person turned down by an employer or college felt free to blame their failure not on their own abilities but on some imagined black or brown person who unfairly took "their" slot. By the 1980s conservatives began to loudly complain of "reverse discrimination," the supposed growing problem of well-qualified whites being passed over in favor of unqualified and undeserving minorities.

However, following the nation's conservative shift in the 1980s, and with President Reagan naming four conservative justices, the Supreme Court grew less tolerant of programs aimed at boosting opportunities for people of color. It struck down union contracts that attempted to overcome the historic effects of seniority systems that benefited those hired under regimes of systematic discrimination by protecting racial minorities during layoffs. It reconsidered its former tolerance for minority set-aside programs and struck down such a program in Richmond, Virginia, a place where, Justice Sandra Day O'Connor said, there was insufficient evidence of past discrimination. In 1995, it struck down a federal minority subcontracting program very similar to the one it had found constitutional in 1979. (One difference between the cases was that the first African American on the court, liberal justice Thurgood Marshall had been replaced by Clarence Thomas, a black conservative who wrote, "it is irrelevant whether a government's racial classifications are drawn by those who wish to oppress a race or by those who have a sincere desire to help those thought to be disadvantaged...government-sponsored racial discrimination based on benign prejudice is just as noxious as discrimination inspired by malicious prejudice...")

By the 1990s, few remnants of the earlier affirmative action programs survived. When a majority of the court stepped back from a historic ruling restraining employers from using hiring tests irrelevant to the job but that had

Figure 14.12 Maryland Univ. Campus scene, Jan. 1964.

the effect of screening out people of color, Justice Harry Blackmun writing in his dissent wondered whether any of his colleagues "still believes that race discrimination... is a problem in our society, or even remembers that it ever was." Today there are still vestiges of federal contracting rules require businesses to make good-faith efforts to hire or subcontract with minorities in proportion to their representation in their sectors.

One area where some element of race-conscious effort to achieve equity remained was in college admissions. Many colleges in the 1990s devised various systems to boost the admissions of students of color. Since the Bakke decision of 1977 made it clear that numerical quota systems could not pass judicial review, most universities assessed application portfolios and used complex rating systems that took into account a broader picture of an individual than just test scores, grade point averages, and class rankings. In such systems, race is just one factor among many other variables and adds a light thumb to the scale of admissions. In the most recent federal case alleging "reverse discrimination" against a white student on the part of the University of Texas at Austin, lawyers for the white woman denied admission, Abigail Fisher, estimated that

UT's admission system increased black enrollment at the university by only 33 students out of a freshman class of 6000. (Moreover, they also admitted that Ms. Fisher would not have made the enrollment cut even had she been black or Latina.)

Institutions of higher education successfully defended their affirmative action programs by arguing that the situation of higher education is unique, in that universities are not just correcting past injustices but promoting better learning environments. An abundant amount of research has shown that in a globalized multicultural world, a diverse student body is vital to modern education. The Supreme Court has upheld these multicultural and diversity arguments and allowed universities to recognize race as a factor in admissions in *Grutter v. Bollinger* (2003), and most recently in *Fisher v. University of Texas* (2016), even when it has denied that same ability to most other government entities.

Though affirmative action programs had been deeply curtailed by the courts, in the mid-1990s conservative political action committees organized campaigns to pass legislation and constitutional amendments in various states that flatly outlawed all systems of racial preference. The first of these, California's Proposition 209, was pushed hard by the state's Republican governor, Pete Wilson, who viewed opposition to affirmative action as his springboard to the Whitehouse. Proposition 209 passed narrowly in 1996 and prohibited any benefits or policies specified by race, including college admissions, financial aid, government contracting and hiring, and public assistance or housing. From California, anti-affirmative action activists won similar campaigns in Washington State, Michigan, Nebraska, Arizona, and most recently in Oklahoma, while such referenda failed in Missouri and Colorado.

Anti-affirmative action protests even spread to college campuses, as conservative groups held "affirmative action bake sales" where they charged whites more for cookies than people of color, and raised money for "whites-only" scholarships. Bake sale protesters expressed their belief in abstract liberal ideals of equality and fairness, and libertarian principles that there should be no artificial impediments to reward for talent and merit. But many observers also pointed out that such protests were also based on the denial that racism remained an ongoing force in American society. Moreover, by portraying whites as a group subject to victimization, just as minority racial and ethnic groups

are, these protests reinforce a white racial consciousness and white identity, the very elements that have historically been the source of institutional racism.

Since the 1980s, white complaints against "reverse racism" have multiplied even as the scope and reach of affirmative action programs that could conceivably have impacted some whites have been sharply curtailed by Congress, state legislatures, referenda, and the courts. In August of 2017, President Trump's Attorney General Jeff Sessions, ordered the creation of a new unit of the civil rights division of the Justice Department to root out discrimination against whites in higher education. Researchers have investigated the reasons behind this puzzling contradiction that whites feel racism directed at them to be increasing.

One explanation is that whites equate the increasing equality of people of color as racism directed against them. This perception stems from the perception of many whites, especially white men, that racial and gendered advantages widely enjoyed by them in the past (such as easy admission to selective schools, the passing of jobs to friends and family, or speedy promotions) were deserved and customary. As one group of researchers found, whites also tend to see racism as a 'zero-sum game,' a situation in where if racism decreases for one group it must necessarily increase for another.

Figure 14.13 Unemployment office, Baltimore, Maryland, Jan. 1975.

Using a national poll conducted in 2011, these social scientists found that whites believed that as racism toward black Americans has decreased since the 1950s, racism towards white people has increased proportionately. Polls find that most white Americans believe African Americans are "better off" finding a job than whites. Overwhelmingly, whites polled indicated that they believed that racial bias against whites was a more common problem in the 2000s than racial bias against blacks. Underlying this dynamic of whites perceiving themselves as an oppressed racial group is implicit bias that wildly inflates white perceptions of the size of minority communities (see chapter 9).

Studies seem to suggest that many whites view the racial discrimination that long oppressed blacks and the patchwork of programs aimed at increasing the representation of racial minorities in workplaces or schools as being morally equivalent. Such beliefs are problematic because they overlook the profound difference between discrimination that is the result of an intention to harm, demean, and isolate a group of people and discrimination that is the inadvertent consequence of efforts to overcome systemic racism. Racism as practiced in America since its founding has been aimed at racial subordination and motivated by hate and malice. Disappointed white applicants of affirmative action programs cannot claim that their disadvantages were driven by contempt or an effort to exploit them.

In fact, as political scientist Randall Kennedy has pointed out, various groups are preferred and advanced over others in our society without complaint. Veterans are given preferences in employment and government benefits, universities give benefits to alumni and advantages to their children in admissions, colleges deploy a lavish amount of resources on their athletes that other students do not enjoy and discriminate in their fee structures against out-of-state students (who may also be favored in admissions for the same reason). Sometimes the college marching band is lacking a tuba-player and will admit one over an academically better trombonist simply because they have enough trombones and the band sounds better with a tuba.

Moreover, as affirmative action sputters on weakly, for the most part only in the realm of education, it is important to remember that it does so because universities make the case that affirmative action is not a matter of equality or civil rights, nor is it an effort to redress past discrimination or promote equal access to higher education. Courts have long abandoned such rationale for these programs. Rather colleges now argue that recruiting a diverse student body is critical to their institutional mission in the 21st century. Having more opportunities to interact with students who have cultural backgrounds and racialized experiences different from one's own, they argue, is fundamental to the learning and personal broadening they were founded for.

When disgruntled white applicants to colleges point to their test scores and GPA to claim they "would have gotten in but for affirmative action," they miss the point. Having experienced the world from the other side of the racial divide is itself a desired and useful element in a resume, not some artificial marker allowing unearned promotion. Surveys have shown that many whites like to think of their own achievements as having "earned" their passage through various gates and assent up ladders of education and career. But, in fact, many positions, whether university seats or jobs, are not laurels bestowed to reward individual merit, but are mission-driven projects serving a broader social interest.

This is not to say that affirmative action programs are without problems. Scholars have identified two important and unintended consequences of affirmative action programs that have serious and long-term social implications.

First, the existence of even a small number of weak affirmative action programs gives any white person who is passed over for a job, a promotion, a university slot, or any other public good, the excuse to claim that they "lost" "their" seat or their job unfairly to a less qualified person of color. Today, roughly only the top fifth of selective colleges and universities practice any sort of systematic racial preference policies. One national survey found that these programs add the equivalent of about half of a point to an applicant's GPA, increasing an applicant's chances of gaining admission by eight to ten percent. Looking at it from the other perspective, since only 15% of applicants to these elite schools would be accepted in any case, the boost given to minorities at most disadvantages 3% of white applicants, though one can be sure that most of the rest of the 82% disappointed white applicants believe that they were injured by affirmative action. The more than four out of five university students who attend less elite schools are not impacted by affirmative action policies at all.

Today, about 200,000 companies that have more than 50 employees and win contracts with the federal government worth $50,000 or more are covered by various nondiscrimination regulations dating back to the Johnson administration. Chief among these are the following requirements:

> Prepare and submit an "Affirmative Action Report" that details what steps the company takes to ensure protected groups are not discriminated against. This report has to be filed within 120 days of obtaining the contract and must be renewed annually.

> The company must maintain employment records for all employees that includes gender, race, ethnicity, and veteran's status data.

Notices that the company is an "equal opportunity employer" must be posted and noted on employment advertisements.

All contracting companies must allow inspectors from the Office of Federal Contract Compliance to enter their business premises and inspect employment records without prior notice.

None of these requirements amount to much in the practical day-to-day world of business.

During the Obama administration, staffing for the Office of Federal Contract Compliance (OFCC), the agency responsible for enforcing these rules, was severely cut back. The number of OFCC employees dropped by nearly 20%. As a result, only 2% of government contractors have their records audited for compliance in any given year. Once a company passes a review it is exempt from further audits for two years. Since 2010, of the 2% of companies audited, the OFCC found violations in 1% of cases, or a couple dozen per year. Of those companies found in viola-

Figure 14.14 OFCCP logo

tion, prosecutions are exceedingly rare, amounting to one percent of violations, and of these 99% of violators simply sign agreements to improve their practices. The handful of companies actually referred for prosecution rarely face the ultimate penalty, disqualification from obtaining government contracts, a death penalty applied to an average of one obstinate company per year. It is so unlikely that any company will face consequences for noncompliance with affirmative action reporting rules that 85% of companies sent a notice of audit don't even bother to return the necessary paperwork within the 30 day limit for such responses.

A review of OFCC regulatory activities by the agency that watches other agencies, the Government Accountability Office (GAO) concluded in 2016, "While OFCCP conducted compliance evaluations for about 2 percent of all contractors in its jurisdiction, it is not able to determine the extent contractors are complying with

equal employment opportunity requirements because of weaknesses in the contractor selection process. Instead, OFCCP relies on federal contractors to voluntarily comply with equal employment opportunity requirements, and some contractors may not be completing certain required activities…"

In spite of the fact that affirmative action rules are so weak that they are described as "voluntary" by the GAO, polls of white Americans reveal that most believe that they suffer mightily from "reverse discrimination." Today a majority of whites polled believe that prejudice against white people is a larger social problem than prejudice against black people. One recent study found that 38% of white people reported that they had personally suffered from racial discrimination (not surprisingly, such feelings of white affliction followed political lines, with evangelicals, southerners, and conservatives more likely to feel aggrieved). Another study found that 40% of whites say that they themselves, or someone they know, has been passed over in college admissions in favor of a less qualified minority applicant. Of course, such perceptions and complaints usually evaporate when the complainant is simply asked, 'how do you know the person who got the job (or admission, or contract, or whatever) had lesser qualifications? Did they show you their resume?'

The second damaging effect of the existence of any affirmative action program is that the abilities and qualifications of any people of color who rise to positions of prominence are questioned and their achievements are discounted. Because a small number of racial minorities have been advantaged by such programs, a cloud of stigma and suspicion is cast over all people of color. Experiments in controlled settings have demonstrated that the credentials and resumes of people of color are assumed to have less value by test subjects who hear the words affirmative action mentioned than by those who do not. Worse, other studies have shown that when primed by words such as "affirmative action" or "preferential treatment" test subjects were far more likely to associate people of color with racial stereotypes.

White complaints about "reverse racism" mask the extent of actual ongoing racism. If "reverse racism" was actually a prevalent problem its trace should show up in employment statistics. But all indices point in the other direction. African Americans and Latinos are underrepresented in STEM (science, technology, engineering, and medicine) careers by nearly half. Though 11% of the workforce was black and 15% Latino in 2011, black STEM employment was just 6% and Latino 7%. Whites, who constitute 72.4% of the workforce, continue to be highly overrepresented in high-paying, high-profile professions, such as lawyers and judges (86.4%), professors (81.7%), accountants (76%) and chief executive officers (87.9%). African Americans, who are 11.8% of the workforce, are underrepresented in all professional categories, such as physicians and surgeons (4.7%), pharmacists (5.3%), lawyers (4.6%) and CEOs (3.4%). Latinos are 9.9% of the workforce but are 5.3% of medical doctors and 4.3% of lawyers. People of color are vastly overrepresented on the other end of the job spectrum, as more than a third of the nation's two million janitors are black or Latino, as are nearly half of the one million housekeepers, and a third of the nation's three million cashiers, bus drivers, and laborers. Skilled trades that require training in technical programs remain largely white: 91% of tool and die makers and airline pilots are white, as are 80% of carpenters, boilermakers, construction equipment operators, millwrights, and machinists. Skilled work that is messy, dirty or dangerous is one exception to this rule as more than third of hazardous material removers are black or Latino, as are cement masons and butchers. Finally, whites continue to enjoy advantages in promotion as nearly 80% of the workers promoted to be first-line supervisors are white.

Instances of discrimination are hard to measure, but sociologists have developed a number of indicators of its continuing force. Surveys of people of color find consistent reporting of employment discrimination. Such studies done around the time of the 2000 census found that one-third of African Americans and one-fifth of Latinos and Asians responded that they had personally been denied a job or promotion because of their race. Statistical analyses of large employment datasets have shown that blacks spend significantly longer searching for jobs and experience longer periods of unemployment compared to whites with comparable qualifications and experience.

Laboratory studies of mock hiring situations found that when subjects were asked to evaluate job applicants with equally sufficient (but neither notably high or poor) qualifications, study participants were nearly 70% more likely to hire the white job seeker. Field experiments where job applications, resumes, or housing applications were sent out with identical credentials except for black or white sounding names, or well-known white or black neighborhood addresses, (known as 'paired-match' studies) have predictably resulted in fewer callbacks for interviews or showings for applicants assumed to be African American or Latino/a. A paired-match study of forty-three wait-staff jobs in fine New York City restaurants in 2010 found that black applicants were hired about half as often as white applicants with identical resumes and were offered wages 12% lower on average than whites. The list of such studies is too extensive to review here.

The End of Color-blindness

Just after noon on July 16, 2009, the distinguished Harvard professor, Henry Louis Gates, Jr., returned to his Cambridge, Massachusetts, home after a long trip. He had trouble with the lock and with the help of his cab driver managed to unjam the door and enter his house. A white woman who happened to be walking by was alarmed at the sight, according to the police report, of "two black males with backpacks...trying to force entry," and called the police. Officer James Crowley, who was also white, was nearby and responded. Stepping onto Professor Gates' porch Crowley could see Gates inside, knocked and ordered him to come out. Gates showed Sergeant Crowley his drivers' license and Harvard I.D. and asked the officer his name. Gates claimed Crowley ignored him, while Crowley claims he responded politely while the professor loudly yelled at him. Whatever the case, Crowley handcuffed Professor Gates on his own porch in front of a gathering crowd of onlookers and arrested him on charges of disorderly conduct. Gates was held for four hours at the police station before being released.

Gates' celebrity, the spectacle of a black Harvard professor being arrested for breaking into his own home, the issue of racial profiling, and the fact that Gates' account of the event and that of the arresting policeman were at odds, all combined to propel this story into the national news cycle. A few days later a reporter asked newly elected President Obama what he thought about it and Obama answered:

> I don't know, not having been there and not seeing all the facts, what role race played in that. But I think it's fair to say, No. 1, any of us would be pretty angry; No. 2, that the Cambridge police acted stupidly in arresting somebody when there was already proof that they were in their own home. And No. 3, what I think we know separate and apart from this incident is that there is a long history in this country of African-Americans and Latinos being stopped by law enforcement disproportionately. That's just a fact.

The president's comments ignited a backlash from police associations who accused him of using race as a divisive issue and disrespecting police officers. The leader of one of the nation's largest police unions criticized Obama saying, "The president's alienated public safety officers across the country with his comments," while the head of the Cambridge police union stated bluntly, "That was totally inappropriate. I am disgraced that he is our

Figure 14.15 President Obama, Henry L. Gates, Jr., and Sergeant James Crowley in the White House Rose Garden, July 2009.

commander-in-chief..." The head of the Fraternal Order of Police in Florida argued that Obama had injected race into a situation where it didn't belong, saying, ""By reducing all contact between law enforcement and the public to the color of their skin or ethnicity is, in fact, counterproductive to improving relationships..."

As the media attention to Obama's observation that race played a role in the incident grew into a frenzy, the White House scrambled to contain what was becoming a political issue. Republican legislators demanded the president apologize and began using the issue to paint the president as being prone to seeing racism everywhere. To settle the uproar, President Obama invited Professor Gates and Officer Crowley to Washington to hash out their differences, a meeting that became known as the "Beer Summit" because the event was intentionally framed as an informal one by being held in the White House garden over glasses of beer.

Keen observers noted that the Beer Summit marked a turning point in both President Obama's public stance toward issues of racism and white America's attitude toward President Obama. For his part, stung by the intense backlash to his mild comments that simply noted that police had been racist in America's past, for the next four years Obama shied away from discussing race or racism. Judging by polling numbers, white Americans were deeply disturbed that their black president would shatter the illusion of color-blindness by pointing out the obvious.

Obama remained careful to tiptoe around issues of racism until July of 2013 when a jury acquitted George Zimmerman, the self-appointed neighborhood watchman who shot and killed Treyvon Martin, an unarmed Florida teenager who had been walking near his own home. Zimmerman's release prompted a deep national debate about forms of racism, especially within the criminal justice system, that to many now seemed more obvious than they had been before. President Obama held a news conference and told the nation:

You know, when Trayvon Martin was first shot I said that this could have been my son. Another way of saying that is Trayvon Martin could have been me 35 years ago. And when you think about why, in the African American community at least, there's a lot of pain around what happened here, I think it's important to recognize that the African American community is looking at this issue through a set of experiences and a history that doesn't go away.

There are very few African American men in this country who haven't had the experience of being followed when they were shopping in a department store. That includes me. There are very few African American men who haven't had the experience of walking across the street and hearing the locks click on the doors of cars. That happens to me -- at least before I was a senator. There are very few African Americans who haven't had the experience of getting on an elevator and a woman clutching her purse nervously and holding her breath until she had a chance to get off. That happens often.

And I don't want to exaggerate this, but those sets of experiences inform how the African American community interprets what happened one night in Florida. And it's inescapable for people to bring those experiences to bear. The African American community is also knowledgeable that there is a history of racial disparities in the application of our criminal laws -- everything from the death penalty to enforcement of our drug laws. And that ends up having an impact in terms of how people interpret the case.

Now, this isn't to say that the African American community is naïve about the fact that African American young men are disproportionately involved in the criminal justice system; that they're disproportionately both victims and perpetrators of violence. It's not to make excuses for that fact -- although black folks do interpret the reasons for that in a historical context. They understand that some of the violence that takes place in poor black neighborhoods around the country is born out of a very violent past in this country, and that the poverty and dysfunction that we see in those communities can be traced to a very difficult history.

And so the fact that sometimes that's unacknowledged adds to the frustration. And the fact that a lot of African American boys are painted with a broad brush and the excuse is given, well, there are these statistics out there that show that African American boys are more violent -- using that as an excuse to then see sons treated differently causes pain.

I think the African American community is also not naïve in understanding that, statistically, somebody like Trayvon Martin was statistically more likely to be shot by a peer than he was by somebody else. So folks understand the challenges that exist for African American boys. But they get frustrated, I think, if they feel that there's no context for it and that context is being denied. And that all contributes I think to a sense that if a white male teen was involved in the same kind of scenario, that, from top to bottom, both the outcome and the aftermath might have been different.

Now, the question for me at least, and I think for a lot of folks, is where do we take this? How do we learn some lessons from this and move in a positive direction? I think it's understandable that there have been demonstrations and vigils and protests, and some of that stuff is just going to have to work its way through, as long as it remains nonviolent…

With these remarks, President Obama detailed how race remained relevant in 21st century America. White Americans who had voted for him, partly out of the feeling that doing so would prove that racism no longer existed, now felt betrayed. The comforting myth of American color-blindness fell to pieces over the coming years as media carried more news of unarmed black men and women killed by police and these murders sparked protests that in several areas escalated into full-blown riots, such as in Baltimore and Ferguson, Missouri.

In the years leading up to the 2016 presidential election, white Americans became more comfortable talking about race and responsive to racial and ethno-nationalist ideas. The candidacy of Donald J. Trump accelerated and harnessed this trend. Once in office, president Trump continued to ratchet up his only lightly veiled appeals to white identity and fears. His refusal to condemn nazi marchers, whose rally in Charlottesville Virginia in the summer of 2017 left one counter-protester dead and many injured, alarmed many, even in his own party.

As President Trump neared the end of his first year in office, the frequency of his signalling intolerant racial and ethnic messages to his white base increased. In a single week around the 2017 Thanksgiving holiday he greeted Navajo World War Two veterans at the White House, choosing as the backdrop for their group photo a painting of Indian-fighter and signer of the Indian Removal Act, Andrew Jackson. He then referred to Democratic Senator Elizabeth Warren as "Pocahontas" in his remarks to the war heroes. A couple of days later the President retweeted videos of Muslims beating Christians and smashing Christian idols that were from a far-right nationalist English group whose leader had recently been charged with harassing

Muslims. As 2017 neared its conclusion, the president's attacks on prominent people of color became more frequent, first black NFL players for kneeling during the national anthem, then the widow of Sgt. La David Johnson, a black special forces soldier killed in Africa, then Frederica Wilson, a black Congresswoman, capping it off by calling Congressman John Lewis "all talk" and "no action." Lewis was once gravely injured by a policeman smashing his baton over his head on the Selma bridge during a march for voting rights in 1965.

American society in the 21st century balances on an odd tension between its ideals and its reality. Most all Americans, white, black, or brown, publicly embrace the vision of America as a nation welcoming and accepting of all people, no matter their race or ethnicity. In our public discourse, one of the worst things someone can be called is a "racist." Americans value fairness and equal opportunity regardless of one's background more highly than almost any other ideals. Yet, in spite of these beliefs, America remains a deeply divided country where people considered to be different races live apart and experience the daily weight of their racial assignment with dramatic, even radical, particularity.

Those Americans who identify as white are least likely among all racialized groups to understand how being racially different in America continues to tilt life's road into a steeper incline. They tend to focus on the formality of law, its color-blind letters, rather than its unequal application and effects. More than other groups, white folks tend to downplay the importance and legacy of the past in shaping opportunities in the present. Unfortunately, America is most truly color-blind when it comes to facing the nature of its own history: that America was born as a racist nation that grew to international power by enslaving Africans and conquering native peoples and that white Americans were boosted to their privileged economic and political position by government policies that gave them lopsided opportunities and vast subsidies unavailable to people of color. America will not become the just and equitable society it believes itself to be until it recognizes its own past, until it chooses not to recoil from that mirror but to see the truth that it reflects.

Figure 14.16 President Donald Trump listens to museum director Lonnie Bunch during a tour on Tuesday, February 21, 2017, of the National Museum of African American History and Culture in Washington, D.C.

"A More Perfect Union," Speech by Barack Obama
March 18, 2008

Then Democratic Illinois Senator Barack Obama, delivered the following speech in Philadelphia in which he discussed the media criticisms of his advisor and pastor, Rev. Jeremiah Wright, who was condemned for making remarks that were interpreted as blaming the U.S. for bringing the terrorist attack of Sept. 11 upon itself. This speech, known as Obama's "More Perfect Union" speech was an unusually frank discussion of racism by a presidential candidate.

"We the people, in order to form a more perfect union ..." 221 years ago, in a hall that still stands across the street, a group of men gathered and, with these simple words, launched America's improbable experiment in democracy. Farmers and scholars, statesmen and patriots who had traveled across an ocean to escape tyranny and persecution finally made real their declaration of independence at a Philadelphia convention that lasted through the spring of 1787.

The document they produced was eventually signed but ultimately unfinished. It was stained by this nation's original sin of slavery, a question that divided the colonies and brought the convention to a stalemate until the founders chose to allow the slave trade to continue for at least 20 more years, and to leave any final resolution to future generations.

Of course, the answer to the slavery question was already embedded within our Constitution—a Constitution that had at its very core the ideal of equal citizenship under the law; a Constitution that promised its people liberty and justice and a union that could be and should be perfected over time.

And yet words on a parchment would not be enough to deliver slaves from bondage, or provide men and women of every color and creed their full rights and obligations as citizens of the United States. What would be needed were Americans in successive generations who were willing to do their part—through protests and struggles, on the streets and in the courts, through a civil war and civil disobedience, and always at great risk—to narrow that gap between the promise of our ideals and the reality of their time.

This was one of the tasks we set forth at the beginning of this presidential campaign—to continue the long march of those who came before us...I chose to run for president at this moment in history because I believe deeply that we cannot solve the challenges of our time unless we solve them together...This belief comes from my unyielding faith in the decency and generosity of the American people. But it also comes from my own story.

I am the son of a black man from Kenya and a white woman from Kansas. I was raised with the help of a white grandfather who survived a Depression to serve in Patton's Army during World War II and a white grandmother who worked on a bomber assembly line at Fort Leavenworth while he was overseas. I've gone to some of the best schools in America and lived in one of the world's poorest nations. I am married to a black American who carries within her the blood of slaves and slaveowners—an inheritance we pass on to our two precious daughters. I have brothers, sisters, nieces, nephews, uncles and cousins of every race and every hue, scattered across three continents, and for as long as I live, I will never forget that in no other country on Earth is my story even possible.

It's a story that hasn't made me the most conventional of candidates. But it is a story that has seared into my genetic makeup the idea that this nation is more than the sum of its parts—that out of many, we are truly one.

Throughout the first year of this campaign, against all predictions to the contrary, we saw how hungry the American people were for this message of unity. Despite the temptation to view my candidacy through a purely racial lens, we won commanding victories in states with some of the whitest populations in the country. In South Carolina, where the Confederate flag still flies, we built a powerful coalition of African-Americans and white Americans.

This is not to say that race has not been an issue in this campaign. At various stages in the campaign, some commentators have deemed me either "too black" or "not black enough." We saw racial tensions bubble to the surface during the week before the South Carolina primary. The press has scoured every single exit poll for the latest evidence of racial polarization, not just in terms of white and black, but black and brown as well.

And yet, it has only been in the last couple of weeks that the discussion of race in this campaign has taken a particularly divisive turn.

On one end of the spectrum, we've heard the implication that my candidacy is somehow an exercise in affirmative action; that it's based solely on the desire of wide-eyed liberals to purchase racial reconciliation on the cheap. On the other end, we've heard my former pastor, Jeremiah Wright, use incendiary language to express views that have the potential not only to widen the racial divide, but views that denigrate both the greatness and the goodness of our nation, and that rightly offend white and black alike...

But the remarks that have caused this recent firestorm weren't simply controversial. They weren't simply a religious leader's efforts to speak out against perceived injustice. Instead, they expressed a profoundly distorted view of this country—a view that sees white racism as endemic, and that elevates what is wrong with America above all that we know is right with America...

[But] I can no more disown him than I can disown the black community. I can no more disown him than I can disown my white grandmother—a woman who helped raise me, a woman who sacrificed again and again for me, a woman who loves me as much as she loves anything in this world, but a woman who once confessed her fear of black men who passed her by on the street, and who on more than one occasion has uttered racial or ethnic stereotypes that made me cringe.

These people are a part of me. And they are part of America, this country that I love...

Understanding this reality requires a reminder of how we arrived at this point. As William Faulkner once wrote, "The past isn't dead and buried. In fact, it isn't even past." We do not need to recite here the history of racial injustice in this country. But we do need to remind ourselves that so many of the disparities that exist between the African-American community and the larger American community today can be traced directly to inequalities passed on from an earlier generation that suffered under the brutal legacy of slavery and Jim Crow.

Segregated schools were and are inferior schools; we still haven't fixed them, 50 years after Brown v. Board of Education. And the inferior education they provided, then and now, helps explain the pervasive achievement gap between today's black and white students. Legalized discrimination—where blacks were prevented, often through violence, from owning property, or loans were not granted to African-American business owners, or black homeowners could not access FHA mortgages, or blacks were excluded from unions or the police force or the fire department—meant that black families could not amass any meaningful wealth to bequeath to future generations. That history helps explain the wealth and income gap between blacks and whites, and the concentrated pockets of poverty that persist in so many of today's urban and rural communities.

A lack of economic opportunity among black men, and the shame and frustration that came from not being able to provide for one's family contributed to the erosion of black families—a problem that welfare policies for many years may have worsened. And the lack of

basic services in so many urban black neighborhoods—parks for kids to play in, police walking the beat, regular garbage pickup, building code enforcement—all helped create a cycle of violence, blight and neglect that continues to haunt us.

This is the reality in which Reverend Wright and other African-Americans of his generation grew up. They came of age in the late '50s and early '60s, a time when segregation was still the law of the land and opportunity was systematically constricted. What's remarkable is not how many failed in the face of discrimination, but how many men and women overcame the odds; how many were able to make a way out of no way, for those like me who would come after them.

For all those who scratched and clawed their way to get a piece of the American Dream, there were many who didn't make it—those who were ultimately defeated, in one way or another, by discrimination. That legacy of defeat was passed on to future generations—those young men and, increasingly, young women who we see standing on street corners or languishing in our prisons, without hope or prospects for the future. Even for those blacks who did make it, questions of race and racism continue to define their worldview in fundamental ways. For the men and women of Reverend Wright's generation, the memories of humiliation and doubt and fear have not gone away; nor has the anger and the bitterness of those years. That anger may not get expressed in public, in front of white co-workers or white friends. But it does find voice in the barbershop or the beauty shop or around the kitchen table. At times, that anger is exploited by politicians, to gin up votes along racial lines, or to make up for a politician's own failings...

And occasionally it finds voice in the church on Sunday morning, in the pulpit and in the pews. The fact that so many people are surprised to hear that anger in some of Reverend Wright's sermons simply reminds us of the old truism that the most segregated hour of American life occurs on Sunday morning. That anger is not always productive; indeed, all too often it distracts attention from solving real problems; it keeps us from squarely facing our own complicity within the African-American community in our condition, and prevents the African-American community from forging the alliances it needs to bring about real change. But the anger is real; it is powerful. And to simply wish it away, to condemn it without understanding its roots, only serves to widen the chasm of misunderstanding that exists between the races.

In fact, a similar anger exists within segments of the white community. Most working- and middle-class white Americans don't feel that they have been particularly privileged by their race. Their experience is the immigrant experience—as far as they're concerned, no one handed them anything. They built it from scratch. They've worked hard all their lives, many times only to see their jobs shipped overseas or their pensions dumped after a lifetime of labor. They are anxious about their futures, and they feel their dreams slipping away. And in an era of stagnant wages and global competition, opportunity comes to be seen as a zero sum game, in which your dreams come at my expense. So when they are told to bus their children to a school across town; when they hear an African-American is getting an advantage in landing a good job or a spot in a good college because of an injustice that they themselves never committed; when they're told that their fears about crime in urban neighborhoods are somehow prejudiced, resentment builds over time.

Like the anger within the black community, these resentments aren't always expressed in polite company. But they have helped shape the political landscape for at least a generation. Anger over welfare and affirmative action helped forge the Reagan Coalition. Politicians routinely exploited fears of crime for their own electoral ends. Talk show hosts and conservative commentators built entire careers unmasking bogus claims of racism while dismissing legitimate discussions of racial injustice and inequality as mere political correctness or reverse racism.

Just as black anger often proved counterproductive, so have these white resentments distracted attention from the real culprits of the middle class squeeze—a corporate culture rife with inside dealing, questionable accounting practices and short-term greed; a Washington dominated by lobbyists and special interests; economic policies that favor the few over the many. And yet, to wish away the resentments of white Americans, to label them as misguided or even racist, without recognizing they are grounded in legitimate concerns—this too widens the racial divide and blocks the path to understanding.

This is where we are right now. It's a racial stalemate we've been stuck in for years. Contrary to the claims of some of my critics, black and white, I have never been so naïve as to believe that we can get beyond our racial divisions in a single election cycle, or with a single candidacy—particularly a candidacy as imperfect as my own.

But I have asserted a firm conviction—a conviction rooted in my faith in God and my faith in the American people—that, working together, we can move beyond some of our old racial wounds, and that in fact we have no choice if we are to continue on the path of a more perfect union.

For the African-American community, that path means embracing the burdens of our past without becoming victims of our past. It means continuing to insist on a full measure of justice in every aspect of American life... And it means taking full responsibility for our own lives—by demanding more from our fathers, and spending more time with our children, and reading to them, and teaching them that while they may face challenges and discrimination in their own lives, they must never succumb to despair or cynicism; they must always believe that they can write their own destiny.

Ironically, this quintessentially American—and yes, conservative—notion of self-help found frequent expression in Reverend Wright's sermons. But what my former pastor too often failed to understand is that embarking on a program of self-help also requires a belief that society can change.

The profound mistake of Reverend Wright's sermons is not that he spoke about racism in our society. It's that he spoke as if our society was static; as if no progress had been made; as if this country—a country that has made it possible for one of his own members to run for the highest office in the land and build a coalition of white and black, Latino and Asian, rich and poor, young and old—is still irrevocably bound to a tragic past. But what we know—what we have seen—is that America can change. That is the true genius of this nation. What we have already achieved gives us hope—the audacity to hope—for what we can and must achieve tomorrow.

In the white community, the path to a more perfect union means acknowledging that what ails the African-American community does not just exist in the minds of black people; that the legacy of discrimination—and current incidents of discrimination, while less overt than in the past—are real and must be addressed, not just with words, but with deeds, by investing in our schools and our communities; by enforcing our civil rights laws and ensuring fairness in our criminal justice system; by providing this generation with ladders of opportunity that were unavailable for previous generations. It requires all Americans to realize that your dreams do not have to come at the expense of my dreams; that investing in the health, welfare and education of black and brown and white children will ultimately help all of America prosper...

Boys atop billboard, Crowley, Louisiana, Oct. 1938. Photo by Russell Lee.

GLOSSARY OF TERMS (edited)

from National Institutes of Health, Office of the Director, Scientific Workforce Diversity
diversity.nih.gov/find-read-learn/glossary

Advocate
Someone who speaks up for her/himself and members of his/her identity group; e.g., a woman who lobbies for equal pay for women.

Ally
A person of one social identity group who stands up in support of members of another group; typically, a member of a dominant group standing beside member(s) of a targeted group; e.g., a male arguing for equal pay for women.

Benevolent prejudice
A superficially positive type of prejudice that is expressed in terms of positive beliefs and emotional responses, which results in keeping the group members experiencing prejudice in inferior positions in society, and can help justify any hostile prejudices a person has toward a particular group. Though well-intended, this type of prejudice is widely considered to produce negative effects on those it targets.

Bias
Prejudice; an inclination or preference, especially one that interferes with impartial judgment.

Categorization
The natural cognitive process of grouping and labeling people, things, etc. based on their similarities. Categorization becomes problematic when the groupings become oversimplified and rigid; e.g., stereotypes.

Cognitive dissonance
The mental stress or discomfort experienced by an individual who holds two or more contradictory beliefs, ideas, or values at the same time; performs an action that is contradictory to one or more beliefs, ideas, or values; or is confronted by new information that conflicts with existing beliefs, ideas, or values.

Cognitive diversity
Including individuals with differences in thought and problem-solving processes.

Color blind
The belief in treating everyone "equally" by treating everyone the same; based in the presumption that differences are by definition bad or problematic, and therefore best ignored; e.g., "I don't see race, gender, etc."

Culture
A social domain that emphasizes the practices, discourses, and material expressions, which, over time, express the continuities and discontinuities of social meaning of an experience held in common.

Discrimination
Actions, based on conscious or unconscious prejudice, which favor one group over others in the provision of goods, services, or opportunities.

Disparity
A significant difference between groups; typically used to describe the condition of being unequal.

Diversity
The range of human differences, including but not limited to race, ethnicity, gender, sexual orientation, age, social class, physical ability or attributes, religious or ethical value system, national origin, and political beliefs.

Dominant culture
The cultural values, beliefs, and practices that are assumed to be the most common and influential within a given society.

Explicit bias
Conscious attitudes and beliefs about a person or group. Often, these biases and their expression arise as the direct result of a perceived threat. When people feel threatened, they are more likely to draw group boundaries to distinguish themselves from others.

Fundamental attribution error
A common cognitive action in which one attributes his/her own success and positive actions to his/her own innate characteristics ("I'm a good person") and failure to external influences ("I lost it in the sun"), while attributing others' success to external influences ("he had help") and failure to others' innate characteristics ('they're bad people"). This operates on the group level as well, with the in-group giving itself favorable attributions, while giving the out-group unfavorable attributions, as way of maintaining a feeling of superiority. A "double standard."

Gender
The socially constructed concepts of masculinity and femininity; the "appropriate" qualities accompanying biological sex.

Identity
Conception, qualities, beliefs, and expressions that constitute a person (self-identity) or group (particular social category or social group).

Implicit association test (IAT)
This measures attitudes and beliefs that people may be unwilling or unable to report; e.g., you may believe that women and men should be equally associated with science, but your automatic associations

could show that you (like many others) associate men with science more than you associate women with science.

Implicit bias
A form of bias that occurs automatically and unintentionally, that nevertheless affects judgments, decisions, and behaviors (also known as nonconscious or unconscious bias).

Inclusion
Involvement and empowerment, where the inherent worth and dignity of all people is recognized. An inclusive organization promotes and sustains a sense of belonging; it values and practices respect for the talents, beliefs, backgrounds, and ways of living of its members.

In group bias
The tendency for groups to "favor" themselves by rewarding group members economically, socially, psychologically, and emotionally in order to uplift one group over another.

Institutional racism
A pattern of social institutions — such as governmental organizations, schools, banks, and courts of law — giving negative treatment to a group of people based on their race.

Intergroup conflict
Tension and conflict which exists between social groups and which may be enacted by individual members of these groups.

Marginalized
Excluded, ignored, or relegated to the outer edge of a group/society/community.

Microaggression
A subtle but offensive comment or action directed at a minority or other nondominant group that is often unintentional or unconsciously reinforces a stereotype; e.g., "No, where are you really from?" or "You don't act like a black person."

Multiplicity
The quality of having multiple, simultaneous social identities; e.g., being male and Buddhist and working class.

Multiracial
An individual that comes from more than one race.

Multiethnic
An individual that comes from more than one ethnicity.

People of color
A collective term for men and women of Asian, African, Latin, and Native American backgrounds; as opposed to the collective "White" for those of European ancestry.

Personal identity
Our identities as individuals, including history, personality, name, and other characteristics that make us...different from other individuals.

Prejudice
A preconceived judgment about a person or group of people; usually indicating negative bias.

Racism
Prejudiced thoughts and discriminatory actions based on differences in race/ethnicity.

Saliency
The quality of a group identity of which an individual is more conscious and which plays a larger role in that individual's day to day life; for example, a man's awareness of his "maleness" in an elevator with only women.

Sex
Biological classification of male or female based on genetic or physiological features, as opposed to gender.

Social identity
This involves the ways in which one characterizes oneself, the affinities one has with other people, the ways one has learned to behave in stereotyped social settings, the things one values in oneself and in the world, and the norms that one recognizes or accepts governing everyday behavior.

Spotlighting
The practice of inequitably calling attention to particular social groups in language, while leaving others as the invisible, de facto norm; e.g., "black male suspect" versus "male suspect" (presumed white) or "WNBA" as opposed to "NBA" (presumed male).

Stereotype
Blanket beliefs and expectations about members of certain groups that present an oversimplified opinion, prejudiced attitude, or uncritical judgment. They go beyond necessary and useful categorizations and generalizations in that they are typically negative, are based on little information, and are highly generalized.

Stereotype threat
The psychological threat felt when a person is performing an action or is in a situation that aligns with a negative stereotype about their group.

Worldview
The perspective through which individuals view the world; comprised of their history, experiences, culture, family history, and other influences.

References

Preface
Anne Mangen, Bente R. Walgermo, and Kolbjørn Brønnick. "Reading Linear Texts on Paper Versus Computer Screen: Effects on Reading Comprehension." *International Journal of Educational Research*, vol. 58, (2013), pp. 61-68.

Introduction
Joseph Ellis, *American Creation: Triumphs and Tragedies at the Founding of the Republic* (New York: Knopf, 2007).

Several of Jefferson's slaves later dictated their memoirs to reporters who published them as books. One of the more interesting is by Isaac (slaves were not generally allowed last names apart from that of their owners) published as *Memoirs of a Monticello Slave* (Univ. of Virginia Press, 1951). A full text version is available at: https://archive.org/details/memoirsofamontic031158mbp

How to Think
Patrick J. Keane, *Emerson, Romanticism, and Intuitive Reason: The Transatlantic "light of All Our Day"* (Univ. of Missouri Press, 2005), p. 204.

The Danger of Common Sense
National Science Foundation, https://www.nsf.gov/statistics/seind14/index.cfm/chapter-7/c7s2.htm.

Antoine Arnauld, *The Port-Royal Logic*, ed. and trans. by Thomas Spencer Baynes, (Edinburgh: James Gordon, 1861), p. 268.

White or Caucasian?
In this book, all terms referring to race are uncapitalized. Many writing stylebooks, including the one used by most major media outlets, the AP Stylebook, mandate capitalizing nationalities and terms such as "Caucasian" but not "white" or "black" when used as either a noun or adjective.

The Anthropological Treatises of Johann Friedrich Blumenbach, Thomas Bendyshe, ed., (London: Anthropological Society, 1869), p. 269.

Joe R. Feagin, *The White Racial Frame: Centuries of Racial Framing and Counter-Framing* (New York: Rutgers Press, 2013), 47-49.

Nell Irvin Painter, *The History of White People* (New York: Norton, 2010), pp. 83-84.

L. Colange, *The Standard Encyclopedia* (Standard Encyclopedia Co., 1899), p. 842.

Raj Bhopal, "White, European, Western, Caucasian, or What? Inappropriate Labeling in Research on Race, Ethnicity, and Health," *American Journal of Public Health*, 88:9, pp. 1303-1307.

Raj Bhopal, "The Beautiful Skull and Blumenbach's Errors: The Birth of the Scientific Concept of Race," *BMJ : British Medical Journal* 335.7633 (2007), pp. 1308–1309.

Thomas Teo, "Psychology Without Caucasians," *Canadian Psychology*, 50:2 (2009), 91-97. A 2004 study in *Nature Genetics* found nearly two-thirds of a sample of scientific papers used racial terms, like 'Caucasian' in an uncritical and unscientific manner. *Nature Genetics*, 36:6 (2004), p. 541.

Hispanic or Latino/Latina?
Ann Brown & Eileen Patten, "Statistical Portrait of Hispanics in the United States," Pew Research Center, Apr. 29, 2014. http://www.pewhispanic.org/2014/04/29/statistical-portrait-of-hispanics-in-the-united-states-2012/ accessed Feb. 4, 2015.

Campbell Gibson and Kay Jung, "Historical Census Statistics on Population Totals by Race (1790 to 1990) and by Hispanic origin (1970 to 1990) for Large Cities and Urban Places," (September 2002) Working Paper Number: POP-WP056, U.S. Census Bureau. http://www.census.gov/library/working-papers/2002/demo/POP-twps0056.html accessed Feb. 4, 2015.

G. Cristina Mora, "Cross-Field Effects and Ethnic Classification: The Institutionalization of Hispanic Panethnicity, 1965 to 1990," *American Sociological Review*, 79:2 (April 2014), pp. 183-210.

Nicholas De Genova & Ana Y. Ramos-Zayas, "Latino Racial Formations in the United States: An Introduction," *Journal of Latin American Anthropology*, 8:2 (2008), pp. 2-16.

Mark Hugo Lopez, "Hispanic or Latino? Many Don't Care Except in Texas," Pew Research Center, Oct. 28, 2013. http://pewrsr.ch/19MvGh1 accessed Feb. 2, 2015.

Oriental or Asian?
Dina G. Okamoto, *Redefining Race: Asian American Panethnicity and Shifting Ethnic Boundaries* (New York: Russell Sage Foundation, 2014).

Native American or Indian?
James Taylor Carson, "American Historians and Indians," *The Historical Journal*, 49:3 (Sep., 2006), pp. 921-933.

Edmundo O'Gorman, *The Invention of America: An Inquiry into the Historical Nature of the New World and the Meaning of its History* (Bloomington: Indiana Univ. Press, 1961).

Carol Chiago Lujan, "American Indians and Alaska Natives Count," *American Indian Quarterly*, 38:3 (Summer 2014), pp. 319-341.

Jack D. Forbes, "The Hispanic Spin: Party Politics and Governmental Manipulation of Ethnic Identity," *Latin American Perspectives*, 19:4, (Autumn, 1992), pp. 59-78.

Hilary N. Weaver, "Indigenous Identity: What Is It, and Who Really Has It?," *American Indian Quarterly*, 25:2 (Spring, 2001), pp. 240-255.

From African to Colored to Negro to Black

Herb Boyd, Autobiography of a People: Three Centuries of African *American History Told By Those Who Lived It* (New York: Doubleday, 2000), p. 5. Some sources claim that Columbus' pilot, Pedro Alonso Niño, was Black. However, other sources dispute this. See Elinor Des Verney Sinnette, *Arthur Alfonso Schomburg, Black Bibliophile and Collector: A Biography* (Detroit: Wayne State University Press, 1989), pp. 79-80. Robin D. G. Kelley, Earl Lewis, *To Make Our World Anew: Volume I: A History of African Americans to 1880* (Oxford University Press, 2005).

Patrick Rael, *Black Identity and Black Protest in the Antebellum North* (Chapel Hill: Univ. of North Carolina Press, 2002), pp. 89-90. "The Star Spangled Banner," was designated as America's national anthem in 1931. Rael, pp. 90-91.

Robert Benjamin Lewis, *Light and Truth: Collected from the Bible and Ancient and Modern History Containing the Universal History of the Colored and Indian Race…* (Boston, 1844), p. 342.

Patrick Rael, *Black Identity and Black Protest in the Antebellum North* (Chapel Hill: Univ. of North Carolina Press, 2002) pp. 109-112.

Tom W. Smith, "Changing Racial Labels: From "Colored" to "Negro" to "Black" to "African American," *The Public Opinion Quarterly*, 56:4, (Winter, 1992), pp. 496-514.

Randall Kennedy, *Nigger: The Strange Career of a Troublesome Word* (New York: Pantheon, 2002).

Jennifer L. Hochschild & Brenna Marea Powell, "Racial Reorganization and the United States Census 1850–1930: Mulattoes, Half-Breeds, Mixed Parentage, Hindoos, and the Mexican Race," *Studies in American Political Development*, 22:1 (2008), pp. 59-96.

Ben L. Martin, "From Negro to Black to African American: The Power of Names and Naming," *Political Science Quarterly*,106:1 (Spring, 1991), pp. 83-107.

G. Smitherman, *Talkin' and Testifyin': The Language of Black America* (Houghton Mifflin, 1977).

Henry Louis Gates, Jr., *Loose Canons: Notes on the Culture Wars* (Oxford University Press, 1993), p. 134.

Ben L. Martin, "From Negro to Black to African American: The Power of Names and Naming," *Political Science Quarterly*, 106:1 (Spring, 1991), pp. 83-107.

Brian Palmer, "When Did the Term Negro Become Taboo?" Slate, Jan. 10, 2011. http://www.slate.com/articles/news_and_politics/explainer/2010/01/when_did_the_word_negro_become_taboo.html.

Elizabeth Compton, Michael Bentley, Sharon Ennis, Sonya Rastogi, *2010 Census: Race and Hispanic Origin Alternative Questionnaire Experiment: Final Report* (Decennial Statistical Studies Division and Population Division, U.S. Census Bureau, 2013), pp. ix and 54. http://www.census.gov/2010census/pdf/2010_Census_Race_HO_AQE.pdf.

Chapter 1: Race and Ethnicity

What is Race?

Jared Sparks, *The Works of Benjamin Franklin: Containing Several Political and Historical Tracts Not Included in Any Former Edition, and Many Letters, Official and Private, Not Hitherto Published* (London: Benjamin Franklin Stevens, 1882), vol. 2, p. 372.

Dictionary of Races or Peoples, Reports of the Immigration Commission #662 (Washington: Government Printing Office, 1911), 32.

Race in the U.S. Census

Jason G. Gauthier, *Measuring America: The Decennial Censuses from 1790 to 2000* (Washington, DC: Dept. of Commerce, 2002), p. 6.

Dvora Yanow, *Constructing 'Race' and 'Ethnicity' in America: Category-Making in Public Policy and Administration* (Armonk, NY: M.E. Sharpe, 2003).

What is Ethnicity?

Theories of Ethnicity: A Classical Reader, Werner Sollors, ed. (New York: New York University Press, 1996), pp. x-xi.

Milton M. Gordon, *The Scope of Sociology* (New York: Oxford University Press, 1988), pp. 119, 130-131.

Michael Omi and Howard Winant, *Racial Formation in the United States* (New York: Routledge, 2015, 3rd ed.), pp. 21-31.

J. T. M. "Supreme Court of Michigan. The People v. William Dean." *The American Law Register*, 14:12 (1866), pp. 721–732.,

Pierre L. van den Berghe, *Race and Racism: A Comparative Perspective* (New York: Wiley, 1967), pp. 9-10.

Ideas of Difference in the Ancient World

Frank M. Snowden, Jr. *Before Color Prejudice: The Ancient View of Black* (Cambridge, MA: Harvard Univ. Press, 1983).

Ivan Hannaford, *Race: The History of an Idea in the West*, (Baltimore: Johns Hopkins University Press, 1996).

Genesis, 9:20 - 9:27.

Principal Navigations, Voyages, Traffiques and Discoveries of the English Nation, collected by Richard Hakluyt, (New York, Macmillan, 1904), vol. VII, pp. 252-253.

Blumenbach quoted in Londa Schiebinger, "The Anatomy of Difference: Race and Sex in Eighteenth-Century Science," *Eighteenth-Century Studies*, 23:4 (1990), pp. 387–405.

The Curse of Ham

Craig Koslofsky, "Knowing Skin in Early Modern Europe, c. 1450–1750," *History Compass*, 12:10, 2014, pp. 794-806.

Slavery and the Idea of Races

Blumenbach quoted in Londa Schiebinger, "The Anatomy of Difference: Race and Sex in Eighteenth-Century Science," *Eighteenth-Century Studies*, 23:4 (1990), pp. 387–405.

Chouki El Hamel, "The Register of the Slaves of Sultan Mawlay Isma'il of Morocco at the Turn of the Eighteenth Century,"

The Journal of African History, 51:1 (2010), pp. 89-98.

Revolution, Race, and the Enlightenment

Bill Ashcroft, "Language and Race," *Social Identities,* 7:3 (2001), pp. 311-328.

Chapter 2: Human Variation

The Human Genome

Richard Lewontin, "The Apportionment of Human Diversity," *Evolutionary Biology,* 6 (1972), pp. 391–398. See also K.L. Hunley, G.S. Cabana, and J.C. Long, "The Apportionment of Human Diversity Revisited," *American Journal of Physical Anthropology,* 160 (2016), pp. 561–569.

Text of Press Conference, June 26, 2000, White House, Office of the Press Secretary, "Courtesy: National Human Genome Research Institute" http://www.genome.gov/10001356

Jun Z. Li, et al. "Worldwide Human Relationships Inferred from Genome-Wide Patterns of Variation." *Science* 319.5866 (2008), pp. 1100-4.

Jinchuan Xing, W. Scott Watkins, Adam Shlien, Erin Walker, Chad D. Huff, David J. Witherspoon, Yuhua Zhang, Tatum S. Simonson, Robert B. Weiss, Joshua D. Schiffman, David Malkin, Scott R. Woodward, Lynn B. Jorde, "Toward a More Uniform Sampling of Human Genetic Diversity: A Survey of Worldwide Populations by High-Density Genotyping," *Genomics,* 96:4 (October 2010), pp. 199-210.

Adam Hochman, "Racial Discrimination: How Not to do it," *Studies in History and Philosophy of Biological and Biomedical Sciences,* 44.3 (2013), p. 278.

David Serre, and Svante Pääbo, "Evidence for Gradients of Human Genetic Diversity within and among Continents." *Genome Research,* 14.9 (2004), pp. 1679-85.

Clines versus Clusters (or Clades)

Stephen Ousley, Richard Jantz, and Donna Freid. "Understanding Race and Human Variation: Why Forensic Anthropologists are Good at Identifying Race," *American Journal of Physical Anthropology,* 139.1 (2009), p. 68.

Smith, S., J. Meik, and J. Fondon. 2013. "The Utility of Domestic Dogs in Assessing Human Morphological Variation," *HOMO: Journal of Comparative Human Biology* 64, (3), p. 163.

P. Villa, W. Roebroeks, "Neandertal Demise: An Archaeological Analysis of the Modern Human Superiority Complex," *PLoS ONE* 9(4): (2014) e96424. doi:10.1371/journal.pone.0096424.

Wolpoff, Milford H. "How Neandertals Inform Human Variation," *American Journal of Physical Anthropology,* 139:1 (May 2009), pp. 91-102.

N.A. Rosenberg, J.K. Pritchard, J.L. Weber, H.M. Cann, K.K. Kidd, L.A. Zhivotovsky, et al. , "Genetic Structure of Human Populations," *Science,* 298 (2002), pp. 2381–2385.

Koffi N. Maglo, Tesfaye B. Mersha, and Lisa J. Martin. "Population Genomics and the Statistical Values of Race: An Interdisciplinary Perspective on the Biological Classification of Human Populations and Implications for Clinical Genetic Epidemiological Research." *Frontiers in Genetics,* 7 (2016), p. 22.

The Myth of the Evolutionary Tree

A.R. Templeton, "Biological Races in Humans," *Studies in History and Philosophy of Biological and Biomedical Sciences,* 44:3 (2013), pp. 262–271.

Koffi N. Maglo, Tesfaye B. Mersha, and Lisa J. Martin., "Population Genomics and the Statistical Values of Race: An Interdisciplinary Perspective on the Biological Classification of Human Populations and Implications for Clinical Genetic Epidemiological Research." *Frontiers in Genetics,* 7 (2016), p. 22.

Human Origins

Kirk E. Lohmueller, "The Distribution of Deleterious Genetic Variation in Human Populations," *Current Opinion in Genetics & Development,* 29 (2014), pp. 139-146.

Elise Eller, John Hawks, and John H. Relethford. "Local Extinction and Recolonization, Species Effective Population Size, and Modern Human Origins," *Human Biology,* 81:5-6 (2009), pp. 805-24.

Some anthropologists once argued that this same evidence could also support the theory that human races evolved independently rather than having a common African origin. But, as it turns out, for this theory to hold water the ancient African human population must have been several orders of magnitude larger than current data indicates or the behavior of early human populations (in terms of migrations, local extinctions, etc.) has to have conformed to a very narrow set of parameters. Elise Eller, John Hawks, and John H. Relethford. "Local Extinction and Recolonization, Species Effective Population Size, and Modern Human Origins," *Human Biology,* 81:5-6 (2009), pp. 805-24.

Brenna M. Henn, L. L. Cavalli-Sforza, and Marcus W. Feldman. "The Great Human Expansion," *Proceedings of the National Academy of Sciences,* 109:44 (2012), pp. 17758-64.

Michael C. Campbell, and Sarah A. Tishkoff. "The Evolution of Human Genetic and Phenotypic Variation in Africa," *Current Biology,* 20.4 (2010), pp. R166-73.

Nicole Creanza, et al. "A Comparison of Worldwide Phonemic and Genetic Variation in Human Populations," *Proceedings of the National Academy of Sciences,* 112:5 (2015), p. 1265.

Brenna M. Henn, L.L. Cavalli-Sforza, Marcus W. Felman, "The Great Human Expansion," *Proceedings of the National Academy of Sciences of the United State of America,* 109:44 (Oct. 30, 2012), pp. 17758-17764.

Janet Kelso, Kay Prüfer, "Ancient Humans and the Origin of Modern Humans," *Current Opinion in Genetics & Development,* 29: (Dec. 2014), pp. 133-138.

Daniel Rayner, David Bulbeck, and Pathmanathan Raghavan. "Races of Homo Sapiens: If Not in the Southwest Pacific, then Nowhere," *World Archaeology,* 38.1 (2006), pp. 109-32.

Mathias Currat, Estella S. Poloni, and Alicia Sanchez-Mazas. "Human Genetic Differentiation Across the Strait of Gibraltar," *BMC Evolutionary Biology*, 10:1 (2010), p. 237.

Deepti Gurdasani, et. al., "The African Genome Variation Project Shapes Medical Genetics in Africa," *Nature*, 517, (15 January 2015), pp. 327–332.

J.K. Pickrell, N. Patterson, P.R. Loh, M. Lipson, B. Berger, M. Stoneking, B. Pakendorf, D. Reich, "Ancient West Eurasian Ancestry in Southern and Eastern Africa," *Proceedings of the National Academy of Sciences*, 111, (2014), pp. 2632-2637.

Luca Ermini, Clio Der Sarkissian, Eske Willerslev, Ludovic Orlando, "Major Transitions in Human Evolution Revisited: A Tribute to Ancient DNA," *Journal of Human Evolution*, 79 (February 2015), pp. 4-20, http://dx.doi.org/10.1016/j.jhevol.2014.06.015.

Guido Brandt, et. al., "Ancient DNA Reveals Key Stages in the Formation of Central European Mitochondrial Genetic Diversity," *Science*, (11 October 2013), 342 (6155), pp. 257-261.

Non-Cordance of Traits

C. C. S. Cerqueira, V.R. Paixão-Côrtes, F.M.B. Zambra, F.M. Salzano, T. Hünemeier and M.C. Bortolini, "Predicting Homo Pigmentation Phenotype through Genomic Data: From Neanderthal to James Watson," *American Journal of Human Biology*, 24 (2012), pp. 705–709.

Ewelina Pośpiech, et al. "Gene-Gene Interactions Contribute to Eye Colour Variation in Humans," *Journal of Human Genetics*, 56.6 (2011), pp. 447-55.

Taichi A. Suzuki, and Michael Worobey, "Geographical Variation of Human Gut Microbial Composition," *Biology Letters*, 10:2 (2014), p. 2013.

Wenqing Fu and Joshua M. Akey. "Selection and Adaptation in the Human Genome," *Annual Review of Genomics and Human Genetics*, 14 (2013), pp. 467-89.

Etienne Patin, et al. "Natural Selection has Driven Population Differentiation in Modern Humans," *Nature Genetics*, 40.3 (2008), pp. 340-5.

Skin Color

Nina G. Jablonski & George Chaplin, "Human Skin Pigmentation as an Adaptation to UV Radiation," *Proceedings of the National Academy of Sciences of the United State of America*, 107 supp. 2 (May 11, 2010), pp. 8962-8968. There is some evidence that latitude and climate may not have operated alone in producing selection pressures based on Vitamin D levels. Some researchers speculate that a general shift in diets due to the rise of agriculture and an increasing density of population, making for greater hazard for weakened immunity, also played a role. B. S. Razib Khan and R. Khan. 2010. "Diet, Disease and Pigment Variation in Humans," *Medical Hypotheses*, 75:4 (2010), pp. 363-367; Brian McEvoy, Sandra Beleza, and Mark D. Shriver. "The Genetic Architecture of Normal Variation in Human Pigmentation: An Evolutionary Perspective and Model," *Human Molecular Genetics*, 15 Spec No 2. Review Issue 2 (2006), pp. R176-81.

Marlijn L. Noback, Harvati Katerina, and Fred Spoor, "Climate-related Variation of the Human Nasal Cavity," *American Journal of Physical Anthropology*, 145:4 (2011), pp. 599-614.

Emilia Huerta-Sánchez, et al., "Genetic Signatures Reveal High-Altitude Adaptation in a Set of Ethiopian Populations," *Molecular Biology and Evolution*, 30:8 (2013), p. 1877.

Forensic Science

H. Walsh-Haney, "Can Grave Secrets Be Revealed via Analysis of Bare Bones? How Kathy Reichs's Fiction Novels Feed the Public Perception of Forensic Anthropology," *American Anthropologist*, 113 (2011), pp. 650–652.

Script excerpt adapted from that posted on the fan blog site "Forever Dreaming" http://transcripts.foreverdreaming.org/viewtopic.php?f=9&t=14525.

Ariane Lange, "'Bones' Has Been Making the Same Mistake for 10 Seasons," *Buzzfeed News*, Apr. 8, 2015. https://www.buzzfeed.com/arianelange/bones-race-forensic-anthropology?utm_term=.uxwbxk27E#.se2Da0QJr accessed Dec. 28, 2016.

Linda L. Kleppinger, *Fundamentals of Forensic Anthropology* (John Wiley & Sons, 2006), pp. 134-135.

P.R. Husmann and D.R. Samson, "In the Eye of the Beholder: Sex and Race Estimation using the Human Orbital Aperture," *Journal of Forensic Sciences*, 56 (2011), pp. 1424–1429.

Joseph T. Hefner, "Cranial Nonmetric Variation and Estimating Ancestry," *Journal of Forensic Science*, 54:5 (Sept. 2009), pp. 985-995.

Ingrid Sierp and Maciej Henneberg. "Can Ancestry be Consistently Determined from the Skeleton?" *Anthropological Review*, 78:1, (2015), pp. 21-31.

Heather J.H. Edgar, "Testing the Utility of Dental Morphological Traits Commonly used in the Forensic Identification of Ancestry." *Frontiers of Oral Biology*, 13 (2009), pp. 49.

Jing Guo, et al. "Variation and Signatures of Selection on the Human Face," *Journal of Human Evolution* 75 (2014), p. 143.

Noreen von Cramon-Taubadel and Heather F. Smith. "The Relative Congruence of Cranial and Genetic Estimates of Hominoid Taxon Relationships: Implications for the Reconstruction of Hominin Phylogeny," *Journal of Human Evolution*, 62:5 (2012), p. 640.

Brian McEvoy, Sandra Beleza, and Mark D. Shriver. "The Genetic Architecture of Normal Variation in Human Pigmentation: An Evolutionary Perspective and Model," *Human Molecular Genetics*, 15 Spec No 2, Review Issue 2 (2006), pp. R176-81.

Norman J. Sauer, "Forensic Anthropology and the Concept of Race: If Races Don't Exist, Why are Forensic Anthropologists so Good at Identifying them?" *Social Science & Medicine*, 34.2 (1992), pp. 107-11.

Lyle W. Konigsberg, Bridget F.B. Algee-Hewitt, and Dawnie Wolfe Steadman, "Estimation and Evidence in Forensic Anthropology: Sex and Race," *American Journal of Physical Anthropology*, 139 (2009), pp. 77–90

Stephen Ousley, Richard Jantz, and Donna Freid. "Understanding Race and Human Variation: Why Forensic Anthropologists are Good at Identifying Race," *American Journal of Physical Anthropology,* 139:1 (2009), p. 68.

Angi M. Christensen, Nicholas V. Passalacqua, Eric J. Bartelink, *Forensic Anthropology: Current Methods and Practice* (Elsevier, 2013), p. 223.

Ancestry Testing
Euny Hong, "23andMe Has a Problem When it Comes to Ancestry Reports for People of Color," *Quartz,* (Aug. 26, 2016), http://qz.com/765879/23andme-has-a-race-problem-when-it-comes-to-ancestry-reports-for-non-whites/ accessed Dec. 29, 2016.

Katarzyna Bryc, et al. "The Genetic Ancestry of African Americans, Latinos, and European Americans across the United States," *American Journal of Human Genetics* 96.1 (2015), pp. 37–53.

Deborah A. Bolnick, Duana Fullwiley, Troy Duster, Richard S. Cooper, Joan H. Fujimura, Jonathan Kahn, Jay S. Kaufman, Jonathan Marks, Ann Morning, Alondra Nelson, Pilar Ossorio, Jenny Reardon, Susan M. Reverby, Kimberly Tallbear, "The Science and Business of Genetic Ancestry Testing," *Science* (Oct. 19, 2007), pp. 399-400.

The American Society of Human Genetics Ancestry Testing Statement, November 13, 2008. http://www.ashg.org/pdf/dtc_statement.pdf/

Mark A. Jobling, Rita Rasteiro & Jon H. Wetton, "In the Blood: The Myth and Reality of Genetic Markers of Identity," *Journal of Ethnic and Racial Studies,* 39:2 (Dec. 2015), pp. 142-161.

Medicine
Celeste Condit, Alan Templeton, Benjamin R. Bates, "Attitudinal Barriers to Delivery of Race-Targeted Pharmacogenomics among Informed Lay Persons," *Genetics in Medicine: Official Journal of the American College of Medical Genetics,* 5:5, (Sept. 2003).

Mildred K. Cho and Pamela Sankar, "Forensic Genetics And Ethical, Legal And Social Implications Beyond The Clinic," *Nature Genetics,* 36, (2004):, pp. S8-S12.

Jonathan Kahn, "The Troubling Persistence Of Race In Pharmacogenomics," *Journal Of Law, Medicine & Ethics* 40:4 (2012), pp. 873-885.

Jonathan Kahn, *Race in a Bottle: The Story of BiDil and Racialized Medicine in a Post-Genomic Age* (Columbia Univ. Press, 2013), pp. 177-180.

Quote in Jerome Kagan, "Equal time for Psychological and Biological Contributions to Human Variation," *Review of General Psychology,* 17:4 (2013), pp. 351-357.

Pamela Sankar, Mildred K. Cho, and Joanna Mountain, "Race and Ethnicity in Genetic Research," *American Journal of Medical Genetics,* Part A, 143A:9, (2007), pp. 961-970.
Asia Friedman and Catherine Lee., "Producing Knowledge About Racial Differences: Tracing Scientists' Use Of 'Race' And 'Ethnicity' From Grants To Articles." *Journal Of Law, Medicine & Ethics,* 41:3, (2013), pp. 720-732.

Genetic Sampling Bias
P. Sankar, M.K. Cho, and J. Mountain, "Race and Ethnicity in Genetic Research," *American Journal of Medical Genetics,* 143A:9 (2007), pp. 961–970.

"European samples also served..." quote in S.M. Fullerton, J.H. Yu, J. Crouch, et al., "Population Description and Its Role in the Interpretation of Genetic Association," *Human Genetics,* 127:5 (2010), pp. 563-572.

Alice B. Popejoy & Stephanie M. Fullerton, "Genomics is Failing on Diversity," *Nature* 538:7624 (October 112, 2016).

Chapter 3: Racial Science

Scientific Classification
The Anthropological Treatises of Johann Friedrich Blumenbach, Thomas Bendyshe, ed., (London: Anthropological Society, 1869), p. 269.

Quoted in *The Boston Magazine,* Jan. 1785, p. 17.

Bruce Dain, *A Hideous Monster of the Mind* (Cambridge, Mass.: Harvard University Press, 2002), p. 23.

William Stanton, *The Leopard's Spots: Scientific Attitudes Toward Race in America, 1915-59* (Chicago: The University of Chicago Press, 1960).

Winthrop Jordan, *White Over Black: American Attitudes Toward the Negro, 1550-1812* (Chapel Hill: University of North Carolina Press, 1968), ch. 13.

John Wood Sweat, *Body Politic: Negotiating Race in the American North, 1730-1830* (Baltimore: John Hopkins Univ. Press, 2003).

Shane White, "We Dwell in Safety and Pursue Our Honest Callings,': Free Black in New York City, 1783-1810," *The Journal of American History,* 75:2 (Sept. 1988), 457.

Craig Steven Wilder, *Covenant With Color: Race and Social Power in Brooklyn* (New York: Columbia University Press, 2000).

The Boston Medical and Surgical Journal, Aug. 19, 1835, p. 34; Sept. 2, 1835, p. 64; Oct. 1849, p. 187.

American Medical Recorder, Jan. 1824, 158; Review of J.C. Prichard, *Researches into the Physical History of Mankind,* by J.C. Prichard, M.D., in *Littell's Living Age,* July 16, 1859, p. 152.

Sutton in *The Western Journal of Medicine and Surgery,* Oct. 1852, p. 308.

Restine in *Medical and Surgical Reporter,* July 10, 1897, p. 33.

Monogenesis and Polygenesis
Johnson quoted in Craig Koslofsky, "Knowing Skin in Early Modern Europe, c. 1450–1750," *History Compass,* 12:10, 2014, pp. 794-806.

Buffon, "Of the Degeneration of Animals," in *Barr's Buffon: Buffon's Natural History,* vol. 10 (London: H.D. Symonds, 1797), pp. 1-26, and "General Views of Nature," Ibid., pp. 324-325; "a kind of weak automaton" in Count de Buffon, *The Natural History of Quadrupeds*, vol. 2 (Edinburgh: Nelson & Brown, 1830), p. 39; also quoted in Lee A. Dugatkin, *Mr. Jefferson and the Giant Moose: Natural History in Early America* (Chicago: University of Chicago Press, 2009), p. 27.

Edward Long, *The History of Jamaica* (London: T. Lowndes, 1774), vol. 2, pp. 356, 335.

Waitz quoted in Robert J.C. Young, *Colonial Desire: Hybridity in Theory, Culture and Race* (New York: Routledge, 2005), pp. 6-7. References to 20th century debates on hybridity are from Young, p. 8.

Human Exhibitions

On Calichoughe, Tim William Machan, *What is English?: And How Should We Care?* (Oxford, UK: Oxford University Press, 2013), pp. 175-176.

Rosemary Wiss, "Lipreading: Remembering Saartjie Baartman." *Australian Journal Of Anthropology* 5.1/2 (1994), p. 11.

Sadiah Qureshi, "Robert Gordon Latham, Displayed Peoples, and the Natural History of Race, 1854–1866," *The Historical Journal*, 54:1 (2011), pp. 143-166

Andrew S. Curran, *The Anatomy of Blackness: Science and Slavery in an Age of Enlightenment* (Baltimore: Johns Hopkins University Press, 2011).

Londa Schiebinger, "The Anatomy of Difference: Race and Sex in Eighteenth-Century Science," *Eighteenth-Century Studies*, 23:4 (1990), pp. 387–405. See also Selig, R. A. "Africans in Early Modern Germany, *German Life*, Jan. 31, 1997, pp. 3, 39.

Observation of Baartman in *The Life and Correspondence of Charles Mathews...by Mrs. Mathews*, Edmund Yates, ed., (London: Routledge, Warne, and Routledge, 1860), p. 385.

Carol E. Henderson, "AKA: Sarah Baartman, the Hottentot Venus, and Black Women's Identity." *Women's Studies,* 43:7 (2014), pp. 946. See also Rosemary Wiss, "Lipreading..." pp. 11-41.

Cuvier quote from Jonathan Glover, "Moreau avec Couvier, Kant avec Sade: Saint Domingue, Sara Baartman, and the Technologies of Imperial Desire," in *Race and Displacement: Nation, Migration, and Identity in the Twenty-First Century*, Maha Marouan and Merinda Simmons, eds., (Tuscaloosa: University of Alabama Press, 2013), p. 177.

Qureshi, Sadiah. "Peopling The Landscape: Showmen, Displayed Peoples And Travel Illustration In Nineteenth-Century Britain," *Early Popular Visual Culture* ,10.1 (2012), pp. 23-36.

Andreassen, Rikke. "Representations Of Sexuality And Race At Danish Exhibitions Of "Exotic" People At The Turn Of The Twentieth Century." *NORA: Nordic Journal Of Women's Studies* 20.2 (2012), pp. 126-147.

Rikke Andreassen, *Human Exhibitions: Race, Gender and Sexuality in Ethnic Displays* (New York: Routledge, 2016).

Rikke Andreassen, "The 'Exotic' as Mass Entertainment: Denmark 1878-1909," *Race & Class*, 45:2 (2003), pp. 21-38.

John Conolly, *The Ethnological Exhibitions of London* (London: John Churchill, 1855), pp. 5, 29-30.

Anatomy

Andrew S. Curran, *The Anatomy of Blackness: Science & Slavery in an Age of Enlightenment* (Baltimore: Johns Hopkins University Press, 2011), p. 2.

Dictionaire des sciences médicales, par une société de médecins et de chirurgiens, C.L.F. Panckoucke, ed. (Paris, 1817), p. 257.

Bartholomew Parr, *The London Medical Dictionary* (London: J. Johnson, 1809), pp. 395, 755-759.

Soemmering's description of buttocks from Julien-Joseph Virey, *Natural History of the Negro Race*, transl. by J.H. Guenebault (Charleston, SC: D.J. Dowling, 1837), pp. 2-6.

Charles White claimed in his *An Account of the Regular Gradation in Man* (1790) that the radius and ulna were an inch longer in Europeans on average.

Johnson, "Parturition in the Negro Race," *The American Journal of Obstetrics*, 8:1 (May 1875), p. 122.

Craniometry

Stephen Jay Gould, *The Mismeasure of Man* (New York: W.W. Norton, 1981).

The Emperor's New Clothes: Biological Theories of Race at the Millennium (New Brunswick, N.J.: Rutgers University Press, 2001).

Medical Experimentation

Quote by Crook in Stephen C. Kenny, "Power, Opportunism, Racism: Human Experiments Under American Slavery, *Endeavour*, 39:1 (March 2015), pp. 10-20.

Martineau quote in Savitt, Todd L. "The Use of Blacks for Medical Experimentation and Demonstration in the Old South," *The Journal of Southern History*, 48:3 (1982), pp. 331-48.

Hornblum, A. M. "They Were Cheap and Available: Prisoners as Research Subjects in Twentieth Century America." *BMJ: British Medical Journal* 315.7120 (1997), pp. 1437–1441.

Cutler quote in Angel R. Rodriguez, "Infectious Imperialism: Race, Syphilis, and Human Experimentation in Guatemala City, 1946-1948," (Ph.D. Diss., Univ. of California, Santa Barbara, 2014), p. 28.

Shamim M. Baker, Otis W. Brawley, Leonard S. Marks, "Effects of Untreated Syphilis in the Negro Male, 1932 to 1972: A Closure Comes to the Tuskegee study," 2004, *Urology*, 65:6 (June 2005), pp. 1259-1262.

P.A. Lombardo & G.M. Dorr, "Eugenics, Medical Education, and the Public Health Service: Another Perspective on the Tuskegee Syphilis Experiment." *Bulletin of the History of Medicine*, 80:2 (2006), pp. 291-316.

One notable exception was the plutonium human experiments

secretly done by the U.S. government, but even that was estimated to involve one-quarter black subjects, a rate double that of the population. Harriet A. Washington, *Medical Apartheid: The Dark History of Medical Experimentation on Black Americans from Colonial Times to the Present* (New York: Knopf, 2008), p. 222; see also Eileen Welsom, *The Plutonium Files: America's Secret Medical Experiments in the Cold War* (New York: Random House, 2010).

A.M. Hornblum, "They Were Cheap and Available: Prisoners as Research Subjects in Twentieth Century America." *BMJ: British Medical Journal* 315.7120 (1997): 1437–1441.

J.M. Harkness, "Prisoners and Pellagra." *Public Health Reports* 111.5 (1996):, pp. 463–467.

Allen M. Hornblum, *Acres of Skin: Human Experiments at Holmesburg Prison: A Story of Abuse and Exploitation in the Name of Medical Science* (NY: Routledge, 1998).

Susan Lederer, *Subjected to Science: Human Experimentation in America before the Second World War* (Baltimore: Johns Hopkins University Press, 1995).

Darwin & Lamarck

Schoijet, Mauricio. "The Metatheory Of Scientific Revolutions And The History Of Biology." *Nature, Society & Thought* 18.2 (2005): 233-239.

George W. Stocking "Lamarckianism in American Social Science: 1890-1915." *Journal of the History of Ideas*, 23:2 (1962), pp. 239–256.

Conway Zirkle, "The Early History of the Idea of the Inheritance of Acquired Characteristics and Pangensis," *Transactions of the American Philosophical Society*, 35, pt.2, (1946), 91-151.

Charles E. Rosenberg, "The Bitter Fruit: Heredity, Disease, and Social Thought in Nineteenth-Century America," in *Perspectives in American History*, 8 (1974), pp. 189-235.

Mary Ellen Bogin, "The Meaning of Heredity in American Medicine and Popular Health Advice, 1771-1860," (Ph.D. Cornell Univ., 1990).

Paul-Gabriel Boucé, "Imagination, Pregnant Women, and Monsters, in Eighteenth Century England and France," in *Sexual Underworlds of the Enlightenment*, G.S. Rousseau and Roy Porter, eds., (Chapel Hill: Univ. of North Carolina Press, 1988), 86-100.

Aleš Hrdlička, "The Old White Americans," Extract from the *Proceedings of the Nineteenth International Congress of Americanists*, Washington, December, 1915, (n.p.; 1917), 582-601.

Ales Hrdlicka, "A Descriptive Catalog of the Section of Physical Anthropology: Panama-California Exposition, 1915," (San Diego, CA, 1914), p. 11, San Diego Public Library. See also Samuel Redman, "Remembering Exhibitions on Race in the 20th-Century United States." *American Anthropologist*, 111:4, (2009), pp. 517–518.

Intelligence and "IQ"

P. Habets, I. Jeandarme, K. Uzieblo, "Intelligence is in the Eye of the Beholder: Investigating Repeated IQ Measurements…" *Journal of Applied Research in Intellectual Disabilities*, 28:3 (2015); B. Benyamin, B. Pourcain, O.S. Davis, G. Davies, N. Hansell, M. Brion, "Childhood Intelligence is Heritable, Highly Polygenic and Associated with FNBP1L," *Molecular Psychiatry*, 19:2 (2014), pp. 253-258.

Ken Richardson, *Genes, Brains, and Human Potential: The Science and Ideologies of Intelligence* (New York: Columbia University Press, 2017).

Elaine E. Castles, *Inventing Intelligence: How America Came to Worship IQ* (Santa Barbara, Cal.: Praeger, 2012).

A. Okbay, J. Beauchamp, M.A. Fontana, J.J. Lee, T. Pers, "Genome-wide Association Study Identifies 74 Loci Associated with Educational Attainment," *Nature: International Weekly Journal of Science*, 533:7604 (2016), pp. 539-542.

R.J. Sternberg, E.L. Grigorenko & K.K. Kidd, K. K.. "Intelligence, Race, and Genetics," *American Psychologist*, 60:1 (2005), pp. 46-59.

Edwin G. Boring, Edwin G. "Intelligence as the Tests Test It," *The New Republic*, 35:444 (1923), p. 35.

Adam Miller, "The Pioneer Fund: Bankrolling the Professors of Hate," *The Journal of Blacks in Higher Education*, no. 6, (1994), pp. 58-61; William H. Tucker, "A Closer Look at the Pioneer Fund: Response to Rushton," *Albany Law Review*, 66:4, (2003), pp. 1145; William H. Tucker, "Bankrolling Racism: "Science" and the Pioneer Fund," *Race and Society*, 4:2, (2001), pp. 195-205.

William H. Tucker, ""A Scientific Result of Apparent Absurdity": The Attempt to Revise Goddard," *Ethnic and Racial Studies*, 22:1 (1999), pp. 162-1

Eugenics

Pat Shipman, *The Evolution of Racism: Human Differences and the Use and Abuse of Science* (Cambridge, Mass.: Harvard University Press, 1994), p. 128.

"harsh and cruel…" quote in Grant Gilmore, *The Age of American Law* (New Haven, Conn.: Yale University Press, 2014), p. 44.

Adam Cohen, *Imbeciles: The Supreme Court, American Eugenics, and the Sterilization of Carrie Buck* (New York: Penguin Press, 2016), p. 225.

U.S. Supreme Court, *Buck v. Bell*, 274 U.S. 200 (1927).

Price, Gregory N., and William A. Darity. "The Economics of Race and Eugenic Sterilization in North Carolina: 1958–1968." *Economics and Human Biology*, 8:2 (2010), pp. 261-272

Lira, Natalie. "Of Low Grade Mexican Parentage:" Race, Gender, and Eugenic Sterilization in California, 1928-1952 (Ph.D. Diss., University of Michigan, 2015).

Elana R. Gutiérrez, *Fertile Matters: The Politics of Mexican-Origin Women's Reproduction*, (Austin: University of Texas Press, 2008).

David M. Perry, "Our Long, Troubling History of Sterilizing the Incarcerated," (The Marshall Project, July 26, 2017).

Cracks in the Wall of Race
Brinton quote in Lee D. Baker, "Columbia University's Franz Boas: He Led the Undoing of Scientific Racism." *The Journal of Blacks in Higher Education*, no. 55, 2007, p. 79.

Theophile Simar, *Etude Critique sur la Formation de la Doctrine de Races…* (1922).

Lewis, Herbert S. "The Passion of Franz Boas," *American Anthropologist*, 103:2 (2001), pp. 447-467.

Marianne Sommer, "Biology as a Technology of Social Justice in Interwar Britain: Arguments from Evolutionary History, Heredity, and Human Diversity," *Science, Technology, & Human Values*, 39:4 (July 2014), pp. 561-586.

Julian Huxley, Alfred Cort Haddon, *We Europeans: A Survey of 'Racial' Problems* (London: Jonathan Cape, 1935), p. 162.

David Mills, *Difficult Folk: A Political History of Social Anthropology* (New York: Berghahn Books, 2008), 131. See also, Myles W. Jackson, "The Biology of Race: Searching for No Overlap," *Perspectives in Biology and Medicine*, 57:1 (Winter 2014): 87–104.

Berthold Laufer, Preface to *The Races of Mankind*, (Field Museum of Natural History, 1933).

Jennifer Schuessler, "Races of Mankind Sculptures, Long Exiled, Return to Display at Chicago's Field Museum," *New York Times*, Jan. 20, 2016.

Tracy L. Teslow, "Representing Race to the Public: Physical Anthropology in Interwar American Natural History Museums," (Ph.D. Diss., Univ. of Chicago, 2002).

"United Nations Educational, Scientific and Cultural Organization," *International Organization*, 3:2 (1949), pp. 354-56.

UNESCO, Statement on Race, Paris, July 1950.

Anthony Q.Hazard, "A Racialized Deconstruction? Ashley Montagu And The 1950 UNESCO Statement On Race." *Transforming Anthropology*, 19.2 (2011), pp. 174-186.

Sauer, Norman J. "Forensic Anthropology and the Concept of Race: If Races Don't Exist, Why are Forensic Anthropologists so Good at Identifying them?" *Social science & Medicine* 34.2 (1992), pp. 107-11.

Goran Štrkalj, "The Status of the Race Concept in Contemporary Biological Anthropology: A Review," *Anthropologist*, 9:1 (2007), pp. 73-78.

Goran Strkalj and V. Solyali. "Human Biological Variation in Anatomy Textbooks: The Role of Ancestry," *Studies on Ethno-Medicine*, 4:3 (2010), pp. 157-161.

Goran Strkalj, Muhammad A. Spocter, and A. Tracey Wilkinson. "Anatomy, Medical Education, and Human Ancestral Variation," *Anatomical Sciences Education*, 4:6 (2011), p. 362.

Chapter 4: Founding the Racial Republic
America Before Columbus
Nagamitsu Miura, *John Locke and the Native Americans: Early English Liberalism and Its Colonial Reality* (London: Cambridge Scholars Publishing, 2013), p. 151.

M. Raghavan, M. Steinrucken, K. Harris, S. Schiffels, S. Rasmussen, M. DeGiorgio, et al. "Genomic Evidence for the Pleistocene and Recent Population History of Native Americans." *Science*, vol. 349, no. 6250, (2015).

Why Columbus?
Frederick Dunn, "On the Antiquity of Malaria in the Western Hemisphere," *Human Biology*, 37:4, (December 1965) pp. 385-393.

Alfred W.Crosby, *The Columbian Exchange: Biological and Cultural Consequences of 1492* (Westport, CT: Greenwood Publishing 1972).

Swedlund, Alan C., et al. *Beyond Germs: Native Depopulation in North America*, (Tuscon, AZ: The University of Arizona Press, 2015); David S. Jones, "Virgin Soils Revisited," *William and Mary Quarterly* 60 (October, 2003), pp. 703–42.

William Cronon, *Changes in the Land: Indians, Colonists, and the Ecology of New England* (New York: Macmillan, 2011), p. 90.

Native Slavery
Michael Guasco "To "Doe Some Good upon Their Countrymen": The Paradox of Indian Slavery in Early Anglo-America," *Journal of Social History*, 41:2 (Winter, 2007), pp. 389-411

Catherine M. Cameron, "The Effects of Warfare and Captive-Taking on Indigenous Mortality in Postcontact North America," in Swedlund, Alan C., et al. *Beyond Germs: Native Depopulation in North America* (Tuscon: The University of Arizona Press, 2015).

Thomas D. Morris, *Southern Slavery and the Law, 1619-1860* (Chapel Hill: Univ. of North Carolina Press, 2004), p. 20.

Alan Gallay, *The Indian Slave Trade: The Rise of the English Empire in the American South, 1670-1717* (New Haven: Yale University Press, 2002), p. 299.

James F. Brooks, *Captives and Cousins: Slavery, Kinship, and Community in the Spanish Borderlands* (Chapel Hill: The University of North Carolina Press, 2002).

Colonization and Slavery
David Eltis, *The Rise of African Slavery in the Americas* (Cambridge University Press, 1999).

Saldaña-Portillo, María J. ""Wavering on the Horizon of Social Being": The Treaty of Guadalupe-Hidalgo and The Legacy of Its Racial Character in Americo Paredes's George Washington Gomez." *Radical History Review*, 89:1, (2004), pp. 135-164.

Vernon Valentine Palmer, "The Origins and Authors of the Code Noir," *Louisiana Law Review* 56:2 (Winter 1996), 363-407.

English Slavery

John Craig Hammond, "Slavery, Sovereignty, and Empires: North American Borderlands and the American Civil War, 1660–1860." *The Journal of the Civil War Era* 4.2 (2014): 264-98.

Edmund Morgan, *American Slavery, American Freedom* (New York:W.W. Norton, 1975).

Commodity Slavery

Lorenzo Johnston Greene, *The Negro in Colonial New England, 1620-1776*, (New York: Columbia University Press, 1942), p.68-69.

Charter of Georgia, 1832, in *The Federal and State Constitutions, Colonial Charters, and Other Organic Laws of the United States*, Benjamin Perley Poore, ed. (Washington, D.C.: Government Printing Office, 2n ed. 1878), pp. 369-370.

Indian Land and the American Revolution

G.S. Rowe, "The Frederick Stump Affair, 1768, and its Challenge to Legal Historians of Early Pennsylvania." *Pennsylvania History*, 49:4 (1982), pp. 259-288.

Jeremy Engels, "Equipped for Murder": The Paxton Boys and "the Spirit of Killing all Indians" in Pennsylvania, 1763-1764." *Rhetoric and Public Affairs*, 8:3 (2005), pp. 355-381.

Ben Kiernan, *Blood and Soil: A World History of Genocide and Extermination from Sparta to Darfur* (Yale Univ. Press, 2008), p. 323.

The Writings of Thomas Jefferson: being his autobiography, correspondence, reports, messages, addresses, and other writings… (Taylor and Maury, 1853), vol. 4, p. 177.

Brantz Mayer, *Tah-gah-jute: or, Logan and Cresap, An Historical Essay* (Albany: Joel Munsell, 1867).

Gary B. Nash, *The Unknown American Revolution: The Unruly Birth of Democracy and the Struggle to Create America* (New York: Viking, 2005).

"The sale of lands…" quote in John Gottlieb Ernestus Heckewelder, *A Narrative of the Mission of the United Brethren Among the Delaware and Mohegan Indians* (Philadelphia: McCarty & Davis, 1820), p. 130.

"I am very anxious to hear…" quote in "Extract of a Letter from London, July 23," *The Pennsylvania Gazette*, September 28, 1774.

"As to America…" quote in "Extract of a Letter from London, June 30," *The Pennsylvania Gazette*, September 28, 1774.

"What Course shall we pursue…" quote in *The Pennsylvania Gazette*, October 12, 1774.

"extending the province of Quebec…" quote in "POSTSCRIPT TO THE PENNSYLVANIA GAZETTE. No. 2393," in *The Pennsylvania Gazette*, November 2, 1774.

Harper, Rob. "Looking the Other Way: The Gnadenhutten Massacre and the Contextual Interpretation of Violence." *The William and Mary Quarterly,* vol. 64, no. 3, 2007., pp. 621-644.

Gregory Ablavsky, "The Savage Constitution." *Duke Law Journal* 63.5 (2014): 999-1089.

Land mania quotes in Blaakman, M. A., "Speculation Nation: Land and Mania in the Revolutionary American Republic, 1776-1803," (Ph.D. Diss., Yale Univ., 2016), pp. 4, 6.

Walter Hart Blumenthal, *American Indians Dispossessed: Fraud in Land Cessions Forced Upon the Tribes* (Philadelphia: George MacManus Co., 1955), pp. 48-51.

A Revolution for Slavery

Gerald Horne, "Negro Insurrection and Foreign Invasion: Slavery, 1776 and the Founding of the United States." *Black Renaissance/Renaissance noire*, 12:1 (2012), pp. 114-151

Lorenzo Johnston Greene, *The Negro in Colonial New England* (New York: Atheneum, 1969).

Samuel Eliot Morison, "The Commerce of Boston on the Eve of Revolution," *American Antiquarian Society Bulletin*, Apr. 1922, pp. 24-51.

Ronald Bailey, "'Those Valuable People, the Africans': The Economic Impact of the Slave(ry) Trade on Textile Industrialization in New England," in *Meaning of Slavery in the North*, Martin H. Blatt and David R. Roedgier, eds., (New York: Taylor & Francis, 1999).

The Somerset Case

Gerald Horne, *The Counter-Revolution of 1776: Slave Resistance and the Origins of the United States of America* (New York: New York University Press, 2014).

A. Leon Higgenbotham, Jr., *In the Matter of Color: Race and the American Legal Process, The Colonial Period* (New York: Oxford University Press, 1978).

Alfred W. Blumrosen and Ruth G. Blumrosen, *Slave Nation: How Slavery United the Colonies & Sparked the American Revolution* (Naperville, Ill.: Sourcebooks, Inc., 2005).

"will occasion a greater ferment…" quote in "Letter from Cologne," June 12, *The Virginia Gazette*, Aug. 27, 1772.

"every evil..." quote in Letter "Cologne," June 12, *The Virginia Gazette*, Aug. 27, 1772.

"I must now then apprize your Lordship…" quote in "Considerations on the Negro Cause," *The Virginia Gazette*, Nov. 12, 1772.

The latest editions of the following textbooks were surveyed: Brinkley, *Unfinished Nation* (McGraw Hill); Divine, *America Past and Present* (Prentice Hall); Faragher, *Out of Many* (Prentice Hall); Henretta, *America's History* (Bedford/Macmillan); Kennedy, The American Pageant (Houghton Mifflin/Cengage); Norton, *A People and a Nation* (Houghton Mifflin/Cengage); Tindall, *America: A Narrative History* (Norton).

Thomas B. Allen, *Tories: Fighting for the King in America's First Civil War* (New York: HarperCollins, 2010), pp. pp. 152-153, 154.

Gary B. Nash, *The Unknown American Revolution: The Unruly Birth of Democracy and the Struggle to Create America* (New York: Viking, 2005), pp. 160, 162, 165.

Chernoh M. Sesay Jr. "The Revolutionary Black Roots of Slavery's Abolition in Massachusetts." *The New England Quarterly*, 87:1 (2014), pp. 99-131.

L. Scott Philyaw, "A Slave for Every Soldier: The Strange History of Virginia's Forgotten Recruitment Act of 1 January 1781." *The Virginia Magazine of History and Biography*, 109.4 (2001), pp. 367-86.

Max Farrand, *Records of the Federal Convention*, (1911), Vol. 1, pp. 247, 567.

Kenneth Morgan, "George Washington and the Problem of Slavery," *Journal of American Studies*, 34:2 (2000), pp. 279-301.

Joseph Plumb Martin, A Narrative of Some of the Adventures, Dangers and Sufferings of a Revolutionary Soldier... (Glazier, Masters & Co., 1830), p. 42.

Dunmore's Proclamation

Thomas B. Allen, *Tories: Fighting for the King in America's First Civil War* (New York: HarperCollins, 2010), pp. 152-154.

Gary B. Nash, *The Unknown American Revolution: The Unruly Birth of Democracy and the Struggle to Create America* (New York: Viking, 2005), p. 160-165.

"I do hereby..." quote in Gary B. Nash, *The Unknown American Revolution: The Unruly Birth of Democracy and the Struggle to Create America* (New York: Viking, 2005), p. 162.

"there is not a man..." quoted in Gary B. Nash, *The Unknown American Revolution: The Unruly Birth of Democracy and the Struggle to Create America* (New York: Viking, 2005), p. 162.

Edward Countryman, *Enjoy the Same Liberty: Black Americans and the Revolutionary War* (Lanham, Maryland: Rowman & Littlefield Pub., 2012), pp. 47-49.

Jefferson runaway ad in A. Leon Higgenbotham, Jr., In the *Matter of Color: Race and the American Legal Process, The Colonial Period* (New York: Oxford Univ. Press, 1978), p. 383.

Independence in a Slave Republic

"an Ethiopian..." quote in James A. Rawley and Stephen D. Behrendt, *The Transatlantic Slave Trade: A History* (Univ. of Nebraska Press, 2005), p. 307.

Kenneth C. Davis, *The Hidden History of America at War: Untold Tales from Yorktown to Fallujah* (Hachette Books, 2015).

Judith L. Van Buskirk, *Standing in Their Own Light: African American Patriots in the American Revolution* (Norman: University of Oklahoma Press, 2017), pp. 186-188.

R.J. Cottrol and R.T. Diamond, "the 2nd-Amendment - Toward an Afro-Americanist Reconsideration," *Georgetown Law Journal*, 80:2 (1991), pp. 309-361.

Carl T. Bogus, "The Hidden History of the Second Amendment," *U.C. Davis Law Review*, 31:2 (1998), pp. 309.

Pinckney quote in Paul Finkelman, "Slavery and the Constitutional Convention: Making a Covenant with Death," in Robert Beeman, et. al., eds., *Beyond Confederation: Origins of the Constitution and National Identity* (Chapel Hill: University of North Carolina Press, 1987), p. 193.

Pinckney quote in *The Records of the Federal Convention of 1787*, Vol. 3, Max Ferrand, ed., (New Haven, Conn.: Yale Univ. Press, 1911), p. 446.

Gerald Horne, *Negro Comrades of the Crown: African Americans and the British Empire Fight the U.S. before Emancipation* (New York: New York University Press, 2012).

Battle of New Orleans, War of 1812 American Muster and Troop Roster List (National Park Service U.S. Department of the Interior)https://www.nps.gov/jela/learn/historyculture/upload/Battle-of-New-Orleans-Muster-Lists-final-copy-01062015.pdf; for estimates of blacks in Jackson's army twice as large as the muster lists, see James Oliver Horton and Lois E. Horton, *Slavery and the Making of America* (New York: Oxford university Press, 2005), pp 81–83.

The Treaty Myth

Susan Scheckel, *The Insistence of the Indian: Race and Nationalism in Nineteenth-Century American Culture* (Princeton, NJ: Princeton Univ. Press, 1998).

Philip J. Deloria, *Playing Indian* (New Haven, CT: Yale Univ. Press, 1998).

Anthony F C Wallace, and Timothy B. Powell. "How to Buy a Continent: The Protocol of Indian Treaties as Developed by Benjamin Franklin and Other Members of the American Philosophical Society." *Proceedings of the American Philosophical Society*, 159:3 (2015), pp. 251.

H. Knox to G. Washington, June 15, 1789, in *American State Papers: Documents...* vol. 4, (Washington, DC: Gales & Seaton, 1832), pp. 12-13.

Robert F. Berkhoffer, Jr., *The White Man's Indian: Images of the American Indian from Columbus to the Present* (New York: Knopf, 1978), pp. 149-151.

Karim M. Tiro, "The View from Piqua Agency: The War of 1812, the White River Delawares, and the Origins of Indian Removal," *Journal of the Early Republic*, 35:1 (2015), pp. 25.

Slavery in the Northern Territories

Christopher P. Lehman, *Slavery in the Upper Mississippi Valley, 1787-1865* (McFarland, 2011), pp. 5-8.

"Almost a Free State: The Indiana Constitution of 1816 and the Problem of Slavery." *Indiana Magazine of History* 111:1 (2015), pp. 64-95.

Darrel Dexter, *Bondage in Egypt: Slavery in Southern Illinois* (Cape Girardeau, MO: Southeast Missouri State Univ. Press, 2011).

Letters of Delegates to Congress: Vol. 4, May 16, 1776 - Aug. 15, 1776 John Adam's Notes of Debates, p. 593.

Christopher Malone, *Between Freedom and Bondage: Race, Party, and Voting Rights in the Antebellum North* (New York: Routledge, 2008), p. 9.

James J. Gigantino II. ""The Whole North is Not Abolitionized": Slavery's Slow Death in New Jersey, 1830–1860." *Journal of the Early Republic* 34.3 (2014), pp. 411-37.

Harvey Amani Whitfield, *The Problem of Slavery in Early Vermont, 1777-1810*, (Barre, VT: Vermont Historical Society, 2014).

Katherin Conlin, "Dinah and the Slave Question in Vermont," *Vermont History* 21:4 (1953), pp. 289-292.

Chapter 5: An Empire for Slavery

George Washington, President and Enslaver

Cassandra Pybus, *Epic Journeys of Freedom: Runaway Slaves of the American Revolution and Their Global Quest for Liberty* (Boston: Beacon Books, 2006).

Henry Wiencek, *An Imperfect God: George Washington, His Slaves, and the Creation of America* (New York, Farrar Straus Giroux, 2003).

Kenneth Morgan, "George Washington and the Problem of Slavery." *Journal of American Studies* 34:2 (2000), pp. 279-301.

Linda Allen Bryant, *I Cannot Tell a Lie: The True Story of George Washington's African American Descendents* (iUniverse Star, 2004).

John Craig Hammond, "Slavery, Sovereignty, and Empires: North American Borderlands and the American Civil War, 1660–1860," *The Journal of the Civil War Era*, 4:2 (2014), pp. 264-98.

Cotton

Lehman Bros.: One Brother Owned 7 Slaves in 1860," *USA Today*, Feb. 21, 2002. http://usatoday30.usatoday.com/money/general/2002/02/21/slave-lehman-bros.htm; "Fifteen Major Companies You Never Knew Profited From Slavery," *Atlanta Black Star*, Aug. 26, 2013. http://atlantablackstar.com/2013/08/26/17-major-companies-never-knew-benefited-slavery/7/ ; Katty Benner, "Wachovia Apologizes for Slavery Ties," *Money*, June 2, 2005. http://money.cnn.com/2005/06/02/news/fortune500/wachovia_slavery/ ; "Lawsuit Chases Companies Tied to Slavery," *Fox News*, Mar. 27, 2002. http://www.foxnews.com/story/2002/03/27/lawsuit-chases-companies-tied-to-slavery/ .

Michael Lobban, "Slavery, Insurance And The Law." *Journal Of Legal History* 28:3 (2007), pp. 319-328.

Jane Webster, "The Zong In The Context Of The Eighteenth-Century Slave Trade." *Journal Of Legal History* 28:3 (2007), pp. 285-298.

America and Transatlantic Human Trafficking

David Head, "Slave Smuggling by Foreign Privateers: The Illegal Slave Trade and the Geopolitics of the Early Republic." *Journal of the Early Republic*, 33:3 (2013), pp. 433-462.

Slavery and Western Expansion

Sven Beckert, *Empire of Cotton: A Global History* (New York:

Alfred A. Knopf, 2014).

Edward Baptist, *The Half Has Never Been Told : Slavery and the Making of American Capitalism* (New York : Basic Books, 2014).

Robert H. Gudmestad. *A Troublesome Commerce: The Transformation of the Interstate Slave Trade*, (Baton Rouge: Louisiana State University Press, 2004).

Mary Chestnut's Civil War, C. Van Woodward, ed., (New Haven, CT: Yale University Press, 1981), p. 29.

Harriet Ann Jacobs, *Incidents in the Life of a Slave Girl* (Boston, 1861), pp. 97-98.

The Cherokee Treaties

Richard Peters, *The Case of the Cherokee Nation Against the State of Georgia* (Philadelphia: John Grigg, 1831), appendix 2.

Ratification of the Agreement Between the United States and Georgia (Washington, DC: W. Duane & Son, 1802), p. 8.

Garrison, Tim A., *The Legal Ideology of Removal: The Southern Judiciary and the Sovereignty of Native American Nations*, (Athens: University of Georgia Press, 2002).

Jodi Boyd, *The Transit of Empire:Indigenous Critiques of Colonialism* (Minneapolis: University of Minnesota Press, 2011).

U.S. Supreme Court, *Cherokee Nation v. Georgia*, 30 U.S. 5 Pet. 1 1 (1831)

Indian Removal

Cass and Monroe quotes from Tiro, Karim M. "The View from Piqua Agency: The War of 1812, the White River Delawares, and the Origins of Indian Removal," *Journal of the Early Republic*, 35:1 (2015), pp. 25.

John Robert Irelan, *The Republic: Or A History of the United States of America* (Chicago: Fairbanks and Palmer, 1888), vol. IX, p. 153.

Memorial of the chiefs and delegates of the Wyandot Indians, praying payment of the value of their improvements ceded to the United States by the treaty of March 17, 1842 (U.S. Senate, 29th Cong., 1st Session, 473 S.doc.136); *Communication from Acting Commissioner of Indian Affairs, on claims of certain Wyandotte Indians* (U.S. Senate, 53rd Cong., 2nd Session, 3171 S. Misc Doc.233).

S.C. Bolton, "Jeffersonian Indian Removal and the Emergence of Arkansas Territory," *The Arkansas Historical Quarterly*, 62:3 (2003), pp. 253-271.

Cody Lynn Berry, "Territorial Capitalism: Early Arkansas Banking and Indian Removal, 1819 - 1860," (M.A. Thesis, University of Arkansas at Little Rock, 2016).

Slavery and Capitalism

Lee A. Craig, Thomas Weiss, "Hours at work and total factor productivity growth in nineteenth-century U.S. agriculture," in Kyle D. Kauffman (ed.) *New Frontiers in Agricultural History* (Advances in Agricultural Economic History, Volume 1, 2000) Emerald Group Publishing Limited, pp. 1 - 30.

Judith K. Schafer, "Details are of a most Revolting Character": Cruelty to Slaves as seen in Appeals to the Supreme Court of

Louisiana." *Chicago-Kent Law Review*, 68:3 (1993), pp. 1283.

Robert W. Fogel, *Without Consent or Contract: The Rise and Fall of American Slavery* (New York: Norton, 1989), p. 85.

Mark M. Smith, *How Race is Made: Slavery, Segregation, and the Senses* (Chapel Hill: University of North Carolina Press, 2006), pp. 22-23.

"In the management of negroes…" quote in "On the Management of Negroes," *The Farmer's Register: A Monthly Publication* (Shellbanks, Virginia), Feb. 1834, p. 564.

Myths of the Civil War
"I am not, nor ever have been…" quoted in http://www.bartleby.com/251/41.html

Eric H. Walther, *The Shattering of the Union: America in the 1850s* (Lanham, Maryland: SR Books, 2004), p. 143.

"I have declared a thousand times…" quote in Robert W. Johannsen, *Lincoln, the South, and Slavery: The Political Dimension* (Baton Rouge: Louisiana State University Press, 1991).

Russell McClintock, *Lincoln and the Decision for War: The Northern Response to Secession* (Chapel Hill: University of North Carolina Press, 2008), p. 98.

Declaration of the Immediate Causes Which Induce and Justify the Secession of South Carolina… (Charleston: Evans & Cogswell, 1860).

An Address Setting Forth the Declaration of the Immediate Causes Which Induce and Justify the Secession of Mississippi… (Jackson: Mississippian Book and Job Printing Office, 1861).

Alexander Stephens quote in *American Annual Cyclopedia…of the Year 1861* (New York: D. Appleton & Co., 1868), p. 129.

John F. Marszalek, *Lincoln and the Military* (Carbondale: Southern Illinois University Press, 2014), p. 22.

John David Smith, *Lincoln and the U.S. Colored Troops* (Carbondale: Southern Illinois University Press, 2013), pp. 12-14, 23.

Frederick Douglass quote on civil war in *The Equality of All Men Before the Law…* (Boston: Geo C. Rand & Avery, 1865), p. 37.

W.E.B. Du Bois, *Black Reconstruction in America*, (New York: Atheneum, 1969, org. 1935).

Chapter 6: Inventing Indians

Berger, Bethany R. "Red: Racism and the American Indian," *UCLA Law Review*, 56:3 (2009), pp. 591.

Dyar, Jennifer. "Fatal Attraction: The White Obsession with Indianness," *Historian*, 65:4 (2003), pp. 817.

Becoming Red
John Smith quote in Kupperman, Karen Ordahl. "Presentment of Civility: English Reading of American Self-Presentation in the Early Years of Colonization." *The William and Mary Quarterly*, 54:1 (1997), pp. 193–228.

Schiebinger, Londa. "The Anatomy of Difference: Race and Sex in Eighteenth-Century Science," *Eighteenth-Century Studies*, 23:4 (1990), pp. 387–405.

The Noble Savage
Paine quote in Thomas Paine, "Agrarian Justice," in *The Life and Writings of Thomas Paine*, Daniel E. Wheeler, ed., (Vincent Parke & Co.: New York, 1908), pp. 10-11.

"The Barbarous races…" quote in Miles A. Powell, Vanishing America: Species Extinction, Racial Peril, and the Origins of Conservation (Cambridge, Mass.: Harvard University Press, 2016), pp. 20-21.

From Innocent Primitive to Savage Beast
Rebecca Anne Goetz, *The Baptism of Early Virginia: How Christianity Created Race* (Baltimore, Maryland.: Johns Hopkins University Press, 2015), pp. 59-60.

Susan Juster, *Sacred Violence in Early America* (Philadelphia: University of Pennsylvania Press, 2016), p. 122.

Ronald Takaki, "The Tempest in the Wilderness: The Racialization of Savagery," *The Journal of American History*, 79:3 (1992), pp. 892–912.

John Demos, *Remarkable Providences: Readings in Early American History* (Boston: Northeastern University Press, 1991), pp. 6-7.

Alden T. Vaughan, *New England Frontier: Puritans and Indians, 1620-1675* (Norman: University of Oklahoma Press, 1995), pp. 110-111.

Nagamitsu Miura, *John Locke and the Native Americans: Early English Liberalism and its Colonial Reality* (Newcastle upon Tyne, UK: Cambridge Scholars Publishing, 2013).

David W. Miller, *The Taking of American Indian Lands in the Southeast: Territorial Cessions and Forced Relocations, 1607-1840* (New York: McFarland, 2011), p. 174.

Alfred A. Cave, *Lethal Encounters: Englishmen and Indians in Colonial Virginia* (Santa Barbara, Cal.: ABC-CLIO, 2011), p. 126.

David Malet, *Biotechnology and International Security* (Lanham, Maryland: Rowman & Littlefield, 2016), p. 16.

Richard Middleton, *Pontiac's War: Its Causes, Course and Consequences* (New York: Routledge, 2012), p. 110.

Benjamin Madley, "Reexamining the American Genocide Debate: Meaning, Historiography, and New Methods." *American Historical Review*, 120:1 (Feb. 2015), pp. 98-139.

Wilbur R. Jacobs, *Dispossessing the American Indian: Indians and Whites on the Colonial Frontier* (New York: Charles Scribner's Sons, 1972), p. 119.

"Introduction to Human Trophy Taking: An Ancient and Widespread Practice," by Robert J. Chacon & David H. Dye, in Chacon & Dye, eds. *The Taking and Displaying of Human Body Parts as Trophies by Amerindians* (New York: Springer Publishing, 2007), p. 22.

Indians and American Identity
Philip J. Deloria, *Playing Indian* (New Haven, Conn.: Yale

428

University Press, 1998).

Shari M. Huhndorf, *Going Native: Indians in the American Cultural Imagination* (Ithaca, N.Y.: Cornell University Press, 2001).

The Vanishing Indian Myth
Jennifer Dyar, "Fatal Attraction: The White Obsession with Indianness," *Historian*, 65:4 (2003), pp. 817.

John S. Henderson, et al. "Chemical and Archaeological Evidence for the Earliest Cacao Beverages," *Proceedings of the National Academy of Sciences of the United States of America*, 104:48 (2007), pp. 18937-18940.

Marin Trenk, "Religious Uses of Alcohol among the Woodland Indians of North America." *Anthropos*, 96:1 (2001), pp. 73–86.

John Smalley and Michael Blake. "Sweet Beginnings: Stalk Sugar and the Domestication of Maize," *Current Anthropology*, 44:5 (2003), pp. 675–703.

W.J. Rorabaugh, *The Alcoholic Republic: An American Tradition* (New York: Oxford Univ. Press, 1979), pp. 5-10; "Recorded Alcohol Per Capita Consumption, from 2000," *World Health Organization, Global Information System on Alcohol and Health* (GISAH), last update: May 2016.

Brian W. Dippie, *The Vanishing American: White Attitudes and U.S. Indian Policy* (Middletown, CT: Wesleyan University Press, 1982), pp. 124-126; Fifteenth Congress, Sess. 2, Ch. 83, Mar. 3, 1819.

Roy Harvey Pearce, *Savagism and Civilization: A Study of the Indian and the American Mind* (Berkeley: University of California Press, 1988, org. 1953), pp. 192-193.

The New England Society Orations: Addresses, Sermons, and Poems Delivered Before the New England Society in the City of New York, 1820-1885, Cephas Brainerd, Eveline Warner Brainerd, eds., Vol. 2, (New York: Century Co., 1901), pp. 297-298.

Robert F. Sayre, *Thoreau and the American Indians* (Princeton University Press, 1977), p. X.

James P. Collins, "Native Americans in the Census, 1860–1890," *Prologue Magazine*, 38:2 (Summer 2006).

"Indians in the United States in 1853, With The Number, in 1789 and 1825, Showing their Location," in *The Seventh Census of the United States: 1850*, Appendix, James Dunwoody Brownson De Bow, Superintendent, (Washington, D.C.: Government Printing Office, 1853), p. xciv.

"Indians In The States and Territories Retaining Their Tribal Character Not Enumerated In The Eighth Census, 1860," in *Report on Indians Taxed and Indians Not Taxed in the United States* (Washington, D.C.: Government Printing Office, 1894), p. 18.

Benjamin Madley, "Reexamining the American Genocide Debate: Meaning, Historiography, and New Methods." *American Historical Review*, 120:1 (Feb. 2015), pp. 98-139.

The West
Ronald W. Walker, Richard E. Turley, Glen M. Leonard, *Massacre at Mountain Meadows* (Oxford University Press, 2011).

Brendan C. Lindsay, *Murder State: California's Native American Genocide, 1846-1873* (University of Nebraska Press, Lincoln, 2012), pp. 24-28.

The War of the Rebellion: A Compilation of the Official Records of the Union and Confederate Armies (Washington, D.C.: Government Printing Office, 1885), vol. 13, p. 684.

Christopher J. Pexa, "Transgressive Adoptions: Dakota Prisoners' Resistances to State Domination Following the 1862 U.S.–Dakota War." *Wicazo Sa Review*, 30:1 (2015), pp. 29-56.

Allan D. Cooper, *The Geography of Genocide* (University Press of America, 2008), p. 145.

John M. Coward, "Creating the Ideal Indian: The Case of the Poncas," *Journalism History*, 21:3 (1995), pp. 112.

"In every tribe of Indians there are..." quote in Zylyff, *The Ponca Chiefs: An Indian's Attempt to Appeal from the Tomahawk to the Courts* (Boston: Lockwood, Brooks & Co., 1880), pp. 61-62.

Helen Hunt Jackson, *A Century of Dishonor: A Sketch of the Government's Dealings with Some of the Indian Tribes* (Boston: Little, Brown & Co., 1889).

The Dawes Act of 1887 and Assimilation
Brian W. Dippie, *The Vanishing American: White Attitudes and U.S. Indian Policy* (Middletown, CT: Wesleyan University Press, 1982), pp. 196, 281.

Bethany R. Berger, "Red: Racism and the American Indian," *UCLA Law Review*, 56:3 (2009), pp. 591; Dippie, 195.

Sally Jenkins, *The Real All Americans: The Team That Changed a Game, a People, a Nation* (New York: Broadway Books, 2008).

Indians in Popular Culture
Rebecca Jaroff, "Opposing Forces: (Re)Playing Pocahontas and the Politics of Indian Removal on the Antebellum Stage," *Comparative Drama*, 40:4 (Winter 2006- 2007), pp. 483-504.

Lydia Maria Child, "Appleseed John," *St. Nicholas: Scribner's Illustrated Magazine for Girls and Boys*, 7:2 (June 1880), p. 604.

William Kerrigan, "The Invention of Johnny Appleseed." *The Antioch Review*, 70:4 (2012), pp. 608–625.

Merskin, Debra. "Winnebagos, Cherokees, Apaches, and Dakotas: The Persistence of Stereotyping of American Indians in American Advertising Brands," *Howard Journal of Communications*, 12:3 (2001), pp. 159-169.

White Jealousy of the 'Savage'
Gail Bederman, *Manliness & Civilization: A Cultural History of Gender and Race in the United States, 1880-1917* (Chicago: University of Chicago Press, 1995).

John Kasson, *Houdini, Tarzan, and the Perfect Man: The White Male Body and the Challenge of Modernity in America* (New York : Hill and Wang, 2001).

Philip J. Deloria, *Playing Indian* (New Haven, Conn.: Yale University Press, 1998).

Shari M. Huhndorf, *Going Native: Indians in the American Cul-*

tural Imagination (Ithaca, N.Y.: Cornell University Press, 2001).

Daniel C. Beard, *The Boy Pioneers: Sons of Daniel Boone* (New York: Charles Scribner's Sons, 1909), pp. v-vi.

"The forests were infested..." quote in Daniel C. Beard, *The Boy Pioneers: Sons of Daniel Boone* (New York: Charles Scribner's Sons, 1909), p. 20.

"No one who studies man's..." quote in E.T. Seton, introduction to Warren H. Miller, *Camp Craft, Modern Practice and Equipment* (London: B.T. Batsford, 1915).

Carol Spindel, *Dancing at Halftime: Sports and the Controversy Over American Indian Mascots* (New York: NYU Press, 2002), pp. 92-95.

Jennifer Guiliano, *Indian Spectacle: College Mascots and the Anxiety of Modern America* (New Brunswick, N.J.: Rutgers University Press, 2015).

Movie Indians
Angela Aleiss, *Making the White Man's Indian: Native Americans and Hollywood Movies* (Westport, Conn.: Praeger, 2005).

Michael R. Fitzgerald, "The White Savior and His Junior Partner: The Lone Ranger and Tonto on Cold War Television (1949–1957)," *The Journal of Popular Culture*, 46:1 (2013), pp. 79-108

"The Origin of the Lone Ranger," (Jun 30 1948), https://sites.google.com/site/microphoneplays/home/loneranger.

Dustin Tahmahkera, *Tribal Television: Viewing Native People in Sitcoms*, (Chapel Hill: The University of North Carolina Press, 2014), pp. 1-4.

The Indian New Deal
The Problem of Indian Administration: Report of a Survey Made at the Request of Honorable Hubert Work, Secretary of the Interior... Feb. 21, 1928, Institute for Government Research Staff, Lewis Meriam, Dir. (Baltimore: Johns Hopkins Press, 1928), pp. 22-23.

Carol C. Lujan, "American Indians and Alaska Natives Count: The US Census Bureau's Efforts to Enumerate the Native Population," *American Indian Quarterly*, 38:3 (2014), pp. 319-341.

Russell Thornton, "Tribal Membership Requirements and the Demography of 'Old' and 'New' Native Americans," *Population Research and Policy Review*, 16: 1/2 (1997), pp. 33-42.

http://www.slate.com/articles/news_and_politics/history/2015/04/staten_island_for_sale_the_munsee_indians_sold_staten_island_under_duress.2.html

Dana Rubin, "The Real Education of Little Tree," *Texas Monthly*, Feb. 1992; McGurl, Mark. "Learning from Little Tree: The Political Education of the Counterculture," *The Yale Journal of Criticism*, 18:2 (2005), pp. 243.

Finis Dunaway, *Seeing Green: The Use and Abuse of American Environmental Images* (Chicago: The University of Chicago Press, 2015), p. 79.

Angela Aleiss, "Iron Eyes Cody: Wannabe Indian," vol. XXV, *Federation Internationale des Archives* (FIAF), 1999, p. 31.

Chapter 7: Inventing Blackness

Nancy Shoemaker, *A Strange Likeness: Becoming Red and White in Eighteenth-Century North America*, (New York: Oxford University Press, 2004), p. 129.

Mechal Sobel, *The World They Made Together: Black and White Values in Eighteenth-Century Virginia* (Princeton, NJ: Princeton University Press, 1987), pp. 66-67, 166-168,

"No body wishes..." Jefferson quote in *The Nature of Difference: Sciences of Race in the United States from Jefferson to Genomics*, Evelynn M. Hammonds & Rebecca M. Herzig, eds. (Cambridge, Mass. The MIT Press, 2008), document 2.3.

The Hardening Lines of Race
"nearer to the brute..." Winthrop D. Jordan, *White Over Black: American Attitudes Toward the Negro, 1550-1812* (New York: Penguin Books, 1968), p. 500.

Jenna M. Gibbs, *Performing the Temple of Liberty: Slavery, Theater, and Popular Culture in London and Philadelphia, 1760–1850* (Baltimore, Maryland: The Johns Hopkins University Press, 2014), p. 1-5.

"Among the productions..." quote from the article, "Monthly Dramatic Review," in *The Polyanthos* (Boston), Mar. 1, 1813, p. 51.

Carroll Smith-Rosenberg, *This Violent Empire: The Birth of an American National Identity*, (Chapel Hill, NC: University of North Carolina Press, 2010), ch. 8.

Matthew Carey, *A Short Account of the Malignant Fever, Lately Prevalent in Philadelphia . . .* (Philadelphia, 1794).

Jacquelyn C. Miller, "The Wages of Blackness: African American Workers and the Meanings of Race during Philadelphia's 1793 Yellow Fever Epidemic," *Pennsylvania Magazine of History and Biography*, 129:2 (April, 2005), pp. 163-194.

The Rise of Whiteness
Nancy Shoemaker, *A Strange Likeness: Becoming Red and White in Eighteenth-Century North America*, (New York: Oxford University Press, 2004), p. 129.

Morgan Godwyn, *The Negro's and Indians Advocate* (London, 1680), p. 83.

Jay Fliegelman, *Declaring Independence: Jefferson, Natural Language & the Culture of Performance* (Stanford Cal.: Stanford University Press, 1993), pp. 160-163.

The Works of Benjamin Franklin, Jared Sparks, ed., vol. 2 (Chicago: Townsend Mac Coun, 1882), pp. 320-321.

Bridget T. Heneghan, *Whitewashing America: Material Culture and Race in the Antebellum Imagination* (Jackson: University Press of Mississippi, 2003), pp. 4-5, 10-11.

The Rise of the Sambo Stereotype
William Drayton, *The South Vindicated from the Treason and Fanaticism of the Northern Abolitionists* (Philadelpia: H. Manly, 1836), pp. 232-233.

Evelyn Glenn, "Racial Ethnic Women's Labor: The Intersection of Race, Gender and Class Oppression," *Review of Radical Political Economics*, 17:3 (1985), pp. 86-108.

William L. Van Deburg, *Slavery & Race in American Popular Culture* (Madison: University of Wisconsin Press, 1984), pp. 22-23. See also Joseph Boskins, *Sambo: The Rise & Demise of an American Jester* (New York: Oxford Univ. Press, 1986) and W.T. Lhamon, Jr., *Raising Cain: Blackface Performance from Jim Crow to Hip Hop* (Cambridge, MA: Harvard University Press, 1998).

Frederick Douglass, *My Bondage and My Freedom* (New York and Auburn: Miller, Orton & Mulligan, 1855), pp. 117 and 332.

"(My slaves) break and destroy more…" quote in Eugene Genovese, *Roll Jordan Roll: The World the Slaves Made* (New York: Vintage Books, 1974, org. 1972), p. 300.

Douglas R. Egerton, *Gabriel's Rebellion: The Virginia Slave Conspiracies of 1800* (Chapel Hill: University of North Carolina Press, 1993).

"It is not to the military skill alone…" quote in *The National Recorder* (Philadelphia), Nov. 25, 1820, p. 344.

Alfred L. Brophy, "The Nat Turner Trials," *North Carolina Law Review*, 91:5 (2013), pp. 1864.

John W. Cromwell, "The Aftermath of Nat Turner's Insurrection," *The Journal of Negro History*, 5:2 (1920), pp. 208–234.

Racism in the North

Alexis de Tocqueville, *Democracy in America*, 3rd ed., (New York: Scatherd & Adams, 1839), vol. 1, p. 357.

Leon Litwack, *North of Slavery: The Negro in the Free States* (Chicago: University of Chicago, 1961), pp. 93-94. "In virtually every phase…" p. 97.

The Invention of Blackface Minstrelsy

W.T. Lhamon, Jr., *Raising Cain: Blackface Performance from Jim Crow to Hip Hop* (Cambridge, MA: Harvard University Press, 1998), p. 17.

Thomas F. De Voe, *The Market Book*, vol. 1, (New York, 1862), p. 344.

Eric Lott, *Love and Theft: Blackface Minstrelsy and the American Working Class* (New York: Oxford University Press, 1993), p. 51-52.

The Knickerbocker; or New York Monthly Magazine (New York) 48:2 (Aug. 1856) p. 215.

Minstrelsy and the Working Class

David Roediger, *The Wages of Whiteness: Race and the Making of the American Working Class* (New York: Verso Press, 1991), p. 118;

Annemarie Bean, James V. Hatch, Brooks McNamara, eds., *Inside the Minstrel Mask: Readings in Nineteenth-Century Blackface Minstrelsy* (Hanover, NH: Wesleyan University Press, 1996), p. 93.

William J. Mahar, *Behind the Burnt Cork Mask: Early Blackface Minstrelsy and Antebellum American Popular Culture* (Urbana:

University of Illinois Press, 1999), p. 10.

Rice quote in Douglas A. Jones, *The Captive Stage : Performance and the Proslavery Imagination of the Antebellum North* (Ann Arbor: University of Michigan Press, 2014), p. 9.

The Country Courier (New York), Jan. 16, 1817, p. 193.

David S. Reynolds, *Mightier Than The Sword: Uncle Tom's Cabin and the Battle for America* (New York: Norton, 2011), pp. 77-83.

Rev. H. Easton, *A Treatise on the Intellectual Character and Civil and Political Condition of the Colored People of the U. States* (Boston: Isaac Knapp, 1837), pp. 41-42.

Claiming Citizenship Through Whiteness

Samuel F.B. Morse, *Foreign Conspiracy Against the Liberties of the United States* (New York: American and Foreign Christian Union, 7th ed., 1855), p. 24.

Robert Knox, *The Races of Men: A Fragment* (Philadelphia: Lea & Blanchard, 1850), p. 213.

Ray Allen Billington, "The Burning of the Charlestown Convent," *The New England Quarterly*, 10:1 (1937), pp. 4–24.

James P. Byrne. "The Genesis of Whiteface in Nineteenth-Century American Popular Culture," *MELUS*, 29: 3/4 (2004), pp. 133–149.

The Spectre of Miscegenation

Randall Kennedy, *Interracial Intimacies: Sex, Marriage, Identity, and Adoption* (New York: Vintage, 2004).

Sidney Kaplan, "The Miscegenation Issue in the Election of 1864," *The Journal of Negro History* 34.3 (1949), pp. 274-343.

Ariela J. Gross, "Litigating Whiteness: Trials of Racial Determination in the Nineteenth-Century South," *Yale Law Journal*, 108 Yale L.J. 109 (Oct. 1998).

Burmeister quote in *Images of Blacks in Ameican Culture: A Reference Guide…* Jessie Carney Smith, ed., (Westport, CT: Greenwood Press, 1988), p. 38.

From Sambo to Savage

"British Philanthropy and American Slavery," *De Bow's Review*, (Mar. 1853), p. 263.

Amanda Frisken, "Obscenity, Free Speech, and "Sporting News" in 1870s America," *Journal of American Studies*, 42:3 (2008), pp. 537-577.

Marilyn M. Mehaffy, "Advertising Race/Raceing Advertising: The Feminine Consumer(-Nation), 1876-1900," *Signs*, 23:1 (1997), pp. 131.

Children's Books

Alice Walker, "Uncle Remus, No Friend of Mine," *Southern Exposure*, (Summer 1981), pp. 29-31.

Peggy Russo, "Uncle Walt's Uncle Remus: Disney's Distortion of Harris's Hero," *Southern Literary Journal* 25 (1992), pp. 19-32.

The Collected Works of Langston Hughes, Christopher C. De Santi, ed., vol. 9, (Columbia: University of Missouri Press, 2002), p. 50.

Selma Lanes, "Children's Books: Dr. Dolittle Innocent Again," *New York Times*, Aug. 28, 1988. See also Jesse M. Birtha, "Images of Blacks in Children's Books," in *Images of Blacks in American Culture: A Reference Guide...* Jessie Carney Smith, ed., (Westport, CT: Greenwood Press, 1988), pp. 191-234.

Booker T. Washington Comes to Dinner
Dewey W. Grantham, "Dinner at the White House: Theodore Roosevelt, Booker T. Washington, and the South," *Tennessee Historical Quarterly*, 17:2 (1958), pp. 112–130.

Edmund Morris, *Theodore Rex* (New York: Random House, 2001), p. 55. Edgar Murphy quoted in Robert J. Norrell, "When Teddy Roosevelt Invited Booker T. Washington to Dine at the White House," *The Journal of Blacks in Higher Education*, 63 (2009), pp. 70–74.

"When I asked Booker..." quote in Joseph Bucklin Bishop, *Theodore Roosevelt and His Time*, vol. 1 (New York: Charles Scribner's Son's, 1920), p.166.

"A perfectly stupid..." quote in Thomas G. Dyer, *Theodore Roosevelt and the Idea of Race* (Baton Rouge: Louisiana State University Press, 1980), p. 110.

Rise of Mass Media
"A War of Images," Janette L. Dates & William Barlow, in *Split Image: African Americans in the Mass Media*, Dates & Barlow, eds., (Washington, DC: Howard University Press, 1990), pp. 14-15.

M.M. Manring, "Aunt Jemima Explained: The Old South, the Absent Mistress, and the Slave in a Box," *Southern Cultures*, 2:1 (1995), pp. 19-44.

John F. Dovidio and Samuel L. Gaertner, "Changes in the Expression and Assessment of Racial Prejudice," in Harry Knopke, et al. *Opening Doors: Perspectives on Race Relations in Contemporary America*, (Tuscaloosa: University of Alabama Press, 1991).

Movie-Made Blackness
Susan Gubar, *Race Changes: White Skin, Blackface in American Culture* (New York: Oxford University Press, 1997).

Donald Bogle, *Toms, Coons, Mulattoes, Mammies, and Bucks: An Interpretive History of Blacks in American Films*, (Continuum, New York, 1994).

James Baldwin, *Collected Essays* (New York: Library Classics, 1998), p. 494.

Amos N' Andy
Ebony, Oct. 1961, pp. 66-73.

Chapter 8: Making the Alien
John Higham, *Send These To Me: Immigrants in Urban America* (Baltimore: Johns Hopkins University Press, Rev. ed. 1984).

New York Times, June 21, 1884, p. 4.

The Founders Immigration Policy
The Records of the Federal Convention of 1787, Vol. 3, Max Ferrand, ed., (New Haven, Conn.: Yale Univ. Press, 1911), p. 440.

Gerald L. Neuman, "The Lost Century of American Immigration Law (1776-1875)," *Columbia Law Review* 93:8; (1993).

Anna O. Law, "Lunatics, Idiots, Paupers, and Negro Seamen–Immigration Federalism and the Early American State," *Studies in American Political Development* 28:2 (2014), p. 107.

Mexican Americans
John C. Pinheiro, ""Religion without Restriction": Anti-Catholicism, All Mexico, and the Treaty of Guadalupe Hidalgo," *Journal of the Early Republic*, 23:1 (2003), pp. 69-96.

Evelyn Nakano Glenn, *Unequal Freedom: How Race and Gender Shaped American Citizenship and Labor* (Cambridge, Mass.: Harvard University Press, 2002), pp. 158-161.

John G. Bourke, "The American Congo," *Scribner's*, May, 1894, pp. 590-609.

Linda C. Noel, *Debating American Identity: Southwestern Statehood and Mexican Immigration* (Tuscon: University of Arizona Press, 2014). "I oppose the blending..." quote in *Congressional Record-Senate*, Jan. 18, 1905, p. 1010.

"the population of the New Mexican portion..." quote in *Congressional Record-Senate*, Mar. 8, 1906, p. 3508.

Ninth Census, The Statistics of the Population of the United States, embracing the tables of race, nationality... vol. 1 (Washington: Government Printing Office, 1872), pp. 12, 47, 50.

"I doubt if there is a more intelligent..." and "the common and usual homes..." in *Congressional Record-Senate*, Mar. 8, 1906, pp. 3513-14.

"Now...what are some..." quote in *Congressional Record-Senate*, Mar. 8, 1906, p. 3521.

The End of White-Only Citizenship
Journal of the Senate of the United States of America, 1789-1873, July 4, 1870, pp. 955-959; *Burlington Weekly Free Press* (Burlington, VT), July 15, 1870, p. 1.

Ian F. Haney López, *White By Law: The Legal Construction of Race* (New York: NYU Press, 1996), p. 43.

Chinese Immigrants
Christopher W. Merritt, Gary Weisz, and Kelly J. Dixon. ""Verily the Road was Built with Chinaman's Bones": An Archaeology of Chinese Line Camps in Montana," *International Journal of Historical Archaeology*, 16:4 (2012), pp. 666-695.

Deenesh Sohoni. "Unsuitable Suitors: Anti-miscegenation Laws, Naturalization Laws, and the Construction of Asian Identities," *Law & Society Review* 41.3 (2007), pp. 587–618.

Ronald Takaki, *A Different Mirror: A History of Multicultural America* (Boston: Back Bay Books, 1993, rev. Ed. 2008), pp. 188-189.

D.E. Wrobleski, "The Archaeology of Chinese Work Camps on the Virginia and Truckee Railroad," (Ph.D. Diss. University of Nevada-Reno, 1996).

Sue F. Chung, *The Asian American Experience: In Pursuit of Gold : Chinese American Miners and Merchants in the American West*, (Urbana: University of Illinois Press, 2011).

"The workers camps were well stocked..." quote on p. 276. "The Chinese in Nevada: A Historical Survey, 1856-1970," *Nevada Historical Society Quarterly* 25:4 (Winter, 1982), pp 237-285.

Anti-Chinese Movement
Evelyn Glenn, *Unequal Freedom: How Race and Gender Shaped American Citizenship and Labor*, (Cambridge, Mass.: Harvard University Press, Cambridge, Mass, 2002).

Claudia Sadowski-Smith, "Unskilled Labor Migration and the Illegality Spiral: Chinese, European,and Mexican Indocumentados in the United States, 1882–2007," *American Quarterly*, 60:3 (September 2008), pp. 779-804

Stereotypes of Asian Men and Women
""The new citizen is a Chinaman..." *The New York Herald*, Nov. 28, 1878, p. 5

"And how does it feel..." *The New York Herald*, Nov. 30, 1878, p. 3.

"To the Editor of the Herald...." *The New York Herald*, May 7, 1877, p. 4.

Qingsong Zhang, "The Origins of the Chinese Americanization Movement: Wong Chin Foo and the Chinese Equal Rights League," in Chan, S., Wong, K.S., *Claiming America: constructing Chinese American Identities during the Exclusion Era*, (Philadelphia: Temple University Press, 1998).

Japanese Immigrants
"...the naturalization abroad" in *San Francisco Chronicle*, Nov. 26, 1920.

Brian J. Gaines, and Wendy K. Tam Cho. "On California's 1920 Alien Land Law: The Psychology and Economics of Racial Discrimination," *State Politics & Policy Quarterly*, 4:3 (2004), pp. 271-293.

"Alien Land Laws and Alien Rights," *Papers presented by. Charles F. Curry, House of Representatives, 69th Cong., 1st Sess., Doc. 89* (Washington: Government Printing Office, 1921), p. 41.

Courts View Asians as Perpetually Foreign
Lucy E. Salyer, "Baptism by Fire: Race, Military Service, and U.S. Citizenship Policy, 1918-1935," *The Journal of American History*, 91:3 (2004), pp. 847–876.

Ichizo Sato v. Harry W. Hall, Supreme Court of California, 191 Cal. 510; 217 P. 520; 1923 Cal. July 26, 1923. See also Robert Arden Wilson and Bill Hosokawa, *East to America: A History of the Japanese in the United States* (New York: Morrow 1980), p. 247.

Hidemitsu Toyota's internment records can be found at Department of Justice, Claims Division, 1933-1953, Series: World War II Japanese Internee Cards , 1941 - 1947; Record Group 60: General Records of the Department of Justice, 1790 - 2002.

Toward a Racial Quota System
Ali Behdad, *A Forgetful Nation: On Immigration and Cultural Identity in the United States* (Duke University Press, 2005).

Nicholas Wisseman, "'Beware the Yellow Peril and Behold the Black Plague': The Internationalization of American White Supremacy and Its Critiques, Chicago 1919." *Journal of the Illinois State Historical Society*, 103:1 (2010), pp. 43–66.

Calvin Coolidge, "Whose Country Is This?" *Good Housekeeping* (Feb. 1921), p. 13-14, 106, 109.

Report of the President of the Carnegie Institution of Washington for the Year Ending October 31, 1921, p. 118.

Charles Hirschman and Elizabeth Mogford, "Immigration and the American Industrial Revolution From 1880 to 1920," *Social Science Research* 38.4 (2009): 897–920.

Jennifer Guglielmo and Salvatore Salerno, *Are Italians White?: How Race is made in America* (New York: Routledge, 2003); James R. Barrett and David Roediger, "Inbetween Peoples: Race, Nationality and the "New Immigrant" Working Class," *Journal of American Ethnic History*, 16:3, (1997), pp. 3; Desmond King, *Making Americans: Immigration, Race, and the Origins of the Diverse Democracy* (Cambridge: Harvard University Press, 2000); Matthew F. Jacobson, *Barbarian Virtues: The United States Encounters Foreign Peoples at Home and Abroad, 1876-1917* (New York: Hill and Wang, 2000).

Japanese Internment
Gen. DeWitt quote in Frank Yu, *Yellow: Race in America Beyond Black and White* (New York: Basic Books, 2002), p. 96. See also Juan González, Joseph Torres, *News for All the People: The Epic Story of Race and the American Media* (New York: Verso Books, 2010), p. 275.

"I am for immediate removal..." quote in Kimi Cunningham Grant, *Silver Like Dust: One Family's Story of America's Japanese Internment* (Pegasus Books, 2013).

William Manchester, *The Glory and the Dream: A Narrative History of America, 1932-1972* (New York: Little Brown & Co., 1974), pp. 299-301.

Timothy P. Maga, "Ronald Reagan and Redress for Japanese-American Internment, 1983-88," *Presidential Studies Quarterly*, 28:3 (July 1998), pp. 606-619.

Imperialism and Immigration
"not an act of justice..."; "...one island near"; "generally full-blooded white..."; ...It can be easily imagined,"; "to see the wage-earner" quotes in José A. Cabranes, *Citizenship and the American Empire: Notes on the Legislative History of the United Citizenship of Puerto Ricans* (New Haven: Yale University Press, 1979), p. 14.

"There is certainly no power..."; "It is obvious..." quoted in Juan R. Torruella, "Ruling America 's Colonies: The Insular Cases," *Yale Law & Policy Review*, 32:1 (2013), pp. 62, 71.

Elliot Young, *Alien Nation: Chinese Migration in the Americas From the Coolie Era Through World War II* (Chapel Hill: University of North Carolina Press, 2014), p. 99.

Oscar Handlin, *A Pictorial History of Immigration* (New York: Crown, 1972).

The Question of Refugees

Howard De Witt, "The Watsonville Anti-Filipino Riot of 1930: A Case Study of the Great Depression and Ethnic Conflict in California," *Southern California Quarterly*, 61:3 (1979), pp. 291–302.

Bruce W. Dearstyne, "Echoes of history in U.S. refugee policy," *Albany Times-Union*, Aug. 6, 2016.

United States Holocaust Memorial Museum, "Voyage of the St. Louis," Holocaust Encyclopedia, https://www.ushmm.org/wlc/en/article.php?ModuleId=10005267#seealso

Mexican Americans in the 20th Century

Tom I. Romero II. "Observations on History, Law, and the Rise of the New Jim Crow in State-Level Immigration Law and Policy for Latinos," *American Quarterly* 66:1 (2014), pp. 153-160.

Mai M. Ngai, *Impossible Subjects: Illegal Aliens and the Making of Modern America* (Princeton: Princeton University Press, 2004), p. 72.

Manuel G. Gonzales, *Mexicanos: A History of Mexicans in the United States* (Bloomington: Indiana University Press, 2009), p. 151.

Mark Overmyer-Velázquez, "Good Neighbors and White Mexicans: Constructing Race and Nation on the Mexico-U.S. Border," *Journal of American Ethnic History*, 33:1, (Fall 2013), pp. 5-34.

The Rise of Mexican-American Activism

Zaragosa Vargas, *Labor Rights are Civil Rights: Mexican American Workers in Twentieth-Century America* (Princeton University Press, 2007).

Patrick Carroll, *Felix Longoria's Wake: Bereavement, Racism, and the Rise of Mexican American Activism* (Texas: University of Texas Press, 2003).

David Cook-Martín, and David Fitz Gerald. "Liberalism and the Limits of Inclusion: Race and Immigration Law in the Americas, 1850–2000," *The Journal of Interdisciplinary History* 41.1 (2010), pp. 7–25.

A Civil Rights Revolution in Immigration Law

Mae M. Ngai "The Civil Rights Origins of Illegal Immigration," *International Labor and Working-Class History*, 78:1 (2010), pp. 93-99.

Lon Kurashige, *Two Faces of Exclusion: the Untold History of Anti-Asian Racism in the United States* (Chapel Hill: University of North Carolina Press, 2016), pp. 212-213.

Rosalind S. Chou and Joe R. Feagin, *The Myth of the Model Minority: Asian Americans Facing Racism* (Boulder, CO: Paradigm Publishers, 2008).

Marisa Abrajano and Zoltan L. Hajnal, *White Backlash: Immigration, Race, and American Politics* (Princeton, N.J.: Princeton University Press, 2015), p. 1.

Daniel Victor, "What, Congressman Steve King Asks, Have Nonwhites Done for Civilization?," *New York Times*, July 18, 2016.

Greg Toppo, Rep. "Steve King blasted for 'our civilization' tweet," *USA Today*, Mar. 12, 2017.

Mallory Shelbourne, "King defends controversial tweet: 'I meant exactly what I said," *The Hill*, Mar. 13, 2017.

Amanda Taub, "White Nationalism Explained," *New York Times*, Nov. 21, 2016. http://nyti.ms/2eWt9wA; http://www.npr.org/2016/11/17/502413784/journalist-says-steve-bannon-had-a-years-long-plan-to-take-down-hillary-clinton.

Ronald Inglehart, and Pippa Norris, "Trump, Brexit, and the Rise of Populism: Economic Have-Nots and Cultural Backlash," (July 29, 2016), HKS Working Paper No. RWP16-026. Available at SSRN: https://ssrn.com/abstract=2818659.

Chapter 9: Prejudice & Identity

Daniel Bernoulli, "Exposition of a New Theory on the Measurement of Risk," *Econometrica*, 22:1 (Jan., 1954: originally 1738), pp. 23-36. See also, Kahneman, Daniel; Tversky, Amos, "Choices, Values, and Frames," *American Psychologist*, 39:4 (Apr 1984), pp. 341-350.

Wilbur Zelinsky, *The Enigma of Ethnicity: Another American Dilemma* (Iowa City: University of Iowa Press, 2001).

"Kyle," Ancestry.com, (2015), https://youtu.be/2J5n8kzpbCs

Jeff Selle and Maureen Dolan, "Black Like Me? Civil Rights Activist's Ethnicity Questioned," *Coeur d'Alene/Post Falls Press*, June 11, 2015.

Eric Ruiz, "All Rachel Dolezal Did Was Show That Race and Identity Are Complicated," Apr. 14, 2017, *Observer* (New York).

Rachel Dolezal (with Storms Reback) *In Full Color: Finding My Place in a Black and White World* (Dallas, TX: BenBella Books, Inc., 2017). On the reaction to those equating "transracial" to "transgender" see Greg Piper, "Sorry for Comparing Transgenders to Rachel Dolezal, Feminist Journal Tells Outraged Mob," *The College Fix*, May 2, 2017.

Erik Erikson, *Childhood and Society*; also Medovoi *Rebels: Youth and the Cold War Origins of Identity*; Butler *Gender Trouble*.

William I. Thomas, "The Psychology of Race-Prejudice," *The American Journal of Sociology*, 9:5 (Mar. 1904), pp. 593-611.

"It is the practical question..." quote in Alfred Hold Stone, "Is Race Friction Between Blacks and Whites in the United States Growing?" *The American Journal of Sociology*, 13:5 (Mar. 1908), pp. 676-697.

W.E.B.Du Bois' response is included in W.F. Wilcox, "Discussion of the Paper By Alfred H. Stone, 'Is Race Friction Between Blacks and Whites in the United States Growing and Inevitable?'" *American Journal of Sociology*, 13:6 (May 1908), pp. 820-840.

E.S. Bogardus, "Social distance and its Origins," *Journal of Applied Sociology*, 9 (1925), pp. 216-226.

Colin Wark and John F. Galliher, "Emory Bogardus and the Origins of the Social Distance Scale," *The American Sociologist*,

38:4 (Dec. 2007), pp. 383-395.

Group Position Theory

J.F. Dovidio and S.L. Gaertner, "Intergroup Bias," in Fiske, Gilbert, Lindzey, eds. *Handbook of Social Psychology,* Vol. 2. (Hoboken, NJ: Wiley. 5th ed., 2010), pp. 1084–1121.

Blumer, Herbert. "Race Prejudice as a Sense of Group Position." *Sociological Perspectives,* 1:1 (1958), pp. 3-7.

Pettigrew, Thomas F. "Regional Differences in Anti-Negro Prejudice," *The Journal of Abnormal and Social Psychology,* 59:1 (1959), pp. 28-36; Thomas C. Wilson, "Interregional Migration and Racial Attitudes," *Social Forces* 65 (1986), pp. 177-86.

Mark A. Fossett, and K. J. Kiecolt, "The Relative Size of Minority Populations and White Racial Attitudes." *Social Science Quarterly,* 70:4 (1989), pp. 820-835; Michael W. Giles, "Percent Black and Racial Hostility: An Old Assumption Reexamined," *Social Science Quarterly,* 58:3 (1977), pp. 412–417.

Social Identity Theory

Gordon W. Allport, *The Nature of Prejudice* (Cambridge, Mass.: Addison-Wesley, 1954).

Yehuda Amir, "The Role of Intergroup Contact in Change of Prejudice in Race Relations." in *Towards the Elimination of Racism,* edited by P. Katz (New York: Pergamon, 1976).

Thomas Pettigrew, "Generalized Intergroup Contact Effects on Prejudice." *Personality and Social Psychology Bulletin* 23 (1997), pp. 173-185.

Ethnic Groups and Boundaries. The Social Organization of Culture Difference, Fredrik Barth, ed., (Oslo: Universitetsforlaget, 1969; reissued Long Grove, IL: Waveland Press, 1998).

Rogers Brubaker, Mara Loveman, and Peter Stamatov. "Ethnicity as Cognition," *Theory and Society,* 33:1 (2004), pp. 31-64.

Personal and Social Identity

Stuart Hall, "Cultural Identity and Diaspora," in *Identity: Community, Culture, Difference,* Jonathan Rutherford, ed. (London: Lawrence & Wishart,1990).

George Herbert Mead, "The Self," in *Identities: Race, Class, Gender, and Nationality,* Linda Martín Alcoff and Eduardo Mendieta, eds., (Malden, Mass.: Blackwell, 2003), pp. 32-40.

Belonging and Identity

Gaither, Sarah E., et al. "Social Belonging Motivates Categorization of Racially Ambiguous Faces," *Social Cognition,* 34:2 (2016), p. 97.

System Justification Theory

Gramsci quoted in J. van der Toorn and J.T. Jost, "Twenty Years of System Justification Theory: Introduction to the Special Issue on "Ideology and System Justification Processes" *Group Processes & Intergroup Relations,* 17:4 (2014), pp. 413-419.

John T. Jost, Mahzarin R. Banaji, and Brian A. Nosek. "A Decade of System Justification Theory: Accumulated Evidence of Conscious and Unconscious Bolstering of the Status Quo," *Political Psychology,* 25:6 (2004), pp. 881-919.

M.J. Brandt, "Do the Disadvantaged Legitimize the Social System? A Large-Scale Test of the status–legitimacy Hypothesis," *Journal of Personality and Social Psychology,* 104:5 (2013), pp. 765-785.

Alison Blodorn, et al. "Understanding Perceptions of Racism in the Aftermath of Hurricane Katrina: The Roles of System and Group Justification," *Social Justice Research,* 29:2 (2016), pp. 139-158.

Whiteness as Identity

Richard Dyer, *White,* (New York & London: Routledge, 1997).

Peggy McIntosh, "White privilege and male privilege: A personal account of coming to see correspondence through work in women's studies," (org. 1988) in *Privilege and Prejudice: Twenty Years with the Invisible Knapsack,* Karen Weekes, ed., (Newcastle upon Tyne, England: Cambridge Scholars Pub., 2009).

David S. Owen, "Towards a Critical Theory of Whiteness," *Philosophy & Social Criticism,* 33:2 (2007), pp. 203-222.

Robert W. Terry, "The Negative Impact on White Values." in *Impacts of Racism on White Americans,* edited by Benjamin P. Bowser and Raymond G. Hunt. Beverly Hills, (CA: Sage, 1981), pp. 119-151.

Black Views of Whiteness

"white people...do not imagine…" quoted in bell hooks, *Black Looks: Race and Representation* (New York: Routledge, 2014, org. 1992), p. 169.

"a vast amount of…" quote in James Baldwin, *The Fire Next Time* (New York: Knopf, 2014, org. 1963), p. 90.

"What Shall We Do With The White People?," by William J. Wilson, in David Roediger, *Black on White: Black Writers on What It Means to Be White* (New York: Schocken Books, 1998), p. 61.

Double Consciousness

W.E.B. Du Bois, *The Souls of Black Folks,* 3rd ed. (Chicago: A.C. McClurg & Co., 1903), p. 3.

Mikhail Lyubansky and Roy J. Eidelson. 2005. "Revisiting Du Bois: The Relationship Between African American Double Consciousness and Beliefs about Racial and National Group Experiences," *Journal of Black Psychology* 31 (2005), pp. 3-26.

Baldwin, *The Fire Next Time,* (New York: Knopf, 2014, org. 1963), p. 115.

Embodiment and Identity

Henri Tajfel, *Social Identity and Intergroup Relations,* (Cambridge: Cambridge University Press, 1982).

Sonia Roccas and Marilynn B. Brewer. 2002. "Social Identity Complexity," *Personality and Social Psychology Review* 6 (2002), pp. 88-106.

Frantz Fanon, *Black Skin, White Masks,* trans. by Charles Lam Markmann, (New York: Grove Press, 1967), pp. 116, 110-112.

"Negroes in this country…" quote in Baldwin, *Fire Next Time,*

(New York: Knopf, 2014, org. 1963), p. 20.

The Clark Doll Experiments

Kenneth B. Clark & Mamie P. Clark, Racial Identification and Preference in Negro Children, in *Readings in Social Psychology*, Newcomb & Hartley, eds. (New York: Henry Holt, 1947).

Brown v. Board of Education of Topeka, Kansas, 347 U.S. 483 (1954) 347 U.S. 483.

Phillip Jordan, Maria Hernandez-Reif, "Reexamination of Young Children's Racial Attitudes and Skin Tone Preferences," *Journal of Black Psychology*, 35:3 (April 14, 2009), pp. 388 - 403.

Intersecting Identities

Ange-Marie Hancock, *Intersectionality: An Intellectual History* (New York: Oxford University Press, 2016).

Patricia Hill Collins and Sirma Bilge, *intersectionality* (Malden, Mass.: Polity Press, 2016).

Devon W. Carbado, "Colorblind Intersectionality," *Signs*, 38:4 (2013), pp. 811-845.

D.R. Williams, N. Priest, & N.B. Anderson, "Understanding Associations among Race, Socioeconomic Status, and Health: Patterns and Prospects," *Health Psychology*, 35:4 (2016), pp. 407-411; Tiffany N Brannon, Gerald D Higginbotham, Kyshia Henderson, "Class Advantages and Disadvantages are not so Black and White: Intersectionality Impacts Rank and Selves, *Current Opinion in Psychology*, vol. 18 (2017), pp. 117-122.

Stereotypes

Michael Pickering, *Stereotyping: The Politics of Representation* (New York: Palgrave, 2001).

Walter Lippmann, *Public Opinion*, (New York: Harcourt, Brace and Co., 1922), pp. 81, 90.

How Stereotypes Cause Harm

Susan Opotow, "Moral Exclusion and Injustice: An Introduction," *Journal of Social Issues*, 46:1 (1990), pp. 1-20.

Monica McDermott, *Working Class White: The Making and Unmaking of Race Relations* (Berkeley: University of California Press, 2006).

Matt Wray, *Not Quite White: White Trash and the Boundaries of Whiteness* (Durham, NC: Duke University Press, 2006).

Social Representation Theory

Serge Moscovici, in C. Herzlich, *Health and Illness: A Social Psychological Analysis* quoted in Miles Hewstone & J.M.F. Jaspars, "Intergroup Relations and Attribution Processes," in *Social Identity and Intergroup Relations*, Henri Tajfel, ed., (Cambridge University Press, 2010), p. 113.

Peter Berger and Thomas Luckmann, *The Social Construction of Reality: A Treatise in the Sociology of Knowledge*, (Garden City, NY: Anchor Books, 1966).

Michael Omi and Howard Winant, *Racial Formation in the United States* (New York: Routledge, 1986).

Wagner, Wolfgang. "Introduction: Aspects of Social Representation Theory." *Social Science Information*, 33:2 (1994), pp. 155-161.

Identity and Stereotype Threat

Claude M. Steele and Joshua Aronson, "Stereotype Threat and the Intellectual Test Performance of African Americans," *Journal of Personality and Social Psychology*, 69:5 (1995), pp. 797-811.

Claude M. Steele, "A Threat in the Air: How Stereotypes Shape Intellectual Identity and Performance," *American Psychologist*, 52:6 (1997), pp. 613-629.

Charlotte R. Pennington, et al. ,"Twenty Years of Stereotype Threat Research: A Review of Psychological Mediators," *PloS One*, 11:1 (2016).

Jim Blascovich, et al. ,"African Americans and High Blood Pressure: The Role of Stereotype Threat," *Psychological Science*, 12:3 (2001), pp. 225-229.

Min-Hsiung Huang, "Race of the Interviewer and the Black–White Test Score Gap," *Social Science Research*, 38:1 (2009), pp. 29-38.

Gregory M. Walton, Steven J. Spencer and Sam Erman, "Affirmative Meritocracy," *Social Issues and Policy Review*, 7:1 (2013), pp. 1-35.

Michael Inzlicht and Toni Schmader, *Stereotype Threat: Theory, Process, and Application* (New York: Oxford University Press, 2012).

Jeff Stone, et al., "Stereotype Threat Effects on Black and White Athletic Performance," *Journal of Personality and Social Psychology*, 77:6 (1999), pp. 1213-1227.

Chapter 10: Race & Perception

Race in the Unconscious Mind

Robert E. Rankin and Donald T. Campbell. "Galvanic Skin Response to Negro and White Experimenters," *The Journal of Abnormal and Social Psychology*, 51:1 (1955), pp. 30-33.

Frank R. Westie, and Melvin L. De Fleur. "Autonomic Responses and their Relationship to Race Attitudes," *The Journal of Abnormal and Social Psychology*, 58:3 (1959), pp. 340-347.

C. J. Vander Kolk, "Physiological Reactions of Black, Puerto Rican, and White Students in Suggested Ethnic Encounters," *The Journal of Social Psychology*, 104:First Half (1978), pp. 107.

John T. Cacioppo, et al. "Electromyographic Activity Over Facial Muscle Regions can Differentiate the Valence and Intensity of Affective Reactions," *Journal of Personality and Social Psychology*, 50:2 (1986), pp. 260-268.

Scott Vrana, and David Rollock. "Physiological Response to a Minimal Social Encounter: Effects of Gender, Ethnicity, and Social Context," *Psychophysiology*, 35:4 (1998), pp. 462-469.

Tiffany A. Ito and Keith B. Senholzi, "Us Versus them: Understanding the Process of Race Perception with Event-Related Brain Potentials," *Visual Cognition*, 21:9-10 (2013), pp. 1096-1120.

The Cognitive Economy

Sonia K. Kang and Galen V. Bodenhausen, "Multiple Identities in Social Perception and Interaction: Challenges and Opportunities," *Annual Review of Psychology*, 66 (Jan. 2015), pp. 547-574.

Tiffany A. Ito and Bruce D. Bartholow. "The Neural Correlates of Race," *Trends in Cognitive Sciences*, 12:12 (2009), pp. 524-531.

Leda Cosmides, John Tooby, Robert Kurzban, "Perceptions of Race," *Trends in Cognitive Sciences*, 7:4 (April 2003), pp. 173-179.

Jonathan B. Freeman, et al. "Looking the Part: Social Status Cues Shape Race Perception," *PloS One*, 6:9 (2011).

Andrew M. Penner and Aliya Saperstein. "How Social Status Shapes Race," *Proceedings of the National Academy of Sciences of the United States of America*, 105:50 (2008), pp. 19628-19630.

A.M. Penner and A. Saperstein, "Engendering Racial Perceptions: An Intersectional Analysis of How Social Status Shapes Race," *Gender & Society*, 27 (2013), pp. 319–344.

A. Noymer, A.M. Penner and A. Saperstein, "Cause of Death Affects Racial Classification on Death Certificates," *Plos One* 6 (2011), p. e15812.

Language and Perception

William A. Foley, "The Languages of New Guinea," *Annual Review of Anthropology*, 29 (2000), pp. 357-404.

Recent research indicates that color perception is highly influenced by language but curiously only in the right visual field. Terry Regier, Paul Kay, "Language, Thought, and Color: Whorf was Half Right," *Trends in Cognitive Sciences*, 13:10 (Oct. 2009), pp. 439-446.

O. Ozturk, S. Shayan, U. Liszkowski & A. Majid, 2013, "Language is Not Necessary for Color Categories," *Developmental Science*, 16:1 (2013), pp. 111-115.

Bem P. Allen, (1996), "African Americans' and European Americans' Mutual Attributions: Adjective Generation Technique (AGT) Stereotyping," *Journal of Applied Social Psychology*, 26 (1996), pp. 884–912.

Priming Stereotypes

J.L. Eberhardt, P.A. Goff, V.J. Purdie, P.G. Davies, "Seeing Black: Race, Crime, and Visual Processing," *Journal of Personality and Social Psychology*, 87 (2004), pp. 876–93.

Allison L. Skinner and Jacob E. Cheadle. "The "Obama Effect"? Priming Contemporary Racial Milestones Increases Implicit Racial Bias among Whites," *Social Cognition*, 34:6 (2016), pp. 544-558.

Gaither, Sarah E., et al. "Sounding Black Or White: Priming Identity and Biracial Speech," *Frontiers in Psychology*, 6 (2015), pp. 457.

A.J. Banks and M. A. Bell, "Racialized Campaign Ads: The Emotional Content in Implicit Racial Appeals Primes White Racial Attitudes," *Public Opinion Quarterly*, 77:2 (2013), pp. 549-560.

Vincent Cicchirillo, "Priming Stereotypical Associations: Violent Video Games and African American Depictions," *Communication Research Reports*, 32:2 (2015), pp. 122-131.

Ryan J. Hurley, et al. "Viewer Ethnicity Matters: Black Crime in TV News and its Impact on Decisions regarding Public Policy," *Journal of Social Issues*, 71:1 (2015), pp. 155-170.

Danielle M. Young, Justin D. Levinson and Scott Sinnett., "Innocent Until Primed: Mock Jurors' Racially Biased Response to the Presumption of Innocence" *PLoS One*, 9:3, (2014).

Jon Hurwitz and Mark Peffley, "Playing the Race Card in the Post-Willie Horton Era: The Impact of Racialized Code Words on Support for Punitive Crime Policy," *The Public Opinion Quarterly*, 69:1 (2005), pp. 99-112.

Developmental Understanding of Race and Racism

Katherine D. Kinzler, Elizabeth S. Spelke, "Do Infants Show Social Preferences for People Differing in Race?" *Cognition*, 119:1 (April 2011), pp. 1-9.

Lawrence A. Hirschfeld, "Do Children have a Theory of Race?" *Cognition*, 54:2, (1995), pp. 209-252.

"children develop…" quote in L.A. Hirschfeld, "The Child's Representation of Human Groups," *Psychology of Learning and Motivation*, 31 (1994b), pp. 133- 185.

Stephen M. Quintana, "Children's Developmental Understanding of Ethnicity and Race," *Applied and Preventive Psychology*, 7:1 (Winter 1998), pp. 27-45.

Clark McKown, and R.S. Weinstein, (2003). "The Development and Consequences of Stereotype-Consciousness in Middle Childhood," *Child Development*, 74:2 (2003), pp. 498 – 515.

Clark McKown, "Age and Ethnic Variation in Children's Thinking About the Nature of Racism," *Journal of Applied Developmental Psychology*, 25:5, (Sept.–Oct. 2004), pp. 597-617.

Benjamin Balas, Jessie Peissig, Margaret Moulson, "Children (But Not Adults) Judge Similarity in Own- and Other-Race Faces by the Color of their Skin," *Journal of Experimental Child Psychology*, 130 (February 2015), pp. 56-66.

Benjamin Balas, Charles A. Nelson, "The Role of Face Shape and Pigmentation in Other-Race Face Perception: An Electrophysiological Study," *Neuropsychologia*, 48:2 (Jan. 2010), pp. 498–506.

'Own Race Bias' Effect

Gustave A. Feingold, "The Influence of Environment on Identification of Persons and Things," *Journal of the American Institute of Criminal Law and Criminology*, 5:1 (1914), pp. 39-51.

C.A. Meissner, and J.C. Brigham, "Thirty Years of Investigating the Own-Race Bias in Memory for Faces - A Meta-Analytic Review," *Psychology Public Policy and Law*, 7:1 (2001), pp. 3-35.

Implicit Bias

Anthony G. Greenwald, Debbie E. McGhee and Jordan K.L. Schwartz, "Measuring Individual Differences in Implicit Cognition: The Implicit Association Test," 74 Journal of Personality and Social Psychology," 74 (1998), pp. 1464-80.

Justine E. Tinkler, "Controversies in Implicit Race Bias Research: Controversies in Implicit Race Bias Research," *Sociology Compass*, 6:12 (2012), pp. 987-997.
Anthony G. Greenwald, Mahzarin R. Banaji and Brian A. Nosek, "Statistically Small Effects of the Implicit Association Test can have Societally Large Effects," *Journal of Personality and Social Psychology*, 108:4, (2015), pp. 553-561.

Ivy W. Maina, Tanisha D. Belton, Sara Ginzberg, Ajit Singh and Tiffani J. Johnson, "A Decade of Studying Implicit Racial/Ethnic Bias in Healthcare Providers Using the Implicit Association Test," *Social Science & Medicine*, (May, 4, 2017).

Chloe FitzGerald and Samia Hurst, "Implicit Bias in Healthcare Professionals: A Systematic Review," *BMC Medical Ethics*, 18, (2017).

David R. Upton and C. E. Arrington, "Implicit Racial Prejudice Against African-Americans in Balanced Scorecard Performance Evaluations," *Critical Perspectives on Accounting*, 23:4-5 (2012), pp. 281-297.

Arusha Gordon and Ezra D. Rosenberg, "Barriers to the Ballot Box: Implicit Bias and Voting Rights in the 21st Century," *Michigan Journal of Race & Law*, 21:1 (2015), pp. 23.

Richard Alba, Rubén G. Rumbaut, and Karen Marotz. "A Distorted Nation: Perceptions of Racial/Ethnic Group Sizes and Attitudes Toward Immigrants and Other Minorities," *Social Forces*, 84:2 (2005), pp. 901-919.

Charles A. Gallagher, "Miscounting Race: Explaining Whites' Misperceptions of Racial Group Size," *Sociological Perspectives*, 46:3 (Fall 2003), pp. 381-396.

Cara Wong, "'Little' and 'Big' Pictures in our Heads: Race, Local Context, and Innumeracy about Racial Groups in the United States," *The Public Opinion Quarterly*, 71:3 (2007), pp. 392-412.

Robert Kunovich, "Perceptions of Racial Group Size in a Minority-Majority Area," *Sociological Perspectives*, 60:3 (2017), pp. 479-496.

The Justification-Suppression Model of Bias

"as helping scenarios contained…" quoted in Donald A. Saucier, Carol T. Miller and Nicole Doucet, "Differences in Helping Whites and Blacks: A Meta-Analysis," *Personality and Social Psychology Review* 2005, 9:1 (2005), pp. 2–16.

Zachary W. Brewster, Michael Lynn and Shelytia Cocroft, "Consumer Racial Profiling in U.S. Restaurants: Exploring Subtle Forms of Service Discrimination Against Black Diners," *Sociological Forum*, 29:2 (2014), pp. 476-495.

Perceptual Segregation

Russell K. Robinson, "Perceptual Segregation," *Columbia Law Review*, 108:5 (2008), pp. 1093-1180.

Jessica C. Nelson, Glenn Adams, and Phia S. Salter, "The Marley Hypothesis," *Psychological Science*, 24:2 (2012), pp. 213-218.

Robin DiAngelo, "White Fragility," *International Journal of Critical Pedagogy*, 3:3 (2011), pp. 54-70.

Ashley W. Doane and Eduardo Bonilla-Silva, *White Out: The Continuing Significance of Racism*, (New York: Routledge, 2003).

Race as Action

W.E.B. Du Bois, *The Souls of Black Folk: Essays and Sketches* (Chicago: A.C. McClurg, 8th. ed., 1909), p. 2.

David M. Katzman, *Seven Days a Week: Women and Domestic Service in Industrializing America* (New York: Oxford University Press, 1978), pp. 73-75.

"Blacks, I realized…" Sallie Bingham quoted in bell hooks, *Black Looks: Race and Representation* (New York: Routledge, 2014, org. 1992), p. 168.

William Shakespeare, *As You Like It*, Act II, Scene VII.

Chapter 11: Economics of Inequality

The Meritocratic Principle

"On Views of Race and Inequality, Blacks and Whites Are Worlds Apart," Pew Research Center, June 27, 2016.

Eileen Patten, "Racial, gender wage gaps persist in U.S. despite some progress," Pew Research Center, (July 1, 2016), http://www.pewresearch.org/fact-tank/2016/07/01/racial-gender-wage-gaps-persist-in-u-s-despite-some-progress/# .

Bernadette D. Proctor, Jessica L. Semega, and Melissa A. Kollar, *Income and Poverty in the United States: 2015 Current Population Reports*, (U.S. Census Bureau: Sept. 2016), p. 7.

"2012 Job Patterns for Minorities and Women in Private Industry," 2012 EEO-1 National Aggregate Report, U.S. Equal Employment Opportunity Commission, http://www1.eeoc.gov/eeoc/statistics/employment/jobpat-eeo1/2012/index.cfm#select_label

"State and Local Government Information (EEO-4), 2011 National Employment Summary," Equal Employment Opportunity Commission, http://www.eeoc.gov/eeoc/statistics/employment/jobpat-eeo4/2011/table1/table1.html

Devah Pager and Hana Shepherd, "The Sociology of Discrimination: Racial Discrimination in Employment, Housing, Credit, and Consumer Markets," *Annual Review of Sociology*, 34 (2008), pp. 181-209.

T. Shapiro, T. Meschede, and S. Osoro, *The Roots of the Widening Racial Wealth Gap: Explaining the Black–White Economic Divide* (Waltham, Mass.: Institute on Assets and Social Policy, Brandeis University, 2013).

Jennifer A. Richeson and Samuel R. Sommers, "Toward a Social Psychology of Race and Race Relations for the Twenty-First Century," *Annual Review of Psychology*, 67:1 (2016), pp.

439-463.

Hyeyeon Cicconi-Eggleston, "An Examination of Hiring in the U.S. Private Sector: Ethical Considerations in Hiring Decisions," (Ph.D. Diss. ,University of Maryland, 2014), pp. 5-7.

Kathryn Dill, "Study: Half Of All Available Jobs Are Never Advertised," *Forbes*, Aug. 20, 2014.

Meschede, Tatjana, et al. "Wealth Mobility of Families Raising Children in the Twenty-First Century," *Race and Social Problems*, 8:1 (2016), pp. 77-92.

Algernon Austin, "The Unfinished March: An Overview," Economic Policy Institute (Washington, DC, June 18, 2013), http://www.epi.org/publication/unfinished-march-overview/

Larry M. Logue and Peter Blanck, ""Benefit of the Doubt": African-American Civil War Veterans and Pensions," *The Journal of Interdisciplinary History*, 38:3 (2008), pp. 377-399.

Convict Leasing and Forced Labor

One Dies, Get Another: Convict Leasing in the American South, 1866-1928 (University of South Carolina Press, 1996).

Scott R. Nelson, *Steel Drivin' Man: John Henry, the Untold Story of an American Legend* (New York, Oxford University Press, 2006).

Pete Daniel, "Up from Slavery and Down to Peonage: The Alonzo Bailey Case," *The Journal of American History*, 57:3 (Dec. 1970), pp. 654-670.

U.S. Supreme Court, *Bailey v. Alabama*, 219 U.S. 219 (1911).

Adam Cohen, *Imbeciles: The Supreme Court, American Eugenics, and the Sterilization of Carrie Buck* (New York: Penguin Press, 2016), p. 236.

Paul D. Moreno, Black Americans and Organized Labor: A New History (Baton Rouge: Louisiana State University Press, 2006).

"...we found that" quote in Karin A. Shapiro, *A New South Rebellion: The Battle Against Convict Labor in the Tennessee Coalfields, 1871-1896* (Chapel Hill: University of North Carolina Press, 1998), p. 52.

Third Biennial Report of the Inspectors of Convicts...1888 to 1890, (Montgomery, Al.: Brown Printing Co, 1890), p. 97.

William S. Kiser, *Borderlands of Slavery: The Struggle Over Captivity and Peonage in the American Southwest* (Philadelphia: University of Pennsylvania Press, 2017).

Douglas A. Blackmon, *Slavery By Another Name: The Re-Enslavement of Black Americans from the Civil War to World War II* (New York: Doubleday, 2008).

"Year after year..." quote in Patrick O'Daniel, *When the Levee Breaks: Memphis and the Mississippi Valley Flood of 1927*, (Charleston, S.C.: The History Press, 2013).

Classical Economics and Racism

John R. Commons, *Races and Immigrants in America* (New York: MacMillan, 1907), p. 150.

"If a white man gets…" quote in David R. Roediger and Elizabeth D. Esch, *The Production of Difference: Race and the Management of Labor in U.S. History* (New York: Oxford University Press, 2012), p. 63.

Edna Bonacich, "A Theory of Ethnic Antagonism: The Split Labor Market," in *The American Working Class: Prospects for the 1980s*, Irving Louis Horowitz, John C. Leggett, and Martin Oppenheimer, eds. (New Brunswick, N.J.: Transaction Books, 1979), pp. 73-93; see also Ralph Fevre, *Cheap Labour and Racial Discrimination* (Brookfield, VT: Gower, 1984), p. 148.

Devah Pager and Diana Karafin, "Bayesian Bigot? Statistical Discrimination, Stereotypes, and Employer Decision Making," *The Annals of the American Academy of Political and Social Science*, 621 (2009), pp. 70–93.

"we were overwhelmed..." quote in Joleen Kirschenman, and Katherine Neckerman,"We'd love to hire them, but . . . : The meaning of race for employers," in *The Urban Underclass*, ed. Christopher Jencks and Paul E. Peterson, (Washington, DC: Brookings Institution, 1991), pp. 203-234.

Last Hired First Fired

Michelle Haberland, *Striking Beauties: Women Apparel Workers in the U.S. South, 1930-2000* (Athens: The University of Georgia Press, 2015).

"the Negro is an undesirable…" quote in Robert H. Zeiger, *For Jobs and Freedom: Race and Labor in America Since 1865* (Lexington: University Press of Kentucky, 2007), p. 102.

Herbert Hill, *Black Labor and the American Legal System: Race, Work, and the Law (*Washington, D.C.: The Bureau of National Affairs, Inc., 1977).

Color Bars to the Medical Professions

Thomas J. Ward, Jr., *Black Physicians in the Jim Crow South* (Fayetteville: The University of Arkansas Press, 2003).

Hubert A. Eaton, *Every Man Should Try* (Wilmington, N.C.: Bonaparte Press, 1984);

Robert Baker, Harriet Washington, Ololade Olakanmi, Matthew K Wynia, "African American Physicians and Organized Medicine, 1846-1968: Origins of a Racial Divide," *JAMA The Journal of the American Medical Association*, 300:3 (August 2008), pp. 306-13.

Harriet A. Washington; Robert B. Baker, Ololade Olakanmi; Todd L. Savitt, Elizabeth A. Jacobs, Eddie Hoover, Matthew K. Wynia, "Segregation, Civil Rights, and Health Disparities: The Legacy of African American Physicians and Organized Medicine, 1910-1968," *Journal of the National Medical Association*, 101:6, (June 2009), pp. 513-527.

Ira Katznelson, When Affirmative Action was White: An Untold History of Racial Inequality in Twentieth-Century America, (New York: Norton, 2005), p. 34.

Education

Celeste K. Carruthers and Marianne H. Wanamaker, "Separate

and Unequal in the Labor Market: Human Capital and the Jim Crow Wage Gap," *NBER Working Paper,* No. 21947 (Cambridge, Mass.: National Bureau of Economic Research, January 2016).

Ronald E. Butchart, *Schooling the Freed People: Teaching, Learning, and the Struggle for Black Freedom, 1861-1876* (University of North Carolina, Chapel Hill, 2010), p. 1.

Thomas Barton abductor quote in Butchart, *Schooling the Freed People*, p. 176.

J. A. Hardin, *Fifty Years of Segregation: Black Higher Education in Kentucky, 1904-1954* (Lexington: The University Press of Kentucky, 2015).
Christopher J. Lucas, *American Higher Education: A History* (New York: St. Martin's Griffin, 1994), p. 164.

"Equal Protection of the Laws in Public Higher Education," United States Commission on Civil Rights (Washington, D.C.: Government Printing Office, 1961).

Charles C. Bolton, *Hardest Deal of All : The Battle Over School Integration in Mississippi, 1870-1980* (University Press of Mississippi, 2007).

Thomas A. Upchurch, *Legislating Racism: The Billion Dollar Congress and the Birth of Jim Crow* (Lexington: University Press of Kentucky, 2015), ch. 2.

Celeste K. Carruthers and Marianne H. Wanamaker, "Separate and Unequal in the Labor Market: Human Capital and the Jim Crow Wage Gap," *NBER Working Paper,* No. 21947 (Cambridge, Mass.: National Bureau of Economic Research, January 2016).

R.A. Margo, *Race and Schooling in the South, 1880-1950: An Economic History* (Chicago: The University of Chicago Press, 1990).

Gary Blasi, "Advocacy Against the Stereotype: Lessons from Cognitive Social Psychology," in *Critical Race Realism: Intersections of Psychology, Race, and Law* (New York: The New Press, 2008), pp. 45-63.

Civil War Pensions

Peter David Blanck, Michael Millender, "Before Disability Civil Rights: Civil War Pensions and the Politics of Disability in America," *Alabama Law Review*, 52:1 (Fall 2000), pp. 1-50.

Larry M. Logue and Peter Blanck, ""Benefit of the Doubt": African-American Civil War Veterans and Pensions," *The Journal of Interdisciplinary History*, 38:3 (2008), pp. 377-399.

Shari Eli and Laura Salisbury, "Patronage Politics and the Development of the Welfare State: Confederate Pensions in the American South," *Journal of Economic History*, 76:4 (December 2016), pp. 1078-1112.

Aid for Mothers

"tended to restrict…" Winifred Bell, quoted in Deborah E. Ward, *The White Welfare State: The Racialization of U.S. Welfare Policy* (Ann Arbor: Univ. of Michigan, 2005), p. 90.

Harrison quote in Mary Poole, *The Segregated Origins of Social Security: African Americans and the Welfare State* (Chapel Hill: University of North Carolina Press, 2006), p. 37.

David R. Roediger, Working Toward Whiteness: How America's Immigrants Became White: The Strange Journey from Ellis Island to the Suburbs (New York: Basic Books, 2005).

Aid to Farmers

"America's Diverse Family Farms: 2016 Edition," *Economic Information Bulletin* No. 164, Economic Research Service, USDA (Dec. 2016).

"Farm Demographics," *2012 Census of Agriculture: Highlights*, ACH12-3 (May 2014), Nat. Agric. Statistics Service, USDA.

Negro Population, 1790-1915, Bureau of the Census, Department of Commerce, (Government Printing Office, 1918), pp. 461, 503, 505.

Revised Statutes of The United States, 43rd Cong., 1st sess. (1873), Sec. 2302, p. 424.

Jason Pierce, *Making the White Man's West: Whiteness and the Creation of the American West* (Boulder: University Press of Colorado, 2016).

Richard Edwards, "Why the Homesteading Data Are So Poor…" *Great Plains Quarterly* 28 (Summer 2008), pp. 181-190.

George Lipsitz, *How Racism Takes Place* (Philadelphia: Temple University Press, 2011), p. 2.

Canaday, Neil, Charles Reback, and Kristin Stowe. "Race and Local Knowledge: New Evidence from the Southern Homestead Act," *The Review of Black Political Economy*, 42:4 (2015), pp. 399-413.

Neil Canaday and Charles Reback, "Race, Literacy, and Real Estate Transactions in the Postbellum South," *Journal of Economic History,* 70:2 (June 2010), pp. 428–45.

Adrianne Petty, "The Jim Crow Section of Agricultural History," in Bennett, Evan P., Debra A. Reid, eds., *Beyond Forty Acres and a Mule: African American Landowning Families since Reconstruction* (Gainesville: University Press of Florida, 2012), p. 27.

Valerie B. Grimm, "Between Forty Acres and a Class Action Lawsuit Black Farmers, Civil Rights, and Protest against the U.S. Department of Agriculture, 1997–2010," in Bennett, Evan P., Debra A. Reid, eds., *Beyond Forty Acres and a Mule: African American Landowning Families since Reconstruction* (Gainesville: University Press of Florida, 2012), p. 273.

United States Commission on Civil Rights, "Equal Opportunity in Farm Programs: An Appraisal of Services Rendered by the United States Department of Agriculture," (Washington: Govt. Printing Office, 1965), p. 8.

Grim, Valerie. "Black Participation in the Farmers Home Administration and Agricultural Stabilization and Conservation Service, 1964-1990," *Agricultural History*, 70:2 (1996), pp. 321–336.

Pete Daniel, *Dispossession: Discrimination Against African American Farmers in the Age of Civil Rights* (Chapel Hill: University of

440

North Carolina Press, 2013).

Rural Electrification

Jill Jonnes, *Empires Of Light: Edison, Tesla, Westinghouse, And The Race To Electrify The World* (New York: Random House, 2004), p. 79.

Harvey K. Newman, "Race and the Tourist Bubble in Downtown Atlanta," *Urban Affairs Review*, 37:3 (2002), pp. 301-321.

Conor M. Harrison, "Power For All? Electricity and Uneven Development in North Carolina," (Ph.D. Diss., University of North Carolina, Chapel Hill, 2014)

Carl Kitchens, Price Fishback, "Flip the Switch: The Spatial Impact of the Rural Electrification Administration 1935-1940," *NBER Working Paper* No. 19743 (December 2013).

Encyclopedia of African American History, 1896 to the Present: From the Age of Segregation to the Twenty-First Century, Paul Finkelman, ed. (New York, Oxford University Press, 2009), vol. 4, p. 436.

Leah S. Glaser, *Electrifying the Rural American West: Stories of Power, People, and Place* (Lincoln: University of Nebraska Press, 2009).

The G.I. Bill

Maggie Rivas-Rodriguez, B. V. Olguín, eds., *Latina/os and World War II: Mobility, Agency, and Ideology* (Austin: University of Texas Press, 2014), p. xvi.

"The Army and Diversity," Center of Military History, U.S. Army, http://www.history.army.mil/html/faq/diversity.html#asian.

Ira Katznelson, *When Affirmative Action was White: An Untold History of Racial Inequality in Twentieth-Century America*, (New York: Norton, 2005).

George Lipsitz, *How Racism Takes Place* (Philadelphia: Temple University Press, 2011), pp. 2-4.

"On Views of Race and Inequality, Blacks and Whites Are Worlds Apart," Pew Research Center, June 27, 2016.

Whiteness as Property

Harris, Cheryl I. "Whiteness as Property," *Harvard Law Review*, 106:8 (1993), pp. 1707-1791.

"Although to publish in a newspaper of a white woman that she is a Negro imputes no mental, moral or physical fault for which she may justly be held accountable to public opinion, yet in view of the social habits and customs deep-rooted in this State, such publication is calculated to affect her standing in society and to injure her in the estimation of her friends and acquaintances. That such a publication is libelous per se is supported by the very great weight of authority," *Bowen v. Independent Publishing Co. Supreme Court of South Carolina* (February 6, 1957), 230 S.C. 509 (1957).

William Hoffer, "Plessy v. Ferguson: The Effects of Lawyering on a Challenge to Jim Crow: Plessy v. Ferguson," *Journal of Supreme Court History*, 39:1 (2014), pp. 1-21.

Plessy quotes from Cheryl I. Harris, "Whiteness as Property," *Harvard Law Review*, 106:8 (1993), pp. 1707–1791.

Chapter 12: The Color of Politics

"A man with a ballot…" quote in "The Constitutional Amendment," *The National Anti-Slavery Standard*, Mar. 20, 1869.

Jeff Manza and Christopher Uggen, *Locked Out: Felon Disenfranchisement and American Democracy* (New York: Oxford Univ. Press, 2006), p. 42.

Judgment in the U.S. Supreme Court Case Dred Scott v. John F.A. Sanford, March 6, 1857; Case Files 1792-1995; Record Group 267; Records of the Supreme Court of the United States; National Archives.

Phyllis F. Field, *The Politics of Race in New York: The Struggle for Black Suffrage in the Civil War Era* (Ithaca, N.Y.: Cornell University Press, 1982), p. 199.

The Constitution vs. Force

1866 Civil Rights Act, "An Act to protect all Persons in the United States in their Civil Rights, and furnish the Means of their Vindication," 14 Stat. 27-30, April 9, 1866.

Creeping Disenfranchisement

David Southern, *The Progressive Era and Race: Reaction and Reform, 1900-1917*, (Wheeling, Ill.: Harlan Davidson, 2005).

J. Morgan Kousser, *Colorblind Injustice: Minority Voting Rights and the Undoing of the Second Reconstruction* (Chapel Hill: University of North Carolina Press, 1999), pp. 20-21.

Henry McNeal Turner quote in Thomas A. Upchurch, *Legislating Racism: The Billion Dollar Congress and the Birth of Jim Crow* (Lexington: University Press of Kentucky, 2015), p. 21.

Xi Wang, *The Trial of Democracy: Black Suffrage and Northern Republicans, 1860-1910* (Athens: University of Georgia Press, 1997), pp. 257-259.

Richard B. Sherman, *The Republican Party and Black America: From McKinley to Hoover, 1896-1933* (Charlottesville: University Press of Virginia, 1973).

Edwin T. Arnold, *What Virtue There Is in Fire: Cultural Memory and the Lynching of Sam Hose* (Athens: University of Georgia Press, 2009), pp. 31-33.

Complete Disenfranchisement

Adam Cohen, *Imbeciles: The Supreme Court, American Eugenics, and the Sterilization of Carrie Buck* (New York: Penguin Press, 2016), pp. 233-235.

Benjamin R. Justesen, *George Henry White: An Even Chance in the Race of Life* (Baton Rouge: Louisiana State University Press, 2001), p. 311.

Deborah Grey White, *Ar'nt I a Woman?: Female Slaves in the Plantation South* (rev. ed., New York: Norton, 1999), p. 188.

McGuire, Danielle L. "'It Was like All of Us Had Been Raped': Sexual Violence, Community Mobilization, and the African

American Freedom Struggle," *The Journal of American History*, 91:3 (2004), pp. 906–931.

Taft quoted in Paul Frymer, *Uneasy Alliances: Race and Party Competition in America*, (Princeton, N.J.: Princeton University Press, 1999), p. 84.

Racial Discrimination and the Courts

R. Volney Riser, *Defying Disfranchisement: Black Voting Rights Activism in the Jim Crow South, 1890-1908* (Baton Rouge: Louisiana State University Press, 2010).

James W. Loewen, *Sundown Towns: A Hidden Dimension of American Racism*, (New York: Touchstone Books, 2005), p. 94.

White Primaries

Steven F. Lawson, *Black Ballots: Voting Rights in the South, 1944-1969* (New York: Columbia Univ. Press, 1976).

Gerrymandering

J. Morgan Kousser, *Colorblind Injustice: Minority Voting Rights and the Undoing of the Second Reconstruction* (Chapel Hill: University of North Carolina Press, 1999).

Immigrant Voting Rights

Alexander Keysar, *The Right to Vote: The Contested History of Democracy in the United States* (New York: Basic Books, 2000), pp. 27-28, 110-112, 337-8.

Native Voting Rights

Stephen D Bodayla, "'Can An Indian Vote?': Elk v Wilkins, A Setback for Indian Citizenship," *Nebraska History,* 67 (1986), pp. 372-380.

The Era of Avoidance

Niall Palmer, "More than a Passive Interest," *Journal of American Studies*, 48:2 (May 2014), pp. 417-443.

"fill such jobs…" quoted in Douglas B. Craig, *After Wilson: The Struggle for the Democratic Party, 1920-1934* (Univ. of North Carolina Press, 1992), p. 174.

Christopher Brian Booker, *The Black Presidential Nightmare: African-Americans and Presidents, 1789–2016* (Xlibris, 2017).

Samuel O'Dell, "Blacks, the Democratic Party, and the Presidential Election of 1928: A Mild Rejoinder." *Phylon*, 48:1 (1987), pp. 1-11.

"it does not matter…" quoted in Antonie L. Joseph, *The Dynamics of Racial Progress: Economic Inequality and Race Relations Since Reconstruction*, (New York: Routledge, 2005), p. 98.

Richard B. Sherman, *The Republican Party and Black America: From McKinley to Hoover, 1896-1933* (Charlottesville: University Press of Virginia, 1973).

Jeremy D. Mayer, *Running on Race: Racial Politics in Presidential Campaigns, 1960-2000* (New York: Random House, 2002), p. 46.

Ian Haney López, *Dog Whistle Politics: How Coded Racial Appeals Have Reinvented Racism and Wrecked the Middle Class* (New York: Oxford University Press, 2014), p. 20.

Steven F. Lawson, *Black Ballots: Voting Rights in the South, 1944-1969* (New York: Columbia University Press, 1976).

Michael K. Fountroy, *Republicans and the Black Vote* (Boulder, CO: Lynne Reinner Publishers, 2007).

"…I say to you…" quote from Jimmy Carter, Inaugural Address, Jan. 12, 1971, Carter Presidential Library.

"The sound of Lester…" quoted in Jeremy D. Mayer, *Running on Race: Racial Politics in Presidential Campaigns, 1960-2000* (New York: Random House, 2002), p. 127.

"Perhaps part of Reagan's appeal…" Jeremy D. Mayer, *Running on Race: Racial Politics in Presidential Campaigns, 1960-2000* (New York: Random House, 2002), p. 165.

"You start out in 1954…" quote in Rick Perlstein, "Exclusive: Lee Atwater's Infamous 1981 Interview on the Southern Strategy," *The Nation*, Nov. 13, 2012.

Rebecca Kaplan, *CBS News*, November 4, 2012, 11:04 PM.

J. Eric Oliver, *The Paradoxes of Integration: Race, Neighborhood, and Civil Life in Multiethnic America*, (Chicago: University of Chicago Press, 2010).

Belkhir, Jean A. "Afterword. Race, Gender, Class Lessons from the 2008 Presidential Election," *Race, Gender & Class*, 15:3/4 (2008), pp. 127-138.

Tolbert, Caroline J. "Mini Symposium: Race and the 2008 Presidential Election," *Political Research Quarterly*, 63:4 (2010), pp. 860-862.

Greenwald, Anthony G., et al. "Implicit Race Attitudes Predicted Vote in the 2008 U.S. Presidential Election," *Analyses of Social Issues and Public Policy*, 9:1 (2009), pp. 241-253.

Tom Scocca, "Eighty-Eight Percent of Romney Voters Were White: The GOP candidate's race-based, monochromatic campaign made him a loser," *Slate*, Nov. 7, 2012.

Moses Frenck, "Black Delegates at GOP Convention at Lowest Level in History," *Diversity Inc.*, July 20, 2016 http://www.diversityinc.com/news/black-delegates-gop-convention-lowest-level-history/

David A. Bositis, "Blacks and the 2012 Republican Convention," Joint Center for Political and Economic Studies (Washington, DC: 2012) http://jointcenter.org/sites/default/files/Blacks%20and%20the%202012%20Republican%20National%20Convention.pdf

Thomas Wood, "Racism Motivated Trump Voters More Than Authoritarianism," *Washington Post*, Apr. 17, 2017.

Alec Tyson and Shiva Maniam, "Behinds Trump Victory: Divisions by Race, Gender, Education," (Pew Research Center, Nov. 9, 2016) http://www.pewresearch.org/fact-tank/2016/11/09/behind-trumps-victory-divisions-by-race-gender-education/

Avidit Acharya, Matthew Blackwell, and Maya Sen, "The Political Legacy of American Slavery," *Journal of Politics* (Feb. 2016).

Structural Disenfranchisement

Neil Malhotra, Connor Raso, "Racial Representation and U.S. Senate Apportionment," *Social Science Quarterly*, 88:4, (Dec. 2007), pp. 1038-1048.

Jamin Raskin, "Lawful Disenfranchisement: America's Structural Democracy Deficity," *American Bar Association Magazine*, 32:2 (Spring 2005).

Felon Disenfranchisement

Jeff Manza and Christopher Uggen, *Locked Out: Felon Disenfranchisement and American Democracy* (New York: Oxford University Press, 2006).

Michelle Alexander, *The New Jim Crow: Mass Incarceration in the Age of Colorblindness* (New York: The New Press, 2010).

Atul Bhattarai, Emily Ericksen, and Boris Litvin, "Anatomy: Race and Incarceration," *World Policy Journal*, 33:1 (2016), pp. 12-13.

Robert DeFina and Lance Hannon, "The Impact of Mass Incarceration on Poverty," *Crime & Delinquency*, 59:4 (2013), pp. 562-586. In fact, the actual swing in terms of poverty statistics would have been closer to 20% because government statistics do not count those in prison as being in 'poverty' though the vast majority were in this status before they were sentenced. Best estimates are that published poverty rates were artificially 10% lower because of the exclusion of inmates during this period.

Jack Glaser, *Suspect race: Causes and Consequences of Racial Profiling* (New York: Oxford University Press, 2014).

Chapter 13: Engineering Segregation

Before Housing Segregation

Paul A. Gilje, "The Baltimore Riots of 1812 and the Breakdown of the Anglo-American Mob Tradition," *Journal of Social History*, 13:4 (1980), pp. 547-564.

David Grimsted, "Rioting in Its Jacksonian Setting," *The American Historical Review*, 77:2 (1972), pp. 361-397.

John M. Werner, *Reaping the Bloody Harvest: Race Riots in the United States during the Age of Jackson, 1824-1849* (New York: Garland, 1986).

Silas N.T. Crowfoot, "Community Development for a White City: Race Making, Improvementism, and the Cincinnati Race Riots and Anti-Abolition Riots of 1829, 1836, and 1841," (Ph.D. Diss., Portland State University, 2010).

"Riot in Cincinnati..." quoted in Crowfoot, Silas N. T. *Community Development for a White City: Race Making, Improvementism, and the Cincinnati Race Riots and Anti-Abolition Riots of 1829, 1836, and 1841*, p. 207.

John Runcie, ""Hunting the Nigs" in Philadelphia: The Race Riot of August 1834," *Pennsylvania History*, 39:2 (1972), pp. 187-218.

"That all Chinamen be expelled..." quoted in Carranco, Lynwood. "Chinese Expulsion from Humboldt County." *Pacific Historical Review*, 30:4 (1961), pp. 329-340.

"a concerted movement..." quote in Alexander Saxton, *The Indispensable Enemy: Labor and the Anti-Chinese Movement in California* (Berkeley: University of California Press, 1971), p. 209.

Sucheng Chan, "Chinese Livelihood in Rural California: The Impact of Economic Change, 1860-1880," *Pacific Historical Review*, 53:3 (1984), pp. 273-307.

Ethnic Cleansing in the North

Elliot Jaspin, *Buried in the Bitter Waters: The Hidden History of Racial Cleansing in America* (New York: Basic Books, 2007).

James W. Loewen, *Sundown Towns: A Hidden Dimension of American Racism*, (New York: Touchstone, 2005).

Lewinnek, Elaine. *The Mortgages of Whiteness*, (New York: Oxford University Press, 2014).

"I want to explain to you..." quote in Elaine Lewinnek, *The Mortgages of Whiteness*, (New York: Oxford University Press, 2014), p. 158.

C.K. Doreski, "From News to History: Robert Abbott and Carl Sandburg Read the 1919 Chicago Riot." *African American Review*, vol. 26, no. 4, 1992, pp. 637–650.

"Keep the Negro in his place..." and ""members of any race..." quotes in Elaine Lewinnek, *The Mortgages of Whiteness*, p. 171.

Michael D'Orso, *Like Judgment Day: The Ruin and Redemption of a Town Called Rosewood*, (New York: G.P. Putnam's Sons, 1996).

Edward Gonzalez-Tennant, *Archaeological Research and Public Knowledge: New Media Methods for Public Archaeology in Rosewood, Florida*, (University of Florida, Ph.D. Diss., 2011).

R.T. Dye, "Rosewood, Florida: The Destruction of an African American Community." *The Historian*, vol. 58, no. 3, 1996, pp. 605-622.

Tulsa Race Riot: A Report by the Oklahoma Commission to Study the Tulsa Race Riot of 1921, (Oklahoma, Feb. 21, 2001).

Alfred L. Brophy, *Reconstructing the Dreamland: The Tulsa Race Riot of 1921 : Race, Reparations, and Reconciliation*, (New York: Oxford University Press, 2003).

James S. Hirsch, *Riot and Remembrance: The Tulsa Race War and its Legacy*, (Boston: Houghton Mifflin Company, 2002).

20th Century Housing Segregation

Richard Rothstein, *The Color of Politics: A Forgotten History of How Our Government Segregated America* (New York: Liveright, 2017).

"ordinance for preserving peace..." quote in Garrett Power, "Apartheid Baltimore Style: The Residential Segregation Ordinances of 1910-1913," *Maryland Law Review* 42 (1982), pp. 289.

Christopher Silver, "The Racial Origins of Zoning in American Cities," in Thomas Manning, June and Marsha Ritzdorf, eds.

Urban Planning and the African American Community: In the Shadows, (Thousand Oaks, CA: Sage Publications, 1997).

Racial Covenants

"The Welles-Bowen Company, 1908-1968," (Unpublished manuscript, n.d.), pp. 3, Toledo-Lucas County Public Library; "At no time shall any lot in Westmoreland…" quote in "Westmoreland Declaration of Restrictions," *Register of Deeds*, vol. 503, pp. 1-7, Lucas County Recorder's Office; "Toledo Real Property Survey," (Toledo Metropolitan Housing Authority: Works Progress Administration Project #17971, Final Report, 1939), pp. 23-25, Toledo-Lucas County Public Library.

"a realtor should never be…" quote in Douglas Massey and Nancy A. Denton, *American Apartheid: Segregation and the Making of the Underclass*, (Cambridge, Mass.: Harvard University Press, 1993), p. 37.

Charles Bird, Elio D. Monachesi, and Harvey Burdick. "Infiltration and the Attitudes of White and Negro Parents and Children," *The Journal of Abnormal and Social Psychology*, 47:3 (1952), pp. 688-699.

Federal Public Housing Policy

Edward G. Goetz, *New Deal Ruins: Race, Economic Justice, and Housing Policy* (Ithaca, N.Y.: Cornell University Press, 2013), esp. ch. 1.

"With their low-rise profiles…" quote in Joseph Heathcott, "Myth #1: Public Housing Stands Alone," in *Public Housing Myths: Perception, Reality, and Social Policy*, Nicholas Degan Bloom, Fritz Umbach, and Lawrence J. Vale, eds., (Ithaca, N.Y.: Cornell University Press, 2013), p. 34.

"the quality of the hardware was so poor…" quote in Katharine G. Bristol, "The Pruitt-Igoe Myth," *Journal of Architectural Education,* 44:3 (1991), pp. 163-171.

"least desirable…" quote in D. Bradford Hunt, "Myth #2: Modernist Architecture Failed Public Housing," in *Public Housing Myths: Perception, Reality, and Social Policy*, Nicholas Degan Bloom, Fritz Umbach, and Lawrence J. Vale, eds., (Ithaca, N.Y.: Cornell University Press, 2013), p. 52.

Statistics on black urban population growth in Mark H. Rose and Raymond A. Mohl, *Interstate: Highway Politics and Policy since 1939*, (Knoxville: The University of Tennessee Press, 2012), pp. 103-104.

"very few blacks live in Minnesota…" quoted in Mark H. Rose and Raymond A. Mohl, *Interstate: Highway Politics and Policy since 1939*, pp. 108-109.

Redlining

"if a neighborhood is to retain stability…" quote in Richard Rothstein, *The Color of Politics: A Forgotten History of How Our Government Segregated America* (New York: Liveright, 2017), p. 8.

Douglas S. Massey, "Origins of Economic Disparities: The Historical Role of Housing Segregation," in *Segregation: The Rising Costs for America*, James H. Carr and Nandinee K. Kutty, eds.,

(New York: Routledge, 2008).

"is virtually 100% white…" quote in James W. Loewen, *Sundown Towns: A Hidden Dimension of American Racism*, (New York: Touchstone, 2005), p. 49.

Daniel T. Lichter, Domenico Parisi, and Michael C. Taquino, "Toward a New Macro-Segregation? Decomposing Segregation within and between Metropolitan Cities and Suburbs," *American Sociological Review*, 80:4 (2015), pp. 843-873.

Housing Discrimination in the 21st Century

Devah Pager and Hana Shepherd, "The Sociology of Discrimination: Racial Discrimination in Employment, Housing, Credit, and Consumer Markets," *Annual Review of Sociology*, 34 (2008), pp. 181–209.

Martin Garrett, Land Use Regulation: The Impacts of Alternative Land Use Rights (New York: Praeger Publishers, 1987).

William Fischel, "An Economic History of Zoning and a Cure for its Exclusionary Effects," *Urban Studies*, 41:2 (2004), pp. 317-340.

Peter Ganong and Daniel Shoag, "Why Has Regional Income Convergence in the U.S. Declined?" Harvard University, January 2015, http://scholar.harvard.edu/files/shoag/files/why_has_regional_income_convergence_in_the_us_declined_01.pdf

"Housing Development Tool Kit," White House, Sept. 2016, https://www.whitehouse.gov/sites/whitehouse.gov/files/images/Housing_Development_Toolkit%20f.2.pdf

Index of Dissimilarity in Douglas S. Massey, "Origins of Economic Disparities: The Historical Role of Housing Segregation," in *Segregation: The Rising Costs for America*, James H. Carr and Nandinee K. Kutty, eds., (New York: Routledge, 2008), Table 2.1, p. 42.

Table 5-2, "Residential Segregation Indexes for Blacks or African Americans by Characteristics of Selected Metropolitan Areas: 1980, 1990, and 2000," *Racial and Ethnic Residential Segregation in the United States: 1980-2000: Census 2000 Special Reports*, (Washington, D.C., Aug. 2002), p. 64.

Lawrence D. Bobo, Camille Z. Charles, Maria Krysan, and Alicia D. Simmons, "The Real Record on Racial Attitudes," in Peter V. Marsden, ed., *Social Trends in American Life: Findings from the General Social Survey since 1972*, (Princeton: Princeton University Press, 2012), p. 45-50.

John Iceland and Gregory Sharp, "White Residential Segregation in U.S. Metropolitan Areas: Conceptual Issues, Patterns, and Trends from the U.S. Census, 1980 to 2010," *Population Research and Policy Review*, 32:5, (2013), pp. 663-686; John Iceland, "Beyond Black and White - Metropolitan Residential Segregation in Multi-Ethnic America," *Social Science Research*, 33:2 (2004), pp. 248-271.

Mary J. Fischer, "Shifting Geographies: Examining the Role of Suburbanization in Blacks' Declining Segregation," *Urban Affairs Review*, 43:4 (2008), pp. 475-496.

Maria Krysan and Reynolds Farley, "The Residential

Preferences of Blacks: Do they Explain Persistent Segregation?" *Social Forces*, 80:3 (2002), pp. 937-980.

Richard Wright, et al. "Patterns of Racial Diversity and Segregation in the United States: 1990-2010," *Professional Geographer*, 66:2, (May 2014), pp. 173-182.

John Iceland, Daniel H. Weinberg, and Erika Steinmetz, U.S. Census Bureau, Series CENSR-3, *Racial and Ethnic Residential Segregation in the United States: 1980-2000* (Washington, D.C.: U.S. Government Printing Office, 2002), p. 63.

Lichter, Daniel T., Domenico Parisi, and Michael C. Taquino. "Toward a New Macro-Segregation? Decomposing Segregation within and between Metropolitan Cities and Suburbs," *American Sociological Review*, 80:4 (2015), pp. 843-873.

Chapter 14: The Color-Blind Era

Nichelle Nichols, *Beyond Uhura: Star Trek and Other Memories* (New York: G.P. Putnam's, 1994), pp. 160, 196, 308.

Opinion surveys results in John F. Dovidio and Samuel L. Gaertner, "Changes in the Expression and Assessment of Racial Prejudice," in Harry Knopke, et al. *Opening Doors: Perspectives on Race Relations in Contemporary America*, (Tuscaloosa: University of Alabama Press, 1991).

Lawrence D. Bobo, Camille Z. Charles, Maria Krysan, and Alicia D. Simmons, "The Real Record on Racial Attitudes," in Peter V. Marsden, ed., S*ocial Trends in American Life: Findings from the General Social Survey since 1972*, (Princeton: Princeton University Press, 2012), p. 45-50.

R.G. Fryer Jr., "Guess who's been coming to dinner? Trends in interracial marriage over the 20th century," *Journal of Economic Perspectives*, 21 (2007), pp. 71–90.

G. Hitsch, A. Hortacsu, D. Ariely, "What makes you click? An empirical analysis of online dating. UCSC Economics Department Seminars Paper 3 (2004) http://repositories. cdlib.org/ ucsc econ seminar/winter2005/3

Color-Blind Racism

MTV/David Binder Study, Executive Summary, 2014. http://d1fqdnmgwphrky.cloudfront.net/studies/000/000/001/DBR_MTV_Bias_Survey_Executive_Summary.pdf?1398858309

Anna Sulan Masing, "I Don't See Race," between the lines (blog), Sept. 6, 2014, https://researchingbetweenthelines.wordpress.com/2014/06/09/i-dont-see-race/

The Marley Effect

The literature on the "digital divide" is voluminous. Kathy D. Tuck, Dwight R. Holmes, "Library/Media Centers in U.S. Public Schools: Growth, Staffing, and Resources," (Washington, D.C.: National Education Association, 2016).

Tina L. Heafner and Paul G. Fitchett, "An Opportunity to Learn US History: What NAEP Data Suggest regarding the Opportunity Gap.(National Assessment of Educational Progress)," *High School Journal*, 98:3 (2015), pp. 226.

Marley and Williams, "Buffalo Soldier," (Island Records, 1983).

"Accurate knowledge…" quote in Jessica C. Nelson, Glenn Adams, Phia S. Salter, "The Marley Hypothesis," *Psychological Science*, 24:2 (2012), pp. 213 - 218.

Eduardo Bonilla-Silva, *Racism Without Racists: Color-Blind Racism and the Persistence of Racial Inequality in the United States*, (Lanham, Maryland: Rowman & Littlefield, 3rd ed., 2010).

Crocker, Jennifer, et al. "Belief in U.S. Government Conspiracies Against Blacks among Black and White College Students: Powerlessness Or System Blame?" *Personality and Social Psychology Bulletin*, 25:8 (1999), pp. 941-953.

Jessica C. Nelson, et al. ,"The Role of Historical Knowledge in Perception of Race-Based Conspiracies," *Race and Social Problems*, 2:2 (2010), pp. 69-80.

Joe R. Feagin, *The White Racial Frame: Centuries of Racial Framing and Counter-Framing* (New York: Routledge, 2009).

Elizabeth Landers, "Pence: 'Too much talk' of institutional, racial bias in law enforcement," *CNN*, Sept. 22, 2016. http://www.cnn.com/2016/09/22/politics/charlotte-mike-pence-police-shootings/index.html

Besiki L. Kutateladze, et. al. "Cumulative Disadvantage: Examining Racial and Ethnic Disparity in Prosecution and Sentencing," Criminology, 52:3 (2014), pp. 514-551. See also, Carlos Berdejó, "Criminalizing Race: Racial Disparities in Plea Bargaining," *Boston College Law Review*, vol. 59 (2018) (Forthcoming).

Daniel Lathrop and Anna Flagg, "Killings of Black Men by Whites are Far More Likely to be Ruled "Justifiable"" (The Marshall Project, August 14, 2017).

United States Supreme Court, BEARDEN v. GEORGIA, (1983) No. 81-6633, Decided: May 24, 1983.

Mario Salas and Angela Ciolfi, *Driven by Dollars: A State-By-State Analysis of Driver's License Suspension Laws for Failure to Pay Court Debt* (Legal Aid Justice Center, Fall 2017), p. 4. "California no longer will suspend driver's licenses for traffic fines," *Associated Press*, June 29, 2017.

Jim Norman, "Confidence in Police Back at Historical Average," Gallup News, July 10, 2017.

"Big Racial Gap As Americans Say No To Anthem Protests," Quinnipiac University National Poll, Oct. 11, 2016. https://poll.qu.edu/national/release-detail?ReleaseID=2387

Chris Bederman, "Transcript: Colin Kaepernick Addresses Sitting During Nationa Anthem," *Ninerswire*, Aug. 28, 2016. http://ninerswire.usatoday.com/2016/08/28/transcript-colin-kaepernick-addresses-sitting-during-national-anthem/

Kyna Hamill, ""The story I must tell": "Jingle Bells" in the Minstrel Repertoire," *Theatre Survey*, 58:3 (Sept. 2017), pp. 375-403.

Theodore R. Johnson, III, "Recall That Ice Cream Truck Song? We Have Unpleasant News For You," *NPR*, May 11, 2014. https://www.npr.org/sections/codeswitch/2014/05/11/310708342/recall-that-ice-cream-truck-song-we-have-unpleasant-news-for-you

All Ford quotes from Emery C. Warnock, "The Anti-Semitic Origins of Henry Ford's Arts Education Patronage." Journal of Historical Research in Music Education, 30:2 (2009), pp. 79-102. Robyn Pennacchia, "America's Wholesome Square Dancing Tradition is a Tool of White Supremacy," Quartz, December 12, 2017. https://qz.com/1153516/americas-wholesome-square-dancing-tradition-is-a-tool-of-white-supremacy/

Mixed Race Identity

K. R. Humes, N. A. Jones, R. R. Ramirez, Overview of Race and Hispanic Origin: 2010 (Washington, DC: Census Bureau, 2011).

M.C. Thornton, M. C., "Policing the borderlands: White- and Black-American newspaper perceptions of multiracial heritage and the idea of race, 1996–2006," Journal of Social Issues, 65 (2009), pp. 105–127. http://dx.doi.org.ezproxy.bgsu.edu:8080/10.1111/j.1540-4560.2008.01590.x

Victoria Bynum, "'White Negroes' in Segregated Mississippi: Miscegenation, Racial Identity, and the Law," The Journal of Southern History 64:2 (May 1998), pp. 247-276.

F. James Davis, Who is Black?: One Nation's Definition, (College Station: Penn State University Press, 10th ed., 2010), pp. 9-10.

Racial Profiling

"Black, White, and Blue: Americans' Attitudes on Race and Police," (Roper Center for Public Opinion Research, Cornell University, 2016), https://ropercenter.cornell.edu/black-white-blue-americans-attitudes-race-police/

Rich Morin and Renee Stepler, "The Racial Confidence Gap in Police Performance," (Pew Center, Sept. 29, 2016), http://www.pewsocialtrends.org/2016/09/29/the-racial-confidence-gap-in-police-performance/

Tammy R. Kochel, David B. Wilson and Stephen D. Mastrofski, "Effect of Suspect Race on Officers' Arrest Decisions," Criminology, 49 (2011), pp. 473–512.

"Contacts Between Police and the Public, 2005," U.S. Department of Justice, Office of Justice Programs, Bureau of Justice Statistics Special Report, at http://bjs.ojp.usdoj.gov/content/pub/ascii/cpp05.txt

Jeff Rojek, Richard Rosenfeld and Scott Decker, "Policing Race: The Racial Stratification of Searches in Police Traffic Stops," Criminology, 50:4 (2012), pp. 993-1024.

"A person of one race…" quote in Lawrence P. Tiffany, Donald M. McIntyre, Daniel L. Rotenberg, Detection of Crime: Stopping and Questioning, Search and Seizure, Encouragement and Entrapment, (New York: Little, Brown, 1967), p. 20.

Tracey Maclin, "Terry and Race: Terry v. Ohio's Fourth Amendment Legacy: Black Men and Police Discretion," St. John's Law Review, 72 (1998), pp. 1271-1387.

I.B. Capers, "Policing, Race, and Place," Harvard Civil Rights-Civil Liberties Law Review, 44:1 (2009), pp. 43.

David A. Harris, "The Reality of Racial Disparity in Criminal Justice: The Significance of Data Collection," Law and Contemporary Problems, 66:3 (Summer, 2003), pp. 71-98.

Consumer Racial Profiling

Andrea Elliott, "Macy's Settles Complaint of Racial Profiling for $600,000," The New York Times, Jan. 14, 2005, pp. B1.

Elahe Izadi, "Barneys Will Pay $525K to Settle Racial Profiling Allegations," Washington Post, Aug. 11, 2014.

Dean A. Dabney, Richard C. Hollinger, and Laura Dugan. "Who Actually Steals? A Study of Covertly Observed Shoplifters," Justice Quarterly, 21:4 (2004), pp. 693-728.

Correlational Racism

John Hartigan Jr., "Millenials for Obama and the Messy Antic Ends of Race," Anthropology Now, 2:3 (December 2010), pp. 1-9.

Alice O'Connor, Poverty Knowledge: Social Science, Social Policy, and the Poor in Twentieth-Century U.S. History (Princeton N.J.: Princeton University Press, 2001).

Daniel Patrick Moynihan, The Negro Family: The Case for National Action (Washington, DC: Office of Policy Planning and Research, U.S. Department of Labor, 1965).

William Julius Wilson, The Truly Disadvantaged: The Inner City, the Underclass, and Public Policy (Chicago: University of Chicago Press, 1987).

Nathan Glazer and Daniel Moynihan, Beyond the melting pot ; the Negroes, Puerto Ricans, Jews, Italians, and Irish of New York City (Cambridge, Mass.: M.I.T. Press, 1963).

James T. Patterson, "Moynihan and the Single-Parent Family: The 1965 Report and its Backlash," Education Next, 15:2 (2015), pp. 6.

Daniel P. Moynihan, "Memorandum to the President," Jan. 16, 1970, Nixon Presidential Library, https://www.nixonlibrary.gov/virtuallibrary/releases/jul10/53.pdf

Imani Perry, More Beautiful and More Terrible: The Embrace and Transcendence of Racial Inequality in the United States (New York: NYU Press, 2011).

Dalton Conley, "Getting Into the Black: Race, Wealth and Public Policy," Political Science Quarterly, 114:4 (Winter 1999/2000).

Affirmative Action

Terry Lichtash, "Ives-Quinn Act–The Law Against Discrimination," St. John's Law Review, 19:2 (1945), pp. 170-176.

"I don't think we can undo the past…" quote in Public Papers of the Presidents of the United States: John F. Kennedy, Jan. 1 to Nov. 22, 1963 (Washington: Office of the Federal Register, National Archives and Records Service, 1964), p. 624.

"It is impossible to create a formula…" quoted in Nancy McLean, Freedom is Not Enough: The Opening of the American Workplace (Cambridge, Mass.: Harvard University Press, 2008), pp. 55-56.

Lyndon B. Johnson: "Commencement Address at Howard University: "To Fulfill These Rights.",", June 4, 1965. Online by Gerhard Peters and John T. Woolley, The American Presidency Project. http://www.presidency.ucsb.edu/ws/?pid=27021.

"an affirmative responsibility to counteract…" Wirtz quoted in David Hamilton Golland, *Constructing Affirmative Action: The Struggle for Equal Employment Opportunity* (Lexington: University Press of Kentucky, 2011), pp. 172-173.

Craig Steven Wilder, *A Covenant with Color: Race and Social Power in Brooklyn 1636-1990* (New York: Columbia University Press, 2000), pp. 229-230; "wanted was a chance to earn a decent living…" quoted in Nancy McLean, *Freedom is Not Enough: The Opening of the American Workplace* (Cambridge, Mass.: Harvard University Press, 2008), p. 90.

"any preferential approach postulated on racial…" quoted in Randall Kennedy, *For Discrimination: Race, Affirmative Action, and the Law* (New York: Pantheon, 2013), p. 35.

United States Supreme Court, *Adarand Constructors, Inc. v. Peña*, 515 U.S. 200 (1995)

David R. Dietrich, "Racially Charged Cookies and White Scholarships: Anti-Affirmative Action Protests on American College Campuses," *Sociological Focus*, 48:2 (2015), pp. 105-125.

Michael L. Norton, Samuel R. Sommers, "Whites See Racism as a Zero-Sum Game That They Are Now Losing," *Perspectives on Psychological Science*, 6:3 (2011), pp. 215-218.

"better off" see David Shipler, *A Country of Strangers: Blacks and Whites in America* (New York: Vintage Books, 2008), p. 411.

Charlie Savage, "Justice Dept. to Take On Affirmative Action in College Admissions," *New York Times*, Aug. 1, 2017. https://www.nytimes.com/2017/08/01/us/politics/trump-affirmative-action-universities.html

Roland G. Fryer, Jr., Glenn C. Loury, "Affirmative Action and Its Mythology," National Bureau of Economic Research, *NBER Working Paper*, No. 11464 (June 2005) JEL No. J7.

Faye J. Crosby, Aarti Iyer, and Sirinda Sincharoen, "Understanding Affirmative Action," *Annual Review of Psychology*, 57:1 (2006), pp. 585-611.

"While OFCCP…" quote and OFCCP data in "Equal Employment Opportunity: Strengthening Oversight Could Improve Federal Contractor Nondiscrimination Compliance," GAO-16-750 (Government Accountability Office, Sept. 2016).

Michael I. Norton and Samuel R. Sommers, "Whites See Racism as a Zero-Sum Game that they are Now Losing," *Perspectives on Psychological Science*, 6:3 (2011), pp. 215-218.

L.N. Borrell, D.R. Jacobs, D.R. Williams, M.J. Pletcher, T.K. Houston, C.I. Kiefe, "Self-reported racial discrimination and substance use in the coronary artery risk development in adults study," *American Journal of Epidemiology*, 166:9 (2007), pp. 1068-1079.

Damon Mayrl and Aliya Saperstein, "When White People Report Racial Discrimination: The Role of Region, Religion, and Politics," *Social Science Research*, 42:3 (2013), pp. 742-754.

Roland G. Fryer, Jr. and Glenn C. Loury, "Affirmative Action and Its Mythology," *NBER Working Paper*, No. 11464 (June 2005), JEL No. J7.

Thomas J. Kane, "Racial and Ethnic Preferences in College Admissions," *Ohio State Law Journal*, 59:3 (1998), pp. 971.

Affirmative action testing mentioned in Randall Kennedy, *For Discrimination: Race, Affirmative Action, and the Law* (New York: Pantheon, 2013), p. 117.

Liana Christin Landivar, "Disparities in STEM Employment by Sex, Race, and Hispanic Origin," (U.S. Department of Commerce, Economics and Statistics Administration, U.S. Census Bureau, Sept. 2013).

Employment data extracted from EEO-CIT02R EEO 2r. Detailed Census Occupation by Sex, and Race/Ethnicity for Residence Geography, Citizen - All Detailed Occupations at the National Level, 2006-2010, (U.S. Census Bureau).

Marc Bendick, Rekha E. Rodriguez and Sarumathi Jayaraman, "Employment Discrimination in Upscale Restaurants: Evidence from Matched Pair Testing," *The Social Science Journal*, 47:4 (2010), pp. 802-818.

The End of Color-blindness

'Disgraceful': Cops Angry After Obama Slams Arrest of Black Scholar, Fox News, July 24, 2009. http://www.foxnews.com/story/2009/07/24/disgraceful-cops-angry-after-obama-slams-arrest-black-scholar.html

Jamelle Bouie, "The Professor, the Cop, and the President," Slate, Sept. 21, 2016. http://www.slate.com/articles/news_and_politics/the_next_20/2016/09/the_henry_louis_gates_beer_summit_and_racial_division_in_america.html

Remarks by the President on Trayvon Martin, The White House, Office of the Press Secretary, July 19, 2013. https://obamawhitehouse.archives.gov/the-press-office/2013/07/19/remarks-president-trayvon-martin

Eli Rosenberg, "Andrew Jackson was called 'Indian killer.' Trump honored Navajos in front of his portrait," Washington Post, Nov. 28, 2017; Eileen Sullivan and Maggie Haberman, "Trump Shares Inflammatory Anti-Muslim Videos," New York Times, Nov. 29, 2017.

448

Photo Credits

Preface
P-1 photo by Tim Messer-Kruse

Introduction
I-1 Thinker, photo by James Enge.

I-2 "Use your noodle," Library of Congress, POS-US.H84, no. 11

I-3 Black and white people in the District of Columbia, 1962. Photo by Marion Trikosko, Library of Congress, LC-DIG-ppmsca-41015.

I-4 Engraving of five skulls of different races, from J. Blumenbach, *De generis humani varietate nativa* (Gottingen: Vanderhoek, 1795). Wellcome Library, London.

I-5 'Boardwalk benches with shade,' 1978, photo by John Margolies. Library of Congress, LC-DIG-mrg-09920.

I-6 Watching the children's parade at the Charro Days fiesta, Brownsville, Texas, 1942. Photo by Arthur Rothstein. Library of Congress, LC-USF33-003662-M3.

I-7 'Young man with Puerto Rican flag,' 1970. Photo by Frank Espada, Library of Congress, LC-DIG-ds-02977.

I-8 Wedding Photograph of Wong Lan Fong and Yee Shew Ning, Jan. 27, 1927. Record Group 85: Records of the Immigration and Naturalization Service, 1787 - 2004, National Archives and Records Administration.

I-9 Gilbert Redsleeves of the White Mountain Apache, photographed in Pueblo, Colorado, at a gathering of North American Native People, 2015. Photo by Carol Highsmith, Library of Congress, LC-DIG-highsm-33856.

I-10 Selma Burke with her portrait bust of Booker T. Washington. Schomburg Center for Research in Black Culture, Photographs and Prints Division, The New York Public Library.

I-11 Rev. Jesse Jackson, 1983. Photo by Warren Leffler. Library of Congress, LC-DIG-ppmsc-01277.

I-.12 Palace Amusements, Asbury Park, New Jersey, 1978, photo by John Margolies, Library of Congress, LC-DIG-mrg-09512

p. 23 W.E.B. (William Edward Burghardt) Du Bois, May 1919. Photo by C.M. Battey.

Chapter One
1-1 Rachel Dolezal speaking at a Spokane, WA, rally in May 2015. Photo by Aaron Robert Kathman.

1-2 School Children, Atlanta, GA, 2014, photo by Amanda Mills. Centers for Disease Control.

1-3 "Caucasian Types," H.G. Wells, The Outline of History: Being a Plain History of Life and Mankind (New York: Macmillan, 1921), p. 144.

1-4 Poster: "Have your answers ready…" 1917. Library of Congress, LC-USZC4-8370.

1-5 'U.S. Census taking--Wisconsin Indians, 1911.' Photographer unknown. Library of Congress, LC-USZ62-124436.
1- Marchand d'esclaves (slave market), by Victor Giraud, 1900-1920. Library of Congress, LC-DIG-det-4a26597

1-6 St. Patrick's Day Girl, photo by Benjamin Miller, publicdomainpictures.net

1-7 'Bavarian Manor, Papa Bear,' 1977. Photo by John Margolies. Library of Congress, LC-DIG-mrg-10557.

1-8 A Moorish Couple on Their Terrace by Eugène Delacroix, 1832. Metropolitan Museum of Art, New York City.

1-9 Didacus Valades, *Rhetorica Christiana*, 1579.

1-10 Marchand d'esclaves (slave market), by Victor Giraud, 1900-1920. Library of Congress, LC-DIG-det-4a26597

1.11 "The Chain of Nature," 1802. Welcome Library, London.

Montage p. 43 (clockwise from top left):
"Types of Mankind: or Ethnological Researches... by J. C. Nott and G. R. Gliddon" (1854) p. 71; Paul Topinard, Elements d'anthropologie generale (Paris, 1885), p. 988. Wellcome Library, London; Title page of journal *Eugenics*, U.S. National Library of Medicine, National Institutes of Health; Man taking Bertillon measurements of the cranium for the New York City Police Dept., 1908. Library of Congress, LC-USZ62-50068.

Chapter Two
2-1 Pencil sketch of the DNA double helix by Francis Crick from 1953. Crick Papers, Wellcome Library, London.

2-2 The first printout of the human genome displayed at the Wellcome Library, London. Photo by Russ London.

2-3 An illustration of an evolutionary tree of humans from H.G. Wells, *An Outline of History,* 1921.

2-4 Human migration routes out of Africa. Photo by Darryl Leja, National Human Genome Research Institute, National Institutes of Health.

2-5 Plaster face casts of Nias islanders by J.P. Kleiweg de Zwaan, circa 1910. Photo by Jane023.

2-6 Median facial goniometer of M. Broca, from Paul Topinard, *Anthropology* (London, Chapman and Hall Philadelphia, J.B. Lippincott and Co., 1878), p. 345.

2-7 Skull of European and of Australian from, *A system of Legal Medicine*, Allan Hamilton and Lawrence Godkin, eds., (New York: E.B. Treat, 1894), Vol. 1, p. 62.

2-8 Man examining skulls, Harris & Ewing, 1926. Library of Congress, LC-DIG-hec-34192.

2-9 The Genealogical Tree, illustration by Geo. Heiss, n.d. Library of Congress, LC-DIG-pga-01537.

2-10 Women waiting to see the doctor on a Saturday morning in San Augustine, Texas, in 1939. Photo by Russell Lee. Library of Congress, LC-USF33-012155-M4.

2-11 CCDG banner image. Photo by Ernesto Del Aguila III, National Human Genome Research Institute. NIH.

2-12 Photo by Ernesto Del Aguila III, National Human Genome Research Institute. NIH.

Chapter Three

3-1 Illustration from Julien J. Virey, *Histoire Naturelle du Genre Humain* (Brussels: Aug. Wahlen, 1826), vol. 20, p. 39. Wellcome Library, London.

3-2 'Royal Aquarium. G.A. Farini's leopard boy! Spotted black, white and yellow, from head to foot.' Advertisement for exhibition, (New York: S. Booth & Co., n.d.). Wellcome Library, London.

3-3 "Love and beauty--Sartjee the Hottentot Venus," by Christopher Crupper Rumford (England), 1811. Library of Congress, LC-USZ62-137332.

3-4 Poster advertising the exhibition of the Hottentot Venus (London: Chester, 1810). Wellcome Library, London.

3-5 Guy de Chauliac giving an anatomy lesson, 1300-1370. From Guy de Chauliac, *La grande chirurgie* (Biblioteque Universitaire Montpellier), Folio 14 verso. Wellcome Library, London.

3-6 Samuel George Morton. The Miriam and Ira D. Wallach Division of Art, Prints and Photographs: Print Collection, The New York Public Library.

3-7 J. Marion Sims, published by *N.Y. Medical Journal*, 1900. Library of Congress, LC-USZ62-120407.

3-8 Participants in the Tuskeggee Syphilis Study, 1932. Centers for Disease Control.

3-9 Jean Baptiste Pierre Antoine de Monet de Lamarck, The Miriam and Ira D. Wallach Division of Art, Prints and Photographs: Print Collection, The New York Public Library.

3-10 "Steps in Mental Development...The Binet-Simon Measuring Scale for Intelligence," 1915

3-11 William Charles Flynn, a winner of perfect "eugenic baby" contests, ca. 1910-1915. Library of Congress, LC-DIG-ggbain-19313.

3-12 Third International Congress of Eugenics held at American Museum of Natural History, New York, August 21-23, 1932, (Baltimore: Williams & Watkins, 1934). Wellcome Library, London.

3-13 Stop forced sterilization, by Rachael Romero, San Francisco Poster Brigade, 1977. Library of Congress, LC-DIG-ppmsca-43321.

3-14 Franz Boas, ca. 1915.

3-15 Illustration from *The Races of Mankind*, (Field Museum of Natural History, 1933).

3-16 UNESCO General Conference, Nov, 1952, Record Group 286: Records of the Agency for International Development, 1948-2003, National Archives.

p. 87 Charles B. Davenport, photo by Marceau (New York, 1914) The National Library of Medicine, National Institutes of Health.

p. 88 Stanford-Binet test questions from J. E. Wallace Wallin, "A Practical Guide for the Administration of the Binet-Simon Scale for Measuring Intelligence," Psychological Clinic, 5:7 (Dec 15, 1911), pp. 224-225.

Chapter Four

4-1 The landing of the Pilgrims at Plymouth, Mass. Dec. 22nd 1620 (New York: Currier & Ives, 1876). Library of Congres, LC-USZ62-3461.

4-2 "Unus Americanus ex Virginia," by Wenceslaus Hollar, 1645. Metropolitan Museum of Art, New York City.

4-3 "The March of Myles Standish, "Standish the Stalwart it was, with Eight of his Valorous Army Led by Their Indian Guide, By Hobomok, Friend of the White Men." Miriam and Ira D. Wallach Division of Art, Prints and Photographs: Photography Collection, The New York Public Library.

4-4 "Exchanging citizens for horses, 1834" Schomburg Center for Research in Black Culture, Manuscripts, Archives and Rare Books Division, The New York Public Library.

4-5 "Branding Slaves," William O. Blake (Columbus, Ohio: 1859). Schomburg Center for Research in Black Culture, Manuscripts, Archives and Rare Books Division, The New York Public Library.

4-6 "Have you pray'd tonight, Dedesmona?" plate 12 from Othello (Act 5, Scene 2) *Quinze Esquisses à l'eau forte dessinées et gravées* par Théodore Chasseriau (1844, reprinted 1910). Metropolitan Museum of Art, New York City.

4-7 "The brave old Hendrick, the great Sachem or chief of the Mohawk Indians…" The Miriam and Ira D. Wallach Division of Art, Prints and Photographs: Print Collection, The New York Public Library.

4-8 Logan finding his murdered family. Wood engraving ca. 1873. Library of Congress, LC-USZ62-60816.

4-9 Boston Tea Party. Matthias Christian Sprengel, *Allgemeines historisches Taschenbuch, oder Abriss der merkwürdigsten neuen Welt-Begebenheiten: enthaltend für 1784 die Geschichte der Revolution von Nord-America* (Berlin: Haude & Spener, 1784). Metropolitan Museum of Art, New York City.

4-10 George Washington (with his servant Billy Lee), painting by John Trumbull, 1780. Metropolitan Museum of Art, New York City.

4-11 "Blow for blow," by Henry L. Stephens, 1863. Library of Congress, LC-USZC4-2523.

4-12 The British surrendering their arms to Gen. Washington after their defeat at YorkTown, October 1781. Painting by John Francis Renault (Tanner, Vallance, Kearny & Co. 1819). Library of Congress, LC-DIG-pga-02820.

4-13 Gnadenhutten massacre. John Warner Barber, *Historical, Poetical and Pictorial American Scenes;...* (New Haven, CT: J.H Bradley, Publishers, 1851), p. 77.

4-14 Penn's Treaty with the Indians, ca. 1788. Metropolitan Museum of Art, New York City.

4-15 The Chief of the Little Osages, watercolor by Pavel Petrovich Svinin, 1811–1813. Metropolitan Museum of Art, New York City.

4-16 Articles of Confederation and Perpetual Union between the states… (Williamsburg: J. Dixon & W. Hunter, 1778). Library of Congress, LC-USZ62-59464.

4-17 Arthur St. Clair, painting by Charles Willson Peale, 1780. Metropolitan Museum of Art, New York City.

4-18 Figure 4.18 "America," by Edward Williams clay, 1841. Library of Congress, LC-USZ62-89745.

4-19 Portrait of Frederick Douglass, n.d. Schomburg Center for Research in Black Culture, Photographs and Prints Division, The New York Public Library.

Chapter Five

5-1 George Washington--The farmer, painting by Junius Stearns (Paris : Lemercier, c1853). Library of Congress, LC-DIG-pga-02419.

5-2 General Toussaint L'Ouveture, n.d. Library of Congress, LC-DIG-pga-13038.

5-3 Drawing of an English slave ship, possibly the Brookes, 1839. Schomburg Center for Research in Black Culture, Photographs and Prints Division, New York Public Library.

5-4 Map of the former territorial limits of the Cherokee Nation, 1884. Lionel Pincus and Princess Firyal Map Division, The New York Public Library.

5-5 Cherokee War Chief. Illustration from James Cowles Prichard, *The Natural History of Man...* (London: H. Baillière, 1845), plate XXXII. Wellcome Library, London.

5-6 Silhouette Portrait of John Marshall, by William Henry Brown 1844. Metropolitan Museum of Art, New York.

5-7 Yaha-Hajo. A Seminole chief. Lithograph by J.T. Bowen (Philadelphia: Daniel Rice & James G. Clark, c1842). Library of Congress, LC-DIG-pga-07610.

5-8 The Coffle Gang, 1864. Schomburg Center for Research in Black Culture, Manuscripts, Archives and Rare Books Division, The New York Public Library.

5-9 Old Slave Market, Charleston, S. C. The Miriam and Ira D. Wallach Division of Art, Prints and Photographs: Photography Collection, The New York Public Library.

5-10 *Affleck's Southern Rural Almanac, and Plantation and Garden Calendar, for 1854.* (Washington, Adams County, Mississippi, 1854). Advertisement in front matter.

5-11 "The Scourged Back - The furrowed and scarred back of Gordon, a slave who escaped from his master in Mississippi and made his way to a Union Army encampment in Baton Rouge, Louisiana, 1863." Schomburg Center for Research in Black Culture, Photographs and Prints Division, The New York Public Library.

5-12 Illustration in, *Authentic and Impartial Narrative of the Tragical Scene which was witnessed in Southampton County* (New York, 1831). Library of Congress, LC-USZ62-38902.

5-13 "Freedom to the slaves," lithograph by Currier & Ives, probably between 1863 and 1870. Library of Congress, LC-USZC2-2366.

15-14 Contrabands Aboard U.S. Ship Vermont, Port Royal, South Carolina, 1861. Photo by Henry P. Moore. Metropolitan Museum of Art, New York City.

5-15 Black Soldier in Camp, photo possibly by Alexander Gardner, 1863. Gilman Collection, Metropolitan Museum of Art, New York City.

5-16 Willis Winn, a former slave, with horn with which slaves were called, near Marshall, Texas. Photo by Russell Lee, 1939. Library of Congress, LC-USF33-012187-M4.

5-17 Harry Stephens and family. Photo by G. Gable, 1866. Metropolitan Museum of Art, New York City.

5-18 A slave auction in Richmond, Virginia (Illustrated London News, Sept. 27, 1856). Wellcome Library, London.

Montage p. 159 (clockwise from top left):
"Model No. 202. Young men's three-button notch lapel sack." Science, Industry and Business Library: General Collection, The New York Public Library; Tee Pee Drive-in Restaurant sign, Route 17. Photo by John Margolies, 1979. Library of Congress, LC-DIG-mrg-0153; "The Jap." Music Division, The New York Public Library; "Emmet Professional Harmonicas," 1887. Library of Congress, LC-USZ62-87637.

Chapter Six

6-1 Natural inhabitants, male and female, of the Antilles of America standing under a pawpaw tree. From Jean Baptiste Du Tertre, *Histoire generale des Antilles habitées par les François* (Paris: T Iolly, 1667), vol. 2, p. 356. Wellcome Library, London.

6-2 Philip alias Metacomet, chief of Wampanoags, copy of engraving by Paul Revere (Newport: Thomas Church, 1772). Library of Congress, LC-USZ62-96234.

6-3 "Sauvage du NO. de la Louisiane" (native of New Orleans, Louisiana). Ilustration in P. Santini, *Atlas universel dressé sur les meilleurs cartes modernes* (Venise: Chez M. Remondini, 1776). Library of Congress, LC-USZ62-45593.

6-4 "Redmens' Diploma Legendary & Historical Chart" for the Society of Red Men," (Philadelphia: Burk & McFetridge, c1889). Library of Congress, LC-DIG-pga-03413.

6-5 Henry W. Longfellow, photo by Frederick Gutekunst (Philadelphia, c. 1876). Library of Congress, LC-DIG-ppms-ca-39898.

6-6 Hiawatha's departure (New York: Currier & Ives, c1868).

Library of Congress, LC-DIG-pga-04874.

6-7 Stick Indian Natives of Copper River, members of Bellums Indian Tribe, near Kotsina Crossing, Alaska, 1899. Schrader Collection, United States Geological Survey.

6-8 Execution of the thirty-eight Sioux Indians at Mankato Minnesota, December 25, 1862. Library of Congress, LC-DIG-pga-03790.

6-9 Ponca Indians between 1865 and 1880. Brady-Handy Photograph Collection, Library of Congress, LC-DIG-cwp-bh-04295.

6-10 Government school for Indians on the Pawnee reservation, n.d.. The Miriam and Ira D. Wallach Division of Art, Prints and Photographs: Photography Collection, The New York Public Library.

6-11 Group portrait of the Carlisle Indian School football team, 1899. Photo by John N. Choate. Library of Congress, LC-USZ62-125089.

6-12 Harris, Beebe & Co.: The Pocahontas Chewing Tobacco (New York: Hatch Lithograph Co., 1868). Library of Congress, LC-USZC4-1071.

6-13 Jonathan Chapman, illustration in *A History of the Pioneer and Modern Times of Ashland County.* (Philadelphia: J. B. Lippincott & Co., 1862).

6-14 Boy Scouts - Outside tent with headdresses, c. 1935-1945. Manuscripts and Archives Division, The New York Public Library.

6-15 Washington Redskins start training. Washington, D.C. Aug. 28, 1937. In air, left to right: Millner (Notre Dame), Rentner (Northwestern) and Peterson (West Virginia-Wesleyan). Photo by Harris & Ewing. Library of Congress, LC-DIG-hec-23282.

6-16 Movie poster for "The Way of the Redman Blood of his Fathers" (Chicago: Goes Lithograph Co., 1914). Library of Congress, LC-DIG-ppmsc-04342.

6-17 Sign in bar window, Sisseton, South Dakota, 1939. Photo by John Vachon. Library of Congress, LC-USF33-T01-001661-M3.

6-18 Longest Walk Indian Teepee at the Washington Monument grounds, July 11, 1978. Photo by Warren Leffler for U.S. News & World Report Magazine. Library of Congress, LC-DIG-ds-00753.

6-19 RCA black/white Indian Head test card, used from 1940 until the advent of color television.

6-20 Actor "Iron Eyes" Cody, 330-CFD-DM-SC-91-09083 National Archives and Records Administration.

6-21 U.S. Census Poster, 2010. National Archives. 6094476

p. 189 Washington Irving, c1861, Library of Congress, LC-USZ62-4238.

p. 190 Mrs. Good Bear, photo by Edward Curtis, 1908, Library of Congress, LC-USZ62-96195

p. 193 Red Cloud, photo by Edward Curtis, 1905, Library of Congress LC-USZ62-66856

Chapter Seven

7-1 Watson and the Shark by John Singleton Copley, 1778. (Detroit Publishing Co., c. 1912). Library of Congress, LC-DIG-det-4a25973.

7-2 The Battle of Bunker's Hill, lithograph by Johann Gotthard Muller after painting by John Trumbull, 1798. Library of Congress, LC-DIG-pga-02211.

7-3 Right Rev. Richard Allen (c. 1902). Schomburg Center for Research in Black Culture, Jean Blackwell Hutson Research and Reference Division, The New York Public Library.

7-4 "De ole Kentucky home--far away" (New York: Currier & Ives, c1885). Library of Congress, LC-USZC2-3216.

7-5 "Mammy," n.d. The Miriam and Ira D. Wallach Division of Art, Prints and Photographs: Photography Collection, The New York Public Library.

7-6 "The Two Platforms," campaign poster from 1866 Pennsylvania gubernatorial race. Library of Congress, Broadside Collection, portfolio 159, no. 9, LC-USZ62-32498.

7-7 "Jim Crow" 1836. Jerome Robbins Dance Division, The New York Public Library.

7-8 White man in blackface, photo by Frances B. Johnston, ca. 1890-1910. Frances Benjamin Johnston Collection, Library of Congress, LC-USZ62-47073.

7-9 "The Irish declaration of independence that we are all familiar with." Illustration by Frederick B. Opper in *Puck*, 13:322, (May 9, 1883). Library of Congress, LC-DIG-ppmsca-28386.

7-10 Fannie Virginia Casseopia Lawrence, a Redeemed Slave Child, 5 years of age, 1863. Schomburg Center for Research in Black Culture, Photographs and Prints Division, The New York Public Library.

7-11 "Alligator Bait," n.d.. Schomburg Center for Research in Black Culture, Art and Artifacts Division, The New York Public Library.

7-12 "The original child's book. Kids of many colors," ca. 1895-1911. The Miriam and Ira D. Wallach Division of Art, Prints and Photographs: Art & Architecture Collection, The New York Public Library.

7-13 "Ten Little Niggers," (London: Dean & Sons,1867).

7-14 Booker T. Washington, ca. 1890-1910. Library of Congress, LC-USZ62-119898.

7-15 "The coon with the big white spot," ca. 1895. Music Division, The New York Public Library.

7-16 "Aunt Jemima's pancake flour," n.d. Art and Picture Collection, The New York Public Library.

7-17 "The Birth of a Nation." Gus (played by white actor Walter Long in blackface) in a scene from director D. W. Griffith's 1915 movie. Schomburg Center for Research in Black Culture,

Photographs and Prints Division, The New York Public Library.

7-18 Spencer Williams playing Andy in the Amos n' Andy Show, n.d. George Grantham Bain Collection (Library of Congress), LC-B22- 516-3.

7-19 Publicity photo from the television program *Mayberry R.F.D*, Dec. 1968. Wikipedia Commons.

7-20 "Birth Of A Nation." Billy Rose Theatre Division, The New York Public Library.

Chapter Eight

8-1 Aerial view of Lady Liberty's feet and pedestal, Statue of Liberty, Liberty Island, Manhattan. Photo by Jack Boucher, 2006. Library of Congress, HAER NY,31-NEYO,89--348.

8-2 "Miscegenation," photo by Fitz W. Guerin, 1902. Library of Congress, LC-USZ62-74311.

8-3 Charles Sumner, photo by Mathew Brady, ca. 1861-1874. Library of Congress, LC-USZ62-128709.

8-4 "A Chinese Vegetable Peddler, San Francisco, Cal.," ca. 1898-1931.The Miriam and Ira D. Wallach Division of Art, Prints and Photographs: Photography Collection, The New York Public Library.

8-5 Photograph of Golden Spike Ceremony at Promontory, Utah, May 10, 1869. National Archives and Record Administration.

8-6 Duplicate Certificate of Identity -- Anna May Wong. Records of the Immigration and Naturalization Service, 1787-2004, National Archives and Record Administration.

8-7 Barnum and Bailey, By the Hair of their Heads (Cincinnati: The Strobridge Litho. Co., 1916).

8-8 Examining Passengers Aboard Ships, Vessel is the Shimyo Maru, Angel Island, California, 1931. Department of the Treasury. Public Health Service, 7452281, National Archives and Record Administration.

8-9 Immigration Interview on Angel Island, 1923. Department of the Treasury. Public Health Service, 7452280, National Archives and Record Administration.

8-10 Americans all! Victory Liberty Loan, by Howard Chandler Christy, 1919. Library of Congress, LC-USZC4-5845.

8-11 Tokutaro Slocum in front of the Japanese American Citizens League headquarters, before leaving for internment camps, 1942, photo by Clem Albers. Department of the Interior, War Relocation Authority, 536805, National Archives and Record Administration.

8-12 "At a Russian boarding house, Homestead, Pa., 1909." The Miriam and Ira D. Wallach Division of Art, Prints and Photographs: Photography Collection, The New York Public Library.

8-13 "An Alien Anti-Dumping Bill" in The Literary Digest, May 7, 1921, p. 13. Library of Congress, LC-USZ62-44049.

8-14 "Jap Trap," World War II Posters, 1942-1945, Records of the Office of Government Reports, 1932-1947, National Archives and Record Administration.

8-15 Japanese families form a line outside Civil Control Station, San Francisco, Apr. 25, 1942. Photo by Dorothea Lange. Department of the Interior. War Relocation Authority, National Archives and Record Administration.

8-16 "White squadron," (Currier & Ives, 1893). Library of Congress, LC-DIG-pga-00970.

8-17 Filipino lettuce field laborer. Imperial Valley, California, 1939. Photo by Dorothea Lange. Library of Congress, LC-USF34-019341-E.

8-18 Border Patrol Agents Blocking a Road in Gainesville, Florida, 1926. Records of the Immigration and Naturalization Service, 1787-2004, National Archives and Record Administration.

8-19 Mexican Farm Workers Applying for Farm Labor in the U.S. through the Braceros Program, ca. 1942-1945. Department of Agriculture,Office of the Secretary, Office of Information, 7452192. National Archives and Record Administration.

8-20 Man in the Solidarity Day march, holding a picket sign, 1981. Photo by Frank Espada. Library of Congress, LC-DIG-ds-02975.

8-21 President Lyndon B. Johnson delivers his speech before signing the Immigration Act, Liberty Island, New York City, Oct. 3, 1965.

8-22 Battle Group Poland Soldiers Attend Historic Presidential Visit to Poland, photo by SPC Kevin Wang, Defense Video Image Distribution System.

Montage p. 253 (clockwise from top left): Identification Photograph on Affidavit "In the Matter of Wong Kim Ark," Native Born Citizen of the United States, filed with the Immigration Service in San Francisco prior to his May 19 departure on the Steamer "China." US District Court- San Francisco Admiralty (Habeas Corpus) Case 11198. Department of Justice. Immigration and Naturalization Service. San Francisco District Office. 296479, National Archives and Record Administration; "Model No. 130. Medium fitting three-button style; Model No. 131. Medium fitting two-button style; Model No. 132. Medium fitting double-breasted style; Models for businessmen." Science, Industry and Business Library: General Collection , The New York Public Library; "Cotton hoer near Clarksdale, Miss., June 1937." Schomburg Center for Research in Black Culture, Photographs and Prints Division, The New York Public Library.

Chapter Nine

9-1 Protest against the integration of Central High School at the Arkansas capitol, Aug. 20, 1959. Photo by John Bledsoe. Library of Congress, LC-U9- 2908-15.

9-2 African American children on way to PS204, 82nd Street and 15th Avenue, pass mothers protesting the busing of children to achieve integration, 1965. Photo by Dick DeMarsico. Library of Congress, LC-USZ62-134434.

9-3 Unidentified man in a studio photograph seated before two mirrors placed at right angles to provide five images, ca. 1866-1899. Library of Congress, LC-USZ62-136902.

9-4 Young women modeling, 1902. Library of Congress, LC-USZ62-74356.

9-5 Segregation in Albany - street scenes, Aug. 17, 1962. Photo by Warren Leffler. Library of Congress, LC-DIG-ppmsca-41020.

9-6 Model No. 702. Young men's two-button notch lapel style, n.d. Science, Industry and Business Library: General Collection, New York Public Library.

9-7 James Baldwin at the March on Washington, D.C., 1963. U.S. Information Agency. Press and Publications Service, 2803443, National Archives and Record Administration.

9-8 The Miriam and Ira D. Wallach Division of Art, Prints and Photographs: Photography Collection, The New York Public Library. "Jay Street, No. 115, Brooklyn." The New York Public Library Digital Collections. 1936.

9-9 Bella Abzug, Betty Freidan, and Billy Jean King accompanying torch relay runners in Houston, n.d. 220-WC-30H, National Archives and Record Administration.

9-10 Walter Lippmann, Photo by Harris & Ewing, ca. 1905-1945. Library of Congress, LC-H25- 247207-T.

9-11 Hillbilly Hot Dogs, West Virginia Route 2, May, 9, 2015. Photo by Carol Highsmith. Library of Congress, LC-DIG-highsm-31849.

9-12 Seaman Chanthorn Peou of San Diego, Calif., takes his Scholastic Aptitude Test (SAT). U.S. Navy photo by Photographer's Mate 3rd Class Jason T. Poplin.

p. 277 Advertisement for Pears' Soap, 1899. Library of Congress, LC-USZ62-86352

Chapter Ten

10-1 Woman taking polygraph test. Photo by Ed Westcott, Department of Energy, National Archives and Record Administration.

10-2 René Descartes, *L'Homme... et un traitté de la formation du foetus du mesme autheur* (Paris: Charles Angot, 1664), p. 79. National Library of Medicine, National Institutes of Health.

10-3 Fritz Kahn, *Das Leben des Menschen* vol. 2 (Stuttgart, 1926). National Library of Medicine, National Institutes of Health.

10-4 Generating ideas, digital artwork by Bill McConkey. Wellcome Library, London.

10-5 First grade class, Albemarle Road Elementary School, Charlotte, North Carolina, Feb. 21, 1973. Photo by Warren Leffler. Library of Congress, LC-U9- 27230-15A.

10-6 Learning and Memory, illustration by Bill McConkey. Wellcome Library, London.

10-7 'Figure 1. The influence of status cues on race categorization,' in J.B. Freeman, A.M. Penner, A. Saperstein, M. Scheutz, N. Ambady, "Looking the Part: Social Status Cues Shape Race Perception," PLoS ONE 6:9 (2011).

10-8 "Autism," photo by Darryl Leja, National Human Genome Research Institute.

Montage p. 297 (clockwise from top left): Soldier standing guard at 7th and N Street, N.W., Washington, D.C., after the uprising following the assassination of Martin Luther King, Jr., Apr. 8, 1968. Photo by Warren Leffler. Library of Congress, LC-DIG-ppmsca-04301; Police Hall of Fame, 1980. Photo by John Margolies. Library of Congress, LC-MA05- 6883; Manpower: Negro bomber plant workers, 1942. Schomburg Center for Research in Black Culture, Photographs and Prints Division, The New York Public Library; Behind the camera during filming at a CBS news, 1967. Photo by James Kavallines. Library of Congress, LC-USZ62-116176.

Chapter Eleven

11-1 Scene at Smithland, Kentucky, 1935. Schomburg Center for Research in Black Culture, Photographs and Prints Division, The New York Public Library.

11-2 Man posing as Uncle Sam stands near the White House on a cold January day in Washington, D.C., n.d. Photo by Carol Highsmith. Library of Congress, LC-DIG-highsm-14669.

11-3 Georgia convicts working on a road in Oglethorpe County, May 1941. Photo by Jack Delano. Library of Congress, LC-USF33-020863-M3.

11-4 Cotton Pickers with Knee Pads, Lehi, Arkansas, 1938. Photo by Russell Lee. Metropolitan Museum of Art, New York.

11-5 Labor protesters, Jan. or Feb. 1930. Photo by Harris & Ewing. Library of Congress, LC-DIG-hec-35732.

11-6 AFL Labor Leaders, Timothy Healy, William B. Fitzgerald, William D. Mahon, Hugh Frayne and Louis Fridiger, ca. 1916. Library of Congress, LC-DIG-ggbain-22332.

11-7 Workers at the Stockham Pipe & Fittings Company, Birmingham, Alabama, ca. 1950. Library of Congress, HAER ALA,37-BIRM,45--13.

11-8 A. Philip Randolph, 1964. Photo by Ed Ford. Library of Congress, LC-USZ62-126849.

11-9 "United We Win," World War Two Poster, Office for Emergency Management. Office of War Information. Domestic Operations Branch. Bureau of Special Services. 513820 National Archives and Record Administration.

11-10 Dr. W.G. Anderson, Albany, Georgia, Aug. 18, 1962. Photo by Warren Leffler. Library of Congress, LC-DIG-ppmsca-41024.

11-11 Children and teacher, Annie Davis School, near Tuskegee, Alabama, 1902. Photo by Benjamin F. Johnston. Library of Congress, LC-USZ62-78481.

11-12 Texas School, Nov. 1965. Photo by Warren Leffler. Library of Congress, LC-DIG-ppmsca-41710.

11-13 "The Veteran," by Thomas Waterman Wood, 1866. Metropolitan Museum of Art, New York City.

11-14 Woman porter with her gear, 1917. Library of Congress, LC-USZ62-46395.

11-15 "Negro sharecropper and son..." 1939. Schomburg Center for Research in Black Culture, Photographs and Prints Division, The New York Public Library.

11-16 "Millions of acres. Iowa and Nebraska. Land for sale on 10 years credit..." (Buffalo. N. Y. 1872). Library of Congress Printed Ephemera Collection; Portfolio 134, Folder 13.

11-17 Wife of Sharecropper, Lee County, Mississippi, 1935. Photo by Arthur Rothstein. Library of Congress, LC-USF33-T01-002050-M5.

11-18 Community leaders in AAA (Agricultural Adjustment Administration) meeting at courthouse to discuss the next year's program. Eufaula, Oklahoma. Photo by Russell Lee. Library of Congress, LC-USF34-035258-D.

11-19 Rural Electrification Administration Poster by Lester Beall, ca. 1930s. U.S. Department of Agriculture. Library of Congress, LC-USZC4-14736.

11-20 Tuskegee airmen attending a briefing at Ramitelli, Italy, Mar. 1945. Photo by Toni Frissell. Library of Congress, LC-DIG-ppmsca-13260.

11-21 Woman and man looking at a house under construction in Arlington, Virginia, Aug. 1966. Photo by Warren Leffler. Library of Congress, LC-DIG-ds-06707.

11-22 Man at the Jekyll Island Club Hotel, 1990. Photo by John Margolies. Library of Congress, LC-DIG-mrg-10371.

11-23 Letters to President Eisenhower from Ava Ayecock and Jackie Robinson. Lyndon Baines Johnson Presidential Library, National Archives and Records Administration.

p. 333 Black street worker in Chicago. Photo by John H. White, 1970. EPA, NARA 556187.

Chapter Twelve

12-1 Congress voting the Declaration of Independence, from unfinished painting by Robert Edge Pine and Edward Savage, early 19c. Library of Congress, LC-USZ62-6078.

12-2 Roger B. Taney, ca. 1855-1865. Library of Congress, LC-BH82- 402 A.

12-3 The Fifteenth Amendment and its results, drawn by G.F. Kahl (Baltimore: Schneider & Fuchs, 1870). Library of Congress, LC-DIG-pga-02587.

12-4 Ku Klux Klan, Watertown, N.Y., Division 289, 1870. Library of Congress, LC-USZ62-122392.

12-5 'This is a white man's government, Democratic Platform, by Thomas Nast, 1868. Library of Congress, LC-USZ62-121735.

12-6 Cartoon used in the campaign for the ratification of the North Carolina disfranchising constitution that shows Negro vampire bat rising from a 3rd party ballot box, 1900. Library of Congress, LC-USZ62-42764.

12-7 Hon. George H. White, 1902. Schomburg Center for Re-

search in Black Culture, Manuscripts, Archives and Rare Books Division, The New York Public Library.

12-8 Founding members of the Niagara Movement, 1905. Schomburg Center for Research in Black Culture, Photographs and Prints Division, The New York Public Library.

12-9 Warren G. Harding, Aug. 31, 1920. Library of Congress, LC-USZ62-130975.

12-10 Flyer, "The Ku Kliux Klan Invites You to the Portals," ca. 1904 - 1937. National Archives and Record Administration, HD1-88014257.

12-11 John Collier, U.S. Indian commissioner, appears before Senate Indian Affairs Committee. Washington, D.C., June 10, 1940. Library of Congress, LC-DIG-hec-28781.

12-12 1964 Democratic National Convention, Atlantic City, New Jersey. Photo by Warren Leffler. Library of Congress, LC-DIG-ds-05242.

12-13 Marian Anderson at the dedication of a mural commemorating her free public concert on the steps of the Lincoln Memorial in 1939, in the Department of Interior Auditorium on January 6, 1943. Photo by Roger Smith. Library of Congress, LC-USE6-D-007911.

12-14 Barry Goldwater, Sept. 1962. Photo by Marion Trikosko. Library of Congress, LC-DIG-ppmsca-19601.

12-15 Pres. Nixon with Sammy Davis, Jr., new member of National Advisory Council on Economic Opportunity, July 1971. Photo by Marion Trikosko. Library of Congress, LC-DIG-ppmsca-31145.

12-16 Official portrait of President-elect Barack Obama on Jan. 13, 2009. Photo by Pete Souza. National Archives and Record Administration.

12-17 Trump Taj Mahal, 2000. Photo by John Margolies. Library of Congress, LC-DIG-mrg-08841.

12-18 Bunk and toilet at the West Virginia State Penitentiary, Moundsville, West Virginia, that operated from 1876 to 1995. Photo by Carol Highsmith. Library of Congress, LC-DIG-highsm- 32032.

12-19 The Confrontation, Selma, Alabama, 1965. Artist Franklin McMahon. Library of Congress, LC-DIG-ds-03217.

p. 363 President George W. Bush and Laura Bush dance at an inaugural ball, January 20, 2001, in Washington, D.C. George W. Bush Presidential Library and Museum. (P74-31)

Chapter Thirteen

13-1 The Burning of the Coloured Orphan Asylum, Aug. 15, 1863. Print Collection, Miriam and Ira D. Wallach Division of Art, Prints and Photographs, The New York Public Library.

13-2 The Anti-Chinese Riot in Denver, Oct. 31, 1880. Engraving by N.B. Wilkins, in Frank Leslie's illustrated newspaper, vol. 51 (1880 Nov. 20), p. 189. Library of Congress, LC-USZC2-760.

13-3 "Damage done by a bomb thrown into a building at

3365 Indiana Avenue killing a six-year-old Negro girl." From Chicago Commission on Race Relations, The Negro in Chicago (1922). Schomburg Center for Research in Black Culture, Jean Blackwell Hutson Research and Reference Division, The New York Public Library.

13-4 Greenwood after attack on June 1st, 1921, Tulsa, Okla. Library of Congress, LC-DIG-anrc-14737.

13-5 Family arriving in Chicago from the Deep South, 1922. From Chicago Commission on Race Relations, The Negro in Chicago (1922). Schomburg Center for Research in Black Culture, Jean Blackwell Hutson Research and Reference Division, The New York Public Library.

13-6 Picket line at Mid-City Realty Company, South Chicago, Illinois, July 1941. Photo by John Vachon. Library of Congress, LC-USF33-016150-M1.

13-7 Poster by Record Section, Suburban Resettlement Administration, Dec. 1935. Library of Congress, LC-USF34-001025-C.

13-8 Techwood Homes, Building No. 16, 488-514 Techwood Drive, Atlanta, Fulton County, GA, ca. 1930s. Library of Congress, HABS GA,61-ATLA,60S--5.

13-9 "First Negro family moving into Sojourner Truth homes, Feb. 1942." Photo by Arthur Siegel. Library of Congress, LC-DIG-fsa-8d45109.

13-10 Sign with American flag "We want white tenants in our white community," directly opposite the Sojourner Truth housing project. Photo by Arthur Siegel. Library of Congress, LC-USW3-016549-C.

13-11 Youths Play Basketball at Stateway Gardens' Housing Project on Chicago's South Side, the Complex has Eight Buildings with 1,633 Apartments, May 1973. Photo by John White. National Archives and Records Administration, 412-DA-13710.

13-12 Central Expressway Leading South into Dallas, May 1972. Photo by Bob Smith, National Archives and Records Administration, 412-da-5277.

13-13 Redline Map for Richmond, Virginia, Home Owners' Loan Corporation, ca. 1935. National Archives and Records Administration, 6104124

13-14 Sign advertising FHA subsidized suburban housing. 1940s. Photo by Lee Russell. Library of Congress, LC-USF34-039357-D.

13-15 The sprawl of suburbs in McCordsville, a northern suburb of Indianapolis, Indiana, 2016. Photo by Carol Highsmith. Library of Congress, LC-DIG-highsm-40877.

13-16 Cleveland, Ohio, May 1965. Photo by Thomas O'Halloran. Library of Congress, LC-DIG-ppmsca-49913.

13-17 Graphic model of the dissimilarity index. U.S. Census Bureau, Housing and Household Economic Statistics Division Last Revised: October 31, 2011

Chapter Fourteen

14-1 Lyndon B. Johnson and Rev. Dr. Martin Luther King, Jr. in the cabinet room, White House, Mar. 18, 1966. Photo by Yoichi Okamoto. Lyndon B. Johnson Presidential Library, A2133-10.

14-2 Protest is Patriotic Solidarity with Colin K Freeway Overpass Bannering, photo by Rick Barry, Sept. 29, 2017.

14-3 "Team fast to the pole," Currier & Ives, 1883, Library of Congress, LC-DIG-pga-09936.

14-4 Ice cream truck, Washington, D.C., 1942. Photo by John Ferrell. Library of Congress, LC-USF34-011541D.

14-5 "Team fast on the snow," Currier & Ives, 1883, Library of Congress, LC-DIG-pga-09935.

14-6 Saturday night square dance, Weslaco, Texas. Photo by Arthur Rothstein, 1942. Library of Congress, LC-USF34-024976.

14-7 New Jersey policeman, 1978. Photo by John Margolies, Library of Congress, LC-MA05-9719.

14-8 Banner outside the Minneapolis Police Department fourth precinct following the officer-involved shooting of Jamar Clark on November 15, 2015. Photo by Tony Webster.

14-9 Daniel Patrick Moynihan at a two-way television conference between business leaders and the Nixon administration sponsored by the Chamber of Commerce, Mar. 26, 1969. Photo by Thomas O'Halloran. Library of Congress, LC-DIG-ds-01507.

14-10 Members of the graduating class at Howard University listening to President Johnson deliver the commencement address, June 4, 1966. Photo by Yoichi Okamoto. Lyndon B. Johnson Presidential Library, A603-10A.

14-11 "Meany and big labor the enemies of workers everywhere." Wilfred Owen Brigade Poster, 1975, designed by Rachael Romero. Library of Congress, POS - US .S1592, no. 37.

14-12 Maryland Univ. Campus scene, Jan. 1964. Photo by Warren Leffler. Library of Congress, LC-DIG-ppmsca-41584.

14-13 State unemployment office, Baltimore, 1975. Photo by Thomas O'Halloran, Library of Congress, LC-DIG-ds-00754.

14.14 OFCCP logo, U.S. OFCCP.

14-15 President Obama, Henry L. Gates, Jr., and Sergeant James Crowley in the White House Rose Garden, July 2009.

14-16 President Donald Trump listens to museum director Lonnie Bunch, Feb. 21, 2017. Photo by Shealah Craighead.

p. 415 Boys atop billboard, Crowley, Louisiana, Oct. 1938. Photo by Russell Lee. Library of Congress, LC-USF3301-011738-M2.

p. 447 Birmingham, Alabama, 1937. A billboard. Photo by Arthur Rothstein. Library of Congress, LC-USF33-T01-002393-M3

Index

Made in the USA
Columbia, SC
08 March 2021